Social problems of urban man

THE DORSEY SERIES IN ANTHROPOLOGY
AND SOCIOLOGY

EDITOR   ROBIN M. WILLIAMS, JR.   *Cornell University*

Social problems of urban man

ELMER H. JOHNSON
Professor of Sociology and Criminal Justice
Center for the Study of Crime, Delinquency, and Corrections
Southern Illinois University

1973 THE DORSEY PRESS Homewood, Illinois 60430
Irwin-Dorsey Limited Georgetown, Ontario

First Printing, January 1973

ISBN 0–256–01124–9

Library of Congress Catalog Card No. 72–83996

Printed in the United States of America

To Carol Holmes Johnson

Preface

The urbanization of this age is placing remarkable demands on both individuals and communities to adjust to unprecedented circumstances. Social problems have grown in size and complexity, but the changes unleashed by urbanization also have increased the chances for significant reforms. I do not argue that urbanization is the *only* social trend, but I have decided to emphasize this trend as a reasonable choice among alternative strategies for clear presentation of a diverse collection of public problems. Because urbanization is intimately involved with developments in technology and demography, early chapters are devoted to these three vital dimensions of each of the social problems taken up later. Incidental to their function in providing background, each of these early chapters presents public problems particularly associated with urbanization, technology, or demography.

Throughout the text each chapter presents a number of themes and concepts. The themes are summarized at the end of each chapter while the important concepts are italicized to attract special attention. In addition, a brief review and definition of sociological principles is offered. In sum, I have endeavored to create a textbook for the student, one which will free the instructor to explore particular aspects of the topics for his class.

The study of social problems is a means of orienting the student to alternative careers and to more advanced courses specializing in a particular field of study within a discipline. Various chapters would have particular interest to students planning to be teachers, engineers, clinical professionals, social or correctional workers, medical practitioners, lawyers, or businessmen. At the same time, certain chapters are introductions to more advanced courses in the sociologies of crime, race, communications, recreation, medicine, technology, population, and urbanism. However, I do not claim to present an exhaustive analysis or to rival those books devoted to advanced study of a specialized field of sociology.

Finally, I have the privilege of acknowledging my intellectual and personal debts to those who participated directly or indirectly in the arduous tasks of producing a book. Of course, I assume responsibility for the inadequacies. To avoid straining the tolerance of the reader, I shall abstain from acknowledging individually my debts to my own teachers and several generations of students, many of whom challenged me to sharpen my own insights. Special acknowledgment is given Connie Venable for very valuable bibliographic research on educational issues. Among those providing editorial counsel, Robin M. Williams, Jr., John F. Galliher, Judson Landis, and Curt Johnson merit special mention. A number of persons labored in typing the manuscript and in assisting in research at Morris Library, Southern Illinois University, Carbondale. My greatest personal debt is to my wife, to whom I dedicate this book in appreciation of her tolerance and faith, which made the task of writing manageable.

Carbondale, Illinois   ELMER H. JOHNSON
January 1973

Contents

Sociology and social problems 1

In the more than forty years that I have been associated with universities—as a student, a faculty member, and an administrator—there has never been a time when students have been as concerned as they are now with the university, its purposes, and their role in the university's structure and functioning. . . . The questions they raise not only go to the heart of the university's traditional involvement with teaching, research, and public service but bear directly on the governance and purpose of the university. . . . Their dissatisfaction with the university fits into larger concerns about the problems of our society and the world, and many of their questions are particularly focused on the way the university relates to these problems.[1]

THE CONCEPT OF SOCIAL PROBLEMS

With these words, William H. Sewell introduces his analysis of unrest on university campuses. Chapter 13 of this book will take up the problems of higher education; here his words are used to lend substance to a presentation of the assumptions of this book. What *are* social problems? *How* should they be studied?

Objective condition and subjective definition

In a classic paper on social problems, Fuller and Myers categorize a *social problem* as a condition which is defined by a considerable number

[1] William H. Sewell, "Students and the University," *American Sociologist*, Vol. 16 (May 1971), p. 111.

of persons as a deviation from some social norm which they cherish. Each social problem is seen as having two general elements. First, there is an objective condition which can be verified by impartial and trained observers. Second, there is a subjective definition of that condition as constituting a threat to certain cherished values.[2] The interpretation of this compact statement is the purpose of this chapter. The statement places the study of social problems in the province of social norms. Therefore, this chapter includes a review of sociological concepts relating norms to the development of human personality, the fitting of individual behaviors into a social scheme, and the maintenance of order so that individual and group goals are achieved. Social problems are related to the dependence of man as a social animal upon rules of his own making in his coping with the environment.

As one of the two general elements of a given social problem, the *objective condition* constitutes the facts of the situation. Frequently, "facts" are seen as existing autonomously and free of distortion from sources outside themselves. Actually, however, a unit of information is significant only when it is fitted together with other units. The very process of fitting facts together to form a conclusion adds something beyond the "natural" quality of the fact. Therefore, it is unreasonable to assume that any human condition qualifies as "objective" when it is judged against a rigorous conception of freedom from interpretation. The "objective condition," then, encompasses the facets of a problem situation which are, or conceivably could be, free of controversy. Impartial and competent observers can determine the rate of enrollment increase in universities, for instance, or what kinds of universities and academic departments are experiencing the highest enrollment rates, the proportion of faculty with advanced degrees, the proportion of faculty specializing in noninstructional responsibilities, the relative importance of large lecture classes in instruction, the employment of computer processing in assigning students to courses and testing them, and similar general dimensions of university administration. The social problem, however, emerges only when these objective conditions are found wanting in a fashion which generates public controversy. This is the second general element of a social problem, the *subjective definition* of a threat to certain cherished values. As we shall see, there are important questions about *who* defines the objective condition as a threat to cherished values, but for now, the crucial point is that somehow there *is* a subjective definition by which the objective condition is conceived as a threat. That is, the objective condition is evaluated against social standards and found to constitute a societal problem which must be remedied.

For example, one of the cherished values of higher education is recogni-

[2] Richard C. Fuller and Richard R. Myers, "The Natural History of a Social Problem," *American Sociological Review,* Vol. 6 (June 1941), pp. 320–28.

tion of individual differences among students, each of whom is to be instructed personally in an environment which provides guidance without demanding intellectual conformity for its own sake. It would appear that the statement of this value would be free of controversy, but general agreement evaporates once discussion moves beyond bland platitudes. With the growth of enrollment and with the increasing complexity of instruction, controversies emerge over how to finance the university, how to determine who is a competent instructor, how to process the flood of students requiring personalized counseling as the number of students per faculty member increases, and how to maintain democratic decision making when the number and variety of participants exceeds the capacity of face-to-face relationships. Quite often resort to the standardized methods of large-scale administration brings in the computer, a troop of administrators, and the handling of students much like so many objects moving along a factory assembly line. When this happens the objective condition of the university becomes defined as a problem in its conflict with the cherished value of higher education.

example of a social problem.

Societal basis of social problems

In speaking of a *societal* problem, we should emphasize that the issues considered in the following chapters are significant in that they involve society as a system of groups and institutions which constitute an established order.[3] The conduct of individuals is most evident when we consider departures of behavior from social expectation. The word *societal*, however, directs attention to the contribution to such behavior of the modes for organizing behavior for the sake of social order. (It appears paradoxical to identify social organization as a source of its own disturbance, but Chapter 2 will deal with this apparent paradox.)

Bernard cites one dimension of *societal* problems in the perception of the suffering of victims of a problem by persons not immediately involved in the suffering.[4] She traces the rise of this dimension to the latter 18th century when industrial towns produced inhuman living and working conditions, when the newly enriched middle classes demonstrated humanitarian concerns, and when the social sciences encouraged a faith that problems *could* be overcome. The rhetoric of campus unrest today includes demands that instruction be relevant to the issues of the larger society. This rhetoric, its spokesmen claim, reflects an abhorrence of inhuman conditions which the university, in keeping with humanitarian values, should also protest. Although not always articulated, the rhetoric implies

[3] Jessie Bernard, *Social Problems at Midcentury* (New York: Dryden Press, 1957), pp. 89–90. She points out the clumsiness of referring to "societal" problems throughout her book because of the broad use of the word "social" in the literature. We will follow her precedent by using "social" as though it is the equivalent of the more precise term "societal."

[4] Ibid, pp. 90–102.

a faith that the problems of the university and of the larger society *can* be overcome. Similarly, the very study of social problems is *societal* in its recognition of difficulties that undesirable conditions raise for persons other than ourselves.

Another dimension of *societal* problems is their involvement in the units which constitute the organization of society. Heidt and Etzioni point out that the solution of social problems requires *societal* efforts because the unguided social processes of individuals and personal groups have little effect. Effective treatment requires concerted action by society because frequently the problem's seeming intractability—and even its very existence —lie in the failure of members of the society to participate authentically in its solution.[5] Thereby, the search for causes of social problems and the explanation of the definition of particular conditions as constituting social problems should include the units which constitute the organization of the society which is being "victimized."

When this is done, the study of the problems of higher education is diverted from virtually exclusive attention to the conduct of "radical" students, "self-serving" professors, "ritualistic" administrators, and other individuals who have been the target of hostile criticism. The *societal* aspects of social problems involve the social and cultural arrangements within which these various individuals operate in the affairs of higher education. Their behaviors as individuals could be disturbing to other persons, but the affairs of higher education become a public issue as these behaviors are symptomatic of the discrepancies between (1) the outcome of the social arrangements within which these individuals perform as social beings and (2) the general expectations of their outcome.

Behind most instances of campus unrest are a number of issues involving the structure and governance of the university. For instance, who should have a voice in running the university: the faculty, the students, the administrators, the board of trustees, the alumni, and the categories of groups and individuals providing financial support? How should this voice be provided? What is the proper priority among the various goal goals the university is supposed to achieve? Is the university relevant to the conditions of contemporary life? These are a few of the questions raised. The objective conditions of higher education are expressed in the social structure by which authority and duties are allocated among the human beings who occupy positions in the university as an organization. These conditions are experienced personally in such events as classroom instruction, a student's contacts with his advisor, procedures in registering for courses, and faculty meetings. When such events bring sufficiently widespread dissatisfactions of great intensity, a social problem may emerge as a public issue because the sequence of these discrete events

---

[5] Sarajane Heidt and Amitai Etzioni (eds.), *Societal Guidance: A New Approach to Social Problems* (New York: Thomas Y. Crowell Co., 1969), pp. 1–2.

reveals the inadequacies of the current social arrangements within the university.

RECOGNITION AND RESPONSE TO PROBLEMS

In every age at least some of the people believe they live in particularly difficult times. We, of course, in our era of intense discontent, self-examination, and even self-condemnation, are no exception. Is this a time of particular stress and strain? Future generations will have the advantage of hindsight to judge, but the visibility of today's social protest, sometimes bursting into violence, indicates that there are unusually strong demands that something be done about current social problems.

Social problems are expressive of the mood of the times which, in turn, reflects social conditions as measured by the expectations of the people. Even long-existing social problems, such as crime, are expressive in the intensity of the concern they arouse of current evaluations. In this sense, Bernard points out, the idea of a social problem does not arise until people feel that something should be done about the condition they see as undesirable. The appearance of a given social problem indicates that basic decisions have been made: The condition has been recognized as constituting a social problem, and it has been decided that something must be done to eliminate or ameliorate the problem. There remains, however, the decision on *what* to do.[6]

Rise of public issues

Instead of emerging full-blown, social problems are described as developing over time through several stages: awareness, policy determination, and reform. To begin with, the residents of a given locality become aware that certain acute conditions threaten values they cherish. Fuller and Myers, for example, cite the complaints in Detroit in the 1920s and 1930s about residential trailer communities for their unsightliness, noise, odors, immorality, crime, and depreciation of property in their environs. These initially random protests gain in intensity and organization with growing demands that something be done to remedy the situation. Next, in the policy determination stage, debate rages among conflicting interest groups over whether or not the condition threatens cherished values and/or how reform is to be undertaken. Finally, in the reform stage the solution agreed upon is put into action to become part of the institutionalized patterns of the community. In the case of Detroit's trailer communities, the city prohibited their location in certain areas and imposed licensing and special public health rules in areas where they were permitted.[7]

---

[6] Jessie Bernard, "Social Problems of Decision," *Social Problems,* Vol. 6 (Winter 1958–59), p. 212.

[7] Fuller and Myers, "The Natural History of a Social Problem," pp. 321–27.

Is awareness of a social problem enough? "Be reasonable, Harry. You just *can't* stay in bed until they get rid of air pollution, traffic congestion, stickups, strong-arming, and all that!"

A review of the newspapers of any decade will disclose a succession of public controversies characteristic of that particular period. Recent examples include "mercy killings" by physicians, the need for air-raid shelters for each family in the nuclear age, duplicity by contestants on television quiz shows, corruption of business and political leaders, hazards created by the design of automobiles, alleged Communist sympathies of officials in U.S. government, fluoridation of public water, control of national life by a "military-industrial complex," and so on. Some of these issues appear suddenly and then disappear from general public attention. Others rise recurrently but differ in particulars. Some others persist.

Virtually any condition could conceivably become a social problem. Indeed, it is not even necessary that the condition actually exist. With the advantage of hindsight, for example, we can state that Senator Joseph McCarthy's ardent search for "Communists" in U.S. government was based chiefly on fantasy and distortion. (Becker notes that the inhabitants of Salem, Massachussetts, once saw nonexistent witches as a pressing community problem.)[8] Conversely, widespread anxiety and distress caused by a given condition does not guarantee that societal action will be undertaken to correct it. Long before racial discrimination, wanton destruction of natural resources, pollution of our rivers and atmosphere, victimization of the poor, handling of alcoholics as though they are criminals, and inhumane treatment of the mentally ill became targets for collective concern, all of these conditions existed.

Why, then, are some conditions defined as sufficiently undesirable to constitute a social problem? And why do only *some* of the conditions so defined become targets for widespread *societal* action undertaken to remedy them? The answers are to be found among the parameters outlined below.

Societies differ in the perceptions of their people toward the *possibility* of overcoming conditions adverse to their interests. Etzioni distinguishes between the *active society* and the *passive society* in exploring the conditions under which a people are able to shape the patterning of social life.[9] The active society has a greater capacity to influence its own functioning because of superior collection and use of knowledge, effective decision making by its leaders, mobilization of its resources to convert power into action, and a continuously revised congruence of preferences (consensus) among the groups composing the society. Lacking these characteristics, the passive society is more a pawn of its own traditions and less capable of remolding its social patterns to cope with social problems.

If a society's members are to begin the stages through which treatment of a problem proceeds, they must have the means to become informed

[8] Howard S. Becker (ed.), *Social Problems: A Modern Approach* (New York: John Wiley & Sons, 1966), pp. 5–7.
[9] Amitai Etzioni, "Toward a Theory of Societal Guidance," *American Journal of Sociology,* Vol. 73 (September 1967), pp. 173–87.

about the particular condition, to evaluate it as unacceptable, and to act collectively on the basis of that evaluation. In other words, they must have the motivation and the means for action. The characteristics of the "active society" are useful for analysis of the basis of this motivation and the means for action.

Knowledge as lever to change

Knowledge has been an important ingredient in the *growing awareness* of undesirable conditions, increasing demand for their correction, and mobilization of effort to overcome them. Fatalism in the face of adversity breeds on ignorance of possible alternatives. The development of knowledge increases the *means* for such change as well as expanding *awareness* that revision of previously accepted practices is necessary.

Applied science has given medicine unprecedented potential to overcome disease and forestall death. The technology which is the foundation of an urban-industrial society holds promise of overcoming poverty and want. Extension of formal education and development of mass communications have increased the proportion of the population aware of society's general conditions and have given that increased proportion a basis for evaluating events outside the sphere of their direct experiences. All of these factors have combined to bring about the paradox of increased dissatisfaction even when the bulk of the underprivileged have a better lot than their equivalents in earlier centuries. In the areas of race relations, health care, and poverty, the concept of *relative deprivation* helps explain this apparent paradox in that knowledge of the advantages gained by others increases your own expectations.[10] In explaining the increased concern about crime, the President's Crime Commission cites the effect of a higher level of expectation of underprivileged groups on the standard of performance set for police:

One change of importance in the amount of crime that is reported in our society is the change in the expectations of the poor and members of minority groups about civil rights and social protection. Not long ago there was a tendency to dismiss reports of all but the most serious offenses in slum areas and segregated minority groups districts. The poor and the segregated minority groups were left to take care of their own problems. Commission studies indicate that whatever the past pattern was, these areas now have a strong feeling of need for adequate police protection. Crimes that were once unknown to the police, or ignored when complaints were received, are now much more likely to be reported and recorded as part of the regular statistical procedure.[11]

[10] For discussion of relative deprivation, see Chapter 6.
[11] President's Commission on Law Enforcement and Administration of Justice, *The Challenge of Crime in a Free Society* (Washington, D.C.: U.S. Government Printing Office, 1967), p. 25.

Power and social problems

Power has been defined by Max Weber as the chance of a man or a number of men to realize their own will in a communal action even against the resistance of others who are participating in the action.[12] Power implies that men and groups differ in possession of the elements which are the raw material of power: public esteem, capacity to influence the behavior of other groups through persuasion or coercion, possession of financial resources and essential knowledge, and occupancy of positions of authority in the organizations within the community.

The possibility that a given condition will become the target of societal reform effort must be assessed against the distribution of power among the groups in the given community. Action is more likely when the groups with greater power recognize the condition as a community problem and are motivated to convert their potential power into reform action.

Problems generate reform efforts because man has the ability to improve or modify the conditions under which he lives. He can build towering skyscrapers, demolish mountains, minimize the impact of climate, erode the barriers of distance in travel and communications, and otherwise bend the forces of nature to his needs, convenience, and even comfort. A man-made environment, however, can also cause serious difficulties— witness traffic congestion, air and water pollution, the devastation of war, population problems, and so on.

The existence of social problems implies uncertainties about how man's technological prowess is to be utilized. Perhaps the uncertainties reflect a conviction that unintelligible paradoxes rule out reasonably effective solutions. The definition of a condition as a social problem, however, indicates a faith that solutions are within the scope of human effort. The uncertainties then involve determination of how utilization of technological power violates cherished norms and what should be done about the violations. Debate should mobilize thoughtful consideration and objective analysis; frequently, however, conflicts among special interest groups lead to controversies ranging from simple disagreements to belligerent disputes.

Decision making and consensus

In the decision-making process associated with social problems, Gamson sees power involved in two general ways.[13] First, from the perspective of partisans in a controversy, power refers to how the financial rewards, privileges, and social gratifications are distributed among the individuals and groups of the community.

---

[12] Max Weber, *From Max Weber: Essays in Sociology,* trans. Hans H. Gerth and C. Wright Mills (New York: Oxford University Press, 1946), p. 180.
[13] William A. Gamson, *Power and Discontent* (Homewood, Ill.: Dorsey Press, 1968), pp. 2–18.

Underprivileged groups have problems of poverty, racial prejudice, inferior access to health care and psychiatric services, underrepresentation in the political processes, and overrepresentation among persons penalized by the system of criminal justice. Their plight stems in large measure from their inferior access to the elements of power and, consequently, their low participation in the decisions crucial to their own fate. Alleviation of their plight depends on growth of concern among the groups with superior power, the gaining of greater power among the underprivileged themselves through improved organization and leadership, and the identification of their problems with issues also adversely affecting the groups with superior power. Because such developments draw opposition from groups holding advantages in the status quo, reform involves conflict and dissension within the community.

Second, from the perspective of the leadership in a society, power is the ability of a society to mobilize and generate resources to attain the goals of the society. Leadership tries to utilize its power to achieve these goals most efficiently while at the same time avoiding conflicts among competing parties which would undermine the community consensus.

As a social mechanism, democracy is supposed to implement decision making in a style that will provide participation by a wide spectrum of special-interest groups without endangering the stability of society as a whole. Lipset notes that a stable democratic system requires both minimal force applied by contending special-interest groups and maximal consensus if it is to permit peaceful use of power in the decisions made in controversial issues.[14] Cleavages among groups may lend flexibility to the social structure when changed conditions erode the effectiveness of traditional arrangements in meeting human needs. But struggles for power must be inhibited sufficiently to preserve the basis of consensus by which the special-interest groups mutually maintain the social order. Then the power held by authorities become an instrument for objective analysis of the nature of a community problem, and enables the working out of accommodations by which reform is accomplished with a minimum weakening of the social-psychological bonds of the community while at the same time implementing the program of reform.

ORIENTATION IN STUDYING PROBLEMS

Some observers interpret student unrest as the work of a "handful of hard-core radicals" out to demolish the university itself and the larger social structure it serves. This extreme position entails an assumption that

---

[14] Seymour Martin Lipset, "Political Sociology," in Robert K. Merton, Leonard Broom, and Leonard S. Cottrell, Jr. (eds.), *Sociology Today: Problems and Prospects* (New York: Basic Books, 1959), p. 92.

all is well with the university as it is and that elimination of the "maladjusted minority" is the answer. From another perspective, however, student unrest merits serious study to determine whether it is a barometer of fundamental difficulties which require remedying if the university, or any social institution relevant to the problem, is to serve human purposes under contemporary conditions. Consistent with the latter perspective, our analysis of social problems is intended to include the relevant social institutions among the possible sources of deviations between what *is* and what is *supposed* to be.

Objectivity and skepticism

As chancellor of the Madison campus of the University of Wisconsin in a period of great unrest, William H. Sewell (whose words led off this chapter) was a participant in many highly emotional situations in the 1960s in which there was fundamental disagreement among factions drawn from the students, faculty, university administration, trustees, officials of other elements of government, and the general public. A considerable number of persons in the Madison community became concerned enough to participate in a public controversy, and in the late 1960s campus dissension spilled over at times into passionate confrontation, sometimes into violence, as evidence of sharp differences in interpretation of issues and what to do about them.

By including the established patterns of the university among the sources of its problems, Chancellor Sewell took the second perspective. Thereby, he demonstrated a constructive form of skepticism whereby familiar assumptions were scrutinized in the pursuit of truth. Second, he assumed that the deficiencies of the university situation could be remedied. Third, he looked beyond the incidents on the campus in an effort to trace their sources to social trends in society at large.

Skepticism frequently is considered destructive in intent and consequences because sacred traditions are not honored for their own sake, nor are familiar practices accepted simply because they are comfortable. Valid analysis and effective remedial action against social problems, however, require that no possible target of inquiry be arbitrarily excluded from scrutiny. By questioning the university organization which comprised his professional habitat, Sewell demanded intellectual justification for activities in which he had leadership responsibility. He insisted that the questions raised by students bore directly on functions and governance of the university. The reader is invited to cultivate similar objectivity in the study of problems which also involve him personally.

The study of social problems particularly tests objectivity because it involves the student in a search for explanations for failures of social arrangements and the departures of categories of persons from the social norms which lend order to community life. Such a search is often betrayed by a negativistic skepticism which portrays the entire social structure as corrupt and/or posits a predominance in its population of maladjusted and rebellious persons.

Social trends as clues to reform

In contrast, the skepticism we regard as constructive is reformist in that the existing social institutions (such as the university) are regarded as essentially healthy if the discrepancies between accepted ideals and current practices can be remedied.

Rather than being employed as an end in itself, this kind of skepticism is a means of determining where correction is required and feasible. Reformism is optimistic in that the undesirable conditions are not deemed to be inevitable and incorrigible. Sewell found room for optimism that universities can be strengthened to serve their avowed purposes. Among the reform strategies he suggested were further decentralization of authority, creation of new and smaller colleges, establishment of experimental colleges, undergraduate tutorials, and compassionate administration of policies developed with the participation of students. He emphasized the need for long-term reform effort because hard-line positions by extremists of the right and left were obstructing the goodwill and broad participation necessary to work out mutually accepted solutions.[15]

Solutions to social problems are further complicated by the seating of a particular social problem in aspects of social life which at first glance appear to have nothing to do with the problem. Actually, each specific problem is so involved with others that the researcher into one will almost invariably come face to face with another researcher busily analyzing another problem. Too, lessons learned in the study of one problem sometimes provide insights for the study of what appears to be a new and distinctive social issue. The social scientist gains such advantages because he raises his sights above the immediate situation to seek the rhythms of human behavior which occur in many settings and under a variety of situations. He assumes that the search for explanation will take him beyond what is accessible to the casual observer of the events of the moment.

For example, is student unrest a barometer of something more profound than an emotional explosion ignited by a "handful of hard-core radicals?" Anticipating our Chapter 13, we find Sewell citing three recent trends which have contributed both directly and indirectly to estrangement of students. First, the increased size and complexity of universities reflect the great value Americans place on making education available to all who are able to profit from it—but administrative complexity and impersonal relationships with students stem to a large extent from the great size of enrollments. Second, the unprecedented importance of applied science to con-

---

[15] Sewell, "Students and the University," pp. 116–17.

temporary technology has deeply involved the university in scientific research and development—an involvement so deep as to raise questions
whether or not teaching is receiving sufficient priority.[16] Third, some questions are also raised by the expansion of university services to private and
public agencies off the campus. All of these trends affect the university's
nature and functions and its relationships with students, and meanwhile,
changes in society have altered the nature of students themselves.[17] Their
experiences differ from those of previous generations of students because
their families, communities, and the larger society have been exposed to
a dynamic, more affluent, and increasingly urban society.

REVIEW OF SOCIOLOGICAL CONCEPTS

The difficulties of the contemporary university are grounded in large
measure, then, in the social trends shaping the society as a whole. And
thus the sociological study of social problems becomes an analysis of how
society operates to serve human purposes through a man-made sociocultural environment. To weld individual behaviors into the social organization known as society, norms are the particularly human means of giving
order and predictability to the search by individuals for gratification of their
personal and social needs. Social problems arise through general recognition that somehow the workings of this organization do not bring the
results that compliance with the norms are supposed to bring. A crisis
brings these workings to such an unusual degree of attention that it gives
the "practical" man reason to examine the basis of a society he usually
leaves to philosophers and social theorists. In this book we will employ
the social problems of our day to focus attention on sociological concepts
as tools for making sense out of the crisis of contemporary urban society.

Culture, norms, and values

Among the creatures relying on relationships with their fellows to cope
with their environment, man is unique in his heavy emphasis on social
norms as the means of fitting individual behaviors together into a social
scheme. *Social norms* are rules of conduct which specify what a human
being in a given culture should or should not do as a member of his group.
The important element of *should* injected into human behavior means that
we are supposed to judge our own behavior and the behavior of others
according to standards accepted by the groups within which we associate
with one another.

The idea of "should," Blake and Davis point out, has two important

---

[16] See Chapter 4, pp. 104–7.
[17] Sewell, "Students and the University," pp. 111–16.

implications.[18] First, the word suggests the possibility that actual behavior will differ from expectations; therefore, the departure of individuals from social norms is more usual among human beings than concerns over various forms of social deviance would indicate. Second, when actual behavior differs from expectations, some group effort—social control—must be undertaken to attempt to bring about conformity to the norms generally accepted as vital to the group's continued existence.

The infant becomes human by acquiring through learning the social heritage of his group—the *culture* consisting of all the knowledge, beliefs, values, norms, and technology developed by his people in their history. Robin Williams says that culture is to social behavior what gene pools are to living organisms. Both contain potentiality for a great variation in unique combinations of basic elements to produce great differences among individuals in outcomes—but both carry a set of rules which produce patterns among the outcomes.[19]

Values, Williams declares, are standards of desirability employed as criteria for preference or as justifications for proposed or actual behavior. Values are abstractions couched in terms of "good" or "bad," "beautiful" or "ugly," "appropriate" or "inappropriate," etc. They comprise criteria for norms which constitute more specific rules of conduct. The basic values of a given culture provide a description of the thought patterns which shape the orientation of a people toward the world and a summary of the system of norms by which they evaluate behavior. The American culture is characterized by broad value orientations such as the following (delineated by Williams): We are conditioned to emphasize personal achievement, especially in an occupation, and to engage strenuously in the hustle and bustle of work; a humanitarian concern and helpfulness for the underprivileged sometimes conflicts with a rugged individualism which assumes that one's own efforts largely determine his destiny; "efficiency" is admired; there is a preference for "practical" usefulness of objects and ideas; "bigger and better" are favored themes in an optimistic view that "progress" is both desirable and inevitable; and, finally, great premium is placed on material comfort, equality of opportunity, and personal freedom.[20]

The term *socialization* is applied to the process by which the child learns the standards of his group's culture through contacts with siblings, playmates, and other persons with whom he associates. From the ready-made cultural environment he inherits from the past, the child learns the norms as measuring rods for his own behavior and for evaluating the behavior of others. Norms are defined as *legitimate* when the individual

[18] Judith Blake and Kingsley Davis, "Norms, Values and Sanctions," in Robert E. L. Faris (ed.), *Handbook of Modern Sociology* (Chicago: Rand McNally, 1964), p. 456.
[19] Robin M. Williams, Jr., *American Society: A Sociological Interpretation* (3d ed.) (New York: Alfred A. Knopf, 1970), p. 26.
[20] Ibid., pp. 27, 452–98.

regards them as binding on his own conduct. He conforms to them because he accepts them as proper; violation of them would be abhorrent to his sense of duty.[21] His own conscience becomes a major vehicle for forestalling his violation of his group's expectations. The content of his conscience is acquired through socialization in the course of his personality development.

Institutions and the social order

Some norms regarded as particularly crucial to the general well-being are supported by widespread agreement by members of the society and maintained by social penalties against transgressors. The patterning of sets of such norms around some human purpose is the basis of *social institutions*. Because institutions are composed of norms, they are not subject to direct observation but are studied through the behavior they elicit in recurrent situations. Examples of social institutions include the family, school, government, and private economic enterprise. Each can be compared to the blueprint for a house. As an overall scheme, the blueprint gives overall significance to the pieces of wood, metal, and other materials needed to build a house. As a concept, the social institution is useful in giving meaning to the norms to form a pattern. The family is such a blueprint for making sense out of a host of norms concerned with controlling sexual relations, relating the behaviors of husband and wife to family obligations, rearing of children, allocation of household tasks, and other purposes served by the family as a sphere of recurrent social behavior. The various social institutions of a society are related to one another to compose a normative framework for the society as a whole.

Although it is an abstraction which cannot be smelled or touched, the social institution has great influence in shaping behavior. The family institution is a set of guidelines which channels the sex drive to support the preservation of society in selection of one's mate, in maintaining a constancy of relationship between man and woman in the status of husband and wife, in producing and caring for children and in providing for their socialization, and otherwise in patterning family behavior in keeping with social values. In the economic realm, other institutions provide guidelines through such ideas as private property, money as a medium of exchange, wage payment for work, duty to support your dependents, and the premium placed on ambition.

If they function ideally, the social institutions collectively fit together to serve as the operative bases of the social order.[22] If they function ideally, families teach children to be dedicated and competent employees

[21] Max Weber, *The Theory of Social and Economic Organization,* trans. A. M. Henderson and Talcott Parsons (New York: Oxford University Press, 1947), pp. 124–25.
[22] See J. O. Hertzler, *Social Institutions* (Lincoln, Neb.: University of Nebraska Press, 1946), pp. 39–48.

of businesses and factories and prepare them to follow the teachings of the church. If they function ideally, businesses and factories provide the income essential to constructive family life. We say "if they function ideally" to suggest that, since institutions are essentially conservative in their emphasis on the value of the ways of the past and on preserving the social order, they tend to provide behavioral guidelines which are always somewhat out of joint with contemporary conditions. Institutions serve human purposes by providing the normative basis by which individuals can advance the interests of individuals and groups through cooperation with others.

Collectively, social institutions provide a structure within which social control operates. Through development of habits and conditioning of attitudes through socialization, an individual's behavior is channeled according to his statuses and roles within groups. In relationships with other persons a person occupies _a social status_ (his social position such as father, wife, dean, professor, student, etc.). Attached to each social position is a _social role_ as a set of expectations against which performance in a given status is evaluated. The norms of particular role-statuses are illustrated by the expectations that a mother place the interests of her children before her own, that a military officer be courageous and certain in his decisions, and that an employee be punctual and efficient in carrying out instructions.

Means of promoting conformity

As measuring rods for behavior, the norms are the content of social control by which the individual is persuaded or compelled to conform to group expectations. _Social control_ refers to the social forces which are brought into play to prevent or oppose deviation from the norms. Sociologists distinguish between informal and formal controls.

Informal controls rely on mores and public sentiment that operate more or less unconsciously within the fabric of daily life. They are exhibited through the contemptuous glance, derisive laugh, or pregnant silence when punishment is required. The approving smile is an example of rewarding behavior. Because they operate within the context of daily life without usually ruffling the regular flow of social intercourse, the application of informal social controls brings relatively little psychological pain.

Formal controls are deliberately formulated and consciously implemented to regulate behavior in specified aspects of life through agencies specifically designed to perform regulating functions. For example, the policeman is a formal control agent who has been assigned the duty of consciously enforcing deliberately formulated criminal laws. His enforcement activities involve clear-cut events (such as an arrest) which stand out from the daily routines of life.

The usefulness of the concept of social control is most evident in social problems most visibly associated with deviance: crime, drug abuse, alcoholism, and sexual deviance. These behaviors are deviant in that they are evaluated as markedly in conflict with norms of the dominant culture. The need to exert external control over them appears obvious. Other social problems less apparent than individual deviance, however, also involve social control. The impact of social and technological change, for example, is reflected in the breakdown of racial segregation as a subterranean social control system. The so-called "law-and-order" crisis reflects the shortcomings of the criminal law as a formal control substitute for the informal controls of family and neighborhood. Even the health-care crisis exemplifies the inadequacies of the control mechanisms, since it now seems clear that physicians and their professional associations have dominated delivery of medical services. As we shall see in Chapter 18, the complex technology of medicine and fundamental changes in the environment of medical practice have eroded the informal control of the patient-physician relationship so as to outmode the traditional image of the "kindly family physician."

Deviant behavior and the defects of organizations would probably not come to public notice and require application of formal controls if there were satisfactory operation of the informal controls of conscience, socialization, and the penalties imposed within the routine life of social institutions. One common denominator of the social problems considered in this book is their reflection of the greater reliance of contemporary urban society on formal controls. Strains have been created in city life by cultural heterogenity, social change, population density, mobility, and other factors undermining traditions supporting informal controls. Rapid technological change has undermined the effectiveness of family and neighborhood and has released individual effort to acquire prestige and personal satisfactions through economic consumption. Population density cloaks deviance in anonymity. Population heterogeneity saps the effectiveness of common socialization to one set of cultural values and norms. Chapters 3 and 4 will consider these factors in greater detail, but their implications bear on the particular problems to be examined.

HOW DIFFERENT ARE THE DEVIANTS?

Among the reasons for at least casual interest in social problems is curiosity about the disreputable behavior of rather "strange creatures" in the subterranean aspects of life in the community, though more penetrating examination of these "strange creatures" and their "subterranean" world can be disturbing to the person who has such stereotyped preconceptions. Students on tours of prisons, for instance, frequently comment: "They don't look so different," or "This place is a lot like the army." The first observation invites the question whether or not conviction for one incident of behavior is sufficient grounds for evaluating the total personality of a person. The second observation may stem from a rejection of regimentation which is found in military life. Closer analysis could concentrate on the similarities between prisons and those social establishments that treat people around the clock as blocks of identical "things" according to rules which they have little, if any, voice in formulating.[23]

The objective of this section is to promote a similar movement beyond the preconception that social deviance is markedly different from what appears to be otherwise universal social conformity. Sharp distinctions between the "good" and the "bad" simply do not exist in the real world. In pursuing this objective, this section will include the following themes as among the premises of later chapters:

¶ People defined as deviant are not as dissimilar from nondeviants as implied by the arbitrary conception of them as "incorrigible and dedicated criminals," "dope fiends," "sex perverts," and other general labels which classify them as something other than human.

¶ Nonconformity comes in a range of shadings rather than being sharply distinct from the behavior of "decent, law-abiding citizens." Violations of social norms from a continuum from heinous crimes to technical violations which are largely unnoticed and extremely unlikely to bring even mild censure. The conception of deviants as totally "bad" according to the standards of the dominant culture overlooks the transgressions of the "decent" people and the difference among the "disreputable" people in the ultimate significance to the society of their deviance.

The "abnormality" of deviants

It has been frequently assumed that there is something inherent in deviants which sets them off sharply from "normal" and "respectable" people. You are supposed to be able to tell who is a criminal by distinguishing features of his physiology or genetic characteristics. Poverty and unwed motherhood have been attributed to feeblemindedness probably carried in the hereditary strain of families whose names pop up recurrently in the files of the local public welfare office and police station. Drug addicts and school truants have been described as possessing distinguishing personality characteristics (such as seclusiveness, suggestibility, and lack of self-assurance) which mark them as different from "normal" people.

Durkheim was a pioneer in pointing out the exaggeration in this drawing of sharp distinctions between the outcasts and the "respectables." In his study of suicide, he found the behavior of "problem" people is merely an exaggerated form of common practices. The daredevil toys with death

---

[23] See the analysis of "total institutions," by Erving Goffman, "On the Characteristics of Total Institutions: The Inmate World," in Donald R. Cressey (ed.), *The Prison: Studies in Institutional Organization and Change* (New York: Holt, Rinehart Winston, 1961), pp. 15–67.

although trying to avoid it; a hero risks his life for his companion; the sickly man endangers himself by neglecting his body. These ways of acting resemble genuine suicide in that they entail risks known to the individual but not deterrent to his behavior.[24]

In attempting to make sense out of events which occur in bewildering profusion, man resorts to generalizations which emphasize the similarities among unique events. In making these generalizations, he must focus attention on only certain of the characteristics which apparently all such events share. In thus narrowing the range of his attention, he risks fitting his selected items into a conceptual whole which does not capture the genuine meaning of the events. Exaggeration of the differences between deviants and nondeviants has been such an error. The consequence has been misinterpretation of the causes of deviance and its significance for the social order.

Gradations of nonconformity

Ideal patterns are constantly held up to the individual as models for his behavior. The images of the "perfect husband," the "model citizen," the "ideal soldier," etc., are presented as models for the novice. The *real patterns* are the behavior models actually followed by group members as they respond to situations in real life.[25] The ideal patterns do not correspond with actual behavior. They convey principles only of what should be done if situations are considered in the abstract.

Complete conformity to idealized rules is at least as exceptional as extreme nonconformity. Rather than arguing that a sharp line exists between the "good" people and the "enemies" of society, it is more realistic to conceive a range of gradations between the extremes of conformity and nonconformity. Human affairs and human personality come in too great a variety to be captured neatly by arbitrary rules. As Wrong says, the individual is not completely molded by the norms of the pertinent culture.[26] The relationship between social demands, personal attitudes towards the demands, and actual conduct comes in many varieties, even in the most stable societies. Norms indicate a *range* of acceptable behaviors rather than providing exact guidelines for specific situations. Turk brings up another important point by his hypothesis that several members of a given group will be in greater agreement regarding what another member should do than regarding what each should do himself.[27] Internal-

---

[24] Émile Durkheim, *Suicide: A Study in Sociology,* trans. John A. Spaulding and George Simpson (New York: Free Press, 1951), pp. 45–46.

[25] Modified from Ralph Linton, *The Study of Man* (New York: D. Appleton-Century Co., 1936), pp. 99–103.

[26] Dennis H. Wrong, "The Oversocialized Conception of Man in Modern Sociology," *American Sociological Review,* Vol. 26 (April 1961), pp. 183–93.

[27] Herman Turk, "An Inquiry into the Undersocialized Conception of Man," *Social Forces,* Vol. 43 (May 1965), pp. 518–21.

ization of norms, then, is more effective in making us agents for enforcing conformity than in policing our own behavior.

All versions of nonconformity should not be equated with behavior contrary to the social order. After all, the inventor, the charismatic political leader, the great artist, and other innovative heroes break rules in establishing precedent. The versions of nonconformity fall at various points along a continuum of evaluations of the degree of threat they are supposed to pose for the social order. The location along the continuum is determined according to several criteria: the particular priority given the value threatened by the deviant, the prestige and general reputation he enjoys, and the perception of the potential contribution the particular form of nonconventional behavior holds for society as a whole.

To show the differential significance to society of various kinds of norm violations, Merton distinguishes between nonconforming and aberrant behavior.[28] The *nonconformist* announces his dissent publicly, challenges the legitimacy of the norms he rejects, and advocates substitution of new norms for those he considers morally suspect. He is likely to be viewed as an unselfish crusader by conventional citizens even if they do not share his opinions. He may be a reformer in the sense that he focuses attention on the discrepancies between actual practice and the high moral principles the society sets as ideals. The *aberrant person* conceals his transgressions from public scrutiny, violates norms without questioning their legitimacy, and attempts to escape the penalties for violating norms without proposing changes in them. The aberrant is believed to be out to satisfy his private interests or to express his private cravings without regard for improving the state of the moral order.

By fitting normality within a sociocultural context, this conception of nonconformity has great flexibility in capturing the significance of deviance. Redlich sees the problem of normality posed by the questions "Normal for what?" and "Normal for whom?" [29] The moderately inadequate executive poses a greater problem than the worker in a position of little responsibility. The man clad in swimming trunks in church in winter is abnormal but not the man on the beach in the summer. A sense of stress when in confined space might be experienced by an astronaut but not usually by, say, a cowboy.

Over time, the criteria for evaluation changes so that the "misfit" of yesterday may be a cultural hero of today. Television, for example, portrays the wandering cowboy as a folk hero, but the portrayal is very selective. Paradoxically, this cowboy of the past shares many of the char-

[28] Robert K. Merton, "Social Problems, and Sociological Theory," in Robert K. Merton and Robert A. Nisbet (eds.), *Contemporary Social Problems* (3d ed.) (New York: Harcourt Brace Jovanovich, 1971), pp. 829–32.

[29] F. C. Redlich, "The Concept of Health in Psychiatry." in Alexander H. Leighton, John A. Clausen, and Robert N. Wilson (eds.), *Explorations in Social Psychiatry* (New York: Basic Books, Inc., 1957), p. 155.

acteristics of today's migrant farm laborer, who draws a generally negative evaluation. The excessiveness of this evaluation is suggested by Hoffer in his report of his experiences in working among transient farm laborers. He found many lacked self-discipline and ability to endure the monotony of "steady" jobs. They had not made good. Some were slaves of their appetites. Some were outcasts and ex-jailbirds. All craved change which would bring luck. Nevertheless, a thought came to Hoffer: These were the qualities of the pioneers who settled the frontier in the course of their drinking, fighting, gambling, and wenching. Men with superior ability shaped the nation but so did the misfits with their willingness to take a chance in a virgin continent.[30]

ORGANIZATIONS AND DEVIANCE

Gradations of behavior between complete conformity and nonconformity are found among organizations as well as among individuals. Deviations within legitimate organizations include thefts of employees in which the employer is victimized and transgressions against other organizations and customers in which the organization is the perpetrator.[31] Our point is that deviance occurs *within* legitimate organizations, not that such organizations are characteristically or usually deviant. Again our objective is to provide evidence that social problems are not simply a matter of the deviance of individuals whose nonconformity, in and of itself, demonstrates their inability to discipline their behavior within *any* organization. This section is organized around three themes:

¶ Nonconformity includes the violations of norms within the patterns of a given organization which are supposed to achieve socially approved purposes. Here the focus is on violations by individuals who essentially are dedicated to the purposes of the legitimate organizations within which they function. The very fact that this deviance comprises part of the normal life of the organization must be enough to create uncertainty among those persons who see deviance as bizarre behavior and personal disorganization by *individuals.*

¶ Nonconformity also includes the normative evasions of organizations themselves. In conflict with the common assumption that deviants are personally disorganized individuals, we find instances of organizations engaging systematically in violation of values held sacred in the society.

¶ Finally, deviance paradoxically can serve the interests of the society upon which it presumably preys. These services are indirect and usually

---

[30] Eric Hoffer, "The Role of the Undesirables," *Harper's Magazine,* Vol. 205 (December 1952), pp. 79–84.

[31] See: Norman Jaspan and Hillel Black, *The Thief in the White Collar* (Philadelphia, Pa.: J. B. Lippincott Co., 1960): Erwin O. Smigel and H. Laurence Ross (eds.), *Crimes Against Bureaucracy* (New York: Van Nostrand Reinhold Co., 1970).

not the purpose of the deviant. They raise, however, the remarkable question of whether or not a society without deviance is a genuine possibility.

Institutionalized evasions

Between conformity and outright antisocial behavior lies the grey area of patterned evasion of rules. The term *institutionalized evasion* refers to provision by a social system for regularized violation of its rules when particular circumstances make compliance an obstacle to other socially desirable consequences. Motion pictures and television series often center around the theme that confidence-game tactics make the organization work. The "moonlight requisitions" of clever enlisted men provide the revered commander means to win the battle while the "ridiculous" supply lieutenant vainly undertakes to enforce the bureaucratic procedures required by the book. Here violations of generally accepted rules are accepted tacitly and perhaps even approved by those supporting these rules.

This form of nonconformity however, carries a risk if the person toying with the rules is found out or steps outside the sphere within which his transgressions are judged to be of ultimate benefit to the social system. Several factors affect the probability that these patterned evasions of norms will be eliminated: the degree of vested interest of the individuals and/or organization in the evasion, the intensity of the demand for the illicit goods and services, and the qualities of the social situation within which the evasions occur.[32] Examples of the latter factor are the amount of surveillance the violator receives, the amount of discretion in decision making his job requires, the ardor with which the violated norm is supported by the fellow participants in the given enterprise, and the side effects of reform on the efficiency of the organization.

As one illustration of institutionalized deviance, Bensman and Gerver employ a factory situation.[33] In aircraft wing assembly, screws may often not be properly inserted due to poor design. The tap, an illicit but extremely hard screw, forces alignment with the nut at the risk of bending the wing plate or losing holding power. The tap may also be a means of concealing a structural defect. New workers are secretly taught the technique, but indiscriminate or obvious use is subject to worker censure. Under pressure to accelerate production and to gain worker approval as a "good egg," the foremen are ambivalent toward rigorous suppression of the tap. In collusion with the workers to evade the inspectors, the foremen go through the ritual of punishment when the worker is caught.

Since use of the tap is a serious transgression, deviance operates to

[32] Williams, *American Society,* pp. 426–27.
[33] Joseph Bensman and Israel Gerver, "Crime and Punishment in the Factory: The Function of Deviancy in Maintaining the Social System," *American Sociological Review,* Vol. 28 (August 1963), pp. 588–98.

support a social system rather than simply being individual nonconformity. The transgression is performed under rules imposed by the workers and foremen. The technique and associated norms are learned. Because the use of the illicit means serves purposes of those charged with preventing use of the tap, the official definition of the act as criminal is insufficient to implement punitive reactions. When the forbidden behavior serves purposes regarded as constructive, the enforcers will not implement punishment.

Institutionalized evasion breeds on the mundane relationships within an organization. Its patterns are learned through example and are excused by the evaders as a form of defense against the organization. Kemper speaks of reciprocal deviance and parallel deviance. In *reciprocal deviation* the subordinate violates company expectations in retaliation for its failure to recognize his meritorious service or for its inflation of his work load beyond original agreement without commensurate reward. His retaliation may be cheating through extra days off, tardiness, and similar relatively minor transgressions. Grudges against employers, however, have also been motives for thefts and embezzlement. In *parallel deviance* the subordinate apes the violation of the boss. In personifying the organization, the unscrupulous superior lends apparent legitimacy to the violations of the subordinate.[34]

Organizationally implemented evasion

The study of deviance, Reiss contends, should include the transgressions of organizations as well as the deviance of individuals who comprise their membership. He distinguishes two kinds of institutionalized evasion. As discussed above, patterning can arise largely from the aggregative effect of individuals deviating from norms. Their transgressions are favored by low risk of detection and rather ambivalent attitudes toward their behavior. Reiss refers to another kind of deviance whereby a more elaborate and complex organizational system promotes mass evasion.[35] As examples of organized deviance among otherwise legitimate organizations, Reiss refers to employing organizations which discriminate against minorities even though such actions are contrary to civil rights laws. School boards also have failed to comply with legal and fiscal requirements.

Sutherland defines *white collar crime* as a crime committed by a person of respectability and high social status in the course of his occupation. His analysis refutes the belief that crime is necessarily associated with poverty or with the social and personal inadequacies associated with poverty. However, more to our immediate purpose, he cites the offenses of busi-

[34] Theodore D. Kemper, "Representative Roles and the Legitimation of Deviance," *Social Problems,* Vol. 13 (Winter 1966), pp. 293–97.

[35] Albert J. Reiss, "The Study of Deviant Behavior: Where the Action Is," *Ohio Valley Sociologist,* Vol. 32 (Autumn 1966), pp. 1–12.

nesses in illegal restraint of trade, discriminatory pricing, violations of patents and copyright laws, misrepresentation in advertising, unfair labor practices, and financial manipulations.[36]

Working within structures resembling those of giant corporations, criminal syndicates are the prime example of systematic normative evasion as the deliberate intent of an organization. Intricate conspiracies are carried on over many years to gain huge profits through control over the supply of illegal goods and services. Gambling, loan sharking, narcotics, and other forms of vice are profitable because of a demand for illegal goods and services among millions of Americans. The President's Crime Commission has described the consolidation of previously fragmented units into a national illicit industrial organization to control a mass market. Techniques of corruption and enforcement are used to protect operations against interruption and to instill organizational discipline. Organized crime flourishes only where it has corrupted local officials who occupy positions of responsibility in the legitimate social order. However, control efforts are also handicapped by difficulties in obtaining proof, fragmentation of law enforcement, and public ambivalence.[37]

Contributions to social order

It is clear that certain kinds of deviants break the social rules because, at least in their own belief, they have a mission to improve social conditions or otherwise benefit mankind. The reform of established practices calls for a remarkable objectivity toward a social world to which the person has been conditioned through socialization during the development of his personality. The reformer must have a deep-seated conviction that his cause is just if he is to be persistent in the face of entrenched habit, passivity of his fellow citizens, and the complexity of the social structure supporting the conditions he would change. Therefore, it is understandable that reformers are described as disturbers of the peace, trespassers on forbidden ground, and assaulters of human complacency.[38] Other innovators are found among inventors, artists, social critics, sports heroes, entertainers, etc. Although such persons may irritate defenders of the status quo, these innovators qualify as "aberrant" nonconformists as Merton defined them in our earlier discussion. Their nonconformity represents a deliberate attempt to improve the condition of mankind. (Other kinds of deviants may claim that their transgressions serve the interests of the community by

[36] Edwin H. Sutherland, *White Collar Crime* (New York: Holt, Rinehart and Winston, 1949); also see Gilbert Geis (ed.), *White Collar Criminal* (New York: Atherton Press, 1968).

[37] President's Commission on Law Enforcement and Administration of Justice, *The Challenge of Crime,* Chapter 7.

[38] Arthur M. Schlesinger, *The American as Reformer* (Cambridge, Mass.: Harvard University Press, 1951), p. 66.

providing jobs for policemen, judges, and prison officials, but such a claim, of course, is not to be taken seriously.)

As a moral example, the deviant provides an opportunity for others to present themselves as defenders of "decency" and *their* conception of the moral order. Doubts about one's own commitment to the protected morality may be cloaked under the strong hostility expressed against the transgressor. The essential point is that such opposition unites the members of the community against the deviant to create at least the impression of a widespread commitment to the sacred norms. The development of common bonds under patriotic sentiments in wartime is a prime example of the social-psychological unification of a people through common opposition to an enemy.

Durkheim identifies deviance as an important source of this moral cohesion. He believes a crimeless society to be a sociological impossibility. Because of the diversity of factors shaping human personality, some persons will inevitably violate norms. But even if absolute conformity to norms could be achieved, Durkheim fears that society would lose the flexibility of innovation by which adjustments can be made to keep the social structure current with conditions. If serious crimes such as murder were to vanish in a hypothetical society of saints, the abhorrence aroused against such crimes would be shifted to less serious offenses.[39]

The encouragement of community consensus through opposition against the deviant has, however, adverse consequences, as witness the problems of applying various kinds of therapy in overcoming crime, drug abuse, alcoholism, sex deviance, mental illness, and racial discrimination. George Herbert Mead notes that hostility emphasizes the common characteristics of the violators of threatened values and thereby erases from the minds of the defenders of these values the qualities which make different the individual deviants who have been lumped in the category of "enemy." We cannot concurrently hate the criminal and accord him the compassion and understanding essential to accepting the rehabilitated criminal as one of us. Aggressive defense of the value of private property runs counter to the understanding of the conditions under which the person became an armed robber.[40] Later we will further consider the negative consequences of hostile reactions to deviants in the problems of unwed motherhood, incest, and homosexuality (Chapter 9), school dropouts (Chapters 12), campus unrest (Chapter 13), racial prejudice and discrimination (Chapters 14 and 15), administration of criminal justice (Chapters 16 and 17), differential utilization and depersonalization of health services (Chapter 18), aggravation of mental illness as "residual deviance"

[39] Émile Durkheim, *The Rules of Sociological Method,* trans. Sarah A. Solovay and John H. Mueller (Chicago: University of Chicago Press, 1938), pp. 67–71.
[40] George Herbert Mead, "The Psychology of Punitive Justice," *American Journal of Sociology,* Vol. 23 (March 1918), pp. 591–92.

and differential treatment according to class status (Chapter 19), and the stigmatization of drug users and alcoholics (Chapter 20).

Another frequently unintentional service of deviants is performed through their marking of the boundaries of acceptable behavior. Every group must establish some line of demarcation between the acceptable and the forbidden among the host of behaviors which occur, especially when the traditional norms do not fit new circumstances exactly. The norms themselves are products of an accumulation of decisions by the community in censuring one kind of behavior, tolerating another, and rewarding others. As a tangible symbol of the rejection of certain behaviors, the deviants of the day stand as boundary markers for the limits of tolerance of transgressions.[41]

Deviance serves as a barometer of changes in the structure of a society. The criminal law expresses the values of the dominant group able to protect its social and economic interests through legislative power. When political changes reflect new social and economic developments, revised definitions of crimes and new administrative policies are a barometer of a new attitudinal climate within which certain kinds of behavior are evaluated to be deviant. Aubert illustrates this possibility in a gradual change in the Norwegian social structure brought about with the rise of the labor movement to political power and the decline of the business group. White-collar offenses become subject to the criminal law. However, to pacify the businessmen for sake of social peace, the implementation of these laws has been slow.[42]

SUMMARY

Social problems arise because man is a sociocultural creature. He creates a sociocultural organization to regulate his own conduct and as a device for utilizing natural resources in the service of individual and group needs. This creation may be the source of problems when the reality of social relationships diverges markedly from the circumstances expected on the basis of his ideals. Poverty, for example, constitutes such a discrepancy. However, an undesirable condition does not qualify as a social problem unless two other factors are present. There must be faith that the elimination of the discrepancy is within the range of human attainment, and the groups occupying strategic places in the society's power structure must be convinced that collective action must be taken. In other words, the very definition of a given condition as a social problem is a sociocultural phenomenon.

[41] Kai T. Erickson, *Wayward Puritans: A Study in the Sociology of Deviance* (New York: John Wiley & Sons, 1966), pp. 8–13.

[42] Vilhelm Aubert, "White Collar Crime and Social Structure," *American Journal of Sociology,* Vol. 58 (November 1952), p. 269.

The emphasis on the sociocultural basis of social problems is the central theme of this book. The next chapter adds more substance to this introduction, and the theme will be found in chapters taking up particular problematic areas. Perhaps there is reassurance in the myth that social problems are simply the product of "problem people" who upset the operations of an "effective" and "good" society, and in questioning this myth, we may add to the perplexity raised in some minds by community problems. But the definition of a *social* problem implies a particular concern with the operation of society in terms of both cause and effect. The word "problem" also can be defined as a question proposed for solution. In that sense, the following chapters will undertake a search for understanding of questions in the faith that they are susceptible to explanation and that man has the potential to deal with them.

FOR ADDITIONAL READING

Harry Elmer Barnes and Howard P. Becker, *Social Thought From Lore to Science* (Boston, Mass.: D. C. Heath, 1938), Chapter 13.

Earl H. Bell, *Social Foundations of Human Behavior* (New York: Harper & Brothers, 1961), Chapter 13.

Herbert Blumer, "Social Problems as Collective Behavior," *Social Problems,* Vol. 18 (Winter 1971), pp. 298–306.

Alexander L. Clark and Jack P. Gibbs, "Social Control: A Reformulation," *Social Problems,* Vol. 12 (Spring 1965), pp. 398–415.

Lewis A. Coser, "Some Functions of Deviant Behavior and Normative Flexibility," *American Journal of Sociology,* Vol. 68 (September 1962), pp. 172–81.

F. James Davis, *Social Problems* (New York: Free Press, 1970).

Harry Gold and Frank R. Scarpetti (eds.), *Combating Social Problems: Techniques of Intervention* (New York: Holt, Rinehart & Winston, 1967), pp. 14–15.

Georges Gurvitch, "Social Control," in Georges Gurvitch and Wilbert E. Moore (eds.), *Twentieth Century Sociology* (New York: The Philosophical Library, 1945), pp. 267–96.

August B. Hollingshead, "The Concept of Social Control," *American Sociological Review,* Vol. 6 (April 1941), pp. 217–24.

Paul B. Horton and Gerald R. Leslie, *The Sociology of Social Problems* (4th ed.: New York: Appleton-Century-Crofts, 1970).

Robert E. Lane, "The Decline of Politics and Ideology in a Knowledgeable Society," *American Sociological Review,* Vol. 31 (October 1966), pp. 649–62.

Richard T. LaPiere, *A Theory of Social Control* (New York: McGraw-Hill, 1954).

Douglas A. Parker, "On Values and Value Judgments in Sociology," *American Sociological Review,* Vol. 32 (June 1967), pp. 463–66.

Talcott Parsons, *The Social System* (New York: Free Press, 1964), Chapters 7, 11.

Robert Perrucci and Marc Pilisuk, "Leaders and Ruling Elites: The Interorganizational Bases of Community Power," *American Sociological Review,* Vol. 35 (December 1970), pp. 1040–57.

John R. Seeley, "The Making and Taking of Problems: Toward an Ethical Stance," *Social Problems,* Vol. 14 (Spring 1967), pp. 382–89.

Gresham M. Sykes, "The Differential Distribution of Community Knowledge," *Social Forces,* Vol. 29 (May 1951), pp. 376–82.

Explanations for 2
social problems

Urban society today raises unprecedented challenges to mankind. The last half century has produced a spectacular increase in the number of urban places with more than 50,000 inhabitants. The administrative limits marking city boundaries have lost their sociological relevance because modern metropolises have flooded the outside areas and urban culture has come to be shared by Americans outside city boundaries. Mankind, Gottmann says, is reshaping its habitat. The rapidity and massive scale of urbanization produce changes in the nature of the city's problems and increasingly emphasize the need for penetrating analysis and intelligent planning if human needs are to be met.[1]

URBAN SOCIETY: THE CENTRAL THEME

Studies of the problems of the city frequently have been preoccupied with "disorganization," as though rural society were the "natural" setting of mankind. This emphasis overlooks the interdependence of city life with the broader society in drawing food, raw materials, and population. Through such interdependence the city is strongly affected by the society within which it develops and is maintained. The metropolis has its particular problems—for example, deterioration of the central city, financial defi-

[1] Jean Gottmann, *Economics, Esthetics, and Ethics in Modern Urbanization* (New York: Twentieth Century Fund, 1962), pp. 2–10.

cits by concurrent expansion in demands for services and the flight to the suburbs of the people and economic enterprises best prepared to pay taxes, the difficulties of managing a complex, large-scale social system, and the inefficiencies of fragmented local government in the face of problems national or regional in scope.

Even for these problems so readily identified with the city, analysis reveals that the life of the city is shaped within a broader, embracing society. This book takes urban society as the central theme in analysis of social problems. Poverty, crime, health care, drug abuse, environmental erosion, technological unemployment, and racial problems are national in their impact on a society marked by urbanization and in the resources which must be mobilized to deal with them.

Public issues of the social structure

The concept of deviance as assigned status will be the subject of the final section of this chapter. Usually, the term *societal reaction* is associated with the idea that the labeling of a person as a deviant aggravates a given social problem. Stigmatization presses the casual law violator into becoming a dedicated criminal and complicates the task of winning the voluntary participation of the drug addict in rehabilitation programs. In the second meaning more germane here, *societal reaction* refers to the workings of the social structure in response to a condition generally recognized as socially undesirable. Under the first meaning of the term, the agencies of organized society play important functions in expressing public attitudes through official actions taken against persons labeled as deviant. Beyond this, these agencies are part of the mobilization of the units of the social structure—a *societal reaction*—to deal with conditions, including certain deviant behaviors, defined as social problems.

When problems elicit a *societal* response, difficulties of individuals have become what C. Wright Mills has called "public issues of the social structure" which "transcend the local environments of the individual and the range of his inner life." [2] One man out of a job and one married couple obtaining a divorce are the "troubles" of individuals within the range of their immediate relationships with others. Such troubles can be widespread in the community because a collectivity of individuals suffer similarly, but, unemployment becomes a "public issue of the social structure" only when it is recognized as involving the economic and social institutions of the community in the problem of poverty which has implications for the well-to-do as well as the poor themselves. Divorce is a societal matter in that a high rate of marital dissolution may be interpreted as a symptom of the difficulties of the family as a social institution in maintaining the

[2] C. Wright Mills, *The Sociological Imagination* (New York: Oxford University Press, 1959), pp. 8–9.

social structure through socialization of the young, preventing or coping effectively with emotional tensions, and procreation of the next generation.[3]

The experiences of contemporary Americans are shaped within a society dominated by an urban culture, marked by an industrial technology, and subject to demographic trends reflecting the qualities and behaviors of the people. We assume that the impact of today's technology and population trends is crucial to the study of the problems of urban society. In providing means of supporting large concentrations of people, industrial technology provides evidence of man's inventive genius in bending nature to serve his needs. However, as Chapter 4 will document, the acceleration of American technology has raised crucial questions as to whether such great power can be handled socially and ethically to the ultimate benefit of mankind. Demography deals with fertility, mortality, and migration. Although analysis of population rates appears rather sterile to some, and to the casual observer seems to be without social relevance, changes in these demographic characteristics have a profound effect on urban society, as Chapter 5 will demonstrate.

The relative satisfaction of material needs in a population, as Nisbet says, does not guarantee elimination of all deprivations and frustrations. With material improvement, a greater proportion of the population will feel greater urgency in the real realm of social and spiritual needs for cultural participation, social belonging, and personal status. The faith in the potentiality of technology will sharpen frustration when these needs are not met. Previously, men found a sense of community in their personal relationships within the family, neighborhood, church and local work groups. These intimate groups provided the individual a place within the social order that gave meaning to his activities. The authority which lent order to these groups was rooted in the rhythms derived from the past and was based ultimately on the consent of the persons under it. With the growth of large-scale society, however, these traditional primary relationships have become less functionally relevant. Nisbet argues that many of our contemporary discontents stem from man's search for personal identity and security within large-scale organizations.[4]

Urbanization has raised a central question. In the light of the concentration of diverse populations in relatively small geographical spaces, how can a sense of community be engendered to link the individual socially to the overall organization upon which he is functionally dependent but from which he is psychologically distant? Some critics of contemporary society interpret Nisbet's argument as support for a negative answer to the central question. However, as Chapter 3 will point out, primary groups

---

[3] See Chapter 8.
[4] Robert A. Nisbet, *The Quest for Community* (New York: Oxford University Press, 1953), pp. 21–23, 49–51.

persist in urban society and bureaucratic administration holds advantages as well as disadvantages, depending on how it is employed. Furthermore, Chapter 21 will present strategies which have been suggested as means of supplying a more positive answer.

Alienation and contemporary life

The contemporary arts and social criticism carry a recurrent theme of the individual uprooted, without a secure place in society, and without personal commitment in a world he evaluates as lacking worthy moral foundations. It is a theme of alienation describing frustration, anxiety, and insecurity. It stands in sharp contrast to Western culture's earlier description of the confident, self-sufficient individual as the motor of progress, advocate of righteousness, and defender of freedom. Describing a youthful revolt of great diversity, Roszak claims there is a common thread in the rejection of a technological totalitarianism he describes as burying human creativity and personal involvement under a rationalism that has organized society to maintain the efficiency of the productive apparatus.[5] Gerson attributes alienation to characteristics of urban society which include submission to the mechanical controls of industrial technology. The impersonal rationality of bureaucratic organization is found in institutions outside the economic realm, as well. Science and secularism have sapped religious faith and brought a disenchantment with the myths which previously enlisted men within the social institutions. Conspicious consumption has lost much of its former justification as the reward for accomplishment through work.[6]

As a term, *alienation* is useful in describing what goes on in the mind and emotions of some kinds of people, but Seeman sees it more as a code word, like "law and order," which tells us more about the user's style than about the substance of issues. We suggest further that a blanket indictment of contemporary technology oversimplifies complex issues (to be presented in Chapter 4).[7] Elsewhere, Seeman outlined some versions of its meaning.[8]

First, *powerlessness* refers to the expectation of the individual that his own behavior cannot determine the social outcome he seeks. This notion emerged from Karl Marx's contention that capitalism, in separating manual

[5] Theodore Roszak, *The Making of a Counter Culture* (Garden City, N.Y.: Doubleday & Co., 1969).

[6] Walter M. Gerson, "Alienation in Mass Society: Some Causes and Responses," in Clifton D. Bryant (ed.), *Social Problems Today: Dilemmas and Dissensus* (Philadelphia, Pa.: J. B. Lippincott Co., 1971), pp. 25–29.

[7] Melvin Seeman, his review in *American Journal of Sociology,* Vol. 77 (September 1971), pp. 351–53, of Richard Schacht, *Alienation* (Garden City, N.Y.: Doubleday & Co., 1970).

[8] Melvin Seeman, "On the Meaning of Alienation," *American Sociological Review,* Vol. 24 (December 1959), pp. 783–91.

workers from influence over means of production, had made them power-less. Seeman would depart from polemics and direct the idea of powerlessness to the pessimism the individual has that he can influence events in political, industrial, or other spheres of the larger social order. Racial riots have been explained under the concept of alienation, and the creation of "black power" has been advocated as a means for remedying the racial discrimination seen as a source of alienation.[9]

The second version of alienation, *meaninglessness,* emphasizes the uncertainty of the individual about what he ought to believe. Whereas powerlessness emphasizes a feeling that control of outcomes is beyond an individual's grasp, meaninglessness refers to his feeling that he cannot explain events or predict what the future holds. The decline of the work ethic has made leisure a social problem by weakening motivational bonds between occupation and other spheres of life. There is a prospect that at least a large share of Americans no longer has to labor strenuously and continually to acquire the benefits of an advanced technology. If work, which has traditionally been the core of an ethic of self-justification and accomplishment, has lost its moral force, can some new ethic be provided to give meaning to an individual's life? [10]

Third, *isolation* indicates an "apartness from society" whereby the individual places low personal priority on the goals or beliefs typically highly valued in the given society. Usually this refers to the intellectual who is detached in his own motivation from the usual quest for economic rewards. Isolation is also characteristic of the rebel against the established order. From this perspective stems much of the concern over the possible deterioration of "high culture" by mass communication media.[11]

Fourth, *self-estrangement* refers to a conception of oneself as an alien. One's own personality becomes an instrument of an alien purpose. The salesman finds that his job requires behavior which he regards as out of keeping with his conception of himself. He makes an instrument of himself for purposes which do not enlist his full personal commitment. Although he stands apart from himself as a salesman, he behaves as one for the sake of rewards outside of this activity; for example, the benefits he gains through the income earned. Mass production technology has been described as depriving the worker of his autonomy and thrusting him into work roles denying him personal satisfactions. Scientists debate whether they can remain aloof from the application of their research findings which are alien to their personal values.[12]

Fifth, Seeman finds a *normlessness* theme of alienation referring to a breakdown or loss of effectiveness of social norms in regulating individual conduct. The social structure is supposed to provide the individual a basis

[9] See Chapter 15.
[10] See Chapter 11.
[11] See Chapter 10.
[12] See Chapter 4.

for predicting the outcome of his interaction with other persons and to provide a regularity of social behavior. Later in this chapter we will consider *anomie,* a concept developed by Émile Durkheim and refined and elaborated by Robert K. Merton, which is relevant here. Seeman believes alienation as "normlessness" converges with anomie in the loss of commonly held standards and the development of instrumental, manipulative attitudes. The alienated individual believes that socially unapproved behaviors are required to achieve given goals.

In society's responses to member needs, Etzioni distinquishes between authentic and inauthentic responses. In *authentic responses,* the appearance of a response to member needs is supported by an underlying structure. Claims of racial tolerance, for example, are supported by an employing organization through its hiring and promotion practices. In *inauthentic responses,* the appearance of response is only a symbolic front for an underlying rejection of member needs. Claims of racial tolerance would be only surface conformity to ideals; in reality the employing organization would practice exclusion of minority groups.[13] We adopt this distinction to suggest that the violation in practice of norms given lip service breeds a mistrust of organizations and of other persons with whom the individual interacts.

DEVIANCE AND SOCIAL DISORGANIZATION

Although there are descriptive linkages between social problems and the several versions of alienation, "normlessness" is the most pertinent to our study. It directs attention to the relationship between norms and social problems in terms of both deviance and social disorganization. The concept of social deviance focuses on the individuals who comprise the population of problems. The concept of social disorganization concentrates on the social structure affected by the problems.

Nature and consequences of deviance

Instead of regarding the deviant as only an individual, the sociologist emphasizes the normative systems according to which the "deviant" receives responses from the community, and according to which he evaluates his own behavior. This statement implies·that "normative systems" include the possibility of a deviant subculture providing a different evaluation than that characteristic of the dominant culture as expressed in its criminal law, administrative codes, and policies of public and private agencies.

[13] Amitai Etzioni, "Basic Human Needs, Alienation, and Inauthenticity," *American Sociological Review,* (Vol. 33 (December 1968), pp. 880–81.

Deviant behavior, Cohen says, is behavior violating institutionalized expectations—that is, expectations which are shared and recognized as legitimate within a social system.[14] He calls attention to implications of this definition. Although deviance obviously can upset the tranquility of a community, the deviants are not necessarily pathological or otherwise abnormal in personality or behavior.[15] The emphasis in the definition on "departure from institutional expectations" implies that study of the various kinds of deviance also involves normative conformity. In our terms, the study of social deviance is the study of the societal factors revealed by their failure to operate successfully (in the case of the deviant himself) and of the societal reactions to the deviant conduct.

Deviance can produce social disorder by upsetting the reciprocal agreements through which an aggregate of individuals are able to coordinate their behaviors. Already we have seen that bending of rules is to be expected,[16] but at some point the quantity and/or quality of rule violations exceed the capacity of the families, economic enterprises, or other social units in a society to maintain stability. When there is high probability that the other fellow will fail to carry out his side of a role bargain, essential faith in the workings of the social system is eroded. Why follow the rules when you gain insufficient benefits and the other fellow may even exploit you?

Conversely, social disorder provides a fertile setting for expression of deviant tendencies. The workings of the social system, especially in a time of a high rate of social change, can contribute to faulty and inappropriate socialization of persons. Even when the individual is schooled properly in role expectations, new social conditions may render his conformity with outmoded norms to be less efficient in gaining satisfactory outcomes.

Deviant behavior does not necessarily constitute social disorganization because the transgression may not interrupt the flow of cooperative activities which enable the society to achieve its purposes. The society continues to function in spite of some crime, sexual irregularities, and other forms of deviance. The norms continue to be supported by penalties intended to minimize the effects on cooperative activities. Cohen compares this to the ejection from a baseball game of the player who strikes another player; the game itself proceeds. Disorganization does occur, however, if the game is ended by the ejection of so many that a full team cannot be put on the field. Deviant behavior, then, *can* produce social disorganization but does not do so necessarily.[17]

In some respects deviance may be a necessary price for preservation

---

[14] Albert K. Cohen, "The Sociology of Social Disorganization and Deviant Behavior," in Robert K. Merton, Leonard Broom, and Leonard S. Cottrell, Jr., *Sociology Today: Problems and Prospects* (New York: Basic Books, 1959), pp. 462–63.

[15] See "How Different Are Deviants?" Chapter 1, pp. 17–21.

[16] See Chapter 1.

[17] Cohen, "Sociology of Social Disorganization," pp. 476–77.

of the institutional order.[18] First, institutionalized evasion of the rules may advance the purposes of the legitimate organization. Second, deviance may provide flexibility to the social order if today's nonconformist becomes a model for accepted role performance in the new conditions of tomorrow's social order. Third, deviance may serve as a safety valve by preventing the excessive accumulation of frustration and discontent when social regulation appears excessive or when legitimate provision for satisfaction is insufficient.

Psychological discomfort is inevitable to some degree in every society because of the many pressures and difficult demands made upon individuals in their social roles. Usually, societies provide some means for management of tensions arising from conflict between the interests of individuals and the interests of the group. These means may include statuses or subcommunities to shelter eccentric, vulnerable, and disturbed persons. However, social structures differ in the degree and nature of such provisions.[19]

Tolerance and differential responses

The severity of societal reaction to a given type of misconduct is related to the seriousness with which it is regarded within a hierarchy of norms. *Tolerance* here refers to the degree to which a particular kind of deviance is permitted to proceed without the active intervention of other persons, as individuals or as a collectivity, to oppose, suppress, or eliminate the misconduct.

Criminal law and administrative codes were framed and are administered in reference to the relative importance placed on various forms of misconduct. To be considered binding on the conduct of individuals, the laws and administrative codes must be accepted as "proper" and "good" according to the moral values held by society in general. If the law does not enjoy this general moral support, enforcement becomes difficult, if not impossible, since it relies substantially on attitudes in the community to stimulate law observance as a matter of conscience.

Only human beings define, regulate, and control the behavior of their fellow beings, Lemert says.[20] People feel for or against things; culture is an abstract concept without such capacity. Groups are networks of social interaction through which control of behavior occurs, but the group's priority of norms is not the equivalent of the priority employed by the individuals in their daily behavior, nor are the norms idealized in the "official" morality necessarily the same as those which influence the daily behavior of individuals. This difference can be observed when the morality

---

[18] See Chapter 1, pp. 21–26; also Albert K. Cohen, *Deviance and Control* (Englewood Cliffs, N.J.: Prentice-Hall, 1966), pp. 6–11.

[19] See Chapter 19, pp. 476–77.

[20] Edwin M. Lemert, *Human Deviance, Social Problems, and Social Control* (Englewood Cliffs, N.J.: Prentice-Hall, 1967), p. 5.

verbalized in public is compared with the private practices of individuals with respect to gambling, use of alcohol, misuse of other people's property, sexual behavior, and so on.

The discrepancy between private and official morality raises the possibility that the public will over time change its negative reaction to what is now considered unacceptable conduct. There is the further possibility that the policies of government and other organizations in society will be changed as they respond to a new climate of moral evaluation.

The possibility of change in sternness of reaction can be illustrated through the concept of *tolerance quotient.* In this fraction the numerator is a measure of the amount of some disapproved conduct in a community, while the denominator is a measure of the degree of tolerance the residents have for that conduct.[21] At some level of relationship between the measures, the community will endure prostitution, drug use, illegitimacy, and other forms of deviance. The probability that a given form of disapproved behavior will be defined as a social problem depends on changes in the relationship between the numerator and denominator. The incidence of the behavior may be increased sufficiently to exceed the prevalent level of tolerance, or greater social visibility may reflect redoubled public attention given offenses which had not departed in quantity or quality from the state at which they previously attracted relatively little concern. Finally, concurrent decrease or increase in both numerator and denominator may cancel each other out in varying degrees.

The popular perception of the threat of deviance is not necessarily accurate. Schur notes that the relatively harmless aspects of deviation do not receive wide attention. Opponents of reform tend to deemphasize the real effects of opiates on the addict's behavior, the relative safety of most hospital abortions, and the great variety of behavior among homosexuals.[22] Injection of heroin into a vein arouses little concern when a nurse acts under a physician's instructions, but injection arouses great fears when it is associated with images of attacks by drug-crazed men on a lonely street. The fact that addicts, when criminal, engage primarily in petty theft does little to dilute this fear.[23]

Significance of social disorganization

Social disorganization has been defined as a decrease of the influence of existing social rules upon individual members of the group.[24] A society

[21] Edwin M. Lemert, *Social Pathology* (New York: McGraw-Hill Book Co., 1951), pp. 57–58.

[22] Edwin M. Schur, *Crimes without Victims* (Englewood Cliffs, N.J.: Prentice-Hall, 1965), p. 175.

[23] Howard S. Becker, "Deviance and Deviants," *Nation,* Vol. 201 (September 20, 1965), p. 115.

[24] William I. Thomas and Florian Znaniecki, *The Polish Peasant in Europe and America,* 2 vols. (New York: Alfred A. Knopf, 1927), pp. 1852–55.

is considered "disorganized" when the unity of the group declines because the institutionalized patterns of behavior are no longer effective and the social controls over individual behavior break down. Chapter 1 summarizes the basis for synchronizing the behavior of individuals into the normative framework of social institutions and roles and statuses within groups which compose the society.

Social problems involving deviance develop because of the failure of people to live up to the requirements of their statuses in the society, but, Merton says, social disorganization involves the faulty organizations of these statuses in a reasonably coherent social system.[25] Social disorganization theories associate social problems with such matters as social change, disharmony among groups composing society, value conflicts, and inadequacies of normative guidelines to individuals which diminish the effectiveness of social organization.

Social disorganization is a relative term. Because a society exists only if the relationships within it are organized, the term suggests some *degree* of disorganization. In fact, Ibrahim prefers "disorganization in society," a term which concentrates attention on the effects of conflicts among socially organized groups who are segments of the society.[26] Social disorganization is relative also in that it is one of the stages of transition from organization through disorganization to reorganization through which a society proceeds. In the organization stage, some groups become restive and protest the conditions they find unsatisfactory in the contemporary social order. Upholders of the status quo strive to curb disintegration of this order. In the disorganization stage, recognition spreads that social problems exist, and some remedial or reform efforts are undertaken. In the reorganization stage, some new social order is established to prepare the way for a new cycle.[27]

As a concept, social disorganization is also relativistic when used to indicate that only conformity is organized and that drug abuse, crime, unwed motherhood, and other forms of deviance are evidence of an absence of socially patterned behavior. The concept becomes a vehicle for a conservative view that deviance is simply personal disorganization of antisocial individuals unable to accommodate themselves to any form of social discipline. Actually, deviance may be socially organized, although the purposes sought and/or the means employed run counter to the moral values of the dominant group. Chapter 1 presented evidence that deviants

---

[25] Robert K. Merton, "Social Problems and Sociological Theory," in Robert K. Merton and Robert Nisfet (eds.), *Contemporary Social Problems* (3d ed.; Harcourt Brace Jovanovich, 1971), p. 823.

[26] Azmy Ishak Ibrahim, "Disorganization in Society, But Not Social Disorganization," *American Sociologist,* Vol. 3 (February 1968), pp. 47–48.

[27] Ernest W. Burgess, "Social Problems and Social Processes," in Arnold M. Rose (ed.), *Human Behavior and Social Processes* (Boston, Mass.: Houghton Mifflin Co., 1962), pp. 385–86.

and nondeviants resemble each other in many ways and that deviance exists within legitimate organizations. A description of the slum as "disorganized" ignores its structure of social relationships which is organized around various combinations of discrete systems of conventional and deviant values. Cloward and Ohlin refer to "illegitimate opportunity structures" whereby criminal behavior is derived from stable accommodations between "adult carriers of conventional and of deviant values."[28] For example, through bribery of officials the criminal systematically avoids punishment and through "fences" the thief has an outlet for stolen goods.

CONTINUITY OF SOCIETY

Earlier we noted that socially problems are societal in two general respects.[29] First, the suffering of others becomes a condition which is deemed an appropriate public issue of the social structure. That is, recognition of a social problem involves the perception that undesirable conditions have an impact beyond the persons experiencing them most directly. Thereby, the problem is seen as worthy of effort from the society as an organized collectivity. Second, the intractability of problems and even their existence are attributed to the operation of the social structure. Problems of poverty, inadequate health care, and deficient education reflect the inferior access of some groups to the benefits of an advanced culture and a highly productive technology. Problems of community disorganization are then related to differential participation of groups in decision-making processes.

Social problems may be regarded as *societal* to the extent that they affect the continuity and survival of a society and its effectiveness in providing for the needs and desires of its members. Davis lists as *societal necessities* the common needs which must be met if any society is to survive as a going, living system. The population must be maintained through provision of nutriment, protection against injury, and reproduction of new members. There must be some division of function among the population as a scheme for allocating tasks and responsibilities. Group solidarity must be maintained through motivation of contacts between members, mutual tolerance among members, and resistance to outsiders. In sum, the social system must be preserved through a continuity of patterned relationships over the generations so that the society can be an instrument for member needs.[30]

---

[28] Richard A. Cloward and Lloyd E. Ohlin, *Delinquency and Opportunity* (Glencoe, Ill.: Free Press, 1960), pp. 154–59.
[29] See Chapter 1.
[30] Kingsley Davis, *Human Society* (New York: Macmillan Co., 1949), pp. 28–31.

Maintenance of population

A society obviously cannot exist without members. The population must be maintained through production and distribution of food, shelter, and other requirements for life. There must be sufficient reproduction to guarantee that there will be future generations. From the perspective of continuity of society as a purpose in itself, maintenance could be considered as a matter of physical survival of people. However, the other societal necessities imply that the maintenance of population involves an enlistment of individuals and groups in organized activities at a motivation level beyond a quest for individual physical survival.

The maintenance of the population is measured against social expectation of the particular culture. Current U.S. issues of poverty and racial discrimination center around a concept of relative deprivation which refers to the experiencing of privation and want in comparison with the imagined or actual lot of some other person or group. By suggesting the cultural nature of poverty and social discrimination, the concept moves these problems from the level of physical survival to the level of social aspirations which distinguish human beings from other creatures. A rising tide of expectations is associated with the potentiality of a highly productive economy for maintaining a high standard of living.

Similarly, the population problem of the United States does not now consist of a lack of numbers adequate to provide future generations, nor a rate of growth so great that it poses a threat of lack of means for subsistence. Rather than the prospect of physical deprivation produced by excessive population growth, Americans are concerned that both a high standard of living and the quality of the physical environment will be undermined.[31]

Division of function

Some social scheme appears necessary for the allocation of the tasks and responsibilities whereby needs are met through the cooperation of individuals and groups with one another. The system of roles and statuses is such a scheme; through it, individual behaviors are fitted into the mosaic of group life. The system of roles and statuses can promote social disorganization, especially in a dynamic society, through obscure definition of roles and through role conflicts which create disorder in spite of the individual's effort to conform to expectations.

The social structure can contribute to its own disorganization when the prescribed roles for a given individual are inconsistent with one another. When a person plays two or more roles, *role conflict* is the product of

[31] See Chapter 5.

the clash of the normative content of one role with the normative content of another. Behavioral conflict, Bates says, saps the effectiveness of the group in two ways.[32] The behavior called for by one norm, if performed, would cancel out the behavior called for by another norm. The father works long hours and is a dedicated subordinate in his employee role to support his child, but his absence from home runs counter to his parental duty to guide the child and show personal concern. Second, the person may be required to do at the same time two mutually exclusive things or to do something which automatically makes it impossible to do something else also required. The teen-ager, for example, is expected to "think for himself" and yet be obedient to his parents.

Urban society has conditions favorable to role conflict. It has heterogeneity of both population and cultural norms. The complexity of its occupations, groups, and class structure places individuals in social positions where they are subject to conflicting claims. Intergenerational conflict has attracted special notice with the growth of teen-age subcultures which have been described as standing in normative conflict with the family and school as adult-dominated institutions. Migration and movement up and down the social class ladder place individuals in statuses with role norms to which they have not been socialized.

Heavy reliance on formal controls may be attributed to failure of informal controls to elicit satisfactory role performance. A reliance on formal controls implies bureaucratic administration which, in turn, requires more deliberate training of personnel and coordination of their specialized activities in a consciously designed system of roles and statuses. The coordination of various consciously designed systems is difficult to achieve in a complex and interdependent urban society and provides further opportunities for role conflict.

Solidarity of the group

Cooperation within the social scheme is dependent on some mode of social interaction among members of the society to bind them into a community sharing a common life. The central task of sociology, Wirth believes, is the study of the consensus which group life influences the behavior of men. The mark of any society is the capacity of its members to understand one another and to act in concert to achieve common goals through common rules of behavior.[33] For the United States to exist as a nation, the behavior of millions of Americans must show regularity and coordination within a complex network of differing group affiliations. This

[32] Frederick L. Bates, "Some Observations Concerning the Structural Aspect of Role Conflict," *Pacific Sociological Review,* Vol. 5 (Fall 1962), p. 79.
[33] Louis Wirth, "Consensus and Mass Communication," *American Sociological Review,* Vol. 13 (February 1948), pp. 2–4.

society is possible because there is some degree of sharing of normative orientations, of continuous communication among the persons composing its population, and of constraints which lend predictability and patterning to behavior. Thereby, it operates as a social system.

With the growth of an interdependent large-scale society, highly advanced technologically, vast concentrations of power and complicated administrative machinery have developed. Wirth sees the future of democracy depending on whether or not effective two-way communication can be maintained between the leaders and the membership of giant political and economic structures. Through sharing a culture to which they have been socialized, the members of a society are supposed to enlist voluntarily in joint behavior. Chapter 3 will consider qualities of urban life which require more conscious engineering of consent among the governed. Inherent in urban problems of crime, management of city affairs, health care, and so on is the question of whether or not the strategies of bureaucracy and formal control lend themselves to maintaining social relationships among citizens so they are bound together into a community.

Wirth suggests that the possibility of building consensus among diverse groups lies in the capacity of their members to grope toward common understanding through communication with each other even when common experiences are scanty and superficial. He regards mass communications (analyzed in our Chapter 10) as of unprecedented importance in holding society together through dissemination of knowledge and elimination of apathy. However, there are problems of censorship and concentrated control of communication media.[34]

The social system must be perpetuated, at least in general character. Williams regards social systems, including modern nation-states, as relatively enduring sets of interrelated institutions that provide recurrent patterns for survival and reproduction of populations. Therefore, the societal necessitities already listed add up to the regularity and predictability of behaviors which make society an instrument for serving human purposes. Williams sees the stability of American society being maintained through *dynamic* processes of social integration whereby the sets of interrelated institutions endure in the face of diverse interests and the many changes impinging on differentiated but interdependent groups included within society. Rather than exhibiting a high degree of orderliness in more specific events, the social system persists through procedural agreements on how to maintain coordination in the midst of conflicts between special-interest groups and localized disruptions.[35] From these conflicts and disruptions emerge recognition of certain conditions as social problems. To an important degree, conflicts and disruptions are symptoms of social changes

[34] Ibid., pp. 10–12.
[35] Robin M. Williams, Jr., *American Society: A Sociological Interpretation* (3d ed.; New York: Alfred A. Knopf, 1970), pp. 584–87.

Wisconsin Department of Health and Social Services

A society cannot exist without members. If any society is to survive, it must provide nutriment, protection against injury, and for the reproduction of new members. However, the social problems of contemporary America attest that physical survival is only one of the necessities. These problems reflect the complexities of maintaining group solidarity and an effective allocation of tasks and thus a basis for cooperation among diverse peoples.

challenging the capacity of the social system to accommodate itself to new conditions in its environment.

SOCIAL CHANGE: A PREVALENT FORCE

When the social environment is modified so that the previous balance of social relationships is upset, we have *social change*. The sources of this change include the natural environment (climate, soil characteristics, mineral resources, and so on), demography (birth, death, and migration trends), technology (the sociocultural mode of converting natural resources to serve human needs), or the social structure. The term *social change* indicates that its relevance to social problems lies in its relationship to the organization of society. Subsumed under the concise list of sources are a host of more specific factors affecting the context within which the society operates. These factors are subject to variation from place to place and from time to time, thereby affecting their relationship with one another. Since society does not operate in a vacuum, the relevance of contemporary social arrangements is continually being tested by changes in the relationships among persons and groups.[36]

Inevitable but variable in rate

Change is inherent in the very structure which lends society its stability and persistence. Stability is a matter of equilibrium among forces of change, and the equilibrium in itself is impermanent and relative. The flesh-and-blood people who populate society are not fully socialized to its norms. Their unique experiences and the contingencies of their particular time in history affect their interpretations of the norms inherited from the past. Too, the norms attached to their roles and statuses are characterized by sufficient lack of specificity to permit some tolerance of deviance in behavior and to accommodate some conflict in interpretations among role performers.

As Moore reminds us, there are major characteristics of human societies and there are strains in social systems themselves which assure the probability of change.[37] The socialization processes are subjected to uncertainties by differences among families in child rearing, even for successive children in the same family and for various families in the same position in the social structure. Biological differences among individuals are combined with personality differences to accentuate the possibility of variations in the consequences of socialization. Because norms do not offer

[36] For more extended analysis, see Richard T. LaPierce, *Social Change* (New York: McGraw-Hill Book Co., 1965), especially Chapter 7.

[37] Wilbert E. Moore, "A Reconsideration of Theories of Change," *American Sociological Review*, Vol. 25 (December 1960), pp. 810–18.

specific role guidelines, they are flexible in the face of new social circumstances. Changes in the birth and death rates affect the composition of the rising generation to alter the distribution of population among the social classes and other social categories. Economic scarcities of goods and services strain the traditional relationships between groups of similar importance. There is an insufficiency of loyalty to equal the total demands of various competing social groups. Shifts in political, economic, and social loyalities will affect the fulcrum of power in the community to bring on the controversies associated with social problems.

Times of rapid social change are especially likely to produce behavior out of keeping with the norms of the dominant culture. New situations are often inappropriate settings for traditional norms in guiding individuals toward personally satisfactory solutions. The norms learned during childhood in one setting may not fit the circumstances experienced in other settings in adolescence and adulthood. Individuals differ in their predisposition to cast off old forms of behavior and to accept new ones, but opportunities to learn new ways are not equivalent among all groups. Rapid social change may upset the social interaction within groups which would otherwise provide means of modifying the norms to fit the new circumstances.

Type of social organization as a factor

Sociologists have seen distinctions in the types of social organization which affect the rate of change. One polar type is characterized by similarities among members of the society. This type has been given various labels: _Gemeinschaft,_[38] mechanical solidarity,[39] and sacred society.[40] A strong identification among members is developed through efficient socialization to their culture and an intimacy is developed over a protracted period of living with one another. A small number of members encourages intensive intimacy. The organization of economic activities is such that each man performs about the same tasks as the other fellow, and this low degree of division of labor provides a similarity of work experience.

Because the group is isolated from dissimilar groups, few strangers appear to challenge the customs and beliefs which the elders pass on to the rising generation. The traditional ways are defined as sacred, the innovator as profane. Heavy reliance is placed on informal social controls derived from efficient internalization of group norms through socialization.

---

[38] Ferdinand Töennies, _Fundamental Concepts of Sociology,_ trans. Charles P. Loomis (New York: American Book Co., 1940), pp. 21–22.

[39] Émile Durkheim, _The Division of Labor in Society,_ trans. George Simpson (Glencoe, Ill.: Free Press, 1947), p. 100.

[40] Howard Paul Becker, _Man in Reciprocity_ (New York: Frederick A. Praeger, 1956), pp. 191–93.

The low degree of division of labor, the homogeneity of belief, and the isolation from competing ideas combine to deter change.

The other polar type derives its social cohesion from differences among the group members. It has been called, alternatively, _Gesellschaft,_[41] organic solidarity,[42] and secular society.[43] The members are tied together by an interdependence of self-interests and differing roles. A high division of labor creates a situation in which a number of specialists concentrate on a particular kind of work or segment of the total process of production. For example, all the items composing a completed automobile are fashioned by a wide range of specialists frequently working in sites separated physically from one another. These items then are assembled in one place to make automobiles. The distribution and sale of the completed automobiles are carried out by a number of other specialists who compose an organization lending ultimate significance to production by placing the finished product in the hands of consumers.

The many roles have a mutual interdependence, but the relationships between persons are restricted to a specific segment of total social life. The relationships tend to be impersonal, although an etiquette for the sake of efficient manipulation of one another may call for at least a superficial appearance of personal concern. Traditions are less effective than in a _Gemeinschaft_ in evoking conformity in a relatively automatic manner because persons are likely to weigh ends and means in a conscious process. Ease of contact with other groups exposes members to new and unfamiliar ideas and beliefs and contributes to a heterogeneity of socialization experiences in preparing children for adult behavior. Innovation tends to be welcome because resistance to change is at a minimum. The high level of division of labor, the heterogeneity of cultural norms, and the greater prevalence of change make for a social stability based more on a moving equilibrium than on a constancy of past social arrangements.

The United States has been particularly prone to change because of qualities linked to its history and because of the _Gesellschaft_ character of its urban society. A relative lack of rigid class lines has been congenial to social mobility under an individualistic ideology that declares that the talented and ambitious should be free to find their place in society. Till just a few centuries ago, the North American continent had not been previously exposed to Western technology, and thus it provided remarkable economic opportunities. Immigrants brought a variety of traditions with them to contribute to a cultural heterogeneity which loosened the grip of traditions of their particular native culture.

---

[41] Töennies, _Fundamental Concepts of Sociology,_ p. 23.
[42] Durkheim, _Division of Labor in Society,_ p. 131.
[43] Howard Paul Becker, _Man in Reciprocity,_ pp. 193–95.

Evaluation of change

Americans tend to be ambivalent toward change. Many citizens mourn the passing of familiar and traditional ways that they identify with a previous "golden age" in which "wise forefathers" were infallible. Change is identified with the rise of "alien" forces and the corruption of the "American way of life." However, as Chapter 4 will note, the American faith in "progress" welcomes the idea of "bigger" and "better" accomplishments toward some superior future. In fact, this faith opposes as unthinkable any policy of restricting technological development out of ethical and social considerations.

Social change, LaPiere points out, is significant in that it occurs outside the regular patterns of organized society.[44] In fact, social organizations resist change as deleterious to the consistencies in their environment that they have been designed to manage. In this respect, change may be evaluated as a form of deviance and it is likely to be associated with persons who are unorthodox by the organization's standards. The evaluation of social change by theorists is related to their conception of how society is held together. Among sociologists, the evaluation of change falls at various points between two polar positions which have been described as *order theories* and *conflict theories*.[45] As abstractions, the two categories underestimate the major agreement that both consensus and conflict are continually present in American society.

Order theories (and these are predominant among sociologists) see the society unified through a normative consensus derived from a shared culture and agreements on values. Society is supposed to have a relatively persistent and stable structure in which behaviors in families, economic groups, churches, schools, and so on occur in regular patterns to produce a smoothly operating social system. The integration of these elements is attributed to consensus, that is, a general agreement among the members on the norms fundamental to the group's continued existence.

Although adherents to such theories hold diverse views, varying in emphasis, there is a tendency among them all to regard social change as deleterious to the social order. Social problems are likely to be attributed to a breakdown of the social order, and deviance from the obligatory norms is conceived as being held in check by social controls safeguarding this order. In some instances, deviants would be seen as persons out of adjustment with their legitimate social roles.

Conflict theories see society as a product of accommodations among

---

[44] LaPiere, *Social Change,* p. 39.

[45] Ralf Dahrendorf, *Class and Class Conflict in Industrial Society* (Stanford, Calif.: Stanford University Press, 1959), pp. 157–62; John Horton, "Order and Conflict Theories of Social Problems as Competing Ideologies," *American Journal of Sociology,* Vol. 71 (May 1966), pp. 701–21, including commentaries of Bert N. Adams and Robin M. Williams, Jr.

continually contesting groups with opposing goals and perspectives. Social change and social conflict is supposed to exist in an indefinite number of places at once. These theorists argue that contemporary society is maintained through force and constraint maintained by the dominant group. Interpreting Georg Simmel's writings, Coser finds conflict between groups serving purposes other than the social disruptions and intergroup tensions usually associated with conflict. Through hostility directed at other groups, the individual's ties to his own group are strengthened. In fact, social conflict always denotes social interaction requiring agreement that an issue exists and that disagreements should be controlled within limits. Paradoxically, aversions are means of maintaining social stability under conditions of changing distributions of power, wealth, and status. Adversaries of yesterday find common interests today to maintain stability of the total social order through changes in the power structure.[46]

Social problems are explained as the failure of the current order to meet changing individual needs as a product of the exploitative practices of the dominant group which subvert the natural growth of human personality. Social change is supposed to arise from the alienation produced by exploitation and to be a means of reorganizing the social order to bring it in line with human needs. Deviance is seen as a means of transforming existing relationships into a better form.

HOW SOCIETY CONTRIBUTES TO PROBLEMS

Sociology treats social problems as expressions of the workings of the social and cultural systems of society. The individual, whether a deviant or not, whether a full participant in society's affairs or not, and whether a recipient of the full benefits of the services a modern community is supposed to provide or not, is a product of learned behavior within the context of a normative system which transforms an aggregate of individuals into an organized group. Deviance becomes defined as a social problem when departures from the norms are seen as threatening this social order. Drug addiction, crime, and mental illness become subjects for reactions from other members of the community and the formal organizations assigned primary responsibility in dealing with such deviance. From the perspective of the social order, the deviance is seen as upsetting to the social system that synchronizes behaviors within the community. However, any scheme whereby individual behaviors are currently synchronized may be the source of social problems by promoting the probability of deviance or by failing to meet societal necessities. The high rate

[46] Lewis A. Coser, *The Functions of Social Conflict* (New York: Free Press, 1956), pp. 33–38, 121–37.

of change characteristic of urban society is a central source of disturbance in keeping the social organization current with human needs.

There are several theoretical approaches which have been taken to indicate the ways in which social and cultural systems are factors in the existence of social problems, and it is time now to discuss them.

Deregulation of the individual

From one perspective, deviant behavior is released by the breaking of the conventional order which has held individuals in check. In explaining the social factors behind suicide, for instance, Durkheim refers to "anomic suicide" which results from the lack of regulation of the individual by society. He applies the term *anomy* (or *anomie*) to a condition of lack of regulation by the cultural norms, as when crisis or abrupt social transition undermines the normative system supporting the society.[47]

As a sociocultural creature, man has appetites beyond those unleashed by his organic constitution such as hunger and sex. Therefore, Durkheim says, man's desires surpass the means at his command for their gratification. Unless his desires are limited by some source external to him, man will experience great restlessness. The norms of his society operate as such a limitation. When the controls of the moral order are removed, the restlessness is released to make the individuals intolerant of all other limitations he will encounter. "All the advantages of social influence are lost so far as they are concerned; their moral education has to be recommenced."[48]

An abrupt growth of power and wealth has such an effect, Durkheim believes, because the traditional ways of distributing rewards and privileges are upset by the greater scale of social resources. Previous limits on human aspirations are lifted for some people who previously were curbed by the moral order. The abrupt growth of power and wealth of society strains the patterns of relationships which had been characteristic, and the new conditions require that a new system of moral limitations be established to regulate behavior. Time is required for a new public conscience to be developed to distribute privileges and rewards to limit the aspirations of men in keeping with the maintenance of social order. Meanwhile, the securing of power and wealth deceives men into believing that they depend only on themselves and produces a state of "anomy" where the previously operating norms no longer regulate man's behavior. Durkheim saw this situation of normlessness as a consequence of the disruption of the sociocultural basis of society.

[47] Émile Durkheim, *Suicide: A Study in Sociology,* trans. John A. Spaulding and George Simpson (Glencoe, Ill.: Free Press, 1951), pp. 246–54.
[48] Ibid., p. 252.

Contradictions in society

The properties of the social system are more directly related to deviance in the idea of "socially structured strain." In his own theory of *anomie,* Merton extends Durkheim's concept of "deregulation" to attribute deviance to the operation of society.

"Social structures," Merton says, "exert a definite pressure upon certain persons in the society to engage in nonconformist rather than conformist conduct." [49] He makes two distinctions. First, the culture holds out certain objectives (ends) for members of the society. For example, in American schools, television, newspapers, and other instruments for conveying messages about the purposes of life, a persistent theme is that materialistic "success" is a proper objective. Second, society provides an opportunity structure within which the culturally shaped aspirations are to be achieved. In a culture encouraging individuals to dream of a better life for themselves, the realization of the dream depends on the realities of the social structure. How much room *is* there at the "top" for those theoretically qualified by personality and special training? How much turnover *is* there among the occupants of the top positions to make room for newcomers? How is essential training acquired and what determines who gets the training? In other words, the social means of attaining the culturally shaped ends are structured within the given society.

Socially structured strain occurs when the social means block the culturally shaped ends to create a contradiction. Legitimate avenues for economic and social opportunity are not equally available to all members of society in spite of the myths of American democracy. Conformity to role expectations does not bring the rewards held out by the American culture because of differential opportunity to gain a quality education. Poverty and racial discrimination illustrate such structural strain in that the workings of society itself operate in conflict with the ideology of equal opportunity for all.

Merton specifies five typical patterns of adjustment in the face of this structural strain. In *conformity,* the individual accepts both cultural ends and restrictions on social means actually available to him. The other four patterns comprise deviance. Under *ritualism,* the high cultural ends are scaled down by the individual and the approved social means are followed slavishly. One example would be a clerk in the lower-status level of a bureaucracy who compulsively follows "company rules" without questioning their ultimate meaning.

Under *innovation,* the cultural goals are accepted but not the moral restrictions on means proscribed by the legitimate social structure. The quest for "success," power and wealth is undertaken in keeping with

[49] Robert K. Merton, *Social Theory and Social Structure* (Glencoe, Ill.: Free Press, 1949), pp. 125–28, 134–46.

cultural goals, but criminal or unethical practices are employed as means. *Rebellion* involves rejection of both cultural ends and the legitimate means as the radical individual aspires to revise the social order. Chronic drunkards, drug addicts, psychotics, and vagrants would be examples of persons undertaking *retreatism.* These people drop out of the competition for rewards to be *in* society but not *of* it.

Cloward and Ohlin make a valuable modification of Merton's means-ends theory by pointing out that an illegitimate opportunity structure exists in addition to the social structure which Merton cites as serving as a barrier against certain groups achieving the cultural goals held out to all.[50] Among others, Whyte has noted that the slum area is not disorganized; rather, the social organization of the slum does not mesh with the structure of the society around it. Slum youth must choose between two worlds: the world of business and politics controlled by upper-class people, and the slum world of rackets and politics based on support of local people.[51]

Culture and social problems

Given the size and complexity of American society, one would expect a number of relatively autonomous groups to be included and a variety of cultural values to be found. Beneath a common allegiance to the same national authority and to very broad cultural values, there are appreciable differences in language, religion, racial attitudes, child-rearing techniques, occupational attitudes, and so on.[52] A number of explanations for social problems, then, start with the fact of cultural heterogeneity in a socially differentiated and dynamic society.

In the days of heavy immigration, social disorganization tended to be attributed to *cultural conflict* stemming from the divergence of the standards and codes of certain ethnic groups from those of the dominant group. Sellin explained crime and delinquency in terms of such conflict, the shift of immigrants from a rural to an unfamiliar urban environment, and their movement from a well-organized, homogeneous society to a disorganized heterogeneous society.[53] There was special interest in the children of immigrants, who were supposed to be particularly prone to deviance because they became marginal people unsocialized to the "old" culture of their parents and yet not adhering to the "American" norms.

A subculture approach has been employed to explain distinctive behavior among the poor, criminals, slum-dwellers, delinquents, racial minorities, illicit drug users, college students, alcohol drinkers, adolescents, and

[50] Cloward and Ohlin, *Delinquency and Opportunity,* pp. 150–60.

[51] William Foote Whyte, *Street Corner Society* (enlarged ed.; Chicago: University of Chicago Press, 1955), pp. 272–74.

[52] Williams, *American Society,* p. 415

[53] Thorsten Sellin, *Cultural Conflict and Crime* (New York: Social Science Research Council, 1938), pp. 83, 130.

sexual deviants. *Subculture,* Roach and Gursslin say, has been used in two senses.[54] First, the term has been used to refer to the *cause* of the behavior associated with a given problem. For example, the poor are supposed to exhibit distinctive behavior and attitudes because they learn a subculture of poverty which is passed down through the generations to lend regularity to their behavior and attitudes as a distinctive and persistent group. Second, the term has been used as a *description* of regularities in action and thought in the given group. These regularities may be the product of similarities in current experiences of the group members rather than an indication of distinctive cultural content relayed down a chain of generations. (One difficulty with the subculture approach, is that it does not distinquish between subcultures. Juvenile delinquents, for example, may also represent higher or lower socioeconomic subcultures, ethnic or racial subcultures, or an adolescent subculture.)

Deviance which appears to be subcultural in cause may stem from the social-psychological influences of common experiences in an immediate environment and may be linked through norms with the larger culture. Yinger hypothesizes a *contraculture* wherever the normative system of a group contains, as a primary element, a theme of conflict with the values of the total society.[55] The personalities of the group members are congenial to development and maintenance of this conflict, and the norms of the group can be understood only in reference to the allegedly larger culture. The alleged slow and inefficient work of the rural black in the South, for example, may be a malingering reaction to racial discrimination, while the distinctive behavior of adolescents reverses the values of an adult-dominated culture to express the tensions accruing from the marginal status of this age group. The hostility of the delinquent gang is a product of blocked ambition expressed in gang norms opposite to the dominant culture's emphasis on neatness, self-discipline, respect for private property, and so on.

In slum areas, Cohen sees a delinquent subculture persisting through transmission of beliefs, values, and knowledge down a succession of juvenile groups. Finding himself at the bottom of the prestige rankings of the middle class which dominates socioeconomic opportunity, a slum boy accepts the values of a delinquent subculture as the solution. These values are nonutilitarian, malicious, and negativistic; in other words, the opposite of the middle-class values which are being rejected by these rejected slum youths.[56]

Cloward and Ohlin believe that access to illegitimate means provides

[54] Jack L. Roach and Orville K. Gursslin, "An Evaluation of the Concept 'Culture of Poverty'," *Social Problems,* Vol. 45 (March 1967), pp. 386–87; see our Chapter 7.
[55] J. Milton Yinger, "Contraculture and Subculture," *American Sociological Review,* Vol. 25 (October 1960), pp. 625–35.
[56] Albert K. Cohen, *Delinquent Culture: The Culture of the Gang* (Glencoe, Ill.: Free Press, 1955), pp. 25–28.

relief to slum youth from pressures arising from limitations on access to legitimate means, and access to illegitimate means is seen as likely to produce a delinquent subculture.[57] Street gangs provide a form of age-grading by which boys "graduate" into older age gangs in successive stages of learning and performing deviant roles. Through contacts with criminals, dealers in stolen goods, police, politicians, and bail bondsmen, the adolescent learns the skills and folklore of the illegitimate world.

When the slum does not provide an accommodation between conventional and deviant cultures, the lack of an illegitimate opportunity structure leads to a *conflict subculture*. The violence of delinquent gangs expresses frustrations magnified by lack of opportunity and the inhibitions which would be imposed by the criminal enterpreneurs. When both legitimate and illegitimate opportunities are unavailable, the slum youth may adhere to a *retreatist subculture* because of his double failure. Identified largely with illicit drug use, this subculture is composed of individuals who withdraw into a world more restricted than the conventional or delinquent cultures. They learn the lore of drug use and means of making connections to obtain drugs. They develop a new pattern of associations and values related to drug use as a means of resolving anxiety and guilt through abandonment of the struggle for a place in the larger world.

Value conflicts and disorganization

Another aspect of culture is social value. In the course of experience people have come to prefer some things over others and have come to apply certain standards by which they make choices among objects or alternative courses of action in terms of such preferences. Americans judge things, beliefs, and social behavior through a screen of major value orientations. Personal achievement is stressed, with intensive activity and "work" honored as values in themselves. The individual is held in high regard, yet the emphasis on self-reliance occurs in a cultural environment which concurrently expresses a humanitarian concern for troubled people. Freedom from external and arbitary restraints is sought, yet—at the same time—there are pressures for external conformity. If this sketchy summary suggests that American value orientations are not consistent with one another, it is meant to.[58]

The very definition of a given condition as "undesirable" implies judgments on the basis of values. To define a housing problem in terms of the absence of inside plumbing is to apply the value judgment that inside plumbing is something every human being should have. To define crime in terms of taking goods without purchase is to accept the idea of private

---

[57] Cloward and Ohlin, *Delinquency and Opportunity*, pp. 161–86.
[58] For more complete discussion of American value orientations, see Williams, *American Society*, pp. 452–98.

property as a central value. Such a recognition of certain conditions as undesirable, together with the particular nature of those conditions, is related to the values characteristic of a given culture. The study of American social problems includes the study of American values and their contradictions.

As abstractions, values may be logically incompatible without creating social disorder, Turner says.[59] Although they are products of ongoing behavior, values acquire an existence partly independent of life activities once they become generalized conceptualizations stated in absolute terms. Because they are generalized, values are incomplete in designating exact guidelines for the variety of unique events. They become more symbolic of a generalized agreement that, for example, freedom of speech is sacred—whereas in actual practice, censorship, legal restriction of public gatherings, and ordinances against disturbance of the peace are also legitimatized. This logical inconsistency does not run counter to societal consensus, Turner explains, because the values acquire an empirical content in the culture which defies logic but is the basis of latent understandings. Also, logical inconsistency among values is usually likely to be sociologically irrelevant because the values are insulated from one another in practice. The "love for fellow man" heard on Sunday is divorced from the quest for profits the rest of the week because religious and business activities are compartmentalized.

Social disorganization, Turner contends, is related to value conflict when social values are called on to support contradictory patterns of behavior in *actual situations.* Attainment of one value in practice either violates or interferes with the attainment of other values. Therefore, to maintain social order, inconsistent norms must be insulated from one another, and groups with differing norms must be isolated from one another. Social change engenders value conflicts when previously isolated groups are placed in contact with one another, when previously compartmentalized activities are brought in social conjunction, or when special-interest groups differ in their willingness to relinquish old values which formerly legitimatized now outmoded courses of action. For example, industrialization, decline of regional isolation, migration, and increased knowledge of the world outside the individual's direct experience have undermined the patterns of compartmentalization which maintained racial segregation. In the contemporary problem of urban poverty, the values of charity and subsistence relief run counter to the need to maintain a high level of economic consumption for contemporary industrial technology.

The complex social structure of urban society creates social situations in which the discrepancies among major value orientations generate social

---

[59] Ralph H. Turner, "Value-Conflict in Social Disorganization," in Mark Lefton, James K. Skipper, Jr., and Charles H. McCaghy (eds.), *Approaches to Deviance* (New York: Appleton-Century-Crofts, 1968), pp. 24–31.

problems. Subsequent chapters in this book will provide illustrations. The reduction of the workweek and the greater number of retired persons in today's U.S. society have raised leisure to the stature of a social problem. Emphasizing activity and work as values, the work ethic persists—and runs counter to the broader distribution of leisure (Chapter 11). Development of mass communication media offers an unprecedented distribution of knowledge congenial to democratic values but, at the same time, poses the problems of concentrated ownership and "efficient" exploitation of economic opportunities by private enterprise (Chapter 10). Educational institutions are caught between demands for "efficiency" in preparing large groups of students for slots in the job system and yet recognizing them as unique individuals (Chapters 12 and 13). Racial discrimination flies in the face of humanitarianism, equality of opportunity, and emphasis on the worth of the individual, yet discriminatory practices are built into the ideological framework of society (Chapters 14 and 15). The spirit of individualism persists in criminal justice and medicine. The roots of our criminal law are in an individualism which fills prisons with petty offenders while largely overlooking white-collar offenders and the transgressions of large enterprises (Chapter 17). Medicine clings to the image of the physician in private practice and intimate supportive relationships with his patients in spite of a new context of medical practice dominated increasingly by teams of specialists in bureaucratic organizations (Chapter 18).

DEVIANCE AS ASSIGNED STATUS

Repeatedly the following chapters will refer to the price in social stigmatization imposed on persons associated with social problems. The welfare client is expected to accept the dishonor of failure. Lower-income groups receive less personalized and continuous medical care than those with greater financial resources. A theme of deviance is added to the theme of incompetence in the handling of mental illness. (The magnitude and intensity of deviant behavior may be attributed in large measure to the evaluations made of deviants by other persons, including the agents of the social structure.)

Some sociologists have employed the concept of deviance to focus attention on the social processes by which certain individuals become evaluated as deviants. Erikson defines *deviance* as conduct "which the people of a group consider so dangerous, or embarrassing or irritating that they bring special sanctions to bear against the persons who exhibit it." [60] Erikson asks us to consider the part played by other people in the appearance of deviance. To him, deviance is a property (trait or attribute) *con-*

---

[60] Kai T. Erikson, *Wayward Puritans: A Study in the Sociology of Deviance* (New York: John Wiley & Sons, 1966), p. 6.

ferred upon that behavior by the people who come in direct or indirect contact with it.

Deviance is conceived as a social process through which a social audience interprets behavior as deviant, defines persons who so behave as a certain kind of deviant, and responds to them in a manner deemed appropriate for that kind of deviant.[61] Certain behaviors are defined as "strange," "abnormal," "criminal," "crazy," and so on. As a consequence, the individual so labeled is placed in a deviant *status* whereby he is subjected by the social organization to the experiences which are deemed appropriate for his particular kind of deviant.

Property conferred by an audience

The definition focuses attention on the relationship between the individual's behavior and standards applied to behavior for his status in the particular social system. The emphasis is on this relationship rather than on the behavior per se because deviance is viewed as a property conferred upon this form of behavior by a social audience rather than as a property inherent in the behavior in and of itself.[62]

Theft, injection of drugs, and abortion are nonconformist acts in reference to norms against which the acts can be compared. Persons other than the actor (the audience) evaluate his act and render a judgment on its appropriateness. This social audience is composed of individuals involved in the immediate situation, but there is also a much larger number of less direct participants in the creation and maintenance of the set of norms being applied in the judgment. This larger audience has given legitimacy to the norms being applied.

Because his act is judged to depart significantly from the relevant norm, the act of theft results in the actor being placed in the social position of a thief, as evaluated by the audience. Because he is placed in the *status* of thief, he becomes eligible to receive the societal reactions deemed appropriate for a thief. The theft *plus* the placing of him in the status of thief initiate the sequence of societal reactions, such as arrest by the police, conviction in court, and commitment to prison. Usually, the deviant act is supposed to shock the public conscience, and the public reaction is seen as a product of the deviant act (in this case, theft). Taking a different tack, Durkheim says that it is the shock of public conscience which makes the act a crime because we reprove it.[63]

In emphasizing the transaction between some group and the rule-breaker, Becker is more concerned with the process whereby certain characteristics of deviants cause the group to create and employ the

[61] John T. Kitsuse, "Societal Reaction to Deviant Behavior: Problems of Theory and Method," *Social Problems,* Vol. 9 (Winter 1969), p. 248.
[62] Erikson, *Wayward Puritans,* pp. 6–7.
[63] Durkheim, *The Division of Labor in Society,* p. 81.

judgment that these individuals are deviants than he is with the personal and social characteristics of the individuals so judged. "Whether an act is deviant, then, depends on how other people react to it." In fact, the individual may be branded as a deviant when actually he has not broken the rule. Others may break the rule and still evade the conferring of the deviant status.[64]

Differentiation of act and personality

The definition of deviance distinguishes between the act and the personality of the actor.[65] It does not insist that the deviant is a pathological creature simply because he has departed from norms of high priority. Rather, most deviants are regarded as psychologically and physiologically normal. The deviant act does not capture all qualities of his total personality and all his behavioral repertoire. As Cohen asserts, it is essential to realize that the deviant, the abnormal, the psychopathic, and the deplorable do not necessarily come wrapped in a single package.[66]

The conferring of a property by an audience is prevalent in relationships with strangers by any group lacking opportunity to know them as full and well-rounded personalities. To react to strangers in social situations, we make quick judgments on the basis of their external qualities such as dress, dialect, or physical appearance. In reacting to other persons, we tend to code their behavior selectively, simplifying what we perceive. What we have come to assume about a certain category of persons is brought into play when we judge that a particular stranger should be lumped in that category. If we assume that women drivers are unreliable, we judge Miss Jones to be a poor driver because she is a woman.

In Goffman's terms, the stranger is given a *virtual social identity* in that certain characteristics are imputed to him.[67] It is assumed that he has certain personal attributes. His genuine attributes constitute his *actual social identity*. The discrepancy between these two kinds of identities taints and discounts the individual when the attributes ascribed are discreditable. The Greeks used "stigma" to refer to brands burned on the body and other bodily signs designed to advertise that the bearer should be avoided as a slave, a criminal, or a traitor. Now, Goffman asserts, the term has come to be applied more to the disgrace itself than to the bodily evidence of it.

In terms of deviance, then, *stigmatization* involves the imputation of

---

[64] Howard S. Becker, *Outsiders: Studies in the Sociology of Deviance* (New York: Free Press, 1963), pp. 9–12.

[65] See "The 'Abnormality' of Deviants," Chapter 1.

[66] Albert K. Cohen, "The Study of Social Disorganization," Merton et al., *Sociology Today*, p. 463.

[67] Erving Goffman, *Stigma: Notes on the Management of Spoiled Identity* (Englewood Cliffs, N. J.: Prentice-Hall, 1963), pp. 1–5.

imperfections to the individual beyond the specific one which caused him to be recognized by the audience as being different. The specific misconduct of the deviant makes him different from those not engaging in this kind of deviance and calls attention to him. This undesirable difference becomes the basis of judgments of him as thoroughly bad, dangerous, or weak. Discrepancies between virtual and actual social identity, then, are raw material for undermining the deviant's place in legitimate society.

The labeling concept emphasizes the initiating by the audience of the labeling process, with the deviant's participation receiving less attention. Lorber, however, points to possibilities that the deviant may also participate in the labeling process rather than being simply a passive target. The deviant may invite labeling by conveying an impression which he hopes will lead to the imposition of a certain label by his audience. Lorber cites the individual who exploits feigned or actual illness for sake of sympathy, avoidance of work, monetary benefits, or other secondary gains accorded the patient.[68]

Screening and differential responses

In seeing deviance as a property conferred upon the actor, the definition calls attention to the screening whereby only some of the actors are handled as deviants. A crucial issue is *why* only some of the deviants are subjected to the actions of the social control agents. Why are extreme measures taken against only *some* illegitimate mothers, *some* excessive drinkers, *some* property offenders, and so on? Why is there such strong action taken in one specific incident when it reflects only a portion of the actor's total attitudes and behavior?

Erikson suggests that the moment of deviation may become the measure of a person's position in society.[69] The deviant resembles categories of nondeviants in most respects. Even the worst criminal will resemble noncriminals in table etiquette, style of dress, recreational interests, or other forms of behavior expected of conventional persons. His violation of norms is frequently shared by other persons who are not regarded as proper subjects for jailing or hospitalization. There are law violators and persons suffering mental illness who never receive official attention. Therefore, rather than focusing exclusively on the deviant's behavior, Erikson directs attention to the screening process whereby the community sifts and codes the many details of behavior to which it is witness. Only certain forms of behavior draw the label of deviant.

The conferring of deviance as a property, we have already noted, carries the probability that the rulebreaker will be treated as though he

---

[68] Judith Lorber, "Deviance as Performance: The Case of Illness," *Social Problems,* Vol. 14 (Winter 1967), pp. 302–10.
[69] Erikson, *Wayward Puritans,* p. 6–8.

were alien in all respects. The convicted criminal is regarded as though he were totally dangerous. The drug addict is treated as though he were totally disorganized as a personality. The poverty-stricken man is seen as weak-willed. The societal reaction to the deviant goes beyond the punishment or therapy which would be justified logically by his deviance per se. Other aspects of his personality and a larger sphere of his behavior are also subject to negative evaluation.

Under his term *degradation ceremonies*, Garfinkel refers to relationships between persons whereby the public identity of an individual is reduced in the scale of respectability.[70] Every society provides organized means of inducing shame and guilt, thereby systematically motivating "proper" behavior. Garfinkel emphasizes the *public* nature of degradation ceremonies whereby moral indignation is expressed against behavior considered blameworthy. In effect, a public curse is delivered to reconstitute the identity of the person into something new, different, and less worthy in the eyes of his condemners. The degradation is stimulated by some event (perhaps a crime) which causes the perpetration to appear to be "out of the ordinary." The deviant event and the perpetrator are judged by the audience to qualify in every respect as an example of the particular behavior which is ardently condemned. He is judged to be another example—in all respects—of "the" drug addict, "the" thief, "the" negligent parent and so on.

Because the denunciation takes on a public character, it has great impact on the self-image of the perpetrator and on his reputation within the community. It is a ceremony in that it is part of the workings of a social system. The denouncer portrays himself as acting as a public figure: the judge imposing a prison sentence, the psychiatrist certifying the patient as mentally ill, and so on. Rather than acting according to his personal views, the denouncer is invested with authority to speak in the name of values of the community and thereby place the deviant outside the pale of the legitimate order.

In studies of inmates of prisons, mental institutions, and facilities for other kinds of problem people, there is reference to filtering of admissions according to criteria other than those officially stated. The selective processes whereby individuals end up in such institutions tend to draw heavily from the lower social classes, minority groups, categories of individuals with reputations for being problems, and persons judged as unorthodox by prevailing community standards. Inmate populations differ from noninmate populations in qualities which indicate that their characteristics reflect the operation of screening procedures according to criteria extraneous to the criminality, mental disorder, and other behavior which is supposed to justify commitment to the particular institution.

[70] Harold Garfinkel, "Conditions of Successful Degradation Ceremonies," *American Journal of Sociology*, Vol. 61 (March 1956), p. 420–24.

This form of screening explains the fluctuations from time to time and place to place in the commitment of individuals to correctional establishments. A given crime will draw punishments which vary in severity when the laws of various states are compared. Drives against gambling, vagrancy, drunkenness, sexual offenses, and other forms of deviance tend to be sporadic. These variations indicate that the intensity of screening is not constant. For example, fluctuations in the number of persons in mental hospitals and prisons do not necessarily measure the incidence in the community of mental illness or crime. Changes in institutional population are more likely to reflect changes in administrative processes whereby decisions are made on who goes to the institutions.

Process of becoming deviant

Deviance is seen as the product of a process which involves the responses of other people to the behavior. Usually, deviant motives are regarded as essential preconditions of deviant behavior. The use of illicit drugs is supposed to come after the person acquires motives to use drugs. Becker reverses the arrangement to argue that the deviant behavior in time produces the deviant motivation.[71] He illustrates his point through a study of marihuana users. Vague desires and curiosity entice the individual to use marihuana. Effective use, however, requires learning of the correct technique to produce the effects of "feeling high," to connect the symptoms with the drug, and to perceive the effects as pleasant. This learning involves him with marihuana users whose responses to his behavior are ingredients in the process of becoming a user.

Because he is called and treated as a deviant, the individual may come to see himself as a deviant, although he had not so conceived himself when he first transgressed. Lemert distinguishes between primary and secondary deviance. For a wide variety of reasons, the individual may engage in deviance, but he does not necessarily conceive of himself as a deviant. He may be a drug user without conceiving himself as eligible for the label of "drug addict." The housewife may engage in shoplifting, but not see herself as a thief. Thus, *primary deviance* is disapproved conduct without enlisting the self-identification of the transgressor with the deviant role. In *secondary deviance,* the person assumes deviant roles *after* he has been assigned to a deviant status through the societal reaction to his transgression. He reorganizes his attitudes toward himself and assumes deviant roles in coping with the problems created by the societal reaction.[72]

The distinction between primary and secondary deviance raises the issue of whether or not tentative rulebreaking is a valid harbinger of future

---

[71] Becker, *Outsiders,* pp. 41–58.
[72] Lemert, *Human Deviance, Social Problems, and Social Control,* p. 17.

deviance, perhaps of even more serious nature. With respect to mental illness, Scheff cites evidence showing that most primary deviance is amorphous and uncrystallized, and much of the behavior is transitory and prevalent among ostensibly "normal" persons. Then why is primary deviance stabilized to become characteristic of the individual's behavior? The conventional answer emphasizes the deviant's contribution to confirmed deviance. Scheff offers another possibility. The definition of questionable cases as mental disorders converts transitory incidents into commitment of the individual to playing the role of the mentally ill.[73]

The existence of primary deviation is indicated by a process to which Lemert attaches the term *risk taking*.[74] Some problem traps an individual in a network of conflicting normative claims. Among the alternative solutions, he selects one which carries the risk of being defined as antisocial, although this outcome is not inevitable. The risk exists because the individual does not control all the factors determining the outcome. If he has "bad luck," subsequent events will lead to an interpretation of his behavior as antisocial because he did violate norms to which strong penalties are attached. However, if the dice of chance roll in his favor, he continues to be defined as an honest man in keeping with his own self-image. His interpretation has some justification because the social system does provide for patterned evasion of its own rules when the ultimate objectives of the system are served. (Chapter 1 considered this paradox under the term "institutionalized evasion.")

As an example, Lemert cites building contractors who, in anticipation of scheduled construction loan payments, may write checks for their workers without sufficient funds on bank deposit. Caught between payroll claims and an immediate cash shortage, the contractor endeavors to solve his problem through a solution which risks charges of fraud if the loan payment does not arrive in time to make the checks valid. The timing of the loan payment is out of his control and will determine his "luck."

Something gets built into the psyche of the deviant when he is penalized for his primary deviation, because there is an imputation of special character qualities in classifying him as a deviant. For example, the physically handicapped person is assigned to a status which has significance beyond the handicap in and of itself. In the popular view, the crippled person is abnormal and incapable of performing as worker, parent, husband, and so on. When accepted by the physically handicapped man, these attitudes exaggerate the dimensions of the physical limitations he actually has. A form of *social processing* operates whereby self-conceptions emerge through a pattern of interactions with people. In a series of transactions,

[73] Thomas J. Scheff, *Being Mentally Ill: A Sociological Theory* (Chicago: Aldine Publishing Co., 1966), pp. 51–54.
[74] Lemert, *Human Deviance, Social Problems, and Control*, pp. 11–12.

the individual may find himself defined as a "failure" or a "troublemaker" in school, military service, a series of jobs, and his other experiences with authority figures.

SUMMARY

As a prologue to the study of major social problems in more detail, this chapter has looked at the underlying themes of sociological analysis. The central theme is that urban *society* is the setting which fundamentally marks the contemporary character of these problems. The study recognizes the dominance of urban culture, the broad influences of an industrial technology, and the profound implications of demographic trends. The next three chapters will consider in turn each of these secondary themes.

The various social problems reflect the difficulties of democratic decision making and of delivering the quality of services now expected of urban society in the United States. These difficulties of urban life have caused some social critics to describe alienation as the primary mental state of our day. The existence of this sense of "normlessness" directs our attention to the definition of deviance and social disorganization as differing orientations to the fundamental importance of social norms in the functioning of society and to assessing the implications of departures from the norms. Society exists because of adherence to its norms by members for the sake of its services in meeting their needs. Society's existence is predicated on "societal necessities" which, in turn, make the range of social problems relevant to the study of a society experiencing a high rate of social change. Finally, we summarized several theoretical approaches which attempt to explain deviance and social disorganization as products of socially organized behavior as well as phenomena sapping the effectiveness of the contemporary form of social organization.

FOR ADDITIONAL READING

Robert Blauner, *Alienation and Freedom: The Factory Worker and His Industry* (Chicago: University of Chicago Press, 1964).

David J. Bordua, "Recent Trends: Deviant Behavior and Social Control," *Annals of American Academy of Political and Social Science,* Vol. 369 (January 1967), pp. 149–63.

Marshall B. Clinard, *Sociology of Deviant Behavior* (3d ed.; New York: Holt, Rinehart & Winston, 1968), Chapter 3.

Albert K. Cohen, "Deviant Behavior and Its Control," in Talcott Parsons (ed.), *American Sociology: Perspectives, Problems, Methods* (New York: Basic Books, 1968).

Kenneth W. Eckhardt, "Deviance, Visibility, and Legal Action: The Duty to Support," *Social Problems,* Vol. 15 (Spring 1968), pp. 470–77.

T. C. N. Gibbens and R. H. Ahrenfeldt (eds.), *Cultural Factors in Delinquency* (Philadelphia, Pa.: J. B. Lippincott Co., 1966).

William J. Goode, "A Theory of Role Strain," *American Sociological Review,* Vol. 25 (August 1960), pp. 483–96.

John P. Hewitt, *Social Stratification and Deviant Behavior* (New York: Random House, 1970).

Eric and Mary Josephson, *Man Alone: Alienation in Modern Society* (New York: Dell Publishing Co., 1962).

John Lofland, *Deviance and Identity* (Englewood Cliffs, N.J.: Prentice-Hall, 1969).

Charles H. McCaghy, James K. Skipper, Jr., and Mark Lefton (eds.), *In Their Own Behalf: Voices from the Margin* (New York: Appleton-Century-Crofts, 1968).

Reece McGee, *Social Disorganization in America* (San Francisco, Calif.: Chandler Publishing Co., 1962).

Pertti J. Pelte, "The Differences Between 'Tight' and 'Loose' Societies," *Transaction,* Vol. 5 (April 1968), pp. 37–40.

Edwin M. Schur, "Reactions to Deviance: A Critical Assessment," *American Journal of Sociology,* Vol. 75 (November 1969), pp. 309–22.

Jerry L. Simmons, *Deviants* (Berkeley, Calif.: Glendessary Press, 1969).

Austin T. Turk, *Criminality and the Legal Order* (Chicago: Rand McNally, 1969).

Leslie T. Wilkins, *Social Deviance* (Englewood Cliffs, N.J.: Prentice-Hall, 1965).

3 Urban society as a setting of problems

New York (May 6, 1964) (Associated Press). A nude, ravished girl fled screaming from her attacker to the very threshold of a Bronx office building, where she pleaded with onlookers to help her. But some 40 of them failed to aid her. Patrolman Norman Brown recounted the latest tale of metropolitan indifference Tuesday in Bronx Criminal Court. There George Coughlin, 26, married and the father of two children, was held in $7,500 bail as the daylight rapist who attacked Olga Romero, 18, on Monday afternoon. Coughlin denied the charge.

Said Brown: "Forty people could have helped that girl yesterday, but none of the jerks helped her."

The slim, 5-foot victim was overpowered in a second-floor office of a building on busy East Tremont Avenue in the Bronx. She was at work alone as a telephone operator. Her assailant threatened her with a razor, beat her, stripped her, and raped her. She finally broke free and fled down the stairway, screaming: "Help me, help me! He raped me, he raped me!"

About 20 persons were attracted by her cries. They rushed to the doorway of the building, but made no move to help the girl. Miss Romero fell the last few steps to the first-floor landing, where her attacker pounced on her, wrapped his jacket around her and tried to force her back upstairs. Again the girl screamed: "Help me, help me! I've been raped." By this time the crowd of onlookers had grown to 40. But they stood silent and immobile, heedless of the girl's pleas. Finally Brown and Patrolman Edmond Woods, attracted by the girl's screams, arrived on the scene.

· · · · ·

Police have complained increasingly of late of the failure of New Yorkers to assist assault victims, lest they become involved in distasteful situations. Last March Catherine Genovese, 28, was stabbed to death on a quiet Queens residential street

64

after dark. Police said at least 38 neighbors heard her cries for help but ignored them.

London (January 21, 1965) (United Press International). A 12-year-old girl flung a broken bottle under the tires of the getaway car of armed bank robbers. Three truckers raced through crowded Piccadilly to capture a robbery suspect and cart him off to the police station in their truck. A yacht designer smashed his new automobile against the stolen Mercedes of an escaping prisoner.

All over Britain the public, aroused by an unprecedented outbreak of underworld violence, was heeding the advice of a high Scotland Yard official to "have a go" when they saw a crime being committed. Assistant Commissioner Randolph Bacon qualified his New Year's Day suggestions that the public tackle criminals, however. He did not mean it to apply to everyone in every case. Alarmed civic organizations—with visions of unarmed citizens shot and beaten in vain battles—have in recent days qualified it still further.

· · · · ·

Martin Ennals of the National Council for Civil Liberties warned that there were legal dangers in tackling suspects. He told of a friend who beat off a man attacking his brother—and was himself arrested and fined for assault. The *Sunday Citizen* in a front-page editorial charged Bacon was "encouraging unarmed and untrained citizens to tackle gunmen. The odds against the citizen getting away alive are high, against escaping uninjured are higher, against making a dent in the crime statistics graph astronomical."

· · · · ·

The newspaper said citizens had a duty to help a policeman under attack but in other cases they would be wiser to take cover and make accurate notes. It pointed out that banks instruct their clerks never to be foolishly brave against a gunman.

Nevertheless in the first ten days in January after Bacon's press conference there was public help against criminals. On January 4 a carload of six bandits armed with a shotgun, revolver, hammers, and iron bars raided a bank. Bill Smith, 43, a passerby, threw bottles through the front and rear windows of the getaway car while another pedestrian, Brian Corneleoues, hammered at the driver with a wrench. Only expert work by the driver—he kept moving the car backwards and forwards—saved him but his accomplices broke off the raid after scooping up only $2,240. As the bandits piled into the car Linda Phillips, 12, . . . aimed a broken bottle at the wheel of the car in the hope of puncturing a tire. "I read about the Scotland Yard appeal to help people being attacked," said Linda, "and I just had a go."

· · · · ·

Two days later an escaped convict, John Marson, with a hostage in his stolen car, screamed into the capital at 130 miles an hour pursued by police. He was reversing out of a police trap when yacht designer Alfred Myline, 46, rammed him with his new Ford Corsair and brought him to a halt. "I knew I was going to wreck my new car," Myline said, "but you don't often get a chance like that." Marson hid in the areaway of a nearby building and shot two policemen. Residents . . . pelted him with bottles and furniture until he was captured.

CITY AS A SETTING FOR PROBLEMS

Through the centuries the city has been a whipping boy, blamed for the ailments of a particular time or indicted by critics as the locus of evil. The first news story quoted above presents the urbanite as the passive witness of a crime in spite of pleas for aid by the victim. Instead of closing ranks against a common enemy, the onlookers avoid getting involved in other people's business. "After all," they may have been thinking, "this is what we pay police to handle."

The second news story offers a more attractive description of urbanites. As the story unfolds, however, the problem is seen to be more complicated than a simple matter of individual perversity. Is the average citizen equipped to cope with the violent criminal? In an event which erupts before his eyes, can the urbanite quickly assess who is the villain and who is the hero when he lacks previous acquaintance with the participants or understanding of the event? If he attacks the screaming girl's pursuer, he may learn later that she was a mental patient fleeing her husband. Carried to an extreme, citizen action can become vigilanteeism. Assumption of unauthorized responsibility has brought violence and disorder in labor-management controversies, racial dissension incidents, and many other adversary situations.

Issues raised by urban society

The American city is being challenged to demonstrate that it can provide education and economic opportunity for its millions. Can the city absorb blacks and Puerto Ricans into its economy and democratic political process as it did previous waves of migrants? In a culture in which job and material possessions are the primary means of fixing social status, can the city find the means of shaping well-rounded personalities? Can the city's heterogeneous collection of individuals be converted into a human community? Will means be found to cope with difficulties raised by the combination of an advanced technology and a mass population?

With the growing dominance of city life, the search for answers to these questions must be quickened. In 1965 144 million people lived in our cities. By 1980 this figure will rise to 198 million. By the end of the century 85 percent of a population of 300 million will be urban and concentrated on less than a tenth of the total area of the nation.

The rise of the urban society has made national in scope the social problems previously identified as almost exclusively those of the city. Poverty, racial conflict, crime, and pollution no longer are exclusive difficulties of the metropolis, as witnessed by the increasing involvement of the national government in attempts toward a solution and by the growing awareness of the inadequacy of purely local efforts. In many ways social problems are assuming an international character as the concept of community becomes more a social psychological entity.

As we shall see, urbanism has certain social characteristics, related to size and density of the city's population, which color the way people behave toward one another. They promote the possibility of deep-seated disagreements on what constitutes proper behavior, the loss of effectiveness of traditions in regulating conduct, and an obscuring of the long-term purpose in our lives. In these ways they favor development of a form of thought wherein man regards social conditions and problems as products of human behavior and, thereby, subject to improvement through efforts of men. There is a higher probability that urban man will define a wider range of undesirable conditions as appropriate subjects for protest and remedial action. In short, urban psychological and sociological conditions produce an array of social problems in addition to those which arise from the direct effects of population congestion.

Technological and demographic dimensions

The next two chapters will select for special attention two dimensions of social analysis of particular relevance to urban society. Chapter 4 will be devoted to the technological developments fundamentally interrelated with the emergence of the contemporary city. Chapter 5 will focus on the demographic trends which have been responses to the forces unleashed by urbanism and industrialism.

By employing a progressively efficient technology to transform natural resources, modern industrialism has raised the prospect of an age of unprecedented satisfaction of man's material needs. Technology has made feasible the growth of urban populations and has drawn its workers and consumers from these concentrated populations. The twin forces of urbanization and industrialization, however, are testing man's capacity to develop the social arrangements whereby this prospect of a golden age will become a reality. The existence of serious social problems attests to failure to meet the challenge so far. The test requires new habits, new patterns of human relationship, and the rearrangement of individuals and groups within an appropriate social organization. We are participating in a vast range of experimentation trying to fit the technological potentialities into a scheme for attainment of the long-held dream of a "perfect" society.

Serious questions are being posed about the sufficiency of natural resources and the effects of technological exploitation on the quality of the natural environment under the pressure of population growth. Demographic trends constitute world problems when the rate of reproduction in any part of the world affects the welfare of the rest of the world's population. What kind of world is being passed on to future generations?

Will the earth become the equivalent of a space capsule occupied by more people than its environment can sustain? Can the rape of the natural environment be continued unchecked without endangering the recycling of air, water, and materials which sustain life? Within the context of demography, can the number of "passengers" be increased indefinitely?

The demographic factors of death, fertility, and migration rates are crucial to the study of urbanism. Population growth is a product of the relationship between death and birth rates. The growth of the city has been largely a product of migration from other regions, which adds to the heterogeneity of the urban population. Death rates involve the health problems of the city, and the relationship between birth and death rates affects the characteristics of the population. This, in turn, determines the dimensions of the social problems to be examined in subsequent chapters. For example, the "baby boom" after World War II ultimately brought heavy enrollment pressures on the schools because, as this population bulge moved through the ages, there was an unprecedented number of pupils to be served progressively by the elementary, secondary, and higher educational institutions.[1]

URBANISM AND SOCIAL CORRELATES

Urbanization is a fundamental dimension in the social problems considered in this book because its influence extends beyond the city. Through the process of urbanization, the distinctive patterns of living associated with urbanism radiate outside political boundaries to permeate all of society. An urban *society* has been produced.

The *city* has been defined sociologically as a relatively dense and permanent settlement of heterogeneous individuals.[2] Wirth regards the city's large number of inhabitants as the primary factor in unleashing the social characteristics of urbanism as a way of life. These characteristics include population heterogeneity, specialization in behavior, anonymous and impersonal relationships, and standardization of life. In analyzing these characteristics, we are endeavoring to understand how urbanism has had great impact on how man lives and associates with his fellows. Analysis of each of these characteristics will convey the impression that urban man has lost all sense of intimacy with his fellows. This exaggeration is one of the inadvertent costs of concentrated analysis of each of a series of factors. We shall endeavor to lend balance to this discussion by pointing out finally that the elements of primary group life do persist.

[1] See Chapter 5.
[2] Louis Wirth, "Urbanism as a Way of Life," *American Journal of Sociology,* Vol. 44 (July 1938), pp. 1–24.

Heterogeneity of population

Because large populations are built up chiefly through migration, the city includes many people who do not have common traditions. This mixture of people with differing backgrounds and beliefs upsets the working of informal controls, which rely on persuasion and habit to motivate individuals to behave in keeping with the interests of the group. Mores and public sentiments are most effective when all persons have learned the same norms through the process of socialization during childhood when the conscience is developed. A contemptuous glance has meaning when all the individuals who witness it have lived with one another over a long period of time; when they have not, the sharing of common sentiments is less likely. With more contacts with strangers, the influence of family and neighborhood is less dominant.

The diversity of people in a city increases reliance on deliberately designed mechanisms for regulating the behavior of individuals and groups because there is an insufficient sharing of common sentiments as a basis for informal controls. Heterogeneity contributes to greater use of the criminal law and bureaucratic administration as means of formal control.

Heterogeneity of population is conducive to change because residents of an area are exposed to ideas imported from other cultures through the arrival of migrants. Constructively, outmoded habits and paralyzing beliefs may be challenged to permit residents to adjust themselves more effectively to ways of improving their economic status or extending the range of alternatives in earning a living, enjoying leisure time, coping with disease, and similar recurrent aspects of life. Less constructively, the arrival of strangers can release prejudice and economic competition. When the isolation of differing peoples is broken, Williams points out, the conflicting interpretations have a potentiality for raising social problems not present when they did not confront one another directly in social interaction.[3] People come into conflict concerning what is the "right" way to behave. Individuals are subjected to competing claims from the dominant culture and their particular subculture.

Specialization of function and behavior

The large size of the population of a city favors the development of specialization. The city has many facets of life and any one individual participates in only some of them. Specialization encourages a diversity of life patterns. The lawyer and the policeman, for example, probably belong to different kinds of churches, live in different residential sections, have different recreational patterns, and so on. Such specialists can make

[3] Robin M. Williams, Jr., *American Society: A Sociological Interpretation* (3d ed.; New York: Alfred A. Knopf, 1970), p. 416.

their contribution to the community and enjoy its benefits because of population size. In a city there is a sufficient number of persons interested in chamber music or other avocations to form groups; there may be enough gourmets to make specialized food shops profitable.

A division of labor is created in that the total process of production or delivery of services is broken down into specialities. Each of a wide variety of workers performs his specific tasks as the automobile is assembled in the factory. The salesman sells only vacuum cleaners, say, and depends on many other specialists to produce, process, and distribute food so that it ends up on his table. Such a division of labor permits an individual to benefit from a broader range of services than his own knowledge and capabilities provide. By employing specialists such as physicians and mechanics, the individual can benefit from the techniques of an advanced culture without learning them or even being aware of their full meaning. With a greater variety of specialized activities, the individual theoretically can match his occupation and his avocations to personal interests. The plumber or mechanic presumably prefers to work on mechanical devices, while the minister or accountant can satisfy his interest in more abstract matters. The individual can choose between postage stamp collecting or golf as a hobby because specialists provide the services each avocation requires.

Specialization contributes to a "good life" in the city by providing the individual with a diversity of ways to act, to express himself, and to develop his potentialities. However, as Haworth warns, specialization removes a sense of community from life. Segmented contacts among individuals narrows their orientation away from the larger social universe which gives significance to the contacts. "By promoting a plurality of individual worlds, specialization dissolves the continuity of persons, their sense of living a common life and having common concerns." [4] The clerk and customer are bound together in a relationship of short duration because each needs the other to gratify his own purpose in a commercial transaction. This dependence is one of reciprocity of the moment rather than one binding them together in a broad spectrum of common interests. In moving through a series of these narrowly defined specialized relationships, the urbanite has little grasp of the whole life of the city.

In a social order characterized by a heterogeneous population and diversity in behavioral codes, there is greater likelihood of confusion among several alternatives for proper behavior in a given situation. For example, a student observes his friend cheating on an examination. Should he report his friend in keeping with the school's honor system? Or should he be loyal to the code which forbids tattling on friends? As another example, suppose that a clerk gives the wrong change in your favor.

[4] Lawrence Haworth, The Good City (Bloomington, Ind.: Indiana University Press, 1966), p. 19.

Should you keep the money because only fools pass up something for nothing? The clerk is bonded, and that is why insurance companies are in business. Then, too, if you return the money, you will call the attention of the store management to the error, to the clerk's detriment. Or should you return the money in keeping with your parents' teachings? The moral dilemmas can be overwhelming to the individual who is sensitive to all facets of an environment characterized by rapid tempo and multiplicity of events.

Anonymity and impersonality

The most frequent complaint against the city is that it's not "friendly." In an urban mob the individual pretends that an elbow pressed into his ribs is not attached to the body of a person with feelings and personal needs.

High population density erodes a sense of personal identity, with effects which include loneliness and a loss of a sense of belonging. Individuals can be seen eating alone in the all-night restaurants. In movie theaters individuals, elbow to elbow, laugh and cry together in the dark. When the film ends and the lights come on, the common emotions disintegrate into anonymity and impersonality. The loss of identity may explain the excessive interest focused on actors, television personalities, professional athletes, and similar cultural heroes who seem to express a semblance of sustained interest in the "little guy."

On the other hand, this very anonymity is the crux of personal freedom. The apparent lack of interest in others releases the individual from heavy pressures toward conformity which would be present when he is highly visible to the people about him. He depends on other people for the goods and services essential to his needs and gratifications, but, if he can pay for what he wants, his responsibility to others can end with payment in many cases. He pays to enter a theater, shooting gallery, sports arena, or night club and becomes another faceless patron. However, he does not have to go through the trouble of winning the acceptance of the other patrons or to engage in the accommodative process of fitting himself into their expectations (except in highly generalized ways). A frequent complaint against urbanites is that they do not participate actively in dealing with public issues and that nonparticipation is corrosive of democracy. On the other hand, nonparticipation suggests that, compared with earlier rural societies, urbanism permits the freedom to participate minimally.

In self-defense against the multiplicity of events and moral judgments encountered in a heterogeneous society, the urbanite acquires a selective sensitivity to all that is happening about him. He gets used to the noise of traffic and, in an equivalent of tunnel vision, withdraws his attention from the bulk of the persons crowded about him. His selective sensitivity insulates him from the full impact of the confusion of judgments and the bombardment of stimuli from multiple events available for observation. From a negative perspective, we are describing what has been called the callousness of urbanites who can step across a prone body blocking the entrance to a subway without determining whether the man is drunk or a victim of a heart attack.

Simmel sees this selective sensitivity as part of the intellectuality which has enabled man to employ science to enrich his life.[5] The scientific method focuses attention on the *patterns* of events rather than on the full uniqueness of each concrete event. This focusing of attention enables the human mind to develop principles which predict future events and permit their explanation. Organization of urban life is feasible because a large number of people apply general principles in relationships with one another. For example, money is a medium of exchange whereby rewards for a man's labor can be converted into a wide range of goods and services he acquires from the work of a host of other persons. Money is based on a rational agreement that pieces of paper are the equivalent of a wide variety of things which can be used directly to serve the owner's interests. Money is a symbol which implements the patterning of the sequence of events which comprise our economic system. But this focusing of attention deprives the persons or objects being observed of their full uniqueness in that their similarities are emphasized. This results in the impersonality which treats persons as if they were elements in mathematical formulas. However, Simmel says, the urbanite thus gains protection against being overwhelmed by the intensification of nervous stimulation in urban life.

Impersonality and anonymity also favor a democracy, since individuals are less likely to be judged according to their parents' lower class status and more likely to be evaluated on the basis of behavior and appearance in relatively immediate and casual contacts. Rigid social class lines can most easily be maintained when each class enjoys intimate relationships within family, peer groups, and other settings which permit drawing reliable distinctions between members and nonmembers. The anonymity and impersonality of urban life gives the social climber greater opportunity to take advantage of symbols such as residential address, kind of automobile, style of dress, mode of speech, and kind of manners to gain the acceptance he seeks.

Sjoberg argues that industrialization, migration, and other social forces associated with urbanization have fundamentally changed the social class structure of the United States. Distinctions in possession of automobiles, attractive clothing, and other material objects have been reduced by inflation, usually high levels of employment, and expansion of welfare programs. The greater education of white-collar workers provides them less income advantage over factory workers and craftsmen. Distinctions in

[5] Georg Simmel, *The Sociology of Georg Simmel* (trans. Kurt H. Wolff) (New York: Free Press, 1950), pp. 409–22.

dress and language have been reduced. The dominance of the business elite has been challenged by the rise of government and labor leaders. Expansion of education has brought forth new kinds of professional groups.[6]

Standardization of behavior

More transactions can be handled in a given period of time if customers or clients are regarded as though they are identical in needs and personality. When there are large numbers of clients, they tend to have sufficient similarities to fall into a limited number of pigeonholes. The salesman finds the same questions being asked by a succession of customers. In personality characteristics, the customers are then seen as types—the person who is looking without buying, the haggler over prices, the fellow who prefers prestigious style over economy, and so on. The experienced salesman quickly judges the type of customer he is confronting and uses the sales strategy he regards as most effective for this type. When his judgment is accurate, both he and the customer are able to handle the sales transaction in a simple, quick, and direct fashion. The customer enjoys prompt and efficient service when his needs neatly fit into one of the preconceived categories.

In every society the individual is expected to conform to group customs even when his particular situation does not fit neatly into standardized expectations. When the customs of his tribe demand the heroism of a warrior from all adult males, the young man finds himself out of step when he regards hand-to-hand combat without enthusiasm. The customs become a straitjacket for him. In urban society, the large size of the population lends particular force to the standardization of behavior, even though the wider variety of customs increases the probability of divergence of individual orientations and the perspective characteristic of the community as a whole. Members of earlier tribes had been exposed to a common culture which would inhibit the development of individual divergences from the general cultural perspective. The urban society provides a greater range of services in which the consumer presents himself for a brief period to a specialist with whom the consumer is unlikely to have had prolonged exposure in the past. Confronting each other as strangers, the two are more likely to treat each other in standardized terms.

When the individual falls outside the range of standardized molds, he encounters special frustrations. Travel schedules are tailored usually to the flow of the bulk of passengers. When a traveler has atypical requirements, he faces long delays in making connections or must take roundabout routes. If he objects to standardized menus, fried foods, and bland season-

---

[6] Gideon Sjoberg, "Are Social Classes in America Becoming More Rigid?" *American Sociological Review,* Vol. 16 (December 1951), pp. 775–83.

ing, the traveler finds little pleasure in most restaurants and their assembly-line kitchens. Radio, television, and the newsstands present a largely standardized fare. Urban shopping districts are very similar in general appearance and kinds of goods offered.

IMPLICATIONS FOR ORGANIZATION

The several characteristics of urbanism as a way of life produce results which potentially can either serve the interests of individuals or be a source of their frustration. The total effect of these characteristics has been to move man from a social environment within which his social relationships are largely primary group in quality to a social environment within which large-scale, consciously developed organizations serve his needs without the same level of fusion of individualities through emotional identification characteristic of primary associations. The trend from a primary-group society to a bureaucratically organized society is relative rather than total. Primary groups continue to be present in urban society, but the basis of community has been changed fundamentally under the impact of urbanism. This section is devoted to an exploration of this change.

Primary groups still persist

In contributing the idea of *primary group* to the concepts of sociology, Cooley saw the primary group as populated by relatively few members and characterized by relative permanence of its relationships. The primary group generates social intimacy and a fusion of individualities in a common whole.[7] Unlike the consciously developed organizations found particularly in urban society, the primary group admits its members through birth and personal affections rather than by imposing rational standards such as the civil service examinations used to select members of governmental bureauracies.

Primary-group members are welded together by a fusion of concerns for one another as individuals per se. In a business, university, or other formal organization, any emotional identification among employees is supplemented by written codes and specification of job obligations. As the most prominent example of the primary group, the family includes a wide range of relationships, while the secondary group, the converse of the primary group, covers a more circumscribed range of relationships. In the family the mother serves as cook, nurse, manager of tensions of other family members, intermediary with the school, moral instructor, and so on. In contrast, the store clerk performs limited and specified functions for the customer.

[7] Charles H. Cooley, *Social Organization* (New York: Shocken Books, 1962), p. 23.

Although urban characteristics have weakened the bonds of family and neighborhood, primary group life has not vanished in the city. Migrants from rural areas frequently retain habits of intensive social participation within a neighborhood.[8] Urban heterogeneity itself produces cultural islands wherein persons share ethnic, social-class, religious, or occupational similarities which buttress the influence of the geographical neighborhood in making residents feel a sense of common interest. Within the expanse of a huge metropolis these cultural islands are isolated from one another to strengthen neighborhood loyalties.

Bell finds in his San Francisco study that relatives continue to be a significant and important source of support and friendship.[9] Neighborhoods differ in degree of participation among residents according to socioeconomic and family characteristics, but the neighborhood has not disappeared. Bell believes the less personal secondary contacts have added to rather than supplanted by the primary contacts.

In a study of Mexico City, Lewis finds peasants adapting to city life with relative ease, although their linkage with their rural traditions persisted. He argues that the processes of urbanization assume different forms and meanings depending upon the prevailing historic, economic, social, and cultural conditions.[10] Caplow finds Guatemala City sharing the basic traditionalism of the surrounding rural environment which permits absorption of many alien practices with comparatively little effect on the shaping of behavior.[11]

General statements on the persistence of primary groups in urban areas should be tempered by recognition of particular characteristics of the subpopulation to which we are referring. A Los Angeles study indicates that type of housing is related to the degree of participation in the family, neighborhood, and other informal groups.[12] Four areas of the city were selected to be similar in the socioeconomic characteristics of residents. However, the residents in the several areas differed markedly in the percentage of women working and of married persons, typical role expectations within the family, and distribution of housing by apartment houses or single-family dwellings. The four areas were ranked along a continuum from an emphasis on single-family dwellings to a preponderance of apartment houses. The greater the emphasis on apartment houses, the greater

[8] See Philip M. Hauser, "Urbanization: an Overview," in Philip M. Hauser and Leo F. Schore (eds.), The Study of Urbanization (New York: John Wiley and Sons, 1965), p. 3.

[9] Wendell Bell, "The City, the Suburb, and a Theory of Social Choice," in Scott Greer, Dennis C. McElrath, David W. Minar, and Peter Orleans (eds.), The New Urbanization (New York: St. Martin's Press, 1968), pp. 137–43.

[10] Oscar Lewis, "Urbanization without Breakdown: A Case Study," The Scientific Monthly, Vol. 75, No. 1 (July 1952).

[11] Theodore Caplow, "The Social Ecology of Guatemala City," Social Forces, Vol. 28 (December 1949), pp. 131–32.

[12] Scott Greer and Ella Kube, "Urbanism and Social Structure: A Los Angeles Study," in Marvin B. Sussman (ed.), Community Structure and Analysis (New York: Thomas Y. Crowell, 1959), pp. 93–112.

was the reliance on formal organizations in social participation. Conversely, single-family dwellings were associated with more participation in informal activities of families, neighborhoods, kinship groups, and fellow workers. Neighborhood ties tended to be stronger in all four areas according to higher ranking of the resident on measures of occupational prestige (white collar versus blue collar), education, and household income.

Increased scale and bureaucracy

Urbanism has had a profound impact on the earlier forms of social organization based on the intimate relationships between individuals captured by the concept of primary group. The sociological characteristics described earlier weaken the bonds that depend on long-term association of persons within a network of familiar traditions. Furthermore, the sheer size of population and the complexity of social relationships require greater reliance on more rational and explicit mechanisms for binding individuals together and integrating groups into a coordinated whole.

Latent in the changes of the modes of organizing social relationships is the influence of increases in the social scale.[13] Technological changes have drastically expanded man's use of nonhuman sources of energy to increase his productivity and his triumph over space through transportation and communication. Physical separation is much less a barrier to social transactions. Men and machines are bound into systems of production and distribution which transcend local, state, and national boundaries. Virtually instantaneously an unprecedented volume of information is available. Locality has lost much of its significance, as organizational networks of businesses, industries, labor unions, and government cover much broader territory. The destinies of people hinge on factors determined largely from outside the immediate community.

Government and economic institutions rely on bureaucracy as an organizational strategy. Diverse specialists are coordinated by drawing jurisdictional lines to define their specific responsibilities and authority within a total set of interrelated activities. Codes of written rules and procedures systematize their activities. Written documents record and transmit the information vital to the activities. By standardizing tasks, the specialist is able to exploit repetitive operations as a way of applying a specialized technique or service of a larger number of units within a given length of time.[14] Weber has pointed to the advantages of a trained bureaucracy.[15] Precise, speedy, and clear-cut solutions to repetitive prob-

---

[13] Scott Greer, *The Emerging City: Myth and Reality,* (New York: The Free Press, 1962), Chapter 2; also see Melvin M. Webber, "The Post-City Age," *Daedalus,* Vol. 97 (Fall 1968), pp. 1091–1110.

[14] Hans H. Gerth and C. Wright Mills (trans. and eds.), *From Max Weber* (New York: Oxford University Press, 1946), pp. 196–98.

[15] Ibid, p. 214.

lems are provided by experts capable of using discretion in their particular jurisdiction without being swayed by personal considerations. Their actions are more likely to be consistent in the long term. Through knowledge of recorded information, their decisions are more likely to be based on fact. Their self-discipline within the rules of the organization reduces the friction among officeholders and advances the organization's objectives with minimum waste. Furthermore, Barnard says, salary and psychological rewards are geared ideally to recognize the differences in difficulty and importance of various tasks and in the amount of training required to be expert.[16] The ambitious person is thereby motivated to qualify himself through training and to stick his neck out to make difficult and important decisions essential to the organization and its clients. When the transactions lend themselves to standardized handling, the bureaucracy can recruit less skillful and trained persons for routine tasks and reserve more complicated jobs for the more able persons.

The disadvantages of bureaucracy lie chiefly in the possibilities of recurrent and routine administration in dehumanizing clients and in placing the convenience of officeholders above the stated purposes the organization is supposed to serve for its clients. Rules are intended to achieve the purposes of the organization, but the pressure on officials to conform to them risks their overconformity to such a degree that the rules become goals in themselves. "It can't be done, fellow, because it's against the rules." Devotion to the rules blocks meeting legitimate purposes which were not envisaged when the rules were drawn up. The bureaucrat develops a loyalty to routines and traditions difficult to ungear when new circumstances require fundamental changes in his attitudes and behavior if the organizational goals are to be achieved and his clients served.[17]

Emphasis on social-psychological community

The rise of bureaucratic organization in part reflects the need for a new basis for integrating individuals and groups into a common effort. Man has relied greatly on the primary association of family, neighborhood, and church to motivate individuals to subject themselves to the discipline necessary for collective effort. Through the intimacy of direct contacts with his fellows, the individual was induced toward self-discipline for the sake of benefits of prestige, the security of knowing his place in the total scheme, and the clarity of definitions of the "good" and the "evil." However, the characteristics of urbanism have eroded the functions of primary

[16] Chester I. Barnard, "Functions and Pathology of Status Systems in Formal Organizations," in William Foote Whyte (ed.), *Industry and Society* (New York: McGraw-Hill Book Co., 1946), pp. 53–59.

[17] See: Robert K. Merton, "Bureaucratic Structure and Personality," in Robert K. Merton, Ailsa P. Gray, Barbara Hockey, and Hanan C. Selvin (eds.), *Reader in Bureaucracy* (Glencoe, Ill.: Free Press, 1952), pp. 361–71.

associations in linking individuals and groups together. Nisbet says that much of the particular character of contemporary human behavior comes from the efforts of men to find in large-scale organizations the values of status and security which were formerly gained in primary associations. He sees the anxiety, insecurity, and alienation found among urbanites as a quest for community in the social-psychological sense.[18]

Usually, *community* is defined as a spatially limited group in a society. Each community has a particular physical setting. Social-psychologically its residents are bound to one another through sharing a common way of life. This definition has two elements crucial to our discussion: territorial and social-psychological. The community has been identified with a particular locality in terms of specific geographical boundaries and the climate, topography, and physical resources of that locality. Martindale would deemphasize the idea of territory and would focus greater attention on the social-psychological bonds whereby the individual derives a sense of place and station within a human collectivity. In this view, a *community* is a set or system of groups sufficient to solve all of the basic problems of ordinary ways of life.[19] The groups within the community are organized for the solution of a specific set of problems. The community has a relation to the natural environment, but under Martindale's definition it is not welded to a fixed point on the earth's surface.

The family was the earliest form of human settlement in that it furnished both the place and the style of life of social interaction which encompassed religion, education, recreation, art, politics, and work. Each of these several kinds of activities involved the individuals with one another within the physical and sociocultural setting of the family. The family was extensive in its membership, including more distant relatives than is the practice today and even including individuals under fictional blood ties. The family gave each member a sense of physical and social place and a set of rights and duties comprising his birthright. These features of early family life, Haworth asserts, provided the continuity and unity which are the definitive traits of every human settlement as a more or less fixed form of life.[20] Individuals live in close proximity to one another, but, of greatest significance, the settlement presents a mode of behavior which involves the life of one person with the lives of others to bind them through interrelationships. The settlement is a whole in that the entire round of life is included in these interrelationships.

The greater scale of urban life has eroded the significance of territoriality in encompassing the sphere of common experience for local residents and

[18] Robert A. Nisbet, *The Quest for Community* (New York: Oxford University Press, 1953), pp. 49–51.
[19] Don Martindale, "The Formation and Destruction of Communities," in George K. Zollschan and Walter Hirsch (eds.) *Explorations in Social Change* (Boston, Mass.: Houghton Mifflin Co. 1964), p. 69.
[20] Haworth, *The Good City,* pp. 13–14.

in providing a reasonable degree of self-sufficiency in meeting their needs. Formal organizations extending outside the local territory reflect the opera- tion of social and economic forces beyond the control of the local commu- nity. The family no longer encompasses all of the affairs which affect the individual fundamentally. Within the community an array of formal organi- zations has been created to perform functions which either were absent or existed in the family settlement in much less developed form. The police, courts, and correctional agencies are designed to preserve the public order and to curb the deviants defined as criminals or delinquents. Private and public welfare agencies provide a range of services to assist and rehabilitate various categories of underprivileged persons. Schools and colleges are dedicated to the wide range of objectives that education is supposed to achieve. Factories, stores, and banks are among the economic institutions which produce and distribute goods and services. These and other social institutions have developed into formal organizations employ- ing the characteristics of bureaucracy. In each organization rules and procedures are developed, functions assigned to cohorts of specialized workers, and jurisdictional lines drawn for each specialist to enable the total activity to be orderly.

Bureaucracy and social problems

From an abstract perspective, bureaucracy appears to be an appropriate scheme for mobilizing collective effort to gratify human needs. Each of the spheres of activity within urban life can be handled by the appropriate organization. Of all the resources available to government, for example, an allocation to public welfare agencies would provide teams of casework- ers assigned their particular tasks to assist the elderly, unemployed, physi- cally handicapped, and dependent children who otherwise would be neg- lected. Theoretically, the bureaucratic organization would bring the most qualified experts into play. Meanwhile, other organizations serve other categories of human needs to comprise a total effort whereby the commu- nity represents a means of serving its citizens.

The disadvantages of bureaucracy, already cited, operate against the achievement in reality of its idealized efficiency in meeting human pur- poses. Designers of bureaucratic procedures must cope with the host of variables involved in human behavior and the intersection of the activities of various bureaucracies. The bureaucracy attempts to give order to the work of its range of employees and to meet the demands of its clients by predicting the behavior and problems pertinent to its operation. Orderly operation is supposed to stem from accurate prediction of the events which occur. Changes in the environment of the bureaucracy, however, undermine the accuracy of prediction. Overlooked factors can have unan- ticipated consequences in behavior of employees and/or clients.

In the several social problems considered later in this book, the effectiveness of bureaucracies is germane to the delivery of services. Schools and colleges face formidable organizational problems in providing the kinds of education the dynamic and complex urban world requires. Faced with formidable responsibilities sometimes in conflict with one another, educational institutions are sharply criticized for placing the "efficiency" of factorylike production over recognition of the individualized needs of students for instruction relevant to today's world. Similarly, public welfare, medical, and mental health services are failing to meet pressing problems because of inflexible procedures and obsolete traditions. Law enforcement, courts, and corrections are troubled with serious problems in curbing crime in an urban society which places heavy reliance on the criminal law to meet a variety of social problems and concurrently expects an unprecedented quality of task performance.

Meanwhile, bureaucratic organization is being subjected to an increasing demand that the broad participation of citizens in democratic decision making be characteristic of urban society. Such a form of organization does not lend itself readily to wide-scale participation because of its reliance on standardized procedures and regularized allocation of authority to specialized personnel. It will be difficult to adjust bureaucracies to alleviate the isolation of the poor and minority groups from the mainstream of community life.

COMPLEXITY AND FRAGMENTATION

The increasing size of metropolitan areas and their population has been accompanied by the rise of complex problems of government. The redistribution of population from rural areas to urban concentrations has brought imposing problems of management. Very large cities are increasingly subject to internal diseconomies: congestion, increasing separation of residential areas from working areas, and haphazard arrangement of land uses through urban sprawl. Urban governments face financial stringencies of increasing severity.

Crisis of central city

Since World War II metropolitan growth has been rapid, but largely through rapid population increase in outlying areas with little increase (sometimes a decline) in the central area. Reductions in central city population have been selective. The young, employed, well-to-do, and white are heavily represented in the movement to the suburbs, leaving behind the aged, unemployed, poor, blacks, and other underprivileged groups.

Decentralization has been encouraged by several technological and economic changes. New efficiencies in transportation and communication have reduced the advantages of central locations near water ports, railroad terminals and lines, and mass transit facilities. Changes in production methods require spacious, single-story plants. Data processing and communications require fewer white-collar workers and permit their location in offices in outlying areas. Currently, the greatest density of employment is in the central cities, but it appears that these peaks will be eroded steadily to spread employment more evenly throughout the city and suburbs. Perhaps the future shape of the city will be that of a doughnut, with the peripheral areas holding the bulk of the jobs.[21]

When new worthwhile jobs have been created in the central city, they have been largely white-collar in nature and unsuitable for the majority of the inhabitants of the inner core. The drawing of suburbanites to these jobs has aggravated traffic congestion and the pressure for provision of municipal services.

The movement to the suburbs aggravates the financial crises of the central city. When the middle class leave their downtown residences, the major land users in the metropolitan core become commercial and industrial enterprises, governmental centers, and slums. The latter siphon off municipal expenditures without commensurate contributions to revenue. As the core becomes an educational or civic center, tax-exempt property increases. Municipal expenditures for services tend to rise more rapidly than the taxes to be gained through economic growth even when expansion of the local urban economy is feasible. Beginning with a heavy burden of debt, the urban administration is restricted by a rural-minded state legislature in the search for broader tax and borrowing authority. Rebuilding the city in physical and organizational terms calls for massive bulldozing of buildings, redirection of highways, creation of major public transit systems, and bullying people out of familiar ways of life.

Fragmentation of government

A crucial dimension in the organizational dilemma is the fragmentation of local government in the face of growing pressure for the provision of public services. The individual and family cannot exist in the city without a great many public services and government controls assuring the welfare and safety of the community. Rising public expenditures in central urban areas reflect involvement of local government in health and welfare services for the poor, in the educational services which will affect the chances for improving the lot of disadvantaged people, and the legacy of obsolete housing and public facilities. Meanwhile, the newer sections of the metropolis experience heavier demands for public services, especially schools, from mounting populations.

The fragmentation of local government is a natural product of the

---

[21] John F. Kain, "The Distribution and Movement of Jobs and Industry" in James Q. Wilson (ed.), *The Metropolitan Enigma* (Cambridge, Mass.: Harvard University Press, 1968), pp. 27–29.

Massachusetts Investors Growth Stock Fund
Photo by Stephan M. Zubricki

Symbols of the past and present. The massive City Hall of Boston frames historic Faneuil Hall. The $21.6 million structure is symbolic of the complexities of managing a large-scale society. To encourage a sense of wide-spread involvement in the processes of government, architects provided an open public court and easy entry to the building.

American nostalgia for the small and provincial town as the natural home of democracy. Because small towns are associated with the settlement of the nation, local autonomy strikes a sentimental chord.[22] In the small government the individual citizen could participate effectively in deciding the local problems he could understand and experience personally. As cities grew in size, their problems multiplied and assumed dimensions which were increasingly difficult to handle locally. Slums, congestion, public disorder, and the influx of immigrants strained the social fabric. The impersonality of urban relationships eroded the efficiency of custom in maintaining order. Provision of water, sanitation, lighting, and police protection became formidable problems of management.

The dominant factor in the collapse of local government as the core of democracy has been the ending of the sociological and economical independence of the town and city. Each locale has become an economic specialist exporting goods it is particularly equipped to produce and importing the other kinds of goods it needs. Nevertheless, time after time, voters reject proposals to create municipalities or create some federal unit to modify traditional autonomy.

Urban sprawl and the suburbs

The manner of growth called "urban sprawl" has drawn strong criticism from urban planners. It is characterized by areas of essentially urban character at the urban fringe which are scattered, strung out, or adjacent to underdeveloped sites. Urbanization is seen as running wild, leapfrogging over empty land without planning and systematic development. Substantial tracts of raw land are bypassed to scatter urban development over the rural landscape. The price, says Whyte, is bad aesthetics and bad economics.[23] Poorly designed developments and a billboard jungle blight areas. Excessive distances for utility lines and paved roads inflate the costs. Lack of zoning prevents intelligent location of industries.

The unsystematic expansion of the city has been attributed to a number of factors. Recognition of the need for planning comes too late to reserve appropriate space for parks, landscaped industrial districts, and other specialized uses. Various special-interest groups fail to take joint action. The 1930s brought government guarantees to create a national mortgage market favorable to suburban home building. Jacobs sees a linkage between suburban growth and economic starvation of the central city. She contends that during the 1930s reformers of all political persuasions favored suburbs because of the traditional nostalgia for small-town life over the presumed moral inferiority of the city. The New Deal Greenbelt approach

[22] Robert C. Wood, *Suburbia: Its People and Their Politics* (Boston, Mass.: Houghton Mifflin Co., 1958), pp. 20–46.
[23] William H. Whyte, Jr., "Urban Sprawl," in *The Exploding Metropolis* (Garden City, N.Y., Doubleday and Co., 1958), pp. 117–24.

would build a whole community on cheap land and then demolish the vacated urban slums.[24] Fragmentation of land ownership impedes the possibility of area planning by private entrepreneurs.

Urban sprawl also has been traced to merchant builders who standardized homes, packaged them, and arranged for rapid distribution through easy financing. Anxious to cope with the post-World War II housing shortage, federal lending agencies favored standardized housing design, landscaping, and placement on lots.[25] Whereas the land speculator buys land only to hold it for later profits, the merchant builder adds value to the land through mass production of housing by crews who move from house to house to perform specialized tasks within a system of division of labor.[26]

Movement to the suburbs

Among the causes for the movement to the suburbs are the shortage of housing in the city, desire for homeownership, search for higher status, and improvements in communication and transportation, which made possible greater distances between home and workplace. The crowded living, anonymity, and impersonal government of the city were repugnant to many of the migrants. An additional factor is especially germane to the fragmentation of government. The nostalgic image of small-town life is one of the magnets for migrants. Some critics of the city hope the suburb will be a means of reviving the sense of community lost in the megalopolis. The ideology of grass-roots democracy is cited to defend small political units as the expression of popular rule close to home. However, the myths associated with suburbia differ markedly from the realities.

The suburbs' array of small government units invites the confusion of overlapping service systems and insufficient tax bases. Each suburban government maintains it own police force, fire station, health department, library, and welfare service in a mosaic of suburban principalities. Overall costs are increased and efficiency is eroded, with each government unit bearing the expenses of separate purchases and the duplication of administrative and political overhead.

The myths associate suburbia with a middle-class way of life which tends to be standardized but at a level of material well-being and respectability. There are images of winding streets, two-car garages, bicycles, ranch-type schools, much "neighboring," evening bridge, child-raising by Spock, the morning station-wagon race of commuters for the 7:12 train, active participation in local civic affairs, and college-educated young cou-

[24] Jane Jacobs, *The Death and Life of Great American Cities* (New York: Random House, 1961), p. 310.

[25] Peter Blake, *God's Own Junkyard* (New York: Holt, Rinehart & Winston, 1964), p. 17.

[26] Edward P. Eichler and Marshal Kaplan, *The Community Builders* (Berkeley, Calif.: University of California Press, 1967), pp. 144–47.

Burgeoning urban conglomerations. Critics of "urban sprawl" see urbanization running wild, leapfrogging over empty land without planning or systematic development.

ples on their way up the status ladder. Residents are supposed to be similar in age, income, occupation, education, position in the family cycle, and type of housing. These similarities are supposed to bind the residents together to strengthen a sense of community.

Berger asks: Why should a group of tract houses, mass-produced and quickly thrown up on the outskirts of a large city be sufficient to generate a uniform way of life? [27] In his study of a new tract suburb created by the building of a new automobile assembly plant in California, he found a consciousness of material well-being and respectability. However, there was a lack of pronounced striving, status anxiety, or orientation to the future. Tastes seemed untouched by "suburbia" in the white-collar style. Berger sees mobility of an entire social stratum, rather than evidence of individual social mobility. He suggests that organized well-paid industrial workers have taken over the "respectable" style of the old middle class without inheriting the yearning for further movement up the ladder of class status.[28]

The migrants to suburbia bring with them the cultural equipment for building an urban society but they also adopt, at least initially, some of the qualities of the society they find in the country. In this sense the suburban society has something of both urban and rural societies.[29] The suburban society combines in several models according to qualities of residents as differentiated by social class, occupation, age, education, point in the family cycle, and so on. In their search for suburban housing, the migrants express their particular qualities in making choices among the alternative suburbs in terms of their particular values and the range of alternatives available within their financial resources.

Apparently the move to the suburbs results in few and minor changes in the way of life. If changes do occur, they stem from the aspirations which were held before the move. Such aspirations could include yearnings for homeownership, more living space, access to better schools, closer proximity to workplace, expanded social life, and opportunity for fuller participation in organizational activity. Other kinds of changes are more directly the result of the move. Living in a single-family house, rather than in an apartment or row house, brings more privacy, a chance to improve one's own house and yard, and the possibility of more joint family activity. The newness of the community increases social activities, at least initially, but Gans finds the move to suburbia in itself has little direct influence on behavior patterns. He discounts the theory that changes in the physical characteristics of a community will bring vital changes in ways of life. The changes must be directed at the social, economic, and political

[27] Bennett M. Berger, *Working-Class Suburb: A Study of Auto Workers in Suburbia* (Berkeley, Calif.: University of California Press, 1960), p. 7.

[28] Ibid, pp. 92–98.

[29] S. D. Clark, *The Suburban Society* (Toronto, Can.: University of Toronto Press, 1966), pp. 8–13.

structure, rather than relying heavily on physical design of housing and other facilities.[30]

What to do about it?

The building of new cities has been advocated as the most promising way out of the dilemmas of urbanism. Instead of relying on a policy of drift which culminates in the urban sprawl of unplanned expansion, new cities would be designed in relatively unsettled areas. Instead of building expensive high-rise structures, such new cities would build along the horizontal dimension to avoid the adverse consequences of high population density. The plan is deemed feasible because recent technological and transportation trends have eased the dependence on particular locales. It is argued that new communities will decrease the distance to work and save public cost for transportation, utility lines, school busing, and so on. However, these savings would require a population density greater than that of conventional suburbia.

Weaver contends that the creation of a simple, uniform, and symmetrical organizational structure is unlikely. The rational proposals of professional urban planners are not matched by attitudes among the citizenry. Pragmatic and proximate adjustments are more likely than comprehensive remedies because of the absence of a widespread, popular perception of urban problems or any general consensus about dealing with them. It is more likely, Weaver believes, that progress in problem solutions will be attained by leaders operating within the framework of contemporary metropolitan organizations. Success will depend on the development of a more widespread and effective sense of membership in the community among the diverse groups.[31]

Haworth distinguishes "housekeeping" from the function of the city in coping with dislocations of its life.[32] Under housekeeping he places the service responsibilities allocated to the city government because they are required and cannot be provided by individuals or private enterprises. The function of coping with social problems would not be necessary if the first function were performed efficiently. The second function appears with failures to revise the institutional structure. Haworth would divert attention from the inadequacies of public housing to the question of why public housing is necessary at all. The housing crisis reflects failures of the present system of financing and constructing homes to meet the needs of certain segments of the population. He sees traffic congestion as a symptom of the failure of the city to perform its housekeeping function. The usual

[30] Herbert J. Gans, "Effects of the Move from City to Suburb," in Leonard J. Duhl (ed.), *The Urban Condition* (New York: Basic Books, 1963), pp. 184–98.

[31] Robert C. Weaver, "Major Problems in Urban Planning," in Duhl, *The Urban Condition*, pp. 98–110.

[32] Haworth, *The Good City*, pp. 43–46.

response is to facilitate the flow of traffic and thereby aggravate the congestion at the sources and destinations of vehicles. Haworth suggests that proper housekeeping would reduce this glut by dispersing over more space the activities which generate the heavy traffic in certain areas.

The major alternative directions for fiscal reform, Netzer suggests, are increased federal and state aid for many urban activities, improved administration of property tax, and metropolitan-wide nonproperty taxes. Included in the latter would be user charges for water and sewage treatment, degree of use of highways, and parking. Failure to apply user charges saddles property tax payers with the cost of dealing with air and water pollution.[33]

SUMMARY

The central theme of this book is that urbanism is prominent among the factors which have raised and aggravated social problems. An increasing share of America's population is living in cities. This occupancy of relatively compact areas has added to the difficulties of dealing with poverty, crime, mental and physical illness, race relations, and so on. Bureaucratic organizations are strained to meet the concurrent demands for efficient delivery of services and widening participation of citizens in decision making. The increased scale of urban society tests the capacity of man to organize his collective efforts to meet social problems. The metropolis is subject to fragmented organization, impoverishment of the central city, and sprawling development of the suburbs. The city draws migrants because of the economic opportunities it appears to offer.

FOR ADDITIONAL READING

Bennet M. Berger, "The Myth of Suburbia," in Roland W. Warren (ed.,), *Perspectives on the American Community* (Chicago: Rand McNally, 1966), pp. 167–78.

Alvin Boskoff, *The Sociology of Urban Regions* (New York: Appleton-Century-Crofts, Inc., 1962).

Morris Davis and Sol Levine, "Towards a Sociology of Public Transit," *Social Problems,* Vol. 15 (Summer 1967), pp. 84–91.

John Fischer, "Planning for the Second America," *Harper's Magazine,* Vol. 239 (November 1969), pp. 21–26.

Harlen W. Gilmore, *Transportation and the Growth of Cities* (Glencoe, Ill.: Free Press, 1953).

[33] Dick Netzer, "Financing Urban Government," in Wilson, *The Metropolitan Enigma,* pp. 85–88.

Harold F. Kaufman, "Toward An Interactional Conception of Community," *Social Forces,* Vol. 38 (October 1959), pp. 9–17.

Allen V. Kneese, "Why Water Pollution is Economically Unavoidable," *Transaction,* Vol. 5 (April 1968), pp. 31–36.

Rene Konig, *The Community,* trans. Edward Fitzgerald (London: Routledge and Kegan Paul, 1968).

John Lear, "Green Light for the Smogless Car," *Saturday Review,* Vol. 50 (December 6, 1969), pp. 81–86.

Norton E. Long, "The Local Community as an Ecology of Games," *American Journal of Sociology,* Vol. 64 (November 1958), pp. 251–61.

William McCord, *The Springtime of Freedom* (New York: Oxford University Press, 1965).

Robert M. MacIver, *Community: A Sociological Study,* (New York: Macmillan Co., 1928).

Pete M. Mann, *An Approach to Urban Sociology* (London: Routledge and Kegan Paul, 1965).

Wilfred Owen, *Cities in the Motor Age* (New York: Viking Press, 1959).

Fred Powledge, "The Flight from City Hall, *Harper's Magazine,* Vol. 239 (November 1969), pp. 86–96.

Peter H. Rossi and Robert A. Dentler, *The Politics of Urban Renewal* (New York: Free Press of Glencoe, 1961).

Gideon Sjoberg, "Comparative Urban Sociology," in Robert K. Merton, Leonard Broom, and Leonard S. Cottrell, Jr. (eds.), *Sociology Today: Problems and Prospects,* (New York: Basic Books, 1959), pp. 334–59.

Roger Starr, *Urban Choices: The City and Its Critics* (Baltimore, Md.: Penguin Books, 1967).

Urban and Rural America: Policies for Future Growth, (Washington, D.C.: Advisory Commission on Intergovernmental Relations, April 1968).

Raymond Vernon, *The Myths and Reality of Our Urban Problems* (Cambridge, Mass.: Joint Commission for Urban Studies, 1962).

Robert Walker, *The Planning Function in Urban Government,* (Chicago: University of Chicago Press, 1964).

Morton and Lucia White, *The Intellectual versus the City* (Cambridge, Mass.: Harvard University Press and the M.I.T. Press, 1962).

Robert C. Wood, *1400 Governments* (Cambridge, Mass.: Harvard University Press, 1961).

4 Technology: Friend or foe?

Americans are supposed to be fascinated by pizza tossing and automobile assembly lines because they like to see things made. Our interest in mechanization is cited to explain the honor given athletes who are machinelike in boxing, track, and team sports. Similarly, we are supposed to see beauty in synchronized machinery but be slow to recognize the beauty of a medieval church. The sheer volume of identical items spewing from the assembly line draws admiration because quantity is emphasized. The massive building or gigantic city evokes pride, while small, graceful, or modest things draw less attention.[1]

NATURE AND EFFECTS OF TECHNOLOGY

The above description risks exaggeration because Americans come in too wide variety to be captured fully in such a simplistic explanation. However, our purpose is to illustrate that the machine technology does color our view of the world. Mechanization is only one of the values which link industrialism with urbanism to shape life in the United States. As a major force operating in conjunction with urbanism, technology is an appropriate subject for this chapter because of its involvement in the

[1] Richard Muller-Freienfels, "The Mechanization and Standardization of American Life," In Logan Wilson and William L. Kobb (ed.) *Sociological Analysis* (New York: Harcourt, Brace & Co., 1949), pp. 146–51.

problems considered later in the book. Furthermore, this chapter will deal with several problems derived directly from technology.

The technological revolution is a key element in what Boulding has called the second great transformation in the history of mankind.[2] The first transition was from precivilized society and began some five or ten thousand years ago. It brought an agriculture surplus to feed urban populations. It emancipated man from the struggle for sheer physical survival sufficiently to enable him to develop the cultural and political components of a civilization. In the second transformation, industrial technology, science, and a stream of knowledge have brought man to the brink of an age where he is confronted with a central issue: Can he adjust his social arrangements for constructive use of the enormous power he has in dealing with nature? This question underlies a set of social problems involving the interaction of technology and society and the impact of our technology on the natural environment.

Nature of our technology

Over the centuries man has scored progressively greater success in converting natural resources to serve his needs. A *technology* is a particular mode of organizing human behavior and the cultural equipment for that purpose. A given technology contributes to the totality of a people's way of behaving so that raw materials are collected from the environment and converted into tools, containers, foods, clothing, shelter, means of transportation, and other material necessities. Examples of technologies are hunting, herding of animals, fishing, various types of agriculture, and various types of industrial production. Each technology is a cultural screen established by man between the natural environment and himself to extend his capacity to transform that environment.

We are likely to identify technology as a drill press or computer because it can be seen and touched. However, this cultural equipment is most significant in that it is tangible evidence of the ideas and forms of human organization which a people employ to convert the natural resources to serve their needs. Bell points out that our technology is "a systematic, disciplined approach to objectives, using a calculus of precision and measurement and a concept of system."[3]

Each technology includes a complex of techniques and an organization of the human beings utilizing the techniques. Techniques have been defined as the "tactics of living" which are more significant in terms of the fundamental ideas behind them than in the particular tangible form in

---

[2] Kenneth Boulding, *The Meaning of the Twentieth Century* (London: George Unwin and Unwin, 1965), pp. 1–2.

[3] Daniel Bell, "Toward the Year 2000; Work in Progess," *Daedalus,* Vol. 96 (Summer 1967), p. 643.

which the ideas are expressed.[4] In utilizing techniques men may work either alone or in groups with a division of tasks appropriate to the characteristics of a given technique. The techniques and their associated organization are patterned by the culture. In turn, the technology contributes to the shaping of culture through its influence on the social interactions from which cultural innovation emerges.

The industrial revolution was characterized by the substitution of powered machine production for handicrafts, increased efficiency of water transportation, development of new kinds of land transportation, and more rapid transmission of information. The substitution of machines for tools took work from the home (its site under domestic production) and brought the dominance of the factory as a method of industrial organization. Production had to be located where nonhuman power and access to raw materials and markets were favorable. Machines could be grouped in a central building for greater efficiency in linking them together for integrated performance of tasks. Supervision of workers could be improved to reduce irregularities in quality and quantity of work.

Early in the twentieth century mass production was introduced.[5] Under the concept of continuous flow, the materials move through a series of steps of processing. Workers perform the same task over and over in a specialization of jobs. The assembly-line brings the job to a worker who stays in one place. World War II brought automatic transfer machines which handle a piece of work, put it in proper position, fasten it in place, perform some operation on it, release it, and move it on to the next position. *Automation* involves automatic control in that the machine's own operation serves to regulate it to conform to predetermined objectives. A deviation from a desired quality activates a feedback readjustment. Electronic computers are provided information upon which machines act. Machines can thus control output, choose between alternative courses of action, and correct themselves for changes in qualities of the product, machine wear, and so on. They can start, stop, accelerate, decelerate, count, inspect, test, remember, compare, and measure qualities such as space and temperature.

Cybernation involves the application of automation to the processing of material and the application of computers to symbols. Wiener invented the term "cybernetics" to encompass the study of messages as a means of controlling machinery and society, and the development of computing machines and other such automata.[6] The explosive growth of scientific knowledge has produced incredibly sensitive measuring instruments, versatile powered controls as suggested above, means of transmitting infor-

[4] Oswald Spengler, *Man and Techniques* (New York: Alfred A. Knopf, 1932), p. 10.
[5] Walter Buckingham, *Automation: Its Impact On Business and People* (New York: Harper & Row, 1961), pp. 6–13.
[6] Norbert Wiener, *The Human Use of Human Beings* (Garden City, N.Y.: Doubleday & Co., 1956), p. 15.

mation electronically, and lightning-fast analysis of data. Automation has been defined as "any continuous and integrated operation of a production system that uses electronic and other equipment to regulate and coordinate the quantity and quality of production." [7] By subsuming automation under the broader term cybernation, we indicate this general technological development has impact beyond the factory assembly line to affect many other organized activities.

Direct and derivative effects

Technological change and social change are associated with one another. We cannot be certain about the order of their appearance or the precise nature of the effect of one upon the other, but the fact that they are associated is important in itself. Ogburn distinguishes between the direct and derivative effects of inventions.[8] *Direct effects* are those changes arising from the making and using of inventions. To use a vaccine for poliomyelitis, it must be produced and distributed. Therefore, factories are created and the habits of customers are changed. *Derivative effects* are less immediate and are obviously linked with the product in and of itself. The rise in the popularity of the automobile reduced the passenger traffic of railroads, brought forth the motel and suburban shopping centers, contributed to the consolidation of rural schools, and so on.

Included among derivative effects are events which are unanticipated. When economic enterprises are only casually integrated, the consequences of a change in marketing practices or the introduction of a new product cannot be predicted solely through knowledge of the innovating entrepreneur. Although unanticipated consequences are not necessarily undesirable, the unforeseen event requires readjustments likely to exceed the competence and resources of the original innovator. Derivative effects magnify the difficulties of planned change even when the innovators are ethical and altruistic. Generally, the pathological consequences of technological change have been the inability or failure to foresee, and prepare for, its social consequences.

Cybernation has unique qualities when compared to previous labor-saving inventions. Killingsworth cites the broad range of applications offered by automation and computers, both introduced at a particularly rapid pace. Cooperation with the laboratory scientist has become a necessity for industry and business if they are to take advantage of these rapid and complex developments. Earlier labor-saving inventions were introduced in industries undergoing rapid growth and provided the greater productivity required by a fast expanding market. Now such inventions

---

[7] Buckingham, *Automation,* p. 6.
[8] William F. Ogburn, "How Technology Causes Social Change," in Francis R. Allen, Hornell Hart, Delbert C. Miller, William F. Ogburn, and Meyer F. Nimkoff, *Technology and Social Change* (New York: Appleton-Century-Crofts, 1957), pp. 19–20.

are more likely to improve productivity at the cost of reduction in the number of people employed because industry has a lower rate of market growth.[9]

EVALUATION OF TECHNOLOGY

Is technology a friend or foe of man? Since technological change has profound ramifications for every facet of life, we should expect evaluations to range from prophecies of dismal doom to predictions of an age of unprecedented accomplishments. Among those who have evaluated modern technologies, three general groups are delineated by DeCarlo.[10]

With their central responsibilities in managing various facets of contemporary society, leaders of business, labor, and government emphasize the preservation of the values and attitudes of the past which have contributed to the success of their particular organization. They seek a structuring of technological change to minimize effects on their organizations through some balance between stability and change.

As critics of the management of the current social system, intellectuals emphasize the impact of technological change in reshaping social institutions and relationships by creating a potentiality for abundance of goods and services, needs for a higher efficiency in planning and leadership, a greater necessity for formal education and training to gain access to socioeconomic opportunity, and the new problems of maintaining a democratic society in the face of growing size and influence of formal organizations.

Scientists and specialists in technological development are likely to emphasize the changes to come in the sphere of materials and gadgetry. They are prone to expect man to reshape his attitudes and values to adjust to the conditions of a new technological environment.

Three sets of attitudes

In the view of those who see technology as the foe of man, it takes away jobs by making hard-won skills obsolete and eliminating opportunities for the unskilled. It is supposed to eliminate the joy of creativity by assigning men repetitive tasks which are only a fragment of a total productive process the laborer cannot comprehend as a whole. The machine is seen as the master of men as symbolized by the call of the factory whistle, the surveillance of the punch card, and the standardization of service through the time tables of mass transportation.

Concern over the implications of burgeoning technology frequently

---

[9] Charles C. Killingworth, "Automation, Jobs, and Manpower," in Louis A. Ferman, Joyce L. Kornbluh, and Alan Haber (eds.), *Poverty in America* (rev. ed.; Ann Arbor, Mich.: University of Michigan Press, 1968), pp. 259–73.

[10] Charles R. DeCarlo, "Perspectives on Technology," in Eli Ginzberg (ed.), *Technology and Social Change* (New York: Columbia University Press, 1964), pp. 21–24.

brings forth the recommendation that its development be halted. This solution, however, must be balanced against the need for more efficient technologies to meet human problems. The population explosion raises the question of whether or not minimum dietary needs of the peoples of the world can be met without technological innovations. But is the meeting of minimum needs the objective sought by Americans? The "war on poverty" suggests that the goal would be extending the material advantages of an advanced technology to a larger proportion of the population to provide a "decent" living. If this goal were set for the world as a whole, a ninefold expansion in production would be required.[11]

From a second perspective, modern technology is lauded as the motor of progress through its raising of per capita income, extending goods and services to an unprecedented share of the population, and breaking the monopoly of the wealthy on many conveniences and even luxuries by producing cheaper copies. Gadgets and pushbuttons come into more homes and workplaces to reduce drudgery and bring greater access to leisure-time activities to a broader segment of the population. Technology is pictured as a worker of miracles in overcoming the limitations of the physical environment and in overcoming the problems of man.

Thirdly, technology has been described as a neutral force which opens opportunities man may use to his benefit or disadvantage because it operates within the sociocultural environment in shaping its application in meeting human and social goals. Kranzberg and Pursell believe this moral neutrality of technology is overstated because it does set constraints upon human choice.[12] A given technology provides a bridge to move man from point A to point B. Once man sets foot on this bridge, he must go from point A to point B under circumstances determined to an important degree by the nature of the technology. For example, a later chapter on mass communication media points out that these technologies require heavy financial investment and large audiences, which raise issues of concentrated ownership and possible deterioration of cultural content.[13]

Kranzberg and Pursell see technology liberating man from a constant struggle with nature for his own survival and providing an abundance of goods, but technology also limits the individual's control over production and distribution and lends itself to exploitation of men by other men. The contribution of technology to many social problems, nevertheless, calls for social inventions to curb its use to encourage human greed and shortsightedness.

Certain characteristics of the social impact of technology, Michael

---

[11] Henry H. Villard, "The Need for Technological Change," in Dean Morse and Aaron W. Warner (eds.), *Technological Innovation and Society* (New York: Columbia University Press, 1966), pp. 158–59.

[12] Melvin Krazberg and Carrol W. Pursell, Jr. (eds.), *Technology in Western Civilization,* Vol. 2 (New York: Oxford University Press, 1967), pp. 705–6.

[13] See Chapter 10.

warns, make difficult the framing of solutions to the problems raised.[14] The accumulated effects frequently have been under way for some time before solutions are sought. The last chapter provided as examples the traffic chaos brought by the automobile. The erosion of the environment is another illustration. When the solution entails fundamental changes in attitudes or creation of a new kind of labor force, there is a time lag in the shaping of attitudes and the reformulation of educational systems consistent with the new conditions.

Culture and social structure are much slower than technological development in responding to new conditions. Time is required for public opinion to form agreement that a given condition qualifies as a social problem and merits collective effort for solution. Furthermore, the past is unlikely to provide a precedent for framing a solution because the complexity of American technology and the expectations of contemporary people differ markedly from earlier situations. Ancient Greece is an inappropriate analogy for interpreting the contemporary problem of leisure, because the shorter work day of masses of workers, including women, was not a factor in the leisure enjoyed by a small Greek elite.

Involvement in fundamental values

The involvement of technology in social problems raises questions about the priorities of various social goals and the control of innovation to serve the ultimate interests of people in general. Among a people particularly prone to expect change, it is odd that Americans should be described as conservative in assessing technological innovation. However, Riesman sees the American belief in *progress* to be conservative in its unquestioned acceptance of the inevitability of technological innovation. Consequently, many Americans see as inconceivable the curbing of aggressive technology or the questioning of growth for its own sake.[15]

Our commitment to the inevitability of "progress" illustrates the permeation of technology through American values. The introduction to this chapter emphasized our keen interest in mechanization and our admiration of sheer quantity. Another illustration is our reliance on *rationalism,* the application of reason to the solution of problems and the search for knowledge. Technological research and development proceeds through judicious selection of what appear to be the most efficient procedures to achieve a given purpose through minimum expenditure of resources and energy. We tend to extend this attitude toward inanimate objects to our dealings with one another. Our "hard-headed" emphasis on "facts" in human relations frequently conflicts with the humanitarianism we like to believe is an American characteristic.

[14] Donald N. Michael, "Some Speculations on the Social Impact of Technology," in Morse and Warner, *Technological Innovation and Society,* pp. 121–26.
[15] David Riesman, "Leisure and Work in Post-Industrial Society," in Eric Larrabee and Rolf Meyersohn (eds.), *Mass Leisure* (Glencoe, Ill.: Free Press, 1958), pp. 366–67.

The American's romance with his automobile is a prominent example of the influence of technology. One sign of the automobile's remarkable place in our set of values was the ruling of a majority of public welfare agencies during the depression of the 1930s that ownership of an automobile would not disqualify a person from receiving public assistance. To search for odd jobs a man needed a vehicle to cover distances beyond foot travel. The vehicle could be used to acquire income. Even more significant was the justification that deprivation of an automobile would undermine a man's self-respect.[16]

Materialism has been identified as one of the central values of our age. As a medium of exchange, money makes possible the rapid and easy transactions whereby our intricate economic system can operate. A man can specialize as an automobile mechanic because the farmer, bread baker, and other specialists produce the goods and services he does not produce for himself. The mechanic's work produces income which, through money as a common denominator, can be converted into the particular goods and services he requires. As a target for human aspiration, money is an invaluable tool for motivating behavior to maintain the overall economic system.

Money exchange concurrently has contributed to personal freedom and the erosion of social obligations. Not having to depend on family and neighbors to provide crucial services, the individual with money can withdraw from their control. He can pay for food, clothing, shelter, and services without obligating himself to future reciprocal services or conformity to social standards beyond the immediate transaction. Theoretically he can choose to stand alone without the supports of custom and group habits and complete with his peers in achieving his own aspirations. But his dependence on money encourages the growth of materialism wherein money becomes an end in itself. Furthermore, his emancipation from custom may be perverted into personal exploitation of the cooperative arrangements which money exchange promotes. Carried to an extreme, materialism can produce a form of social cannibalism.

Space exploration as an issue

The permeation of technological determinism in our values is currently involved in the debate over the merits of heavy investment in space exploration. On the one hand, the accomplishments of physical scientists and engineers strain the imagination. On the other hand, critics question a set of national priorities which allocates so much treasure and effort to probe a universe far removed from the scene of serious social problems.

Why explore space? A frequent answer is "because it is there." The spirit of courageous adventure is supposed to be sufficient justification for

[16] Simeon Strunsky, *The Living Tradition* (New York: Doubleday, Doran & Co., 1939), p. 174.

probing the unknown environment of space. Perhaps the men riding the fire-tailed technological dragon capture the individualistic heroism of the frontier lawman facing alone the forces of evil on a dusty street of a frontier town. However, the television picture of men picking up rocks on the stark surface of the moon is a more accurate portrayal of the significance of the massive effort. These men are carefully trained technicians gathering information on the properties of planets, the behavior of the solar system, and the fundamental laws of the universe.

The debate over space research qualifies in some respects as an illustration of judgments based on immediate benefits which overlook the long-term benefits of pure research. The collaboration of the physical sciences has opened the way to tackling fundamental problems previously inaccessible. Tremendous discoveries are in prospect concerning such matters as atmospheric pollution, the earth's gravitational field, the chemistry of life, the forces affecting the weather, and many others.[17]

In more immediate terms, space research has had payoffs in commercial and military applications. Compounds of hydrazine, used in liquid propellants, are used in pharmaceuticals. Solenoid valves for rocket engines are used in home furnaces. Coating of metals improves or inhibits transfer of heat and strengthens resistance to wear. Miniaturization of electronics has been of widespread advantage to consumers. Military applications include reconnaissance, early warning of enemy strikes, and ejection of explosive devices against earth targets.[18]

The admirers of space exploration have the weakest justification when they argue that this example of technological determination will in some vague manner produce an age of reason without war and strife. The common effort is supposed somehow to bring all mankind into an altruistic consensus. The argument overlooks the rivalry with the Soviet Union which stimulated the American effort and the competition for nationalistic prestige and power. Michael objects to the simplistic equating of escape from the earth by rocket with escape from the earth's present and future problems. Human behavior is too grounded in sociocultural settings to be accessible to the wand of the good fairy of space technology.[19]

TECHNOLOGY AND SOCIAL ORGANIZATION

Industrialization and urbanization have been twin forces in the rise of contemporary urban society. Urbanism has been both a contributor to and

[17] See Homer E. Newell and Leonard Jaffe, "Impact of Space Research on Science and Technology," *Science,* Vol. 157 (July 7, 1967), pp. 29–39.

[18] Hugh Odishaw (ed.), *The Challenges of Space* (Chicago: University of Chicago Press, 1962), pp. 3–6, 315–16.

[19] Donald N. Michael, "Prospects of Human Welfare: Peaceful Uses," in Lincoln P. Bloomfield (ed.), *Outer Space: Prospects for Man and Society* (Englewood Cliffs, N.J.: Prentice-Hall, 1962), pp. 62–63.

a product of technological developments.[20] Revolutions in food production and industrialization made available the surpluses whereby the urban populations could acquire necessities by means other than their own direct labor. With the growth of trade and of networks of transportation and communication, the human community was released from the limitations of a local territory. By providing a means of supporting population clusters, industrial technology has contributed to urban growth. Conversely, urban concentrations have provided the labor force and consumers for industry.

Amassing of population has accelerated the demands on technological innovation to meet needs brought by the complexity of social structure and the large scale of social organizations. Through a common relationship with population concentrations, urbanism and industrialism have given urban life the sociological characteristics analyzed earlier: heterogeneity of population, specialization of behavior, anonymous and impersonal relationships, and standardization of life.

Effect on social institutions

Technology has influenced the nature of contemporary social organization by substituting more individualistic striving to gain a paycheck in place of duty to the kinship group. By contributing to the growth of urban society, industrialism has weakened traditional family ties and eroded emotional identifications with the neighborhood.[21] The high turnover of residents of a neighborhood lessens probability of emotional ties developed through long-term association. Technological considerations favor high turnover when the labor force must be moved where the work is. When jobs are mechanized, such as farm work, the workers rendered surplus are pressed to migrate where they are told employment can be found. Technology might create new industries to attract migrants. Improvements in standard of living or conversion of residential areas into industrial or commercial sections also favor migration.[22]

Nevertheless, Litwak and Szelenyi note, technological society encourages the development of nationally based industry, mass media, and nationally based educational norms, which in turn promote a common language and culture. The professional in a large-scale bureaucratic organization develops an occupational milieu which provides a common basis for adjusting personal lives to different physical settings. Perhaps this situation is a prototype for a greater prevalence of personal planning for

---

[20] See Paul Meadows, "The City, Technology, and History," *Social Forces,* Vol. 36 (December 1957), pp. 141–47.

[21] Bert F. Hoselitz, "The City, the Factory, and Economic Growth," in Paul K. Hatt and Albert J. Reiss, Jr. (eds.), *Cities and Society* (Glencoe, Ill.: Free Press, 1957), pp. 549–52.

[22] Eugene Litwak and Ivan Szelenyi, "Primary Group Structures and Their Functions: Kin, Neighborhood, and Friends," *American Sociological Review,* Vol. 34 (August 1969), pp. 466–67.

adjustment to new neighborhoods. The local institutions (church, school, and voluntary groups) could speed the welcoming and indoctrination of newcomers into the neighborhood norms. In short, Litwak and Szelenyi argue, the neighborhood can survive in spite of high membership turnover, but in some new form.

Family relations are altered as the occupational role is separated from the family role in terms of physical locales and the experiences shared by the members of the family. Employment away from the home diffuses the experiences of the individuals composing the family. Money payments for work separate consumption from productive activities. Occupation rises and kinship declines as status determinants.

In the political sphere, the territorial diffusion of markets erodes the effectiveness of local control and intensifies the power of centralized administrative and political agencies in an age when transportation and communication technologies have expanded the human community beyond local boundaries. The base of potential political power spreads to wider groups in the society. The establishment of political order is complicated by the need to achieve consensus among a cadre of special-interest groups. The rapid pace and manifold derivative effects of technological change lend further emphasis to the need to narrow the time lag between recognition of a given social problem and the implementation of a remedial strategy. The quality of political and moral leadership is of particular importance in confronting problems requiring technical knowledge and a capacity to interpret the counsel (not necessarily consistent) of experts drawn from specialized fields of physical science, social science, industry, labor unions, and so on.

Autonomy of the individual

By contributing to the vast scale and pervasiveness of man-made events, technology has complicated our idealization of the individual. The vast bureaucracies and the scale of the problems associated with the use of elaborate technology dwarf the individual when he asks: "What can I do to correct the conditions I abhor and fear?"

Michael suggests three typical responses.[23] Limited by the amount of information and stimuli a human being can process at a given time, some people are selectively involved. They pick the issues and things to which they respond and for which they feel responsibility. Therefore, their meaningful alternatives for action are fewer than the scope of information technology can provide about itself for democratic resolution of the issues it raises. Another reaction is to opt out of the "big system" and seek some simpler, direct segment of the social universe where face-to-face relationships are more characteristic. The third reaction is violence or forms of

[23] Michael, "Prospects of Human Welfare," pp. 134–35.

protest which sidestep the legal or ethical constraints of the urban technological system.

Privacy has been defined as a right of the individual to decide for
himself how much he will share his thoughts, his feelings, and the facts
of his private life.[24] The right to privacy is intimately associated among
American values with inalienable rights to dignity, self-respect, and freedom of action within broad limits set to maintain an essential social order.
On the other hand, protection of the right of privacy must be accommodated to an equally important right to protect the community against
conduct of the individual which would place its interest in serious jeopardy. Vital issues are raised in the enforcement of criminal laws to protect
the community without unduly invading privacy or violating civil rights.
Another important need is to discover new knowledge essential to man.
Research into human behavior is an important area where the right of
privacy must be balanced against learning of reliable facts useful to mankind in the long run.

Threats to privacy and civil rights can be produced by miniature microphones and recording equipment, wiretaps, closed-circuit television cam-
eras, two-way mirrors, and parabolic microphones for long-distance
eavesdropping. Computers have made it possible to assemble information
on millions of individuals from credit ratings, insurance investigations,
collection agencies, and employers.[25]

Pharmacology and electronics have brought technological developments which aggravate value conflicts in relationships between the individual and the state. Either to control or to free the mind, drugs are
grouped as tranquilizers, sedatives, stimulants, antidepressives, and psychoactive (that is, inducing altered states of consciousness).[26] Drugs have
the potential to treat troubled minds, but they also raise social issues by
involving government in the control of their antisocial uses. Control of the
mind also can involve extraction of information under circumstances im-
periling privacy and civil rights.

Impact on work environment

Modern technology has the potential to fundamentally alter the
social-psychological basis of roles. Automation is likely to increase the
service occupations as factory production is taken over by computer-
directed machines. Service jobs tend to have qualities seen as "feminine,"

---

[24] "Privacy and Behavioral Research" (Preliminary Summary of Report of Panel on
Privacy and Behavioral Research), *Science,* Vol. 155 (February 3, 1967), p. 536.
[25] Myron Brenton, *The Privacy Invaders* (Greenwich, Conn.: Fawcett Publications,
1964).
[26] Johathan O. Cole, "Drugs and Control of the Mind," in John G. Burke (ed.), *The New
Technology and Human Values* (Belmont, Calif.: Wadsworth Publishing Co., 1966), pp.
267–75.

such as cultivation of the interest of customers instead of demonstrating physical prowess or psychological aggressiveness. Work will appear to be less masculine. With shorter hours, the greater prevalence of leisure will undermine the work ethic.[27] The sitting posture becomes more characteristic in a sedentary society where man sits in a chair to supervise automatic machines, to operate a bulldozer, to telephone, and to travel.[28]

The psychological costs of industrialism generally have been compared adversely to a romanticized view of the life of craftsmen—who comprised only a fraction of the medieval labor force. Although exaggerated, this view does reflect the increased expectations that work should be a source of personal satisfaction. There is evidence that the majority of workers in most occupations are at least moderately satisfied with their jobs. However, the degree of satisfaction varies with the presence in the occupation of qualities which lend themselves to the worker's control.[29]

A study of Detroit factory workers found mental-health scores declined consistently with occupational status from upper semiskilled jobs through ordinary semiskilled to routine, repetitive jobs. Comparatively high mental health was associated with these characteristics: use of the worker's abilities to stimulate his interest, sense of accomplishment, personal growth, and self-respect; positive feelings in regard to income and a sense of financial security; low pace, intensity, and repetitiveness of work operations; positive supervision and human relations on the job; genuine opportunities for advancement and increased prestige. Generally, workers had a moderately positive attitude toward work and the job—neither acute discontent nor enthusiasm.[30]

Cybernation potentially can have great impact on the organization of work.[31] With it, the type of work performed and the relationships among jobs are changed. The interdependence of man and machines reduces physical handling of materials, but requires greater alertness to catch difficulties in the work processes. The physical distance between work stations is increased with the result that the amount of contact among workers decreases. Thereby, the development of friendships and of a sense of team membership is reduced. Worker morale and satisfaction with work may be undermined. Supervisory skills are tested in human relations and in

[27] See Chapter 11 on erosion of the work ethic.

[28] Herbert Collins, "The Sedentary Society," *Scientific Monthly*, Vol. 79 (November 1954), pp. 285–92.

[29] Robert Blauner, "Work Satisfaction and Industrial Trends in Modern Society," in Walter Galenson and Seymour M. Lipsett (ed.), *Labor and Trade Unionism* (New York: John Wiley & Sons, 1960), pp. 339–60.

[30] Arthur Kornhauser, *Mental Health of the Industrial Worker: A Detroit Study* (New York: John Wiley and Sons, 1965), pp. 261–66.

[31] Floyd C. Mann, "Psychological and Organizational Impacts," in John T. Dunlap (ed.) *Automation and Technological Change* (Englewood Cliffs, N.J.: Prentice-Hall, 1962), pp. 50–55.

technical skills essential to meet demanding schedules without machine breakdown. The cleanliness and safety of the workplace tends to be improved.

Smaller work forces mean less opportunity for promotion. The specialization of tasks reduces the possibility of promotion through moving into another work activity without special training. The possibility of unemployment through obsolescence of a given job creates insecurity in times of rapid technological skills, but advanced technology usually means higher pay and greater prestige on a scale related to greater demands of work tasks. Large capital investments are likely to require around-the-clock operations and these expose some employees to work schedules discordant with usual living patterns. Labor unions generally have accepted the "high wage-low labor cost" doctrine favorable to technological innovation. Work rules are employed to assure that the worker receives his share of the benefits from innovation. In some instances, the rules serve as "featherbedding," whereby favored workers gain advantages unrelated to their productivity.

Advocates of technological innovation predict displaced workers will find new job opportunities created because increased production will stimulate sales through lower prices. Michael reports estimates range from 4,000 to 40,000 displacements a week from cybernation along. But no clear answer on the effects on jobs is available. New jobs are created by cybernation, such as programmers, special-skill maintenance men, and subprofessionals who relieve highly trained professionals of routine tasks in processing data or dealing with clients; and the growth of leisure time offers the prospects of many new kinds of jobs. However, the net effect is difficult to determine. Employees are not likely to be fired immediately because of humanitarian and public-relations considerations. Rather, the labor force is reduced "silently" through failure to replace retired workers or those who quit.[32]

The consequences of new technologies, Michael says are most significant in relation to alterations in the future job market. Cybernation is recognized as a threat to unskilled and semiskilled jobs which are sought by a growing army of competitors reinforced by school dropouts, women returning to the work force, illiterates, mental inadequates, the young, the vocationally untrained, and persons displaced from other jobs. However, inroads also are being made on the skilled jobs of metalworkers, welders, machinists, clerical and office workers, engineers in relatively routine jobs, and so on. Middle-level managers face prospects of displacement by computers for routine decision making. Meanwhile, the shift has been from blue-collar productive jobs to white-collar service jobs. However, cybernation may become appropriate for many service tasks, including the

[32] Donald N. Michael, "The Impact of Cybernation," in Krangberg and Pursell, *Technology in Western Civilization,* pp. 659–63.

use of household robots. Fiberglass boats and artificial turf for athletic fields are examples of innovations that eliminate service jobs.

The problem of diffusion of technological innovation, Hollomon says, is crucial to the effective social use of science and economic growth.[33] He notes that about a tenth of one percent of American manufacturing companies perform 80 percent of industrially sponsored research and development and account for 60 percent of the sales of all manufacturing companies. The disparity in research activities between large and small companies reduces market competition and reduces the productivity and profits of smaller firms. To undertake innovation, the small company faces disadvantages because of the costs of research and the investments necessary to benefit.

THE UNIVERSITY AND RESEARCH

The historic missions of the university have been the preservation, development, and transmission of knowledge. Now the universities also play vital functions in research for technological innovation. As research entrepreneurs, universities compete for governmental and private funds, and, thereby, acquire a stake in the status quo of the established society.

The university needs the government's financial support for science, but unresolved issues stem from its response to the government's need for university research. Can the university expand its research activities without shortchanging the education of students in an age when quality instruction is of special importance? How can a competent faculty be assembled and retained in the face of industry's competition for research talent? As a community with heavy ethical obligations to society in general, how can the university select research topics appropriate for linking technological innovation to the long-term interests of mankind? Can the university accept funds for research under terms of the granting agency and still preserve essential freedoms? [34]

Ideological issues and the campus

The twentieth century has transformed the relationship between science and war because development of technology is increasingly dependent upon advances in basic knowledge about the physical world. The scientist has been catapulted into the arena of policymaking because he possesses specialized and relevant skills and information. He has been

[33] J. Herbert Hollomon, "Science, Technology, and Economic Growth," in Norman Kaplan (ed.) *Science and Society* (Chicago: Rand McNally, 1965), p. 523.
[34] Charles V. Kidd, "The American Universities and Federal Research," in Kaplan, *Science and Society,* p. 414.

moved from the position of benevolent outsider to valuable insider because he is perceived by the public as a disinterested party and a miracle worker and because he perceives himself as an agent of nature and of problem solving. His influence is derived, in the public's mind, from his aloofness from big business, shabby practices, and uncertainty in thought. However, difficulties of this image of what Wood calls "an apolitical elite" are suggested by criticisms that scientists fail to recognize the special expertise of the political process in accommodating competing objectives and that scientists are pressed to move outside the proper sphere of their technical expertise.[35]

Disputes over the functions of the university in technological innovation express deep-seated ideological differences which exist on the campus as well as in society at large. In a widely quoted comment, C. P. Snow notes the existence of "two cultures" which convey "a curious distorted image of each other."[36] Nonscientists see scientists as shallowly optimistic and unaware of man's condition. However, Snow believes that physical scientists recognize tragedies in individual life in such matters as undernourishment and premature death, but they also believe something can be done by man to improve the human lot. Because scientists are particularly apt to come from poor families, they have "the future in their bones." Scientists believe "literary intellectuals" are totally lacking in foresight, peculiarly unconcerned with their brother men, and in a deep sense anti-intellectual. Snow sees these intellectuals as more traditional because literature changes more slowly than science. He calls them "natural Luddites" inclined to oppose technological innovation. In noting this gulf in understanding, Snow's chief concern is that education tends to further this ideological conflict at the same time that common effort has become more essential.

The linking of technological research and production with the military establishment has involved the university in sharp criticism of what has been called a "military industrial complex," diverting a major share of the nation's talent and treasure into warfare as opposed to solution of social problems.[37] Governmental requirements have stimulated conflicts concerning the loyalty of research personnel and the secret classification of findings. The university has been cast in the unsatisfactory role of exploiter in contract negotiations over indirect costs of administration, library services, building maintenance, and the like. Research assistantships have lent

---

[35] Robert C. Wood, "Scientists and Politics: The Rise on an Apolitical Elite," in Robert Gilipin and Christopher Wright (eds.), *Scientists and National Policy-Making* (New York: Columbia University Press, 1964), pp. 41–72.

[36] C. P. Snow, *The Two Cultures and a Second Look* (Cambridge, Eng.: Cambridge University Press, 1965), pp. 1–22.

[37] See John Kenneth Galbraith, *How to Control the Military* (Garden City, N.Y.: Doubleday, 1969), Sidney Lens, *The Military-Industrial Complex* (Philadelphia, Pa.: Pilgrim Press, 1970), and Seymour Melman, *Our Depleted Society* (New York: Holt, Rinehart & Winston, 1965).

themselves to diverting students from serious study and career preparations into prolonged work on fairly mundane research problems.[38]

Critics argue that research and policy-making roles place the scientist
in support of a status quo repugnant to the intellectual. "Posing as disinterested scholars, we perform policy research for powerful organizations in
our society, providing them with knowledge they need to influence or
control their problems. We have placed our expertise at the disposal of
the establishment, letting the development of our field be guided by the
needs of those who can pay for our time."[39]

Because of the sheer scale of research projects, Weinberg warns that
expenditure of great funds may be deemed an equivalent of the profound
thought science requires, that administrative demands may outweigh
scientific creativity, and that the value of publicity in acquiring funds may
lend a journalistic triviality to "scientific" reports. He sees Big Science

---

4 Sociologists Back Strikers

Four. . . . University sociologists have joined striking employees in the
labor dispute at the Gateway Army Ammunition plant. . . . The four said
they would carry picket signs, help obtain legal assistance and help workers
determine eligibility for food stamps. It may be unlawful for workers themselves to set up a formal picket line because the walkout has not been
sanctioned by the union.

"We just went down and talked to some of them who were standing on
the sidewalk and said we wanted to support them. . . . We're not there to
mediate, or to study them. We're supporting them on their own conditions
—as more bodies for the picket line, not as social scientists. . . . Five years
ago a sociologist would have been down there saying we want to write this
up . . . That's building an academic career by climbing on the backs of the
people being studied. We disavow aloof professionalism and the kind of
so-called objectivity which calls for distorting data so as to reach a predetermined conclusion."

Blue collar workers and academic scholars have a community of interest
in that both are dealing with the problems of oppressive bureaucracy, the
four said. Both groups, they said, are dependent on military spending, although at the same time craving peace; both are under control of boards
of directors composed of the same persons. (They envisage) a growing
alliance between student radicalism and labor. Plant workers not only permitted the sociologists to attend union meetings, but promised to support
student agitation (they said) . . . .

St. Louis Post-Dispatch, Vol. 91, No. 268 (October 5, 1969), p. 25A.

[38] J. Stephan Dupre and Stanford A. Lakoff, *Science and the Nation: Policy and Politics*
(Englewood Cliffs, N.J.: Prentice-Hall, 1962), pp. 43–63.

[39] Quoted by Howard M. Vollmer, "Toward a Sociology of Applied Science," *American
Sociologist,* Vol. 4 (August 1969), p. 248.

diverting university faculties from their essential function as professors into research entrepreneurs specializing in administrative, housekeeping, and publicity functions.[40]

As an employee, the scientist encounters role conflicts which vary with the demands placed upon him by the degree of research freedom provided, his ethics, and the subject of his investigation. Whereas science demands a selfless dedication to objective truth, the employee is expected to produce consistently on the job, to be "efficient" in utilization of resources, adjust to the authority of superiors in the organization, and discipline his behavior within the rules of the employing organization.[41]

Scientist versus actionist

Their contributions to the development and application of technologies involve physical scientists in ethical and social matters which bring into sharp debate their traditional role as scientists. The social implications of technological innovation exert similar pressures on social scientists to take on the actionist role. The *scientist* engaged in pure research plays the circumscribed role of the specialist applying his particular theoretical and methodological skills to seek the fundamental principles explaining the "why" and "how." He seeks truth regardless of his personal views. His view is long-term, and he believes that "the greatest utility of his work lies in its contribution to the richness of man's intellectual and cultural heritage, rather than in the direct application of scientific knowledge to social problems." [42] As a scientist he can testify on the facts he has determined objectively and reliably. He cannot go beyond his specific findings to say that a particular action *should* be taken.

Neutrality in research is essential to the reliability of findings and the apolitical status of the scientist as public expert. However, neutrality is not the equivalent of commitment to the status quo. The very pursuit of truth concerning the social problems associated with technological aspects of society sometimes places the scientist in conflict with defenders of the status quo. He is likely to expose unfounded myths about the workings of the social institutions in the implementation of technological innovation. He may prove that sacred institutions are important sources of the social problems. As Glazer puts it, the social scientist outrages the "respectable segments of society by attacking that which should be upheld and defended and by explaining that which should be attacked and suppressed." [43]

---

[40] Alvin M. Weinberg, "Impact of Large-Scale Science on the United States," in Kaplan, *Science and Society,* pp. 552–54.

[41] Morris I. Stein, "Creativity and the Scientist," in Kaplan, *Science and Society,* pp. 335–36.

[42] Howard Waitzkin, "Truth's Search for Power: The Dilemmas of the Social Sciences," *Social Problems,* Vol. 15 (Spring 1968), p. 409.

[43] Nathan Glazer, "The Ideological Uses of Sociology," in Paul F. Lazarsfeld, William H. Sewell, and Harold L. Wilensky (eds.). *The Uses of Sociology* (New York: Basic Books, 1967), p. 76.

The *actionist* emphasizes his civic responsibility as he sees it. Whereas the scientist adopts a neutral stance, the actionist takes sides and plunges into political bargaining to effect the reform he advocates. Because the social scientist is well-informed on the nature of social problems, he is urged to become directly involved in efforts to ameliorate them:

"We are nauseous over the continual replication of meaningless, microscopic quantifications . . . . from sterile, neutral, non-involved, objective research sociologists. . . . It is imperative for sociologists to analyze precisely what is sick in American society and then to act to . . . heal American society." [44]

Advocates of action participation by social scientists argue that involvement in the "life-heat of the interactions" of problem situations provides a profound understanding not accessible to outside and dispassionate observers, shut out from the lives of people they study. Furthermore, it is contended that usual research has little impact because the persons who populate the problem situations are denied expertise in understanding the source of the problem and in framing strategies to reshape the social system which continues the problem.[45]

The rhetoric of the actionist argument has appeal to many scientists, although in the long run the actionist role would eliminate the place and function of science and the university within the total system. The rhetoric reflects the literary intellectual's ambivalence about physical science, as described by Snow, which underestimates the scientist's commitment to humanity. The appeal of the actionist's argument is derived from the scientist's awareness of the ethical conflicts latent in policy-making and applied research functions. However, since the university has been committed to service to rational purposes, the issue is respect for ethical obligations rather than substitution of a fundamentally different role. Furthermore, action plunges the university into a political maelstrom, diverting it from its primary educational mission, jeopardizing the economic basis upon which students gain the physical and intellectual resources of the university, and threatening vital academic freedom from all points of the political spectrum.

DRAIN ON NATURAL ENVIRONMENT

Each technology is a strategy for converting natural resources to satisfy human needs. The consequences of our technology on the quality of the natural environment have produced fears for the future of mankind. The magnitude of the ecological crisis results from a combination of population

[44] Henry Etzkowitz and Gerald M. Schaflander, "A Manifesto for Sociologists: Institution Formation—A New Sociology," *Social Problems,* Vol. 15 (Spring 1968), pp. 399–408.
[45] Ibid.

density, increasing consumption of natural resources, and the previous neglect of the consequences of ruinous exploitation of the environment. Heavy demands placed on the environment by each individual in a burgeoning horde of urbanites lead to various forms of pollution. Directly or indirectly, the average city dweller uses 150 gallons of water, 4 pounds of food, and 19 pounds of fossil fuel per day. This consumption is converted into 120 gallons of sewage, 4 pounds of refuse, and 1.9 pounds of air pollutants.[46]

New dimensions to pollution

Fundamental value conflicts are latent in the controversies over methods of converting natural resources to human use. Industrial pollution means job opportunity and community prosperity. Agricultural pesticides which threaten wildlife also hold down costs of producing food. The erosion of the quality of the environment is directly related to the growing demand for fossil fuel used to power air conditioners, automobiles, and other aspects of the "good life." Elimination of pollutants involves higher taxes and increased costs of products. Will the average citizen be willing to surrender some of the benefits of technology and pay the costs?

The overcoming of pollution requires a revision of human priorities. Bates argues that an enlightened self-interest must be substituted for the general assumption that man's own immediate needs and convenience hold unquestioned priority over the complex and intricate ecological balance of nature. In creating an artificial system to serve his needs in conflict with nature, man raises hazards to himself. Unanticipated consequences emerge which require further use of chemicals or machinery to maintain a precarious balance.[47]

Man's pollution of his environment is not new, but new factors have been added by ruinous exploitation and by the obnoxious residues of things we make and use. Cut-and-get-out logging operations result in inadequate fire protection, soil erosion, downstream flooding, and loss of habitat for wildlife. Overuse of farm land and single-crop plantings exhaust soil fertility and create erosion. Strip mining can create unsightly spoil banks and rubbish dumps. Rivers have become open sewers.

Previously the natural processes of the environment remedied these consequences. Now the technology, the higher productivity, and the greater size and concentration of populations exceed the capacity of these natural processes. Raising of the gross national product burns more coal and oil to discharge more sulphur dioxide into the air. Higher production

[46] Abel Wolman, "The Metabolism of Cities: Water and Air," in H. Wentworth Eldredge (ed.), *Taming Megalopolis,* Vol. I (New York: Frederick A. Praeger, 1967), p. 57.
[47] Marston Bates, *The Forest and the Sea* (New York: Random House, 1960), pp. 259–62.

of paper means more trash, and more new automobiles contribute to the piles of old junked vehicles. Advancing technology produces new kinds of poisons in the city and farm.[48]

The average American throws away more as time passes. In 1930 it was 650 pounds, 500 of which was combustible. By 1960 the per capita figure had risen to 1,100 pounds of combustible refuse. At that rate the total annual production of combustible waste will be 175 million tons by the year 2000, sufficient to bury all of Washington, D.C., in 30 feet of trash.[49] Concurrently, as a society, Americans are becoming less tolerant of environmental deterioration. Rising standards of expectation have contributed to the definition of the polluted environment as a social problem.

Although the specter of vanishing resources has risen in light of the tremendous appetite of modern technology for raw materials and the dilemmas associated with the population explosion, studies indicate that widespread scarcity is not in prospect.

Technology offers means of coping with the problem of supply by new abilities to upgrade old resources; examples are fertilization of cropland and concentration of low-grade iron ore into taconite pellets. New resources may be discovered, such as plastics, nuclear fission, and previously inaccessible oil in offshore and arctic regions. Resources may be utilized more efficiently; wood waste is used in pulp mills and to make pressed board. Other resources and techniques may be substituted; aluminum replaces copper and air cooling replaces water cooling. Technology has provided means of assuring a sufficiency, especially if higher costs are accepted. However, in the process, technology has degraded the quality of the natural environment through air and water pollution by discharge of wastes and through deterioration of the land.[50]

The social problems associated with natural resources, then, are the matter of facing up to the variety of effects of technological growth upon the nature-man relationship. The natural environment is only part of what one generation passes on to another, Barnett asserts. Knowledge, technology, capital institutions, and economic institutions are also part of the heritage which can become instrumentalities for meeting the interests of future generations. The social problems lurk in the conflict of values which are behind the destruction of natural beauty, failures in the system of income distribution, breakdown in waste disposal, and other problems of urban agglomerations.[51]

[48] Roger Revelle, "Pollution and the Cities," in James A. Wilson (ed.), The Metropolitan Enigma (Cambridge, Mass.: Harvard University Press, 1968), pp. 92–93.

[49] Today and Tomorrow in Air Pollution (Washington, D.C.: Public Health Service, 1968), p. 11.

[50] Hans H. Landsberg, "The U.S. Resource Outlook: Quantity and Quality," Daedalus, Vol. 96 (Fall 1967), pp. 1034–57.

[51] Harold J. Barnett, "The Myth of Vanishing Resources," Trans-action, Vol. 4 (June 1967), pp. 6–10.

Air pollution and the automobile

The automobile loses about 15 percent of the fuel energy it uses, emitting about three pounds of carbon monoxide and two ounces of nitrogen for each gallon of gasoline burned. Revelle estimates that the automobiles in Los Angeles county alone produce sufficient nitrogen oxides a year to fertilize the entire county with 70 pounds per acre. Motor vehicle exhaust also discharges large amounts of lead, which tend to concentrate in soils and plants near major highways and add to the lead burden in human bodies. Transportation accounts for about 60 percent of air pollution in the United States compared to 30 percent from electric power generation and industry. The emitted particles and sulphur dioxide become part of atmosphere inversion layers. When warm air forms a lid over cold air beneath, the pollutants are held close to the ground. When fresh air is not brought in, the combination of high population density and high rate of fossil fuel consumption raises the possibility of a shortage of air.[52] Smog causes eye and respiratory ailments, reduced visibility, damage to certain vegetation, and damage to certain materials such as rubber.

Suggested solutions include reduced emissions from internal combustion engines, fewer automobiles in operation at a given time, treatment of the polluted air, and substitution of some other kind of energy. A collection system for air pollution emissions is impossible because direct venting to the open air comes from every house, motor vehicle, factory, and power plant. Certain devices can remove fly ash when coal and oil are used in large volume, but control of small and numerous home furnaces is a formidable task. The problem of unburned hydrocarbons and carbon monoxide of automobiles is even more difficult. Substitution of natural gas reduces the emissions resulting from bituminous coal and fuel oil. Atomic power plants do not produce the particulate and gaseous emissions of fossil fuels, but the radioactive byproducts must be considered.

Pollution of water

Pollution of water is another consequence of industrial and technological development. Between 1960 and 1980 it is anticipated that industry will increase its use of water by 146 percent, and water use for irrigation will gain by 18 percent. By 1980 the amount of water used in cities will be more than 12 times the 1900 level. In addition to population increases, these trends reflect bathrooms, modern kitchens, home laundries, and air conditioners as symbols of a higher standard of living.[53]

[52] Revelle, "Pollution and the Cities," pp. 98–105.
[53] *Social Development: Key to the Great Society* (Washington, D.C.: U.S. Department of Health, Education and Welfare, 1966), p. 27.

Urban congestion in the suburbs. The American's love affair with the automobile has had derivative effects, including the spread of urban traffic congestion and the billboard jungle to satellite villages. Here most of the vehicles have one occupant as they creep along narrow State Highway 54 south of Atlanta, Georgia.

Since water can be reused, the chief problem is quality rather than quantity. Under conditions of balance between man and the natural environment, bacteria convert human wastes into harmless substances and the river cleanses itself. When this balance is upset, organic sludges and other suspended solids settle to the bottom and stimulate bacterial production of toxic substances.

The condition of Lake Erie illustrates the consequences of dumping the sewage, chemicals, oils, and detergents of an urban population into even a very large body of water. Power plants, steel mills, chemical companies, food processors, rubber companies, and urban sewage have made the lake a cesspool. In Cleveland the inflammable ooze has made the Cuyahoga River a fire hazard. An excess of nutrients has produced great growths of algae to impair the oxyzen supply, especially in the deeper water during the summer. The fish catch has declined sharply, with sheepshead and carp assuming greater proportional importance. The increasing burden of organic wastes threatens to convert the lake into a huge swamp.[54]

Water pollution is a social problem in that solutions depend heavily on fundamental changes in attitutes of individuals and organizations. Recognition of the problem must be followed by willingness to change habits of an earlier day when natural processes were sufficient to overcome the effects of water pollution. However, more substantial and systematic efforts are necessary. Revelle suggests a number of measures.[55] Industrial action can be encouraged by tax incentives for pollution abatement and rapid amortization of waste treatment equipment. Standards must be set for maximum allowable amounts of pollutant discharges. Research should determine more accurately the effects of various pollutants on human beings, animals, and plants. Governmental agencies can test and demonstrate advanced control systems for entire communities. Special agencies are required to handle regional waste disposal and pollution control on an integrated basis. The public should be systematically informed on pollution problems.

Dilemmas of transportation

Man has exploited his inventive genius to move from foot travel and the horse to the train, automobile, airplane, and space vehicle. In the course of producing swarms of mechanical bugs, he has shown less genius in coordinating these forms of transportation, and here the accumulation of highly concentrated masses of population has been a central factor.

As long as cities were small, narrow streets were sufficient for horse-drawn carriages and wagons. Now large traffic arteries are essential to

[54] Peter Schrag, "Life on a Dying Lake," *Saturday Review,* Vol. 52 (September 20, 1969), pp. 19 ff.
[55] Revelle, "Pollution and the Cities," pp. 127-28.

siphon thousands of people in and out of the urban centers. Widening of streets is complicated by the hemming in of the streets by costly buildings. Skyscrapers pack thousands of people into a narrow horizontal area but increase the traffic and parking problems.

The jumbo jet accelerates the boom in air traffic, which has made long-distance travel in a brief time available to an increasing number of people. This quantitative success has imposed problems of congestion and delays in group transportation, terminals, and stacking of aircraft awaiting opportunity to land.[56] Most terminals were designed for a day when air travel was dangerous, glamorous, and for a select few. The sensational rise in air passenger traffic and technological progress in aircraft design have outstripped the logistic support.

The demand pattern for urban transportation is changing in response to the dispersion of economic opportunities away from the central city.[57] The great needs for transport facilities will come in the rapidly expanding metropolitan rings and suburbs rather than in the central business district. Barring racial discrimination, the typical urban commuter has a choice between spending more for transportation and less for housing, if quality is held constant. Persons with higher incomes and/or larger families normally vote for more spacious housing at the cost of greater traveling. Lower income people working downtown accept higher residential density for cheaper transportation or very long trips for the sake of housing advantages. Furthermore, the private automobile offers personal comfort and flexibility in scheduling travel to one's convenience.

The decline in number of passengers per automobile accelerates the growth of vehicular traffic even more than the concentration of population. Meanwhile, mass transit loses passengers and suffers resistance to fare increases and trimming of services to curb financial deficits. The automobile's voracious appetite for space requires land for broader highways and parking lots without producing sufficient revenue through property taxes. The building of vast road networks arouses opposition when scenery and historical sites are threatened. The automobile exacts a heavy toll of life and injury. Meanwhile, the civil and criminal courts are jammed with traffic cases.[58]

Although no panacea for the transit problems of the city has been found, many proposals have been advanced. Zoning might create lines of high-density population to feed transit systems. Chicago has built tracks in the center of expressways. Improved comfort, reliability, and speed of service are supposed to increase willingness of people to ride commuter trains and pay higher fares, especially when space is provided for suburban

[56] Evert Clark, "Stack-ups, Breakdowns, Hang-ups, and Hope," *Saturday Review,* Vol. 52, (January 4, 1969), pp. 34.
[57] John R. Meyer, John F. Kain, and Martin Wahl, *The Urban Transportation Problem* (Cambridge, Mass.: Harvard University Press, 1965).
[58] Mitchell Gordon, *Sick Cities* (New York: Macmillan Co., 1963), pp. 16–62.

parking. By reserving curbside lanes for buses, downtown transit time is accelerated. Heavy investment in new subways and commuter lines requires subsidies which have been defended on grounds that property values are raised.

SUMMARY

Technology is a cultural screen man establishes between himself and the natural environment to convert resources to his needs. Through the centuries man has scored such success in technological development that he has reached a point when he questions the worthiness of his own creation. However, the issues now being debated are less attributable to the techniques of technology than they are to the cultural values and social priorities with which man applies them. The unprecedented interest in these issues is directly related to the new dominance of urban society. The city is reaping the adverse consequences of automobile congestion and pollution of air and water. The values and institutional patterns of urban life are strongly influenced by industrial technology. The world of work has been affected fundamentally. The growing affiliation of the university with technological innovation raises far-reaching questions concerning its future status and function. The ecological crisis illustrates this point because it is a product jointly of population density, rising consumption of natural resources, and the obvious impact on the environment of a greater number of people continuing a traditional neglect of the consequences of the habits of pollution.

FOR ADDITIONAL READING

William W. Brickman and Stanley Lehrer (eds.), *Automation, Education, and Human Values* (New York: School and Society Books, 1966).

Fred Cottrell, *Energy and Society* (New York: McGraw-Hill Book Co., 1955).

Peter F. Drucker, "Worker and Work in the Metropolis," *Daedalus,* Vol. 97 (Fall 1968), pp. 1243–62.

Jacques Ellul, *The Technological Society,* trans. John Wilkinson (New York: Alfred A. Knopf, 1964).

William R. Ewald, Jr. (ed.), Environment for Man: *The Next Forty Years* (Bloomington, Ind.: Indiana University Press, 1967).

Victor C. Ferkiss, *Technological Man: The Myth and the Reality* (New York: George Braziller, 1969).

George M. Foster, *Traditional Cultures and the Impact of Technological Change* (New York: Harper & Row, 1962).

Kyle Haselden and Philip Hefner (eds.), *Changing Man: The Threat and the Promise* (New York: Doubleday, 1968).

Henry Jarrett (ed.) *Environmental Quality in a Growing Economy* (Baltimore, Md.: Johns Hopkins Press, 1966).

Hans H. Landsberg, *Natural Resources of U.S. Growth* (Baltimore, Md.: Johns Hopkins Press, 1964).

Robert Macbride, *The Automated State* (Philadelphia, Pa.: Chilton Book Company, 1967).

Robert S. Nelson and Edward M. Johnson (ed.) *Technological Change and the Future of the Railway* (Evanston, Ill.: Transportation Center at Northwestern University, 1961).

Don K. Price, *The Scientific Estate* (Cambridge, Mass.: Harvard University Press, 1965).

Donald A. Schon, *Technology and Change* (New York: Delacorte Press, 1967).

Robert B. Seligman, *Most Notorious Victory* (New York: Free Press, 1966).

Edward H. Spicer (ed.), *Human Problems in Technological Change* (New York: Russell Sage Foundation, 1952).

John Tebbel, "People and Jobs," *Saturday Review,* Vol. 50 (December 20, 1967), pp. 8–12 ff.

Aaron W. Warner, Dean Morse, and Thomas E. Cooney (eds.), *The Environment of Change* (New York: Columbia University Press, 1969).

George K. Zollschan and Walter Hirsch (eds.), *Explorations in Social Change* (Boston, Mass.: Houghton Mifflin Co., 1964).

The demographic 5
dimension

Two germs are placed in the bottom of a bucket. It takes one hundred hours to fill the bucket when they double their number each hour. When will the bucket be half full? . . . After 99 hours.

In presenting this analogy, Price attempts to capture the essence of the population crisis facing the world because of the persistence of what appears at first glance to be a small rate of growth. His point is not that the United States is already "half full." Rather, he argues, the maintenance of the current standard of living becomes progressively more difficult if the same rate of population growth persists without an improvement in the capacity of technology to provide the ingredients of the standard of living.[1]

POPULATION AND SOCIAL REFORM

In raising the hand of caution against those today who dream of a "perfect society," the contemporary demographer has his predecessor in Thomas Robert Malthus, an English clergyman and amateur economist. In 1793 the Marquis de Condorcet (Marie Jean Antoine Nicholas de Cartetat) wrote a book proclaiming the coming of a perfect society. He saw nature setting no limits on the perfecting of human faculties. Limitless

[1] Daniel O. Price (ed.), *The 99th Hour: The Population Crisis in the United States* (Chapel Hill, N.C.: University of North Carolina Press, 1967), pp. 3–4.

human progress would bring equality in material comfort and security of livelihood. Science and industry would yield support without limit. Moral and intellectual perfection, universal peace, and political liberty would reign. At the same time, William Godwin, an English scholar, expressed similar optimism. To assure universal happiness in an age of reason, he urged the abolishment of all government, so far as it was coercive, and substitution of a society wherein the freedom of individuals would be restricted only by the moral censure of their associates.[2]

Specter of overpopulation

To oppose this unbridled optimism, Malthus in 1798 published *An Essay on Population,* calling attention to a "constant tendency in all animated life to increase beyond the nourishment prepared for it." Whereas the human species would increase geometrically (1, 2, 4, 8, 16 and so on), he said subsistence would increase arithmetically (1, 2, 3, 4 and so on). To keep down the disproportionate increase of population, "positive checks" include causes arising from vice and misery which would shorten the duration of human life through unwholesome occupations, disease, wars, pestilence, and famine, and "preventive checks," which include moral restraint, deferment of marriage, and delay of parenthood until economic support for babies can be provided.[3]

Malthus has been justifiably criticized. Since he could not know of forthcoming technological progress, he underestimated man's potentiality for spurring the increase of subsistence to provide for larger populations. He omitted contraceptive practices as a voluntary check on population growth. (This omission reflected a religious orthodoxy which eroded the objectivity of his evaluation.) Although Malthus had sympathies for the underprivileged, his essay provided support for the conservative logic of laissez-faire. He regarded the provision of poor relief on the basis of number of children to be sheer madness because the policy would encourage population increase without increase in production of food.[4]

Nevertheless, in raising the specter of overpopulation, Malthus called attention to the effects of population factors which must be recognized in any program of social reform. The implementation of utopian plans involves the qualities of the population to be benefited in the new and better era. The measurement of births, deaths, and migration may appear to the casual observer to be unexciting, but population dynamics are at the root of the issues which test the capacity of man to achieve his philosophical and social aspirations.

[2] Harry Elmer Barnes and Howard Becker, *Social Thought from Lore to Science,* Vol. 1 (Boston, Mass.: D. C. Heath and Co., 1938), pp. 473–81.
[3] Thomas R. Malthus *On Population,* Gertrude Himmelfarb (ed.) (2d ed.; New York: Modern Library, 1960), pp. 157–61.
[4] Ibid., pp. xvii–xxvii; also see Warren S. Thompson and David T. Lewis, *Population Problems* (5th ed.; New York: McGraw-Hill Book Co., 1965), pp. 28–30.

Mankind is experiencing unprecedented rapidity of population growth. In the Middle Ages the population doubled over a span of a thousand years. Through famine and disease, the environment restricted population within the capacity of the economics of food gathering, hunting, or farming to meet human wants. Man gave a hand to mortality through war. The nineteenth century brought a modest quickening of population growth to an average one half of one percent per annum. In the early eighteenth century, public health measures began to reduce mortality. Technological developments brought new means of coping with disease and famine. The world population increase was 1.1 percent between the two world wars. Since World War II the rate of increase has climbed to 2.1 percent per annum. The world population of about 3,300 million people is increasing by 70 million a year.[5] Estimates of the world population for the year 2000 range from 5,500 to 7,000 million.

Population growth in the United States

Rapid population growth in the 19th century facilitated the industrial development and emergence of the United States as a world power but, as Stockwell points out, the country today is vastly different from what it was in the 19th century.[6] The pressures being placed on the provision of services for people is indicated by the sociopolitical issues concerning the adequacy of educational facilities, public utilities, housing and hospitals. Population growth is combined with the effects of technological developments and urbanization to create pressures on the natural environment.

Population growth in the United States stems from four demographic conditions.[7] Death rates are among the lowest in the world. Second, a remarkably high proportion of Americans (95 percent) are married at least once in their lifetime. Third, Americans marry at an earlier age than Europeans. Half of the American wives were married before their 21st birthday and about 90 percent before their 25th birthday, and the trend is toward even earlier marriage. In 1960 only 6.9 percent of women aged 30–34 years were single compared with 14.7 percent in 1940. Fourth, U.S. family size clusters within the range of two to four children, with few couples having no children, one child, or more than four children. A larger proportion of married women have children, and the childbearing is completed in a shorter period after marriage than in the previous generation. The birth

---

[5] Halvor Gille, "Recent Trends and Perspectives in World Population Growth," in J. E. Meade and A. S. Parkes (eds.), *Biological Aspects of Social Problems* (New York: Plenum Press, 1965), p. 31.

[6] Edward G. Stockwell, *Population and People* (Chicago: Quadrangle Books, 1968), pp. 8–9.

[7] Lincoln H. Day, "The Population Problem in the United States," in Price, *The 99th Hour,* p. 58.

rates are being maintained by a larger proportion of women having two or three children in spite of the decline in the proportionate importance of very large families.

The sustained population growth of the United States is remarkable, Day points out, because it has been accomplished with family size of only moderate dimensions. Unlike peoples of the nonindustrialized nations, Americans already are making extensive use of birth control methods and most of them can afford to raise three or four children. To reduce the growth rate by voluntary means, it would be necessary to persuade these couples to limit their childbearing to two children, or three at the most.

The American population crisis, then, is unique in several respects. First, the crisis entails the possible erosion of the standard of living rather than the prospect of mass hunger and physical deprivation. In fact, the increased demand for improving the lot of the poor and other under-privileged people involves the population crisis in the difficulty of extending the benefits of an advanced technology to a broader spectrum of the population in the face of the financial burden of child care on many underprivileged people. Second, our excessive population increase is associated with relatively small average family size. Third, a paradox exists in the necessity to persuade couples to have even smaller families when our culture stresses the desirability of parenthood for bringing long-term significance to an individual's life. Fourth, in spite of the concern of some experts over the survival of the family as a social institution, the particular popularity of marriage among young Americans is a cause of the problem of population growth.

The above characteristics of the problem call for greater birth control among a people already making extensive use of fertility restrictions. Some segments of the American people decry what they regard as unparalleled permissiveness in sexual behavior, but what they regard as the immorality of a "sex revolution" can be interpreted as a cultural readjustment to the situation described here as a population crisis. Within this interpretation, there is a logic in sex education in schools, birth control clinics, and liberalization of laws on abortion.

POPULATION FACTORS IN CHANGE

Demography studies people and their behavior as reflected in their patterns of fertility, mortality, and migration. Abstract principles and statistics are the tools of this form of research into fundamental patterns shaping the lives of individuals. The operation of these patterns in large populations is an important facet of the study of social change.

Some social problems are direct consequences of social change measured by demographic statistics. A larger population of aged persons brings problems in income maintenance, utilization of the leisure of the "golden

A population cohort united by common experiences. Harold Richardson (right) and friends gathered around the stove in his general store in East Orange, Vermont. Of roughly similar ages, they are drawn together by having shared the experiences of their particular slice of history.

years," medical care, and housing. A larger population of children and youth aggravates the problems of schools already struggling to provide the type of education required in a changing society. Migration has altered the spatial distribution of blacks to lend new dimensions to racial discrimination and urban poverty.

Other social problems have demographic elements which elude casual observation. The relationships between the individual and government are affected by increased population density. Population growth raises political issues in the allocation of tax revenues, zoning (nominally to safeguard residential areas while providing for industrial development), and housing for the underprivileged and minority groups. For each system of technology there is some limit in the size of population which can be supported at a given standard of living.

Cohort as a concept for insights

The impact of population factors in unleashing profound social changes is revealed through use of the idea of cohort.[8] A *cohort* consists of the aggregate of individuals who share approximately the same birthday. As a particular cohort moves through its particular slice of history, its members experience at about the same time the crucial milestones of life which come at particular points in the continuum of chronological ages. As the individual moves through the sequence of life stages from birth to death, he undergoes along with other persons of similar age the experiences of infancy, childhood, adolescence, schooling, falling in love, finding a job, marriage, parenthood, departure of grown children, retirement, and death.

Each cohort is unique in that it is affected by the historical events and the quality of technology of its particular times. In times of rapid change each cohort experiences a somewhat different sociocultural environment at each of the points along the stages in the sequence of life. Marked by their experiences in the severe economic depression of the early 1930s and in World War II, parents may find it difficult to understand the attitudes of their children's cohort toward spending money, pressure to have their own automobiles, or attitudes toward the military draft. Recalling their thrill at going to the circus, parents may be disappointed over the blasé attitude of their children toward the circus an attitude produced in part by the broad experiences already provided the children through television.

As another consequence of its place in history, each cohort has its qualitative characteristics when compared to other cohorts. These qualitative characteristics include distribution of members according to social class, occupation, race, religion, educational attainment, marital status,

[8] For a more profound analysis, see Norman B. Ryder, "The Cohort as a Concept in the Study of Social Change," *American Sociological Review,* Vol. 30 (December 1965), pp. 843–61.

size of family, previous military experience, tendency to change place of residence, and similar variables. The quality of the cohort in a given geographical area can be affected by migration, birth, and death rates. The differences in qualities of in-migrants versus out-migrants affects the characteristics of the population in such matters as educational attainment, vocational skills, and race. For example, the North has been gaining blacks and other minority groups, and the South has a decreasing proportion of the black population of the United States. A declining death rate increases population size for a given level of birth rates, but the reasons for the decline have an effect on the composition of the total population. The lag of minority groups in reduction of infant mortality rates cancels out at least some of the effect of their higher birth rates. On the other hand, reduction of mortality rates among blacks makes their higher fertility more of a factor in raising their share of the total population.

Implications for social issues

In the major problems to be evaluated in subsequent chapters, the distribution and characteristics of population will have crucial impacts. At first inspection, the analysis of age, sex ratios, and labor force statistics can appear highly technical and detached from social problems, but (as already indicated) such population variables hold an important potential for increased understanding of social issues.

The age of an individual has implications in terms of his probable orientation toward the world, his physiological capabilities, his income potential, the degree of his participation in the labor force, the occupations open to him, and the social groups with which he is most likely to be affiliated. When the age distribution of a population changes, the society undergoes a wide range of readjustments.

For example, a younger population will generate greater demands for schools than for convalescent hospitals and pension programs. Popular music and theater will reflect a greater emphasis on the tastes of the young as an entertainment market. Absolute numbers of juvenile delinquents and teen-age marriages will likely rise.

"Age" may even involve historical changes in physiological as well as cultural factors. For example, during the last 50 to 100 years children have been maturing progressively earlier, according to evidence summarized by Tanner for Europe, North America, some parts of China, and Japan.[9] Adolescents show an increase in average height and the girls an earlier average age of first menstrual period over the years. This trend has implications for earlier age of marriage and possibilities of earlier sophistication than is assumed when adolescents are seen as only older children.

[9] J. M. Tanner, "The Trend Toward Earlier Physical Maturation," in Meade and Parkes, *Biological Aspects of Social Problems*, pp. 40–65.

The *sex ratio* reports the number of males for every 100 females. The sex ratio in the United States has declined from 106 males for every 100 females in 1910 when immigration had contributed an excess of males; in 1965 the U.S. sex ratio was 96.4 males for every 100 females in spite of the birth of more boy than girl babies. For a given area the imbalance of the sexes may reflect differences between the sexes in tendency to migrate. One area may lose more females and another area gain a disproportionate share of females, thus affecting the probability of marriage. The overall trend in the sex ratio partially explains the rise of discontent among women with the employment opportunities they are offered and the lower average compensation they receive for equivalent jobs.

In the area of race relations, the greater social visibility of the problems of blacks has been associated with the increase in their numbers, especially as a consequence of their recent movement into the cities and the North where they are identified with the difficulties of the central city. Their occupancy of central cities gives them strategic power which has not been overlooked by politicians. The migration of blacks and their progress in education and economic terms has made them less amenable to a subordinate status. With the decline of immigration of whites in the United States and the lowering of mortality rates of blacks, blacks are assuming a greater importance as part of the labor force.

Level of income is a sensitive index of the well-being of a population, as our chapter on poverty will demonstrate. The standard of living is associated with the quality and quantity of food, place and condition of housing, living arrangements, possibility of illness and death, and access to educational and vocational training.

The *labor force* includes all persons 14 years and over who are either employed in a paid job or actively seeking a job. The size of the labor force can reflect population growth or an increase in the participation rate of particular groups. An example of the latter is the increasing proportion of women who are gainfully employed, with consequences for child-rearing practices, patterns of family life, and fertility. Labor force studies are also pertinent to problems related to the necessity to reorganize schools, which coincides with changes in skills demanded by emerging technologies, the upgrading of local workers' skills to permit expansion or relocation of factories, and the expansion of jobs to provide for an excess of young adults produced by an earlier "baby boom."

Particular forms of economic specialization influence the social characteristics of the population in a given city. The style of life and the qualities of a population will affect the prevalence and quality of drinking, medical, crime, poverty, and other social problems. Manufacturing increases the proportion of craftsmen, foremen, operatives, and kindred workers producing a fairly high medium income but fewer extremes in income. In contrast, a financial center has an excess of white-collar workers with relatively few manual workers. Here homeownership is especially prevalent, and educational attainment high. There is an excess of older persons and females. Military centers are dominated by the heavily male and mobile character of military personnel. Homeownership is relatively low. The host community emphasizes governmental employment and provision of entertainment and other service functions.[10]

MORTALITY: INDEX OF PROGRESS

There are several reasons for interest in death rates. Variation over the years tells us something about the rate of progress in improving life chances of the citizens in general. When the various segments of the population have different rates, we should be alert to the possibility that the life chances are not being distributed equitably. The existence of "high-risk" groups suggests that remedial actions should be directed especially toward them. In a later chapter the problems of medical care for the poor and the aged will be considered. The possibility of decreasing further the overall death rate depends largely on reduction of mortality among these groups. As death rates decline, the medical care of the survivors will involve the illnesses and physical handicaps of the older age groups to an increasing degree.

Another reason for interest in death rates is that their decline ultimately contributes to the possibility of higher birth rates. Reduction in mortality parodoxically makes a population somewhat younger rather than simply increases the number of older people. Coale explains this reversal of popular expectation.[11] Improvements in health and medicine have had their greatest effect in raising survivorship among the young rather than the old. These young survivors later contribute to parenthood to add further to the numbers of young. Conversely, falling fertility contributes to a higher average age by giving greater relative importance to older people who represent the consequences of earlier higher fertility.

Progress against disease and death

Studies of embalmed bodies from ancient Egyptian tombs found evidence of tuberculosis, pneumonia, spondylitis, gallstones, and trachoma. Greece and Rome were scourged by malaria, bubonic plague, and leprosy. Syphilis is believed to have been brought back from the New World by the sailors of Christopher Columbus. Measles, smallpox, diptheria, scarlet

[10] Albert J. Reiss, Jr., "Functional Specialization of Cities," in Paul K. Hatt and Albert J. Reiss, Jr. (eds.), *Cities and Society* (Glencoe, Ill.: Free Press, 1957), pp. 562–75.
[11] Ansley J. Coale, "How A Population Ages and Grows Older," in Ronald Freedman (ed.), *Population: The Vital Revolution* (Garden City, N.Y.: Doubleday & Co., Inc.: 1964), pp. 49–51.

fever, and other infections were the routine hazards which kept down the population of children in the Middle Ages. The prevalence of such diseases was aggravated when man abandoned nomadism and settled in communities. Then he was confronted by the need to safeguard health through pure water, proper disposal of his excreta, and uncontaminated food.[12]

In the last 150 years modern medicine has gradually discarded its dependence on magico-religious practices and has achieved unprecedented control over disease by reliance on the scientific method. Among the specific developments were the ideas of William Harvey (1578–1657) on the circulation of blood; invention of the microscope, hypodermic needle, and the thermometer; and invention of the stethoscope by René Théophite Laennec (1781–1826), vaccination against smallpox by Edward Jenner (1749–1823), further development of preventive serums by Robert Koch (1843–1910) and Louis Pasteur (1822–95); and the discovery of the X ray by William Röntgen (1845–1923) in 1895.[13] In short, progress in medicine is the story of the advancement of experimental science in physiology, chemistry, physics, and biology.

The greatest medical advances have come in the last 50 to 100 years, too late to explain the sharp reductions of mortality which produced the population explosion of Western Europe. Medicine lagged behind industry and science in the progress achieved in the early 18th century because experimentation with the human body encountered great resistance from the general public and ecclesiastical authorities. Public repugnance against dissection for medical research and instruction was stimulated by images of wanton mutilation and fears that violation of the "sanctity of the human body" would jeopardize resurrection of the dead.

From an aristocratic attitude that working with one's hands is degrading, the medical profession has moved to make laboratory work in the experimental sciences a keystone of medical practice. During the Middle Ages the practical work was performed by surgeons and by apothecaries who had a sharply lower social status than the physicians, who served only the upper classes. Surgeons were itinerants who were also barbers; apothecaries were tradesmen. In the 14th century surgeons began to move toward becoming part of the medical profession. The 17th and 18th centuries began the elevation of the medical profession in public opinion. However, the difference in knowledge between the physician and the quack was shadowy. Medical practices consisted largely of bloodletting and formidable administration of drugs, the effects of which had not been reliably determined.[14]

Factors inherent in medical practice are conducive to delay in accepting

---

[12] F. N. L. Poynter and K. D. Keele, *A Short History of Medicine* (London: Mills & Boon, 1961), pp. 83–91.

[13] Ibid.; also see Bernard J. Stern, *Society and Medical Progress* (Princeton, N.J.: Princeton University Press, 1941), pp. 41–78.

[14] Stern, *Society and Medical Progress,* pp. xi–xii, 13–40.

innovation. The physician in the Hippocratic tradition feels a strong sense of responsibility not to harm the patient by excessive experimentation. Failures with previous patients encourage caution. The safest course is to follow the traditional methods of the time. In the United States medical education did not achieve university status until the end of the 19th century. As recently as 1941, Stern found progress in medical education and licensing standards still insufficient to protect the public against inferior medical services.[15]

The early industrial revolution brought urban masses living in misery but it also brought wealth to some individuals who could then afford to take a benevolent interest in the underprivileged. Humanitarianism developed among the rising middle classes. The more farsighted of the physicians saw the need of institutions to provide for the sick poor, and English humanitarians subsidized the reorganization of hospitals established earlier by churches and helped to build new ones in the 1750s. The Pennsylvania Hospital in Philadelphia was established in 1751. These and other hospitals provided a supply of clinical material for medical research, and thereby provided a basis for later medical advances.[16]

Until modern times herbs, mineral substances, and parts of animals were the central focus of medical teaching. With improvement of chemical techniques, the essential qualities of medical plants were isolated. In 1806 morphine was obtained from opium, and codeine was obtained in 1832. Strychnine was isolated in 1818 from seeds of an Indian tree. Quinine was taken in 1820 from the bark of the cinchona tree. With the rise of pharmacology, synthetic drugs were created.[17] As a major strategy against disease, immunology involved the innoculation with a mild strain of a particular virus to produce a mild case of the disease. Through the work of men like Jenner, Koch, and Pasteur, control was achieved over cholera, anthrax, hydrophobia, diphtheria, typhoid, whopping cough, and scarlet fever. More recently, progress has been made against influenza, poliomyelitis, and measles.

Technology and sanitation

Because until relatively recently, medicine lagged behind the pace of progress in other aspects of life, the explanation for the population growth of western Europe and the United States in recent centuries must be sought elsewhere.

Acute food shortages, such as the Irish potato famine of the 1840s, have been a major cause of high death rates. Less spectacular but equally important is the effect of undernourishment and malnutrition in lowering

[15] Ibid., pp. 79–82, 94–97.
[16] Richard H. Shryock, *The Development of Modern Medicine* (New York: Alfred A. Knopf, 1947), pp. 43–45, 90–93.
[17] Poynter and Keele, *Short History of Medicine,* pp. 98–106.

resistance to disease. Nutritional deficiencies contribute to beriberi, eye difficulties, pellagra, anemia, scurvy, rickets, hemorrhages, stunted growth, and lack of energy. The early population growth of western Europe followed improvements in agricultural techniques which increased availability of food.

Industrialization broadened the distribution of goods to provide the possibility of alleviating want and privation. However, the crowding of population into cities without new provisions for public sanitation exposed people to greater possibility of disease. There were few, if any, provisions for sewage and refuse disposal. The custom of the man of a mixed-sex couple walking next to the curb is a remnant of the day when garbage and excreta was thrown out the window into the street. Long hours, inadequate safety precautions, poor working conditions, and child labor were destructive to health, but social reforms in the late 19th and early 20th centuries decreased illness and death rates.

Improvements in transportation facilitated the distribution of foods and goods but also enhanced the spread of communicable diseases. Dysentry, typhoid, smallpox, typhus, and plague have decimated vast numbers when trade and war spread disease throughout the world. The remedying of these consequences of easier communication awaited the development of public health and sanitation measures.

The 19th century brought improvements in public sanitation. Previously, administrative action had been limited largely to enforcement of quarantine regulations against epidemics. The early introduction of pipes, steam pumps, and water closets sometimes aggravated conditions, as in the case of the contamination of London sewers and water supply after 1785. The draining of swamps was a step forward, but bacteriological discoveries revealed the danger of infected water supplies. In 1892 nearby Altona escaped the cholera epidemic of Hamburg because of its filtering system. Thereafter, most cities constructed either sand or mechanical filter systems as safeguards against cholera, typhoid fever, and other waterborne diseases.[18]

Mortality trends in the United States

The crude death rates in the United States have dropped during the 20th century.[19] Between 1900 and 1921 there was a fairly rapid and substantial decline from 17.2 per 1,000 in 1900 to 11.5 in 1921. Another period of fairly marked decline from 1937 to 1954 brought the rate down to 9.2; this was when sulfa and other new drugs were introduced. Since then the rates again have been relatively stable.

---

[18] Shryock, *Development of Modern Medicine,* p. 212 and pp. 292–93.
[19] The crude death rate is the number of deaths in a given population in a calendar year divided by the number of people in that population and multiplied by 1,000.

Recent decades have recorded a sharp reduction of communicable diseases. Further progress depends on breakthroughs against cardiovascular-renal diseases, cancer, and accidents. The improvements suggest the dimensions of future health problems. Because of higher life expectancy, the medical care of the aged looms as a concern of unprecedented magnitude. Persons who would have died formerly from severe illnesses will add to the load of acute disabling and chronic illness. Hospital admissions and average days of hospital use per person are increasing, partially because of greater use of diagnostic services.[20]

Our later chapter on medical care will cite the paradox of increased effectiveness of medicine coupled with rising discontent with the quality of medical care. Greater use of diagnostic services has been one of the means of forestalling death and reducing the impact of disease. In the course of achieving technical success, the delivery system for medical services has attracted an increased volume of patients and their rising expectation that miracles are everyday events. The conjunction of these two developments explains the paradox. The overtaxing of medical personnel and facilities has brought impersonality and standardized procedures of bureaucratic organization to medical care, a sphere of human activity which is characterized by a demand for the emotional concern described as "tender, loving care."

Nonwhites in the United States have a higher mortality than whites, but the difference is narrowing slightly with a decline in nonwhite death rates since the turn of the century. Since nonwhites have relatively high birth rates, their declining mortality rates adds to their numbers disproportionately to the total population and lends great significance to the social problems related to minorities. The higher death rates of nonwhites is an index of the social and economic deprivation which makes race relations a social problem taken up in later chapters. Their lower standard of living is associated with substandard housing, inferior diet, and inadequate medical care.

PATTERNS OF FERTILITY

As a primary stimulant of human behavior, sexuality has profound impact on the individual in the most intimate and vital recesses of his personality. Later chapters will take up the implications of sexuality within the patterns of family life and in terms of its expression in various forms of sexual deviance. Another important social aspect is the reproductive function of the family, whereby births create a new generation.

[20] Odin W. Anderson and Monroe Lerner, "Measuring Health Levels in the United States, 1900–1958," in Charles B. Nam (ed.), *Population and Society* (Boston, Mass.: Houghton Mifflin Co., 1968), pp. 170–77.

Fertility and social psychology

The influence of social and psychological factors in fertility is suggested in the difference between fertility and fecundity. *Fertility* of a woman refers to the number of children she actually has borne. *Fecundity* refers to the number of children she is biologically capable of having. Physiologically women are capable of bearing children between the ages of about 15 and 49. The average female probably is capable of bearing as many as 15 or 20 children.[21] Since human fertility is much less than human fecundity, the difference indicates that births are being restricted by nonbiological as well as biological factors.

Customs offer inducements to marry and beget children.[22] Marriage is a prerequisite to legitimate sexual intercourse, ownership of land, and claim to respect. In the course of personality development the individual is conditioned to see marriage and parenthood as proper and prized objectives for his life. The old maid and bachelor are commonly regarded as abnormal. Parenthood is a means of achieving many personal goals: salvation of the soul, security in old age, acquiring workers for the farm, preservation of the family's name and lineage, and the gaining of affection. Civic and religious virtue is demonstrated by contributing to the new generation.

Urbanism has played a prominent part in raising inducements against having children, at least a number of children. Individualism favors choices for sake of career or material comforts which tend to delay or limit births. Marriage is more likely to be attractive for the sake of affection and psychological security than as a means of demonstrating one's sense of duty. Limited space in housing and the economic dependence of children replace rural inducements to have children to help with farm work. The inducements for parenthood are weakened in urban society where the family is less prepared to safeguard the individual against disease and want. Occupational success by the individual is a superior road to gratification of personal needs than his status within his family. In sum, urbanism has substituted a small family pattern, including only parents and children, for the earlier pattern of the extended family encompassing a broader range of relatives and exerting greater control over its members.

In cities birth rates are particularly subject to the effects of an individual's personal desires, especially since sexual behavior is expressed in particular privacy. Birth control techniques are effective largely when their use entails foresight and a special resolve to limit births—qualities especially difficult to demonstrate in the highly emotional circumstances of sexual intercourse. The availability of techniques also is a factor. Modern times has extended use of the condom. The pessary and diaphragm

---

[21] Kingsley Davis, *Human Society* (New York: Macmillan Co., 1949), pp. 561–62.
[22] Ibid.

were invented in the last century, while the contraceptive pill has been developed more recently. Research is being conducted on an oral contraceptive to induce temporary sterility in males and on an antipregnancy vaccine for women.[23] However, the rise of new methods of birth control is secondary to the development of a more intensive desire to restrict births among a larger proportion of people. The expanding concern over the quality of the natural environment has placed birth control in a new social perspective. Previously, abortion and birth control were treated as matters largely involving immoral behavior.

Paradox of fertility problem

As already noted, the imminent population crisis in the United States is a paradox. It entails the possible erosion of the standard of living rather than the prospect of physical deprivation. The contemporary concern over the poor and underprivileged minority groups requires that the prospect of abundance offered by our technology be more widely distributed. The costs of technological development to the quality of the natural environment have brought us to the brink of an ecological crisis. Can our technology achieve three purposes at the same time? Can it maintain a high standard of living, distribute it in unprecedented fashion throughout the entire population, and assume the responsibilities of protecting the quality of the natural environment? A burgeoning population would complicate even further an already formidable assignment summarized by this question.

The paradox also involves the reliance of population growth on the small family rather than on a family of more than four children. Americans tend to marry at a relatively young age, have fewer childless wives, and to be more likely to be married. Since large families are not prevalent, birth control practices already are in operation. Therefore, a remarkable feature of the American situation is that the popularity of marriage necessitates persuading couples to employ birth control more rigorously to reduce further family size which would be regarded as already small by the standards of some people, including earlier Americans.

The remarkable features of the American situation have produced a substantial population increase in spite of a long-term decline in birth rates from 30.0 births per 1,000 population in 1910 to 18.7 in 1935 during the Depression. The birth rate increased to 19.4 in 1940 and climbed further during the years after World War II to peak at 24.9 in 1955. Since then it has dropped gradually. However, the remarkable features of American fertility patterns have produced the possibility that the average number of children per family may even be increasing. Such evidence is provided by the number of children bore per 1,000 ever-married women aged 15

---

[23] Stockwell, *Population and People,* p. 90.

through 59. The cohorts of such women born in 1920 or 1930 have higher numbers of children than the cohort born in 1910.[24]

The post-war baby boom

The upsurge in births in the years immediately following World War II produced a remarkably large cohort which strained the resources of the community as it moved through the ages. The schools were particularly strained by unprecedented student enrollments.

The boom was the product of a number of factors.[25] A large deficit of marriages accumulated because of the postponement of marriages during the war and late Depression years. Many women who would have married earlier had their weddings in late 1945 and 1946 and began motherhood in 1947. Prolonged absences of husbands caused extensive postponement of births. Meanwhile, there was a substantial reduction of the age at first marriage to add to the number of married women exposed to the possibility of legitimate motherhood. Furthermore, there was a marked reduction in the interval from marriage to a first birth, the interval between first and second births, and the interval between subsequent births.

Several economic developments in this period contributed to a social-psychological climate favorable to earlier marriage and parenthood. Unemployment compensation and retirement programs were improved and health and accident insurance programs expanded to further a sense of security. Expansion of installment buying provided opportunities to get married, buy a house, and have children in a relatively brief time—by mortgaging the future.

MOBILITY AND CHANGE

In certain respects mobility is an extension of the demographic study of migration. *Horizontal mobility* involves change of residence. *Vertical mobility* refers to the movement of individuals upward or downward in the social structure, the dynamic aspect of social stratification whereby persons are treated in terms of the status position they occupy. The implications of social class are an important dimension of vertical mobility. A prerequisite to vertical and horizontal mobility is *mental mobility,* defined as a willingness or capacity to change ways of acting or thinking.

The three fundamental aspects of mobility are related to social disorganization in their potentiality for removing the individual from familiar

[24] Ralph Thomlinson, *Population Dynamics* (New York: Random House, 1965), pp. 166–68.
[25] Thompson and Lewis, *Population Problems,* pp. 266–70; Stockwell, *Population and People,* pp. 97–98.

grooves of behavior. In conjunction with population size, mobility is an important factor in releasing the sociological characteristics of urbanism.[26]

Migration: Bane or promise?

The movements of people on the surface of the earth are related to social problems. On the one hand, the uprooting of a people from their familiar setting upsets traditional cultural arrangements. It places together peoples who are strangers to one another without the bonds of common beliefs and customs developed through generations of sharing a sense of community. Migration raises the problems of assimilating diverse people, transforming strangers into neighbors. Abandonment of a familiar environment and moving to a new environment tests the emotional and intellectual flexibility of the individual. Higher rates of delinquency, mental illness, and other social malfunctioning are indications of the strain placed on individuals and social institutions.

Because the cities have grown to an important degree through migration, the urban problems associated with normative deviance can be attributed in large measure to the consequences of migration. Less obvious but of prime importance are the effects of migration on the age-sex composition of the population. The prospects for marriage and the birth and death rates are affected by the changes in the proportion of certain age groups through population influx or exodus.

On the other hand, the heightened rate of contacts with differing ideas and behaviors encourages creativity and invention. Migration is a valuable means of balancing the distribution of a population's numbers in accordance with resources. When there are too many people for the economic opportunities in a given area, migration to other places with a need for more workers is a valuable means of benefiting both the individual and society. Migration affects the quality of the population in the region left and the region joined. The departure of young adults leaves the native region with a greater proportion of population representing the very young and the very old. There are fewer employed people to bear the tax burden of educating the young and providing social services to the elderly. Concurrently, the receiving region adds to its labor force. The level of job skill and educational attainment affects the significance of the addition. If the new arrivals are not able to support themselves through employment, the receiving region may only be adding to the burden of its taxpayers.

Migration may be motivated by natural disasters, depletion of resources, overpopulation, and political persecution. These factors push the residents out of their native land. Migration also may be in response to "pull" factors in the other areas which attract people in search of better socioeconomic opportunity or new experience. Peterson defines *free mi-*

---

[26] See Chapter 3, pp. 68–74.

gration as movement motivated by the individual's willingness to risk the unknown of a new home and breaking from a familiar social universe for the sake of adventure, achievement of ideals, or to escape a social system from which he has become alienated.[27] The free migrants are the minority who break ground for the subsequent wave of migrants who compose one of the mass movements which have been a particular mark of American history.

Major migration movements

Mass immigrations from Europe boosted the earlier growth of the nation, accelerated urbanization, and mingled diverse cultures. When immigration was at full tide, the cities of the North drew the bulk of the newcomers, giving this region an advantage in industrialization, whereas the agricultural South remained relatively homogeneous in culture because the peoples from southern and eastern Europe did not dilute the heritage received earlier from northern and eastern Europe.

Although mass immigration has ceased to be the dominant population movement, mobility continues to be a salient American characteristic in terms of migration within the nation's boundaries. One in every five Americans each year lives in a different house than he occupied the previous year. Four broad movements within its boundaries have shaped or are shaping the nation. Migration from east to west broke the earlier barrier of the Appalachian Mountains and brought the settlement of the nation. The recent growth of the West is indicated by a population increase of 39 percent between 1950 and 1960 for the West, 17 percent for the South, 16 percent for the North Central, and 13 percent for the Northeast. Nevertheless, the industrialized Northeast continues to have the greatest population density.

Second, the movement from the farm to the city has transformed the United States into an industrial power. Beyond the effect of the numbers of migrants, this movement reflects the spread of urban values to rural areas. Country people have been exposed to the urbanizing influence of newspapers, city shopping areas, entertainment centers, television, radio, and urban-oriented public education. The selective nature of rural-to-urban migration has drawn heavily from the young who have been reared and educated at the expense of rural residents but now are denied the economic return of the children when they become adult workers. The consequence has been a disproportionate share of the very young and the old among rural residents, while cities have paid a price for any educational and vocational deficiencies the migrants bring with them.

[27] William Petersen, "A General Typology of Migration," *American Sociological Review,* Vol. 23 (June 1958), pp. 256–66.

The third movement, from the South to the North, has special significance because it has expanded the proportional importance of blacks in northern cities. In 1790 ninety percent of U.S. blacks lived in the South under a plantation slave economy. Recent decades have accelerated the dispersal of blacks throughout the nation. The movement was a trickle immediately after the Civil War, but after World War I a number of factors stimulated a migration of greater magnitude. The sharp decline of immigration opened a supply of unskilled and semiskilled jobs in northern industries, and mechanization of agriculture created a surplus of farm labor in the South.

Finally, the movement from the central core of the metropolises to the suburban fringe has profound implications for urban society. We discussed this movement in Chapter 3. Because this movement primarily consists of middle-class whites, it is associated with the development of racial ghettos and the aggravation of poverty in the central city. The aggravation of the problems of the central city is not simply a matter of the influx of the poor. An analysis of the 12 largest metropolitan areas found that both white and black immigrants exceeded the educational and occupational levels of the white nonmigrants of the central city. The lowering of these levels of central city people is attributed almost entirely to the heavy out-migration of whites of higher status.[28]

Vertical mobility and social problems

As an aspect of social change, vertical mobility is a primary dimension in a dynamic society which is committed to democratic values. The "log cabin to White House" myth has lost its relevance except to summarize the principle that one's place in the social structure ideally should reflect his talent and other capacities to serve the community. Social interests would presumably be served by the strivings of individuals to demonstrate their qualifications to perform the prestigious and rewarding tasks which are vital to the community. To make these strivings worthwhile and their persistence likely, room at the top of the status ladder must be provided for talented newcomers.

The absence of vertical mobility can be associated with social problems. A dynamic society requires plastic and versatile reactions to new conditions which are not amenable to the inflexible application of outmoded principles. The free flow of new persons into positions of responsibility mitigates against unquestioned acceptance of traditional ways. Absence of mobility can be a barrier to equal opportunity. Poverty and racial discrimination are among the social problems intimately related to the

---

[28] Karl E. Taeuber and Alma F. Taeuber, "White Migration and Socioeconomic Differences between Cities and Suburbs," *American Sociological Review,* Vol. 29 (October 1964), pp. 718–29.

shutting out of significant segments of the population from social and economic opportunities.

The correlates of class position are subsumed in many social problems. To deny vertical mobility is to preserve differences in life chances reflected in differential access to health and dental services, level and quality of education, and well-rewarded occupation.[29] Differential experiences are associated with proneness to be subject to the systems of criminal justice and public welfare agencies. Class position influences the kind of treatment one receives from storekeepers, teachers, classmates, and public officials. Social class is included among the barriers to communication among groups inhabiting adjacent space. The railroad tracks separate the rich and the poor along psychological and sociological dimensions. The probability of participation in community affairs and of being informed on public issues is affected by class status.

As an important aspect of social change, rapid mobility also creates social problems in that the established order is upset. It may be that the established order should be upset when the institutionalized patterns do not serve their professed purposes, but the replacement of persons in the various levels in social organization is not *necessarily* constructive. Winners in a competitive "rat race," Tumin says, frequently lose their capacity for objective criticism of the organizations they join. Instead, they may turn conservative in gratitude for the privileges they have gained. The very rapidity of social mobility operates against the inculcation of a sense of ethics against the "cult of the fast buck" whose expediency and search for personal payoffs operate against genuine improvement of the organizations.[30] Rapid mobility is conducive to reliance on standardized and overt symbols of status as criteria of social worthiness. Therefore, personal ethics and specialized competence are less likely to be criteria for evaluating the credentials of climbers than their immediate appearance and the quality of their possessions.

Vertical mobility tends to disrupt personal social controls based on the family and neighborhood because the individual is likely to establish new sets of interpersonal relationships as he moves up and down the status scale. His socialization as a child in one class usually does not prepare him for adult roles in another class. Unless he acquires more appropriate norms through more deliberate socialization in the course of his education or through new, less formalized experiences, vertical mobility will bring considerable stress and strain for the individual. Acceptance by others in his new social position may elude him because he does not feel natural in his social setting and lacks the necessary social skills. He must rationally fit himself into unfamiliar social situations and assume new roles. The

[29] Louis Kriesberg, "The Relationship between Socio-economic Rank and Behavior," *Social Problems,* Vol. 10 (Spring 1963), pp. 334–53.

[30] Melvin M. Tumin, "Some Unapplauded Consequences of Social Mobility in a Mass Society," *Social Forces,* Vol. 36 (October 1957), pp. 32–37.

mental mobility demanded involves individuation whereby each person must make his own decisions and break loose from many of the traditions which usually control behavior.

Special reliance is placed on education as a route upward for a person with ability but limited resources. With greater complexity of society in general, and of the occupational system specifically, the school becomes the gateway to upward mobility through personal achievement. However, as a gateway, the school operates also to restrict vertical mobility by excluding the "unfit" from training. Exclusion on the basis of social characteristics (ethnic background, lack of financial resources, "appropriate" conduct, and previous education) can operate to the disadvantage of persons in lower levels of social status.

Vertical mobility gives vital importance to the evaluation of future contingencies in decision making. The rhythms of institutional life can penalize severely individuals who made faulty decisions early in life although those decisions can be evaluated as socially constructive and personally responsible at the time they were made. The future consequences of present choices are illustrated particularly by the interdependence of formal education and the family cycle, which follows the sequence of wedding, child rearing, departure of the children, the "empty nest," and the final dissolution of the family.[31] If a wrong choice, in terms of future income, is made at the first stage, the right choice becomes progressively more difficult to make at each subsequent stage. If marriage comes at an early age, family responsibilities are likely to interfere with educational and vocational training. Early arrival of children raises obstacles to capital accumulation as a safeguard against financial crises, especially if pregnancy terminates the wife's job.

The choice of the first job establishes a pattern of job movement which is progressively harder to change as family responsibilities grow and as the age of the worker advances. The young husband who has entered the job market before acquiring specialized vocational skills learns later of the consequences on his bargaining power. Parents become caught in the *family-cycle squeeze* when income is insufficient to realize their own aspirations and concurrently meet the family's financial needs, especially when there are a number of children. It appears that the fourth or fifth child is the point of no return for poor families, and the fatalism of poverty is experienced. Family disorganization and dissolution are among the costs of the family-cycle squeeze. The repetition of the consequences of faulty early choices is made more probable by the family's low capacity to provide the children with psychological and economic resources for a better start than their parents enjoyed.

---

[31] Alvin L. Schorr, "The Family Cycle and Income Development," in Louis Ferman, Joyce Kornbluh, and Allen Haber (eds.) *Poverty in America* (rev. ed.; Ann Arbor: Univ. of Michigan Press, 1968), pp. 39–61.

SUMMARY

The study of population is pertinent in several respects to the study of the social problems of urban society. Through population growth and migration the large city has emerged as dominant in our society. This growth is an important dimension in the problems raised by the conjunction of urbanism and modern technology as described in Chapter 4. Population analysis provides worthy objections to hope of a golden age raised by optimists and admirers of our technology. The United States faces a population crisis in the sense of difficulties in maintaining the desired standard of living. Population factors of mortality, fertility, and mobility are important dimensions in the changes which contribute to the social problems considered in this book. This chapter has surveyed the problematic aspects of these population factors as background for study of the major social problems in more detail, a study that begins with an examination of poverty as a difficulty of particular concern to a people who claim to believe in equality of opportunity.

FOR ADDITIONAL READING

Peter M. Blau and Otis D. Duncan, *The American Occupational Structure* (New York: John Wiley and Sons, 1967).

Louis I. Dublin, Alfred J. Lotka, and Mortimer Spiegelman, *Length of Life* (New York: Ronald Press, 1949).

Paul R. Ehrlich, *The Population Bomb* (New York: Ballantine Books, 1968).

Ronald Freedman and Lolagene Coombs, "Childspacing and Family Economic Position," *American Sociological Review,* Vol. 31 (October 1966), pp. 631–48.

Maurice Halbwachs, *Population and Society,* trans. Otis D. Duncan and Harold W. Pfautz (Glencoe, Ill.: Free Press, 1960).

C. Horace Hamilton, "The Negro Leaves the South," *Demography,* Vol. 1, No. 1 (1964), pp. 273–95.

Oscar Handlin (ed.), *Immigration as a Factor in American History* (Englewood Cliffs, N.J.: Prentice-Hall, 1959).

Philip M. Hauser (ed.), *The Population Dilemma* (Englewood Cliffs, N.J.: Prentice-Hall, 1963).

E. P. Hutchinson, *The Population Debate* (Boston, Mass.: Houghton Mifflin Co., 1967).

Jan Lenica and Alfred Sauvy, *Population Explosion: Abundance or Famine* (New York: Dell Publishing Co., 1962).

Katherine and A. F. K. Organski, *Population and World Power* (New York: Alfred A. Knopf, 1961).

Fairfield Osborn (ed.), *Our Crowded Planet* (London, Eng.: George Allen & Unwin, 1963).

William Petersen, *The Politics of Population* (Garden City, N.Y.: Doubleday & Co., 1964).

Samuel A. Stouffer, "Intervening Opportunities: A Theory Relating Mobility and Distance," *American Sociological Review,* Vol. 5 (December 1940), pp. 845–67.

Irene B. Taeuber, "Demographic Transitions and Population Problems in the United States," *Annals of American Academy of Political and Social Science,* Vol. 369 (January 1967), pp. 131–40.

Charles E. A. Winslow, *The Conquest of Epidemic Disease* (Princeton, N.J.: Princeton University Press, 1944).

Louise B. Young (ed.), *Population in Perspective* (New York: Oxford University Press, 1968).

Hans Zinsser, *Rats, Lice and History* (Boston: Little, Brown, and Co., 1935).

6 Poverty: Definition and dimensions

In introducing his poignant account of poverty among mountain people of eastern Kentucky, Caudill describes an eighth-grade graduation in a coal camp school. Two generations had sat at the scarred desks in this dilapidated two-room building with its unpainted walls and leaky roof. Through the worn windows, the seven graduates could look out on a grassless playground in the shadow of an immense slate dump fringed by ramshackle houses. One child had been orphaned by a mining accident. The father of another gasped with silicosis. The fathers of three others had no jobs. The ceremony opened with the singing of "America the Beautiful." [1]

DEPRIVATION AS A SOCIAL PROBLEM

The description implies some of the themes in our review of the associated problems of poverty, housing, and the slum. In Caudill's description of the sources of squalor and demoralization of the mountain people, an important thread is the contribution of the exploitation of Appalachia's coal reserves to feed the industrial technology and urban growth which developed contemporary urban society. In rich detail he describes the stripping of a beautiful land, the economic exploitation of a people who had preserved the ways of their colonial ancestors, the stranding of these

[1] Harry M. Caudill, *Night Comes to the Cumberland* (Boston, Mass.: Little, Brown and Co., 1963), p. xiii.

140

people in stark poverty when the economic boom deflated, and the coming of the dole in the Depression to demoralize wholesale these previously independent and self-reliant people.

Implications for urban society

The mountain people of eastern Kentucky are involved in the economic distress shared by Appalachia, a territory encompassing mountains from Pennsylvania to northern Georgia and Alabama. Appalachia is characterized by high incidence of unemployment, low educational attainment, lack of opportunities in the kinds of occupations producing a decent livelihood, high birth rates, and a heavy out-migration. Beyond the present situation is the difficulty of creating a potential for future economic growth. Great investments are required to create modern roads, hospitals, sewage plants, technical assistance to new business, and vocational training.[2] Caudill describes the legacy of eastern Kentucky in loss of the best quality of timber and coal, the departure of much of the best of human resources, the forced migration of much of the youth produced by continued high fertility, the evaporation of ambition under widespread welfare dependency, and the poverty of educational, medical, and other essential services.

The urban poor are more likely than the rural poor to draw attention. They are somewhat more vulnerable because of the urbanite's sole dependence on cash income. Their concentration in urban slums is more apt to attract attention of the concerned observer than the plight of the poor off the central pathways of transportation. However, this visibility is only relative. Harrington notes the general invisibility of the poor who reside isolated from the usual attention of affluent citizens traveling rapidly along urban throughways over or around the urban slums or along turnpikes which avoid the rutted roads of rural poverty. Cheap clothing conceals the appearance of poverty. The aged and the sick compose a disproportionate share of the poor, and they are less likely to be on the streets accessible for ready observation by the affluent. The poor are politically invisible in that they are relatively inarticulate and not affiliated with organizations which would press effectively for recognition of their interests.[3]

The urban poor are statistically dominant in absolute numbers because of their particular concentration in the 100 largest metropolitan areas of the nation. Although they included only 17 percent of the total population in 1967, these areas drew 42 percent of all poor people. The concentration

[2] Donald A. Crane and Benjamin Chinity, "Poverty in Appalachia," in Leo Fishman (ed.), *Poverty amid Affluence* (New Haven, Conn.: Yale University Press, 1966), pp. 124–49; William J. Page, Jr., and Earl E. Hisyck, "Appalachia: Realities of Deprivation," in Ben B. Seligman (ed.), *Poverty as a Public Issue* (New York: Free Press, 1965), pp. 152–76.

[3] Michael Harrington, *The Other America* (New York: Macmillan Co., 1962), pp. 3–5.

was particularly marked for nonwhites; 11 percent of the whites but 58 percent of the nonwhites in the 100 large cities lived in poverty areas.[4] Nevertheless, rural concentrations of economic deprivations are of serious magnitude in the deep south, Appalachia, the eastern coastal plain, the Ozarks, the Mexican-American areas, the upper Great Lakes, and New England. Rural poverty is a part of the urban problem in the sense that exodus from these rural concentrations aggravates the difficulties of cities in coping with the plight of the undereducated and vocationally unskilled persons.

A paradox of particular importance

For the first time in history, a large-scale society has developed the technical potential to maintain an affluent society. Galbraith has defined an *affluent society* as one characterized by imposed command of physical resources, high standards of private consumption, and freedom from most of the economic uncertainties which previously plagued man.[5] The persistance of poverty in an affluent society is particularly paradoxical in a nation committed to the idea of equality of opportunity. When the workings of the affluent society itself deny equal chances to demonstrate eligibility for social and economic rewards, the words of "America the Beautiful" sound hollow and ironical.

The poor constitute a social problem also in their personification of a drain on the resources of the community. The plight of the mountain people of eastern Kentucky is an illustration of such a waste of natural and human resources. Their socioeconomic situation provides little opportunity to demonstrate their potentiality for strengthening the community through their work, talents, and aspirations. Exploitive utilization of their region's natural resources accrued little economic benefit to the mountaineers and left them with a ravaged land and a community grossly undernourished in educational and social services.

These circumstances are pregnant with possibilities of alienation from the general society. Isolation from the mainstream of the reward system is conducive to apathy, hopelessness, rejection of the work ethic, and chronic dependency. The transmission of such attitudes through the generations constitutes a subculture of poverty which stands in stark contrast to the values of vertical mobility as professed in statements of the "American dream." In our later consideration of the subculture of poverty, the "analgesic subculture" of the mountain people will be a prime example.

[4] United States Department of Commerce, Bureau of Census, *Current Population Reports,* "Characteristics of Families and Persons Living in Metropolitan Poverty Areas: 1967," Series P-60, No. 61, June 30, 1969, pp. 2–3.

[5] John Kenneth Galbraith, *The Affluent Society* (Boston, Mass.: Houghton Mifflin Co., 1958), pp. 1–3.

THE STATE DISCOVERS POVERTY

American history is replete with cycles of national concern for the poor. The concern was humanitarian but also reflected awareness that the lot of the poor was a potential political and economic threat to the affluent, since frustration and unrest breed revolt and social turmoil. Underconsumption threatens overproduction to an industrial system geared to rapid and extensive distribution of goods. Welfare expenditures add to the tax burden of the employed. Chronic dependency erases hope of reducing this burden when the willing and able are denied access to employment.

Cycles of concern for the poor

The existence of the poor has been recognized politically at various times in American history. The pattern reflects an American tendency to launch spasmodic but ambitious efforts to eliminate a given social problem. When the collective enthusiasm wanes, the problem usually continues without widespread recognition. Perhaps changes in the environment of the problem modifies its dimensions sufficiently to weaken its prevalence. Perhaps there is a belief that the undesirable condition has been ameliorated. Perhaps the apparent massiveness of the reform effort is deemed sufficient justification for termination of the campaign. Perhaps, even, genuine improvement has been accomplished in some respects.

The settlement of America was motivated to an important degree by a search for a better life by the underprivileged of Europe.[6] However, as early as the economic panics of 1819 and 1837, the improvement in general living standards under mechanization and the factory system appeared incongruous to many Americans when compared to the evident distress among the working classes. A new poverty accompanied industrialization, urban growth, and immigration as evidenced in slums of the larger cities. Reform measures included establishment of the Association for Improving the Condition of the Poor in 1843, the Homestead Act signed by President Abraham Lincoln, the charity organization societies in many cities in the latter 1800s, and the Progressive Era at the turn of the century (including campaigns for better housing, public health, child-labor regulations, compulsory education laws, and regulation of the liquor trade). The New Deal under Franklin Roosevelt mounted eclectic programs in an attempt to cope with the weaknesses of socioeconomic arrangements revealed by the "Great Depression."

During the 1950s and the early 1960s the problem of poverty received little attention. A rediscovery of poverty culminated in the signing of the

---

[6] For historical review see Robert H. Brenner, *From the Depths* (New York: New York University Press, 1956); Sidney Lens, *Poverty: America's Enduring Paradox* (New York: Thomas Y. Crowell, 1969).

Economic Opportunity Act by President Lyndon B. Johnson in 1964 in a time of prosperity. Levitan partially explains this development as a combination of several studies of social deprivations, several White House memoranda on the needs of the poor, the civil rights movement, and President Johnson's interest in a program to "help people." [7]

Changes in conception of poverty

The conception of poverty and what to do about it have changed over the decades.[8] Under Social Darwinism the lazy and the inefficient were supposed to be at the bottom of the economic ladder as a consequence of the "law of survival of the fittest." Society was conceived as a network of self-sufficient families which provided for their own. Needy persons outside a household (orphans, childless elderly, and the crippled) were provided outdoor relief grudgingly and as a temporary expedient. Although it was agreed the "poor will always be with us," the individual was expected to improve himself through acts of his own will. Charity was thought to be the nurse of idleness. By keeping wages low, laborers would be encouraged to work harder.

At about the turn of the century, the closing of the frontier and the beginning of concern about natural resources brought uneasiness about the possible spread of beggary. The poor were a potentially dangerous class in terms of disease and disorder. The "poor" were seen as different from "paupers." *Paupers* were individuals well adjusted to being on the low end of the socioeconomic scale. Without shame or bitterness, they would not seek independence and a "better life." For the mountaineer, subsistence and some slum dwellers, the lack of wealth, it has been argued, reflects a preference not to pay the psychological costs of the struggle for riches or of adopting the middle-class work ethic of striving.[9] In contrast, the *worthy poor* struggled to improve their lot against circumstances beyond their control: low wages, sickness, industrial accidents, widowhood, and so on.

This distinction separated the problem of poverty from the problem of relief.[10] Because poverty was linked to "miserable and unjust social conditions," there was the possibility that reform measures would reduce the numbers of the poor. The reformers of the Progressive Era pushed through

---

[7] Sar A. Levitan, *The Great Society's Poor Law,* (Baltimore, Md.: Johns Hopkins Press, 1969), pp. 11–18; as a barometer of the rise of interest in poverty, Levitan cites the relatively small sales of Michael Harrington's *The Other America* in 1962 and its heavy sales in 1963.

[8] See: Oscar Handlin, "Poverty from the Civil War to World War II," in Fishman, *Poverty amid Affluence,* pp. 3–17; and Oscar A. Ornati, "Poverty, Affluence, and Opportunity," in George A. Brager and Francis P. Purcell (eds.), *Community Action against Poverty* (New Haven, Conn.: College and University Press, 1967), pp. 29–30.

[9] Theodore W. Schultz, "Public Approaches to Minimize Poverty," in Fishman, *Poverty amid Affluence,* p. 169.

[10] Handlin, "Poverty from the Civil War to World War II," pp. 14–17.

legislative action and social reform to alleviate conditions, pressing the "deserving" poor toward the passive accommodation of the pauper. The New Deal gave more attention to the consequences of the malfunctioning of the economic system revealed by the Depression in the 30s, but the idea still persisted that poverty was an inevitable feature of the American social system based on scarcity. It was not until World War II that the ideas of full employment and universal diffusion of adequate minimum incomes emerged.[11]

By 1960 federal involvement in social welfare included aid for the aged and disabled, aid for children, aid for the needy, and related programs. The Social Security Administration provides pensions for older persons and payments to the totally and permanently disabled. Pensions are also provided the aged not qualifying for social security benefits. Programs are designed to aid the blind, the crippled, and those permanently disabled by disease. Injuries on the job are covered by workmen's compensation. Medicare and Medicaid are intended to provide medical care for the aged and indigent.[12] Programs for children include aid to dependent children, maternity and chid services, and school lunches. Aid for the needy includes unemployment compensation, public works programs for the jobless, grants to counties struck by natural disasters, and general welfare for the indigent. The Veteran's Administration provides pensions, hospitalization, and rehabilitation services. Fellowships and loans are granted to students. Public housing programs are another facet. However, the movement of the United States toward the welfare state is also exemplified by intervention in economic life through subsidies to farmers, loans to businesses, highway construction, and depletion allowances to oil and mining companies.[13]

Rise of the "welfare state"

In summarizing a large literature, Schottland indicates ideas common to various versions of the welfare state: Income should be redistributed to assure minimum standard of living. Equality of opportunity is regarded as essential—in keeping with an ethical mission of the welfare state which proceeds beyond material well-being alone to provide social justice and equality. At least a minimum of social services should be provided for all. Welfare benefits for the underprivileged take on the qualities of a legal right.[14]

These common ideas do not imply that the welfare state draws universal

[11] Ornati, "Poverty, Affluence, and Opportunity," pp. 29–30.
[12] See Chapter 18, pp. 464–65.
[13] Fred Krinsky and Joseph Baskin, *The Welfare State: Who Is My Brother's Keeper* (Beverly Hills, Calif.: Clencoe Press, 1968), pp. 4, 71–72.
[14] Charles I. Schottland (ed.), *The Welfare State* (New York: Harper & Row, 1967), p. 95.

acceptance, exists in a single form, or has been fully implemented. Miller explains that the welfare state exists in the United States only to the extent that there is a limited commitment to clean up some of the social debris produced by the operation of the private economy.[15] Schlesinger notes that Western governments have been driven toward welfarism by fear of losing the loyalty of neglected citizens rather than by sentimental idealism. He sees welfarism as a form of social Machiavellianism designed to prevent the underprivileged from undertaking social revolution.[16]

Disagreements over the nature and significance of the welfare state are indicated by the arguments summarized by Schottland. Opponents argue that the welfare state will destroy the free enterprise system, stifle private business, undermine economic stability through excessive government spending, destroy individual responsibility, and erode democracy by favoring either Communism or dictatorship. Advocates contend that the welfare state is essential to preserving democratic society by ensuring basic freedoms, to relieving distress such as old age or unemployment attributable to broad social factors, to achieving the democratic goal of equality, and to offering a "middle way" between dictatorship and laissez-faire government.[17]

Relative deprivation

The idea of relative deprivation is a product of a revolution of rising expectations and a discontent aroused by recognition of the discrepancy between the socioeconomic conditions of the poor and the high promise of the affluent society. The term *relative deprivation* was coined in a social-psychological study of the American army during World War II.[18] If A, who does not have something but wants it, compares himself to B, who does have it, then A is "relatively deprived" with reference to B. It is not necessary that an individual actually experience a genuine lack in an objective way. The crux of the matter is that he has a sense of deprivation when he compares his lot with some desired standard. His sense of deprivation is dependent on a comparison with the imagined situation of some other person or group.[19]

The values of American culture emphasize certain cultural objectives

---

[15] S. M. Miller, "Youth and the Changing Society," in Irwin Deutscher and Elizabeth J. Thompson (eds.), *Among the People: Encounters with the Poor* (New York: Basic Books 1968), p. 116.

[16] Arthur Schlesinger, Jr., "The Welfare State," in Schottland, *The Welfare State,* pp. 119–20.

[17] Schottland, *The Welfare State,* pp. 150–51.

[18] Samuel A. Stouffer, Edward A. Suchman, Leland C. DeVinney, Shirley A. Star, and Robin M. Williams, Jr., *The American Soldier: Adjustment during Army Life,* Vol. 1 (Princeton, N.J.: Princeton University Press, 1949), p. 125.

[19] W. G. Runciman, *Relative Deprivation and Social Justice* (London, Eng.: Routledge & Kegan Paul, 1966), p. 10; subsequent paragraphs draw on an interpretation of this source.

Office of Economic Opportunity

Reaching out to alleviate medical deprivation. Among the examples of relative deprivation experienced by the poor is their inferior access to medical services. To remedy this situation in two coastal counties of South Carolina, Comprehensive Health Services sends coordinated teams of doctors and nurses to find the sick and promote preventive medicine.

to be proper obligations for individuals and to be the basis for judging the social worth of the individual. Among these are economic self-sufficiency, provision for the material needs of one's dependents through work, occupancy of comfortable housing, and attainment of the highest level of schooling possible with one's intellectual level. When objectives of this sort are not attained, the individual is evaluated negatively and is subjected to a system of rewards and punishments which may be intended to motivate him to behave in keeping with the objectives.

The individual who does not strive for an education may be considered unworthy. His deficient educational attainment closes gates of job opportunity, and he continually encounters situations wherein he is ranked as inferior. His educational deficiencies have widespread effects because his income, his language, his style of dress, the location of his housing, and many other badges of social prestige are related indirectly to his level of schooling. Beyond the costs to his standard of living, inferior schooling sometimes carries a burden of guilt to the individual because he has failed to achieve in a sphere regarded as obligatory. He is a misfit, and he is punished implicitly for having the social and psychological correlates of poverty.

Deprivation refers to the state of being dispossessed of some valued condition. The term "dispossessed" implies that the individual has been motivated to seek the valued condition but he has been denied opportunity to achieve the amenities which are regarded as normal and accepted services. He has a desire for decent housing, for example, in keeping with the cultural goals of his society. Furthermore, he is prepared to achieve decent housing in a manner socially approved by his society.

Under the concept of deprivation, he is dispossessed of means to achieve his purpose because of factors irrelevant to the professed rules which are supposed to regulate the granting of the reward of decent housing. Prejudice may single out his ethnic or racial group to be shut up in a ghetto. Educational provisions may not be made to prepare him for jobs which would afford economic means for purchase of decent housing. His lack of resources may compel him to devote his full energy to survival and render him unable to invest time and resources in improvement of his circumstances. He may not have information on opportunities which could be made available to him. After experiencing a series of defeats, he may be overwhelmed by fatalism in the face of what appears to him to be overwhelming odds.

The concept of relative deprivation, then, emphasizes the cultural nature of poverty in that the poor man's frustrations are derived from his acceptance of the values and norms of society and the severe limitations on his chances to achieve them. His awareness of this discrepancy is sharpened by his learned comparsion between his own situation and that of other persons he has been taught to use as models for his own behavior. The cultural aspect of poverty also refers to secondary effects, such as children being exposed to the social circumstances accompanying deprivation during the crucial early years when basic patterns of personality are established.

The concept of deprivation should be applied to recognize the effects of technological change on the symbols of status and the commonly accepted standards of what constitutes deprivation. For example, the prevalent use of electric refrigerators has made use of a well or an icebox to cool food proper grounds for feeling deprived. The importance of television for being informed in contemporary urban society has made a lack of a set a form of deprivation.

WHO ARE THE POOR?

Poverty is subject to differing statistical definitions and is a relative term. Critics of public welfare programs are prone to cite the relative affluence of the American poor when compared with living conditions and widespread hunger in the Far East. For example, we regard the absence of running water and an inside toilet as constituting substandard housing. A sizable proportion of public dependents are found to possess washing machines, television sets, or automobiles.[20] In comparison with the poor of the Orient, how can these Americans be described as being in want?

Complexities in counting the poor

Definition and measurement differ according to the concept of poverty. Rein identifies three concepts.[21] *Subsistence* emphasizes the provision of sufficient resources to maintain health and working capacity in the sense of survival and capacity to maintain physical efficiency. *Inequality* compares the lot of individuals at the bottom layer of stratified income levels with that of more privileged people in the same society. Their deprivation is relative. *Externality* focuses on the social consequences of poverty for the rest of society, apart from the impact on the poor themselves.

In counting the numbers of the poor, poverty may be seen as income below a level selected as the proper cutoff point. The Council of Economic Advisors defined the poverty line as $3,000 (at 1962 prices) of total money income for families and $1,500 for unrelated individuals. These criteria produced an estimate that 20 percent of American families and 45 percent of unrelated individuals were poor in 1962: 35 million persons. If poverty is conceived as a discrepancy between needed and actual consumption,

---

[20] Herman P. Miller, "The Poor Are Still Here," in Ben B. Seligman (ed.), *Aspects of Poverty* (New York: Thomas Y. Crowell Co., 1969).

[21] Martin Rein, "Problems in the Definition and Measurement of Poverty," in Louis A. Ferman, Joyce L. Kornbluh, and Alan Haber (eds.), *Poverty in America* (rev. ed.; Ann Arbor, Mich.: University of Michigan Press, 1968), p. 116.

however, this estimate is an exaggeration in that it does not recognize nonmoney income (home-produced food and imputed rent), spending of savings, borrowing, receipt of gifts, and consumption of assets. Furthermore, the estimate does not recognize differences among families in number of children, age and sex composition, residence, occupational circumstances, health needs, and obligations toward relatives.[22]

Recently the U.S. census bureau adopted a poverty index developed by the Social Security Administration. This index takes into account family size, number of children, and farm-nonfarm residence as well as the amount of money income. The poverty level is based on an "economy" food plan designed by the Department of Agriculture for "emergency or temporary use when funds are low." Assuming that a family should not have to spend more than a third of its income for food, the cost of food included in the economy plan was used to determine the minimum total income requirements for a given type of family. A household is deemed poor if its total money income falls below this level. For example, in 1968 the poverty threshold for a nonfarm family of four was $3,553. For nonfarm residents it ranged from $1,700 for a female living alone to $5,804 for a family of seven or more persons with a male head of the family.[23]

Since 1960, the census data indicate a sizable decline in the proportion of families living in poverty.[24] In 1969, 24.3 million persons had incomes below the poverty level, compared with 39.5 millions in 1959. About 1 out of 10 families were poor in 1969, compared with 1 out of 5 in 1959. Families headed by a nonwhite were three times more likely to be poor than white families. In other words, nonwhites constituted 31 percent of the poor in 1969, although they comprised only 12 percent of the total population. Poverty persisted especially among families without a male head. Between 1959 and 1969 the number of poor families headed by a man decreased by about one-half, whereas there was no significant change in the number of poor families headed by a woman.

Social patterning of poverty

Identification of the target population for antipoverty programs is obscured by the heterogeneity of the subgroups which make up the poverty-stricken. The poor are drawn from various ethnic and racial groups, the

[22] Robert J. Lampman, "Population Change and Poverty Reduction, 1947–75," in Fishman, *Poverty amid Affluence,* pp. 18–20.

[23] United States Department of Commerce, Bureau of the Census, *Current Population Reports,* "Family Income Advances, Poverty Reduced in 1967," Series P–60, No. 55, August 5, 1969, p.2; United States Department of Commerce, Bureau of the Census, *Current Population Reports,* "Poverty in the United States 1959 to 1968," Series P–60, No. 68, December 31, 1969, p. 11.

[24] United States Department of Commerce, Bureau of the Census, *Current Population Reports,* "24 Million Americans—Poverty in the United States: 1969," Series P–60, No. 76, December 16, 1970, p. 1.

city and the farm, fatherless families and intact families, the young and the old, disabled and able-bodied, employed, underemployed and unemployed, and those born in poverty and those who have dropped below the poverty line.

Analysts refer repetitively to *poverty-linked characteristics* to point out that individuals with certain characteristics have greater risk of being poor. The chances increase as the individual exhibits more of these characteristics: absence of a wage-earner in the family, being nonwhite, age 65 years or more, age 14 to 24 years, being a female, in a family headed by a female, in a family with more than six children less than 18 years of age, unattached to a family, living on a farm, living in the South, education of less than the eighth grade, absence of work experience, and part-time employment.

Through statistical analysis, Ornati demonstrates that the risk of being poor increases with the convergence of several of the poverty-linked characteristics.[25] For example, using 1960 census data, he finds 28.6 percent of the nonwhites had incomes below $2,500. For nonwhites living on farms, the percentage increased to 54.8 percent. For nonwhite females living on farms, the percentage was 86.6.

Since poverty is linked to certain characteristics, Ornati points out that poverty is related to the special circumstances reflected by these sociodemographic factors. If poverty stems from factors related to social structure, remedial measures must be directed against the special circumstances which aggravate the economic plight of the persons possessing these characteristics in spite of the affluence of others.[26] The population of the poor is made up of a wide variety of groups: the mother with dependent child, the elderly person, the vocationally inept, the school dropout, and so on. Therefore, the problems of poverty are not of one piece and require a wide range of strategies, each tailored to all aspects of a situation rather than deficient income alone.

The statistics summarized in Table 6–1 portray some of the patterning in the relative prevalence of poverty among certain categories of the American population. Poverty has impact on members of all races, but blacks have a higher proportion of their numbers below the poverty line in all population categories in the table. Although urban slums are identified with the plight of blacks, the marked difference between the races in nonmetropolitan areas attests to the wider prevalence of poverty among blacks.

The family context of poverty is illustrated by the greater proportion of persons below the poverty line among persons in families with a female head. Family disorganization is associated with absence of a male head

[25] Oscar Ornati, "Poverty in America," in Ferman, Kornbluh, and Haber, *Poverty in America,* p. 36.
[26] Ibid., pp. 37–39.

TABLE 6-1
Percentage below the poverty line in each of population groups differentiated by residence, family status, age, and race for 1969

Family status, age, and race	White				Black			
		Metropolitan				Metropolitan		
	Total	Inside central cities	Outside central cities	Non-metro-politan	Total	Inside central cities	Outside central cities	Non-metro polit.
All persons								
Total	7.3	10.2	5.4	13.5	24.4	24.7	23.2	51.5
Under 25 years.........	7.5	11.1	5.5	12.9	28.4	29.0	26.6	54.5
25-64 years.............	4.7	6.5	3.5	9.9	16.9	17.1	16.1	42.4
65 years-over	18.8	20.9	16.5	30.5	38.9	38.6	40.6	65.7
Unrelated individuals 14 years and over								
Total	27.0	27.5	26.3	42.7	38.3	36.7	50.3	70.0
14-24 years.............	34.6	32.8	37.0	49.4	33.1	30.1	*	*
25-64 years.............	15.9	16.5	15.0	26.5	30.4	29.5	37.5	55.7
65 years-over	39.1	40.4	37.2	54.5	66.1	64.0	*	88.8
Persons in families with male head and male unrelated individuals								
Total	4.4	6.4	3.1	10.4	13.0	12.4	14.8	41.8
Under 25 years.........	4.5	7.0	3.2	10.2	13.7	12.9	16.3	43.8
25-64 years.............	3.1	4.6	2.2	8.3	10.5	10.5	10.7	34.9
65 years-over	11.7	13.1	10.3	23.1	28.5	27.1	34.6	58.8
Persons in families with female head and female unrelated individuals								
Total	28.1	29.1	26.9	39.5	51.0	50.6	53.0	75.3
Under 25 years.........	35.9	38.4	33.5	45.1	58.0	57.6	60.1	78.9
25-64 years.............	17.9	18.0	17.8	27.2	36.9	36.5	39.1	66.5
65 years-over	33.4	34.7	31.5	47.8	55.3	55.5	*	76.8

* Base is insufficient for computation of a percentage.
    Definitions: Metropolitan population is composed of residents of standard metropolitan statistical areas (a country or group of co
tiguous counties which contains at least one city of 50,000 inhabitants or more). The largest city in an SMSA is always a central city; and
or more additional cities may be secondary central cities. The poverty level takes into account such factors as family size, number
children, and farm-nonfarm residence. For example, the poverty threshold for a nonfarm family of four was $3,743 in 1969. Term "u
related individuals" refers to persons 14 years and over (other than inmates of institutions) not living with any relative.
    Source: United States Department of Commerce, Bureau of the Census, *Social and Economic Characteristics of the Population i
Metropolitan and Nonmetropolitan Areas: 1970 and 1960*, Current Population Reports, Special Studies, P23, No. 37, June 24, 197
Table 19.

through death, desertion, divorce, illegitimate births, or institutionalization. The next chapter takes up the impact of dismemberment and divorce. Our later analysis of racial problems will note the high prevalence of mother-headed households among blacks as a mark of family problems fundamental to the persistence of poverty in the black ghetto. Gibbard emphasizes that female-based household is not exclusively a black family form. However, its greater prevalence among both urban and rural blacks is noteworthy in that it tends to perpetuate itself by denying the growing boy a male model to orient him to the male breadwinner role. A girl is exposed to an environment wherein she sees adult males in terms of the unreliable and untrustworthy men moving through her mother's life. The urban job market favors the persistence of this family form because, among the poorly educated and unskilled, women are more likely to be employable than men. Thereby, an important facet in the persistence is the inferior chance of the young men to become employable and be employed.[27]

The category with the highest proportion exposed to poverty is that of individuals outside a family group, with the exception in some instances of the family with a female head. A related pattern, significant in itself, is the high economic vulnerability of persons aged 14 to 24 years or over 65 years. The plight of the aged unattached to a family is particularly demonstrated. Deficient financial resources are a vital aspect of the family's withdrawal from the care of the elderly in a stage of the life cycle when medical problems are aggravated and absence of employment and a valued family role deprives the individual of a sense of personal worth and dignity. Data on the 14–24 year group attest to the special economic vulnerability of youths without access to a family environment. The unemployment and underemployment of youth is a particular social problem, aggravated by their high numbers produced by the "baby boom" following World War II.

How are the poor different?

This brief presentation of poverty-linked characteristics demonstrates that persons making up the poor are different. But what is the significance of these differences? The poor may be a collectivity distinctive from the other collectivities making up American society in that only the poor display certain characteristics. On the other hand, the poor may differ in their greater display of characteristics also found among members of the other groups.

Rossi and Blum surveyed the research studies on the following variables affecting the poor: degree of participation in the labor force; kinds of employment; characteristics of family and community life; degree of knowledge of the larger society; and value orientations in politics, religion, and toward one's own effectiveness in coping with the larger society. Rossi and Blum conclude that the "special" characteristics of the poor are the ones they share with the "blue-collar" component of the labor force. The poor *are* different but in matters of *degree* rather than of kind.[28]

The most obvious common dimension among poor people is lack of satisfactory employment, including unemployment, underemployment, or substandard income for the employed. A recurrent target for campaigns against poverty is increased job opportunities to provide income and to

[27] Harold A. Gibbard, "Poverty and Social Organization," in Fishman, *Poverty amid Affluence,* pp. 52–54.
[28] Peter H. Rossi and Zahava D. Blum, "Class, Status, and Poverty," in Daniel P. Moynihan (ed.), *On Understanding Poverty* (New York: Basic Books, 1969), pp. 39–41.

deal with the adverse psychological consequences of unemployment in a society which defines work as essential to self-respect and meaning to life. However, unemployment is not restricted to the poor. Automation, for example, exerts the impact of technological unemployment on a wide range of occupations as well as on the unskilled.

Furthermore, the poor are not necessarily unemployed. A great deal of poverty comes about as a result of substandard earnings of the employed. Then, too, many of the poor are not employable because of physical or mental illness, infirmities of the aged, and opposition to hiring fit men near retirement age. In families without a male head, the mother is unable to seek work because of the care required for dependent children. Another group is too young for employment in spite of the absence of means of support through their nonaffiliation with a family.

COMPLICATIONS IN FINDING SOLUTIONS

The organization of an effective collective effort to solve the problems of poverty is complicated by the diversity among individuals in the ranks of the poor and by the involvement of the causes of poverty within the fabric of society itself. These complications raise many issues, some of which will be explored in the next chapter. Common to these issues are a number of factors suggested in our previous discussion. Only recently has the idea of relative deprivation seriously challenged traditional views that poverty is the inevitable lot of the "lazy and inefficient" and that poverty is a means of motivating the will to work.

In the United States there is a lingering reluctance to deal with the malfunctioning of social institutions which produce the persistent distress illustrated by Appalachia. The eradication of poverty is handicapped by residual elements of the identification of assistance to the underprivileged with charity and the rewarding of the socially inept. This clinging to the values of individualism, Elman says, has erected what he calls the *poorhouse state:* a system of inadequate payments, grudging services, petty rules tyrannies, and surveillance mechanisms.[29]

Social structure and the pains of poverty

The very social institutions supposed to be beneficial sometimes aggravate the plight of the poor by increasing the strain between them and the larger society. Social services are provided through agencies which utilize bureaucratic procedures to handle the great volume of clients produced by large urban populations and the increasing commitment of government

---

[29] Richard M. Elman, *The Poorhouse State: The American Way of Life on Public Assistance* (New York: Dell Publishing Co., 1966), p. 281.

to respond to the varied social and personal problems of urban society. The potential of bureaucracy is great for serving human needs which come in high volume and repetitiveness, but the characteristics of bureaucracy also lend themselves to blocking the achievement of the worthy purposes of the service agencies.[30]

The poor are particularly vulnerable to the adverse effects of bureaucracy because they are in an uncertain status as applicants for help in a society imbued with a philosophy of self-reliance. This status blocks the participation of the poor in the community decision-making processes in matters which have great significance in their destinies.

Society itself reinforces poverty in ways which must be altered if the lot of the poor is to be improved.[31] Frequently, the poor pay higher retail prices and higher interest rates for credit. Residence in low-income areas means higher rents relative to service received and difficulty in improving owner-occupied homes because of inferior access to mortgage money. There the schools are likely to have the most deficient plants and a disproportionate share of the least qualified teachers. Garbage collection, police protection, and other city services there are of lowest quality. New job opportunities are created in outlying sections of the city difficult to reach by residents of the deteriorated areas in the central city. Educational requirements and racial discrimination are other barriers to finding satisfactory employment.

Barriers to participation and services

The reputation of the poor, as seen by the middle classes, is a major obstacle to their acceptance into full participation in community life and their enjoyment of full benefit of its services. As we have seen, the ranks of the population regarded as poor include a diversity of groups with physical, social, and psychological handicaps. However, collectively they share the common qualities of subnormal access to economic means to obtain a reasonable share of the material and social benefits of what has been billed as an affluent and equalitarian society. Parodoxically, their very dependency on special services to deal with their particular handicaps becomes a barrier to their full participation in community life and their enjoyment of social equality.

To be a welfare client is to accept the mark of failure according to values of self-reliance and the importance of making a contribution to the vitality of the economic system through one's own labor. Since the United States

---

[30] For discussion of strengths and weakness of bureaucratic organization, see Chapter 3, pp. 76–77.

[31] Anthony Downs, *"Who Are the Urban Poor?"* (New York: Committee for Economic Development, 1968), pp. 38–43; Warren G. Magnuson and Jean Carper, *The Dark Side of the Marketplace* (Englewood Cliffs, N.J.: Prentice-Hall, 1968), chapter 2; David Caplovitz, *The Poor Pay More* (New York: Free Press, 1968).

is a middle-class society, Haggstrom contends that there is a readiness to accept findings that the lower classes have particular tendencies toward schizophrenia, character disorders, undisciplined and childlike behavior, little foresight, and hostility. Conversely, when representatives of the poor describe social workers as "phonies" and the community power structure as set against their interests, the claims are discounted as showing the "ignorance" or "opportunism" of the spokesman.[32]

Because they produce little which the community cannot do without, the poor lack collective power in community decision making. Workers can withdraw their labor and shut down an industry, but the poor lack connections with the levers of power to gain a place in bargaining. Their sense of unity is eroded by their diversity, their isolation from one another as groups, and their isolation from the mainstreams of community intercourse because of their scattering in enclaves throughout the nation.[33]

Furthermore, public benefits to the poor are received by *individuals* in a qualification status, which cuts off the poor from eligibility to gain influence in community decision making.[34] Assistance and services are gained on the basis of physical disability or other satisfaction of particular requirements for eligibility, not on the basis of membership in a group such as a labor union. Under the conception that one's contribution to the economic system determines self-respect, this form of qualification for benefits is not congenial to development of a sense of group unity among welfare clients. Furthermore, the clients are vulnerable in presenting their status as grounds for admission to decision making in organizations controlled by the middle class.

Criticisms of bureaucracies

Social services are criticized for inadequacies in terms of amount of allowances, quality of assistance against personal problems, and availability of decent housing. Insufficient coordination among private and public agencies obstructs the accessibility of potential clients to services, especially since agencies tend to specialize in certain services. The orientation of agencies is too frequently toward remedying difficulties that have already developed and policing applicants to make certain legal and organizational requirements are met. Prevention of difficulties receives insufficient attention.[35]

Both the agency employee and his client must operate within sets of

[32] Warren C. Haggstrom, "The Power of the Poor," in Frank Riessman, Jerome Cohen, and Arthur Pearl (eds.), *Mental Health of the Poor* (New York: Free Press, 1964), pp. 205–6.

[33] Warren C. Haggstrom, "Can the Poor Transform the World?" in Deutscher and Thompson, *Among the People,* pp. 67–68.

[34] Richard A. Cloward and Frances Fox Piven, "Politics, the Welfare System, and Poverty," in Ferman, Kornbluh, and Haber, *Poverty in America,* pp. 230–32.

[35] S. M. Miller, "Poverty, Race, and Politics," in Chaim Isaac Waxman (ed.), *Poverty: Power and Politics* (New York: Grosset & Dunlap, 1968), pp. 149–50.

rules and procedures intended to link the activities of the various specialists in the agency with those making up the total system. When the individual presents himself as a client, his personal problem is of pressing urgency—at least in his own view—but he sees himself exposed to routinized activity and formalized relationships confusing to the poor, who are unschooled in the workings of bureaucracy. At the welfare office, the needy person must first obtain from the receptionist an appointment with a caseworker for a more or less distant date. He then confronts the caseworker behind a desk in the agency office. If his case is acceptable, he becomes a part of a weekly cycle of contacts formulated to regularize activities for the sake of the agency as a complex social structure.

Because the agency is apt to specialize in certain kinds of problems and clients, the division of labor among agencies enhances the probability of gaps in services, or what the applicant calls the "run-around." Response is dictated by the built-in tempo of the agency rather than the time dimensions of the client's needs. Delay is not necessarily inappropriate, however, because the client's problems may require careful study by specially competent specialists when the crisis masks more profound difficulties. Hasty response based on pure emotion may bring a handout without affecting the sources of the difficulty. But the person in need is likely to interpret anything less than instantaneous action as bureaucratic pathology and rejection.

Another type of difficulty is the discrepancy between the claims and the performance of agencies. The poor receive less attention and the nonpoor benefit increasingly in the operations of many community service agencies. The troublesome youngster is likely to be excluded and favor given the "good boy." Casework is directed more toward the symptoms, with little attention to the underlying sources of the difficulty. Private social-welfare agencies tend to move away from low-income clients, closing the case at first interview by diverting the client to public agencies, under the principle that a "community agency" should serve all social classes. With the growth of social work as a specialized occupation, occupational prestige motivates a preference for the nonpoor as clients. The trend toward therapeutic-oriented case work favors clients who are motivated to interact effectively with the caseworker, and the lower-class client is less likely to participate effectively with a caseworker oriented toward middle-class values.[36]

The costs of dependency

In keeping with the high value placed on self-reliance, individuals tend to be judged as morally worthy to the degree that they make long-term

---

[36] Richard A. Cloward and Irwin Epstein, "Private Social Welfare's Disengagement from the Poor: The Case of Family Adjustment Agencies," in Brager and Purcell, *Community Action against Poverty,* pp. 40–63.

and arduous effort to achieve a socially acceptable goal. This moral approach identifies the root cause of poverty as an insufficiency of individual effort. A favorite remedy is to encourage the indigent individual to lift himself out of his plight.

This approach of course underestimates the environmental restrictions placed upon the poor, restrictions which favor the persistence of personal habits and institutionalized patterns maintaining dependency.[37] The seasonal nature of some industries and the impact of technological innovation on unskilled and semiskilled jobs lend special uncertainty to the irregularly employed. Experiences of deprivation in childhood undercut development of confidence, interpersonal skills, and knowledge of courses of action to be taken in dealing with a crisis. But even if these psychological handicaps were removed, the poor would still encounter condescending attitudes from agencies benevolent in intention and hostile attitudes from other agencies dedicated to protecting the overall community from the threat they assume the poor pose to the security of property and physical well-being. In either sense, the poor face humiliation in seeking assistance to gain means of helping themselves because the proffering of such assistance too frequently implies a belief that the recipient is inferior.

Such an imputation of inferiority can be present in the offers of assistance from the most benevolent. Moore captures the flavor of this imputation in a story he tells.[38] A minister at a farm migrant-worker camp received a call from a woman who said her club wanted to bring a Christmas dinner out to the camp. He agreed it was a fine idea. "Now tell me," she said. "What do they like to eat?"

The recipient of public assistance risks degradation. Aspects of his behavior usually concealed from public observation now are open to the scrutiny of investigators. His home can be visited and possibly embarrassing questions can be asked. He is not free to dispose of his money as he wishes. He must account to others for his needs and the disposition of his money. As though he were a child, he must show he has spent his money "wisely" according to standards which are not necessarily consistent with the realities of his situation. Paradoxically, the very workers who seek him out to assist him may become agents of his degradation.[39]

One example of the use of public aid for moralistic purposes is offered by Bell in her study of Aid to Families with Dependent Children, a federal-state grant-aid public assistance program authorized under the Social Security Act. To protect the interests and promote the welfare of children, a "suitable home" was deemed essential in the early years of the program. To minimize the change impact of federal funding in arousing protests against federal control, the states were given latitude interpreting eligibility

---

[37] See Haggstrom, "The Power of the Poor," pp. 212–17.
[38] Truman Moore, *The Slaves We Rent* (New York: Random House, 1965), p. 117.
[39] Lewis Coser, "The Sociology of Poverty," *Social Problems,* Vol. 13 (Fall 1965), p. 144.

requirements. The implementation of the program by many states, Bell asserts, converted the "suitable home" policies into vehicles for achieving two purposes. First, the growth of caseload was restricted by favoring an "elite poor" whose behavior coincided with the moral standards of the caretakers. Second, "unsuitability of the home" was sometimes extended to exclude children of illegitimate mothers and to exclude blacks disproportionately since they are particularly exposed to family instability.[40]

SUMMARY

The technological capacity to maintain a high standard of living has made poverty a paradox in a society experiencing a rising level of social expectations. Concurrent with an incomplete movement toward the welfare state, the image of poverty has shifted from Social Darwinism toward the idea of relative deprivation. Here the problem of poverty American style has been shifted from subsistence to inequality of economic opportunity and access to fundamental services and to the consequences of poverty on society at large. The target of anti-poverty programs is obscure because of the diversity of people suffering deprivation. Another complexity involved in mounting a collective effort to relieve poverty is the possible contribution of the social structure to aggravation of the social-psychological costs of poverty. The resort to bureaucratic strategies, the vulnerable status of applicants for assistance, and the environmental restrictions on the poor raise important issues. The next chapter takes up some of them.

FOR ADDITIONAL READING

Bernard Beck, "Bedbugs, Stench, Dampness, and Immorality: A Review Essay on Recent Literature about Poverty," *Social Problems,* Vol. 15 (Summer 1967), pp. 101–14.

Winifred Bell, "Services for People: An Appraisal," *Social Work,* Vol. 15 (July 1970), pp. 5–12.

H. Ben Bogdikan, *In the Midst of Plenty* (Boston, Mass.: Beacon Press, 1964).

Clarke E. Chambers, *Seed-Time of Reform: American Social Services and Social Action, 1918–1933* (Minneapolis, Minn.: University of Minnesota Press, 1963).

Thomas Gladwin, *Poverty U.S.A.* (Boston, Mass.: Little, Brown and Co., 1967).

Nathan Glazer, "Paradoxes of American Poverty," *Public Interest,* Vol. 1 (Fall 1965), pp. 71–81.

[40] Winifred Bell, *Aid to Dependent Children* (New York: Columbia University Press, 1965), pp. 174–86.

Margaret S. Gordon (ed.), *Poverty in America* (San Francisco, Calif.: Chandler Publishing Co., 1965).

Paul Jacobs, "Keeping the Poor Poor," in Leonard H. Goodman (ed.), *Economic Progress and Social Welfare* (New York: Columbia University Press, 1966), pp. 158–84.

Herman P. Miller, *Poverty American Style* (Belmont, Calif.: Wadsworth, 1966).

Martin Rein, "The Strange Case of Public Dependency," *Trans-action,* Vol. 2 (March-April 1965), pp. 16–23.

Richard M. Titmuss, "The Welfare State: Images and Realities," *Social Service Review,* Vol. 38 (March 1963), pp. 1–11.

Adam Walinsky, "Keeping the Poor in Their Place," in Arthur B. Shostak and William Gomberg (ed.), *New Perspectives on Poverty* (Englewood Cliffs, N.J.: Prentice-Hall, 1965), pp. 159–67.

Poverty: Issues 7
and implications

The public welfare department, May says, is the social seismograph of the community.[1] It records the tremors of a faulty school system, the closing of a factory, the layoffs caused by atuomation, and the distinctions made between the racial and social class status of individuals. Although the welfare rolls are commonly regarded as the best indicator of the consequences of poverty, there are others: the systems of medical services, education, and criminal justice—suggesting the interrelationship of poverty with issues which on casual observation would seem to have no connection. Through discussions of housing and slums, this chapter presents some of these issues.

HOUSING AND POVERTY

What makes a house a home? What makes a city a community? The physical locale takes on social-psychological dimensions in terms of its effects on the possibility of residents developing a sense of common identity and of deriving the satisfactions which membership in the community is supposed to bring. The family's dwelling unit and the neighborhood within which it is located are important elements in the problems associated with poverty.

Bad housing is identified by most persons with urban slums. Actually

[1] Edgar May, *The Wasted Americans* (New York: New American Library, 1964), p. 188.

the greatest share of substandard housing exists outside large cities. Even if the presence or lack of plumbing is ignored, more occupied housing is substandard in areas outside the large cities than in them.[2] While the greater prevalence of bad housing outside of metropolitan areas indicates the serious dimensions of rural and small city poverty, the pattern does not indicate a dearth of housing problems for the urban poor.

Home as setting for family life

As the physical setting for family life, the dwelling has a part to play in the social interactions among family members and in the family relationships with the world outside. Riemer cites two trends in reference to the home in urban life.[3] First, there is an effort to arrange for privacy and special purpose rooms inside the family residence. The well-to-do provide for privacy through separate bedrooms, a study, a recreational room, and so on. The poor lack the space for privacy and, certainly, rooms for special functions.

The second trend is toward elimination of specialized activities within the individual dwelling unit and their transfer to community facilities: recreational establishments, laundromats, hospitals, food processing plants, clothing manufacturers, police departments, credit institutions, schools, and so on. Therefore, urban family life is dependent on the quality of the services provided by the environment immediately external to the home. The poor are especially dependent on this environment.

The importance of housing design on the family, furthermore, is suggested by postulation of two polar types of family values.[4] The *familistic type* is characterized by strong in-group feelings, identification with family traditions, common effort of members to achieve family goals, concern whether the family name will continue through the generations, concern for family perpetuation, and joint family effort to protect members against problems from outside the home. The housing should provide for the needs of the housewife role, nursery and child play space, preservation of heirlooms, and special family celebrations.

The *emancipated type* emphasizes personal pursuit of individual goals, individual property with restricted obligations to family welfare, and subordination of interest in problems of other family members. Activities within the dwelling are subordinated, with the home primarily a dormitory for individuals who are oriented to activities outside the house. Personal

[2] Oscar Ornati, *Poverty amid Affluence* (New York: Twentieth Century Fund, 1966), p. 69.

[3] Svend Riemer, "Sociological Perspectives in Home Planning," *American Sociological Review,* Vol. 12 (April 1947), pp. 155–59.

[4] John P. Dean, "Housing Design and Family Values," in William L. C. Wheaton, Grace Milgram, and Margy Meyerson (eds.), *Urban Housing* (New York: Free Press, 1966), pp. 131–35.

privacy is emphasized, and housekeeping services are minimized. Congregate facilities for laundry and food preparation are more acceptable. Day nurseries, joint recreational facilities, and other extra-home provisions modify the social interaction among family members and expose them more to the influences of the external social environment.

In addition to the position of the family in a continuum between these polar types of values, the neighborhood has influence on the attraction of members into relationships outside the home. Dean suggests some of the pertinent factors: the distance between dwellings, the amount of social circulation in stimulating contacts among people, the location of centers where people meet casually, the existence of community facilities, and community leadership to encouraging associations among people.

Linkage of dwelling unit with problems

The housing of the poor raises problems in terms of the space and the physical conditions provided by the housing unit. Secondly, the location of the unit within the city has much to do with the quality of services the residents receive from the community at large.

In urban slums a considerable portion of family life is conducted outside the dwelling unit. Schorr cites studies indicating the close quarters and drabness of dwelling units drives children out into the streets and thus complicates the efforts of parents to control their children.[5] Space does not permit proper sleeping arrangements without excessive crowding and invasion of privacy. Family tensions may be traced in part to insufficient sleep and insufficient provision for withdrawal from quarrels or the noisy radio.

It is doubtful that bad housing in itself is a direct cause of distorted personality and antisocial behavior, but deficient housing does contribute to probability of illness and home accidents. However, the problem of poverty lurks beyond the sanitary and structural deficiencies of dwellings. Self-respect is eroded and cynicism fostered, largely because substandard housing usually is located in decayed neighborhoods inhabited by down-and-out, marginal, and disadvantaged people. Inadequacy of income requires diversion of a sizeable proportion of income to such substandard housing, leaving less for food, health care, and other prerequisites for decent living.[6]

Because substandard housing fails to provide a proper setting for its life, the slum family must turn to Reimer's second function of housing: providing access to services in the community external to the dwelling unit.

---

[5] Alvin L. Schorr, "Housing the Poor," in Warren Bloomberg, Jr., and Henry J. Schmandt (eds.), *Urban Poverty: Its Social and Political Dimensions* (Beverly Hills, Calif.: Sage Publications, 1970), pp. 206–8.

[6] Alvin L. Schorr, *Slums and Social Insecurity* (Washington, D.C.: Department of Health, Education and Welfare, 1963).

Because the environment is that of the slum, the ultimate significance of substandard housing lies in the deficiency of community services provided the slum dweller.

In turning to the environment external to the dwelling unit, the slum dweller is diverted from the familistic type and encouraged to follow the emancipated type. In this way deficient housing contributes to the further weakening of family solidarity. It would be excessive to attribute disorganized families in the slum to deficient housing. Rather, the difficulty lies in the failure of the dwelling unit to serve either of Riemer's functions of proper housing as a physical environment conducive to the effective operation of the family in meeting the needs of its members and serving social purposes. The physical setting is no substitute for the family as a network of social relationships.

What to do about housing?

Three strategies for meeting housing needs have been suggested. Through reduction of the costs of new construction, more people could enter the market. Greater possibilities of housing turnover would facilitate wider choices of location and would hold down cost for owners and renters. Direct subsidies for new housing could be managed to counter imbalances resulting from the turnover system.[7] (Later in this chapter, urban renewal and public housing will be reviewed as solutions to slum housing.)

The homebuilding industry has lagged in exploiting technological innovation for reducing construction costs. This lag is attributable to the large number of small firms, labor's fear of loss of jobs, and the fragmentation of the housing market in a tangle of diverse local building codes. To reduce this lag, several measures have been recommended: easing of local reliance on property taxes, federally financed experimentation in building techniques, and uniform national building codes accommodating the special circumstances of different regions.

Turnover involves a chain of housing transfers initiated when the previous occupants move to new units. In each exchange of housing, the families with lower incomes improve the quality of their shelter. However, limitations on resources of low-income families reduce the usefulness of turnover as a solution to the housing problem. One remedy is use of governmental subsidies for renovation of old dwellings.[8]

Turnover is one means of providing decent housing to minority groups if racial discrimination in the sale and rental of housing can be eliminated. The concentration of blacks and other minority groups in the central core

---

[7] Bernard J. Frieden, "Housing and National Urban Goals: Old Policies and New Realities," in James A. Wilson (ed.), *The Metropolitan Enigma* (Cambridge, Mass.: Harvard University Press, 1968), pp. 187–202.
[8] Ibid., p. 179.

of metropolitan areas, a product of economic and social segregation, is strengthened by the contention that blacks destroy market values of housing if they are able to buy housing outside the ghetto, a contention upon which studies cast serious doubt. Laurenti, for example, finds prices rose in 44 percent of those areas where housing was turned over to blacks, were unchanged in another 41 percent, and declined in the remainder.[9]

SLUM: ITS NATURE AND SIGNIFICANCE

The slum is characterized by poverty, run-down housing, insufficiency of public facilities and services, high population density, a concentration of the poorly educated and vocationally inept, and a high proportion of recent migrants with few financial resources. The significance of the slum lies in the atmosphere of apathy and social isolation lurking beneath its more visible aspects. Rather than its physical manifestation, Gans says, the problem of the slum lies in the economic and social conditions which have produced slum life. Obsolescence of housing, he argues, may be a social problem according to the judgment of middle-class observers, but it is not one from the perspective of slum dwellers.[10]

The location of the slum is a dimension in its economic defects. Although downtown offices and stores and enterprises within the slum provide some work, manufacturing and retailing have moved increasingly to the suburbs to the detriment of residents left in the central city. The flow of economic opportunity has undermined the tax base of the central city at a time when the demand for public services is increasing. The squeeze on the central city has been aggravated by the transfer of private incomes to suburbs concurrently with an increasing proportion of low-income persons in the population of central cities requiring services.

Differential organization and weakened consensus

Criminologists have documented the fact that the slum is not disorganized in the sense of an absence of behavior patterns tying it together into a social structure. Instead, the problem is that it is not meshed with the structure of the society about it.[11] Kobrin reports that, even in areas with high delinquency rates, the criminal culture is challenged by a conventional culture. He suggests that delinquency areas vary in the relative dominance of these two opposing value systems.

[9] Luigi Laurenti, *Property Values and Race* (Berkeley, Calif.: University of California Press, 1960).
[10] Herbert J. Gans, *The Urban Villagers: Group and Class in the Life of Italian-Americans* (New York: Free Press, 1962), pp. 142–55.
[11] William Foote Whyte, *Street Corner Society* (enlarged ed.; Chicago: University of Chicago Press, 1955), pp. 272–73.

At one extreme, highly organized adult criminals manage illicit enterprises and exert indirect control over delinquent gangs in terms of providing criminal career opportunities. The gaining of these rewards necessitates some limitation on violence and destructiveness. At the other extreme, adult criminality is not organized and the conventional values are in open opposition to criminal values. However, probably because of drastic changes in the class, ethnic, or racial characteristics of the slum population, the conventional values are not firmly established. Because neither value system is dominant, delinquency is not subject to restraints by any form of adult social structure, and juvenile offenses take on a wild character.[12]

The sense of unity among a slum's residents is eroded by a preoccupation with the daily problems of survival, lack of the verbal and literary prerequisites to organizational skill, lack of familiarity with formal methods of conducting the business of organizations, and a basic pessimism that improvement is not possible. Any sense of community that exists does so against great odds. Slum residents must cope with bureaucracies controlled from outside their neighborhood and, as discussed above, such operations bewilder slum residents. Urban renewal projects too frequently disperse the residents of previous slums and import deprived families from diverse areas to smash existing institutions. Intergroup tensions are a barrier. Marris finds the slum to be less of a fully integrated community and more of a tenuous group held together by a common hostility to outsiders and a common set of self-justifications as psychological protection against feelings of failure and humiliation.[13]

Rundown neighborhoods can demoralize attitudes and moral fiber through promoting a perception of one's self conducive to pessimism, passivity, and cynicism about people and organizations. However, the relationship between negativistic attitudes and physical conditions is indirect in that the latter symbolize a lack of concern for the well-being of slum residents. The invisibility of the poor to outsiders suggests a powerlessness among residents. Few other than a slum's residents know the look and smell of the slum, Hunter says. These few are likely to be individuals with a specific mission; for example, public welfare investigators, firemen, policemen, building inspectors, and politicians after votes.[14] Bullough argues that ghetto alienation is not only a product of ghetto living but is a vehicle for keeping residents locked into the narrow world of the ghetto. She compares middle-class blacks in the ghetto with middle-class blacks living in a predominately white suburban area. In contrast to the former,

[12] Soloman Kobrin, "The Conflict of Values in Delinquency Areas," *American Sociological Review*, Vol. 16 (October 1961), pp. 657–58.
[13] Peter Marris, "A Report on Urban Renewal in the United States," in Leonard J. Duhl (ed.), *The Urban Condition* (New York: Basic Books, 1963), pp. 126–27.
[14] David R. Hunter, *The Slums: Challenge and Response* (New York: Free Press, 1964), pp. 33–34.

integrated blacks exhibited less alienation and greater expectation that they could control events crucial to their lives. She argues that a sense of powerlessness and the feeling that the world makes no sense deters ghetto blacks from making sustained effort to overcome segregation.[15]

Slums: Hope versus despair

Slums come in several varieties, increasing the risk of overgeneralization concerning the social significance of the slum. Some are *slums of hope* inhabited by persons who see the ghetto as a way station in a movement to a better life. Although not yet benefiting fully from the economic and social advantages of the city, these persons believe that their stay in the slum is only temporary. Some are *slums of despair* because the residents' own attitudes and social circumstances put them at the end of the line in the dumping grounds of society.[16]

The slum of despair is promoted by a constant struggle for economic survival as the product of unemployment, low wages, and irregular work. Resources are insufficient to plan for the future. Miller lists these focal concerns of the lower class: avoidance of *trouble* (usually behavior which is normal by lower-class standards but contrary to the middle-class norms protected by law enforcement and courts); need for *toughness* in physical prowess, masculinity, and bravery in the face of danger; *smartness,* in terms of ability to dupe others through mental rather than physical effort; *excitement* in the form of gambling, "hanging out," alcohol, sex, and music; a feeling that *fate* (exterior and uncontrollable forces) regulates one's destiny; and freedom from external restraints in the sense of *autonomy.*[17]

Fatalism breeds a generalized suspicion of the world outside the neighborhood as represented by the police, school, welfare agencies, and persons of higher social classes in general. Inferior maintenance of buildings and inadequate public services reflect low official concern. Inferior schools, medical services, recreational facilities, and other services impair the environment for child and youth development. Inferior job opportunity feeds a rationalization that low socioeconomic status is the product of cynical and corrupt exploitation of the weak. Slum attitudes make the outsiders a "they" distinct from the "we" of local people, and are characterized by an ambivalence toward behavior defined as deviant by "them." Suspicion obstructs efforts of well-intentioned outsiders to help.

A distinct life style and orientation toward the world promotes a

---

[15] Bonnie Bullough, "Alienation in the Ghetto," *American Journal of Sociology,* Vol. 72 (March 1967), pp. 469–78.

[16] Charles Stokes, "A Theory of Slums," *Land Economics,* Vol. 48, No. 3 (August 1962), pp. 187–97.

[17] Walter B. Miller, "Lower Class Culture as a Generating Milieu of Gang Delinquency," *Journal of Social Issues,* Vol. 14 (March 1958), pp. 5–19.

social-psychological segregation impeding the movement of the poor into the opportunity structure of the larger society.[18] The ghetto aggravates the plight of the poor through a system of exploitation that includes consumer fraud, overpricing, and exhorbitant rentals for substandard housing.[19]

In association with the slum, poverty becomes a trap, a vicious circle maintained by a social structure which requires that the applicant for opportunity be literate, knowledgeable in completing application forms and taking tests, and that he be aware of the existence of opportunities. Lacking power, membership in community organizations, and a bent for active participation in affairs, the poor are unlikely to meet these demands.

The world of skid row

"Skid row" centers around substandard hotels and rooming houses offering inferior facilities at low rates. Skid row areas also provide cheap restaurants, taverns, pawnshops, and missions offering a free meal after religious services. They are populated largely by physically disabled, elderly, or destitute men. Another type of resident ("mission stiffs") prefers skid row because it provides a means of getting by without work. Regardless of the type of man who resides on skid row, he is homeless, has few if any economic resources, and has difficulties in interpersonal relations, with heavy drinking frequently a symptom. Additional groups of residents are criminals, young runaways, working men on a temporary liquor "binge," unstable young men on the "loose," sex perverts, and mentally unstable persons, together with the employees of business enterprises in the area.[20]

Skid row exists because it serves purposes: cheap living accommodations, companionship for elderly men, sanctuary for the rejects of families; availability of cheap liquor, proximity to free medical clinics, public welfare offices, and other services in the center of the city; the advantages provided by the tolerance and anonymity of the slum in evading responsibility and avoiding punishment for past transgressions; and, for a few, skid row residents are easy victims for robbery or pickpocketing.[21]

The population of skid rows appears to be declining over the long term because of greater availability of jobs. There are other explanations, however, which suggest erosion of the functions once served by skid row. The "hard-core" derelicts and unemployables, who are easy prey for muggers, complain of the influx of black hoodlums. Public welfare agencies are placing unattached men in rooming houses outside skid row. Urban

---

[18] Harold A. Gibbard, "Poverty and Social Organization," in Leo Fishman (ed.), *Poverty amid Affluence* (New Haven, Conn.: Yale University Press, 1966), pp. 46–71.

[19] David Caplovitz, *The Poor Pay More* (New York: Free Press, 1968).

[20] Donald J. Bogue, *Skid Row in American Cities* (Chicago: Community and Family Center, University of Chicago, 1963).

[21] Ibid.

renewal sometimes eliminates taverns and other skid-row institutions. Generally, dispersal of homeless men, rather than a significant reduction of their numbers, appears to be occurring.[22]

THREE APPROACHES TO SLUM PROBLEMS

Attempts to cope with the blight and human erosion of slums have tended largely to center around three general approaches: urban renewal projects, public housing, and vitalization of a sense of community.

Urban renewal as a strategy

Urban renewal constitutes the rehabilitation or clearance of deteriorated structures and their replacement with new construction. The federal Urban Renewal Program has had three primary objectives: substandard and other inadequate housing would be eliminated by clearing blighted areas; housing production would be stimulated to lift the pace of the general economy and to expedite development of a viable community; and a decent home for every family would be provided.

The federal program spearheaded a great deal of effort to put new life into the central cities. To be eligible for federal loans and grants, a community is required by the Urban Renewal Administration to submit a "workable program" as measured by certain elements. Adequate standards of health and safety must be established under which dwellings may be lawfully constructed and occupied. A comprehensive community plan must provide a framework for improvement and renewal of housing and for blight prevention to foster sound future community development. The location, intensity, and probable solutions for blight must be analyzed. An administrative organization must fix authority and responsibility for coordinating the overall program, funds must be made available for relocation of displaced families, and representative organizations and neighborhood groups should have opportunity to participate in the development and implementation of the program.[23]

Government reports cite figures on large areas of land cleared, and tens of thousands of structures rehabilitated and displaced families relocated. Projects are cited whereby new government buildings and cultural centers have been created to provide beauty in the central city.[24] Urban redevelopment is supposed to increase the city's tax base, reduce the expense

[22] Howard M. Bahr, "The Gradual Disappearance of Skid Row," *Social Problems,* Vol. 15 (Summer 1967), pp. 41–45.
[23] Martin Anderson, *The Federal Bulldozer* (Cambridge, Mass.: M.I.T. Press, 1964), pp. 17–18.
[24] Jewel Bellush and Murray Hausknecht (eds.), *Urban Renewal: People, Politics and Planning* (Garden City, N.Y.: Doubleday & Co., 1967), pp. 380–89, 400–405.

to the public of social services provided low-income families, and raise the esthetic quality of the central city.

Impact on housing inadequacies

The scope of the tasks contemplated by urban renewal denied the possibility of full success. Greer notes that the federal program tries to deal concurrently with two separate problems: the persistence of substandard housing in the urban core and the relative decline of the central business district in the metropolitan economy.[25] The first problem enlists the support of humanitarians and social reformers who would assist the poor, the second draws the intense interest of people concerned with the prosperity of the inner city in the face of socioeconomic forces favoring the movement of the middle classes and economic opportunity to the suburbs. The federal program provides an opportunity to use the governmental power of eminent domain to take over sufficient blocks of land in the central city for civic centers, cultural centers, and private projects which do not provide housing for low-income people, and in responding to the second problem, urban renewal is consistent with the major trends which are reshaping the function of the central business district. However, the enlistment of the power structure of the central city brings housing reform for the poor into conflict with the values of this power structure and their institutionalized practices which produced the slum in the first place.

Slums are produced, Greer points out, by the concurrence of demand and supply.[26] Persons with limited opportunity for choice demand low-quality housing. Supply is provided by cheap housing concentrated in the urban core. The particular segregation of the poor, the underprivileged, and the rejected in these areas leads their identification with the seamy elements of life. In addition to the financial restrictions, a negative moral evaluation of slum residents aggravates their housing plight. While responsible agents of society respond to the social consequences of segregation of the poor and the images of the residents held by the community external to the slum, the deterioration of the slum reduces tax revenues, and the services of garbage collection, education, public security, and so on decline in quality.

Greer argues that the key element in this process is the limited choice for housing provided slum inhabitants. Racial segregation and insufficient income pack a substantial portion of the urban poor into the slum. Paradoxically, slum clearance decreases the supply of, and increases the demand for, low-quality housing through demolition of the homes of people who are neither provided new housing within their economic means in

---

[25] Scott Greer, *Urban Renewal and American Cities* (Indianapolis, Ind.: Bobbs-Merrill Co., 1965), pp. 128–29.
[26] Ibid., pp. 148–53.

the central city nor permitted by segregation to join the flight to outlying areas. Urban renewal thus *reduces* their already limited range of housing choices.

Gans doubts that elimination of slum housing adds to the economic vitality of the urban core. The shopping of low-income residents is lost because small businessmen are unable to reestablish their stores in other parts of the city, and the financial burden of remaining residents is increased by higher rentals for new apartments and the reduced supply of low-rent housing. Middle-class residents who move in probably already are patrons of the downtown businesses. Along with reduction of the supply of housing for low-income people, clearance destroys neighborhoods as functioning social systems by gutting churches, small businesses, and other neighborhood institutions. The scattering of families is particularly destructive to older people.[27]

Urban renewal has forced many displaced families to move to housing no better than their now gutted former dwellings, which were replaced largely by high-rise apartment buildings for high-income families, Anderson contends. He believes that urban renewal is likely to encourage the spread of slums, that it will merely shift them. He estimates that half of the new construction would have been put up elsewhere in the city if urban renewal had not been undertaken.[28]

Public housing strategy

Publicly subsidized housing draws support as a direct and indirect answer to housing difficulties, because by increasing the range of choice available to the poor, it is a means of breaking their dependence on the worst structures.[29] Governmental control weakens the impact of racial, ethnic, or class prejudice in access to decent housing. Poverty involves a complex of fundamental social factors affecting the status of the aged, inadequate education, unemployment because of technological change, and so on, and public housing can be integrated into a comprehensive attack on this complex of problems—but the scale of such an attack would require governmental coordination.

Public housing strategy faces formidable opposition.[30] It has suffered from a lack of the pervasive and persuasive popular support which stimulates effective change in a democracy. Private builders, lenders, and property owners have exerted adverse political pressures which have placed public housing officials on the defensive. The low-income groups themselves have not demonstrated a strong interest through applications for

[27] Herbert J. Gans, *People and Plans* (New York: Basic Books, 1968), pp. 213–15.
[28] Anderson, *The Federal Bulldozer*, pp. 219–23.
[29] Greer, *Urban Renewal*, pp. 166–70.
[30] Catherine Bauer Wurster, "The Dreary Deadlock of Public Housing," in Wheaton, Milgram, and Meyersohn, *Urban Housing*, pp. 245–51.

admission to public housing projects, and when they do apply they are likely to have no other alternative because of the emergency nature of their housing problem or because they have the status of a public welfare client.

Moreover, the architectural design of publicly subsidized housing is inconsistent with American standards of space, outdoor privacy, and emphasis on the individual home. Public housing's standardized design and authoritarian management policies give an institutional flavor to it which reinforces its charity stigma. Even the gains of nondiscrimination and mixed racial occupancy scored by some projects are threatened by the preponderance of minority families who are subject to slum clearance and relocation and hence are prime candidates for public housing.

Public housing projects as a means of improving living conditions have been criticized for aggravating the dehumanizing effects of poverty. They have been described as cold, impersonal, and cheerless places. Their physical appearance, the imposition of rules on tenant behavior, and the discipline imposed by the project manager contribute to their atmosphere of a domiciliary institution. Deutscher documents the function of the application officer as a gatekeeper who informally screens applicants according to "desirability." Possible criteria used by the gatekeeper include race, dress, speech, manners, and the absence of a father. The key objectives are to avoid "troublemakers" and loss of rent payments.[31] In keeping with the policy of using the project as a halfway house along the route from the slum to decent private housing, income limits are set for occupant eligibility. The consequences are snooping by authorities, duplicity by tenants, discouragement of efforts to seek even modest improvement of income, and the aborting of tenant leadership through occupant turnover.

Strengthening the neighborhood

Although size, density, and heterogeneity of population are complicating factors, metropolitan areas do prevent evidence of neighboring behavior.[32] Can the private purposes of inhabitants be brought in conjunction with public purposes to make the slum neighborhood a basis for a sense of community? Cunningham describes four strategies which have been employed for this purpose.[33]

Under the *neighborhood conservation approach,* the city government strives to reverse housing deterioration and the flight of middle-income families from increased crime and the decline of community services. Private and public funds are utilized in a program intended to develop local

[31] Irwin Deutscher, "The Gatekeeper in Public Housing," Irwin Deutscher and Elizabeth J. Thompson (eds.), *Among the People: Encounters with the Poor* (New York: Basic Books, 1968), pp. 38–52.
[32] See Chapter 3, pp. 74–76.
[33] James V. Cunningham, *The Resurgent Neighborhood* (Notre Dame, Ind.: Fides Publishers, 1965), pp. 116–39.

citizen leadership and participation in neighborhood life. The director of a neighborhood center endeavors to coordinate the employment, clinical, and referral services of public and private agencies. Housing inspectors locate overcrowded families, and attempts are made to relocate them in public housing.

The *social invention approach* focuses on reorganizing the various systems which deliver educational, employment, health, recreational, and welfare services to the neighborhood. Instead of bulldozing deteriorated buildings and seeking to redevelop downtown areas, the emphasis is placed on new organizations, including both public and private sectors, in a movement to revolutionize the relationship of services to the neighborhood.

The *self-determination approach* employed by the Industrial Areas Foundation directed by Saul D. Alinsky is marked by militant demands of neighborhood residents rallied by staff organizers. Job discrimination, rent gouging, overcrowded schools, and other frustrations are raw material for organizing a neighborhood group as a power base against any outside force exerting control over the neighborhood.

The *neighborhood urban extension approach* of ACTION-Housing, Inc., Pittsburgh, works with private builders and lenders to meet the housing needs of families with incomes too high for public housing but too low for the regular private markets. Housing is made available through construction and modernization, and the staff works with local citizens by invitation to involve them in the planning and implementation of a renewal program, thereby encouraging a sense of community. A revolving loan fund provides seed money.

What about the racial ghetto?

What should be done about the racial ghetto? Downs suggests combinations of three classes of alternatives.[34] Nonwhites could either be concentrated in ghettos in continuation of the current pattern, or they could be dispersed throughout the city. Whites and nonwhites could continue to live in isolation from one another in segregated clusters, or they can be scattered randomly among the population in a form of integration. The nonwhites could continue to live under cultural, social, and economic deprivation, or programs can be initiated to enrich their lives.

Because of its ultimate objective of creating a separate black society, the Black Power movement is consistent with the combination of concentration, segregation, and enrichment. By gaining control over areas of heavy black population concentration in central cities, it would transform segregation into a means of political and economic power. Block voting

[34] Anthony Downs, "Alternative Futures for the American Ghetto," *Daedalus,* Vol. 97 (Fall 1968), p. 1344.

and selective use of purchasing power would become tools for bargaining to win concessions from the white majority to improve conditions for the racial minority. Success of this version of the self-determination approach depends on effective mobilization of the vast majority of blacks, but only a minority has been enlisted actively in the civil rights movement. The problems of the black are so intertwined with those of whites that participation of the whites seems essential to solutions. A segregated labor market would deny blacks a range of genuine economic opportunities, and programs of cultural enrichment and educational improvement would be sharply restricted by the lack of economic resources. Total alienation of the white community would have a paralyzing effect.

Downs advocates serious consideration of a dispersal strategy, probably resulting in some blacks becoming residents of largely white areas and other clustering in primarily black neighborhoods.[35] He offers these supporting arguments: Job opportunities will develop increasingly in suburbs rather than in the central cities. Residential dispersal is more likely than racial concentration to provide the community and school environments essential to effective education as an agent of cultural and social enrichment. Solution of the urban housing crisis necessitates dispersal from the central cities. Continuation of impoverished ghettos will lead to intolerable crime rates and the further aggravation of problems associated with racial segregation.

POVERTY: A HERITAGE?

A disturbing prospect is raised by the question of whether or not poverty is the heritage of a permanent class of underprivileged people sharing hopelessness, rejection of the work ethic, and chronic dependency. Harrington raises the question by contending that "they made the mistake of being born to the wrong parents, in the wrong section of the country, in the wrong industry, or in the wrong racial or ethnic group." [36]

Subculture of poverty

The similarities among the poor have caused a number of writers to suggest the existence of a *subculture of poverty*.[37] Lewis describes remarkable similarities among the poor of various nations and regions in the structure of their families, interpersonal relations, their value systems, their orientation in time, and their spending patterns.[38]

[35] Ibid., pp. 1363–65
[36] Michael Harrington, *The Other America* (Baltimore, Md.: Penguin Books, 1963), p. 21.
[37] For bibliography see: Jack L. Roach and Orville K. Gursslin, "An Evaluation of the Concept 'Culture of Poverty,'" *Social Forces,* Vol. 45 (March 1967), pp. 383–84.
[38] Oscar Lewis, "The Culture of Poverty," in Daniel P. Moynihan (ed.), *On Understanding Poverty* (New York: Basic Books, 1969), p. 187.

Will the poor always be with us? Only recently has the idea of relative deprivation seriously challenged traditional views that poverty is the inevitable lot of the "lazy and inefficient." A disturbing question is whether poverty is becoming the heritage of a permanent class of underprivileged people in an age promising abundance.

A useful distinction is made by Roach and Gursslin.[39] Sometimes the term is used as *description* of the similarities in a poverty group in terms of regularities of behavior and patterns of thought, while at other times the term is used to indicate that culture is the *cause* of poverty. (In this instance the contemporary poor would exhibit distinctive behavior and attitudes because of learning of a culture of poverty from the older generation.)

The distinction is useful in that the similarities caught by the descriptive version can be explained without resort to the concept of subculture. Although the membership of the poor changes to an important degree over the generations, the successive generations resemble each other in behavior and values as a product of the common experiences of being underdogs and of being subjected to similar social pressures.[40]

The use of subculture to indicate a cause of poverty requires two conditions to be satisfied.[41] First, it must be transmitted through successive generations, and second, the particular culture pattern must be uniform from generation to generation for the given group. To meet these conditions, Roach and Gursslin say, the given group of poor must have a capacity for effective interaction among its members to transmit common norms to the next generation. This interaction must be sustained with others of their own kind outside the family circle. The characteristic apathy and limited role performance of the poor raise doubts. Furthermore, the diversity of the poor and the social isolation of various groups from one another should be considered.

The universality of a subculture of poverty is questioned by a study of three separate ethnic groups: anglo, black, and Spanish-speaking Americans. Each group was divided between those receiving public assistance and those not receiving public assistance. The respondents were tested on 8 value orientations germane to the subculture of poverty, and in 14 out of 16 instances, the groups differed significantly enough from one another to suggest that the universality of the subculture was not proved.[42]

The prospect of persistent poverty for an already existing subculture justifies concern. A particular group may qualify as a subculture in its own right apart from poverty itself. Then the process of learning cultural norms becomes identified with poverty through the relegation of the group to the lot of chronic dependency. A pertinent example is the effect of economic distress to the folk society of the mountain people of Appalachia. The

[39] Roach and Gursslin, "The Concept 'Culture of Poverty,' " pp. 386–87.

[40] Louis Kriesberg, "The Relationship Between Socio-Economic Rank and Behavior," *Social Problems,* Vol. 10 (Spring 1963), pp. 335–36.

[41] Roach and Gursslin, "The Concept 'Culture of Poverty,' " pp. 387–88.

[42] Lola M. Irelan, Oliver C. Moles, and Robert M. O'Shea, "Ethnicity, Poverty, and Selected Attitudes: A Test of the 'Culture of Poverty' Hypothesis," *Social Forces,* Vol. 47 (June 1969), pp. 405–13.

economic plight in the southern Appalachian mountains, Ball says, is related to an "analgesic subculture." This subculture is associated with behavior standing in sharp contrast to what is regarded as rational in the general American culture.[43] In spite of the frustrations of poverty, squalor, and ill health, the mountain people persist dogmatically in maintaining old customs contrary to what outsiders regard as their own self-interests. Instead of holding their ground against adversity, they regress into anti-intellectualism, literal interpretation of the Bible, entanglement of religious fundamentalism with superstition, squandering of money available, and a dependency on public welfare as a way of life. Physical aggression against available targets is employed in lieu of rational action against the source of problems. Years of stress produce resignation, apathy, and fatalism.

Is today's situation unprecedented?

The potential danger of the slum lies in the possibility that it will become increasingly a place of despair. Slums inhabited by minorities are not new, but there is today a concern that new means of upward mobility will not be provided in sufficient magnitude to replace those means available to earlier slum residents. In one view, earlier immigrants saw poverty as a temporary state, undesirable but necessary to gaining a start on the ladder of increasing opportunity. With the development of contemporary technology, it is argued, the labor market is closed to individuals with the poverty-linked characteristics, offering them little hope for themselves or their children. Since disadvantage breeds disadvantage, the poor are supposed to face unprecedented barriers to employment and social participation.[44]

Although recognizing that the poor may display certain traits in aggravated form and degree of disability, Rossi and Blum argue that the more fortunate working class also has these traits. They find that studies on mobility along the social class ladder fail to support the idea that the American poor generally inherit economic deprivation over the generations. Rather, there is considerable reshuffling of the membership of major occupational groups over the generations.[45]

Citing evidence on the upward mobility experiences of the poor in Newburyport, Massachusetts, a century ago, Thernstrom argues that the contemporary poor are receiving the same fraction of the economic pie

[43] Richard A. Ball, "A Poverty Case: The Analgesic Subculture of the Southern Appalachians," *American Sociological Review*, Vol. 33 (December 1968), pp. 885–95.
[44] Louis A. Ferman, Joyce Kornbluh, and Alan Haber (eds.), *Poverty in America* (rev. ed.; Ann Arbor, Mich.: University of Michigan Press, 1968), pp. xxi–xxii.
[45] Peter H. Rossi and Zahava D. Blum, "Class, Status, and Poverty," in Moynihan, *On Understanding Poverty*, pp. 42–43.

as the earlier poor, but that the total pie has grown substantially.[46] He doubts that upward mobility for the low-skilled worker is more difficult than before. A smaller proportion of the population falls below the poverty line. Sons of unskilled and semiskilled laborers still rise to a higher occupation during their lifetimes than their fathers.

Educational requirements are more rigorous, but educational opportunities have at least kept pace. He cites evidence of unemployment rates for the unskilled in the past exceeding those of today to indicate that unemployment is not a *growing* problem. The plight of the contemporary elderly retired person is unprecedented because earlier higher death rates left relatively few to reach advanced ages. The special impact of racial discrimination, however, justifies genuine alarm over the plight of the black poor, Thernstrom says.[47]

COPING WITH POVERTY

Already some means have been suggested for dealing with bad housing and slums as components of the general problem of poverty. Now we move up the ladder of abstraction to consider strategies for dealing with poverty in general. Three orientations are found among the various strategies. First, the basis flaw is attributed to the poor themselves, who must be encouraged to develop and utilize new capacities to fit themselves into the opportunity system of society. Education and vocational training are prominent among the strategies for investment in human capital to bring the behavior of the poor in conjunction with the expectations of a middle-class opportunity structure.

Second, at the other extreme, poverty is attributed to the failures of society which require correction to bring its socioeconomic system in keeping with the American ideals of democracy and equality of opportunity to demonstrate qualifications for social and economic rewards. Third, between the two extremes, the fault is seen to be in the *operation* of the socioeconomic system. Remedies here center around improvement in the quality of services delivered by private and public agencies, reduction of the adverse consequences of bureaucratic organization, and development of new means of getting income into the hands of the poor without attaching the stigma of charity.

Focus on economic factors

Poverty as a total social condition is only partly an economic matter, but economic measures designed to remedy low income are obviously

[46] Stephan Thernstrom, "Poverty in Historical Perspective," in Moynihan, *On Understanding Poverty,* pp. 171–79.
[47] For discussion of this issue, see Chapter 15, pp. 385–89.

crucial among strategies for dealing with poverty. One approach would be to hope for further economic growth as a means of curbing unemployment. However, as Schultz notes, pervasive economic growth increases income per family, which in turn raises the poverty line in keeping with the concept of relative deprivation. Furthermore, economic growth does not necessarily produce increases in per-family income. He argues that reduction in the prevalence of poverty depends on greater investment in people to correct imbalances stemming from inadequate vocational skills and racial discrimination, and the South's special burden of great dependence on agriculture and an unskilled labor force.[48]

Poverty today, one economist asserts, is largely structural in character in that "it does not automatically disappear as the favored majority becomes steadily more affluent."[49] It is structural in that either the nature of the economic system or of the population of the poor is relatively untouched by general economic progress. Economic growth may benefit the more affluent, but factors such as increased automation forestall distribution of benefits to the unemployed. The prevalence of unemployables among the aged and persons without needed skills would forestall their sharing in new opportunities. The existence of opportunity in one region does not help the immobile unemployed in another area.

Another economic approach would raise wages of unskilled workers through minimum-wage laws and of farmers through high farm price supports. Economists cite difficulties for broadening the distribution of goods when the prices are raised by higher costs without improved efficiency in production. Furthermore, the benefits of these laws are unlikely to accrue to the *very* poor because participation in the labor force is necessary. Farm price supports, for example, have largely worked to the advantage of the wealthy owners rather than to farm laborers or subsistence farmers.[50]

Friedman advocates a negative income tax. When the taxable income of an individual or family falls below a certain figure, the taxpayer would receive a subsidy. He argues that the benefits would emphasize the status of being poor rather than an occupational status (farmer) or age level, which also includes the nonpoor. Furthermore, the approach would operate through the market rather than as another factor affecting the operation of the market.[51] Friedman's negative income tax goes beyond progressive taxation, which imposes higher taxes on the well-to-do to reduce income discrepancies among the social classes, although special deductions for

[48] Theodore W. Schultz, "Public Approaches to Minimize Poverty," in Leo Fishman (ed.), *Poverty amid Affluence* (New Haven, Conn.: Yale University Press, 1966) pp. 173–81.

[49] R. A. Gordon, "An Economist's View of Poverty," in Margaret S. Gordon (ed.), *Poverty in America* (San Francisco, Calif.: Chandler Publishing Co., 1965), pp. 10–11.

[50] Schultz, "Public Approaches to Minimize Poverty," pp. 170–71.

[51] Milton Friedman, *Capitalism and Freedom* (Chicago: University of Chicago Press, 1962), pp. 191–92; also see Christopher Green, "Guaranteed Income Plans—Which One is Best?" *Trans-action,* Vol. 5 (January-February 1968), pp. 49–53.

business expenses and depletion of oil and mineral resources provide loopholes to reduce achievement of this purpose.

The "war on poverty"

In signing the Economic Opportunity Act of 1964, President Lyndon B. Johnson launched what had been heralded as a "war on poverty." Although largely a supplementation of existing programs, the effort embodied several new intellectual propositions centering around investment in human resources. Eckstein lists four basic strategies.[52] Through access to as much good education and training as he could absorb profitably, the individual would gain opportunity to develop his full potentiality; every individual would be made aware of the opportunities open to him and the rewards to be gained through his own efforts; equal opportunity would be available to all on the basis of his job qualifications; and every individual would be exposed to the cultural values of high personal achievement and full use of his potential.*

We will use the "war on poverty" as a rubric under which we will summarize rather briefly some of the trends and issues involved in the current ferment over dealing with poverty as a central social and political concern. Under the Community Action Program (C.A.P.), the Office of Economic Opportunity (O.E.O.) set out to implement the provisions of the 1964 Act for "maximum feasible participation of the residents of the areas and members of the groups served." The objective was to develop *community* action through joint effort of local public officials, voluntary agencies, and representatives of the poor. The concept attracted special interest because it implied a recognition of the need to change the function of poverty within the overall functioning of society.

Partly by design and partly by the force of its innovative thrust, O.E.O. has had great impact on the political establishment.[53] One of its primary missions was to mobilize the poor as a political force for reshaping public institutions. Second, by giving less emphasis to the state level of government, the Economic Opportunity Act became an experiment in federalism whereby the national government related directly to local government. It appears that the framers of the act did not fully recognize the implications of "maximum feasible participation." The responses included militancy among portions of the poor which seriously disturbed community leaders and bureaucracies. The C.A.P. became embroiled in local politics and in dissension over the participation of the poor. Fears of social and political revolution, financed from Washington, stimulated resistance from the political and social establishment. Sincere doubts were expressed that the

[52] Otto Eckstein, "Strategies in the War on Poverty," in Fishman, *Poverty amid Affluence,* pp. 202–3.
[53] Robert H. Davidson, "The War on Poverty: Experiment in Federalism," *Annals of American Academy of Political and Social Science,* Vol. 385 (September 1969), p. 2.

poor has sufficient parliamentary skills, articulateness, administrative know-how, and self-esteem to function constructively in decision making.[54]

Nevertheless, Rubin sees great significance in the incorporation in law for the first time of a notification to the poor that they are capable of taking a hand in their own affairs. The issue of the capability of the poor had been transferred from *whether* to *how* the leaders of the poor would gain a legitimate place in the institutional structure to provide for participation in the decision making of events bearing on their lives.[55]

In spite of doubts about the participation of the poor in community decision making, it has become an accomplished fact in many communities. Positive consequences have been claimed in terms of providing a measure of representation of the poor in community power structures and improved coordination of social services. In encouraging the poor to believe they have a real stake in the community, "maximum feasible participation" offers the possibility of narrowing the gap in understanding between the poor and the nonpoor. Many communities have been awakened to the deep-rooted sources of poverty.[56]

Where the effort fell short

The Office of Economic Opportunity has been severely criticized for lack of coordination, wasted effort, and other consequences of an overly ambitious announcement of objectives. The poverty program has been victimized by the excessive expectations it raised for quick ending of a long-term accumulation of social structure and tradition in maintaining poverty. The resources provided did not match the promises. The responsibilities assigned O.E.O. did not match the scale of income redistribution, public employment, and structural reorganization the promises implied. The local communities were unable to provide sufficient skilled leadership, agreement on resident participation, management of funds, and reorganization of the complex of service bureaucracies operating on a level beyond the local community.[57]

As a participant in the drafting and implementation of the Economic Opportunity Act of 1964, Moynihan was in a position to observe the difficulties.[58] In his judgment, the community-action programs were carried out in such a way as to produce a minimum of the social changes

---

[54] Sanford Kravitz, "The Community Action Program in Perspective," in Bloomberg and Schmandt, *Urban Poverty,* pp. 297–300.

[55] Lillian B. Rubin, "Maximum Feasible Participation: The Origins, Implications, and Present Status," *Annals of American Academy of Political and Social Science,* Vol. 385 (September 1969), pp. 14–29; also see Sanford Kravitz and Ferne K. Kolodner, "Community Action: Where Has It Been? Where Will It Go?" in same issue, pp. 30–40.

[56] Kravitz, "The Community Action Program in Perspective," pp. 301–4.

[57] Ibid., pp. 304–6.

[58] Daniel P. Moynihan, *Maximum Feasible Understanding* (New York: Free Press, 1969), pp. xiii, 144–47.

desired by its sponsors and a maximum increase in the opposition to such change. He describes internal contradictions in the program, interagency jealousies, political bargaining, wide discrepancies between the rhetoric of promise and the low level of performance, and contradictions between conservative and radical formulations of community action. The conservative formulation, he says, is identified with stability, continuity, and coordination of programs for efficient management. The radical formulation emphasizes social change, innovation, and strategies of conflict to involve the poor in policymaking.

The program has been found at fault for having least impact on the segments of the poor in greatest need. As is usual in antipoverty training programs, the war on poverty has been subjected to the dilemma of *creaming* whereby the least disadvantaged among the poor gain the most advantage from training and public employment programs. In the short-run, the "success" of the program is most likely when selection of candidates favors the most trainable and the least alienated. Then those who enter a program are more likely to complete it and emerge into the community as "good workers." But, Miller and Rein point out, a danger lies in the overlooking of the forgotten youth who are not reached by traditional programs when the programs are not devised to meet their needs.[59]

Contrary to its promise to be innovative, the program fell into some familiar traps. The primary thrust has continued to be improvement of the lot of the poor by changing them as individuals to conform to the expectations of the status quo, rather than giving sufficient attention to the existing social arrangements which impinge on the poor. The emphasis on the difficulties of youth is congenial to American values and the faith in education as the gateway to better opportunity. However, can the outlook and life-chances of an individual be changed in the teens without improvement of the family and neighborhood environments within which the personality is developed? Can greater access to education and training suffice without revamping the nature and workings of educational institutions?[60] Furthermore, the strategies ultimately centered around *reduction* of the gap between needs and resources through welfare assistance, remedial education, and other services, rather than striking at the causes of maldistribution of income. Consequently, Ornati finds the strategies embedded in a conception of poverty as subsistence, providing resources for survival alone.[61]

In spite of these telling criticisms, the "war on poverty" should be judged against the background of difficulties it has faced in confronting a long-existing problem. The major gains, Shostak believes, have been in lessons learned and in revision of general conceptions of how to overcome

---

[59] S. M. Miller and Martin Rein, "The War on Poverty: Perspectives and Prospects," in Ben S. Seligman (ed.), *Poverty as a Public Issue* (New York: Free Press, 1965), pp. 294–97.
[60] Ibid., pp. 288–93.
[61] Oscar Ornati, "The Spatial Distribution of Urban Poverty," in Bloomberg and Schmandt, *Urban Poverty,* p. 79.

poverty. The national effort has broadened national consciousness of the poverty problem. It has reduced the initial arrogance of conventional wisdom that poverty is simply a matter of laziness and congenital deficiencies. It has increased recognition of the interrelationship of poverty with all aspects of life. It has played a part in the emergence of a constructive skepticism toward "easy" solutions. It has provided evidence of the appearance of genuine innovation in seeking new bases for employment, revision of education, involvement of professionals, and fuller participation of the poor in the benefits of community life.[62]

SUMMARY

Why be concerned about poverty? The fundamental reason, as this and the preceding chapter on the subject demonstrate, is that it has implications which permeate the entire society and which are expressed in the major social problems to be taken up in the rest of this book. Haworth offers a convenient summary statement by noting that justifications for concern fall under three moral categories: goodness, justice, and prudence. Poverty in the city demonstrates that the quality of urban life falls far short of the "good city" we claim as our ideal. Poverty is a form of social injustice imposed on the poor. Efforts to overcome poverty are prudent for the nonpoor because the ultimate consequences of poverty threaten the well-being of all.[63]

This chapter has focused on deficient housing and the slum as key elements in the overall problem of poverty. Housing is significant largely in terms of its association with the social degradation and deficiency of community services experienced by the poor. Approaches to remedying deficient housing and the slum include urban renewal public housing, and strengthening of the neighborhood. Answers were suggested to the questions: Is poverty inherited through cultural learning? Is our age producing a new class of the permanent poor? What can be done about poverty?

FOR ADDITIONAL READING

Charles Abrams, *Forbidden Neighbors* (New York: Harper, 1955).

Martin Anderson, *The Federal Bulldozer: A Critical Analysis of Urban Renewal, 1949–1962* (Cambridge, Mass.: The M.I.T. Press, 1964).

Kurt W. Back, *Slums, Projects and People* (Durham, N.C.: Duke University Press, 1962).

[62] Arthur B. Shostak, "Old Problems and New Agencies: How Much Change?" in Bloomberg and Schmandt, *Urban Poverty,* pp. 341–60.

[63] Lawrence Haworth, "Deprivation and the Good City," in Bloomberg and Schmandt, *Urban Poverty,* pp. 40–41.

Marshall B. Clinard, *Slums and Community and Development: Experiments in Self-Help* (New York: The Free Press, 1966).

Nelson W. Foote (ed.), *Housing Choices and Constraints* (New York: McGraw-Hill, 1960).

Marc A. Fried, "Is Work a Career?" *Trans-action,* Vol. 3 (September-October 1966), pp. 42–47.

Clarence Funnye and Ronald Shiffman, "The Imperative of Deghettoization: An Answer to Piven and Cloward," *Journal of Social Work,* Vol. 12 (April 1967), pp. 5–11.

David Gottlieb and Charles E. Ramsey, *Understanding Children of Poverty* (Chicago: Social Research Associates, Inc., 1967).

David R. Hunter, "Slums and Social Work or Wishes and the Double Negative," in Bernard Rosenberg, Israel Gerver, and F. William Howton (eds.), *Mass Society in Crisis: Social Problems and Social Pathology* (New York: Macmillan Co., 1964), pp. 594–603.

Jane Jacobs, *The Death and Life of Great American Cities* (New York: Random House, 1961).

Oscar Lewis, *A Study of Slum Culture: Backgrounds for La Vida* (New York: Random House, 1968.

Robert K. Merton, "The Social Psychology of Housing" in Wayne Dennis et al., *Current Trends in Social Psychology* (Pittsburgh, Pa.: University of Pittsburgh Press, 1961), 163–217.

S. M. Miller, Frank Riessman, and Arthur A. Seagull, "Poverty and Self-Indulgence: A Critique of the Non-Deferred Gratification Pattern," in Louis Ferman, Joyce Kornbluh, and Allen Haber (eds.), *Poverty in America* (rev. ed.; Ann Arbor, Mich.: University of Michigan Press, 1968), pp. 416–32.

Maurice Pinard, "Poverty and Political Movements," *Social Problems,* Vol. 15 (Fall 1967), pp. 250–63.

Lee Rainwater, "Fear and the House-As-Haven in the Lower Class," in Bernard J. Frieden and Robert Morris (eds.), *Urban Planning and Social Policy* (New York: Basic Books, 1968), pp. 84–95.

Family: An institution 8 in transition

The collapse of the family is a favorite refrain among those who see American society going to rack and ruin. On the one hand, defenders of what they regard as a sacred and fundamental institution decry divorce, "frivolity" in the undertaking of marriage, "disloyalty" to kin, and "sexual promiscuity." On the other hand, critics of the family indict it as a decadent and patriarchial institution obstructing freedom of sexual expression and shackling individuals in the name of "responsibility."

Although they do not provide sufficient intellectual substance for understanding the workings of this social institution, these conflicting interpretations attest to the importance of the family to the study of social problems.

SOME PRELIMINARY CONSIDERATIONS

The family is regarded as the basic social institution for two reasons. First, it may be the prime mover in determining the nature of life in a given society. (As Udry points out, industrialization has removed the family from the position of prime mover and has profoundly affected family life.) Second, the family is the primary determinant of the life chances of the individual born into it.[1] In the family, the child acquires his initial status, the basic structure of his personality, and his initial resources for making

[1] J. Richard Udry, *The Social Context of Marriage* (Philadelphia, Pa.: J. B. Lippincott Co., 1966), p. 19.

185

his contribution to society as an individual. The family is a unique institution, Goode says, in that almost everyone is both born into a family and establishes his own. Usually family obligations cannot be delegated to others as specialized responsibilities, as they can be in the case of occupation. Furthermore, although participation in family life is not enforced by formal punishment of those who abstain, most persons do take part in family activities.[2]

Place of the family in the social structure

Among social institutions the family has the greatest potential for touching the individual through the most intimate of human experiences. Much of this potential is derived from sexuality. Sexual desires are a part of normal personality, and marriage is a socially approved means of satisfying them. Human sexuality is not simply a biological phenomenon limited to the physical act. The impulse colors the whole of emotional life. Physical attraction, interpreted through a romantic myth, brings most American couples into marriage. A more enduring interdependence is expected to emerge later to provide protection against crises and to insulate the individuals against the corrosion of family relationships by the trivialities and routines of everyday family life. Through an allocation of tasks according to sex roles, family members are supposed to function as a unit and to provide personal advantages to the individuals who compose the unit.[3]

One's own sexual gratification becomes dependent on the consideration of the mood of the other. From this egocentric need for cooperation of the partner, an elaborate network of social norms is supposed to transform physical intimacy into a means of building a family as a social system patterning the interactions among its members. With the coming of children, the closed system of man and wife must accept parental obligations to the new personalities in the home. The bonds of intimacy enclose both parents and children in a network of roles and associated norms that help to provide guidance to the individual as he balances his pursuit of private goals with the necessity to contribute to order within the family.

The basic element in family organization is the husband, wife, and their dependent children; this unit is known as the *nuclear family.* In the *extended family* the nuclear family is the basis of a larger organization. Christensen distinguished several ways in which the extended family includes nuclear families. In the consanguine family, the extension is along the line of parent-child relationships. In polygamy, where one person has more than one spouse, the extension is along the line of husband-wife relationships. The extension may also be accomplished through adoption.[4]

[2] William J. Goode, *The Family* (Englewood Cliffs, N.J.: Prentice-Hall, 1964), p. 4.
[3] Gunnar Boalt, *Family and Marriage* (New York: David McKay, 1965), pp. 2–4.
[4] Harold T. Christensen "Development of the Family Field of Study," in Harold T. Christensen (ed.), *Handbook of Marriage and the Family* (Chicago: Rand McNally, 1964), p. 4.

Frequently, two other related but distinct systems are regarded as though they are identical with the patterned interactions which constitute the family as a social system. The consequence is a blurring of meaning that interferes with penetrating analysis. *Marriage* refers to the mating arrangement between human males and females which is a precondition to the establishment of a family. Christensen emphasizes that marriage is a sociological concept, as distinguished from biological mating, in that it involves normative regulation of sexual behavior and the establishment of responsibilities for the adult mates.[5] Through marriage, entry is gained to the legitimate status of parent. Parenthood is crucial to the care and training of the next generation, making this status of primary concern to the society's long-term interests.

The second system is a *kinship system* consisting of statuses constructed of putative (supposed) or real genealogical relationships. At birth the individual gains rights, privileges, and obligations within a kinship system which defines how descent is determined in regard to property and also relationships with persons occupying particular designated statuses. In patrilineal societies, descent is through the father. In matrilineal descent, it is through the mother. Kinship systems also vary in the range of relatives included in vital relationships and the importance placed on particular statuses such as brothers, uncles, and cousins.[6] Marriage and kinship are related in terms of the fixing of authority in deciding when the single individual shall marry, whom he shall marry, and the conditions of the legal or informal contract. A typical mark of the American family is that the individual has comparative freedom from kin groups in such decisions.

The American family, broadly speaking, expresses sets of cultural values which shape the place of family life in American society and the expectations of most people who participate in this life. Sirjamaki summarizes the sets of cultural values.[7] Marriage is a dominating life-goal for adults of both sexes, as indicated by the unusual popularity of marriage among Americans. Because marriage is seen foremost as the linking of two young people by personal attraction, the marital interaction should be based on personal affection and choice. Personal happiness of husband and wife is supposed to be the mark of a successful marriage, with children commonly considered to be a means of achieving this bliss. Youth is considered the best period of life and its qualities the most desirable. This high esteem for youth is related to a remarkable urge to shelter children from the trials and tribulations adulthood is supposed to bring. Considerable tension is associated with the expectation that the exercise of sex should be contained

---

[5] Ibid., p. 3.

[6] For our purposes we pass lightly over a phenomenon which rivals the complexity of a periodic table of chemical elements. See Morris Zelditch, Jr., "Cross-Cultural Analyses of Family Structure," in Christensen, *Handbook of Marriage and the Family,* pp. 462–500.

[7] John Sirjamaki, "Cultural Configurations in the American Family," *American Journal of Sociology,* Vol. 53 (May 1948), pp. 464–70.

within wedlock. The division of labor within the family presupposes the status of the male as breadwinner and family representative to the external community. Finally, the American emphasis on individualism tends to weaken the unity of the family and loyalty to kin.

Within the environment of these cultural expectations, the American family as a form of social organization is supposed to serve the interests of its members and society. In other words, the family has functions which involve it concurrently in the lives of its members and in the patterns of society. It thus serves as a mediating agent between most individuals and the environment external to the family. However, industrialization and urbanism have removed the family from the position of prime mover of events, as we stated earlier, and has affected its functions profoundly.

Shifts in functions of family

The *protective function* has been shifted to extrafamilial agencies. In urban society the family is poorly equipped to deal with enemies, disease, tainted manufactured food, fire, and crime. The *economic function* of the family has shifted from a largely self-sufficient farm to an economic consumption unit, with the wages of the breadwinner distributed to meet the needs of the members. With the paycheck permitting the individual to purchase goods and services previously acquired through family membership, the urbanite finds marriage less essential to the meeting of his economic needs. Further, because income is acquired by individuals in employment outside the home, the family loses the benefits of common work activities for developing psychological consensus.

Educational and *recreational functions* have been taken over for the most part by other social institutions. When largely an informal and incidental part of family life, education and recreation were among the activities drawing family members together. However, with a wider range and complexity of occupations, transmission of vocational skills from father to son becomes less effective. Formal education has become essential. In contrast to the family, specialized institutions in education and recreation tend to differentiate activities according to age and sometimes according to sex. Thereby, family members frequently go in different directions and have experiences not necessarily binding them to one another.

The school has assumed some responsibilities of *socialization* whereby the child becomes familiar with his culture and competent to live within his society. Nevertheless, the family continues to have major responsibilities for socialization and for its corollary, the *social control function.* As the scene of intimate social relationships with great emotional impact, the family has the potential for instilling a self-discipline in accordance with the rules of the general social order. At the same time, the range of behavior subject to effective parental control has been shortened by the challenge of competing values carried by mass communications, the school, and heterogeneous contacts outside the home.

Through the *affectional function* the individual is supposed to gain the emotional security of belonging to a group which cares about him, worries over his troubles, and applauds his accomplishments. Within the segmental relationships of urban life and the impersonality of bureaucratic organizations, the nuclear family assumes particular importance as a refuge for management of tensions and balancing of the emotional budget. Conversely, the emphasis on personal gratification and the expectation that marriage will bring "happiness" raises the risk of conflicts and tensions within the home. The *reproductive function,* the creation of the next generation, continues to be a paramount contribution of the family, although urban life has brought new incentives for birth control.

FAMILY AND SOCIAL PROBLEMS

Because the family is the primary determinant of the life chances of the individual born into it, analysis of any particular social problem will include the family as an important variable. Already we have emphasized the relationship of the family and its physical and social settings to poverty. Subsequent chapters will trace aspects of this relationship in other social problems.

Family as contributor to problems

The family frequently is blamed for undesirable conditions. Parents are indicted for failure to bring up their children properly. Children are seen as some new breed of hellions who lack respect for sacred traditions. This essentially moralistic and simplistic approach overlooks the changing conditions of the overall social environment within which contemporary families must operate.

Nevertheless, it would be an exaggeration to portray the family as a helpless pawn of forces beyond its control. It retains essential functions in socialization and affection. These functions are significant in the creation and continuity of control mechanisms whereby the individual commits himself to the norms regulating behavior within the other social institutions of urban society. As a setting for intimate relationships, the particular family can encourage the development of a sense of being wanted as insulation against the impersonality of urban life. The child can be oriented to the acceptance of values and compliance with norms which advance his merger of private and public interests in his adult life. Conversely, the particular family may aggravate tensions, impart inappropriate role models, and increase the probability of subsequent deviant behavior.

The relationships within the family circle have potential for conflict among its members. As an intermediary, the family is drawn into the difficulties its members encounter in the larger community. In either case, reactions of particular families to problems are related to its qualities, as well as to factors outside its control.

The family has a repertory of solutions, not necessarily effective, for problems that arise sufficiently often to be expected. The term *crisis* is reserved for a problem that shocks a family because it comes without warning and exceeds the range of the repertoire of solutions. Hill lists three variables which determine whether a given event constitutes a crisis for a given family.[8] First, the crisis situation, or the event itself, imposes hardship. "Hardship" is defined as the temporary paralysis of the family's resources or the loss of such resources by the crisis event. If the family has the means to cope with the problem event, it is not considered a hardship according to this interpretation. (A hardship to one family is not necessarily a hardship to another family.)

Second, the crisis exceeds the resources of the family, its role structure, flexibility, and previous experiences with such problems. The resources include money, rallying of relatives, and adaptability to unprecedented circumstances. Removal of one parent, or other key figure, creates a void in the role system which must be filled by another person if the family is to operate effectively. Will the family as a whole and its constituent members be flexible enough to adapt themselves to this crisis? If the family has previously faced unemployment, bereavement, or other crises, it is more likely to cope effectively. Hill suggests the range of ways in which breakdown of role performance can generate family crises.[9] The family may experience *dismemberment* through widowhood, orphanhood, loss of a child, or separation through hospitalization, imprisonment, or military service of a member. Crises of *accession* involve unwanted pregnancy, return of an unwelcome deserter or absent member, or the addition of a stepparent. Here the familiar modes of role adjustment must be reorganized in the light of the social significance of the particular way a new member is added. In *demoralization* the family suffers loss of morale and unity because the actions of a member produce loss of financial support, progressive dissension, or infidelity.

Third, the family members conceive the event to be a crisis threatening their social position and their goals. Familiar with poverty, one family may define sudden unemployment as the same old story; another family, conditioned to a life of comfort, may be overwhelmed by sudden unemployment. The concept of relative deprivation is pertinent here in that the reaction is related to the particular standard employed by the family in evaluating the problem.[10]

---

[8] Reuben Hill, *Families under Stress* (New York: Harper and Brothers, 1949), p. 9.
[9] Ibid., p. 10.
[10] See Chapter 6, pp. 146–49.

Contributions of the family system

We have concentrated so far on family units to consider, first, some of the variables affecting the capacity of a particular family to cope with a given problem and, second, some of the sociological differences among the crises a particular family is likely to confront. Another perspective is consideration of the relationship between social problems and a family system. The social system of the family is the network of status-roles of the family members which constitutes the structure of their relations.[11] Study of the family as a system offers the advantage of emphasizing the linkages of family problems with the larger structure of society and the common behaviors of groups of particular families in problematic situations. Attention is then concentrated on the similarities among family groups in the patterning of their relations within the family unit and of their relations with groups outside the family. The recurrent patterns of family life are examined for examples of social disorganization in terms of faulty organization of family roles or of a burden of contradictory expectations imposed on family members by forces of change underway in society as a whole.

The conjunction of a family system and the larger social structure is illustrated in the relationship between social class and parent-child relationships. Summarizing studies over a 25-year period, Bronfenbrenner notes that reports consistently found middle-class parents to be more acceptant and equalitarian and working-class parents more oriented toward maintaining order and obedience through great reliance on physical punishments. From about 1930 until the end of World War II, working-class mothers were more permissive in feeding, weaning, and toilet training. After World War II, however, middle-class mothers became the most permissive in these respects.[12]

He attributes this change to the greater access of middle-class parents to books and pamphlets on infant care and child rearing and to the guidance of physicians and counselors. Kohn extends this explanation to suggest that middle-class parents are likely to discuss their children's behavior with friends, neighbors, and teachers because of their greater concern over child-rearing problems. Among working-class parents, their comparative lack of education and more routinized job experiences appear conducive to the retention of familiar methods. Furthermore, the writings of family experts are oriented to middle-class values.[13]

Later in this chapter, the study of the family as a social system will be

[11] See Talcott Parsons, *The Social System* (New York: Free Press, 1951), p. 25.

[12] Urie Bronfenbrenner, "Socialization and Social Class through Time and Space," in Eleanor E. Maccoby, Theodore M. Newcomb, and Eugene L. Hartley (eds.), *Readings in Social Psychology* (3d ed.; Holt, Rinehart and Winston, 1958), pp. 424–25.

[13] Melvin L. Kohn, *Class and Conformity: A Study in Values* (Homewood, Ill.: Dorsey Press, 1969), pp. 5–7.

brought to bear on several issues. Is the American family disintegrating under the conditions of urbanism and industrialism? Courtship and mate selection have undergone changes under these conditions, and some observers express concern that the continuity of the family is threatened by a "fun ideology." Divorce sometimes has been described as clear-cut evidence of the "collapse" of the family system; we shall challenge this simplistic interpretation. The system of family roles is under pressure of changes signaled by issues involving intergenerational conflict, parental roles, employment of mothers, and the problems of the elderly. Changes in sex roles have implications beyond family life; Chapter 9 will consider such matters as the depolarization of sex roles, the weakening of the double standard, and contradictions in the female role.

Resource for solutions

While the family is identified as the locus of personalized and flexible responses to individuals, this identification is not always borne out in practice. It is significant, however, that family status terms are employed in many settings where persons are particularly anxious to indicate close bonds. Colleges, fraternal associations, labor unions, and similar groups frequently speak of "brothers" and "sisters," and ghetto merchants put up "Soul Brother" signs to protect their establishments against looting in riots.

In its socialization function the family has been described as a particularly strategic institution in facilitating adjustment to norms under the impact of change. Vincent cites the importance of the family in modifying norms in the course of socializing the new generation. The family differs from other social institutions in its lack of organized group spokesmen who present a unified resistance to change. The church, schools, and other social institutions have an established elite who are motivated to cry out against the erosion of tradition, but the aggregate of specific parents are largely independent of one another in responding to change.[14]

The family has greater possibilities than bureaucratic agencies for motivating individuals to solve personal problems. The "client" is more likely to move toward greater conformity with group expectations when the "therapist" is identified as a member of the family and "treatment" is not limited to specialized relationships within scheduled sessions. Bureaucracy demands conformity to rules to assure predictable response to an event defined as being one of a class of similar events, and the various tasks of the organization are apportioned among experts who ideally have been selected especially to handle particular tasks. Efficiency so gained, however, exacts a price in varying degrees of depersonalization. As an antidote

---

[14] Clark E. Vincent, "Familia Spongia: The Adaptive Function," in John N. Edwards (ed.), *The Family and Change* (New York: Alfred A. Knopf, 1969), p. 370.

there is increased interest in developing smaller treatment facilities closer to clients' homes in order to recapture a share of the family's sense of personal concern and intimacy. Even within large-scale institutions, elements of family relationships are present in such treatment strategies as group therapy and the therapeutic community.

Litwak and Meyer contend that certain classes of tasks provide no unusual advantage for employment of experts.[15] When special expertise is not required, the family can be brought into programs designed to alleviate community problems. Examples would be many of the daily problems which generate parent-child disputes or marital conflict. Other tasks involve events which do not recur sufficiently to justify training and assignment of experts. For example, even the most progressive public school is not equipped to provide specialized study for the young mathematical or artistic genius.

IS THE FAMILY DISINTEGRATING?

Some authorities have warned that the American family is disintegrating.[16] Increased birth control, promiscuity, divorce, and similar trends have been cited as supporting evidence. Yet Goode, after his analysis of families about the world, concludes that some apparently recent characteristics of family life may actually be repetitions of old social patterns.[17] Similarly, culling the accounts of foreign travelers in the United States in 1850–80, Furstenberg finds reports of strains resulting from the voluntary choice of mates, the abrupt loss of freedom for women at marriage, women's discontent with household responsibilities, and lack of discipline of children.[18]

Nuclear family and social networks

It is useful, Rogers and Sebald say, to distinguish between familism, family integration, and kinship orientation.[19] *Familism* is the subordination of individual interests to those of the family group. *Family integration* is

[15] Eugene Litwak and Henry J. Meyer, "The School and the Family: Linking Organizations and External Primary Groups," in Paul F. Lazarsfeld, William H. Sewell, and Harold L. Wilensky (eds.), *The Uses of Sociology* (New York: Basic Books, 1967), pp. 525–32.

[16] For example, Pitirim A. Sorokin, *The Crisis of Our Age* (New York: E. P. Dutton, 1941), p. 188; Carle C. Zimmerman, *Family and Civilization* (New York: Harper & Row, 1947), p. 632.

[17] William J. Goode, *World Revolution and Family Patterns* (New York: Free Press, 1963), pp. 368–71.

[18] Frank F. Furstenberg, Jr., "Industrialization and the American Family: A Look Backward," *American Sociological Review*, Vol. 31 (June 1966), pp. 326–37.

[19] Everett M. Rogers and Hans Sebald, "A Distinction Between Familism, Family Integration, and Kinship Orientation," *Marriage and Family Living*, Vol. 24 (February 1962), pp. 25–30.

defined as the product of efforts of individual members to increase the rewards and satisfactions of other members. Frequently familism is identified with the extended family which Rogers and Sebald see as kinship orientation. Under this view, family integration is associated with the support of individuals to the wider range of kin outside the boundaries of the nuclear family. In these circumstances giving priority to the interests of the nuclear family over those of the extended family would be evidence of family disintegration. But, Rogers and Sebald assert, family integration can also be a matter of efforts by members to increase the rewards and satisfactions of the *nuclear* family. Then an orientation to kin outside the nuclear family is not necessarily a requirement for family integration. Familism can be demonstrated but only in terms of the nuclear family. If analysis presupposes the desirability of the extended family as the proper form of family life, the extent of family disorganization will be exaggerated for a society based on the nuclear family.

Kephart cites the American characteristic of maintaining ties with relatives on the basis of friendship rather than kinship considerations. This characteristic lends a noncontinuous quality to kinship affiliations as the nuclear families are formed through a series of generations.[20] Then it is more meaningful to see family life in terms of networks of social relationships rather than solely in terms of some notion of a fixed social structure.

In her study of twenty English families, Bott focused on the actual relationships of family members with friends, neighbors, relatives, clubs, shops, places of work, and so on.[21] These relationships external to the family unit assumed the form of a *network,* with each family member having his particular network which did not necessarily correspond with the network of other members. Of greater importance, family X did not have the identical network of family Y. Therefore, the family units collectively did not form an organized group in the sense of being components of a larger social whole (for example, a social class or neighborhood) with common aims, interdependent roles, and a distinctive subculture.

She reports that families differed greatly in the "connectedness" of their networks in the sense that people known by a family know and meet with one another independently of that family. A family was considered "close-knit" when its network included many relationships with other families. It was "loose-knit" when there were few such relationships. Bott finds the degree of connectedness related to the role relationship between husband and wife. When many of the people a person knows interact with one another (close-knit), the husband and wife tend to have segregated conjugal roles, that is, their tasks are markedly differentiated and they have a considerable number of separate interests and tasks.

---

[20] Floyd M. Kephart, *Family in Society* (New York: Dodd, Mead & Co., 1970), p. 203.
[21] Elizabeth Bott, *Family and Social Network* (London, Eng.: Tavistock Publications, 1957), pp. 52–61.

Bott's explanation is that the greater interaction among persons in the network strengthens consensus on norms and that the marriage must accommodate itself to informal pressures from outside the husband-wife relationships. If the bride or groom brings to marriage close-knit networks through which emotional satisfactions continue to be gained, the individual is likely to demand less of the spouse and to obtain help from other people. Popular stereotypes are relevant here: the wife who checks everything with her mother, and the husband who clings to his associations with the "boys." When an individual's network is loose-knit, the smaller degree of interaction is associated with less agreement on norms and more fragmentation of social control and mutual aid. Then the husband and wife are more likely to seek in each other some of the emotional satisfactions and help with familial tasks that couples in close-knit networks can get from outsiders. In short, conjugal roles are less likely to be segregated.

For our study of urban society, this analysis is significant. Although individual members of the family frequently belong to the organized groups characteristic of the institutions, Bott says, the family usually as a whole does not. External institutions control only one aspect of the family's life and do not contain the family in all its aspects. The large scale and complexity of urban social structure fragments its relationships with the family as a whole and produces an individuated family life through differentiation among family members and between families in the social networks. Greater variation among families is possible in family roles and in relationships with relatives and neighbors.[22]

Urban conditions lend more personal choice to relationships with kin. Bott suggests some of the factors affecting expression of personal interest in choices among kin for more intimate relationships.[23] Kinship ties are strengthened when family members share occupational and other economic interests. Geographical mobility is involved in that great distances between residences impede interaction. The families in the study limit their recognition of significant relatives through grandparents and first cousins, and although they differed in the degree of "connectedness" of their kinship networks, all families agreed that each household should be financially independent of others. Personal preference, however, directed the flow of relationships in that particular relatives served as mediators between the nuclear family and other kin. The choice of the "connecting relative" reflected personal likes. Social class distinctions appeared to influence the preferences among relatives.

Is the urban nuclear family isolated?

Some writers have pronounced the nuclear family to be particularly congenial to industrialism. Because each family sets up its own household

---

[22] Ibid., pp. 98–101.
[23] Ibid., pp. 122–48.

and places less reliance on land ownership, migration is more likely to meet the needs of industries in locations not consistent with the traditional residences of the extended families. With less obligation to the extended family, the nuclear family frees the individual to respond to the individual-istic incentives of the pay check and work career opportunities. With greater emphasis on personal satisfactions, the nuclear family helps bal-ance the individual's emotional budget against the strains of the imperson-alized discipline of industrial work systems.[24] However, as Greenfield says, this association between industrialism and the nuclear family should not be interpreted as evidence that industrialism created the nuclear family. He shows that each exists without the presence of the other. Greenfield argues that the nuclear family existed in England and the United States before the rise of urbanism and machine technology. The occupa-tional and other social institutions of industrial technology were adapted to the nuclear family.[25]

Images of the deteriorating American family have received some sup-port from the description of the urban nuclear family as relatively isolated from the kinship system. Derived from this description is a picture of the urbanite as a victim of the collapse of a kin structure incapable of coping with urban conditions. The isolated individual is caught alone and without guidance because the kin structure that had developed in rural society had disappeared under the impact of a complex urban society. Under urban conditions the extended rural family would be unequipped to handle protective, educational, socialization, social control, and other functions.

The interpretation has been challenged on the grounds that the atomis-tic character of urban families has been overstated. Litwak postulates a *modified extended family* composed of a series of nuclear families bound together on an equalitarian basis and providing aid in terms of housing, care of illness, and leisure pursuits. It differs from the "classical" extended family in that the nuclear families need not live close to one another, need not confer occupational privileges to fellow kin, and need not defer to the strict authority of the extended family. It differs from the idea of an isolated nuclear family in that significant and continuing aid is received from the relatives. Litwak finds the modified extended family congenial to industrial-ism. Financial assistance and medical aid are provided the couple attempt-ing to gain upward mobility. With the shrinking of distinctions between social classes through formal education, mass communications, and a general rise in standard of living, upward mobility is less likely to be impeded by inappropriate attitudes and mannerisms learned through so-cialization to a lower-class culture within the extended family.[26]

---

[24] Goode, *The Family*, pp. 108–17.
[25] Sidney M. Greenfield, "Industrialization and the Family in Sociological Theory," *American Journal of Sociology*, Vol. 67 (November 1961), pp. 312–22.
[26] Eugene Litwak, "Occupational Mobility and Extended Family Cohesion," *American Sociological Review*, Vol. 25 (February 1960), pp. 9–21, and "Geographical Mobility and Extended Family Cohesion," *American Sociological Review*, Vol. 25 (June 1960), p. 385.

A number of studies provide evidence of mutual aid between parents and their married children: shopping, care of children, counseling, cooperating with welfare agencies, providing physical care and shelter for the elderly, accommodations for vacationing kin, assistance in search for jobs, and help at weddings, medical crises, and funerals. Sussman and Burchinal see industrialism removing responsibilities for job placement from this network of mutual aid and permitting concentration on social and economic aid to persons in the kin network in a supportive rather than a coercive way. Improved communications and transportation enable the network to operate in spite of geographical dispersion of the relatives.[27]

COURTSHIP AND MATE SELECTION

Obviously, family life and sexual behavior are related. This interrelationship is particularly noteworthy in the sphere of the social patterns whereby mates are selected and new nuclear families established. This sphere involves fundamental value conflicts. Considerable tension is associated with the cultural ideal that the exercise of sex should be within wedlock. Usually all public discussions condemn premarital sex, but recently there has been a wider recognition of discrepancies between private behavior and the professed view that such indulgence is rare. It is rather standard practice in all eras for many of the elders to condemn the youth for departing from the "true and tried" traditions. Now such criticisms are imbued with an uneasiness over increased permissiveness which some persons call a "sexual revolution." Partially, this development reflects the increased prevalence of birth control measures and the increasing challenge to the double standard and the subordinate status traditionally applied to women. These developments are taken up in the next chapter.

Dating as a prelude to courtship

American courtship patterns are particularly subject to rising doubts about an oversimplified, puritanical sexual code. Developments associated with urban society have favored the rise of dating as a social institution preceding courtship to lend even greater freedom to youth in relationships with the opposite sex. American culture has always emphasized personal affection and individual choice over kinship considerations within the extended family, but today the influence of the parental nuclear family is becoming even more questionable.

The emphasis on the nuclear family is not a new development, but the

[27] Marvin B. Sussman and Lee G. Burchinal, "Kin Family Network: Unheralded Structure in Current Conceptualizations of Family Functioning," in Edwards, *The Family and Change,* pp. 141–47.

rise of dating reflects urban conditions which lend greater urgency to the requirement that sex and family-life education be effective for preparing youth for the contingencies of mate selection and family life. The effectiveness of parents as instructors in sex education has always been questionable. In an era of remarkable social and value changes, the provision for such education outside the parental family has become a more pressing issue.

Dating has been defined as a social event in which two young people seek pleasure without any additional commitment. The date is an end in itself and does not necessarily signify further involvement. It provides opportunity for friendly association with a large number of persons of the opposite sex. Through this enlarged range of contacts, occasions for social engagements are enlarged. The rating of the members of the opposite sex for dating desirability is determined by the youth with little, if any, influence of parents.[28]

The cultural stress on the individual and the associated preference for the nuclear family are essential elements of the place of dating in American behavior. Udry sees several social trends behind the emergence of dating as a characteristic of the second decade of this century.[29] The accelerated rate of urbanization at that time complicated the efforts of parents to supervise the lives of adolescents. The circumstances wrought by increased residential mobility undermined the previous patterns whereby eligible mates were located and tested within family and neighborhood life. Dating provides a means for young people to make contacts outside previously dominant patterns, and the network of youth relationships is likely to differ sufficiently from the network of their parents to operate against parents having a significant direct influence over marital choice. The trend toward emancipation of women has reduced the effectiveness of parental control over girls. Youths tend toward reliance on the standards of their peer groups rather than complying passively to the expectations of their parents' generation.

Theoretically, dating can serve the purposes of courtship in an urban society; that is, the individual can judge his prospective marital choice according to the standards of his age group. The effectiveness of these standards for creating stable marriages, however, depends on their appropriateness to subsequent circumstances of marriage, when the couple encounters the mundane problems of financial, household, and parental management. Dating does provide a test for the give-and-take of individuals toward one another, which can be useful for the more directed testing of courtship, and the interpersonal experimentation of dating, followed by courtship, is pertinent to the testing for compatibility and emotional flexi-

[28] Ernest W. Burgess and Harvey J. Locke, *The Family: From Institution to Companionship* (2d ed.; New York: American Book Co., 1953), p. 331.
[29] Udry, *Social Context of Marriage,* pp. 109–10.

bility required by the American ideal that marital interaction should be based on affection and personal choice.

Dating, love, and the family

The functions of dating for mate selection have been identified as a source of marital instability because of a generalized "fun ideology." The term *fun ideology* encompasses a permissive child-rearing style, an emphasis on personal pleasure as the purpose of contacts between the sexes, an exploitation of sexual attraction as the key motivation for selling various industrial products, and a quest for happiness as the fundamental motivation for increasing worker productivity.[30]

Because of its linkage with this fun ideology, the emphasis of dating is on romantic love as the primary basis for mate selection. From infancy Americans are exposed to the romantic love myth which assumes that for every girl there is *the* boy, that they will experience bliss when they know each other, and that they will live happily forevermore. Nursery tales, popular songs, motion pictures, and fiction are saturated with romantic symbols. Romantic love emphasizes sexual attractiveness, emotional response, and companionship. The wife is expected to continue to be physically attractive and sexually stimulating. Husbands and wives are supposed to share thoughts and actions as equal partners. A mutual agreement between the couple is supposed to be the basis of voluntary conformity to marital obligations on the basis of generalized feelings of affection and trust.[31]

Love can threaten the persistence of the parental family, however. The maintenance of the social and economic power of the family into the next generation is jeopardized when the marriage is with a person unprepared to manage family resources and to safeguard its prestige. When the chosen one is from a different locale and social stratum, the probability of continued social contact of the parental family with the married child is reduced.

Societies try to minimize the conflict between love and the family by limiting the range of marital choices to particular groups, restricting contacts of the adolescents and young adults, and supporting the authority of elders in arranging marriages. In American and Western European societies, love is given its greatest latitude, though social control of love is sought through selection of the social circles within which the youngsters move, thereby influencing the quality of the group from which the marital partner

[30] The term is employed by Clark E. Vincent, *Unmarried Mothers* (New York: Free Press of Glencoe, 1961), pp. 6–12; also see Martha Wolfenstein, "The Emergence of Fun Morality," in Eric Larrabee and Rolf Meyersohn (eds.), *Mass Leisure* (Glencoe, Ill.: Free Press, 1958), pp. 86–96.

[31] George A. Theodorson, "Romanticism and Motivation to Marry in the United States, Burma, and India," *Social Forces,* Vol. 44 (September 1965), pp. 20–22.

is selected.[32] In addition to romance, courtship involves decisions affecting one's future and economic position. Selection of the marital partner is likely to be influenced by family background, economic power, and education—in addition to the physical attractiveness and personal qualities related to love.

Love as a basis for marriage should not be evaluated as "madness." Their research findings lead Blood and Wolfe to conclude that most couples "do not fall vaporously in love but test their compatibility through months of companionship." The wives in their study reported they were seldom disappointed with their husbands regardless of the contentions of some experts that marriage for love leads to disillusionment, cooling passions, and taking one another for granted. Such satisfaction, however, was associated with effective communication generally, doing things together, and similarity in age, education, and social status.[33]

Exclusive emphasis on the adverse potentialities of dating and love overlooks the fact of their existence and strength in American society. Why this persistence and strength? Greenfield points to our complex industrial technology which distributes rewards on the basis of personal achievement rather than family status. Production and consumption of material goods take precedence over other activities; money as a symbol is supposed to motivate individuals to fulfill responsibilities. A fundamental question is how to induce rational, calculating, and ambitious individuals to form the nuclear families essential to the performance of vital societal functions. Greenfield suggests that the romantic love complex serves as the reward-motive to induce individuals to make an irrational choice congenial to the societal functions.[34]

ROLES AND FAMILY PROBLEMS

In providing a script of expectations, the system of family roles provides means of guiding family members in relationships with one another and in situations involving persons outside the family circle. When the script is poorly "written" the family can contribute to personal and social problems. The roles may represent discrepancies between cultural demands and biological capacities, as illustrated by the failure to provide culturally for the sex drive of adolescence. The culture may encourage expectations which cannot be satisfied in a subsequent role: the romantic emphasis in courtship, for example, which conflicts with the realities of interaction with

[32] William J. Goode, "The Sociology of the Family," in Robert K. Merton, Leonard Broom, and Leonard S. Cottrell, Jr., *Sociology Today* (New York: Basic Books, 1959), pp. 193–96.
[33] Robert O. Blood, Jr., and Donald M. Wolfe, *Husbands and Wives* (Glencoe, Ill.: Free Press, 1960), pp. 222–31.
[34] Sidney M. Greenfield, "Love and Marriage in Modern America: A Functional Analysis," in J. Ross Eshleman (ed.), *Perspectives in Marriage and the Family* (Boston, Mass.: Allyn and Bacon, 1969), pp. 346–62.

one's spouse. In a time of high population mobility, role training in one subculture may fail to equip an individual for meeting the expectations of a spouse socialized in another subculture.

Parent-child relationships

Parent-youth conflict has been described as a grave problem in American family life. The concept of adolescence as a distinctive age group is fundamental to the idea of conflict between the generations. By emphasizing puberty as the most important period for education, Rousseau prepared the way for the contemporary definition of an age group distinct from either childhood or adulthood. Musgrove notes that this distinction has become the basis of special clothing styles and books oriented to this age category. Reforms of the system of criminal justice and of factory conditions distinguished adolescents from adults as requiring special protections. Youth was to be protected from the elements of unpleasantness of adult life in its full reality.[35]

Why does this concept persist? Two opposing interpretations can be made. First, this age group is regarded as distinctive because the complexity of urban life makes for unusual stress for the adolescent in the twilight zone between childhood and full adulthood. The effectiveness of the family has been eroded in guiding the adolescent in making choices in marriage and occupation. The prolongation of the period of dependence into adolescence and even early adulthood can be interpreted as recognition of the need for more intensive and systematic preparation for adult roles.

The second interpretation places the adults in a less favorable light. Musgrove detects tendencies of the seniors to employ a variety of stratagems for self-protection.[36] Prolonged training regimes can delay the competition of young workers. Musgrove also finds the mature generation directing hostility against the young as a testimony of the latter's potential for power in an age when declining death rates have given them special demographic impact and when technological change provides them with special advantages in vocational competition. In his study in England he finds evidence that adults agree adolescents should occupy a virtually autonomous social sphere segregated from adults. In contrast, the adolescents return less hostility and they value approval of their seniors.

Effects of change and bureaucracies

Adolescence is but one example of our emphasis on age grading by which we make distinctions between nursery school, kindergarten, and

[35] F. Musgrove, *Youth and the Social Order* (Bloomington, Ind.: Indiana University Press, 1965), pp. 33–34.
[36] Ibid., pp. 10–11.

school-aged children. We have "pre-teens," "teens," young married couples, the middle-aged, and senior citizens. Our equalitarian emphasis makes relationships with our peers more comfortable than relationships with persons of dissimilar age and authority. Technological change in our complex industrial society also encourages distinctions according to age whereby employment of the young is delayed until they have necessary skills and the old workers are removed from the labor force before their knowledge becomes obsolete.[37]

The rapid pace of change, David believes, is germane in other ways.[38] The rate of socialization decelerates with advancing chronological age, for example, because cumulative social experience dilutes the impact of a specific learning experience with an increasing store of acquired interpretations. Therefore, the parent's own attitude and values are determined to a high degree by the nature of his socialization experiences in the early phases of his own life. Approximately 20 to 30 years separate the time of the parent's movement through these early life phases and the movement of the child through the same phases. Davis notes the importance of the cultural content each generation experiences during its respective exposure to these phases of life. Perhaps the parent experienced the Great Depression of the 1930s or a major world war in his adolescence, while contemporary living exposes the adolescent to new meanings attached to formal education, access to an automobile, relationships with the opposite sex, choice of vocation, and so on. Thus, rapid social change magnifies the differences between the generations in the cultural content acquired during their respective socializations.

With adults in control of the educational and recreational bureaucracies, there are pressures applied on the adolescent which run counter to his search for identity and his experimentation with developing capacities for intimacy and tenderness. Friedenberg is concerned over the trend toward thrusting adolescents into personality molds designed to create "organization men" whereas adolescence is a period congenial to a high degree of personality differentiation. In pursuit of conformity, the school strives to abolish adolescence by meting out guilt and anxiety to the youth for employing adolescence as the period of search for identity.[39]

Another explanation is offered by Coleman, who sees industrial society segregating the adolescent from other age groups to form a distinctive group.[40] Job training has been transferred from the family to a system of

[37] Elaine Cumming and David M. Schneider, "Sibling Solidarity: A Property of American Kinship," in Seymour M. Farber, Piero Mustacchi, and Roger H. L. Wilson (eds.), *The Family's Search for Survival* (New York: McGraw-Hill, 1965), pp. 142–43.

[38] Kingsley Davis, "The Sociology of Parent-Youth Conflict," in Herman D. Stein and Richard A. Cloward (eds.), *Social Perspectives on Behavior* (New York: Free Press, 1958), pp. 35–44.

[39] Edgar Z. Friedenberg, *The Vanishing Adolescent* (Boston, Mass.: Beacon Press, 1959).

[40] James S. Coleman, *The Adolescent Society* (New York: Free Press of Glencoe, 1961), pp. 2–4, 312–13.

educational institutions and has prolonged the length of time during which adolescents are exposed to experiences focused on their age status. Compelled to carry out most of their important interactions with their own age group, adolescents develop their own language and values. Constituting an important market, adolescents are further drawn to one another by entertainment, music, and other products catering to their tastes.

Coleman's solution to parent-youth conflict would be to bring adolescents back into the home and reduce the pervasiveness of adolescent society. He suggests that the geographical and social mobility of the family be reduced to enhance the integration of the family. He calls for reinstitution of authoritarian control of parents and removal of "implements of adult pleasures" from the hands of children. Berger senses in Coleman's analysis a puritanical aversion for the frivolous and erotic character of adolescent life—and Berger makes more telling points.[41] The content of adolescent life has more relevance to adult futures than Coleman suggests. Rather than qualifying as distinctive subcultures, the values of youth can also be found among adults. For example, the lack of emphasis on academic achievement is not a monopoly of the adolescent. The adult world also provides a seedbed for the search for popularity, athletic achievement, admiration on basis of physical attractiveness, and similar aspects of youth behavior.

The parental roles

Of the two key roles for socialization of children, the mother's role is accorded central attention because of the birth process and of maternal responsibilities. However, the father's role is becoming more active in the daily life of the nuclear family.[42] Fatherhood has two general dimensions in all cultures. In the survival dimension, the father contributes his sperm, takes the role of nurturant father, handles family crises, and serves as a primary link between the family and the larger social environment. In the expressive dimension, the father reassures the children against anxiety and insecurity in management of tensions. Benson argues that trends in urban life have increased opportunities for the father to perform expressive functions.

The role of married women has undergone changes. For the first time, Rossi emphasizes, motherhood is a full-time occupation for adult women because their energies are no longer required for work on the farms or on handicraft production in the home. However, this new dominance of

[41] Bennett M. Berger, "Adolescence and Beyond: An Essay on Three Books on the Problems of Growing Up," *Social Problems,* Vol. 10 (Spring 1963), pp. 394–400; also see William A. Westley and Frederick Elkins, "The Protective Environment and Adolescent Socialization," *Social Forces,* Vol. 35 (March 1957), pp. 243–49.

[42] Leonard Benson, *Fatherhood: A Sociological Perspective* (New York: Random House, 1968), pp. 37–73, 85–89.

the mother role has come when there are fewer reasons for women to confine their life expectations to marriage and parenthood. The woman's average life span has been extended well beyond the years of motherhood, and technological developments in food and clothing production have reduced the need for specialized domestic skills.[43]

Meanwhile, the greater emphasis on the affectional functions of the family has diverted attention toward the wife as comrade. Parenthood is more likely to be a matter of choice and less an exclusive role for married women. The housewife role tends to be deprecated by themes in advertising and mass communications.

Employment of mothers

One of the major trends affecting family roles has been increased participation of married women in the labor force. The proportion with paid jobs doubled from 1900 to 1940 and then doubled again from 1940 to 1960.[44] Between 1940 and 1960, employment of mothers has moved from those who were sole support of their families to those whose husbands are employed in low-income jobs, and finally to those whose family incomes are only slightly below average.[45]

A study of husbands and wives found a number of patterns in employment of wives. College-educated women were more likely to be employed than those with less than a ninth-grade education. Nevertheless, wives of college-educated men were less likely to enter the labor market, possibly because the wives had less education than their husbands and would be qualified only for jobs deemed below the husband's status. The proportion of wives employed declines consistently with number of children. As the children grow, the likelihood of an employed mother increases. As her youngest child becomes older, the employed mother is more likely to move from part-time to full-time employment. Both partners in a marriage tend to score lower in marital happiness when the wife's employment is a response to felt economic necessity than when it is entered on as a free choice.[46]

The employment of mothers is involved in the narrowing of differences between the roles of the husband and wife. Hoffman tested the effects in terms of increased participation of husbands in routine household tasks, changes from male dominance to husband-wife equality, and changes in

[43] Alice S. Rossi, "Equality Between the Sexes: An Immodest Proposal," in Robert J. Lifton (ed.), *The Woman in America* (Boston, Mass.: Houghton Mifflin Co., 1965), pp. 105–6.

[44] Glen G. Cain, *Married Women in the Labor Force: An Economic Analysis* (Chicago: University of Chicago Press, 1966), p. 1.

[45] F. Ivan Nye and Lois W. Hoffman, "The Socio-Cultural Setting," in F. Ivan Nye and Lois W. Hoffman (eds.), *The Employed Mother in America* (Chicago: Rand McNally, 1963), pp. 12–13.

[46] Susan R. Orden and Norman M. Bradburn, "Working Wives and Marriage Happiness," *American Journal of Sociology*, Vol. 74 (January 1969), pp. 392–407.

attitudes toward male dominance. Comparison with families without an employed mother revealed that husbands of working wives participated more in household tasks and in making decisions about routine household matters. However, employment does not affect the family power structure; rather, the male dominance or sharing of decisions pivots on the preexisting attitudes and personalities of the given husband and wife. In fact, the working wife may become less dominant than she was before employment as a means of compensating for the threat offered by the sheer fact of her employment.[47]

The effect of the mother's employment on socialization and care of the children appears to pivot on the form of adjustment made by the husband and wife and with the children. The absence of the mother, in and of itself, is less crucial than the motivation of the mother in seeking employment, the impact of her employment on the masculine image of the father, and how the children interpret her motive for working.[48] She may be using the job as a refuge from home and family, or to ease her tensions, or to give the family a firmer economic base and fuller contacts with its external environment as a means of making the family life more constructive for children.

DIVORCE: EVIL OR REMEDY?

Usually divorce is considered a social problem because it is considered a source of marital instability. Actually it is the final expression of a previous process of marital dissolution. The problem lies in the value conflict which has inhibited the use of divorce as a proper means for terminating marital conflict. The rise in the divorce rate signals social change and suggests that shifts in values have eased previous inhibitions. Over the decades public policy has moved toward greater permissiveness in the use of divorce. Attitudes have been reshaped in concert with emancipation of women, greater physical mobility, a more individualistic basis for mate selection, and increased secularization of life.

Changes in incidence of divorce

In the United States, divorce rates have increased since 1860 (when data first became available). Although exceeded by certain other nations in previous years, the United States has recently had the highest crude

---

[47] Lois W. Hoffman, "Effect of the Employment of Mothers on Parental Power Relations and the Division of Household Tasks," in Seymour M. Farber, Piero Mustacchi, and Roger H. L. Wilson (eds.), The Family's Search for Survival (New York: McGraw-Hill, 1965), pp. 316–26.

[48] Jesse R. Pitts, "The Structural-Functional Approach," in Christensen, Handbook of Marriage and the Family, p. 105.

divorce rate among the larger nations.[49] Contrary to a popular impression, proneness to divorce is inversely related to occupational status, with unskilled workers having the highest rate. Blacks are particularly subject to greater likelihood of divorce as the level of the male's education is increased.[50] Divorces are more common among childless couples. The reduction in the stigma attached to divorce has contributed to an increase in the remarriage rate of divorced people and to occurrence of divorce earlier in marriage.[51]

A variety of societal factors may influence changes in the divorce rate. The preservation of the marriage is less essential to the individual because many previous functions of the family have been assumed by outside agencies. Broader employment of women makes them less dependent on husbands. The moral sanctions against divorce have eased. Urban life enables the individual to escape much of the stigmatization previously attached to divorce. Finally, the declining control of parents over mate selection and the emphasis on romantic love as the basis for marriage contribute to the possibility of marital instability.

As a measure of the strength of the marital bond, divorce rates are not necessarily accurate in showing changes over the years in probability of seeking a divorce. The duration of marriage before divorce is a hidden factor. A trend toward shorter duration would inflate the divorce rate temporarily without necessarily indicating a greater proportion of married couples with unsatisfactory marriages in a given year. Probably the duration of marriage to separation varies according to educational achievement, premarital pregnancy, race, and occupation. Furthermore, the time between separation and final divorce action will vary with length of legal proceedings, attitude of judges, court backlogs, procedural delays, and existence of compulsory conciliation procedures.

In a Wisconsin study, Monahan finds separation occurs to the highest degree in the first year of marriage. Over the years since 1887, the duration of separation increased slightly while the interval from separation to divorce decreased.[52] Consequently, he challenges the reliability of crude divorce rates as evidence that contemporary marriages are breaking up sooner or that marriages have become more fragile.

Consequences following divorce

Considerable personal disorganization is supposed to follow the trauma of divorce. Adjustment to status of being formerly married is likely to bring

[49] William J. Goode, "Family Disorganization," in Robert K. Merton and Robert A. Nisbet (eds.), *Contemporary Social Problems* (3d ed.; New York: Harcourt, Brace & World, 1971), pp. 481–82.

[50] William J. Goode, *After Divorce* (Glencoe, Ill.: Free Press, 1956), pp. 46–55.

[51] Goode, *World Revolution and Family Patterns,* pp. 84–85.

[52] Thomas P. Monahan, "When Married Couples Part: Statistical Trends and Relationships in Divorce," *American Sociological Review,* Vol. 27 (October 1962), pp. 625–33.

its particular tensions and frustrated habits.[53] However, there is a stereo-typed conception that divorce in and of itself is evidence of a neurotic personality doomed to a series of unhappy marriages. Divorce is also supposed to bring unhappiness to the children. Each of these suppositions appears to be an exaggeration.

Goode finds that most divorced women attributed the collapse of their marriages to deep-seated problems, with a long period of conflict preceding the decision to seek divorce. Most reported little if any discrimination against them on the basis of their new status. Usually, they had almost as much income as before. When income was a problem, it had usually also been a problem during the marriage.[54]

The trauma attributed to divorce is captured by the troublesome status of the stepchild, who is propelled into a relationship with a stepparent usually without previous sustained personal involvement and without having a real voice in the events leading to his murky status. At the wedding of his remaining parent, he is out of place in a ceremony which is oriented to the image of a young bride and groom who are novices in marriage. The American culture raises expectations which subject the child to conflicting guidelines for his role performance. Folklore describes the stepchild as the neglected and oppressed victim of a cruel stepparent. How is continuing love and sense of duty to the missing parent to be balanced with similar obligations for the parent who appears to be more interested at the moment in the "stranger"? The child is likely to experience emotional upheaval when pressed to call this person "mother" or "father" to indicate acceptance of this newcomer in the status of the missing parent.[55]

The cultural heritage imposes a burden of emotional tension upon the persons involved in divorce and remarriage. The definition of the unbroken marriage as "normal" confers a burden of tension regardless of the circumstances of a particular divorce. This definition relies on an unexamined belief that the family system is too sacred to be broken regardless of the social chemistry produced in a given household by the convergence of two particular personalities in a conjugal union. Each marriage is subject to a particular combination of social and economic factors. Nevertheless, this unexamined belief would attribute the breaking of the marriage to the inadequacies of the husband and/or wife as individuals. The presence of children is interpreted as justification for particular damning of these individuals for imposing "inevitable" unhappiness on innocent dependents.

The belief that divorce per se is destructive to children is an overdrawn generalization. One study finds that delinquents are as likely to come from disorganized but structurally unbroken homes as they are from broken

---

[53] See Morton M. Hunt, *The World of the Formerly Married* (New York: McGraw-Hill Book Co., 1966).
[54] Goode, *After Divorce,* pp. 15–17, 137–39, 184–89.
[55] Anne W. Simon, *Stepchild in the Family* (New York: Odyssey Press, 1964), p. 131.

homes.[56] Other studies indicate that, although some children suffer extreme trauma from divorce per se, it is difficult even in these cases to determine whether the trauma occurs because of divorce or whether it reflects the conflict preceding the divorce. At any rate, divorce is not, as it is frequently described in folklore, the overwhelming influential factor.[57]

Although dissolution of their marriage had brought difficulties, more than 80 percent of the respondents in a metropolitan study report that divorce had improved the situation for themselves and their children. The children were most likely to show behavior problems when they had always disliked the father or had loved him less after the divorce. When the children had been hardest to handle during the former marriage, the mothers were less likely to favor the father's visits, largely because they saw him as of no help with the children.[58]

THE AGED: GOLDEN OR DECLINING YEARS?

The problems of the aged affect all persons ultimately, assuming they do not die earlier. Some of the aged are isolated from the general rhythm of life and the cycle of community activities, and they thereby form another of the groups shut out from full participation in the community. (Other such groups include prisoners, mental patients, and segregated racial minorities.) The isolation may be in the form of segregation in a special establishment, or it may be in the form of deterioration of the network of intimate associations within family and work groups to which the individual had been habituated in earlier life.

Categorization of the elderly

As the reduction in death rates for earlier ages adds to the number of people over 65, their needs must be given greater attention in public policies concerning hospital and medical planning, adaptation of housing to their special needs, and poverty when employment opportunities dry up. Economic trends indicate a movement toward a welfare state which tends to depart from the traditional pattern in which grandparents are supported by parents. Kreps cites the increased proportion of aged couples who maintain independent living arrangements in spite of the continued decline in the proportion of older men deriving current earnings through participation in the labor force. During this period a significant proportion of the national income has been allocated to nonworking adults through

[56] Charles J. Browning, "Differential Impact of Family Disorganization upon Male Adolescents," Social Problems, vol. 8 (Summer 1969), p. 43.
[57] Lee C. Burchinal, "Characteristics of Adolescents from Unbroken, Broken, and Reconstituted Families," Journal of Marriage and the Family, Vol. 26 (February 1964), pp. 44–51.
[58] Goode, After Divorce.

What does grandparenthood mean? Contrary to a common stereotype, the elderly appear to vary widely in the role they see for themselves in relating to grandchildren. Most of them express satisfaction and pleasure in the relationships. A few offer advice and financial assistance; some seek their own "fun"; others appear infrequently as rather distant figures.

social welfare programs, unemployment compensation, old age benefits, and so on. Some but not all of these allocations represent a transfer of taxes collected from working adults to the elderly. Such transfer payments represent a smoothing out of life earnings outside the control of the individual family.[59]

These trends towards categorization of the elderly raise the possibility that their spectrum of personalities will be overlooked. Videbeck and Knox find unfounded the popular assumption that the senior years, in and of themselves, bring a sharp decline of social participation in family, political, recreational, church, and other domains of life.[60] They report that the degree of participation in the final phase of the human life cycle is influenced by the same factors that influence younger people. Regardless of age, high social participation is associated with urban residence, high educational achievement, prestigious occupations, and favorable socioeconomic status. When high activity is characteristic of an individual's earlier life, he is less likely to show a decline in activity as he becomes older. When he does show such a decline it is associated with factors other than physiological aging. For example, the status of the elderly person undergoes shifts with the departure of grown children and retirement from employment. Since social participation of other ages also is affected by status changes, there is no justification for regarding all of the elderly as identical beings simply because they have the same age.

Another overgeneralization is the portrayal of the elderly as the victims of neglectful adult children who leave them to rock in lonely rooms and to suffer economic deprivation. Blenkner attests that studies fail to produce evidence that the old are neglected or repudiated by their children. Rather, the evidence is that the older person prefers to maintain his independence as long as he can. Only when he can no longer manage for himself, do both he and his children expect the children to undertake services. But though the children feel a strong obligation to assume the "taking care of" function as an affectional and ethical response to emotional need,[61] both the old and their children look to government aid through a system of social security to provide basic economic maintenance.

A study of grandparents presents further evidence of a flexibility among senior citizens denied by the stereotype of dependent and neglected old people. The majority of grandparents expressed only comfort, satisfaction, and pleasure. Some saw grandchildren as making them "feel young

[59] Juanita M. Kreps, "The Economics of Intergenerational Relationships," in Ethel Shanas and Gordon F. Streib (eds.), *Social Structure and the Family: Generational Relations* (Englewood Cliffs, N.J.: Prentice-Hall, 1965), pp. 267–88.

[60] Richard Videbeck and Alan B. Knox, "Alternative Participation Responses to Aging," in Arnold M. Rose and Warren A. Peterson (eds.), *Older People and Their Social World* (Philadelphia, Pa.: F. A. Davis Co., 1965), pp. 37–48.

[61] Margaret Blenkner, "Social Work and Family Relationships in Later Life with Some Thoughts on Filial Maturity," in Shanas and Streib, *Social Structure and the Family*, pp. 48–49.

again"; others reported that grandparenthood provides emotional self-fulfillment beyond parenthood; a few offered financial or advisory assistance to grandchildren; and about one fourth of the respondents acknowledged grandparenthood had little effect on their lives. There were indications that increasing youthfulness of grandparents and emergence of new values is producing changes in grandparent styles. Among grandparents less than 65 years of age there was a greater prevalence of "fun seekers" and "distant figures." The fun seeker relates to the grandchild in a spirit of informality and playfulness, while the distant figure has fleeting and infrequent contact with the grandchild at holidays.[62]

Problems associated with retirement

Retirement from work is a rite of passage, not necessarily marked by a ceremony, which distinguishes productive maturity from nonproductive old age. The significance of retirement differs among individuals in both economic and social terms. For the already impoverished or underemployed, retirement is just one more economic insult. For some of the others, retirement may mean economic deprivation when compared with their financial resources before retirement. The alleviation of economic problems of the aged, then, is combined with meeting the more general problem of poverty already considered.

When work is central to a man's life, retirement threatens his conception of himself as a worthy person and confronts him with the difficulties of using unaccustomed leisure. Changes in industrial technology are eroding the possibility of making work the central anchorage for life. What then, Maddox asks, will be the anchorage point?[63] The American culture blocks an easy answer because of its ambivalence toward leisure time and its emphasis on accumulation of material possessions as a mark of prestige. However, already there are signs that these values are changing and that the social impact of retirement can be eased. The conditions of the elderly among various societies vary according to the resources the elderly command, the functions they perform, and the state of the social organization.[64] When the young are dependent on their property or knowledge, the elderly are in an advantageous position. In our society, however, property is not particularly controlled by the elderly. Technological change and expansion of higher education have opened opportunities frequently favoring young adults and reducing their dependence on the elders of their

[62] Bernice L. Neugarten and Karol K. Weinstein, "The Changing American Grandparent," *Journal of Marriage and Family*, Vol. 26 (May 1964), pp. 199–204.

[63] George L. Maddox, "Retirement as a Social Event in the United States," in John C. McKinney and Frank T. DeVyver (eds.), *Aging and Social Policy* (New York: Appleton-Century-Crofts, 1966), pp. 118–26.

[64] Irving Rosow, "And Then We Were Old," *Trans-action*, Vol. 2 (January–February 1965), pp. 21–26.

families. The elderly are at a disadvantage when technological developments bring about obsolescence of their jobs, and advanced age blocks their search for new jobs and their eligibility for retraining. With the erosion of community ties under the impact of urbanization and residential mobility, the elderly frequently lack the psychological security of stable neighborhoods which provide links with their past. Furthermore, the shift from the traditional extended family has reduced the bonds of mutual dependence which supported obligations of blood relatives to care for the old.

Rosow points out that the later years pose the least problem for those individuals who can maintain their middle-age characteristics in marital status, work, income, and health.[65] The trend toward a greater rate of marital dissolutions signals exacerbated problems of adjustment among the elderly. Wives are more likely than husbands to outlive their spouses, and adjustment to old age is difficult for widows who have been dependent on husbands to manage finances and make other decisions.The proportion of people over 65 in the labor force is declining; many of those elderly persons who continue to work are in self-employed occupations such as farming and small businesses. The overall decline of persons in these occupations increases prospects for a further decline in proportion of persons over 65 who continue to work. Retired people are not maintaining their pro rata share of income and are especially victimized by inflation of living costs. The diseases of old age have not succumbed to medical progress at the same rate as diseases of the young. Physiological deterioration takes its toll, and the crisis in medical services strikes the elderly with particular impact.

Housing for the elderly

Housing raises problems for the elderly if for medical or economic reasons the preferred independent housing arrangement is not feasible. Living with their children raises difficulties for the elderly of intergenerational differences in customs and energy levels, feelings of powerlessness when not the source of guidance and direction, and insufficient space. Independent living arrangements dispersed throughout neighborhoods place the elderly among a population with a range of ages and is consistent with personal independence as a fundamental value.

Planned congregate arrangements under a central management have been a recent development for persons of retirement age capable of managing their own affairs. The facilities provide special services and programs, but they raise several issues. Does concentration in group housing cater to the special needs of the elderly or does it excessively narrow their lives by denying contacts with other ages and social patterns? How does the financial vulnerability of some of the older persons affect access

[65] Ibid.

to group housing appropriate to their needs? What is the optimal size of congregate arrangements to balance services against the impersonal anonymity characteristic of large organizations? How can facilities and services be designed to avoid the extremes of empty idleness and frantic but meaningless activities inconsistent with the social-psychological needs of the residents? [66]

SUMMARY

Some observers see the survival of the family threatened. We prefer to see the family as undergoing a process of adaptation to the impact of changes in its functions and roles within the context of urban society. Although no longer the prime mover of events in that society, the family continues to be a vital institution as a primary determinant of the life chances of the individual born into it. The nuclear family is a crucial concept in analysis of the social problems related to the qualities of the particular family, a family system, and the environment within which family life is being accommodated. The family is seen as a source of personal and social problems, a scene of crises, and a means of coping with problems. Social problems associated with contemporary family life include intergenerational conflict, permissiveness of dating as opposed to courtship under kin group control, divorce and its relationship to marital instability, and the vulnerability of the elderly. In spite of these serious issues, we conclude that the family continues to be a key and viable social institution. Either directly or indirectly, such issues are associated with sex in terms of social status or sexual intercourse. Sexual behavior, of course, is a prime factor in the place and function of the family as a social institution. Therefore, the study of family continues into the next chapter.

FOR ADDITIONAL READING

Bert N. Adams, *Kinship in an Urban Setting* (Chicago: Markham Publishing Co., 1968).

Ruth N. Ashen (ed.), *The Family: Its Function and Destiny* (rev. ed.; New York: Harper & Brothers, 1959).

Jessie Bernard, *Remarriage: A Study of Marriage* (New York: Dryden Press, 1956).

Nelson M. Blake, *The Road to Reno* (New York: Macmillan Co., 1962).

Dorothy R. Blitsten, *The World of the Family* (New York: Random House, 1963).

[66] Daniel M. Wilner and Rosabelle P. Walkley, "Some Special Problems and Alternatives in Housing for Older Persons," in McKinney and DeVyver, *Aging and Social Policy*, pp. 224–52.

J. Louise Despert, *Children of Divorce* (Garden City, N.Y.: Doubleday and Co., 1953).

Jim Egleson and Janet Frank Egleson, *Parents without Partners* (New York: E. P. Dutton & Co., 1961).

George Gleason, *Horizons for Older People* (New York: Macmillan Co., 1965).

Donald A. Hansen, "Personal and Positional Influence in Formal Groups: Propositions and Theory for Research on Family Vulnerability to Stress," *Social Forces,* Vol. 44, (December 1965), pp. 202–10.

William H. Key, "Rural-Urban Differences and the Family," *Sociological Quarterly,* vol. 2 (January 1961), pp. 49–57.

Herman R. Lantz and Eloise C. Snyder, *Marriage: An Examination of the Man-Woman Relationship* (New York: John Wiley and Sons, 1962).

Hope J. Leichter and William E. Mitchell, *Kinship and Casework* (New York: Russell Sage Foundation, 1967).

Donald G. McKinley, *Social Class and Family Life* (New York: Free Press of Glencoe, 1964).

Charles E. Ramsey, *Problems of Youth: A Social Problems Perspective* (Belmont, Calif.: Dickenson Publishing Co., 1967).

Irving Rosow, *Social Integration of the Aged* (New York: Free Press, 1967).

William C. Smith, "The Stepchild," *American Sociological Review,* Vol. 10 (April 1945), pp. 237–42.

Gordon F. Streib and Wayne E. Thompson, "The Older Person in a Family Context," in Clark Tibbits (ed.), *Handbook of Social Gerontology* (Chicago: University of Chicago Press, 1960), pp. 447–88.

Peter Townsend, *The Last Refuge* (London, Eng.: Routledge and Kegan Paul, 1962).

Sex roles and   9
sexual deviance

One writer describes the American male as ruled by women from the moment of birth. Hospital nurses, then mothers and teachers "dictate his every move." Emancipated wives are supposed to make heavy economic and sexual demands which fatigue husbands and raise anxieties that they will not measure up.[1]

In contrast, Friedan describes the American woman as caught in the cultural trappings of a "feminine mystique" centered around the argument that woman should abandon her "envy" and imitation of men and accept her femininity. This "femininity" is defined in terms of sexual passivity, male domination, and nurturing maternal love. By trapping her in the housewife-mother role as *the* route for self-fulfillment, Friedan says, the feminine mystique dooms the American woman to surrender her career aspirations and her desire to be, in her own right, a part of the world outside her well-equipped but isolated kitchen. The cost is widespread discontent and even desperation among educated women with "fine children" and "a lovely new home."[2]

The marked conflict between these two interpretations of the relative social status of the sexes is a barometer of the complexity and importance of shifts in contemporary attitudes toward sex roles and sexual behavior. In both respects institutionalized norms are being questioned intensely in

[1] J. Robert Moskin, "Why Do Women Dominate Him?" in *The Decline of the American Male,* by the editors of *Look* (New York: Random House, 1958), pp. 4, 11–12.
[2] Betty Friedan, *The Feminine Mystique* (New York: Dell Publishing Co., 1963), pp. 37–38.

an urban society which is revising circumstances under which the sexes interact with one another in a broadening range of relationships. Because these shifts in role definitions and values involve the family, this chapter is an extension of matters considered in the last chapter. However we will also take up issues of sexual deviance and redefinition of sex roles which extend beyond the boundaries of the family.

SOCIAL CHANGE AND SEXUALITY

Conspicuous changes in the kind of concerns associated with sexuality have occurred during recent years. The signs of a so-called sexual revolution are seen in a more open attitude and more frank dialogue on matters previously discussed secretly. Court decisions have undermined the censorship previously restricting public distribution of "controversial" novels, magazines, art, motion pictures, and so on. The issue of birth control has taken on new dimensions with fears that continued high fertility will lower the standard of living and the quality of the natural environment. The mass communication media present hard news and documentaries on abortion, homosexuality, unwed motherhood, sex education, venereal disease, prostitution, and similar social problems.

Implications for society and family

Sexuality is a primary stimulant of human behavior. It has profound impact on the individual in the most private and vital recesses of his personality. Sexuality also has great implications for society, which attempts to keep its expression within bounds of societal interests. The importance of sexual interests to both the individual and the society helps explain the prevalence of moral and legal codes which seem intended to harness sexuality to serve social purposes. As systems of institutionalized norms, the family, church, school, and law often have set up norms that would restrict sexual intercourse to husband and wife—thus linking sexuality to the responsibilities of parenthood.

The sexual behavior of human beings is remarkable among mammals in the frequency of copulation. Even more remarkable is the elaboration of sexual conjugation to serve purposes in addition to procreation of the next generation.[3] Human beings differ from other creatures in their dependence on learning of norms to coordinate individual behaviors into a collective whole. The norms concerning sexuality cover a wide range of matters from courtship to symbolism in the arts. Culture also is involved in the development of means to forestall pregnancy as a consequence of sexual intercourse, thereby giving human beings fuller opportunity to separate sexuality from procreation.

[3] Nelson N. Foote, "Sex as Play," *Social Problems,* Vol. 1 (April 1954), pp. 159–61.

Traditionally, legitimate sexual behavior has been identified with parental duty within the confines of marriage and the family. This linking of sexuality solely with procreation and the raising of the new generation has been professed more universally than it has been observed in practice. A discrepancy between the official morality and the practiced morality in some instances has created considerable uneasiness and many varieties of guilt.

The last chapter considered the impact of change on the functions of the family for its members and the society. This impact is relevant to the shift in attitudes toward sexual behavior. The decline of the family as a core of social and economic life has reduced the identification of sexuality with parental duty, especially in an age when high birth rates are considered a source of serious social problems. The American family has been shifting toward affectional and companionate functions which emphasize romantic love and sexual satisfaction for the marital partners. This development is consistent with what Foote describes as the legitimatization of sex as a form of play.[4] Within the context of marriage itself, the human use of sexuality as a source of pleasure is gaining acceptance.

Shifts in attitudes on sex

Shifts in attitudes toward sexual behavior reflect broad changes in the social structure under the impact of urbanization and technological developments. We have already described these changes, but they should be summarized here for emphasis. Perhaps the central area of change is the family's loss of its previous place as the core around which society has been organized. Urban concentrations provide greater anonymity and independence in personal choice away from the intimacy of family life. Selection of a date or mate is more likely to be a personal matter reflecting standards of one's peer group rather than family expectations as expressed by one's parents. With the decline of the family's functions as an economic productive unit, its members depend increasingly for services on social and economic agencies outside the family's immediate control.

The young acquire attitudes towards sex and learn the norms for their sex roles from formal and informal education agencies ranging from their own peers through mass communication media to the sex education courses of the school. The sexual experimentation of youth encounters inhibitions and guilts imposed by the refusal of many adults to recognize new social circumstances. School teachers and other parental surrogates are usually unprepared to handle the psychological problems created by parental failures. Sex education in schools, frequently resisted by parents, is handicapped in overcoming traumatizing experiences of children and in preparing adolescents for sexual surgence and marriage. With the

---

[4] Ibid.

greater freedom of urban society, its youth acquire means of gaining sexual knowledge for easy adjustment to adult sexuality with few of the guilts that had accompanied earlier religious and moral teachings.[5]

A number of specific developments pertinent to attitudes on sex are among those accelerating the pace of social change.[6] Major wars have removed substantial numbers of men from familiar environments and exposed them to the hedonism of the combat soldier and the sexual permissiveness of camp followers. (It would be an error to assume that military service is an unprecedented factor in creating the sex attitudes now emerging, of course, since major wars are a part of our history.) Increased travel has promoted exposure of sexual mores at variance with one's own. Nineteenth-century feminists were pioneers in the struggle for equal rights for women—which included demands for birth control. Sigmund Freud and others were influential in focusing attention on the effects of sexual factors on personality; although Freud emphasized ego-controls, not unbridled expressiveness, the long-run effects of the new psychological interpretations were to open the way for freeing individuals from rigid anxieties and taboos against serious discussion of the subject. The study of sexual behavior has grown in quality, and the findings have been given broadening dissemination.

Consolidating data from several studies, Smigel and Seiden summarize trends in American attitudes. Permissiveness without affection is tolerated decreasingly, with the decline more sharp for men than women. Both sexes favor the standards of abstinence and permissiveness with affection. The percentage of men favoring permissiveness with affection has increased markedly, but for females the percentage has remained about the same.[7] From data derived from a survey of engaged couples, Burgess and Wallin conclude that the proportion of married women who have had premarital intercourse has increased but this increase has been largely only in relations with fiances or future husbands. The similar percentage for men also has increased, but the researchers explain this in terms of sex relations with the future wife only.[8]

Sexual revolution or evolution?

With the greater freedom of social relationships between the sexes in urban society, young people are assuming greater independence from

[5] George Simpson, *People in Families* (New York: Thomas Y. Crowell, 1960), pp. 121–22.

[6] Erwin O. Smigel and Rita Seiden, "The Decline and Fall of the Double Standard," *Annals of American Academy of Political and Social Science,* Vol. 376 (March 1968), pp. 9–11; and Floyd M. Martinson, *Family in Society* (New York: Dodd, Mead & Co., 1970), pp. 256–58.

[7] Ibid., pp. 11–13.

[8] Ernest W. Burgess and Paul Wallin, *Engagement and Marriage* (Chicago: J. B. Lippincott Co., 1953), pp. 350–51.

parents in formulating their own sexual standards. This independence is furthered by concurrent developments of freedom in choices in spending money and in establishing prestige rankings according to criteria set by their own generation. Reiss sees a rise of a new sex code, especially on campuses, which accepts coitus if it occurs in a stable affectionate relationship. The previously covert acceptance has become more overt and widespread, though there are still moral prohibitions against sexual permissiveness without affection—that is, in pursuit of purely "biological sex." [9]

There is evidence that the extent and dimensions of the "sexual revolution" in the United States have been exaggerated. Although increasingly liberal attitudes toward sexual behavior exist among college students of North America, a cross-cultural study indicates that U.S. students continue to be more conservative than their equivalents in England, Germany, and Norway.[10] A comparison of coeds and their mothers reveals significant differences in their attitudes toward the importance of virginity upon entering marriage and toward the acceptability of sexual intercourse during engagement. The greater prevalence of negative attitudes among mothers can be attributed in part to the special concern over their daughters, as an aspect of parental responsibility. Then, too, Bell and Buerkle argue, the greater liberality of the college girl could be a temporary phenomenon characteristic of her age group.[11] However, the change in values does occur in society as a whole but at a less marked rate than suggested by the attitudes expressed by young adults.

Accordingly, Reiss sees more of a normal evolution of values than the abrupt and drastic change suggested by the term "sexual revolution." The greater change has been in sexual attitudes rather than in behavior, he asserts. Increased premarital sexuality is socially patterned in that, when two groups are subject to the same social and cultural forces, the differences in permissiveness are caused by differences in independence of the courtship group from family control. Even when young people have almost full independence in courtship, as in our system, they do not copulate at random. They follow many of the values characteristic of parents and family as a social institution. Among these values are association of sex with affection, choice of partners, equalitarianism between sexes, and so on. There is conflict between the permissiveness of courtship and the pressure of family values against premarital sexuality, but we are witnessing change in values rather than the absence of a social regulation.[12]

[9] Ira L. Reiss, "Consistency and Sexual Ethics," in Edwin M. Schur (ed.), The Family and the Sexual Revolution (Bloomington, Ind.: Indiana University Press, 1964), pp. 86–94.
[10] Eleanore B. Luckey and Gilbert D. Ness, "A Comparison of Sexual Attitudes and Behavior in an International Sample," Journal of Marriage and the Family, Vol. 31 (May 1969), p. 378.
[11] Robert R. Bell and Jack V. Buerkle, "Mother and Daughter Attitudes to Premarital Sexual Behavior, " Marriage and Family Living, Vol. 23 (November 1961), pp. 390–92.
[12] Reiss, "Consistency and Sexual Ethics," and Ira L. Reiss, "How and Why America's Sex Standards are Changing," Trans-action, Vol. 5 (March 1968), pp. 26–32.

Role change and the bachelor father. Additional responsibilities must be assumed by the father of the multiple-child family if the mother dies. Yet his situation is only an exaggeration of the changes in function and responsibility of parents as a result of the movement toward equality between the sexes.

The trend, Kirkendall and Libby argue, is away from an emphasis upon abstinence from nonmarital intercourse as the badge of sexual morality. In place of this emphasis, attention has been diverted to whether nonmarital intercourse involves an interpersonal relationship characterized by a growing sense of responsibility and sincere regard for one's partner. In counterdistinction from intercourse with a prostitute, premarital intercourse is evaluated according to its contribution to the movement of the participants from self-centeredness to broader emotional involvement with one another. The sex act ideally would then become a means of strengthening a relationship based on understanding and insight into the needs of the other.[13]

TWO TRENDS AFFECTING SEX ROLES

While the sexes differ fundamentally in a number of biological ways, cultural conceptions of masculinity and femininity are subject to change. Two of the important changes are a trend toward depolarization of sex roles and toward erosion of the double standard.

Depolarization of sex roles

The more obvious evidence of the depolarization of sex roles is in hair styles and dress. Such evidence of the change in the visible distinctions between the sexes leads Odenwald to fear that a population of "neutrals" is developing.[14] Men have accepted deodorants, scented products and colorful clothing. Women have adopted clothing and shoe styles previously identified as masculine. Winick reports boys and girls frequently have similar toys and reading tastes.[15]

Women have moved into occupations traditionally considered exclusively male: truck driving, professional wrestling, welding, and so on. They have invaded male sanctuaries in bars, billiard establishments, and bowling alleys. Previously, physical strength and muscular skills were given prestige in many occupations identified as "male." Now the ranking of occupations according to prestige places greater emphasis on intellectual capacity and on skills in manipulation of persons and symbols. Man the hunter and builder has been supplanted by the artist, salesman, executive, and other occupations which employ intuitive and social skills previously identified with feminine behavior.[16]

---

[13] Lester A. Kirkendall and Roger W. Libby, "Interpersonal Relationship—Crux of the Sexual Renaissance," *Journal of Social Issues,* Vol. 22 (April 1966), pp. 45–59.

[14] Robert P. Odenwald, *The Disappearing Sexes* (New York: Random House, 1965), p. 3.

[15] Charles Winick, "The Beige Epoch: Depolarization of Sex Roles in America," *Annals of American Academy of Political and Social Science,* Vol. 376 (March 1968), p. 19.

[16] Ibid.

The rise of the companionate family involves democratic values which undermine the patriarchial status which identified maleness with dominance of family decision making. The husband is caught in the value dilemma of striving to share decision-making authority with his wife while coping with his own anxieties that the loss of patriarchial authority signifies that he is less of a dominant and self-assured "man."

Observers of contemporary family life frequently see males threatened by the expectation that they give sexual gratification to their wives. In the previous one-sided arrangement it was the male who was thought to have strong needs to gratify his appetites, with the woman considered as a relatively passive partner. Sex has become a duty, rather than a pleasure, because the male now faces the prospect that he may not perform satisfactorily and no longer will be able to blame an unresponsive wife. In fact, ironically, the husband may find himself trapped by a wife who is *too* responsive and demanding. He may consider himself a victim of the decline of the double standard.

Erosion of the double standard

One important development has been the increased questioning of the traditional *double standard* which condemns sexual intercourse for women but tolerates such behavior for men. This questioning is a symptom of the trend toward equality between the sexes. The double standard assumed that exploitation of women is consistent with "masculinity" of men. This code differentiated between "good" and "bad" women; the "good" were supposed to be the exclusive candidates for wifehood.

The Kinsey data provide evidence of a decline in the double standard. Increasing proportions of females have engaged in premarital intercourse. Those born in the decades of either 1910 or 1920, when compared with older women, have more than twice the probability of having engaged in premarital intercourse. Similarly, married women have had an increase over the decades in percentage of marital copulations leading to orgasm. The proportion engaging in extramarital coitus rises with age to peak in ages 36–40 years. The accumulated proportion is 26 percent compared with 50 percent for males. In spite of the norm against premarital intercourse supposed to be applied with particular force against females, only around 40 percent of the males wanted to marry virgins.[17]

More permissive attitudes give women greater freedom to employ birth control measures. With less fear of pregnancy they have a greater voice in the choice of sex conventions they follow. Their sexual independence

---

[17] Alfred C. Kinsey, Wardell B. Pomeroy, Clyde E. Martin, and Paul H. Gebhard, *Sexual Behavior in the Human Female* (Philadelphia, Pa.: W. B. Saunders Co., 1953), pp. 298–99, 323, 380, 437.

also has been advanced by greater access to employment and careers outside the home. They have less of a need to assume a passive role in courtship and marriage wherein, as a dependent, they must employ covert and manipulative techniques to control the dominant male. Furthermore, greater awareness of the psychology of sex frees the female to acknowledge her own sexual needs, including the possible use of sex as a defense against loneliness.

In urban life some individuals crave a social intimacy they find denied them by anonymity and impersonality. Some of these lonely people may seek through the physical intimacy of casual sex the social intimacy they especially crave. Foote calls this the *counterfeiting of intimacy* because, without the substance of intimacy, sex as a physical act is mutual masturbation. In reality, intimacy is achieved through a wide range of communications between two individuals who expose the inner recesses of their personalities to one another to develop mutual trust and understanding. Foote describes the act of human coitus as a drama which begins with pursuit but, if social intimacy is to be achieved, culminates in the expression of this mutuality through the physical intercourse.[18]

With the erosion of the double standard, the change in the female interpretation of sex has implications for sexual deviance. In his interviews with men, Brenton noticed that some men want women to desire to be treated as whores. To them, the prostitute represents primitive sex as pure eroticism, undiluted by feelings of guilt, fear, sentimental love, respect, and competition. Brenton contends that women have a similar unconscious wish in that the woman wants the man to be compelled into the sexual act by her sexual desirability and her own desire. To the extent that the wife shares this earthy desire, the husband's virility is tested more severely by the need to satisfy his partner. The previous conception of the sex act as a one-sided arrangement for the sole benefit of the male did not require him to meet his partner's vital desires.[19]

The challenge to his potency may make marital sex a threat to the male and raises the possibility of sexual deviance. Aging and psychological difficulties in handling sexual identity can raise formidable barriers for the husband who believes himself to be confronted with recurrent tests of his capacity as an aggressor in marital relationships. The prostitute dedicates herself to the client's wishes. Her image as a professional sex object frees the client of any obligation to please her. The client determines the time of the sex act in keeping with his mood. The transaction is carried out largely to meet *his* desires and is terminated usually as he dictates. Similarly, homosexual contacts usually provide short-term and impersonal relationships without long-term social commitments to the temporary partner.

[18] Foote, "Sex as Play," p. 162.
[19] Myron Brenton, *The American Male* (New York: Coward-McCann, 1966), pp. 188–91.

FEMALE ROLE: NEW CONTRADICTIONS

On several scores women have enjoyed a favorable status in the United States since its establishment. Scarcity of women on the frontier gave them high value, the doors of higher education opened to them early, and industrialization provided some of them with work outside the home, especially after World War I. However, the situation has been contradictory. Women have not drawn the pay scales of men, and their occupations are remarkably similar to those historically held by women: secretaries, typists, clerks, teachers, nurses, and telephone operators. They have been notoriously underrepresented among lawyers, physicians, engineers, and scientists.[20]

Erosion of the place of women

Sex equality, according to Rossi's view, means equal and similar roles of men and women in such spheres as intellectual, artistic, political, and occupational interests and participation. The roles would be complementary only in those spheres dictated by physiological differences between the sexes. The feminist goal of earlier years was adaptation to a masculine role. Rossi sees a new conception of sex equality involving an enlargement of the common ground of the sexes through the cultivation by each of some of the characteristics traditionally associated with the other. Tenderness and expressiveness would be approved for men; personal achievement, workmanship, and constructive aggression would be cultivated in girls.[21]

The contradictions in the current status of American women reflect the erosion of the traditional homemaker status and the failure of women to maintain gains in education and employment which would signal the appearance of a new accepted status.[22] The general trend in this century, Mead contends, has been to limit American women increasingly to the home and to take away functions they used to perform. In ancient times women bathed the dead; now male morticians do this for a profit. Midwifery is the responsibility of male obstetricians, followed by male pediatricians. Male insurance agents visit the widowed and sorrowful people. Care of infirm elderly persons is handled by specialized institutions.[23]

Statistics on occupational trends between 1940 and 1966 show a sharp increase in the number of employed females, Knudsen reports, but women

[20] Carl N. Degler, "Revolution without Ideology: The Changing Place of Women in America," *Daedalus*, Vol. 93 (Spring 1964), pp. 653–63.
[21] Alice S. Rossi, "Equality between the Sexes: An Immodest Proposal," *Daedalus*, Vol. 93 (Spring 1964), p. 608.
[22] For discussion of the employed mother, see Chapter 8, pp. 204–5.
[23] Margaret Mead, "Introduction," in Beverly B. Cassara (ed.), *American Women: The Changing Image* (Boston, Mass.: Beacon Press, 1962), pp. ix–xi.

have held a decreasing share of the professional occupations. Their greatest percentage increase has been in professional occupations in which men had an overwhelming majority. The growth of female employment has been greatest in the lower status occupations and those occupations which were part-time or irregular, and thereby congenial to homemaking responsibilities. Furthermore, as the proportion of females has increased in any occupational category, the discrepancy between the sexes in pay scales widened progressively to the disadvantage of women. Between the years 1940 and 1966, women have fallen behind men in their relative position in median education, share of instructional staffs of elementary and secondary staffs, and share of faculties of institutions of higher education.[24]

Why the status contradictions?

One frequent explanation for the status contradictions of American women presents a "conspiratorial" theme.[25] Women are supposed to be victimized by psychoanalytic concepts that they are "a strange, inferior, less-than-human species" who exist "in terms only of man's love." Social scientists are criticized for strengthening a "feminine mystique" which denies women a career route for their self-fulfillment needs, needs they have as total human beings because of their education and their awareness of events in a dynamic world outside the home. Social scientists describe the female role as essentially complementary to the male role, and sex educators tend to identify the housewife role as "normal" and the appropriate target for women who would avoid personal and social conflicts. The contents of popular magazines and television portray the "happy housewife heroine" dedicated to babies, cooking, and keeping beautiful for her husband.[26]

Rather than seeing a "conspiracy," the Kenistons explain the new concern about the status conflicts of modern women in terms of unprecedented circumstances. When death rates were high and average life-span shorter, the survival of society necessitated the concentration of adult women on responsibilities associated with childbearing. The idleness of women in years beyond childbearing was a minor problem because death rates reduced the proportion of the population surviving to these ages. When the family was the chief unit for economic production, women worked within its boundaries. The demands placed on the mother homemaker have declined as medical advances and industrial technology have revised the functions and activities of families. Meanwhile, the husband's job outside the home has increased his absence from the home, but the

---

[24] Dean D. Knudsen, "The Declining Status of Women: Popular Myths and the Failure of Functionalist Thought," *Social Forces,* Vol. 48 (December 1969), pp. 183–93.

[25] Ellen and Kenneth Keniston, "An American Anachronism: The Image of Women and Work," *American Scholar,* Vol. 33 (Summer 1963), pp. 355–56.

[26] Friedan, *The Feminine Mystique,* pp. 28–32, 100, 117–26.

tensions of the job increase the reliance of some husbands on their wives for emotional sanctuary. The Kenistons believe that the adjustments of contemporary women to these new circumstances have been handicapped by cultural lag in that their parents' conceptions of the female role, so crucial in early socialization of personality, have preserved archaic attitudes within the social psychology of contemporary women.[27]

The "conspiratorial" explanation is overdrawn if it is interpreted as a conscious "plot" to keep the female sex in subjugation. However, that explanation does focus attention on the network of norms and institutionalized practices which channel the experiences and expected behavior of females in ways inconsistent with their full participation in contemporary social life as total human beings. The parallel with the dynamics and consequences of racial discrimination is striking.

Implications of "minority" status

Some time ago Hacker pointed to women as an example of a minority group of people "who, because of their physical or cultural characteristics, are singled out from the others in the society for differential and unequal treatment, and who thereby regard themselves as objects of collective discrimination." In ways similar to the behavior of racial minorities experiencing discrimination, women may be unaware of the extent to which their sex status influences the way others treat them or of the generally low esteem in which their sex group is held. Furthermore, they may believe that differential treatment is *warranted* by the distinctive characteristics of their sex.[28] Goldberg for example, presented to college girls articles carrying names of male and female authors. Identical articles were evaluated less favorably by the girls when the name was female.[29]

The interpretation of women as a minority group is consistent in certain respects with their general tendency to avoid a firm commitment to any crusade for improving their lot as a group. Usually, employed women are more interested in gaining immediate and practical advantages in terms of better employment, abolition of legal and administrative barriers against equal access to job and educational opportunities, day-care centers for children, maternity benefits, more adequate domestic help, and so on. The Women's Liberation movement finds that the winning of adherents involves a conversion process to eliminate "a happy slave mentality." Conversion to the beliefs of the movement, Micossi says, is more likely when the individual recognizes that there are alternatives to the mother-housewife role, feels discrepancies between her actual circumstances and

---

[27] Keniston and Keniston, "An American Anachronism," pp. 364–71.

[28] Helen Hacker, "Women as a Minority Group," *Social Forces,* Vol. 30 (October 1951), pp. 60–61.

[29] Philip Goldberg, "Are Women Prejudiced against Women?" *Trans-action,* Vol. 5 (April 1968), pp. 28–30.

her aspirations, comes to see the social structure as the source of her frustrations, and has a biographical history of defying traditions.[30]

The "apathy" among most women, so frustrating to the adherents of Women's Liberation, is consistent with the American pattern of being more concerned about individual practice than the furthering of an ideological principle. Their greater interest in more immediate gains, Degler says, is consistent with the greater success in the United States of social reforms which have been impromptu and practical without expression in an elaborate ideology.[31] In keeping with this interpretation, research indicates that most women would reject any radical reorganization of the social structure. There are trends among women toward delay of marriage, return to college, and reduction in number of births, which suggest an impromptu and practical bent in their efforts to improve their circumstances as individuals. Lack of strong interest among women persists as a roadblock against commitment to an ideology of full equality between the sexes.[32]

To achieve equality between the sexes, Rossi suggests changes in the patterns of child care, of residence, and education. The employed mother is less able to rely on relatives for childcare because of the increasing geographical and social separation of nuclear families from their parents. The declining availability of domestic help is another complication. Rossi suggests establishment of a network of child-care centers and upgrading of the status of child-care jobs. Because suburbanization increases the geographical distance between home and work, she believes location of residences closer to the business center would ease the conflict between career and motherhood and increase the fathers' participation in the lives of children. To reduce the conditioning of girls away from socialization exclusively for the housewife roles, Rossi recommends that schools expose them increasingly to male teachers, excursions to a variety of workplaces, and the learning of skills now reserved for boys. The general idea would be to reduce the current sex-role stereotyping which distinguishes sharply between man's work and woman's work.[33]

UNWED MOTHERS AND VALUE CONFLICTS

Illegitimacy and incest arouse abhorrence because they fly in the face of moral patterns which identify the community's interests with keeping accepted sexual relations within marriage. This abhorrence of sexual rela-

---

[30] Anita L. Micossi, "Conversion to Women's Lib," *Trans-action,* Vol. 8 (November–December 1970), pp. 82–90.

[31] Degler, "Revolution without Ideology," pp. 663–65.

[32] Jessie Bernard, "The Status of Women in Modern Patterns of Culture," Cynthia F. Epstein and William J. Goode (eds.), *The Other Half: Roads to Women's Equality* (Englewood Cliffs, N.J.: Prentice-Hall, 1970), pp. 15–17.

[33] Rossi, "Equality between the Sexes," pp. 628–46.

tions outside of marriage has contributed to the enactment by many states of criminal statutes against voluntary coition between unmarried adults. Such statutes would extend the coercive force of criminal law to sex offenders with the intention of employing punishment to deter future offenses. Nevertheless, unwed mothers are rarely prosecuted in spite of their pregnancy providing evidence of illegal sexual relationships. This lack of enforcement suggests that value conflicts are present in responses to illegitimacy.

"Fun ideology" as a latent factor

The stigmatization of the unwed mother represents a value conflict by its contrast with the general support given to a "fun ideology" which inadvertently encourages, if not implicitly condones, illicit coition which sometimes culminates in an unwanted pregnancy.[34] Christensen suggests the paradoxical effects of this contradiction. When a culture is more permissive regarding sexual matters, premarital pregnancy is less likely to produce hasty marriage and thereby a higher incidence of later divorce. Forced marriages appear to work against marital success.[35]

Within this emphasis on "fun" as a major personal goal, the dating patterns of urban society exert pressures which can be conducive to illicit sexual relationships. The controls of home and family over contacts among unmarried individuals have been undermined in more fundamental ways than simple failure to control young rebels. Using his concept of role bargaining, Goode explains illegitimacy as a consequence of social forces blocking the function of courtship in keeping pregnancy within marriage.[36] He agrees that unwed motherhood may reflect low conformity to values which would reserve sexual relationships to the married couple. In addition, however, unwanted pregnancy may reflect the vulnerability of the young women in making a courtship bargain when the family cannot provide sufficient wealth and prestige for power in bargaining.

In early anthropological studies, it was emphasized—for example, by Malinowski—that legitimate conception is always preceded by a legal (or "customary") contract of individuals to enter marriage. Thereby, marriage, said Malinowski, is a *licensing of parenthood*.[37] Goode illustrates the linkage between illegitimacy and the lack of social provisions for courtship opportunities to gain this license for parenthood. The alternative decisions

[34] Clark E. Vincent, *Unmarried Mothers* (New York: Free Press of Glencoe, 1961), pp. 6–12.

[35] Harold T. Christensen, "Cultural Relativism and Premarital Sex Norms," *American Sociological Review,* Vol. 25 (February 1960), pp. 31–39.

[36] William J. Goode, "Illegitimacy in the Caribbean Social Structure," *American Sociological Review,* Vol. 25 (February 1960), pp. 21–30.

[37] Bronislaw Malinowski, "Parenthood—The Basis of Social Structure," in Robert W. Roberts (ed.), *The Unwed Mother* (New York: Harper & Row, 1966), pp. 32–34.

to marry or to enter a consensual union are influenced by the social standing of the girl relative to her lover, her personal qualities such as beauty, the likelihood that the couple will suffer social punishment, and the chances of the girl encountering an eligible male in the social circle encompassing her family.

Challenge to the moral order?

The unmarried mother has been popularly regarded as a woman who has willfully violated the conventions and probably is oversexed. The baby is likely to be viewed as only incidental to the "sin." However, since the woman conceived outside of marriage, her motherhood is evidence that she engaged in sexual intercourse in violation of its prohibition outside marriage. In that sense her status as an unwed mother appears to flaunt the conventions. Young rejects the evaluation of willful irresponsibility on grounds that the unwed mother is likely to feel "wicked." [38] However, since the unwed mother does not *necessarily* feel "wicked," a more telling criticism would be that such pregnancy, in and of itself, is not proof of the woman's total commitment to the fun ideology and to a pursuit of sexual experience for its own sake.

The arbitrary identification of unwed mothers with general willfulness ignores their wide distribution through the general population and the wide range of characteristics they exhibit. The unwed mother is represented in every social and economic level. Women without financial and social advantages are more likely, however, to be caught in the net of private and public agencies by which illegitimate births become public knowledge. It is this *public* revelation which raises moral indignation. The stigmatization of unwed mothers revealed as such in public is reinforced by fear of parents that their own daughters will be affected by knowing that illicit coition is not punished. The stigmatization is supposed to be justified by the moral unworthiness and inferior character of unwed mothers, but Vincent reports that the unwed mothers in his Alameda County, California, study were fairly representative in socioeconomic terms of all females of equivalent age, race, and marital status in that county. The majority showed little evidence of subnormal mentality or emotional instability.[39]

Inconsistencies in negative evaluations

Popular folklore assumes that unwed mothers are very young, poor, uneducated, or psychologically disturbed. The lash of censure is directed most against these kinds. Vincent believes that this differential imposition of stigmatization is attributable to the failure of certain unwed mothers to

[38] Leontine Young, *Out of Wedlock* (New York: McGraw-Hill Book Co., 1954), pp. 7–16.
[39] Vincent, *Unmarried Mothers*, p. 262.

serve other approved purposes and to the possibility that their pregnancy will contribute to the burden of the taxpayer.[40] Less censure is directed toward the unwed mother able to meet her difficulties through her own resources. One beneficial side effect of illegitimate births is that foster parents are provided children through adoption. Paradoxically, the lack of demand for black babies for adoption channels this benefit largely toward whites. Furthermore, illegitimate births among urban blacks do not provide economic advantages by adding to the low-paid work force as they did on southern plantations in an earlier era.

The movement toward racial integration enhances prospects that illegitimacy among blacks will be criticized as inconsistent with their moral qualification for equal status. Because of its reliance on public funds, the Aid to Dependent Families program is recurrently attacked on grounds that it "subsidizes" illegitimacy. A value dilemma ensues because the program is intended to safeguard the well-being of babies thrust into adverse circumstances.

Value contradictions are also present in the matter of surrender of the baby for adoption. Failure to keep a baby is frequently interpreted as a lack of mother's love and evidence of willful irresponsibility, but one study indicates that the unmarried mother who *keeps* her baby is more likely to exhibit general "immaturity." Those who surrender their babies were described as exhibiting greater intelligence, independence, and emotional stability. The explanation was that the latter were more aware of the norms of general society and more competent in avoiding further definition of themselves as deviants.[41]

Surrender of the baby was forced by the norms of society, then, although a portion of the members of the society paradoxically censures this action as a rejection of a mother's responsibility. In the study cited above, 62 percent of the black mothers and 21 percent of the white mothers retained their babies. Although direct comparison is hazardous because of the effect of other factors, a study of inmates pregnant at admission to prison finds only 13 percent of the babies born out of wedlock were surrendered for adoption.[42] (A form of chivalry which operates against the imprisonment of women, as compared to men, may have particular force in protecting pregnant women convicted of a crime. Therefore, imprisonment of pregnant women suggests that they were evaluated as *particularly* unworthy and irresponsible. Nevertheless, the existence of special justification for placing a child up for adoption resulted in only a few adoptions among the mother-inmates in the study group.)

[40] Ibid., pp. 12–15.
[41] Wyatt C. Jones, Henry J. Meyer, and Edgar F. Borgatta, "Social and Psychological Factors in Status Decisions of Unmarried Mothers," *Journal of Marriage and the Family,* Vol. 25 (August 1962), pp. 224–30.
[42] Elmer H. Johnson, *Childbirth to Women under Sentence: Characteristics and Outcome* (Carbondale, Ill.: Center for the Study of Crime, Delinquency, and Corrections; Southern Illinois University, July 1969).

INCEST AND THE FAMILY

The prohibition of sexual relations or marriage between designated persons is found in all known societies. However, in his survey of 250 societies, Murdock found variation in the specific family members subject to the prohibition beyond mother and son, father and daughter, or brother and sister. Relatives with whom marriage and intercourse are forbidden in one society are often privileged mates in another. The incest taboo operates with peculiar intensity among sexual prohibitions, but sporadic instances of incestuous intercourse do occur.[43]

Incest may be defined as sexual intercourse between persons of near kindred. Complexities lurk within this apparently simple definition. Goody notes that incest is commonly evaluated from the perspective of our conception of kinship without recognizing the influence of this conception on our evaluation of what incest is and what it signifies for the social order. He employs anthropological studies to illustrate the marked differences among societies in their definition of what social positions are involved in incest and in the degrees of moral horror raised. Using the Ashanti and Tallensi of the African Gold Coast, Goody illustrates the differences between societies which trace descent through the mother (matrilineal) and those which trace descent through the father (patrilineal).[44]

We define *adultery* as voluntary sexual intercourse of a married person with one of the opposite sex. Goody employs the native terms for various sex statuses and forms of sexual intercourse to cite the blurring by the Ashanti and Tallensi of this distinction between adultery and incest. To the matrilineal Tallensi, the greatest horror is engendered by prohibited sexual intercourse with the females of the group. Incest is extended to the immediate female kin. To the patrilineal Ashanti, the greatest horror is aroused by illegitimate intercourse with the wife of another member of the group. Incest covers the wife of a father, brother, or son. With emphasis on the nuclear family, Americans apply their greatest moral horror against incest within the confines of this element of kinship structure.

Possible threat to family stability

Incest raises problems for the family by undermining the conventional ways of determining descent of offspring. What constitutes incest is related to how kinship is determined. Regardless of the definition of kinship in the family organization, however, the birth resulting from an incestuous union is more difficult to handle than births resulting from extramarital inter-

---

[43] George Peter Murdock, *Social Structure* (New York: Macmillan Co., 1949), pp. 284–89, 300.
[44] Jack Goody, "A Comparative Approach to Incest and Adultery," in Bernard Farber (ed.), *Kinship and Family Organization* (New York: John Wiley & Sons, 1966), pp. 54–68.

course. The difficulty stems from the lack of means of giving the infant a recognized place in the family. In most illegitimate births our frequent social "remedy" is the marriage of the unmarried man and woman to legitimatize the birth. However, the incest taboo makes the incestuous birth a primary example of a situation denied this "remedy."

The emotional force of the incest taboo, Davis believes, stems from the great threat posed by incest to the nuclear family as a social organization within which the next generation is provided a protected milieu and is socialized in the earlier years of dependency.[45] Violations of the taboo create sexual rivalry destructive to the balance of the roles of father, mother, brother, and sister which permits the family to serve its functions. The status system is jeopardized when the father concurrently is lover of the daughter who is in a position of dependence and submissiveness. At the same time, the daughter is denied the opportunity to gain the legitimate rewards of a wife through a sexual relationship. In the role of lover, the father exploits the young daughter rather than treats her immaturity and dependency as resources for his responsibilities in the social function of socialization.

For the society as a whole, violation of the taboo interferes with the transfer of the young from their original nuclear family into families wherein they are parents. If the nuclear family were an independent society, the general practice of incest would be socially feasible, but the family is a unit within the larger society, the continuance of which requires the liquidation of the specific nuclear family and the production of personalities to compose the nuclear families of the next generation. The incest taboo serves to regulate the expression of the sex drive in ways consistent with socialization of personality and the strengthening of maturation to assume familial responsibility.[46]

Social context of the problem

Incest operates within a social context which is dominated by the highly intense emotions aroused by the violation. The emotional intensity of this prohibition favors an indiscriminate rejection of these offenders as universally pathological. One consequence is a resort to blanketing a wide variety of incest offenders under the broad but obscure term of "sex criminal." Emotionalism obstructs recognition of the wide variety of social circumstances under which incest occurs, a variety suggested by the five types of incest delineated by Bagley.[47] In *functional incest,* the family is either alone or culturally isolated from the community for reasons such as the

[45] Kingsley Davis, *Human Society* (New York: Macmillan Co., 1949), pp. 401–4.
[46] Talcott Parsons, "The Incest Taboo in Relation to Social Structure and the Socialization of the Child," *British Journal of Sociology,* Vol. 5 (June 1954), pp. 101–17.
[47] Christopher Bagley, "Incest Behavior and Incest Taboo," *Social Problems,* Vol. 16 (Spring 1969), pp. 505–19.

religious persecution of the Mormons until the 1870s; when the mother cannot provide sexual comforts for her husband (because of illness, frigidity, death, or desertion), one daughter may be indulged materially to encourage her to become a new "wife" through a sense of duty. *Accidental* incest occurs in a socially disorganized and/or crowded community when the cultural regulation of behavior declines. In *pathological incest* one or both partners are psychotic or mentally subnormal and cannot understand the existence of moral prohibitions. *Incest through object-fixation* involves the dominant partner's first sexual experience with a child or adolescent. To achieve sexual experience by this preferred means, the parent finds a member of the family to be the most easily available child. *Psychopathic incest* is perpetrated by a dominant parent of apparently normal personality and intelligence. Although a married partner provides a normal sexual outlet, a child is seduced.

In light of the varieties of incest, Bagley protests the uniform imposition of criminal penalties regardless of circumstances or precipitating causes. He suggests that only for psychopathic incest is the application of rigorous penalties appropriate. However, even in this instance Bagley falls into the trap of a vague term which conceals the heterogeneity of individuals and social situations it is supposed to encompass.

If a kinship system is to be maintained, moral censure must be supported by penalties against the transgressor. Punishment through law enforcement, however, lacks the effectiveness of sanctions functioning in the social situations within which incest occurs, because the social situation involves the entire family rather than a single individual. This thesis is supported by qualities of central roles in the incest drama and characteristics of the individuals regulated by these roles. Brother-sister and mother-son incest are certainly both important aspects of the topic, but in this brief review of the literature we will concentrate on father-daughter incest.

Incestuous fathers are frequently described as having grown up amidst parental separation or divorce, and thus with an emotionally deprived childhood. Typically, they lack a criminal record but show manifest difficulties in achieving adult sexuality. Frequently their wives are reported to have promoted the incest by frustrating them sexually and to have encouraged the misconduct at least tacitly. The wives seem to indulge the oldest daughter and encourage her toward maturity beyond her years as a means of foisting responsibility on her. Usually, the wives say they were ignorant of ongoing incest even when evidence was apparent. Researchers have reported collusion of daughters, whose attitudes range from placidity to manifest guilt. However, it is difficult to assess the significance of emotions which may involve admiration for the father or rivalry with the mother.[48]

[48] Irving B. Weiner, "On Incest: A Survey," *Excerpta Criminologica,* Vol. 4 (March–June 1964), pp. 142–49.

In a study of incestuous fathers placed on probation, Kennedy and Cormier find incest was the culmination of a growing crisis in family relationships. The crisis included disappointment and lack of sexual gratification, or the dissolution of a sexual relationship by death or divorce. The presence of an available daughter sometimes was related to the reawakening of an unresolved conflict in a man with incomplete psychosexual development. Because of the family context, Kennedy and Cormier believe, the lack of a prison sentence was advantageous in permitting a healthy outcome through family reconstruction. The cases studied were found to be examples of proper responses to incestuous unions in that they were handled officially as basically acute problems of a family.[49]

HOMOSEXUALITY AS HUMAN BEHAVIOR

Although popularly identified with aberrant sexual behavior itself, homosexuality is actually a condition characterized by a psychosexual propensity towards others of the same sex. Because some persons control their physical urges, their condition is not the equivalent of behavior. Furthermore, some persons without the condition may engage casually in homosexual practices out of curiosity or in exceptional circumstances, such as confinement in a one-sex establishment.[50] The strongly adverse moral responses to sexual relationships between members of the same sex overlook the distinction between the condition and the behavior. This failure suggests that the study of homosexuality is an important facet of the more general topic of deviance of individuals from social expectations associated with sex roles.

The distinction between the condition and behavior points up a basic difficulty in identifying the genuine dimensions of homosexuality as a social problem. The genuine homosexual, expressing the condition, seeks a permanent emotional attachment with another male. This stable arrangement is more conducive to privacy and invisibility from the police than is that of the individual seeking immediate emotional release without regard for his sexual partner. Hence, the person with the homosexual propensity probably is underrepresented in the group captured by the official net.

Estimates of the prevalence of homosexuality have been obtained by other means than official statistics. About 37 percent of males and 13 percent of the females above puberty, Pomeroy estimates, have had at

[49] Miriam Kennedy and Bruno M. Cormier, "Father-Daughter Incest: Treatment of a Family," in Walter C. Reckless and Charles L. Newman (eds.), *Interdisciplinary Problems in Criminology: Papers of the American Society of Criminology,* 1964 (Columbus, Ohio: College of Commerce and Administration, Ohio State University, 1965), pp. 191–96.

[50] Michael Schofield, *Sociological Aspects of Homosexuality,* (Boston, Mass.: Little, Brown and Co., 1965), pp. 147–48.

least one homosexual experience to the point of orgasm. About 13 percent of males and 8 percent of females have had homosexual reactions without overt experience after puberty.[51] However, the privacy of sexual behavior and the stigmatization of homosexuality raises special doubts about any mode of estimating prevalence in the total population.

Relative invisibility of lesbianism

The Kinsey research also indicates that the amount of homosexuality is less among females than males. Only about one half to one third as many females as males were reported as primarily or exclusively homosexual in any age category. Furthermore, a much smaller proportion of the females studied had continued their homosexual activities for as many years as most of the males in the sample. Of the females with any homosexual experience, 29 percent had had more than two partners, compared with 49 percent of equivalent males.[52]

The homosexual activities of females are less likely to attract notice because of the social correlates of the two sex roles and their effects on the possibility of detection. The differences in public reactions to visible deviance also reduce the impact for female homosexuals. Males are expected to be physically strong and dominant and aggressive in interpersonal and sexual relationships. Their vocational activities involve them disproportionally in places outside the home where their behavior is subject to public observation. A scandal for them is more likely to have the possibilities of blackmail and other secondary consequences because a greater proportion of males have occupational careers which are dependent on public reputation.

The movement of women into occupations previously considered monopolies of males has placed women in places of public visibility to a greater degree than in previous decades, but the female status continues to be identified especially with the home where public observation of deviant behavior is unlikely.

Lesbian activities appear to be especially prevalent among prostitutes. Psychoanalytically oriented investigators argue that women who become professional prostitutes are likely to be frigid sexually or to become disenchanted with heterosexual intercourse. Cory disputes these arguments as oversimplifications. Frigidity, he believes, usually becomes a matter of inability to achieve orgasm regularly with customers because of inability to relate emotionally in a positive way. He suggests that daily engagement in a variety of deviations and sheer boredom lower resistance to lesbian overtures.[53]

[51] Wardell B. Pomeroy, "Homosexuality," in Ralph W. Weltge (ed.), *The Same Sex: An Appraisal of Homosexuality* (Philadelphia, Pa.: Pilgrim Press, 1969), p. 8.

[52] Kinsey et al., *Sexual Behavior in the Human Female,* pp. 474–75.

[53] Donald Webster Cory, *The Lesbian in America* (New York: Macfadden-Bartell Corporation, 1965), pp. 143–47.

Three myths about homosexuality

Homosexual males are popularly identified as feminine in mannerisms, vocal inflections, and way of dress; homosexual females are supposed to be swaggering individuals in the "butch" model—but only a minority of homosexuals so qualify. Pomeroy notes that the cowboys and Indian fighters of the West, highly masculine symbols of the 19th century, probably included a larger proportion of homosexuals than any other single group of males.[54]

One study suggests the unreliability of identifying sexual deviants on the basis of observable characteristics. Thirty homosexuals were matched with 30 heterosexuals by age, intelligence quotient, and educational attainment. Projective tests were administered to determine their personality structures. Two expert clinicians evaluated the documents to rate the overall adjustments of the subjects in both groups. The homosexuals and heterosexuals did not differ significantly. Tentatively, Hooker concludes that the forms of homosexuality are too varied to constitute a clinical entity and that homosexuality is within the range of psychological differences among heterosexuals.[55]

Homosexuality is sometimes explained as a pathological condition which existed prior to the deviant behavior. The Wolfenden Report raised doubts that the condition of homosexuality qualifies as a "disease." Unorthodox behavior is not necessarily symptomatic of disease if it is the only symptom that can be demonstrated. Homosexuality does not present the demonstrable physical pathology of disease. A single specific cause of homosexuality has not been determined to establish a chain of causal events leading inevitably to the condition.[56] Comparison of a group of 89 male homosexuals with a control group of 35 unmarried male heterosexuals reveals little difference in prevalence of psychopathology. Despite slightly more psychological disability, the homosexuals were able to achieve an educational, occupational, and economic status similar to the heterosexuals.[57]

Simon and Gagnon emphasize the importance of distinguishing between the sexual practices and the social identity of the deviant as sources of maladjustment.[58] Homosexual behavior per se is not sufficient explanation for any difficulties the deviant may exhibit in coping with the problems

[54] Pomeroy, "Homosexuality," pp. 10–11.

[55] Evelyn Hooker, "The Adjustment of the Overt Male Homosexual," *Journal of Projective Techniques,* Vol. 21 (March 1957), pp. 18–31.

[56] *The Wolfenden Report: Report on the Committee on Homosexual Offenses and Prostitution* (New York: Stein and Day, 1963), pp. 31–33.

[57] Marcel T. Saghir, Eli Robins, Bonnie Walbran, and Kathye A. Gentry, "Homosexuality: III. Psychiatric Disorders and Disability in the Male Homosexual," *American Journal of Psychiatry,* Vol. 126 (February 1970), pp. 1079–86.

[58] William Simon and John H. Gagnon, "Homosexuality: The Formulation of Sociological Perspective," *Journal of Health and Social Behavior,* Vol. 8 (September 1967), pp. 180–81.

of life. Rather, his commitment to obtaining emotional gratification with members of his own sex elicits particular attitudes of other persons toward him. *Because* he is evaluated as psychopathological, he is vulnerable to demoralization, despair, and self-hatred.

Even among men with extensive histories as homosexuals, Simon and Gagnon find evidence of a capacity to cope with problems of life counterindicating psychopathology. They define extensive homosexuality as a minimum of 50 or more incidents and/or contact with 21 or more males. In a group so qualifying, three quarters reported no trouble with the police, and only a fifth had trouble in a milieu where definition as a homosexual is particularly crucial.

Another myth sees the homosexual as the seducer of young children, yet the great majority have no more interest in children than do heterosexuals. Schofield sees child molesters as distinctive in more pronounced heterosexual interests, their failure to mix with homosexuals, less promiscuity, greater tendency toward shame and guilt, preference for more elementary techniques, and initiation of sexual activities at a later stage in life. The offense of child molestation draws particular public aversion because of concern over the impact on the victim. This raises an unusual possibility of the conviction of the innocent person accused of the offense, since a wide variety of relatively innocent behavior can be interpreted as molestation and the charge can stem falsely from the overripe fantasies or various motives of children.[59]

Some sociological dimensions

The term *homosexual community* covers a variety of groups which bind their members through common interests and sometimes friendship. Primarily the group provides acceptance of members as homosexual, relief from anxieties of being penalized, and reassurance that homosexuality is normal according to the group's standards. Within the shelter of the congeniality group, members develop an emotional involvement which tends to induce them to accept its norms. The group provides relationships among peers which dilute sexual drives into other channels than those directly sexual. As an example, "camp" behavior gives the appearance of cultural sophistication which can constitute a special form of communication. Nevertheless, for many, the common interest in homosexuality is insufficient to eliminate barriers of race, social class, occupation, and formal education within the community.[60]

Fearing identification by "straight" society, *secret homosexual groups* emphasize concealment. They consist of a loose confederation of small

[59] Schofield, *Sociological Aspects of Homosexuality,* pp. 149–54; also see John H. Gagnon, "Female Child Victims of Sex Offenses," *Social Problems,* Vol. 13 (Fall 1965), pp. 176–92.
[60] Simon and Gagnon, "Homosexuality," pp. 182–83.

cliques, each of which is united by common specialized interests such as similar occupation and personal tastes. Openly homosexual, *overt homosexual groups* make little effort toward concealment and have a high degree of social isolation from heterosexual activities. The secret homosexuals fear that the overt groups endanger their anonymity, but they are forced into interdependency with overt homosexuals when they seek sexual partners.[61]

Special institutions for homosexuals include "gay" bars, steam baths, public toilets, beaches, coffeehouses, and restaurants which cater to homosexuals or serve as special gathering places. These places are characterized by location in areas with heavy concentrations of homosexuals, high tolerance and relative permissiveness toward various forms of deviant behavior, accessibility for both "straight" and "gay" people as public places, and opportunity for gossip and exchange of information. To gain high profits, *"gay" bars* cater to the social needs of homosexuals, and they provide a cloak of anonymity for secret homosexuals in recruiting partners. The participants acquire clusters of friends to provide congeniality and to instruct novices in the values and expectations of the homosexual world.[62]

In homosexual argot a *"tearoom"* is a public restroom with certain features appropriate for sexual encounters without more than momentary involvement. A study by Humphreys found the features to be easy accessibility, easy recognizability as a likely place for contacts, and, nevertheless, concealment from public visibility. Such public restrooms may be located in department stores, bus stations, libraries, and so on. However, the restrooms of public parks and beaches have gained popularity in the motor age when they are located near a traffic throughway from which a quick stop can be made. Within these physical settings, sexual encounters can be made impersonally with various strangers without social commitment beyond the immediate situation. The brevity of the encounter and one's anonymity reduce the risk of being found out.[63]

Homophile organizations appeared in the United States after World War II as one of the products of a social climate permitting greater candor in discussions of sexual behavior. Greater population mobility and the anonymity of urban life cloaked the homosexual from intensive surveillance by his family and gave him opportunities to seek out his fellows.

[61] Maurice Leznoff and William A. Westley, "The Homosexual Community," *Social Problems,* Vol. 3 (April 1956), pp. 260–63.

[62] Evelyn Hooker, "The Homosexual Community," in James O. Palmer and Michael J. Goldstein (eds.), *Perspectives in Psychopathology* (New York: Oxford University Press, 1966), pp. 357–61.

[63] Laud Humphreys, *Tearoom Trade: Impersonal Sex in Public Places* (Chicago: Aldine Publishing Co., 1970), pp. 2–3, 152–54. (His analysis of the difficulties in conducting research in a highly stigmatized problem topic is particularly useful.)

Sagarin sees the publication of the Kinsey report as a veritable sexual "atom bomb" in that it brought to public attention the fact that literally millions of American males were exclusively homosexual throughout their lives. Learning that there were many others like themselves, Sagarin says, homosexuals spontaneously formed a number of homophile groups. Some, like the Mattachine Society, struggle to alleviate the conditions of the homosexual in society by demanding civil rights and public education. The contradictions among the various segments of the amorphous movement, however, are indicated by other less influential groups, among which are motorcycle groups whose leather jackets suggest masculine strength and whose bike chains symbolize mastery over slaves. "Vanguard" is an organization of young homosexual prostitutes.[64]

Societal reaction to homosexuality

The sex deviant is evaluated by nondeviants as though his total personality and his total behavior are described by that aspect of his sexual conduct which is deviant. Simon and Gagnon point out that the homosexual is "located in a social landscape that has been stripped of everything but his deviant commitment." His choice of another male as his sexual target is the prepossessing interest of nondeviants in interpreting all of his behavior. The presence of homosexuality is seen as prima facie evidence of his major psychopathology. All of the psychological and social aspects are evaluated under a simplistic view that he is identical with other individuals lumped together as homosexuals. His creations in the arts, for instance, are scrutinized for evidence of phallic imagery rather than rated against the conventions of the particular art form.[65]

The hostility of the community, Schofield hypothesizes, has two adverse consequences for the community at large when stigmatized individuals are shut off from "normal" relationships. First, the disruptive influences of homosexuals is greater in accordance with the severity of the external restraints placed on their behavior. Second, the social and economic contributions of homosexuals vary inversely with the hostility shown to them.[66] These consequences stem from the impact of stigmatization in fixing the largely unconscious homosexual tendencies into identification of oneself as a peer of homosexuals. The homosexual is moved from primary deviance to secondary deviance.[67] For some individuals, early floundering to establish sexual identity is transformed into self-commit-

[64] Edward Sagarin, *Odd Man In: Societies of Deviants in America* (Chicago: Quadrangle Books, 1969), pp. 81–83, 89–95.
[65] Simon and Gagnon, "Homosexuality," pp. 177–80.
[66] Schofield, *Sociological Aspects of Homosexuality,* p. 211.
[67] See Chapter 2, pp. 60–61.

ment to a homosexual way of life in absorbing their interests and dominating their search for social colleagues.

Public hostility raises psychological barriers against the homosexual accepting a course of rehabilitation. Lesbians, Cory declares, exhibit anxiety about beliefs that they can be "cured." He attributes this anxiety to fear that public acceptance of their deviance will become more difficult if change is believed possible. This possibility of change forces the lesbian to confront the question of whether she could make it in the straight life. Furthermore, she must abandon her contention that her current way of life is worthy.[68]

PROSTITUTION: COMMERCIALIZED SEX

American traditions identify prostitution with vice crusades, corruption of the young, traffic in women, community disorder, venereal disease, crime, sin, and undermining of the family. Although condemnation has lost some of the stridence of earlier times, prostitution still symbolizes parasitism on the social vigor of the community. It also is identified with commercialism of the sex drive—a result which may be felt to threaten the usefulness of sexual needs in motivating support of the legitimate social order.

Two contrasting policies toward prostitution have been taken by governments. On the European continent the *licensing system* has been typical, under the assumption that vice is inevitable and must be controlled to minimize its antisocial consequences. Brothels and free prostitutes are licensed under obligations to submit to medical examination for control of disease and to conform to regulations intended to reduce public nuisance. Objections to licensing are that it lends legitimacy to vice and to the degradation of women and encourages a profitable trade for brothel-keepers. In the United States and England, the *voluntary system* emphasizes the immorality of prostitution and charges the government with the duty to suppress it. When suppression is impossible, the only course is to leave the practice alone. Changes in the forces affecting supply and demand are relied on to regulate prostitution. Only when gross public indecency and disorder occur does the government take action. In times of large-scale prostitution, the failure to regulate disease can be a serious public problem.[69]

Demand for the prostitute's services

In his 1896 report on prostitution in England and France, Acton regarded prostitution as "an inevitable attendant upon civilized, and espe-

---

[68] Cory, *The Lesbian in America,* pp. 177–78.
[69] William Acton, *Prostitution* (London, Eng.: MacGibbon and Kee, 1968), pp. 140–43.

cially closely-packed population." Whereas the moralists of his day argued that all illicit intercourse is prostitution, whether or not for hire, he limited his definition to the hiring of oneself, openly or secretly, for sex services. As a pioneer investigator, Acton anticipated later researchers by emphasizing that prostitution exists because of a demand for the service. The demand, he said, abounds in large cities where large numbers of unmarried men are collected together and where the sexes are brought in close relations in daily work. "Here always abound idle and wealthy men, with vicious tastes, which they spare neither pains nor expense to gratify. Here also are the needy, the improvident, and the ill-instructed, from whose ranks the victims of sensuality may be readily recruited." [70]

Acton focused attention on a matter not usually noticed in sweeping moral condemnation of the prostitute. As in the case of any service whether approved or condemned, there must be a market of willing consumers and a supply of "workers" ready and able to provide the services in demand. In this sense the prostitute is but the visible symbol of a system of patterned relationships maintained by a demand from customers. What motivates the client to seek out the prostitute? What motivates the woman to become a prostitute? The answers should make provision for the contribution of the society's overall regulation of sex behavior to the breaching of its own prohibition of prostitution.

Psychiatrists, Esselstyn says, see symbolism and unconscious need in clients' search for prostitutes. By possessing a "bad" woman, men may strike back at "good" mothers. Shameful passion may be vented with shameful women. Latent sadism may be expressed. However, less symbolic reasons should also be recognized. Military personnel, traveling businessmen, conventioneers, and other categories of men away from their women are more likely to be clients. Prostitution has the advantages of avoiding the uncertainty and time for "courtship" required in other methods of arranging for illicit sex in an unfamiliar city. It cloaks the prostitute in the erotic imagery of unadulterated passion, satisfies curiosity over "the fallen woman," and offers the thrill of being a temporary participant in a subterranean world. Moreover the prostitute offers means of satisfying an appetite for varied or condemned sexual techniques and of meeting the needs of men unable to obtain partners otherwise.[71]

From interviews of 732 men who had visited prostitutes, Winick concluded that the desire for sexual outlet is overshadowed by symbolic meanings. The respondents were vague in recalling the prostitute explicitly but described her as "unusual" because of her deviant career and her ability to provide special gratification. For many of the respondents, the mechanical delivery of sexual favors was in keeping with the emotional

---

[70] Ibid., pp. 29–32, 126.
[71] T. C. Esselstyn, "Prostitution in the United States," *Annals of American Academy of Political and Social Science,* Vol. 376 (March 1968), pp. 130–31.

passivity they perceived as characteristic of women. Other minor themes were that relations with a prostitute would be cheaper than usual dating, would alleviate fear of impotence, and would circumvent onerous responsibilities associated with other kinds of sexual intercourse.[72]

Since World War II prostitution has become less visible, although it appears that the numbers of prostitutes and their clients have not changed appreciably. Esselstyn offers several explanations. Vice crusades of the past may have driven prostitution underground and encouraged less visible operations. Although suffering from the unreliability of all official crime statistics, reported arrests for prostitution and commercialized vice have increased generally. Decline in the frequency with which men seem to patronize prostitutes suggests that other women are accessible for heterosexual outlet. The rise of call girls indicates that greater tolerance of social deviants in general permits individuals to engage in the profession without the more visible organization of brothels.[73]

American males go to prostitutes less than is popularly believed, the Kinsey report declares. Although some 69 percent of U.S. white males ultimately have such experience, many have no more than one or two experiences. Of all forms of male sexual experience, only some 4 percent is with female prostitutes, the report asserts. The use of prostitutes increases through the teen ages and levels off in the 30s, except for the relatively few unmarried males in later years who have difficulty finding sexual partners. Recourse to prostitutes is more frequent in the lower social classes as measured by educational attainment.[74]

Recruitment and key roles

What motivates a woman to become a prostitute? The question centers attention on the possibility that she is driven by strange passions and antisocial tendencies which set her off from "decent" people. However, the question can also direct attention to the characteristics of our general culture which are consistent with prostitution. Lemert cites such characteristics.[75] Our culture normally disposes women to utilize sex to charm customers, hold jobs, and gain favors in other situations outside of marriage. Sex is a means of balancing her disadvantages in other methods of controlling or manipulating people or of acquiring material rewards. The unresolved tensions of courtship, family, and marriage provide both clients and prostitutes. The inferior marital and job prospects of lower social

[72] Charles Winick, "Prostitutes' Clients' Perceptions of the Prostitutes and of Themselves," International Journal of Social Psychiatry, Vol. 8 (Autumn 1962), pp. 289–97.
[73] Esselstyn, "Prostitution in the United States," pp. 124–25.
[74] Alfred C. Kinsey, Wardell B. Pomeroy, and Clyde E. Martin, Sexual Behavior in the Human Male (Philadelphia, Pa.: W. B. Saunders Co., 1948), pp. 597–601.
[75] Edwin M. Lemert, Social Pathology, (New York: McGraw-Hill Book Co., 1951), pp. 245–47.

classes give their women greater reason for entering prostitution to acquire the income necessary for the material rewards our culture presents as appropriate targets for aspiration. The mass communication media emphasize themes conducive to sexual stimulation which are characteristic of the culture.

The "white slavery" interpretation of the prostitute described her as the unwilling captive of ruthless exploiters who seduced her into a "fate worse than death." Because in actuality the number of volunteers is sufficient to meet the demand, the actual explanation of the prostitute is more complex. The appeal of high income is the most obvious. Other apparent "explanations" are an unhappy love affair, early exposure to a life of sexual permissiveness, lack of acceptable marriage, and engagement in an occupation vulnerable to seduction. Psychiatrists have sought explanations in terms of self-debasement for revenge on parents, unconscious homosexuality, and sadomasochistic impulses. Recent investigators, however, have given less emphasis to the prostitute's loathing of her work or desire to abhor her clients uniformly.[76]

The *call girl* has been called "the elegant prostitute" because she lives on a high economic plane. Call girls dress well to please fastidious clients and to avoid undue attention when entering quality hotels. They claim greater prestige than the streetworker or house prostitute on the basis of their attractiveness, manners, financial status, dress, and apartment. The telephone, sometimes with an answering service, is the essential means of making appointments. Usually recommendations from previous customers, rather than direct solicitation, are the basis of expanding clientele. However, businessmen who provide call girls for their clients serve as voluntary procurers, and call girls also pay fees to professional procurers. Call girls also haunt some cocktail lounges and restaurants, where indirect solicitation depends on an overture from the adventurous client or an introduction through the bartender.[77]

One of the most despised of occupational specialists, the *pimp,* has been described as an economic parasite who violates the expectation that the male is the provider for his woman. Furthermore, he is portrayed as the seducer who recruits young girls into prostitution. The pimp-prostitute relationship, however, exists because of the functions each serves for the other in a social milieu characterized by her illicit occupation. Reitman sees five functions served by the pimp: protection against the prostitute's going to jail, maintaining regularity of her employment through knowledge of this strange "job market," protecting her against violence, instructing her in the business, and serving as her lover.[78] Hirschi adds the sometime

---

[76] Esselstyn, "Prostitution in the United States," pp. 128–30.

[77] Harold Greenwald, *The Elegant Prostitute: A Social and Psychoanalytic Study* (New York: Walker and Co., 1970), pp. 3, 10–18, 24–27.

[78] Ben L. Reitman, *The Second Oldest Profession* (New York: Vanguard Press, 1931), pp. 14–29.

function of posing as her husband to enable the prostitute to conceal her occupation from her relatives and others.[79]

Value orientations of prostitutes

Since the prostitute is scorned, how does she maintain self-esteem? One analysis emphasizes the very isolation of the girl from the dominant culture as a contributing factor. Her alienation makes her more amenable to accepting behavior that is condemned generally. However, since the general values do have some impact on her despite her isolation, she finds justification in attacks on the moral purity of her detractors. She is likely to cite her income as evidence of material success and as the means of unselfish assumption of the financial burden of people dependent upon her.[80]

Jackman and his colleagues describe two principal types of reference-group orientations. The prostitute oriented to a *criminal world contraculture* identifies with criminals and regards "respectable" people as unimaginative and hypocritical. She scorns their "dull" life in comparison with her "exciting" and "luxurious" style of living. Other prostitutes are oriented concurrently to the *dual worlds* of prostitution and of the conventional middle class. Striving to live according to middle-class values, they attempt to repress their illegitimate sexual activity by disassociating themselves from it emotionally. They maintain strong identification with their families and claim their friends are neither criminals nor prostitutes.

In a study of call girls, Bryan describes an *apprenticeship period*, or "turning out" process, whereby novices are immersed in a call-girl subculture in the course of learning how to obtain clients. Since the skills and values are rather simple and quickly learned, the tutelage, under an experienced call girl usually, emphasizes methods of developing clientele through referrals, telephone calls, and fee splitting. The "do's" and "don't's" of relating to customers receive primary attention. Instruction includes how to obtain the fee, how to converse with the client, how to solicit effectively by telephone, and how to observe personal hygiene. Incidental to instruction, a value structure is transmitted on how to gain the most with minimum effort. Because men are viewed as corrupt, or easily corruptible, the "johns" are pictured as easy marks for exploitation. Honesty is described in terms of regard for other call girls and fidelity to the pimp. Concern for the client is supposed to be limited to gaining manipulative benefits. Unnecessary interaction is typically avoided to reduce the length of a "date" for sake of maximizing fees.[81]

[79] Travis Hirschi, "The Professional Prostitute," in William A. Rushing (ed.), *Deviant Behavior and Social Process* (Chicago: Rand McNally, 1969), p. 203.

[80] Norman R. Jackman, Richard O'Toole, and Gilbert Geis, "The Self-Image of the Prostitute," *Sociological Quarterly*, Vol. 4 (April 1963), pp. 150–61.

[81] James H. Bryan, "Apprenticeships in Prostitution," *Social Problems*, Vol. 12 (Winter 1965), pp. 287–97.

In interviews with 52 call girls, Bryan detects the failure of the individuals to absorb these values into their behavior after they are established as professionals. Many of the respondents described their customers as coming in wide variety, rather than in terms of stereotype of the stupid and corrupt "trick." While friendship with some of the "square" clients was reported, the girls expressed considerable distrust of other girls, describing them as exploitive and disloyal. In other words, the knowledge of the call girl ideology was insufficient for winning the personal adherence to an occupational in-group. Bryan explains that the girls do not interact with one another sufficiently to maintain such adherence and that they are sheltered from full impact of the public stigmatization of their occupation. The call girl usually avoids public revelation. Both she and the client pretend that each is performing functions other than solely gratification of physical sexual appetites. The call girl is shielded by the rationalization that the sanctity of marriage is protected through provision of comfort to lonely men and of an outlet for sexual perverts.[82]

CRIMINAL LAW AS RESPONSE

A bewildering array of criminal laws are supposed to keep individuals chaste before marriage and to confine sex activity to marriage thereafter. Few branches of law, Ploscowe says, show such a wide divergence between actual human behavior and the stated legal norms as do sex offense laws. The almost universal disregard for legal prohibitions reflects the realistic impossibility of restricting sexuality through the criminal law. Furthermore, the laws among the states show a wide variety in types of sexual behavior prohibited and in penalties imposed for similar offenses.[83]

Difficulties in enforcement

Lack of order and consistency among the "system" of laws aggravates the inherent unenforceability of laws intended to control behavior which is largely concealed from public observation and strongly motivated from sources inherent in the psychology of individuals and in the fabric of social relationships.

The difficulties of enforcing such a confusion of laws lead to sporadic enforcement. Gerassi describes the prosecution and conviction of a handful of homosexuals in a scandal which stunned the citizens of a western city. The sudden revelation brought demands for severe punishment, but the quality of justice became doubtful as the witch-hunt threatened more

---

[82] James H. Bryan, "Occupational Ideologies and Individual Attitudes of Call Girls," *Social Problems,* Vol. 13 (Spring 1966), pp. 441–50.
[83] Morris Ploscowe, "Sex Offenses: The American Legal Context," *Law and Contemporary Problems,* Vol. 25 (Spring 1960), pp. 215–22.

people than originally anticipated.[84] The prevalence of undetected homosexuality in the community lends a capriciousness to sporadic enforcement when a scandal makes the homosexual vulnerable to blackmail and other crimes when he is afraid to go to the police.

Resort to the criminal law, Hart points out, depends on four important assumptions: [85] First, the punishment of the offender deprives him of the liberties of movement, property, and avoidance of pain. These deprivations, assumed to be wrong to inflict on others without justification, are inflicted on him. Second, the threat of legal punishment is supposed to coerce nonoffenders into obedience. Thereby, the potential offender may be deterred from a free choice to behave against the social interest, but he may also be restricted from experimentations which may be constructive for himself and others. In the sexual realm, both types of restrictions involve matters which are a recurrent and insistent part of daily life. Therefore, compared with theft and murder as accepted crime, the criminalization of sexual behaviors has special impact on the individual. Third, the enforcement of morality encounters difficulties in making distinctions between what content of morality is to be punished by law and what content is not. Is morality as such to be enforced? If not, *which* morality is to be enforced? Fourth, in protecting the individual against himself, the law assumes a form of paternalism which does not necessarily recognize the distinction between advancing the interests of the individual and the imposition of others' opinions of what is "right."

In Great Britain the Wolfenden Report defined the function of the criminal law as "to preserve public order and decency, to protect the citizen from what is offensive or injurious, and to provide sufficient safeguards against exploitation and corruption of others." The Committee denied that the function of law is to intervene in the private lives of citizens, to enforce any particular pattern of behavior, or to attempt to cover all fields of behavior.[86]

Two fundamental distinctions

The application of the criminal law to regulation of sexual behavior is criticized by Fletcher for confusing legality with morality and for overlooking the distinction between private and public moral standards.[87] In telling you what you can or cannot do, the law is specific in regulating certain aspects of overall behavior without delineating the full range of righteousness. In distinction from morality, the law does not prescribe ideals and

[84] John Gerassi, *The Boys of Boise* (New York: Macmillan Co., 1966).
[85] Herbert L. A. Hart, *Law, Liberty and Morality* (Stanford, Calif.: Stanford University Press, 1963), pp. 20–24, 30–34.
[86] *Wolfenden Report,* pp. 23–24.
[87] Joseph Fletcher, "Sex Offenses: An Ethical View," *Law and Contemporary Problems,* Vol. 25 (Spring 1960), pp. 251–56.

a broad range of standards for qualifications as "good." Instead the law *limits* obligation. Morality relies on voluntary and general obedience, but the criminal law would compel compliance through coercion applied in a narrow sphere of behavior. In this sense the law does not build character.

In expressing their moral stance toward sex deviance, the framers of laws risk invasion of areas of private choice where the lack of a general moral consensus undermines effective legal control. A key argument for legal measures against sexual deviance is that the law's business is to protect the continued existence of society by insisting on moral conformity. However, since toleration of freedom is essential to maintaining the social cohesion of the members of the society, the application of the force of the law should be restricted to areas which arouse general public outrage. Dworkin interprets this argument to mean that a general disgust must be supplemented by a genuine threat to the survival of society before legalized punishment of the sexual deviant is in order.[88]

In the face of a plurality of values held by a wide range of subcultures within an urban society, the criminal law is a clumsy instrument for regulating morals in the absence of a common agreement on what is right. The legislator and the officials of criminal justice must thread their way through a confusion of attitudes and prejudices held by various segments of the community to determine what is *the* popular morality to be safeguarded. The variation in moral principles and the ease in concealing private behavior undermine enforcement and open the way to invasion of the personal freedoms upon which the general order is based.

In discussing prosecution for bigamy without deception, Hart suggests the latent complexity of the official interpretation of public outrage and disgust. Cohabitation with another woman by a married man is not punishable in many jurisdictions. He may set up house, distribute wedding cake, and go through other rituals of a valid marriage in an open manner; but when he goes through a ceremony of marriage, he is arrested. Why is the immorality of open sexual cohabitation ignored but official action taken when the ceremony is performed? Perhaps the public nature of the ceremony is an affront to public decency or to religious sensibility? Perhaps the confusion of public records is forestalled. Perhaps such a marriage would result in desertion or nonsupport to the detriment of the couple and the community? Hart cites the common theme that the law is less concerned with immorality than with the nuisance created by a public offense.[89]

Because the control of sexual deviance involves some of the most intimate aspects of personality, preventive measures are often more promising than the later imposition of coercive methods. Imposition of the

---

[88] Ronald Dworkin, "Lord Devlin and the Enforcement of Morals," *Yale Law Journal*, Vol. 75 (May 1966), pp. 988–92.
[89] Hart, *Law, Liberty and Morality*, pp. 38–42.

concept of legality on matters of morality exposes the system of criminal justice to its own corruption in a multivalued urban society. In invading areas of personal conduct usually left to personal choice as shaped by early socialization of personality, the agents of criminal justice are made vulnerable to the unhappy role of guardians of a moral consensus which exists only in fiction.

SUMMARY

As a primary source of human behavior, sexuality is the subject of an elaborate array of moral and legal norms ostensibly intended to make sexual behavior compatible with maintaining the established order. Social change affects the attitudes which stand between the norms and the behavior which is supposed to express the norms. However, attitudes on sexual behavior are being subjected to a remarkable rate of change. Such changes include an increased tolerance of permissiveness with affection, depolarization of sex roles, and erosion of the double standard. Apparently, fundamental trends associated largely with urbanism are involved in an evolution of new sexual standards—but short of the dramatic term "sexual revolution." Some of the effects of this evolution can be traced in a study of several forms of sexual deviance: unwed mothers, incest, homosexuality, and prostitution.

In view of the high degree of moral concern about such deviance, it is not surprising that the criminal law has been rushed in to mend what some consider serious breaks in the defenses against moral choas. Yet criminal law is an inadequate response because it is not designed to cope with the aspects of personality development and expression which are best left to the less coercive institutions of society. At the same time the new sexual codes which are emerging appear to include controls for social responsibility. Study of several forms of sexual deviance suggest that the very population of deviants provides evidence of moral adherence in opposition to pessimistic views of universal moral decay.

FOR ADDITIONAL READING

Robert R. Bell, *Premarital Sex in a Changing Society* (Englewood Cliffs, N.J.: Prentice-Hall, 1966).

Rose Bernstein, "Are We Still Stereotyping the Unmarried Mother?" *Social Work,* Vol. 5 (July 1960), pp. 22–38.

Andrew Billingsley and Amy Tate Billingsley, "Illegitimacy and Patterns of Negro Family Life," in Robert W. Roberts (ed.), *The Unwed Mother* (New York: Harper & Row, 1966), pp. 133–57.

Caroline Bird, *Born Female* (New York: David McKay Co., 1968).

Sara B. Edlin, *The Unmarried Mother in Our Society* (New York: Farrar, Straus and Young, 1954).

Cynthia F. Epstein, *Woman's Place* (Berkeley, Calif.: University of California Press, 1970).

Sidney Goldstein and Kurt B. Mayer, "Illegitimacy, Residence, and Status," *Social Problems,* Vol. 12 (Spring 1965), pp. 428–36.

Shirley M. Hartley, "The Amazing Rise of Illegitimacy in Great Britain," *Social Forces,* Vol. 44 (June 1966), pp. 533–45.

William J. Helmer, "New York's 'Middle-Class' Homosexuals," *Harper's Magazine,* Vol. 226 (March 1963), pp. 85–92.

Martin Hoffman, *The Gay World* (New York: Bantam Books, 1968).

Nora Johnson, "The Captivity of Marriage," *Atlantic Monthly,* Vol. 207 (June 1961), pp. 38–42.

Charles H. McCaghy and James K. Skipper, Jr., "Lesbian Behavior as an Adaptation to the Occupation of Stripping," *Social Problems,* Vol. 17 (Fall 1969), pp. 262–70.

Robin Morgan, *Sisterhood Is Powerful* (New York: Random House, 1970).

Albert J. Reiss, Jr., "The Social Integration of Queers and Peers," in Howard S. Becker (ed.), *The Other Side: Perspectives on Deviance* (New York: Free Press, 1964), pp. 181–210.

Karen T. Romer and Cynthia Secor, "The Time is Here for Women's Liberation," *Annals of American Academy of Political and Social Science,* Vol. 397 (September 1971), pp. 129–39.

Hendrick M. Ruitenbeek, (ed.), *The Problem of Homosexuality in Modern Society* (New York: E. P. Dutton & Co., 1963).

Edward Sagarin and Donal E. J. MacNamara (eds.), *Problems of Sex Behavior* (New York: Thomas Y. Crowell Co., 1968).

David A. Ward and Gene G. Kassebaum, *Women's Prison: Sex and Social Structure* (Chicago: Aldine Publishing Co., 1965).

Gordon Westwood, *Society and the Homosexual* (New York: E. P. Dutton and Co., 1953).

Robert K. Woetzel, "Do Our Homosexuality Laws Make Sense?" *Saturday Review,* Vol. 46 (October 9, 1965), pp. 23–26.

10 Mass communication and mass media

On the night of October 30, 1938, thousands of Americans panicked when they heard a radio dramatization of H. G. Wells' fictional work, *The Invasion from Mars.* A determined man with a shotgun guarded his haystack from alien creatures; half-dressed people rushed out of their residences in a disorderly scramble for sanctuary; mothers rushed to protect children; telephone switchboards were jammed with calls.

A study by Hadley Cantril offers some conclusions on the Orson Welles broadcast of that night which tell us something about the potentiality of mass communication media.[1] Some listeners curbed panic because they checked the fictionalized description against other information they already possessed and made an independent judgment that they were not hearing genuine news events. Others checked other radio stations, newspaper listings of radio programs, looked out the window for spacecraft, and so on. (Some of this second group, however, continued to believe that Martians had landed.) A third group made no effort to check the authenticity of the radio drama because of fright, complete resignation to their apparent fate, or disorganized efforts to escape.

Cantril suggests that the avoidance of panic was associated with critical ability, which he defines as a capacity to evaluate the drama's stimulus in such a way as to understand its inherent characteristics and then to judge and act appropriately. In this respect, certain listeners were able to

---

[1] Hadley Cantril (assisted by Hazel Gaudet and Herta Herzog), *The Invasion from Mars* (New York: Harper & Row, 1966).

250

discern details in the broadcast which did not square with other facts they regarded as trustworthy. They doubted the interpretations apparently offered by the radio actors unless they were verifiable according to the listener's previous knowledge. Critical ability alone, however, was not sufficient to counteract panic, Cantril says, because some intelligent individuals suffered panic and some listening situations were more conducive than others to panic. He finds individuals especially susceptible when they were experiencing job insecurity, had fears aroused by disasters, lacked self-confidence, or were fatalistic. Panic was more likely in situations where the fear of other persons was contagious, where the reported site of the invasion was nearby, or where the individual was separated from his usual family circle.

RELATIONSHIPS TO SOCIAL PROBLEMS

The unanticipated reactions to a radio play suggest that mass communication media hold great power over their consumers, and strong fears have arisen that men will be enslaved through today's unparalleled opportunities to reach millions of minds and stir the emotions of great masses of people through the technologies of radio, television, and the newspapers. On the other hand, the media have been described as servants of man, expanding his ideas and extending his cultural horizons beyond the range of his direct experience. Both of these views, Katz and Lazarsfeld say, draw on the same conception of mass media.[2] An atomistic mass of consumers is supposed to be ready to receive the message and to be stimulated directly and powerfully to react predictably to this presumably overwhelming force.

Intervening factors affecting response

This conception exaggerates the power of mass communication media and underestimates the influence of factors which intervene between the message and the behavior of the media's consumers. As Cantril suggests, the reactions to the 1938 radio play were influenced by the personalities of the listeners in terms of their critical ability and the stresses they felt prior to the broadcast, as well as the nature of the situation within which the broadcast was experienced. The great extent to which responses to messages are shaped by such factors rules out the simple belief that the consumer is a lump of clay to be molded as the propagandist wishes.

As an individual shaped by the beliefs of the various groups to which he has been exposed, the consumer selects from the messages those which

---

[2] Elihu Katz and Paul Lazarsfeld, *Personal Influence* (Glencoe, Ill.: Free Press, 1955), p. 16.

he deems pertinent to his needs. Within the context of his own attitudes, he may interpret a message much differently than the media manager had anticipated. The manager tailors his message to attract the interest of the consumer, and thereby he too is influenced by his own conception of the consumer's orientation to the facts and their meaning. Effective influence comes through preexisting behavior patterns or attitudes, rather than the simple manufacturing of them for the moment, as the exaggerated image of the power of mass media would have us believe.

A great many wants exist in all human beings, Seldes says, without the average man knowing the specific ways in which his wants may be satisfied. The consumer of mass communications, shopping around among the products offered him, becomes aware of a latent want when it is satisfied. A given film may draw a remarkable audience response because of the simultaneous discovery by a great many individuals that a certain want had existed. Similarly, Seldes cites the audiences for radio "soap opera" serials, broadcasts of symphony orchestras, and panels of intellectual experts. The audience for a particular film or television program, he points out, prefers it to available and competing films or programs. The "popularity" of a particular product suggests a preference among available choices rather than an expression of tastes among a full range of choices.[3]

Illustrating the linkage of the message with the consumer's preexisting environment, Davison sees at least three ways in which adjustive behavior can follow communication.[4] Some event or fact can be made known to the individual, such as death in the family or the availability of a new manufactured product. Second, the individual may be reminded of something of which he already was aware but which has particular immediate relevance. The soft-drink commercial, for example, is particularly appropriate in hot weather. Third, attention may be directed toward a new way of patterning relationships to an environment. New information motivates the individual to reassess habitual behavior. For example, driver training or a serious traffic accident may lead to reevaluation of a traffic safety appeal, causing the individual to see the safety belt in a new light.

Solving and creating problems

A central function of mass communications is the dissemination of information. Since information must be presented in some organized form and within some context, the dissemination of information involves the

[3] Gilbert Seldes, "Media Managers, Critics, and Audiences," in David M. White and Richard Averson (eds.), Sight, Sound, and Society (Boston, Mass.: Beacon Press, 1968), pp. 33–38.
[4] W. Phillips Davison, "On the Effects of Communications," in Louis A. Dexter and David M. White (eds.), People, Society, and Mass Communications (New York: Free Press of Glencoe, 1964), pp. 81–89.

WSIU-TV, Southern Illinois University (Myers B. Walker)

Technology and communications in action. Using a complex electronic technology, "News at Five" rapidly transmits to a wide audience the information essential to intelligent decision-making in a democracy.

transmission of culture. Then, too, mass communications are inevitably involved in interpretations of the discrete facts, rather than in conveying sterile and completely neutral information. News may be distorted deliberately by the propagandist to exploit a situation for the special benefit of his client—but the opposite role of a completely value-free reporter does not exist. The very definition of an event as news implies a value decision in that it has been selected from all ongoing events as being worthy of special attention. Consequently, a prominent problem of mass communications is the use of the potentiality of informational dissemination to broaden intelligent decision making among citizens in keeping with democratic ideals. Mass media contribute to the problems of urban society to the degree that their practices deviate from this general objective.

Both the rise and the alleviation of social problems is intimately related to the dissemination of information. A given condition becomes known by the significant decision makers as constituting a serious descrepancy between expectations derived from ideals and the practices found in the community. Recognition of this discrepancy and the resolve to do something about it entail possession of crucial information. Debate over choice of available solutions and the implementation of that choice requires the structuring and mobilization of public opinion in some new way. Since the debates imply fundamental disagreement with past evaluations of the undesirable condition, this process of problem solving involves the establishment of some new agreement whereby community unity can be served. The norms regulating human behavior must be reshaped if the social-psychological community is to remain to support a sense of common destiny.

The communication media are a source of problems in several respects. In times of profound change, they can indiscriminately support the interests of the obsolete status quo. Since they are profit-making enterprises, the media may advance the interests of fellow entrepreneurs, sacrificing their responsibility to the community as a whole. For commercial advantage, they may attract a large audience through sensationalism and catering to debased tastes. Finally, concentration of ownership offers possibilities for consequent abrogation of the media's responsibility. When such problems stimulate cries for censorship and greater governmental regulations, however, the representatives of the media see a problem in threats to the freedom of the press.

The conveying of information in itself injects new dimensions into a situation. The erasing of ignorance brings benefits, but it also can create at least momentary unrest. For example, in school desegregation, deep-seated customs and beliefs must be uprooted and new social standards inserted in their place if minority children are to gain the educational opportunities defined as their constitutional rights. If the internalized beliefs of cit.zens are to coincide with legal definitions, the press has a formidable responsibility in interpreting disputes.

TECHNOLOGIES OF MASS COMMUNICATIONS

In the twentieth century the technological revolution has brought forth the motion picture, radio, and television to supplement printing as a means of capturing the attention of vast audiences. Through these technologies man uses written and/or spoken symbols to affect behavior and to achieve the agreements through which the efforts of individuals can be mobilized collectively to cope with the problems they share. Do these new means of communication bring great benefits to mankind, or do they only ensnarl him in difficulties? The answer lies in how they are employed and the social circumstances within which they are employed.

"Mass" and its implications

The word "mass" suggests something about the circumstances within which the media are employed. These media are particularly useful today because they contact great aggregations of people over broad geographical areas. This population mass includes a wide variety of people who differ in personal interests, beliefs, and styles of life, and who are too numerous to experience each other personally over any reasonable period of time.

"Mass" can also refer to mass production, whereby copies of newspapers, books, and magazines, radio and television sets, and showings of a motion picture can be brought within the buying capacity of a large volume of consumers. The greater the number of consumers for a given total cost of production, the lower is the average cost per consumer.

Technologies have been developed which permit the capture of very large audiences. In 1833 Benjamin Day reduced the price of the *New York Sun* to a cent a copy to capture the volume of readers he could serve as copies spewed more rapidly from the new steam press than from the old-style hand press. By developing a continuous roll of transparent film in 1889, George Eastman served as intermediary between Thomas Edison's "kinetoscope" and today's motion pictures which attract vast audiences from the teeming populations of cities. In 1922 WEAF in New York inaugurated the selling of time, enabling advertisers to reach those early radio enthusiasts who adjusted A and B batteries to amplify the signal of feeble transmitters. The establishment of a standard method of television transmission in 1941 permitted commercial application of a series of earlier inventions beyond the offering of luxury entertainment in taverns and cocktail lounges.[5]

Important social implications emerge from the characteristics of the technologies and the dependence of their commercial exploitation on

[5] Eric Barnow, *Mass Communication* (New York: Rinehart and Co., 1956), pp. 5–9, 13–24, 30–34.

mass audiences. At a central point messages can be prepared in the form of news items, plays, documentaries, musical presentations, and so on. A group of specialists can be assembled at this central place to work as a team in carrying out a wide variety of tasks of artistic creativity, library research, production of dramas, solicitation of advertising, operation of various technological devices, and all the many other kinds of work carried on in newspaper buildings, radio and television stations, and motion picture studios.

The narrow scope of each worker's task gives the communication enterprise the qualities of a factory in that most of the employees tend to concentrate on details of a particular aspect of the total work process. Most of the workers lose touch with consumers of the ultimate product. Workers and consumers are separated by a collective enterprise identified as a motion picture corporation or a broadcasting company. The enterprise replaces a flesh-and-blood artist working for a flesh-and-blood patron. A newspaper reporter becomes more nearly a high order clerk than the colorful figure who, with his feet on the mayor's desk, dictates a story by telephone.

The organizations of mass media are expensive to assemble and operate. They survive financially because large audiences can be collected to be exposed simultaneously to messages tailored to appeal to large numbers of persons. The assemblage of mass audiences is made by appealing to those interests and tastes which are common to most individuals. In other words, the message is one directed to the lowest common denominator rather than one cultivating the interests and tastes which are unique to segments of the total population. The reporting of a bloody crime is more likely to draw widespread immediate interest than an event like the first flight of the Wrights at Kitty Hawk—which contributed to a revolution in transportation.

Differences among the media

The social and psychological impact of the several technologies differs because of difference in reliance on sight and/or sound. The reliance on only one of the senses reduces the impression that the experience is real, although all media deny the consumer the direct participation which would make the event genuinely interpersonal. Newspapers, magazines, books, and pamphlets depend solely on sight, and radio on sound. Television and motion pictures employ both the visual and auditory senses.

The printed media are a limited form of communication because they demand that the reader make the effort to read, select among various materials available, and interpret what he reads within his preexisting attitudes. The greater demand on the reader enables him to contribute his own interpretation of the message. He can select the fare and the time and duration of his reading.

In radio, voice tone and inflection give greater flexibility to communication and extend the possibility of the listener experiencing events personally. However, radio communication has greater influence than print in shaping the probable impact of the message on the consumer. Short of a tape recording, the consumer can not control the timing of the message. Through the combination of sight and sound, motion pictures and television maximize the possibility of personalizing experiences. Concurrently, the communicator has the greatest potential of tailoring the experience to influence the probable interpretation according to the communicator's expectations.

Motion pictures have certain unique characteristics.[6] They are made for a large general audience which must be physically assembled in a large number of clusters at different places but at approximately the same time. For each picture a new audience must be assembled, whereas television, radio, and newspapers have a greater possibility of a more sustained audience. Because of the time and expense required, the production of a film is more complicated than a single radio program or newspaper issue. Furthermore, ticket sales are the revenue source for films, while newspapers and radio stations depend largely on advertising, which is a revenue source less subject to the vacillations of public tastes.

Each of the forms of mass communication encourages or precludes social situations by the physical conditions they impose on the audience. Motion pictures place large numbers of persons together in the dark. Television is conducive to viewing in the home, with family and friends composing the group. The newspaper and novel are usually read alone in a place selected by the individual.

The mass media also differ in the value context within which their consumers judge them. Television viewers, Steiner reports, tend to feel guilty when they conceive TV watching as a relaxation for lazy people who should be doing something else. Reading is not so conceived, though Steiner doubts that a larger share of all printed matter than of all television is "worthwhile." The answer to the paradox may be that reading is done with greater selectivity because of greater range of choice available. Furthermore, reading requires more dedicated pursuit, and usually consumes fewer hours of time.[7]

Television can carry its messsage into virtually any location. This gives it an intrusive quality which provides special pertinence to its packaging of experience. The printed page can mold experience with words and still photographs, but television presents *events* through a combination of visual and auditory presentation of the here and now as selected by its

---

[6] Delbert C. Miller, "Motion Pictures," in Francis R. Allen, Hornell Hart, Delbert C. Miller, William F. Ogburn, and Meyer F. Nimkoff, *Technology and Social Change* (New York: Appleton-Century-Crofts, 1957), pp. 134–36.

[7] Gary A. Steiner, *The People Look at Television* (New York: Alfred A. Knopf, 1963), pp. 56–60.

managers. Selection from the overall sequence of a news happening tends to give undue stress to the sensational aspects, even though the selected portion of the film did occur. On the small screen of the television set, Fairlie asserts, a small band of straggling civil rights demonstrators appears as a disciplined army when selected aspects of the overall event are presented.[8] In this sense, the qualities of television lend themselves to the creation of news without necessarily involving deliberate distortion of the facts. Life in reality evolves slowly, and the selection of a particular phase of that evolution inevitably results in a unreal report.

FUNCTIONS OF COMMUNICATIONS

Societies exist because man is able to substitute symbols for the concrete objects or events experienced personally and directly. Through use of symbols, written and spoken language becomes a means of referring to matters outside of direct experience and of converting a confusing mass of discrete events into a logical order. Particular symbols like "mother" and "rape," for example, assume emotional overtones which shape behavior. These social functions of symbols are possible because the participants have come to attribute similar meanings to each of the symbols. In short, communication through shared symbols is the process whereby individuals become subject to the discipline which makes group life possible (social control) and whereby the society is capable of readjusting the basis from common agreements (social consensus) in face of new circumstances of life (social change).

The term "function" has a number of possible meanings.[9] Two are relevant here. In the sense of "useful activity," it refers to the fulfillment of needs in that the patterned activities of mass media constitute solutions for their consumers. Mass communication media provide information, interpretations, and entertainment for individuals. In the course of these services, the interests of society may also be promoted in terms of the second meaning of "function." This meaning refers to system-determined and system-sustaining activity. The mass media are shaped by the political, social, and economic characteristics of the American society within which they operate. For example, they operate according to the profit-seeking nature of American business firms and are exposed to the political values of American democracy. Simultaneously, the mass media are supposed to contribute constructively to the continued operation of this society.

In a fast-moving and interdependent world, both individuals and the community have special need for the rapid collection and distribution of

---

[8] Henry Fairlie, "The Unreal World of Television News," in White and Averson, *Sight, Sound, and Society,* pp. 128–35.

[9] See Don Martindale, *The Nature and Types of Sociological Theory* (Boston, Mass.: Houghton Mifflin Co., 1960), pp. 442–46.

information about events. Warnings about threats to tranquility at home and abroad are of special importance. Weather forecasts, entertainment listings, shopping announcements, financial facts, obituary notices, and so on are useful to daily living. The political system requires reliable facts if democratic decision making is to exist to any degree. By facilitating consensus and contributing to social control, mass communications provide one of the means of welding the urban population mass into the social order necessary for meeting man's needs.

Advancing community consensus

Social problems involve the evaluation of a given condition as undesirable and the mobilization of collective effort to overcome the difficulty. In these terms it is useful to define public opinion as the consensus achieved through social interaction within a group in the course of its search for a solution to a problem common to its members. Communications constitute networks for transmitting facts and opinions about social issues. Person-to-person communication continues to be of great importance among these networks, but, through their capacity to reach large numbers of people simultaneously, the mass media have an impressive role in the relationship between public opinion and social problems.

Chapter 1 cited the frequently unintentional function of deviants in providing opportunities for marking new boundaries between acceptable and unacceptable behavior when traditional norms do not fit new situations. In transmitting facts and opinions, mass media are vehicles for challenging the validity of old norms and testing the acceptability of alternative norms as the basis of a new community consensus. For example, is drug addiction a criminological or a medical problem? If this question becomes a subject for community controversy, the messages of the mass media have a potential effect on public opinion which, in turn, will influence political decisions.

Although it cannot originate a proposal for overcoming a social problem, public opinion is a barometer of the intensity of concern over an issue and of the general evaluation of competing proposals for solution. The proposal must be formulated by political leaders and/or organized pressure groups. This barometer will reflect a variety of events, not necessarily predictable, which are frequently beyond the control of any faction. Until the crucial events occur and the direction of opinion can be gauged, many political leaders are likely to delay their own commitment. Meanwhile, other leaders and pressure groups committed to a particular solution will endeavor to mold public sentiments.

In reporting life within the locality they serve, radio, television, and the press may function as agents of community cohesion. By tailoring messages to the common elements of the experience of these people, the media can mitigate conflict and promote a constructive search for a new basis of agreement among contending parties. They orient citizens to the local institutions of government, industry, religion, education, and so on. They interpret news from the local perspective as shaped by the community's unique culture, history, and social order.

The integration of communication media within the setting of a locality is illustrated by the recent rise of community newspapers in the suburbs of large metropolises. These newspapers serve local advertisers and readers in ways which would be uneconomical for the larger metropolitan dailies. They cater to the local interests of their readers by emphasizing local issues, reporting events of concern only to the immediate locality, and demonstrating loyalty to the cultural and economic values of special importance to the local readers.[10]

Social control functions

The community exists because the behaviors of individuals constitute a reasonable degree of order in advancing the interests all members are supposed to share. Social control encompasses the total span of mechanisms employed to coerce or persuade individuals to conform to group expectations. Mass media rely on the conveying of information and its interpretation to persuade consumers in an educational process. They are forces in social control through the mobilization of public opinion. When controversial issues arise, they play a part in shaping public opinion to bring collective decision concerning the nature of the problem and the proper course of action to overcome it.

The primary contribution of mass media to social control is the conveying of information. This contribution may be interpreted as either conservative or innovative. As a conservative force, mass media urge respect for the status quo and conformity to taboos which support the present social system. As an innovative force, mass media can accentuate conflict, but they also have the potential for promoting new agreements in a time of rapid change. Through acceptance of new standards as the basis for social control, the community is preserved as a social unity in spite of the effect of change in undermining the foundations of the previous order.

As a conservative force, the mass media maintain the appearance of community unity by omission of information as well as by interpreting events. In the fifties, Breed found a tendency to soft-pedal flaws in the workings of community institutions.[11] News items tended to portray motherhood, patriotism, civic "progress," and the "dedicated" physician as models. The questionable behavior of privileged individuals was likely to receive minimum comment. Policies of mass media differ among commu-

[10] Morris Janowitz, *The Community Press in an Urban Setting* (2d ed.; Chicago: University of Chicago Press, 1967), pp. ix–xi, 60–61.
[11] Warren Breed, "Mass Communication and Socio-Cultural Integration," *Social Forces,* Vol. 37 (December 1958), pp. 109–16.

nities, but Breed's description has become less accurate as a generalization in recent years. In-depth reporting of social issues has become more common in television documentaries and newspapers. In fact, some conservatives have complained about the tendency of the "liberal" press to emphasize flaws in community institutions.

Advocates of a "free press" frequently argue that mass media are inherently innovative because increased knowledge is supposed to be benefical to mankind. Defenders of the status quo reveal their own doubts when they strive to restrict access to crucial information as a means of minimizing dissension and challenges to the interests of the status quo.[12] Beyond the particular concerns of the defender of the status quo, the expansion of knowledge engenders change in itself with unanticipated consequences for social stability when the expectations of the underprivileged are raised and when new groups emerge to challenge the existing balance of power.

Television is particularly likely to stimulate social unrest, Hayakawa argues, because it is very accessible to the underprivileged.[13] Like radio, television does not require its audience to read or write. Perhaps this characteristic explains the more rapid spread of television sets among the uneducated than among educated groups. Because television can be viewed at home, blacks were able to gain entertainment without the degradation of segregated movie theaters. The heavy investment required for television stations, however, prevented one development characteristic of radio: the rise of stations catering to particular audiences. With the reliance on commercials to finance TV programs, blacks watch the appeals to whites to buy this automobile, move to that new suburban development, or have a spotless kitchen. In "babysitting" black children, television may create some black teen-agers deeply resentful of the discrepancy between the reality of segregation and the friendly, happy world portrayed by television.

From the innovative perspective, mass media may serve as an informational agent easing the transition of public opinion toward achieving a new normative consensus in keeping with new social circumstances. Community crises may involve racial conflict, opposition to school consolidation, protest against inadequacies of medical services, labor-management disputes, and so on. Overcoming of such problems frequently requires confrontation of deep-seated suspicions, established habits, and generalized fears. The mass media can be useful in preventing the community from being torn apart by warring factions. Impartial reporting can focus attention on the issues and minimize the possibility that unsubstantiated rumors will inflame passions unjustifiably. The usefulness of the latter service is in-

[12] See Wilbert E. Moore and Melvin M. Tumin, "Some Social Functions of Ignorance," *American Sociological Review,* Vol. 14 (December 1949), pp. 787–95.
[13] S. I. Hayakawa, "Television and the American Negro," in White and Averson, *Sight, Sound, and Society,* pp. 68–74.

dicated by the effectiveness of rumor centers in dampening violence in cities suffering race riots. After the disputes are settled, wounds must be healed if the unity of the community is to be regained on the basis of the new normative consensus.

By bringing deviant behavior into public view, mass media strengthen social control over individual or group nonconformity. As watchdogs over the failures of government and other organizations, the press can protect the public interest and sound alarms against threats to the well-being of the community and its citizens. Publicity itself serves as a device for mobilizing public opinion against transgressions even though the violations were known privately. When known only privately, violations are apt to be tolerated by others to avoid inconvenience and involvement, or because of personal reservations about the right and wrong of the situation.[14] When publicized, the moral lapses of the executive or political leader draw strenuous rejections from individuals who previously had regarded them rather tolerantly. Public disclosure means "everybody" knows about the transgressions, and failure to censure the violator raises questions about one's own moral stance.

MASS MEDIA AND MASS CULTURE

Mass communication media have been accused of undermining the critical faculties of their audiences and favoring blind conformism. The media manager is perched on a delicate balance between meeting the tastes of minority audiences and gaining the economic advantages of capturing a mass audience. The mass media are not directed at the intelligensia, who constitute only a fraction of the potential audience. When the size of audiences is expanded by seeking common denominators of interest, there is a risk that aesthetic tastes will deteriorate.

Deterioration versus cultural surge

In previous centuries the audience for the arts was largely confined to a selected aristocratic elite. Relatively few people were literate, and very few possessed the means to buy books, attend theaters, and travel to art centers. The spread of popular education and the emergence of the new technologies have provided an enlarged market for the arts.

The rise of the possibility for a "cultural democracy" has brought about a heated debate. Critics have lamented the debilitation of culture-bearing elites and the aesthetic values they sustain. The mass media are indicted

---

[14] Paul Lazarsfeld and Robert Merton, "Mass Communication, Popular Taste, and Organized Social Action," in Wilbur Schramm (ed.), *Mass Communications* (Urbana, Ill.: University of Illinois, 1960), pp. 499–501.

as either creators of triviality or exploiters of already existing debased tastes. On the other hand, we may be witnessing an unprecedented distribution of the fruits of a culture which previously was available only to a small elite. What is the significance of a bus station newsstand displaying a seminude woman on the cover of a popular edition of a literary classic? Are the finest products of human creativity being profaned? Are the rough equivalents of medieval peasants being lifted to an intellectual and emotional plateau beyond their grasp before mass production and mass education were developed?

As tools for mass marketing, mass communication media lend themselves to standardization of life. The traveler in search of variety may wonder why he left home. He will find the communication media exposing him to rather standardized experiences. Station identifications will change as he drives along interstate highways, but the same songs and commercials will emerge from his automobile radio. Motels offer newspapers with different mastheads but with the same illustrations, news stories, comics, and columns arranged in slightly different forms. Local theaters present the same motion pictures blazoned on marquees at home. Television conveys network fare which largely repeats the same dramatic plots and entertainment techniques. As Minow puts it: "Too many local stations operate with one hand on the network switch and the other on the projector loaded with old movies." [15]

The culture communicated through mass media, Handlin says, has displaced much of the "popular culture" of earlier days found in vaudeville, newspapers, circuses, and music of the "common" people. He finds the displaced culture has qualities missing in the fare of present mass media. Less structured, it dealt with the world experienced by its audience without imposing self-conscious realism. Through direct contacts, the popular culture encouraged a response from the audience. In the case of newspapers, the writers had rapport with their readers because both sprang from identical social environments and frequently shared common ethnic traditions.[16]

Other observers offer more favorable evaluation. Toffler sees evidence of a "cultural surge" as measured by community theaters, museum attendance, expenditures for art books and lessons, sale of classical records, and so on. He refers to the rise of FM stations offering classical music and other programs on the fine arts and the rise of educational TV stations. Even the financial problems of nonprofit cultural institutions, Toffler says, are the pains of growth, not of a degenerate disease.[17]

[15] Newton N. Minow, "A Vast Wasteland," in Reo M. Christenson and Robert O. McWilliams (eds.), *Voice of the People: Readings in Public Opinion and Propaganda,* (2d ed., New York: McGraw-Hill Book Co., 1967), p. 175.
[16] Oscar Handlin, "Comments on Mass and Popular Culture," in Norman Jacobs (ed.), *Culture for the Millions* (Princeton, N.J.: D. Van Nostrand Co., 1959), pp. 65–67.
[17] Alvin Toffler, *The Culture Consumers* (New York: St. Martin's Press, 1964).

Highbrow, middlebrow, and lowbrow

The culture of a society is experienced selectively by various groups. Analysis of the differences among the social classes of mass society have distinguished between "highbrow," "middlebrow," and "lowbrow" cultures.[18] Associated with enduring and contemporary works of art, *highbrow culture* is identified with acute penetration of perceptions and the subtlety of expressed feelings. Pursuit of truth and beauty is supposed to be the objective, not crass concern for the patron's social prestige and the artist's material prosperity. *Middlebrow culture* is identified with less originality and richness in expression and is "inferior" to highbrow culture in quality and life-span. *Lowbrow culture* offers little original creation and is impoverished in symbolic content. It is supposed to be sterile in thought and superficial in performance.

Is highbrow culture being overwhelmed by the unprecedented means for disseminating middlebrow and lowbrow culture? Theoretically, the modern communication technology permits greater dissemination of highbrow culture, but the economics of this technology requires mass audiences, which are likely to be obtained by appeals to middlebrow and lowbrow cultures. As Shils points out, the chief consumers of highbrow culture are persons in occupations requiring application of high intellectual skills. This segment of today's population, as in the past, is outnumbered among the shapers of public taste by the political and economic elites who are indifferent to highbrow culture. Since highbrow culture has always been under attack, Shils suggests the chief unprecedented threat lies in the possibility that the intellectual classes will be disintegrated by forces which are eroding the sense of community in society generally. These forces include growth of numbers, greater spatial dispersions of populations, and the fragmentation of professional specialists.[19]

Should any deterioration of highbrow culture be interpreted as a tragedy? In one sense, the answer should be yes. Appreciation of the fine arts requires cultivation of acute perceptions and a capacity to recognize distinctions in subtly expressed feelings. Appreciation of certain cultural objects can be associated with the highest qualities of the human mind and spirit. The ways of demonstrating this appreciation will differ over time as man is exposed to new conditions of life and as the means of expressing creativity are developed, but the loss of a capacity for such appreciation would be a tragedy.

However, highbrow culture may also be defined as a form of social snobbery. An in-group minority defines its standards of taste as those of "higher civilization," and this self-styled "elite" may simply exploit distinc-

---

[18] Edward Shils, "Mass Society and Its Culture," in Jacobs, *Culture for the Millions,* pp. 4–6; he uses the terms "superior," "mediocre," and "brutal" cultures.
[19] Ibid., pp. 9, 17–21.

tions between tastes to put down the groups it deems "inferior" without demonstrating valid superiority in terms of standards of appreciation. In the second sense, the erosion of highbrow culture is a false issue. A culture does not exist apart from its society. Culture is functional to its adherents, with aesthetic appreciation for its own sake included as a function. Instead of indicating a decline in the quality of artistic appreciation, the demise of a portion of the artistic heritage may signify a change in the function of the arts within the contemporary society. The crucial question is whether the dominance of a previous elite is being challenged or whether acute perceptions and subtle emotional distinctions are being lost—regardless of the social situation within which they are applied.

With increase in relative economic abundance, Wilensky believes mass taste will gradually improve as participation in mass culture is extended. However, he notes that the highbrow will be subjected to pressures toward conformity through the pervasiveness of mass communications. It will be the rare person who will be able to preserve his unique standards through insulation of himself against these pressures.[20]

CENSORSHIP AND CONTROL

Spokesmen for mass communication enterprises are usually ardent advocates of freedom of the press as fundamental to the preservation of democracy. They argue that, because a democracy must have free trade in information and ideas, the press must have a minimum of external restraint in carrying out its role of protector of freedom. Distortions of fact and other abuses of freedom may occur, but these spokesmen see the total operation of the free press as imposing a test of reason on the power struggles among the groups participating in democratic decision making. The existing government represents a coalition of such groups and the interests of administrators who would impose order for the sake of the objectives of particular programs. Without free expression of private groups, the spokesmen say, the government would protect its own interests and jeopardize the balance of power essential to democratic decision making.[21]

Demands for social responsibility

The image of the solitary, crusading editor is difficult to maintain in the face of the growth of communication bureaucracies and the great power they hold over the flow of ideas. The theory of the free press gives reason

[20] Harold L. Wilensky, "Mass Society and Mass Culture: Interdependence or Independence?" *American Sociological Review,* Vol. 29 (April 1964), pp. 173–97.
[21] See Theodore Peterson, "Why the Mass Media Are That Way," in Charles S. Steinberg (ed.), *Mass Media and Communication* (New York: Hastings House, 1966), p. 62.

for government to be reluctant to impose controls, but in addition to the power available to communication businesses, the appearance of radio and television has added a new dimension. The airwaves belong to the people, rather than being property equivalent to the production and distribution resources of newspapers. The entrepreneurs must make investments to permit broadcasting, but the use of the airwaves is a legitimate concern of the people as a whole. Furthermore, the heavy investment is justified by the economic return from advertising which ultimately is paid for by consumers through addition of advertising costs to the sales price of products.

From several sources come demands that the media managers demonstrate social responsibility in the uses made of the opportunities provided by freedom of the press and a profit-making enterprise. Pressure for censorship statutes has been applied by women's, civic, welfare, and religious organizations to safeguard children and mentally subnormal persons from corruption. Consumer boycotts have been imposed on motion pictures to influence decisions of producers. Another pressure has come from a variety of racial, ethnic, occupational, and avocational groups who contend that their people are portrayed in the negative stereotypes of gangsters, for example, or bungling professionals, irresponsible motorcyclists, or ignorant peasants. From a variety of critics come charges of frivolity, waste of time of consumers, excessive preoccupation with sex and violence, and capricious attitudes toward sacred institutions such as marriage.

The imposition of standards of social responsibility implies that the legitimate search for profits must be limited by principles that safeguard the interests of the citizen-consumers. The Commission of Freedom of the Press advances five ideals which give substance to these principles. A truthful, comprehensive, and intelligent account should be given the day's events in a context which gives them meaning. As common carriers of public discussion, the great agencies of mass communication should provide a forum for the exchange of comment and criticism. Because people make decisions in large part in terms of favorable or unfavorable images, the media should project a representative picture of the constituent groups in society. Similarly, the goals and values of society should be stated and clarified because the media are educational instruments. The demand for information for effective decision making by citizens calls for full access to the day's intelligence.[22]

Such ideals assume that mass media should provide public service and that entertainment should be a secondary function at best. Markel finds the press to be deficient in emphasizing entertainment over presentation of information and objective editorial comment. He laments scanty editorial research and self-analysis and surrender to borrowed opinion and

[22] The Commission on Freedom of the Press, *A Free and Responsible Press* (Chicago: University of Chicago Press, 1947), pp. 20–29, 52–62, 65–68.

slanted "news." [23] Steiner argues that this distinction tends to be over-drawn. While public service tends to be identified with news coverage, providing of information, religious presentation, editorial comment, and similar matters, he believes entertainment should be recognized as a legitimate function. Considering the size of the audience attracted, a motion picture based on the life of a religious leader could have greater educational impact than any sermon. Since entertainment of quality can enrich the aesthetic sensitivities and provoke critical thought, he contends that the conception of public service should be expanded to include it. [24]

Concentration of ownership

Issues of social responsibility and freedom are interlocked with trends in the ownership of media. A significant proportion of cities are served by newspaper, radio, and television facilities owned by one man or one company. A major newspaper or broadcast facility in a city often is a subsidiary within a large business organization headquartered outside the city. In addition to the influence they hold over affiliated stations, the national broadcasting networks own stations in several major cities. Conglomerates collect more than one kind of communications outlet, and may include television, radio, magazines, book publishers, and films. [25]

The trend toward concentration is attributable to a number of factors. Small communities cannot support more than one newspaper. Radio, television, and newspapers compete for the advertising dollar. Modern transportation has increased competition from nearby metropolitan papers and national magazines. Consumers demand more sophisticated products which inflate costs and the need for specialized personnel. These expenses can be borne more efficiently if a larger audience is acquired through national or regional marketing. Advertisers who provide income for the media are primarily interested in obtaining the maximum impact at least average cost. This consideration gives an advantage to newspapers or television stations which draw the largest volume of consumers because production costs do not increase at the same rate as size of audience.

It is hazardous to assume that concentrated ownership brings deficient quality and an abrogation of ethical responsibilities. Although absentee ownership encourages citizens to regard a media outlet as nonrepresentative of local interests, the absentee owner can be free of local financial and political interests. Consequently, he may be inclined to free the media managers to be objective in community controversies. The level of social conscience is a product of personal ethics rather than the exclusive quality of any particular category of ownership. Lack of competition reduces the

[23] Lester Markel, "The Real Sins of the Press," *Harper's Magazine,* Vol. 225 (December 1962), pp. 85–94.
[24] Steiner, *The People Look at Television,* pp. 241–42.
[25] "The American Media Baronies," *Atlantic Monthly,* Vol. 224 (July 1969), pp. 81–94.

pressure to sensationalize presentations to outstrip rivals in attracting audiences. Newspapermen gain relief from deadline pressure and thereby have opportunity to prepare articles more carefully and to avoid premature publication. The media managers may take advantage of relief from financial pressures against taking an unpopular stand or accepting questionable advertising. Because the media try to appeal to as broad an audience as possible, competition in itself does not guarantee responsible use of the power of mass communication.

Assessment of censorship

The censor has few friends in a democracy because he is identified frequently with loss of freedom. Censorship goes hand in hand with the politics of the authoritarian state. Regulations lend themselves to state controls intended to instill ideological conformity and to limit intellectual horizons. Much folklore portrays the administrator of regulations as psychologically abnormal.

At best, censorship operates under severe limitations. Since it functions solely to eliminate the "objectionable," censorship does not contribute to the creation of products of quality. The reliance on formal and circumscribed rules encourages evasion of the objectives of censorship by operating on the fringes of a code. Innuendo becomes a tactic of evasion which can aggravate the very conditions censorship is expected to correct. Because the "forbidden" is attractive, the censor may find he is producing audiences for the violator of the standards he is policing. The complexity and variablility of moral norms defy simple and clear statements of standards free of the private values of the censor or the special interests he represents. Subjective judgments are likely to become the criteria in administration. Then we ask: Who censors the censor? Finally, the premises of censorship tend to exaggerate the influence of mass media in originating antisocial behavior. The prohibited content is likely to reflect patterns of behavior already existent in the society at large.

Nevertheless, the operation of mass media as a business has made them vulnerable to censorship efforts. For example, a ruling of the United States Supreme Court in 1915 made that point in giving legitimacy to film consorship. Moral indignation against films in the early twenties stimulated a rash of legislative proposals for censorship, and the Motion Picture Producers and Distributors of America was established under the direction of Will H. Hayes to stem this tide through self-regulation by the film industry. The efforts of the Legion of Decency of the Roman Catholic Church then stimulated this new organization to tighten its regulations.

After World War II the Supreme Court weakened censorship boards by demanding that the constitutional guarantee of free speech and free press be extended to motion pictures. In *United States* v. *Roth,* the court ruled, for example, that the test of obscenity must be whether, to the average person applying contemporary standards, the dominant theme appeals to "purient interests." [26] The decision brought great confusion because standards of "purient interest" vary grossly from person to person, rural to urban, urban to urban, and region to region. The later *Ginzburg v. United States* decision affirmed the conviction of the publisher of *Eros* magazine on the grounds that the seller had made a "business of pandering to the widespread weakness for titillation by pornography." Here the deliberate pandering for profits intent was added to the criterion of "appeal to purient interests" advanced in the Roth case as a measure for obscenity.[27] There continue to be legal obscurities in the differentiation between the antisocial effects of hard-core pornography and the essential protection of free speech in a culture characterized by great diversity in tastes and moral values.

SUMMARY

The complexities of imposing censorship illustrates the importance of self-regulation by media managers if their strategic position in processing information is to be utilized in keeping with great social responsibilities. This position does not provide the awesome power attributed to them by conceptions of the individual as a helpless pawn of propaganda manipulators. The individual and his situation affect the reaction to the messages conveyed by the media, as do the characteristics of the particular communication technology. Nevertheless, mass communications have important social functions in advancing consensus and supporting social controls. Issues raised include whether high culture is being eroded by mass communication and how to balance freedom of the press against the social responsibilities. Mass communicators also struggle with the question of whether entertainment or advancement of the public "good" should receive priority.

FOR ADDITIONAL READING

Curtis G. Benjamin, "Book Publishing's Hidden Bonanza," *Saturday Review,* Vol. 53 (April 18, 1970), pp. 19–21, 81–82.

Ira H. Carmen, *Movies, Censorship, and the Law* (Ann Arbor, Mich.: University of Michigan Press, 1966).

Francis Chase, Jr., *Sound and Fury: An Informal History of Broadcasting* (New York: Harper & Brothers, 1942).

[26] Bosley Crowther, "Censoring the Movies," in Christenson and McWilliams, *Voice of the People,* pp. 295–301.
[27] See Richard D. Knudten (ed.), *Criminological Controversies* (New York: Appleton-Century-Crofts, 1968), pp. 81–111.

Stanley T. Donner (ed.), *The Meaning of Commercial Television* (Austin, Texas: University of Texas Press, 1967).

Stuart Hall and Paddy Whannel, *The Popular Arts* (London, Eng.: Hutchinson Educational, Ltd., 1964).

Hilde T. Himmelweit, A. N. Oppenheim, and Pamela Vince, *Television and the Child* (London, Eng.: Oxford University Press, 1958).

Nelville M. Hunnings, *Film Censors and the Law* (London: George Allen & Unwin, Ltd., 1967).

Joseph Wood Krutch, "Is Our Common Man Too Common?" in Reo M. Christenson and Robert O. McWilliams (eds.), *Voice of the People: Readings in Public Opinion and Propaganda* (2d ed.; New York: McGraw-Hill Book Co., 1967), pp. 234–42.

Carl E. Lindstrom, *The Fading American Newspaper* (Garden City, N.Y.: Doubleday & Co., Inc., 1960).

Walter Lippman, *Public Opinion* (New York: MacMillan Co., 1957).

Lee Lowenthal, *Literature, Popular Culture, and Society* (Englewood Cliffs, N.J.: Prentice-Hall, 1961).

Jack Lyle, *The News in Megalopolis* (San Francisco, Calif.: Chandler Publishing Co., 1967).

Hortense Powdermaker, *Hollywood: The Dream Factory* (Boston, Mass.: Little, Brown and Co., 1950).

Wilbur Schramn (ed.), *Mass Communications* (Urbana, Ill.: University of Illinois Press, 1960).

————Jack Lyle, and Edwin B. Parker, *Television in the Lives of our Children* (Stanford, Calif.: Stanford University Press, 1961).

Charles R. Wright, *Mass Communication: A Sociological Perspective* (New York: Random House, 1959).

Leisure and 11
recreation

An advertisement promises that a certain book offers secrets whereby the "penny-ante novice" can earn $50,000 a year by playing poker. The reader is asked his goal in poker: "Do you want to get rich, be the biggest winner in the game, gain confidence, punish another player, or just have more fun?" The book is supposed to offer a variety of tips, including how to increase an advantage so greatly that the player can break most games at will; how to avoid winning too fast; how to extract money from opponents; how to keep big losers in the game; how to practice deceit ("only in poker can you do this and remain a gentleman"); how to stimulate poor attitudes in opponents; and how to locate or create new games for bigger profits.

In attempting to entice purchasers, the advertisement inadvertently suggests value conflicts which are expressed in leisure-time activities. Becoming rich is a popular incentive in a materialistic society which blurs the distinction between business speculation and winning through gambling. A competitive society encourages a man to be a "winner" and to outdo the other fellow. Gaining confidence is important when individualism as a value requires a man to stand on his own feet in a competitive world. Having "fun" in poker is congenial to a philosophy that regards the quest for personal happiness as sufficient justification. Latent in these various justifications for poker playing is an agreement that it is worthy pursuit tailored to male tastes, sharpening analytical skills, and refreshing the fatigued and jaded breadwinner. However, opponents of poker may see it as an unworthy pursuit that corrupts morals, wastes resources earned through dedicated labor, and permits the parasitic cardsharp to exploit innocent victims. These conflicting evaluations illustrate the problem of defining the place of leisure among the social behaviors of man.

LEISURE: SIGNIFICANCE AS A SOCIAL PROBLEM

Ever since work ceased to absorb all the capacities and energies of man, recreation has been a part of human behavior. The contemporary age is unique in its potentiality for distributing a large amount of leisure to more than a small elite. Reduction of the work week without loss of productivity has combined more leisure with a high standard of living for a large proportion of the population. The spread of public education and the decline of child labor has increased leisure time for children. Medical advances have added to average life expectancy and the number of retired workers. The automobile and airplane have expanded the use of travel for pleasure, while motion pictures, radio, and television have grown to near universal popularity.

 Qualification as a social problem

It seems paradoxical that leisure should be included among social problems. After all, a critic may ask, why worry over the plight of the dilettante who cannot keep himself amused when undernourishment, disease, appalling housing conditions, and similar serious problems exist? In refutation, opportunities for leisure have been extended to a large proportion of our population, and the issues in the utilization of leisure involve behaviors beyond those of the bored dabbler in life. Prospects are offered of broad participation in the fruits of an advanced civilization or, at least, unprecedented opportunities for self-fulfillment. Leisure is thus an aspect of the "good life" which an age of abundance appears to promise.

Leisure is problematic chiefly in terms of its relevance to many of the social problems analyzed in this book. As we shall see, leisure cuts across the boundaries of economic, family, educational, religious, and other social institutions. In each of these, freedom to follow one's own inclination in leisure-time activities is a part of a trend toward greater permissiveness. Debates rage over whether this trend is toward fulfillment of the democratic ideal of individualism or a collapse into anarchy. The first evaluation makes leisure utilization a part of the study of new motivational systems to link individual and social interests under the conditions of urban life. The second evaluation arouses intense concern reflecting pessimism about the capacity of individuals to make choices consistent with their long-term interests.

The several aspects of the social problem of leisure center around a discrepancy between the expectations suggested by the idea of recreation and the limitations on opportunities to fulfill these expectations. *Recreation* has been defined as an act of experience selected by the individual during his leisure to meet a personal want or desire, primarily for his own satisfaction.[1] The definition implies that the individual has discretion to select a kind of leisure activity according to his own conception of his needs. Grazia would define leisure as freedom from the necessity of being occupied. Although freedom from the necessity to labor is included, his definition implies freedom from necessity to engage in any activity and, conversely, to substitute another activity for its intrinsic pleasure.[2]

Mass leisure in urban society

The concentrated populations of urban society provide a market for recreational programs and commercialized recreation. The recreational programs of government, private agencies, and industrial enterprises can be extensive when a sufficient clientele can be assembled to hold down the per-client cost of operations. Rapid transportation has permitted the restrictions of space and time to be overcome in assembling large groups of customers for spectator sports, cultural events, and other tourist attractions.

The benefits of urban concentrations in extending the range of recreational alternatives must be assessed, however, against the social costs of impersonality in mass packaging of experiences. The selection among, and participation in, standardized events erode the significance of leisure in meeting personal wants for the individual's satisfaction. Leisure takes on the features of anonymity, impersonality, and formalization of social relationships of urban life, although recreation is supposed to serve as relief from these very features. By accepting activities designed by specialists, the consumer risks dependence on others and their structuring of activities which by definition are supposed to be under his control.

Urbanism and the devices of contemporary technology have disrupted traditional leisure pursuits by extending the range of interests available to individuals. Spontaneous and informal neighborhood and family life enclosed a great share of leisure-time activities, and certainly there are still individuals and groups with narrow geographical and cultural horizons. But the greater physical and social mobility of urban life has deprived the local institutions of their previous control over leisure-time activities. As a facet of the increased formalization of life, the school, church, family, governmental recreational units, and character-building associations compete for the participation of individuals and groups in consciously designed recreational programs. This competition reflects the complexity of the

[1] Thomas S. Yukic, *Fundamentals of Recreation* (New York: Harper & Row, 1963), p. 5.
[2] Sebastian de Grazia, *Of Time, Work and Leisure* (New York: Twentieth Century Fund, 1962), p. 13.

The pursuit of leisure. Even in the wide open spaces, recreation can assume the characteristics of mass conformity. The impact of technology on the natural environment poses problems for management of resources in the face of competing claims.

institutional network of urban society. Further, it reflects the special difficulties of organizing leisure because by definition recreation is unstructured activity.

However, the conditions of urban life set restrictions on the expression of personal freedom in recreation. As the effects of population density begin to operate, campers in search of privacy find the public facilities packed like a subway in the rush hours. Lining up at restaurants and theaters becomes more prevalent. Recreational planning becomes complicated because certain points in space are more likely to attract consumers. Yet overloaded swimming pools, for example, are not a simple problem to be solved with more pools when construction costs and the competition for other uses of space must be considered. Studies of peak hours of use may reveal ways of changing habits of consumers.

Besides peak hours, another time pattern associated with overload is what Wilensky calls *bunching of leisure.*[3] The gains in leisure have been concentrated in long weekends, additional holidays, and paid vacations. These offer blocks of time for trips and house maintenance tasks, and are especially convenient for employers in scheduling of work shifts. The concurrent release of hordes of people, however, gives a boom-or-bust pattern to recreational enterprises.

A rich market encourages advertising, which creates large blocks of consumers and thus leads to the standardization of experience. Tourists become flocks of sheep to be herded through 9 countries in 15 days. "Native folk festivals" and one free drink at a "glamorous" night spot are part of the package. The fun and games of the summer resort can take on the qualities of a factory assembly line. Such recreational enterprises probably provide new experiences for some of the consumers, but they depart from the ideal of recreation as a diversion from the standardized mold of the urban life.

"Spectatoritis" as a problem

Critics of mass recreation see a social malady in "spectatoritis." They lament the effects on the physical well-being and the intellectual discernment of audiences watching the performance of others instead of exercising the intellectual or physical powers demanded of participants. Further, in distinguishing between the game and the spectacle, Stone suggests that mass audiences place such emphasis on winning in competitive sports that appreciation of skill and observance of rules is undermined. The game is ennobling of its players, moral through conformity to its rules, yet unpredictable in outcome because of differences in the performance of the individual players. In contrast, the demand for victory at all costs creates

[3] Harold L. Wilensky, "The Uneven Distribution of Leisure: The Impact of Economic Growth on 'Free Time,' " *Social Problems,* Vol. 9 (Summer 1961), pp. 51–52.

a spectacle wherein the skills of the players and the observance of rules are secondary.[4]

Apparently, the extent of "spectatoritis" lends itself to exaggerated estimates. In his study, Graham finds spectator activities do take up a large part of leisure-time activity, but that spectator sports were relatively unimportant.[5] Another study reports that the majority of each level of occupational prestige devotes more leisure time to nonspectator activities.[6]

Observance of an event without physical participation does not necessarily involve the passivity associated with "spectatoritis." Dumazedier speaks of the "active spectator" who is selective in his choice of events to observe and is sensitive to the nuances of the event as it unfolds. This spectator decodes the specific language of the event in a search for hidden meanings. He shares with others what he learns through assumption of the role of objective critic.[7] Dumazedier refers specifically to moviegoers, but his scheme is also applicable to the sports spectator who becomes knowledgeable in the strategy and technical skills of the particular game.

VALUE CONFLICT: WORK ETHIC VERSUS LEISURE

One facet of the problem of leisure is the difficulty experienced by many persons in detaching themselves from the work ethic which links the job with a sense of responsibility and respectable adulthood. Work and recreation are fundamentally different. Work involves self-discipline within an organization, monetary rewards as the basic motivation, a time scheduling of activities, and the necessity to demonstrate particular competencies. Recreation is voluntary, emphasizes self-fulfillment as a reward, usually involves little time scheduling, and places fewer demands on proven competency. Enjoyment of "unearned" leisure for its own sake is inhibited by guilt feelings that the pleasure is "sinful" or "wasteful" unless earned through work.

Decline of work ethic

The work ethic has as its central theme the individual's moral duty to be industrious, continuously "to earn his salt." It took a lot of hard work to clear the wilderness, put up the log cabins, build the railroads, and

[4] Gregory P. Stone, "American Sports: Play and Display," in Eric Larrabee and Rolf Meyersohn (eds.), *Mass Leisure* (Glencoe, Ill.: Free Press, 1958), pp. 261–62.

[5] Saxon Graham, "Social Correlates of Adult Leisure-Time Behavior," in Marvin B. Sussman (ed.), *Community Structure and Analysis* (New York: Thomas Y. Crowell Co., 1959), pp. 338–40.

[6] Alfred C. Clarke, "The Use of Leisure and Its Relation to Levels of Occupational Prestige," *American Sociological Review,* Vol. 21 (June 1956), pp. 301–7.

[7] Joffre Dumazedier, *Toward a Society of Leisure,* trans. Stewart E. McClure (New York: Free Press, 1967), pp. 224–28.

otherwise transform a continent into a new nation. And the harder one works, according to the work ethic, the more moral he is supposed to be. In attempting to explain the rise of capitalism, Max Weber refers to the influence of Protestant doctrine which shaped the personalities of the entrepreneurial middle class. The individual's fate was believed to be already set by God in reference to eventual assignment either to hell or heaven. How could mortal man predict which way he was predestined to go? He looked for signs that God had put him among the elect. Righteous success in this world would be such a sign. Honesty, efficient toil, and self-control were the means to success and ultimate grace. Hard work was the means of demonstrating worthiness in terms of strict self-discipline, rejection of worldly pleasures, and righteous success.[8]

In earlier times the work ethic elicited a set of motivations whereby individuals were induced to perform arduous labor, to discipline their behavior to fit in with the necessities of the overall production activities, and to acquire the skills necessary for the performance of their particular jobs. The moral righteousness of sustained and dedicated work was supported by teachings in the vein of "early to bed and early to rise makes a man healthy, wealthy, and wise." Ambition, loyalty to the employer, punctuality in meeting work obligations, and earning of the "good life" were values emphasized in the home, school and church.

Our technologies have produced a large volume of goods and services by linking workers and machines together in systems regulated by rigid time schedules. As Friedman observes, this disciplining of workers within a time schedule has had two consequences. Through accelerated production, it made possible unprecedented amounts of leisure. Secondly, more to our immediate purpose, a sharp distinction was made between time devoted to work and time not devoted to work. In premachine societies the day was not so sharply divided. Instead, abstinence from work was related to the slow cycles of cultural, seasonal, and social rhythms. With the Industrial Revolution came punctuality and the idea that time free from work is acquired by compressing the portion of the day required for work.[9]

The conditions of contemporary life lend less support to the work ethic in that they question strenuous labor, dedicated performance, and postponement of self-gratification as the behaviors whereby the individual gains control over his destiny, wins recognition of others as a worthy person, and feels a sense of personal accomplishment.[10] The supporting ideology has fallen away from the work ethic. Identification of hard work

[8] See Max Weber, *Protestant Ethic and the Spirit of Capitalism,* trans. Talcott Parsons (London, Eng.: Allen and Unwin, 1930); also R. H. Tawney, *Religion and the Rise of Capitalism* (New York: Harcourt, Brace, 1926); on the meanings of work, a number of valuable excerpts from literature are provided in Sigmund Nosow and William H. Form (eds.), *Man, Work, and Society* (New York: Basic Books, 1962), pp. 9–55.

[9] George Friedman, "Leisure and Technological Civilization," *International Social Science Journal,* Vol. 12, No. 4 (1960), pp. 509–10.

[10] Chapter 4 provides background for these paragraphs.

as *the* crucial moral value has become untenable in an economy relying on mass consumption to keep the production lines in full operation. Sales must be kept sufficient to empty store shelves by persuading customers that immediate gratification of wants is the style. In fact, advertising is dedicated to the proposition the consumers should be persuaded to develop new wants. Easy credit policies, attractive packaging, and strategies in displaying goods are designed to inflame inner desires to acquire the "goodies" mass-production technologies spew out. The incentives to buy *now* and pay later run counter to making personal gratification the carrot on the end of the stick, and this was the basic motivational strategy of the work ethic.

Compartmentalization of job experience from other facets of the employee's life may block identification of work with family, social, and political issues of the community, and other matters which loom large in the individual's perception of what makes life significant in the long run. The standardization of tasks and the minute division of labor in large-scale work organizations raise prospects of dehumanized and goalless work performance. Technological change raises the peril of obsolete skills and being shut out of the training essential to getting through the gateway to current job opportunity. Boredom, discontent, and stunted personal development can be consequences of the worker's feeling that work has no relevance to his primary needs or his gaining control over means of gratifying them.

Ambivalent adjustments

The growing ambivalence toward the work ethic exacts its toll in tensions and in moral uncertainty as to whether it is really proper to enjoy oneself. Short of a moral code which accepts recreation on its own terms, some rationalizations continue to accept the work ethic in some respect. One interim rationalization accepts the sanctity of work and argues that leisure has been earned by previous labor. A second rationalization conceives of recreation as filling a vacuum of boredom left by the absence of work. In both instances, the work ethic seeps into "free" time to abort development of a positive interpretation of leisure as an opportunity for self-realization and new experience.

Ambivalence is also reflected in a breakdown in the distinction between play and work and a trend toward fusion of play with all activities of life. With work no longer identified with virtue and play with sin, Wolfenstein sees entertainment and the capacity to please others as elements in business relations. Then, she says, we worry when we are not having fun in work because we are supposed to enjoy ourselves on the job.[11]

[11] Martha Wolfenstein, "The Emergence of Fun Morality," in Larrabee and Meyersohn, *Mass Leisure,* pp. 86–96.

As indicated by "moonlighting" to absorb released time in a second job, rank-and-file workers show little enthusiasm for greater leisure. Riesman sees them too conditioned to industrialism to abandon their identification of the job with a stable life and a favorable male self-image. Without conviction that it is feasible, he notes that leisure can be made more meaningful by increasing the demands the job places on the worker. The distinction between work and leisure would thereby be strengthened. However, realistically, Riesman sees leisure being used only as a "blotting paper" to absorb energies otherwise untapped.[12] This use is a far cry from the recreational and creative potential of leisure.

If leisure is defined broadly to encompass all activities away from the work place, Margaret Mead finds evidence that home and community service for the sake of children are gaining new emphasis as the primary interest of many couples. Here work becomes the means for a livelihood permitting achievement of satisfactions in home and family. She raises the interesting possibility that the work place may become the sanctuary from the activities of the home in do-it-yourself projects, the turmoil of the children, and the obligations to the PTA and Cub Scouts.[13] Probably other individuals center their lives around fishing, golf, church activities, fraternal organizations, and so on.

RECREATION AND SOCIETY

With growing moral ambivalence toward the work ethic, the bonds between the world of work and the world of nonwork are being weakened. Can leisure serve as some kind of motivational force to contribute toward filling any breach between an individualistic quest for self-gratification and a sense of duty for community interests? Recreation provides payoffs for the individual; he is redeemed from routine and fatigue through activities presumably expressing his individuality. These payoffs emphasize his freedom to make choices. Does his diversion from the cares of his world necessarily dilute his sense of duty to others beyond himself?

Leisure-time activities have important functions in promoting the social order. In fact, Huizinga goes so far as to trace the creation of language, law and order, art, wisdom, and science to the characteristics of play. As voluntary activity, plays differs from "ordinary life" in its value as an activity engaged in for its own sake, the necessity that the player conform to the rules of the particular game to enjoy its benefits, and its emotional satisfactions outside the bounds of the immediate satisfaction of instrumen-

---

[12] David Riesman, "Leisure and Work in Post-Industrial Society," in Larrabee and Meyersohn, *Mass Leisure,* pp. 368–72.

[13] Margaret Mead, "The Pattern of Leisure in Contemporary American Culture," *Annals of American Academy of Political and Social Science,* Vol. 313 (September 1957), pp. 11–15.

tal goals.[14] A man may go bowling for his own pleasure but concurrently he may be contributing to worker morale in his place of employment by experiencing his fellow workers in a new light. Leisure also permits the contemplation essential to penetrating thought conducive to aesthetic and technological invention. In this regard, relief from the necessity to labor for survival offers possibilities of releasing the creative energies of a broader spectrum of human beings. Finally, play has a vital part in the development of personality. As George Herbert Mead points out, play of children is a stage in self-development. As the child plays at being a parent, teacher, policeman, and the like, he learns the rules whereby he becomes a social being.[15]

Unordered use and indefinite norms

Nevertheless, the emphasis on free choice lends certain characteristics to recreational activities which complicate their mobilization to support the social order. Ennis captures these characteristics in describing leisure activities as unordered in their uses and values, as normatively indefinite, and as institutionally interstitial.[16]

Recreation is *unordered in its uses and values* because it can fulfill a variety of functions for the individual. Thereby, the use of leisure is not predictable according to a restricted number of priorities accepted by most individuals. The possibilities for choice are a welcome antidote for the pressures toward rigid conformity which are found by critics of contemporary society, but these possibilities also complicate the channeling of individual energies into paths defined by the community's leaders as socially constructive. Mercurial shifts in recreational interests are conducive to disorder of arrangements intended to derive maximum social benefits from the allocation of resources and services. Resources can be wasted when fads such as miniature golf, say, fade from popularity.

The unordered use of leisure reflects the greater priority granted to spontaneous impulses when institutionalized controls are absent. The family, church, school, and other social institutions are made up of social expectations which advance the probability that the interactions among the individuals will be patterned to benefit the group. In the course of his personality development, the individual has learned to accept these expectations as proper guidelines. If each individual followed only his spontaneous impulses (sudden, unreasoned inclinations to action), anarchy would

[14] Johan Huizinga, *Homo Ludens: A Study of the Play-Element in Culture* (Boston, Mass.: Beacon Press, 1950), pp. 6, 28.
[15] George Herbert Mead, *Mind, Self, and Society* (Chicago: University of Chicago Press, 1934), pp. 150–64.
[16] Philip H. Ennis, "Leisure in the Suburbs: Research Prolegomenon," in William H. Dobriner (ed.), *The Suburban Community* (New York: G. P. Putnam's Sons, 1958), pp. 258–62.

exist in place of the network of predictable relationships which constitute a social order. Unless each individual can reasonably predict the behavior of the other fellow, he cannot adjust his own behavior to be a part of a collective effort.

For example, spontaneous impulses related to the sex urge are harnessed by our culture to relate the sentiment of love to fidelity of a man and a woman to each other in a mystic communion. Sexual intercourse is evaluated in terms of its contribution to the movement of the participants from self-centeredness to broader emotional involvement with one another. We are conditioned by our culture to define the physical and personal attractiveness of potential spouses in certain ways during dating and courtship. Selection of a mate also involves family background, economic status, educational factors, and preferences of one's immediate social circle.

In the sphere of recreation per se, the norms regulating individuals are less definite in inhibiting spontaneous impulses. Today's greater emphasis on freedom of choice obstructs the patterning of recreational behavior into channels regularized over a relatively long period of time. Recreational behavior is channeled, but the norms are less likely to stem from recreation in and of itself than to be imported from other spheres of life such as religion, work, or education. This importation is emphasized in the idea that leisure is institutionally interstitial.

Intersects social institutions

Leisure is *institutionally interstitial* in that it cuts across the boundaries of economic, family, educational, religious, and other social institutions. As a consequence these institutions compete for the financial and moral commitments associated with leisure as a means of promoting interests other than recreation per se. Businesses try to convert recreation into a means of gaining the loyalty and increasing the productivity of workers. The church competes with commercialized recreation to woo the marginal member into full-fledged participation in church activities. Art galleries, symphonies, and book clubs strive to capture the recreational dollar to strengthen "high culture."

Values and motivations associated with other institutional behavior leak into recreation. The prevalence of the work ethic exports the tensions and attitudes of the workaday world to leisure activities to lend themes of compulsiveness and striving for perfection in bridge, for instance, or at golf. Our technological culture favors admiration of the technical efficiency of the well-drilled sports team. The hope for quick riches motivated settlement of the frontier—and now is a basis for gambling. Among the middle classes, individuals seek club membership and frequent prestigious recreational spots to cultivate business relationships.

Possibilities of ordering leisure activities

Leisure activities are unordered in the sense of relative freedom of choice. The choice is made, however, within a range of alternatives and conditions. The choice between poker and bridge is shaped by cultural standards related to social class, occupation, and history of the particular region. Poker tends to be identified as a he-man's game, and bridge with sophisticated tastes. Urban congestion imposes restrictions on such forms of recreation as horseback riding. The volume of clients imposes scheduling on bowling alleys and tennis courts. Leisure activities also compete with other obligations. The employee returns home to find his obligations as father, husband, and homeowner competing with his wish to go fishing or play golf on the weekend.

Leisure activities are unordered only in comparison with such structured spheres of life as the job. It may be possible to facilitate leisure styles which encourage individuals to commit themselves to the values binding the community together. In analysis of mass communications, Seldes points out that the moviegoer has a limited range of choices among films available for his entertainment, and his attendance at a specific film only represents his preference among the films available to him.[17] Along this line of reasoning, Berger would substitute another strategy for futile exhortation of individuals to engage only in recreation deemed "wholesome" by self-appointed moral leaders. He could facilitate the growth of those leisure styles which emerge spontaneously and which lend themselves to mobilization of the individual's commitment to the community's interests. As an example, he cites the transformation of bowling alleys from places of ill repute to respectable places for family fun.[18]

Recreation and behavioral change

Recreation is also conceived as a tool to heighten the subject's motivation to achieve some programmed goal. By converting the social environment into an apparent quest for pleasure, the organization hopes to accelerate the individual's participation in social situations designed to achieve the organization's goals. A group worker in a neighborhood center may try to bring about changes in personality and behavior of potential delinquents through sports and games that, to the boys, are forms of recreation. The school may attempt to accelerate learning through merging educational and recreational activities.

Most leisure activities involve direct relationships with other persons.

[17] Gilbert Seldes, "Media Managers, Critics, and Audiences," in David M. White and Richard Averson (eds.), *Sight, Sound, and Society* (Boston, Mass.: Beacon Press, 1968), p. 38.
[18] Bennett Berger, "The Sociology of Leisure: Some Suggestions," in John Scanzoni (ed.), *Readings in Social Problems* (Boston, Mass.: Allyn and Bacon, 1967), pp. 271–76.

The more complex and numerous these relationships are, the greater the possible influence of the social setting on the play. Then rules emerge to make common and predictable the behaviors of individuals which collectively comprise the play situation. Ethical ideas like fair play and sportsmanship become part of the emotional content. The players are assigned roles and statuses to permit orderly participation. Cooperation is essential if rivalry between competing "teams" is to be possible; therefore, agreement on ethics and roles are vital to link the sets of players into a large situation.

When the individual pursues pleasure through group recreation, he must subject himself to the rules of the group to reap benefits. Leisure activities then hold promise for keeping the individual under control by requiring him to conform to the desired ethics in order to enjoy the benefits he seeks. Under the guise of recreation, the trained worker can approach the street corner boy or the prison inmate by enlisting his own interests in a series of informal relationships which do not smack of therapy. By taking advantage of the rules of the recreational activity, the worker can utilize opportunities to gain insight into the individual's perspectives. Acceptance of the worker as a recreational participant or instructor has the possibility of avoiding the barriers to mutual understandings common among more formalized relationships between therapists and clients.

SELECTION AMIDST CHOICES

Earlier we cited elements in the definition of recreation. It is voluntary, emphasizes self-fulfillment as a reward, usually involves little time scheduling, and, compared with many work tasks, places fewer demands on proven competency. These elements imply that the individual has primary control in determining how he will use his free time. In this sense, selection by the consumer gives leisure-time activities particular potency in advancing the freedom of the individual (which is given high priority among democratic ideals).

Two perspectives for selection

Because of personal and social variables, choices among alternatives fall into grooves rather than exhibit sheer anarchy. Choices are meaningful only if alternatives exist. The imagination and resourcefulness of the individual can extend the range of alternatives, but the availability of alternatives depends largely on what the social environment provides and what the individual has been conditioned to seek in the course of his exposure to the values of his group's culture. Bowling alleys must be available and he must be conditioned to accept bowling as a significant activity if bowling is to be among his alternative choices. Therefore, freedom of choice among leisure-time alternatives is screened by a sociocultural environment. This is illustrated by the value conflicts raised by the persistence of the work ethnic, which may handicap personal adjustment to a greater volume of free time. Here the attitudes acquired from the culture inhibit the effective use of leisure in a socially and personally constructive manner.

In spite of lingering attitudes that they are somehow irresponsible and parasitic, leisure-time activities are as much a part of social and cultural behavior as is earning a livelihood. The pursuit of activities for their own sake (intrinsic ends) is as much a part of human behavior as the pursuit of activities for "practical" or "useful" purposes (instrumental ends). Since the accomplishments of man are derived from his capacity to cooperate with his fellows, it is inevitable that leisure activities will be assessed against the need for orderly relationships if society is to persist. Then selection among alternative choices assumes another dimension. Instead of concentrating solely on the gratification of the individual's wishes, leisure-time activities are evaluated in terms of their consistency with a behavioral code which is supposed to express the interests of the community.

Already we have noted that programs of recreation can entice individuals to join cohorts of clients where preconceived purposes can be attained to a reasonable degree.

The evaluation from a community perspective is illustrated by two models proposed by Winthrop.[19] *Developmental leisure* entails enlargement of the individual's intellectual, spiritual, and cultural horizons. The study of art, reading in philosophy, and comparison of the ways of peoples in other nations are examples of the enlargement of horizons. *Recreative leisure* refers to pursuits concerned at best only incidentally with enlargement of horizons. Using data drawn from several studies, Winthrop sees evidence that development of leisure has not expanded sufficiently to give cheer to those who urge that leisure-time activities increase the prevalence of intelligent citizens in a complex age, though he appears to rule out the functions of recreation in advancing the physical well-being and morale of individuals. The assessment of a particular activity as socially unworthy risks the moral imperialism which imposes the standards of an elite on activities intended to express the volition of the individual or his own group.

Wider range of amusements

Amusements are more numerous, more frequent, and more complex than they were even 20 years ago. This range of choices aggravates problems of selection, especially since individuals do not necessarily have the knowledge and capacity to make appropriate choices. Just as the growth

[19] Henry Winthrop, "Developmental Leisure Time Activity in the United States in Relation to Cultural Ideals," *Journal of Human Relations,* Vol. 14, 2d quarter (1966), pp. 267–72.

of recreational activities has been phenomenal; so too are the changes in the composition of spending for leisure worthy of equal note. The distance of travel has been extended to accelerate contacts with other cultures. Between 1947 and 1963 U.S. automobile travel increased 302 percent, and departures for oversea travel by air and sea rose 443 percent.

Various kinds of recreation may compete with one another and reflect shifts in patronage. The number of U.S. families with television was boosted by 3,500 percent, while average movie attendance dropped 52 percent. Among participation sports, the increases were 258 percent for ten-pin bowling, 72 percent for skiing, 27 percent for golf, and 21 percent for tennis. Visits to museums rose 122 percent and the number of symphony orchestras, 81 percent.[20]

Commercialized recreation

An important facet of the expansion of opportunities for choice has been the remarkable expansion of commercialized recreation. In a business-oriented society, commercialized recreation is as inevitable as the supplying of any commodity. By assembling a large group of consumers, the entrepreneur can gain the profits which are the legitimate purpose of economic activities through manufacture of products or provision of services in demand.

Numerous industries, businesses, and services depend upon recreation in whole or in part. Many thousands of people depend for a livelihood on work in parks, recreation agencies, camps, settlement houses, industrial and other institutional recreation programs, and commercial recreation enterprises. Jobs also are created through the sales of sporting goods, hobby supplies, bicycles and motorcycles, travel trailers, photographic equipment, and so on. Commercialized recreation includes a multitude of other enterprises: athletic teams, theater troupes, dance orchestras, television stations, gambling casinos, resorts, factories for sport equipment, and so on. Occupations have emerged for avocational counselors: travel agents, hotelmen, resort directors, sport coaches, dancing teachers, and so on. The use of the automobile for recreation has contributed to the development of a broad range of services. Drive-in theaters, restaurants, and motels depend on the automobile.

Expenditures for leisure affect community growth, land values, and tax revenues. Recreational opportunities are an inducement for attracting and holding residents. Therefore, industries looking for the site for a new plant consider recreational resources as one of the factors related to employee morale. Municipal parks enhance the beauty of adjacent residential areas and sustain property values. With the establishment of resorts and wildlife areas, previously worthless land has become valuable. Such developments

[20] Peter Henle, "The Quiet Revolution in Leisure Time," *Occupational Outlook Quarterly,* Vol. 9 (May 1965), pp. 7–8.

boost governmental revenue through property taxes, licensing fees, and other taxes. Commercialized recreation offers benefits in addition to its contribution to the economy through profits and employment. It relieves the taxpayer of some costs by placing the financial burden on those who benefit directly from recreational goods and services. City dwellers are provided choices in the use of leisure beyond those alternatives which may be sponsored by government, character-building organizations, and churches. Specialization in some facet of recreation enables the entrepreneur and his employees to provide a better quality of goods or services than the average amateur can provide through his own efforts. Usually the amateur would build a less satisfactory boat, plan a less satisfying tour, or play golf less capably if he relied solely on his own devices and knowledge. As a seller of his work, a person exchanges time for money; as a buyer of recreation, he swaps money for effective use of his time.

Personal and social variables

Choice among leisure activities is related to personality and to social variables such as age, sex, and social class. Havighurst believes the personality qualities of the individual are particularly crucial in determining choice. Leisure activities, Havighurst says, are one of the ways in which an individual expresses his personality needs.[21] Choice of a given form of leisure-time activity serves some purpose such as cultivation of personality growth or maintaining prestige in a particular peer group.

The personal needs of the individual are shaped by social variables. Men drawn from different social classes may share a desire for sociability or for gaining prestige among peers, but the contents of their respective recreations differ according to social variables. The upper-status man may play handball at his club, whereas the lower-class man may go bowling or to his neighborhood bar. Tastes in recreation reflect the effects of educational attainment, financial advantages, family size, and characteristics of residence. Apartment dwellers and occupants of small single-family homes must rely on recreational facilities outside the house, while homeowners may include "do-it-yourself" maintenance and gardening as a form of recreation. Graham reports that urbanites differ from ruralites in greater participation in voluntary associations and church-related activities. In spite of a common belief to the contrary, urbanites engage in frequent visiting and partying. Both urban and rural residents engage in strenuous exercise or spectator activities.[22]

In a Kansas City survey of people aged 40 to 70 years, Havighurst and

[21] Robert J. Havighurst, "The Leisure Activities of the Middle-Aged," *American Journal of Sociology*, Vol. 63 (September 1957), pp. 152–62.
[22] Graham, "Social Correlates of Adult Leisure-Time Behavior," pp. 343–46.

Feigenbaum found two major leisure styles which they define as the over-all patterning of an individual's leisure activities in kind and quality.[23] The *community-centered style* emphasizes use of theaters, other entertainment institutions, fraternal and social groups, and so on. Choices tend to emphasis practical purposes beyond leisure per se according to one's own life interests. Examples are business contacts or demonstration that the individual belongs to some prestigious group. The instrumental use of recreation to make points in the prestige game is not limited to the 40 to 70 age groups. It is predominant in the upper-middle class and upper-lower class. Working class people seldom are community-oriented.

The *home-centered style* pivots around family values. Visits to relatives, church outings, fishing trips, and television watching offer joint participation of family members. Gardening, woodworking, cardplaying, and reading are activities centered about the home. Middle-class people may choose either leisure style.

The selection of leisure activities according to membership in a particular social class, White reports, becomes more pronounced as the individual moves above 18 years of age. Inverse to level of social class is the use of parks and playgrounds, church attendance, community-chest services, museums, and ethnic-racial organizations. Conversely, the higher the class status, the higher the rates in use of libraries, home activities, and lecture-study courses. He suggests that with adulthood, the individual settles in the ways of the class to which he belongs and accordingly selects leisure congenial to his class.[24]

DIFFERENTIAL ACCESS AND FORCED LEISURE

Two paradoxes related to the distribution of leisure time justify caution against the assumption that modern technology has produced opportunities for carefree freedom from labor previously enjoyed only by the "idle rich." One paradox is that leisure is forced on categories of people unprepared to use it to meet a personal want primarily for their own satisfaction. The other paradox is that many of the persons in an advantageous financial position to utilize it effectively have the least leisure time.

These paradoxes stem partially from a failure to distinguish between "spare time" and "free time." Friedman points out that reduction of working hours has lengthened time spared from the pursuit of a livelihood, but that this spare time is not the equivalent of time available to the individual for activities of his own choice.[25] One possibility is that spare

---

[23] Robert J. Havighurst and Kenneth Feigenbaum, "Leisure and Life-Style," *American Journal of Sociology*, Vol. 64 (January 1959), pp. 396–404.
[24] R. Clyde White, "Social Class Differences in the Uses of Leisure," *American Journal of Sociology*, Vol. 21 (September 1955), pp. 145–50.
[25] Friedman, "Leisure and Technological Civilization," pp. 514–16.

time produces no free time because the individual has obligations to the family, church, social groups, and occupational associations.

Paradox in distribution

The gains in leisure have been unevenly distributed among occupations. Private nonagricultural industries have benefited especially but not uniformly. The self-employed executives, professionals, officials, and other civil servants are at a disadvantage, having longer workweeks and greater possibility of year-round employment. In his survey of "long-hours" men, Wilensky finds a third of the high-income group works at least 55 hours a week compared with about a fifth of the less affluent. He sees special significance in the wide variation in hours worked among members of respective occupational groups. Lurking under the general nature of an occupation, he sees the operation of career patterns and specific work milieux. Long hours reflect self-employment, establishment of professional practice, the drive of white-collar workers to cancel out the disadvantage of undereducation, and a preference for income over leisure.[26]

Two classes of seven-day toilers are distinguished by Gunther. The *homogenizing toiler* takes the office home with him and continues to focus on his specialized work career without regard for his family roles. Saturday and Sunday find him engaged in the same activities as the rest of the week. The *variegating toiler* continues to work but at different tasks. He is the "moonlighter," who may actually need additional income from a second job, though the desire for luxury items or amassing of a surplus for sake of security may be the explanation. Nevertheless, there is the probability that commitment to the work ethic has deprived him of contentment in activities other than work.[27]

In a study of professors, advertising men, and dentists, Gerstl reports leisure activities were influenced by the tempo of the occupation. The workhours of the professor are extended by tasks he can perform at home, whereas the dentist cannot perform his tasks there. Although crises occur, the adman has little spillover of office tasks. Professors are remarkable in their absence of expressed desire for relaxation and sports activity. They have little interest in "do-it-yourself" hobbies, a prime interest among dentists. Admen illustrate a vocational orientation in a preference for painting and authorship. Membership in voluntary associations is highest among dentists and lowest among professors, while the daily routines of the admen give them the greatest opportunity to combine recreation with business activities.[28]

[26] Wilensky, "The Uneven Distribution of Leisure," pp. 37–45.
[27] Max Gunther, *The Weekenders* (Philadelphia, Pa.: J. B. Lippincott Co., 1964), pp. 47–56.
[28] Joel E. Gerstl, "Leisure, Taste and Occupational Milieu," *Social Problems,* Vol. 9 (Summer 1961), pp. 79–81.

Among industrial workers, the drive to reduce workhours is related to a desire to be regarded as human rather than an adjunct to machinery. However, without means of using leisure, the further reduction of work-hours draws less enthusiasm. With the rise of commercialized recreation and other consumer tastes requiring money, workers are likely to choose more income when it is offered as an alternative to more free time. Second jobs become more prevalent when payments on the house, automobile, or luxuries stimulate a desire for more money, since workers usually fail to show the postponed gratification and planning foresight of the middle classes. Only a few use increased leisure to prepare themselves for more favorable jobs or to engage in education. Leisure is spent with the family or "with the boys." [29]

Inferior access to creative leisure

With increased ambivalence toward the work ethic, having access to leisure activities is gaining attention as the mark of difference between men and beasts of burden. As indicated by the earlier definition of recreation, access implies freedom to meet a personal want or desire, primarily for one's own satisfaction. Furthermore, the definition implies freedom from necessity to work.

The distinction between "spare time" and "free time" suggests that denial of an adequate income undermines the arbitrary identification of abstinence from employment with the freedoms essential to full-fledged access to creative leisure. Barriers to participation in the labor force make enforced spare time a problem for the involuntarily retired, the intermittently unemployed, and the chronically unemployed. Here the social problem of compulsory leisure is related to occupational obsolescence, involuntary retirement, age discrimination in hiring, and a decline in the number of jobs tailored to older workers. Seasonal and cyclic industries favor underemployment. Unskilled and semiskilled workers are particularly vulnerable to layoffs and loss of jobs through technological change. Wilensky notes the paradox that men with high productivity may work longer hours partly to support the enforced leisure of men in jobs made obsolete.[30]

Ideally, creative leisure involves people in self-sustained activities through their own volition. However, many people lack the psychological capacity to utilize leisure suddenly made available. A prime example is the difficulty of some persons to detach themselves from the work ethic when they retire from their jobs. The sudden break in the familiar rhythm of life based on the job necessitates the filling of a time void with unfamiliar

---

[29] Robert S. Weiss and David Riesman, "Some Issues in the Future of Leisure," *Social Problems,* Vol. 9 (Summer 1961), pp. 79–81.
[30] Wilensky, "The Uneven Distribution of Leisure," p. 47.

activities or activities previously peripheral to the individual's interests. Unless he has developed plans and resources for this unprecedented leisure, the retired worker is cast in the status of a novice, even though he is in the senior years of life.

Probably the greatest irony is the spare time available to inmates of prisons and mental hospitals. As public charges they have relatively little choice in employing the unused time forced upon them. Typically, prisons lack sufficient industries to provide meaningful work for inmates. Educational and organized recreational programs of reasonable quality are available in some correctional institutions to lend some point to confinement, but subterranean gambling, alcoholic binges, and bull sessions about crime usually occupy a large portion of spare time. Too frequently, "museum wards" in mental hospitals rely on television for "baby-sitting." The major barrier to constructive use of this enforced leisure in most custodial institutions, however, is the lack of basic connection of the inmate with the family and employment settings dominant in the community which, presumably, he is being prepared to rejoin. In this regard, the use of enforced leisure usually has no relevance to the enrichment of the individual.

From another perspective, access to creative leisure involves status in aspects beyond recreation per se. The self-defined elite strives to insulate its style of life against groups it regards as socially inferior. By retaining control over who is permitted access to prestigous recreational facilities (such as resorts or social clubs), the elite endeavors to strengthen the sense of belonging among its own members. In the case of the civil rights campaigns of minority groups, the denial of access to public parks, theaters, and restaurants has been identified with discrimination. Thereby, access to opportunities for creative leisure becomes symbolic of full participation in a free society.

SUMMARY

Leisure for greater proportions of the population in a triumph of contemporary technology. This development might provide an unprecedented opportunity for fulfillment of human aspirations, but serious issues center around the difficulties of detaching ourselves from the work ethic to enjoy the freedom of leisure without eroding the social order. Among aspects of the broad social problem of leisure are the difficulties of selecting intelligently among alternative uses of spare time. Another set of questions centers around the differential access to leisure among groups. Furthermore, availability of unused time is not necessarily an opportunity to meet a personal want primarily for one's own satisfaction. The sociological characteristics of leisure-time activities set limits on the possibilities of meeting these problems of leisure and of using recreation as a tool for changing behavior to deal with other social problems.

FOR ADDITIONAL READING

Cleveland Amory, *The Last Resorts* (New York: Harper & Brothers, 1952).

Roger Caillois, *Man, Play, and Games,* trans. Meyer Barash (New York: Free Press of Glencoe, 1961).

Reynold E. Carlson, Theodore R. Deppe, and Janet R. MacLean, *Recreation in American Life* (Belmont, Calif.: Wadsworth Publishing Co., 1963).

Donald Clemmer, *The Prison Community* (New York: Rinehart & Co., 1958), Chapter 9.

Herbert Gans, *People and Plans* (New York: Basic Books, 1968), Chapter 9.

Paul Hollander, "Leisure as an American and Soviet Value," *Social Problems,* Vol. 14 (Fall 1966), pp. 179–188.

Roger Kahn, "Money, Muscles—and Myths," in Eric Larrabee and Rolf Meyersohn (eds.), *Mass Leisure* (Glencoe, Ill.: Free Press, 1958), pp. 264–68.

Walter Kerr, *The Decline of Pleasure* (New York: Simon and Schuster, 1962).

George A. Lundberg, Mirra Kamarovsky, and Marie Alice McInery, *Leisure: A Suburban Study* (New York: Columbia University Press, 1934).

Don Martindale, *American Society* (Princeton: N.J.: D. Van Nostrand Co., 1960), Chapter 18.

Borje Saxberg and Edward Grubb, "Self-Actualization through Work or Leisure?," *Business Quarterly,* Vol. 32 (Spring 1967), pp. 28–34.

A. W. Zelomek, *A Changing America: At Work and Play* (New York: John Wiley & Sons, 1959).

12 Schools and community problems

A teacher asked her class of ninth-grade boys why they refused to read the English literature she assigned. As reply, the boys insisted that the books were "phony."

"Phoniness," Fantini and Weinstein explain, meant one-dimensional characters, unbelievable situations, and dialogue with little, if any, connection with the reality of these children.[1] They describe an *antiseptic curriculum* in which textbooks are likely to depict as reality happy, neat, wealthy, white people in intact and loving families residing in clean, grassy suburbs. There is no crime, practically no disease, and seldom a crisis beyond loss of a pet. In effect, these texts ignore what is disliked in life. In the *nonessential curriculum* children memorize the order of American presidents but are presented few facts on the environments of employment and family life with which they will have to adjust themselves in reality. The school avoids helping the pupils with matters of real concern to them. The *remote curriculum* fails to show the student the relevance of history and nutrition to their lives. The school avoids utilizing what the pupils already know.

These criticisms illustrate the discontent being expressed over the performance of institutions of education. It is not surprising that schools should be criticized. As one of the fundamental social institutions, education is patterned and linked to traditions inherited from the past; the

[1] Mario D. Fantini and Gerald Weinstein, *The Disadvantaged: Challenge to Education* (New York: Harper & Row, 1968), pp. 124–46.

schools contribute to the stability of society and, thereby, resist change. Schools are populated by human beings whose frailties produce discrepancies between expectation and performance, and because the school is assigned grave responsibilities in urban society, its faults are particularly visible.

The criticism of "phony" courses is particularly significant in that it is now regarded seriously. The criteria by which the school is evaluated have become more demanding. Terms such "relevance," "sensitivity," and "cultural deprivation" suggest a testing of the school and its teachers with an intensity reflecting a higher level of expectation. The place and function of schools in urban society have gained enough importance to produce this demanding evaluation. This chapter will consider the implications for elementary and secondary schools, Chapter 13 for colleges and universities.

URBANIZATION AND EDUCATION

The pace and social consequences of urbanization pose critical problems for education. After World War II rapidly increasing school enrollments aggravated the shortages of competent teachers and of classroom space. Even more significant, questions about the quality of education are raised by the heterogeneity of urban populations and the demands for a diverse and well-trained labor force.

Urbanization has brought a major dilemma: With diverse populations concentrated in relatively small geographical space, how can a sense of community be engendered that will link the individual responsibly to the overall social organization upon which he is functionally dependent but from which he is psychologically distant?[2]

Whether prepared or not, the schools have been singled out to provide answers. Education is supposed to bring common agreement in beliefs and attitudes among graduates who had come to the schools from many subcultures and stations in life. Furthermore, schools are ideally expected to pass on the various kinds of knowledge and develop the various skills essential to keeping the intricate social machinery of the city operating.

Place among urban institutions

The modification of the setting of family has placed new responsibilities on the school as an agent for socialization. Migration to cities has given even the rural school a greater responsibility to prepare the individual child for adjustment as an adult to values not integrated within his present life.

The school is supposed to prepare children for a world characterized

[2] See Chapter 3.

increasingly by large-scale and impersonal organizations. At the same time, the organization of schools themselves has been exposed to growing populations of pupils and staffs; the schools are thus confronted with the difficulties of adjusting bureaucratic strategies to activities that are supposed to give special recognition to individual differences. In transmitting the cultural heritage and in shaping the personality of the young, the school serves as an interdependent element within the network of urban institutions. To promote the possibility that social relationships are orderly as a whole, the school is supposed to operate in a fashion consistent with society's other institutions: employing organizations, elements of the criminal justice system, welfare organizations, and so on.

Increasingly, elementary and secondary schools are expected to build a foundation of attitudes and skills which will prepare the young to enter a job market experiencing great technological changes. The school occupies a crucial position as gatekeeper to social and economic opportunity, with awesome potential in determining who gains rewards and whether the graduate will be prepared to assume the responsibilities he acquires. Rather than indoctrination of pupils in moral principles, the influence of the school on the life chances of its graduates rests on the functions of gatekeeper. In a large-scale society dedicated to democracy, this sifting and preparation of human resources is of primary importance to both individuals and the society.

With increased proportions of teen-agers in the high school, the social system of the high school becomes a force in setting off this age group from other age groups as being in a marginal status. Compulsory education is a facet of the school's responsibility in either preparing adolescents for adult roles in a complex urban society or in temporarily protecting adults from competition from youth.[3] In the former sense, the school has become a more important center of adolescent socialization and of coordination with colleges and prospective employers.[4]

In the latter sense, some critics have questioned compulsory education. Mead doubts that *vertical transmission,* the passing on of "tried and true" knowledge, is sufficient in an age requiring very rapid integration of new knowledge into the cultural content being passed on in schools.[5] She would break the monopoly of the school to bring all facets of life into a *lateral transmission* of all information which has just been discovered. Children would receive "primary education" to enable them to be fully human, but "secondary education" would spill over into all experiences beyond the boundaries of the school.

[3] See Chapter 8, p. 201.
[4] John I. Kitsuse and Aaron V. Cicourel, "The High School's Role in Adolescent Status Transition," in B. J. Chandler, Lindley J. Stiles, and John I. Kitsuse (eds.), *Education in Urban Society* (New York: Dodd, Mead and Co., 1962), pp. 75–77.
[5] Margaret Mead, "A Redefinition of Education," in Kalil I. Gegi and James E. Meyers (eds.), *Teaching in American Cultures* (New York: Holt, Rinehart & Winston, 1968), pp. 166–72.

Compulsory school attendance, Friedenberg argues, is no guarantee that the individual pupil will be benefited by acquiring particular competence or occupational benefits. He raises the question of whether or not compulsory school attendance is a violation of civil liberty.[6] Goodman takes an even more extreme position to deny that universal literacy is essential. He sees literacy being used to maintain an "artificial" demand for products of mass production—a demand fed by advertising and mass communication media. Furthermore, he says, illiteracy would make regimentation of people more difficult.[7] His position suffers from the same weakness inherent in the argument that technological innovation should be abolished.[8] To eliminate the adverse consequences of universal literacy or technological innovation, mankind would be denied the benefits each holds.

Technology and education

Industrialization has been an important force in reshaping the environment within which the school must meet its greater responsibilities in sifting and educating its pupils. Labor demands have shifted from physically arduous, unskilled occupations toward jobs requiring higher levels of skills. Goods-producing industries take a declining share of total employees. Service jobs, including trade and government, represent a greater proportion of the labor force. The growth of professional and other white-collar occupations has been particularly marked, and the fastest expanding occupational sectors typically require the highest degree of education and training.[9]

Today's job market provides a broadening range of occupations and demands formal training to a greater degree than in the past. The selection of an occupation has become a vital decision for ambitious youth. Embarkation upon a comparatively long course of training is likely to narrow the possibility of withdrawal from prior choice the further the individual proceeds along the training route. If he does not accept the rigors of training, he is apt to be confronted by sharply delimited job opportunities in later life. His choice and the availability of appropriate training rest in large measure on the quality and range of educational programs available in his community. Because of increased population mobility, his native community (where he receives his education or training) is less likely to be the site of his adult life (where his vocational competence is tested). Thereby, the individual and the national economy are penalized by any serious discrepancies in the quality of educational or training programs between

[6] Edgar Z. Friedenberg, "An Ideology of School Withdrawal," in Daniel Schreiber (ed.), *Profile of the School Dropout* (New York: Random House, 1967), pp. 11–12.

[7] Paul Goodman, "The Universal Trap," Schreiber, pp. 33–34.

[8] See Chapter 4, pp. 94–96.

[9] Herbert Bienstock, "Realities of the Job Market for the High School Dropout," in Schreiber, *Profile of the School Dropout,* pp. 101–25.

his native and adopted communities. Inadvertently or by design, the school polices the social class system of technological society by including individuals and groups among those granted access to opportunity, or by excluding them from the "social elevator."

The training function of education has given it a vital place in modern technological society, but the expanded functions of the school may also be attributed to other consequences of industrialization. Social reforms associated with industrialization resulted in abolition of child labor; the idle children have been diverted to public schools. Contemporary technology requires that the unskilled and many of the semiskilled be reeducated and retrained to fit a dynamic labor market. Without skills in reading, writing, and use of numbers, the individual is handicapped in handling job skill training. The contemporary mass production economy depends on mass consumption; advertising is a major strategy for cultivating new wants and channeling consumption to suit a mass market; and universal literacy thereby becomes a prime prerequisite for successful operation of the contemporary economy and for regulating behavior within a large-scale society. Cybernation raises important issues about the power of the individual in a machine age and how to make complex systems serve the human being. Resort to democratic political processes to cope with such issues requires intelligent, informed citizens.[10]

Technology also has potential for developing tools for education; new educational media include films, filmstrips, language laboratories, tape recorders, teaching machines, and television. The claimed benefits are lower costs of instruction or improved quality of instruction by enabling the pupil to move at his own pace, to follow his own interests, or to permit him the services of a teacher able to concentrate on the interpersonal aspects of teaching.[11] Technology has been a facet of innovative programs which have restructured the school through team teaching, regrouped pupils for greater flexibility in instruction, reordered the use of space, changed course scheduling, and permitted more specialization of teachers. However, "innovative" programs have suffered from expediency, lacked sound psychological principles, avoided reorganization of the school as a social system, and failed to adapt curricular content to the technology. Dehumanized instruction for the sake of cutting costs undermines the effectiveness and prestige of teaching.[12]

[10] See: Chapter 4, pp. 100–101; and Alice M. Hilton, "Cybernation and Its Impact on American Society," in Paul W. F. Witt (ed.), *Technology and the Curriculum* (New York: Teachers College Press, Columbia University, 1968), pp. 1–33.

[11] Philip W. Jackson, "Technology and the Teacher," in H. Thomas James et al., *The Schools and the Challenge of Innovation* (New York: McGraw-Hill Book Co., 1969), pp. 137–42.

[12] Paul Saettler, *A History of Instructional Technology* (New York: McGraw-Hill Book Co., 1968), pp. 355–59. (Recently private enterprise has entered the field of public education to apply "performance contracting" through technology to classroom instruction. See James A. Mecklenberger and John A. Wilson, "Learning C.O.D.—Can the Schools Buy Success?" *Saturday Review*, Vol. 54 (September 18, 1971), pp. 62–65, 76–79.)

INVOLVEMENTS IN SOCIAL PROBLEMS

Since elementary and secondary schools are an important aspect of the local community, they are thrust into controversies of special concern to the local residents. Some issues overlap into educational affairs because school segregation is linked with residential segregation and because education is basic to access to job opportunity. Other issues are more exclusively educational matters of curriculum changes deemed by some groups to be essential to contemporary conditions, of difficulties in financing schools, and of proper functions for the school as a fundamental institution within the community. Regardless of the particular controversy, widespread and intense concern for the young accentuates interest in the school.

Difficulties from external sources

The characteristics of American education and the expectations applied to its operations color the social problems with which it is associated. Elementary and secondary education is universal, comprehensive, and local. Schooling is supposed to serve everyone and to enable any person to achieve the level of education dictated by his ability or inclination. A variety of programs is supposed to provide an appropriate education for every pupil. The schools are expected to be comprehensive in providing curricula ranging from college preparation to trade training. The control and financing of education is complicated by its emphasis on localism and the traditional American suspicion of centralized authority. Thereby, schools suffer from the organizational dilemmas of urban society in terms of the crisis of the central city, the fragmentation of local government, and urban sprawl into the suburbs.[13] Comprehensiveness of educational programs and localism, in combination, add to the diffusiveness of educational goals.

The school has paid a price for insufficient planning to handle the population growth and redistribution of people into urban centers and from the central city into the suburbs. Now schools and individual teachers face the prospects of a declining rate of population growth. Already graduates of colleges of education are experiencing difficulties in finding jobs in a reversal of the earlier demand for more teachers to handle burgeoning pupil populations. What will be the eventual adjustment to a lower rate of gross population increase? Forecasts are hazardous when a general trend is in its early stages, but migration patterns and differential birth rates will surely produce a variety of situations among school systems of the nation. Some school districts will require more buildings and larger staffs; some school buildings will be in excess of enrollment demands. Perhaps

[13] See Chapter 3, pp. 80–87.

easing of the enrollment pressure will bring measures to improve the quality of education in keeping with efforts to eliminate the cultural deprivation associated with poverty and various forms of social discrimination. Since the American population crisis is defined in terms of threats to the standard of living, such efforts would be consistent with the movement toward a welfare state.[14]

In the United States the schools have been assigned a major share of the responsibilities of "Americanizing" the diversity of people immigrating into its society. Similar responsibilities are involved in the assimilation into urban culture of a diversity of internal migrants and in the inculcation of a sense of community among the heterogeneous groups who populate the cities. The content and range of educational programs have reflected the increasing specializations within the larger urban culture. The ghetto crisis has been added to the range of problems reflecting factors beyond the control of the school. The exodus of the middle class to suburbia has intensified the problems of education in the central city as resources have been diverted into the suburban schools and away from the central city schools. The more attractive schools and higher salaries in the suburbs have aggravated the diversion of experienced teachers away from central city schools where superior teachers are particularly required.

Local control has given American education the appearance of a crazy quilt at a time when the broadening scale of urban social structure calls for organizational symmetry if educational experience is to be comparable throughout the nation. Although the right of a local community "to run its own school" has been vigorously defended, the insufficiency of local tax resources stimulates a search for outside help. The cities have depended on state funds to meet escalating costs—and hence have been penalized by the rural dominance of many state governments.

The development of nationwide patterns in education has been promoted by insistence on minimum standards to qualify for federal funds, the use of standardized tests to assess applicants to colleges, introduction of new programs in science and mathematics, and criteria employed by regional accrediting associations. Localism has raised mixed feelings about federal financial assistance. In addition to suspicion of centralization of control, the issue of federal aid is linked with opposition to racial integration, assistance to parochial schools, and resistance of wealthy states to "subsidizing" the less fortunate states.

Maintaining social stability

The school is a *people-processing institution* in that its output is knowledge, skills, and the like, rather than tangible products. As an institution,

---

[14] For discussion of the American population crisis, see Chapter 5, pp. 119–20. The welfare state and cultural deprivation are discussed in Chapter 6, pp. 145–49.

it is supposed to contribute to the continuity of society by transmitting the cultural heritage and shaping individual personalities to promote their adjustment to the social framework. Being an institution, the school reflects the society as it is. Thereby, it has potential for being a conservative force. For example, the operations of the school can be such that the inequities of social class and racial stratification can be maintained through differential distribution of learning opportunities or through the messages conveyed to children inadvertently by attitudes of staff, or deliberately through design of curricula. Through indoctrination of pupils, the school can mold attitudes and select among kinds of knowledge it provides to retard change and to encourage forms of conformity in favor of the status quo.

The most prevalent rationale for heavy public investment in education is to help the individual improve his life chances. However, the interests of the state are at least equally important. In analyzing the debates at 37 constitutional conventions, Garber identifies ideological themes in justifications offered for the state investing in education.[15] One theme was that public education is essential to the political health of the state through cultivating responsibility of the electorate. Other themes linked the economic well-being of the state with public education: Migrants and investment capital would be attracted; work productivity, habits of thrift, and moral virtue were supposed to be enhanced. But the desirability of creating a disciplined citizenry and motivated work force risks the possibility of indoctrination in the particular values of a socioeconomic elite if provision is not made for the varying interpretations existing within a multivalued democratic society.

Educators are agents of cultural indoctrination in that they have a key responsibility for transmitting the knowledge, norms, and skills deemed essential to the continuity of the society. They share this responsibility with the family and the church. In recent times mass communications have risen as an important additional agent. The school, however, bears the largest responsibility. The teacher's job is complicated by the vagueness with which goals are set and by the range of pupil readiness to respond to the school's cultural orientation. The teacher is told to teach "good citizenship," to develop "high ideals," and to inculcate a sense of "high moral values." The implementation of such highly general objectives is pregnant with the possibility of moral imperialism.

School as problem solver

More and better schooling are among the major strategies advocated for alleviating society's difficulties and individual maladjustments. Cremlin

---

[15] Lee O. Garber, *Education as a Function of the State* (Minneapolis, Minn.: Educational Test Bureau, 1934), pp. 4–9.

quotes the wry remark of a friend: "In other countries, when there is a profound social problem, there is an uprising. In the United States we organize a course." [16] In light of the social unrest and demands for reform of the last decade, this observation is not quite as apt as it was, but faith in education as a primary answer still remains.

Usually the school is conceived of as simply dispensing cultural orientations, information, and knowledge developed outside the school. The knowledge explosion has thrust upon educators the responsibilities of incorporating new facts and ideas into the content to be transmitted to the rising generation, however, and today's school curriculum also reflects the perspectives of decision makers outside the school system. (Since culture is inevitably selectively transmitted by persons in closest contact with the learner, however, the teacher influences the interpretations acquired by pupils.)

To be effective in innovation, teachers must require allocation of tasks within a program based on goals and means provided by leaders of the total society. Usually, education is controlled by the more conservative elements of the community, and it is certainly true that it can be used as much to prevent change as to create change. Necessarily, therefore, forces external to the school must support the advocated changes and, for this reason, educational innovations come largely as a response to crises external to the school and to organized pressures outside the field of education.

Although educational deficiencies are characteristic of the underprivileged segments of the population, the popularity of education as a strategy of social reform is not always justified. Raising the level of the young has possibilities of improving their life chances, but it has little significance for the older person shut out from labor force participation. And reform based on educational programs raises great difficulties in implementation; that is, redistribution of resources is resisted because of other considerations also given high priority. For example, schools have reason to encourage the economically more privileged pupils with exceptional talent, and experienced and able teachers must be diverted from activities they may find worthy and satisfying if personnel is to found to carry out the new "reform" programs. Nor does higher educational attainment guarantee that discriminatory practices will cease to handicap the underpriviliged. Finally, as implied previously, the educational system itself is a conservative force and has difficulty in revising its use of familiar criteria in its status-sifting function. [17]

[16] Lawrence A. Cremlin, *The Genius of American Education* (Pittsburgh, Pa.: University of Pittsburgh Press, 1965), p. 10.

[17] S. M. Miller and Pamela Roby, "Education and Redistribution: The Limits of a Strategy," In Robert L. Green (ed.), *Racial Crisis in American Education* (Chicago: Follett Educational Corporation, 1969), pp. 45–55.

Because of the complexities of teaching and learning within a consciously created organization, Schaefer believes that the school must be a producer as well as transmitter of knowledge. In light of the expansion of educational responsibilities, more must be discovered about the mysteries of human learning and the means of internalizing intellectual values. Schaefer argues that lower schools must join the universities in reducing these mysteries for the sake of intellectual health of teachers and improved direction of educational activities. He calls for the drastic reduction of teaching loads and student class time, raising of the authority of the teacher in the school's decision-making process, and recognition that mere administrative tinkering is not the equivalent of educational innovation.[18]

When envisaged as an instrument for overcoming social problems described collectively as the "urban crisis," the school is likely to be expected to tailor educational policies and practices to the needs of the metropolitan community as a whole. The orientation differs from the conception of the school as an autonomous social system. First, it recognizes that the schools are part of a total institutional structure; educational issues are considered to be interrelated with community issues. Second, the urban school is part of a social system extending beyond the district boundaries.

The urban community school has been distinguished from the neighborhood school.[19] The *urban community school* reflects a philosophy that calls for it to be a constructive force in involving parents and citizens in framing school policies and in resolving social issues concerning the school. It takes active part in reshaping and renewing the urban community by adopting appropriate educational policies. In contrast, the *neighborhood school* has traditionally taken a more passive role, reflecting the characteristics of the more narrow geographical area it serves. It draws pupils from an area within a few minutes walk between home and school. Its identification with the immediate neighborhood makes it useful in maintaining racial and social segregation in the guise of protecting the sentimental value of neighborhood.

Havighurst and Levine cite the parallels between improvement of metropolitan government generally and improvement of the structure of the urban educational system.[20] Both require development of decentralized but coordinated subregions to strengthen metropolitan organization, regardless of more local political boundaries. The multiplicity of school districts is an important aspect of the fragmentation of metropolitan government, and the problems of the inner city and racial discrimination

[18] Robert J. Schaefer, *The School as a Center of Inquiry* (New York: Harper & Row, 1967), pp. 1–2, 60–69.
[19] Robert J. Havighurst and Daniel U. Levine, *Education in Metropolitan Areas* (2d ed.; Boston, Mass.: Allyn and Bacon, 1971), pp. 126–31.
[20] Ibid., pp. 199–201.

require the schools to take a lead in reformation of social attitudes and strengthening a sense of community.

ORGANIZATIONAL ASPECTS OF EDUCATION

In the school, learning takes place within patterned relationships, within the authority and decision-making structure of the school, and within a population of students and teachers who constitute a kind of sample of the population of the community. In these ways the school should be a model of the community it serves if its activities are to be pertinent to the conditions of life the graduates will subsequently encounter. But schools will have to come in varying types in a large-scale society characterized by a range of subcultures and differing social circumstances among communities.

Fundamental organizational dilemma

As a part of the institutional structure of the community, the school is supposed to support the socialization function of the family, prepare children for adult roles in industrial and political institutions, and prepare some children for movement into institutions of higher education. At the same time, the school is expected to place special emphasis on individual differences among the pupils and thus lend a personal quality to the schooling experience.

In studying the place of the school in the institutional structure, the organization of the school is evaluated according to the consistency of its policies and procedures with the needs of other institutions. Do its graduates become "good" parents, "efficient" employees, and "responsible" citizens? Are they prepared to be successful in higher education or in further vocational training? Are the local schools organized so their activities are sufficiently consistent with the practices of schools in other communities to comprise (to a reasonable degree) a national educational system in an age when large-scale urban society has eliminated much of the social significance of local political boundaries?

Earlier we noted that local control of schools has produced such great diversity that it is very difficult to characterize *the* American school *system*. The fragmentation of education poses organizational problems of finance and comparability of programs. However, paradoxically, local control also involves centralized authority at this level of government. This centralization raises the possibility that the pathologies of bureaucratic administration will breed inertia when reform is urgently demanded and will breed impersonality and standardized practices in an organization which claims to regard pupils as unique personalities.

With increasing enrollments, staff size, and complexity of operation, the elementary and secondary schools are pressed to adopt bureaucratic administration. This form of administration has important advantages but lends itself to the dehumanizing of people, the treatment of rules as ends in themselves, the substitution of the self-interests of officials for the stated purposes of the organization, and the preservation of outmoded practices.[21] The effectiveness of any form of administration pivots on the attitudes and skills of the personnel directing and implementing its activities. When the personnel is unable to utilize bureaucratic strategies effectively, the disadvantages become characteristic of the school and the school system. The possibilities are suggested by the three models of the school described by Grannis.[22]

Three versions of school organization

The *"family" school*, the most prevalent model, emphasizes the intimate manner of the children's learning with and from each other as in a household, but in a more organized manner to facilitate intellectual and emotional growth. The teacher shares certain interests of the pupils and provides materials and settings to facilitate their solving of problems developing out of their own life. Based essentially on the relatively self-sufficient family of an earlier era, this model implies that both teacher and pupil have been socialized to similar expectations on how parents and children should interact with one another. The divergence of such expectations is especially marked when the middle-class teacher confronts pupils drawn from other special classes. The middle-class teacher tends to see a need to impose discipline for the sake of order. Her expectations of quiet and sustained effort are unlikely to coincide with what the children's previous experience has led them to believe is appropriate behavior. Furthermore, the model underestimates the impact on the family of the discontinuities among the kinds of authority being applied to contemporary children.[23]

The *"factory" school* requires pupils to work on identical material at a uniform pace under standardized grading. Teaching is through rote learning and emphasizes assignments and recitation. Competition in sheer quantity and rate of production is favored over individual initiative and quality of work. Punitive authority has its source in the principal's office and is delegated to teachers. The superintendent is in a role similar to that of an industrial executive who is responsible to his employer for getting certain work done by subordinates he controls under authority delegated to him by the employer. Thereby, the teachers are in a status similar to a factory foreman caught in a conflict of demands from the employer and from the individuals under his immediate supervision.

The *"corporation" school* is oriented to the employment of specialized

---

[21] See Chapter 3, pp. 76–77.
[22] Joseph C. Grannis, "The School as a Model of Society," in Witt, *Technology and the Curriculum*, pp. 103–13.
[23] See Chapter 8, pp. 201–3.

skills and technology in a planned and rational manner, with teachers expected to accommodate their own interests and styles to the teaching team as a whole. Elaborate schemes are developed for evaluating students and for recognition of their variety in interests and capacities. Authority is distributed throughout the staff hierarchy. The necessity for coordination of team teaching imposes restrictions on the time of pupils and their voice in school decisions. The emphasis on collective planning leaves little room for decisions contingent on immediate circumstances and favors a sense of detachment inconsistent with personalized relationships between teacher and pupil. In these ways this model reflects characteristics of urban life—characteristics such as impersonality and the disciplining of behavior to suit organizational interests.

"Cult of efficiency in management"

The "factory" model and, to a lesser extent, the "corporation" model are mirrors of a business-dominated society. Since business values have been dominant in American culture as a whole, this relationship is to be expected. However, Callahan contends that development in the early decades of the century created a "cult of efficiency" which imposed principles of factory management on the schools to such a degree that "economical" administration continues to rule regardless of the quality of education the contemporary society requires.[24]

At the turn of the century U.S. schools were confronted with waves of immigrants to be assimilated into American culture and, at the same time, a great influx of enrollments because of the passage of compulsory school attendance laws. Sharp criticism of the schools coincided with the rising popularity of "scientific management," which contended that industrial productivity can be increased through scientific study of work operation, training of the worker to perform tasks according to rational principles, and managerial planning and supervision of the entire process by management. The ideology of business "efficiency" provided the school administration a means of gaining a constituency for its own protection.[25]

The consequences have been tragic, Callahan asserts, because educators emphasized lowest cost ("the finest product at the lowest cost"). The movement produced administrators who were not educators and strengthened an anti-intellectual climate which favored decisions emphasizing minimization of financial costs. Schools were seen as enterprises rather than as centers of learning.[26]

In asking why education should not be considered an industry, Richmond takes a different tack. Since education is a social process and we

---

[24] Raymond E. Callahan, *Education and the Cult of Efficiency* (Chicago: University of Chicago Press, 1962), pp. 14–28.
[25] Ibid.
[26] Ibid., pp. 246–47.

live in an industrial society, why stop short of acknowledging that the two are interdependent? Men and machines *are* in symbiotic relationship. To justify the costs of education, he cites evidence of a high correlation between educational expenditure and national income. The maintenance of large educational systems is less expensive on a per-unit basis than small systems. If access to education is to be open, costs must be held down; otherwise, the demand for improved education will strain the country's resources.[27]

An interpretation of criticisms

The difficulties of schools are frequently attributed to their administrative characteristics. Janowitz points to misconceptions arising from overgeneralized application of these criticisms.[28] The school system has been found to be so overcentralized that flexible decision making is impossible. However, the authority of the central officials is diffused by legal restraints, vague lines of authority, and difficulties in acquiring information. Although inner city schools are handicapped by a high degree of inflexibility and uniformity of practices, the individual schools suffer more from isolation from other schools, fractionizing the system as a whole.

School administration is criticized for placing excessive emphasis on formal education, formal certification, and professional status, as though they were the equivalent of teacher effectiveness in the classroom. Thereby, the teacher is portrayed as excessively oriented to his "profession" and ill prepared to deal with classroom behavior in its full reality. "Professional" training does not necessarily provide insights in cultural differences among pupils and personalities. Janowitz believes that much of the wear and tear of classroom teaching is due to the fact that the teacher is placed alone before her class without the psychological support and assistance of a work group (such as found in a hospital setting, for instance). In a mobile society the teacher is not even likely to gain work satisfaction through feeling accomplishment by later encountering his successful pupils as adults.

There are sharp criticisms of the application of intelligence and achievement tests to children who are exposed to cultural and social environments that differ fundamentally from those experienced by the middle-class persons who are likely to be models in the framing and administration of such tests. The tests do serve to stigmatize some children and to operate to lower the aspirations of those pupils judged to be inadequate, but Janowitz warns against elimination of any means of evaluating the performance of *teachers* and the *school system*.

[27] W. Kenneth Richmond, *The Educational Industry* (London: Metheun and Co., 1969), pp. 1, 29–39.
[28] Morris Janowitz, *Institution Building in Urban Education* (New York: Russell Sage Foundation, 1969), pp. 24–34.

EQUALITY OF EDUCATIONAL OPPORTUNITY

Because it is a prime vehicle for joining the social mainstream, American public education is in the eye of the social hurricane unleashed by the rising expectations of minorities. The school receives conflicting instructions. On the one hand, it is supposed to respect lower-class values in keeping with the tolerance of democracy. On the other hand, it is expected to change the lower-class child into a middle-class adult for the sake of cultural homogeneity and the pupils' chances for greater economic opportunity.

Difficulties of definition and measurement

It is simpler to state what equality of educational opportunity is *not* than to define what it is. Equality is absent when educational opportunity differs according to the parents' economic circumstances or the child's location in the state. Wise reviews alternative forms of definition.[29]

The *full-opportunity* version assumes that the school should provide the student with every conceivable assistance in developing his abilities. This definition does not, however, recognize that educational resources are limited. The *foundation* version argues that a minimum acceptable quality of education should be guaranteed in dollars to be spent per pupil. The *minimum-attainment* definition asserts that resources should be allocated until every student reaches some accepted minimum level of adjustment. Thereby, the amount spent on pupils could vary according to their educational needs. The *leveling* definition would allocate resources in inverse proportion to the student's ability, with the objective of having all children leave the school with equal chances of success. Conversely, the *competition* version would allocate educational resources in direct proportion to the students' ability under the argument that the greater the ability, the greater should be the student's access to educational resources. The *classification* definition would expend the same amount of resources for every student in a state placed in a certain category. For example, all students rated as being college material would receive the same approximate allocation throughout a state, and all gifted children would receive another standardized allocation.

Traditionally, equality of educational opportunity has been measured by physical and economic factors such as teacher-pupil ratio, per-pupil expenditures, number of volumes in the library, and laboratory facilities. The controversial Coleman Report presented evidence to the contrary and summarized: "Difference in school facilities and curriculum, which are the major variables by which attempts are made to improve schools, are so

[29] Arthur E. Wise, *Rich Schools: Poor Schools* (Chicago: University of Chicago Press, 1968), pp. 146–58.

little related to differences in achievement levels of students that, with few exceptions, their effects fail to appear even in a survey of this magnitude." [30]

The study finds that family background is of great importance in determining student achievement and that this relationship does not diminish with increased years of schooling. Although the characteristics of teachers affect achievement, the teachers tend to be socially and racially similar to their pupils. When the student's own social background is ruled out, the social composition of the student body is the most important influence among school factors. The net result of these findings is that the school is failing to exert the influence, independent of the child's immediate social environment, that should exist if the school is to be a vehicle for equality of educational opportunity. [31]

The Coleman Report states that children from disadvantaged backgrounds benefit from merger with advantaged students, while the latter are not harmed by integration: "If a white pupil from a home that is strongly and effectively supportive of education is put in a school where most pupils do not come from such homes, his achievement is likely to increase." [32]

Coleman fixes the responsibility for achievement on the school in terms of the intensity with which it employs its available resources to exceed the intensity of influences of the underprivileged home and neighborhood. [33] His view represents a sharp shift from the popular view that the school plays a passive role in providing educational opportunity at a level determined by outside budgetary decision makers and by the level of parents' eagerness to take advantage of schooling for their children.

Barriers to achieving equality

Inequality of education exists because of factors built into the institutional fabric and because of patterns of prejudice. Inadequate schools reflect their vulnerability to the adverse consequences of local financing and control of education. Local residents may be incapable, or unwilling, to support schools financially at the level necessary for quality education. Economically privileged groups are usually eager to support schools for their own children, especially when differential education is a means of preserving their privileged position, and these groups tend to dominate decision making in the community, whereas underprivileged groups have relatively little opportunity to assess the quality of education their children

[30] James S. Coleman, Ernest A. Campbell et al., *Equality of Educational Opportunity* (Washington, D.C.: U.S. Government Printing Office, 1966), p. 316.
[31] Ibid., p. 325.
[32] Ibid., p. 22.
[33] James S. Coleman, "The Concept of Equality of Educational Opportunity," *Harvard Educational Review*, Vol. 38 (Winter 1968) pp. 21–22.

are receiving or to compare it with superior brands provided other groups.

The school crisis in the inner city repeats the gross inequities of educational resources among sections of the city and the nation which were also found in earlier eras. The black relationship to ghetto schools differs, however, from that of earlier immigrant ghetto residents. Janowitz sees a new crisis at hand because technological developments have transformed the labor market and made a high school education the requirement for even low-income jobs. Ghetto schools are confronted by the unprecedented responsibility to produce social attitudes, interpersonal competence, and maturity as personality components—in addition to academic and vocational components.[34] Rather than speaking solely of the deterioration of the inner city schools, Janowitz attributes the "new crisis" to the extension of this new responsibility to include the more immediate candidates for the labor force as well as students headed for college.[35]

Rural depressed areas and urban ghettos have difficulty in attracting and retaining higher-caliber teachers. These areas offer less attractive salaries and working conditions and must rely disproportionately on inexperienced instructors with inferior career opportunities. Furthermore, reluctance to accept such positions may reflect the individual's recognition of his lack of preparation to cope with the unfamiliar language, behavior, and norms encountered in these settings. The training of teachers for this assignment usually fails to provide information on the backgrounds and community settings of disadvantaged pupils.[36]

Issues in abolishing segregation

Achievement of educational quality is difficult in and of itself. When this objective is combined with elimination of racial discrimination, the school system faces even greater obstacles in changing practices inherent in the social fabric extending beyond the boundaries of direct and reasonably manageable control of educators. To capture the general dimensions of a complex subject, we employ five focal issues Pettigrew lists as germane to desegration of schools.[37]

Political pressures. The desegregation movement subjects the school system to three sets of political pressures: demands of committed blacks and of white liberals, fears of less-committed and generally upper-status whites, and the resistance of segregationists. School boards are caught between direct black protest and intensified white fears when the boards

---

[34] The failure of the school to meet this responsibility raises the possibility of aggravating the "slum of despair." See Chapter 7, pp. 167–68.

[35] Janowitz, *Institution Building in Urban Education,* pp. 7–10.

[36] B. Othanel Smith, *Teachers for the Real World* (Washington, D.C.: American Association of Colleges for Teacher Education, 1969), pp. 27–29.

[37] Thomas F. Pettigrew, "School Desegregation," in Gegi and Meyers, *Teaching in American Cultures,* pp. 291–96.

initiate changes. The threatened withdrawal of federal monies gives the local boards a means of countering the pressures of segregationists.

What level of government is responsible? Key issues are local control versus need for outside financial assistance and of suburban growth versus inner city deterioration. In determining responsibility for desegregation, these issues raise complex and delicate difficulties over the relative responsibilities of federal, state, metropolitan area, and local district levels of government.

How to do it? A variety of devices has been developed; to implement racially balanced education: redrawing of school lines within a district, pairing of predominately white and black schools, altering the arrangements whereby pupils are channeled from elementary through junior high schools into high schools, placement of new schools near the ghetto, conversion of schools into districtwide specialized institutions, establishment of campus parks, including a variety of programs at many levels, and subsidized transportation to mingle categories of pupils previously separated from one another.

How to blend racial balance and compensatory training? Balancing the racial characteristics of the student body is insufficient for educational equality. Previous practices have lowered standards and achievement found typically in predominantly black schools. Somehow the achievement of racial balance must include provisions for correcting these deficits.

Several strategies are usually advocated. In compensatory and remedial instruction, specially trained teachers enrich preschool experience with emphasis on the development of skills in communication. For older children, class size is reduced, curricula are redesigned to awaken their interest, and specialized teachers are employed. To reduce conflict between the family and school, social workers and teacher aides are employed to reach out into the home. Counselors and vocational guidance workers strive to give proper recognition to the unique problems of the pupil and to ease entry into the job market. Education and work experience are related more directly. Unpaid volunteers and older children help the teacher to improve learning.

How to maximize intergroup acceptance and learning? Once desegregation is accomplished to a reasonable degree, there remains the troublesome matter of achieving intergroup acceptance and learning for all children in an interracial school. Allport notes that contacts between individuals who perceive one another as threats are harmful rather than helpful. The school and teacher have the difficult tasks of encouraging a sense of equality in social status and of avoiding artificial relationships outside of ordinary purposeful pursuits. Contact and acquaintanceship requires the development of team sentiments.[38]

---

[38] Gordon W. Allport, *The Nature of Prejudice* (Garden City, N.Y.: Doubleday Anchor, 1958), pp. 453–54.

STRAINS IN A CENTRAL ROLE: THE TEACHER

The teacher is subject to status dilemmas because his position in the social systems of the community in general and the school in particular does not produce the level of social and economic rewards that his vital functions would suggest they should.

Because of the vital importance of the children, the teacher's work is especially visible in the community. This visibility is associated with a relatively low degree of social distance from the groups who evaluate his work.[39] From their children and their own contact, parents obtain information and opinions. The qualifications of the teacher as an expert are challenged by anti-intellectual traditions, preference for experience over knowledge acquired in abstract form, and the tenuous relationship between the teacher's specific contribution and the overall development of the pupil's personality. The professions of law and medicine maintain professional images by maintaining secrecy over the inner workings of their occupations. Teachers lack this advantage.

Some patterns in the occupation

Certain characteristics of the occupation reflect the status problems of teaching. There is a great amount of geographical mobility among teachers, either within or between school districts, in search of better conditions of work and higher status. For the last decade about 70 percent of those trained for the career actually enter teaching. About 12 percent of all teachers left the field at the end of each academic year in that decade. Some come back, especially women who had dropped out to rear their children,[40] but the supply and quality of elementary and secondary staffs is reduced by this turnover and mobility.

Although high school teachers are about equally divided between the sexes, the predominance of women among elementary teachers results in two thirds of all teachers being female. The predominance of female teachers has brought warnings that the shortage of male figures deprives boys of role models at a crucial stage in personality development. Because teaching salaries are less attractive to men, they seek administrative posts, become part-time teachers through moonlighting, or leave the field. For women, also, teaching is often a temporary occupation before marriage and motherhood. Despite the frequent identification of the teacher as a middle-class person, young teachers are being drawn more from blue-

---

[39] Holger R. Stub, "The Professional Prestige of Classroom Teachers: A consequence of Organizational and Community Status," Robert R. Bell and Holder R. Stub (eds.), *The Sociology of Education: A Sourcebook* (rev. ed.; Homewood, Ill.: Dorsey Press, 1968), pp. 254–55.

[40] B. Othanel Smith, *Teachers for the Real World* (Washington, D.C.: American Association of Colleges for Teacher Education, 1969), pp. 21–22.

collar than white-collar families.[41] Reiss finds that only the lower social classes rank teaching as possessing the prestige accorded other professions.[42]

Although states are requiring increased college training, many still allow persons with less adequate preparation to teach by granting them provisional credentials. In 1966 7 percent of public school teachers had less than four years of college preparation.[43] Even among college-educated teachers, there is evidence that the field of education is not competing successfully with other professions in drawing its full share of high-potential personnel. When national samples of education students are compared with samples of other categories of students in terms of academic achievement, they fall below the liberal arts, science, and engineering categories.[44]

Professionalism and militancy

Teaching qualifies as a profession in that ideally it is based on intellectual competence derived from prolonged and specialized training, involves ethics of public service, and requires a closely knit professional colleagueship. However, professionalism is not necessarily characteristic of a teacher or the particular teaching activity. Although the National Education Association has a code of ethics worthy of a profession, there are not sufficient means of enforcement.[45] Occupational cohesion is eroded by the diversity of activities—from administrators to counselors—which are included under "teaching."

Professionals usually are in a position to regulate their working conditions and standards of renumeration, but teachers as a group lack sufficient power in this regard. Their prestige is sapped by public underestimation of the demands of teaching and the failure of some teachers to offer sufficient qualifications. Teachers are vulnerable economically to the reluctance of local government to raise tax rates. When the school operates as a rigid bureaucracy, the teacher becomes an instrument of a program which requires the clerical and administrative tasks of keeping attendance, correcting papers, maintaining grade records, hall and bus

[41] Ronald F. Campbell, "Teaching and Teachers—Today and Tomorrow," in H. Thomas James et al, (eds.) *The Schools and the Challenge on Innovation* (New York: McGraw-Hill Book Co., 1969), pp. 110–11.

[42] Albert Reiss, *Occupation and Social Status* (Glencoe, Ill.: Free Press, 1961), p. 276.

[43] National Education Association, "Characteristics of Teachers, 1956, 1961, 1966," *NEA Research Bulletin,* Vol. 45 (October 1967) pp. 87–88.

[44] Robert D. North, "The Teacher Education Student: How Does He Compare Academically with Other College Students," in *The Education of Teachers: New Perspectives* (Washington, D.C.: National Commission on Teacher Education and Professional Standards, National Education Association, 1958).

[45] James E. Meyers and Kalil I. Gegi, "Is Teaching a Profession?" in Gegi and Meyers, *Teaching in American Cultures,* pp. 335–49.

duties, and lunchroom supervision. These standardized functions are not professional. Assignment of the teacher to the role of a bureaucratic functionary deprives teaching of the qualities of a creative process requiring independent and trained judgment.

The doubling of the membership of the American Federation of Teachers since World War II reflects the growing militancy of teachers. It is also noteworthy that A.F.T. leaders have called teaching's claim to professional status a curse that isolates teachers from the world of reality and operates against their own interests. Instead, the union leaders insist, teaching is a *craft,* with skills acquired through an apprenticeship and learning on the job.[46] Teachers have demonstrated increasing resolve to have a voice in school affairs and to demand more favorable salaries and working conditions. Stinnett speaks of a "new breed of teachers" coming, with rising levels of competence among teachers derived from better training. Scanty preparation, poor pay, and routine tasks had favored docility among teachers. He also cites the larger proportion of males among teachers, declining average age, effect of increasing size of school districts in increasing a sense of vulnerability, and teacher idealism as causes for greater rejection of passive conformity.[47]

The growing willingness of teachers to join a union is especially noteworthy because it represents a marked change from the former white-collar opposition to unionism. The National Education Association's philosophy emphasizes "professional obligations" as prior to the teacher's pursuit of personal interests. The A.F.T. emphasizes issues such as class size and salary scales and argues that union solidarity is essential to power for effective collective bargaining. Because, as public employees, strikes embroil teachers in possible conflict with public interest, teachers sometime prefer mass refusal to sign new contracts as an alternative strategy.[48]

Another kind of solution to the status dilemma would be creation of a hierarchy of statuses within the school social system, instead of lumping all teachers in the same category. Stub suggest these labels: associate teacher (noncertified), teacher (beginning certified teacher), career teacher (major category of experienced teachers with tenure), and master teacher (those with great teaching abilities and other special skills.) He argues that this arrangement would focus attention on the competence of teachers, increase the range of promotion opportunities for retaining superior teachers, transfer the prestige of college professors to elementary and secondary teachers and open the way for application of professional criteria in evaluation of teachers.[49]

---

[46] T. M. Stinnett, *Turmoil in Teaching* (New York: Macmillan Co., 1968), pp. 158–60.
[47] T. M. Stinnett, *Professional Problems of Teachers,* (3d ed.; New York: Macmillan Co., 1968), pp. 502–4.
[48] Stinnett, *Turmoil in Teaching,* pp. 87–96, 157–85.
[49] Stinnett, *Professional Problems of Teachers,* pp. 265–67.

PREMATURE WITHDRAWAL FROM SCHOOL

With the extension of universal education through high school, dropping out of high school has come to be defined as a social stigma and a major national problem. The pressure to reduce dropout rates comes in spite of the unparalled success of American schools in retaining students. This paradox is attributable to accelerated recognition of the personal and social costs of dropouts in the face of the urban emphasis on literacy, the obsolescence of unskilled and semiskilled jobs, the increased proportion of youths in the total labor force, and the increased concern over the plight of underprivileged minorities. Another paradox is that the greater concern over dropouts creates new problems for the school—which will have to cope with problem pupils who otherwise would be out of the classroom.

Who leave school prematurely?

It would be advantageous if the potential dropout could be identified early. A subsequent career as an inadequate pupil might be forestalled. Incipient problem behavior may be prevented through early diagnosis of psychological difficulties or mobilization of community resources. Attention to such problems may provide evidence of inadequacies of the school itself or of specific members of the staff. Individual needs of a child may be recognized and special resources of the school brought into play.

The difference in test scores is not sufficient to support a reliable conclusion that dropouts are inferior in intelligence. In all probability, however, the dropout is failing when he withdraws, and frequently he is at a lower grade than his age would indicate as appropriate. Because of legal requirements on attendance, he is likely to be sixteen years of age, with a record of irregular previous attendance and low participation in school activities. A majority of dropouts come from low-scale socioeconomic homes.[50]

Since the act of leaving school is a symptom of varied personal and social conditions, Tannenbaum doubts that there is a "typical dropout." Whether or not a pupil stays in school is affected by many social and economic indices: average income, rental rates, teacher salaries, amount of schooling completed by the adults of the neighborhood, proportion of professionals in the community, and per-capita student expenditure. Too frequently, the school lacks the knowledge and skilled personnel to deal with the scholastically weak and emotionally thwarted. The regime of school life is not congenial to pupils unprepared to react effectively to a middle-class dominated curriculum. Conversely, the pupil may lack intellectual firepower and/or emotional readiness no matter how great the teaching energy and good will exhibited by the school.[51]

[50] Bert I. Greene, *Preventing School Dropouts* (Englewood Cliffs, N.J.: Prentice-Hall, 1966), pp. 23–29.
[51] Abraham J. Tannenbaum, *Dropout or Diploma* (New York: Teachers College Press, Columbia University, 1966) pp. 7–15.

Four types are delineated by Miller.[52] The *school-inadequate dropout* has difficulty because of low intellectual functioning or disturbed emotional functioning. Miller believes this to be a small category and intellectual inability to be a minor cause for early withdrawal. The *school-rejecting dropout* regards the school as confining, unuseful, and ego-destructive. Nevertheless, Miller finds such negativism among dropouts to be surprisingly unusual. The *school-perplexed* dropout recognizes education as a means to power and prestige, but he finds the operations of the school beyond his comprehension. Miller finds this category becoming more numerous. The bulk of the low-income dropouts, he says, are of the *school-irrelevant* type who have job goals which require little education. If the latter type is encouraged successfully to stay in school in hopes of better jobs, will enough high-status jobs be available for the increased volume of later applicants? Miller argues that the essence of the dropout problem lies in an increased supply of genuine job opportunities. When dropouts are explained solely as a matter of low individual aspiration, the utlimate price could be more individual frustration and magnified social unrest.

Who fails? The pupil or the school?

The individual qualities of the dropout are pertinent to the problem under study, but (as Miller suggests) the problem is not encompassed by these qualities in and of themselves. Both the pupil and the school are affected by factors external to the school. Unemployment affects the low-income groups markedly because of the special impact on them of automation and other technological developments. The disproportionate increase of the youthful population aggravates their unemployment and increases the number of delinquents. Although the inadequacies of the school are a major facet of the dropout problem, the casual factors are too far-ranging to be subject to correction by the school alone.

Concern over early school withdrawal, Tannenbaum warns, has produced an example of Gresham's law. Primary attention on reduction of dropouts tends to erode academic and behavior standards which are supposed to be recognized by a diploma. When the diploma fails to describe actual performance, it loses its credential value. Tannenbaum fears we are approaching a point where nearly all but extremely deviant adolescents will earn diplomas; thus, high school completion is becoming less and less a mark of achievement.[53]

[52] S. M. Miller, "Dropouts—a Political Problem," in Schreiber, *Profile of the School Dropout,* pp. 184–97.
[53] Tannenbaum, *Dropout or Diploma,* pp. vii–viii.

SUMMARY

The contemporary school has been assigned concurrently the purposes of maintaining the stability of the social order and of implementing changes deemed necessary to overcome social problems. The functions grouped under these general purposes frequently conflict with one another. The complications of achieving equality of educational opportunity and dealing with school dropouts illustrate the difficulties. The balancing of opposing sets of functions is further complicated by the fragmentation of education among local agencies, increasing costs and pupil populations, the explosion of knowledge, and organizational difficulties. The organizational difficulties stem from contrary calls for "efficient" management and individualized instruction. The teacher's role suffers a strain as a consequence. The dimensions of these problems for the school testify to the increasing importance given U.S. elementary and secondary schools in coping with the various difficulties found in urban society. In the next chapter the analysis is continued into the realm of higher education.

FOR ADDITIONAL READING

Robert H. Anderson, *Teaching in a World of Change* (New York: Harcourt, Brace & World, 1966).

William H. Boyer and Paul Marsh, "Are Children Born Unequal?" *Saturday Review,* Vol. 51 (October 19, 1968), pp. 61–63, 73–79.

Wilbur Brookover and David Gottlieb, *A Sociology of Education* (2d ed.; New York: American Book Co. 1964).

James W. Brown and James W. Thorton, Jr., *New Media in Higher Education* (Washington, D.C.: National Education Association, 1963).

Burton R. Clark, "Sociology of Education," in Robert E. L. Faris (ed.), *Handbook of Modern Sociology* (Chicago: Rand McNally, 1964), Chapter 19.

James S. Coleman, *Adolescents and the School* (New York: Basic Books, 1965).

James Bryant Conant, *Shaping Education Policy* (New York: McGraw-Hill Book Co., 1964), Chapters 1, 2 and 5.

Francesco Cordasco, Maurie Hillson, and Henry A. Bullock (eds.), *The School in the Social Order* (Scranton, Pa.: International Textbook Co., 1970).

Robert Havighurst, Paul H. Bowman, Gordon P. Liddle, Charles V. Matthews, and James V. Pierce, *Growing Up in River City* (New York: John Wiley and Sons, 1962).

Nathaniel Hickerson, *Education for Alienation* (Englewood Cliffs, N.J.: Prentice-Hall, 1966).

John Holt, *Why Schools Fail* (New York: Pitman Publishing Corporation, 1967).

August Kerver and Wilfred R. Smith (eds.) *Educational Issues in a Changing Society* (Detroit, Mich.: Wayne State University Press, 1968).

Arthur E. Lean, *And Merely Teach: Irreverent Essays on the Mythology of Education* (Carbondale, Ill.: Southern Illinois University Press, 1968).

Myron Lieberman, *The Future of Public Education* (Chicago: University of Chicago Press, 1960).

Harry L. Miller and Roger R. Woock, *Social Foundations of Urban Education* (Hinsdale, Ill.: Dryden Press, 1970).

Harry A. Passow (ed.), *Education in Depressed Areas* (New York: Teachers College Press, Columbia University, 1963).

Albert J. Reiss, Jr., (ed.) *Schools in a Changing Society* (New York: Free Press, 1965).

Jean I. Roberts (ed.) *School Children in the Urban Slum* (New York: Free Press, 1967).

David Rogers, *110 Livingston Street* (New York: Random House, 1968).

Patricia Caye Sexton, *The American School: A Sociological Analysis* (Englewood Cliffs, N.J.: Prentice-Hall, 1967).

Frederick R. Smith and R. Bruce McQuigg (eds.), *Secondary Schools Today: Readings for Educators* (Boston, Mass.: Houghton Mifflin, 1965).

Higher education 13

"We are people of this generation, bred in at least modest comfort, housed in universities looking uncomfortably to the world we inherit."[1]

These words introduce an official statement of the Students for a Democratic Society, an organization identified with the "new left." Among other claims, the statement describes professors and administrators as withholding moral guidance through sacrifice of controversy to public relations in a society the S.D.S. sees characterized by great discrepancies between moral principle and actual practice. Professors are accused of discrediting passion on grounds that it is "unscholastic" and of "selling their skills in service to the arms race." Students generally are indicted for committing themselves to "business as usual, getting ahead, playing it cool."

This condemnation is one example of the rising crescendo of criticisms directed at higher education. In the 1960s and early 1970s, higher education experienced a period of acute self-criticism and questioning of its operations by critics with diverse political beliefs. The situation was paradoxical in several respects. As in the case of our S.D.S. example, much of the criticism comes from within the ranks of higher education. Faculties of diverse ages, fields, and political beliefs have also expressed serious doubts about existing academic forms and values. The criticisms come at a time when the reliance on the university as means of solving problems

---

[1] "Excerpts from the 'Port Huron Statement,' " in Charles H. McCaghy, James K. Skipper, Jr., and Mark Lefton (eds.), *In Their Own Behalf: Voices from the Margin* (New York: Appleton—Century-Crofts, 1968), pp. 212–22.

of urban society has grown to unprecedented proportions. As the social institution which stakes out the role of objective critic of the society it serves, the university is under fire in an age of widespread ideological conflict when the services of the knowledgeable and objective critic would be particularly useful.

CHALLENGES TO THE UNIVERSITY

For society as a whole, the colleges and universities have been defined concurrently as engines of change and agents for maintaining the stability of a society exposed to rapid and profound social changes. Because either function in itself poses awesome responsibilities and requires mobilization of great resources by an educational system of increasing complexity, there are bound to be organizational strains and discrepancies between expectation and accomplishment. The probability of problems for society at large is magnified when the social processes of higher education are disrupted seriously by conflicting norms and disagreement over the purposes to be sought. Higher education is racing frantically to remain contemporary, Kerr declares, in the face of unprecedented growth in enrollments, shifts in academic emphases necessitated by expansion of the types of professional specialities, and the widening involvement of the university in the daily life of the nation.[2] The events and outcome of this race are of great importance to both the university and the nation it serves.

Adaptability: Expansion plus creativity?

From many sources the university is pressed to become more relevant to the solution of immediate issues. It has been summoned to reverse the environmental decline and to serve directly as an instrument for more equitable distribution of social and economic rewards. Somehow it is supposed to provide intellectual leadership and discover new principles and techniques for meeting social crises. To implement the various strategies, well-trained personnel are supposed to flow from the campuses. An "explosion" of knowledge has intensified the American demand for more and better education. The delayed effects of the post-World War II "baby boom" coincided with a broadening aspiration for higher education, challenging U.S. institutions of higher education in their readiness and capacity to instruct masses of students.

In its responses to the challenges to its adaptability, expansibility, and creativity, the university operates within an environment of heightened visibility. There was less general concern over the problems and inadequa-

[2] Clark Kerr, "The Frantic Race to Remain Contemporary," *Daedalus,* Vol. 93 (Fall 1964), pp. 1051–70.

cies of higher education when it touched the lives of only a small segment of the American people. The profound influence of the university on the workings of an urban and technological society has accentuated the impact of the university's problems and inadequacies.

Perhaps the heightened visibility of higher education will modify the nature of a remarkable paradox Sanford has noted. In American society, many people place little value on learning and intellectual life and have little understanding of academic perspectives. Nevertheless, in this same society a majority of adults regard the experience of college as a virtual necessity for young people. The reconciliation of this paradox lies in the public conception of the benefits of college in terms of social and job advancement rather than in the pursuit of intellectual inquiry. The emphasis on nonacademic benefits explains much of the relative immunity of higher education from widespread public scrutiny of its academic programs.[3]

As the target for a wide range of hopes, the university qualifies as what Barzun calls a *residual institution.* Whatever the individual and society cannot do for themselves is entrusted in a likely institution. Their faith in education and science brings to the university a wide variety of seekers of sociability, business advice, medical care, legal aid, relief from crime and intergroup conflict, and so on. Alma mater finds herself overwhelmed by the feelings she inspires in others, even when she knows her own limitations.[4]

Implications of "college for everyone"

Advocates of "higher education for all" argue that human capacities must be developed to their full potential in an increasingly complex society and to meet the need for intelligent voters. Also, prolonged education has been advocated as necessary in light of the expansion of knowledge and the desire to keep youth off the job market. Counterarguments raise doubts that institutions of higher learning can expand their services and adapt themselves to larger student bodies without deterioration of their quality. It is difficult to train and maintain a sufficient staff of professors and to provide the additional facilities. There are fears that quantitative expansion will necessitate dipping into the lower levels of the student aptitude pool. These fears are counterbalanced to a degree by recognition that previous decades did not bring all high-aptitude youths to the campus and even then students were not universally of high caliber.

However, the issue of student quality depends on the nature of the educational goals. The principle that college is only for the intellectually

[3] Nevitt Sanford, "Higher Education as a Social Problem," in Nevitt Sanford (ed.), *College and Character* (New York: John Wiley, 1964), pp. 3–5.
[4] Jacques Barzun, *The American University* (New York: Harper & Row, 1968), pp. 10–11.

The campus door to opportunity. An "Upward Bound" program helps capable youth obtain a college education at the University of Delaware. Higher education, in turn, has had to cope with serious financial and organizational problems in responding to the demands placed upon it as a gatekeeper to opportunity and the supplier of highly trained personnel.

elite is being challenged by the contention that everyone has the right to higher education. The conversion of the university into an instrument of social equality and technological development, however, runs counter to its previous function of producing an intellectual elite and maintaining a cultural elite. Open admission regardless of educational readiness aggravates the complexities of teaching, especially when the volume of students overwhelms those teachers who are dedicated to quality instruction.

The expansion of colleges has raised difficult issues of finance, which came to a head in 1971. If higher education is conceived as primarily a benefit for the student, it may be argued that he or his parents should bear at least the largest share of the costs. A college education raises potential lifetime earnings and therefore constitutes a good investment for the individual. But if higher education is considered in the national interest for developing human resources, diversion of tax revenues to maintain colleges is justified. To force all students to bear the full cost discriminates against the able student with insufficient economic resources. Finally, however, the rising costs of higher education constitute a drain on the tax dollar at a time when there is mounting pressure for sustained, large-scale efforts to cope with problems such as poverty, environmental pollution, and deterioration of the cities.

Heterogeneity and change

Among institutions of higher education there are huge differences in affluence, preparation of faculty, and selectivity in admission of students. Almost half have not been approved by an official accrediting organization; that is, they have not been subjected to the scrutiny of, or gained the approval of, either a regional association of colleges and universities or a national professional organization. Lack of accreditation does not necessarily indicate that their students fail to learn; it does suggest, however, that there is plenty of room for improvement in many colleges and universities.

Under either private or public control, institutions of higher education include universities, liberal arts colleges, teachers colleges, technical institutes, theological schools, and junior colleges. Their enrollments vary from less than 500 to more than 30,000 students. In the fall of 1969, total enrollment already had exceeded 7 million students and the number of full-time instructional faculty had surpassed 300,000.[5] Significantly, the highest rate of enrollment increase since 1930 has been set by those institutions with more than 3,000 students each.[6]

As a consequence of its diversity of purposes, the "multiversity," as it

[5] "Facts of American Education," NEA Research Bulletin, Vol. 48 (May 1970), pp. 40–41.
[6] John J. Corson, Governance of Colleges and Universities, (New York: McGraw-Hill Book Co., 1960), pp. 5–6.

is labeled by Kerr, has burgeoned from a community of masters and students into a complex series of communities and activities held together loosely by a common name, a common governing board, and related purposes.[7] The boundaries of this set of communities are fuzzy because the university reaches out to perform services for the society beyond the campus. The university is at the center of the growth of knowledge which is permeating government and industry. Heated debates have been waged over "perversion" of science and self-serving "grantsmanship" which advances the careers of some professors but removes them from the classroom. Questions have been raised about the wisdom of universities seeking financial support for research of questionable usefulness to science and at the cost of instruction as the primary mission of the university.[8]

As these criticisms suggest, there are differences of opinion on what the university is and should be. At one extreme the university is viewed as the locale within which able individuals are sheltered from the stresses and transitory issues of the larger world. Within this shelter, these individuals employ their intellectual wares in teaching, research, or study, with only the ties of a scholarly community linking them together in a loose confederation. By dedicating themselves to the long-term pursuit of truth, these individuals contribute to the preservation and expansion of accumulated knowledge to make the university a balance wheel for society in times of change.

At the other extreme, the university is urged to develop a more firm organizational consensus and to deliver practical services to a society beset by serious social problems. It should relieve the manpower shortages which deprive the citizenry, or a significant segment thereof, of the benefits of scientific progress. It should not remain aloof from the value conflicts which threaten to tear society asunder. As a gateway to opportunity, the university is seen as obligated to provide as much education as any individual desires and from which he can profit.

RELATIONSHIPS WITH REST OF SOCIETY

Since the people who populate colleges and universities share values which tend to mark them as different from other people, it would be easy to exaggerate the similarity of beliefs among campus people. Distinctions from the rest of society are suggested by the term "egghead" and the attractiveness of the campus to some persons as a refuge from pressures of the outside world. Large universities have the characteristics of a com-

---

[7] Clark Kerr, *The Uses of the University* (Cambridge, Mass.: Harvard University Press, 1963), pp. 1 and 86–88.
[8] See Chapter 4, pp. 104–8.

munity in terms of their own police forces, dining facilities, housing, and many other services. However, the functions of the university embed it within the structure of society. This interdependence has been strengthened by increased reliance on higher education for specialized personnel and technological research.

The intellectual power of the university safeguards it against being a mere pawn of the forces which impinge on it from the outside. However, it is strongly influenced by the forces which are shaping the outside community and by the ambivalence with which the various groups in that community regard the university. The university depends on the legislature and donors for financial support. Moreover, it must communicate with the larger community if its educational and research programs are to be relevant and if it is to maintain a constituency.

Ambivalence toward intellectualism

The derisive term "egghead" suggests the resentment of many citizens of an educational system which has among its goals the cultivation of an intellectual elite. Hofstadter sees universal admiration for intelligence which works within a framework of limited and specific goals, and thus the educator is praised for cultivating the intelligence of his pupils. Acclaim is less than universal, however, when pupils turn to critical analysis of the ideas which give comfort and moral security to large segments of the population. With the greater complexity of the human environment, the services of the intellectual are of growing importance and give him power and privilege—and because he is needed, he is more fiercely resented. Furthermore, Hofstadter argues, the cosmopolitanism and skepticism of the intellectual are viewed as subversive tendencies by persons who cling to fundamental religious beliefs, isolationist views in foreign affairs, nationalistic sentiments or prejudices, and conservative economic faiths.[9]

A prevalent conflict: Town and gown

The relationship between the college people and the long-term residents of the environing community tend to polarize into a "town versus gown" conflict. Long ago, quarrels between students and townsmen were important in establishing the legal security of medieval universities. The continued existence of such town-gown struggles ever since medieval times suggests that the sources of conflict are more basic than transitory escapades of undisciplined youth. In 1229–31 a tavern squabble over a wine bill culminated in the summoning of troops and the killing of several

[9] Richard Hofstadter, *Anti-Intellectualism in American Life* (New York: Alfred A. Knopf, 1963), pp. 7, 25, 33–34, 42–44.

students of the University of Paris. The masters suspended lectures and then voted to close the university for six years. The French royal court became alarmed over the loss of prestige and trade, and the masters returned in 1231 with a papal document which confirmed the university's right to strike and to punish violation of university statutes through exclusion from the society of masters. Through such privileges, the legal security of the university was established, to be imitated in grants to new universities during the next two centuries.[10]

Some of the basic characteristics of town-gown conflict are amazingly consistent from decade to decade. In a study from the 1930s Rapport gave a description that is relevant to many situations today.[11] Each group he indicates is highly self-conscious with respect to its own prestige and welfare. Each group distorts the real reasons for conflicts with the other by falsifying the facts of the issues. Although many of the faculty are taxpaying residents for a considerable time, the townspeople lump all "university people" together as though they are the equivalent of summer visitors to a resort town. The university group generally restricts its social life to colleagues and generally is ignorant of town affairs. Each group stereotypes the other. University people are accused of disinterest in the town welfare, intent to gain selfish benefits, aloofness, and impractical theorizing. Townspeople are labeled as selfish exploiters, old-fashioned, intellectually sterile, and narrow in vision. When a political issue arouses special concern, each group is particularly wary of the possibility that the other will railroad through a decision favorable to its selfish interest. Although usually the townspeople are called the aggressors in conflicts, Rapport finds the "gown" people equally responsible.

When the university is the predominant employer and generator of local prosperity, the conflict between town and gown is more apparent. In a study of such a situation, Miller reports that resentment against the university stems from the heavy dependence of the town on it for economic support.[12] There is fear that the university will inflate costs of land and rentals and will demand governmental services which are opposed by townspeople and not supported through university funding. Covert quotas are placed on university representation in governmental bodies and on faculty membership in various organizations. Although the unusual capacity of faculties for leadership is recognized, it is preferred that they concentrate attention on books and students. However, the cosmopolitan orientation of most faculties reduces their interest in local affairs and diverts it toward colleagues on the campus and throughout the nation.

[10] Lowrie J. Daly, *The Medieval University* (New York: Sheed and Ward, 1961), pp. 190–93.

[11] Victor A. Rapport, "Conflict in a New England College Town," *Social Forces,* Vol. 17 (May 1939), pp. 527–33.

[12] Delbert C. Miller, "Town and Gown: The Power Structure of a University Town," *American Journal of Sociology,* Vol. 68 (January 1963), pp. 440–41.

Urbanism and the university

Urbanization is undermining the collegiate way of life. Universities located in urban centers are receiving a larger share of burgeoning enrollments than those which are not. This places heavy demands on their instructional, research, and service resources. Additionally, the wider spectrum of specialized occupations of the city has added to the range of curricula in urban schools. Finally, the urban universities have to struggle with limited land space, high costs of acquiring more land for expansion, traffic congestion, inadequate parking space, and urban blight.

The appearance of the urban university has been relatively recent. Many early colleges were established in pastoral settings because of antipathy to towns for their supposed "ensnarling and demoralizing influence." In addition, the Cambridge- and Oxford-trained gentlemen of colonial New England imported the collegiate pattern from England to bring civilization to the barbaric New World, and in the absence of large cities in early America, this pattern of semirural setting became an established norm which has strongly influenced even the contemporary residential college. Rudolph sees the central notion of the *collegiate way* to be that a residential scheme is essential to transform a curriculum, library, faculty, and students into an institution of higher learning.[13] This "way" looks to quiet rural settings, dormitories, dining halls, and a paternalistic faculty and administration in its assigned task of turning "barbarians" into "cultured gentlemen." Beyond studies, such a close community is supposed to expose students to the beneficial influence of one another and to kindly discipline during the passage to adulthood.

With the democratization of higher education, and the enrollment flood, the tendency to prolong adolescence unnecessarily became more apparent than before. Students have become restless under the doctrine of *in loco parentis* which casts them as dependent children and the university as all-knowing parent.

The chancellor of an urban institution predicts a continuation of the explosive growth of the urban university which started after World War II. The tide of students from the lower-middle and lower income levels of society will continue to intensify enrollment pressure, and rising tuition charges and high entrance requirements will require that more youths seek campuses close to their homes. Urban universities have already experienced an explosive growth; state universities not so located are developing campuses in the urban concentrations of their states.[14]

An urban location complicates orderly expansion. Blight, obsolescence, overcrowding, and traffic congestion stultify the campus atmosphere. The

[13] Frederick Rudolph, *The American College and University* (New York: Alfred A. Knopf, 1965), pp. 3–4, 87–89.
[14] J. Martin Klotsche, *The Urban University,* (New York: Harper & Row, 1966), pp. 5–6.

need for inexpensive housing and food has involved some universities, Klotsche says, in the conversion of single-family dwellings into rooming houses and multiple residences. Expansion beyond original campus boundaries involves the university in the controversies of urban renewal —including charges of violating the interests of slum dwellers. Some universities have moved to new locales in search of greater space outside the central city. Others have remained to attempt to cope with the difficulties of bringing about an urban renaissance.[15]

The various kinds of association between the university and the problems of the city may tempt the scholar to lament the erosion of the foundations of the ivy tower, but dissension and involvement in off-campus problems are also symptoms of intellectual ferment, which is one of the qualities of a living university. In an urbanized society, the university must adapt itself to new roles and new circumstances which challenge the pursuit of truth that it has always claimed to be its unique function.

ORGANIZATION AND GOVERNANCE

Higher education is characterized by remarkable decentralization and organizational diversity. It is especially vulnerable to management difficulties while reacting effectively to growing size, scope, and complexity.

Pluralistic decision-making system

When a small body of scholars could decide questions through face-to-face discussion, there was relatively little need for organizational structure and administrative specialization. Although the traditional centering of authority in the faculty continues to be the professed precept, in practice the "clinical efficiency" of formal administration has become dominant. In problems previously subject to the personal attention of faculty members, students must now deal with an expanding bureaucracy staffed by registrars, controllers, deans, guidance counselors, resident managers, placement officers, and so on.

The college or university is a "government" in the sense that, as an organization, it must make rules to govern the conduct and relationships of the individuals banded together within it. Similar to a business, labor union, or military group, the university exists to accomplish something.

The University is unique, however, in that it serves a remarkable diversity of purpose. Its governance is particularly complicated by the dispersion of its activities among many and relatively independent schools, institutes, and departments. Finally, decision-making responsibility is widely diffused beyond the trustees and the president to the faculty as a

[15] Ibid., pp. 61–71.

group, to individual teachers, and to deans, department heads, coaches, and administrative officers.[16]

The man in the middle

The president of a university is midway between a board of trustees which holds final legal authority and a faculty which traditionally was the policy-making body. The board reflects the public conscience and acts as a buffer between the university and the outside community which ultimately provides the university's resources. Ideally the faculty determines which students are admitted, the courses they take, and the standards for their graduation. In practice, this ideal is frequently a fiction. Instead, an array of administrative offices comprises a decision-making structure devoted to "efficiency" in handling the volume of routine tasks.

In reflecting attitudes of the outside society, boards of trustees frequently have difficulty in understanding the orientation of the faculty. The boards vary in the degree of faculty participation they are willing to seek. Moreover, the faculty owes allegiance to academic freedom, which is not necessarily supported by the practices of the organizational structure of the university.

Many devices for review and concurrence would frustrate a dynamic industrial executive. Ideas and judgments are expressed in every department and school. Decisions affect the faculty, administrative officers, students, alumni, trustees, donors, and the governmental agencies off the campus. As the chief executive, the president must rely heavily on consultation in responding to crises because the faculty is particularly sensitive to decisions imposed by administrators. The university president must take the difficult route of gaining willing and effective action from a multitude of groups. Since academic people are more given to free discussion than to quick decision, the president must learn to anticipate problems and issues so that preparations to cope with them can be made through consultation.[17]

FACULTY ROLE: CRUCIAL BUT COMPLICATED

Among all categories of university personnel, the faculty has the greatest potential for determining the ultimate outcome of instruction and research. This potentiality involves the faculty in obligations to frame and implement educational policies. As the person with whom the student has the most frequent and persistent contact, the instructor is the most direct symbol

---

[16] Corson, *Governance of Colleges and Universities,* pp. 9–11.
[17] J. Douglas Brown, *The Liberal University* (New York: McGraw-Hill Book Co. 1969), pp. 12–16.

of the university. Sometimes the instructor is a professor but, in universities with large classes, he is more likely to be a member of the junior staff or perhaps a graduate-student teaching assistant. Then close contact between students and the professor is more myth than reality.

Tensions in professor role

This deviation from expectation is one example of the difficulties encountered in trying to draw clear-cut conclusions on the functions and behavior of the faculty within the social structure of the university. The size of the university staff and student population calls for resort to bureaucratic administration, yet the socialization of the professor during his own education tends him to be ambivalent toward such administration. His personal inclination and his socialization to his role are likely to produce a highly individualistic orientation in an organizational environment becoming increasingly bureaucratic.

The role of the professor centers around freedom to pursue the truth objectively and freely. Such pursuit requires time for meditation, experimentation with ideas, and a process of continual learning. Bureaucratic administration may release much of his time for intellectual activities, but his individualism and intellectual skepticism incline him toward suspicion of the standardization of behavior inherent in such administration. He desires to be free of responsibilities he regards as relatively mundane or trivial, but fulfillment of this desire weakens some measure of the authority he believes he should have over the experiences students have on the campus.

The qualities of its professors are important to the educational environment on any given campus. In addition to his direct impact on students, the professor ideally has a strong influence on educational policies. As Bundy says, the universities belong legally by charter to their governing boards, but a great faculty is the vital center of a great university. The faculty is the necessary center of gravity of policies for teaching, learning, and internal discipline.[18]

Prospects for change in faculty power

The academic profession has been in a strategic position because of two factors. First, the growing reliance by society on the university as the center of increasingly essential knowledge has given new visibility to the specialized competence of the professor. Second, the expanding demand for well-trained professors exceeded the supply in the 1960s. Bundy implies this power has been used by too many professors to advance their

[18] McGeorge Bundy, "Faculty Power," *Atlantic Monthly,* Vol. 222 (September 1968), pp. 42–44.

own careers and to protect themselves from administrative interference with their freedom to pursue their professional interests. Bundy, and probably most professors, would prefer that this power be employed to strengthen the university to fulfill its functions.[19]

However, there is evidence of fundamental changes in the bargaining position of faculties which raise the prospect of a reorientation away from individualism. The early 1970s reversed the supply-demand situation for persons possessing the doctor of philosophy degree. That is, in the 1960s about half of the new doctorates became college or university teachers, but on the basis of several projections of the supply of doctorates, only about a quarter of today's new doctorates will be needed as teachers in higher education. The enrollment decline already found in elementary grades will move progressively through secondary schools and colleges, probably bringing a decline in higher education enrollments by 1982. Confronted by a buyer's market, faculty independence and prospects for promotions will be undermined. To protect their interests, the faculty may move increasingly toward unionization, a most unprecedented development for an occupational group which has been noteworthy for its individualism.[20] Lieberman cites accomplishments of the Senate Professorial Association and the American Federation of Teachers in organizing faculties. He contends: "It is virtually certain that college and university faculties will follow this pattern in the 1970s." [21]

The development of this form of solidarity among faculties for the sake of job security would encourage collective bargaining to strengthen occupational advantages. It would work further against the use of faculty power for strengthening of the university as a whole—the use advocated by Bundy. However, as implied by Bundy's call for organizational altruism, the collective faculty in the time of faculty shortages has been prone to foot-dragging when a college undertakes change. The training, inclination, and job-slot requirements of the typical professor condition him to be a specialist in his academic subject. The reward system of the University encourages him to advance his career through concentration on research and teaching, with little effort to integrate his activities with segments of the organization beyond his own academic department. The greater scale of university operations and the identification of self with colleagues of a specialized discipline have undermined the cohesiveness of the faculty as an ongoing policy-making body. Faculty meetings often become futile rituals and curricula uneasy compromises between competing departmental pressure groups.[22]

---

[19] Ibid.
[20] Dael Wolfle and Charles V. Kidd, "The Future Market for Ph.D.'s," *Science,* Vol. 173 (August 27, 1971), pp. 784–93.
[21] Myron Lieberman, "Professors, Unite!" *Harper's Magazine,* Vol. 243 (October 1971), pp. 61–64, 69–70.
[22] Sanford, "Higher Education as a Social Problem," pp. 10–11.

When frustrated by bureaucracy, the faculty may dream of a university without presidents and deans. However, the economic reality is that faculty salaries, classrooms, secretarial services, and research resources must be provided if the first-rate university is to exist. As the chief executive, spokesman, and symbol of the university, the president has an influential role and function in obtaining funds. In this process he must preserve a form of internal governance congenial to free inquiry.

Issues involving teaching functions

Although teaching is presented as its primary function, the faculty is caught in the emphasis placed on research activities as a badge of competence. Guarantee of job security (tenure) and promotion, vital aspects of career advancement, are governed by evaluations by senior professors and the university administration. Yet academic freedom insulates the teacher from direct observation of his peers. Moreover, teaching effectiveness is difficult to evaluate by any standardized criteria. Research publications, on the other hand are tangible, can be read by evaluators, and their numbers counted. Therefore, a fundamental paradox is that the excellent teacher is unlikely to gain career rewards solely on the basis of his teaching competence.

As a product of the high regard for research, heavy emphasis is placed on scholarly publication as a criterion for faculty promotion and tenure. Research presumably reflects the teacher's engagement in the intellectual inquiry he aspires to develop in students. By it, his own insights into the principles of his discipline are sharpened and his enthusiasm for his discipline refreshed. But research competence must be balanced with skills in the communication process of teaching. Concentration on research tends to favor withdrawal from easy social interaction with students because of limitations on time and the need for undisturbed study and meditation. For the graduate faculty, which teaches the more advanced courses and works with students with specialized interests, research for publication is more consistent with teaching functions than for the undergraduate faculty, which teaches large classes in introductory courses. The heavier teaching load, Hurt says, makes for injustice when the "publish or perish" policy is applied to the undergraduate faculty. Other defects, he argues, are possibilities of undue emphasis on quantity of publications, as opposed to their intellectual merit, and encouragement of a form of "intellectual" snobbery.[23]

The ideal teacher should be lucid, articulate, fair-minded, and competent. Although the particular styles of combining these virtues are too diverse to permit clear definition of the "good" teacher, Adelson presents

[23] Lester E. Hurt, "The Case against 'Publish or Perish,' " in William P. Lineberry (ed.), *Colleges at the Crossroads* (New York: H. W. Williams Company, 1966), pp. 148–53.

some possible models. A *charismatic* teacher has an outstanding and memorable personality and is marked by intellectual strength, uncommon perceptiveness, vivacity of personality, and a deep absorption in his work. When he lacks such qualities, he becomes a narcissistic shaman. As a *"priest,"* the instructor's claims to power are based less on his personal virtues and more on this status as an agent of his academic discipline. He indoctrinates the promising student in the vocabulary and ideas of the discipline and seeks to commit him to a career in that discipline. As a *mystic healer,* the altrustic teacher concentrates on the developmental needs of the student rather than on himself, the subject matter, or the discipline. He endeavors to uncover the latent strengths of the particular student and to correct inner flaws to help him find what is best and most essential within himself.[24]

STUDENTS: STRESSES AND UNREST

The contemporary university fails to demonstrate in action that the student is its foremost interest. The functions of research and public service compete for attention. Other diversions include the tasks of fund raising, maintenance and expansion of plant, attraction of prestigious faculty, and cultivation of a favorable public image. The very tide of student admissions has shifted student-oriented tasks from faculty to bureaus of specialists. A frequent allegation is that this bureaucracy stifles the individuality of students, but we cannot be certain that earlier forms of administration were superior in recognition of individuality.

In a recent study, one group of educators listed nine typical criticisms of higher education: Colleges tend to reinforce rather than alleviate the freshman's transition from his family home to the relatively impersonal milieu of the campus. Impersonal and mechanical instruction extinguish curiosity and lower intellectual aspirations of students. New knowledge on learning and personality growth is frequently ignored in teaching. Too many students are poorly housed and poorly fed. Students are denied sufficient contact with the outstanding scholars among the faculty. Programs tend to be geared to an intellectual elite rather than the majority of students who are prepared to learn. Students are insufficiently involved in shaping the educational environment. The learning opportunities outside campus boundaries are not sufficiently recognized as a means to enhance the relevance of education. The grade-point average is too frequently overemphasized to encourage grim competitiveness.[25]

---

[24] Joseph Adelson, "The Teacher as a Model," in Sanford, *College and Character,* pp. 93–98.

[25] Joseph F. Kauffman, Chairman, *Report of the Committee on the Student in Higher Education* (New Haven, Conn.: The Hazen Foundation, 1968), pp. 13–14.

Stresses in entering college

The effect of college life on students is determined by the resources they bring with them and the nature of the life they find on the campus. To some degree the attitudes of students are shaped by experiences in the institutions of their home communities. The ambitions of parents and the idea of college for everyone have pressed high school seniors into an orientation toward higher education, regardless of personal inclination or readiness. They arrive on campus with varying intellectual capacities, ethical and moral values, and readiness to absorb the knowledge and ideas to which they will be exposed. They bring with them varying aspirations and expectations. Because of the difficulties for the American adolescent of making a career choice and of establishing a sense of self-identity, many will not have a clear understanding of why they are entering college and what they are supposed to do there.

The kind of mobility associated with American higher education places particular strains on mobility-oriented students. While the English use what Turner calls *sponsored mobility,* whereby recruits are chosen by the established elite early in the training process, the American norm is *contest mobility,* wherein elite status is the prize to be taken by the aspirants' own efforts outside of firm control of elites. Contest mobility in American high schools avoids sharp social selection between superior and inferior students. In the absence of a clear distinction between those who will win elite status and those who will not, contest mobility promotes more serious and continuing uncertainty among college students. And because career choices are made relatively late in the overall educational regime, the student is thrust into new circumstances where his earlier socialization may fail to equip him for elite status. Then he faces the tensions of abandoning previous lower-level friends and working out a personal adjustment to social rules of the elite he hopes to join.[26]

Although selective criteria differ among societies, there are certain qualifications which must be met if the elite are to perform their functions in making the society operate effectively. Whatever way the "cream" is defined in terms of individual skills and abilities, only a proportion of the "liquid" is of superior quality. U.S. elementary and secondary schools avoid consistent and persistent screening of pupils for higher education. Even choice of a vocation is deferred until college. The distinction between the successful and the nonsuccessful aspirants for contest mobility comes during college.

In "cooling-out" the unsuccessful student, institutions of higher education follow either a "hard" or "soft" response. When unable through admission standards to weed out those individuals with low probability

[26] Ralph H. Turner, "Sponsored and Contest Mobility and the School System," *American Sociological Review,* Vol. 25 (December 1960), pp. 855–67.

of graduation, some universities protect quality of educational outcome through a heavy dropout rate. Thus, a sizable proportion of students spends only one or two years on the campus under the "hard" selective process. The "soft" reaction provides the student with alternatives through detours into other less demanding curricula or colleges. Preentrance tests divert marginal students into remedial classes. Academic probation provides a marginal status for the low achiever. These strategies are intended to result in the student's eventual realization of his own limitations and are intended to enable him to fit his life plans to them. The features of this "cooling-out" process, Clark says, are provision of alternatives for achievement, gradual disengagement of the student from his original objective, confronting him with the realities of his situation, offering consolation to ease the sense of failure, and avoidance of a sharp definition of standards.[27]

Effects of the official structure

College life, Brownell asserts, has three principles which create discrepancies in the consistent development of the student for participation in society as a whole.[28] The first "corrupting principle" is *delayed function,* whereby the student spends several years storing up knowledge before he returns to the stream of life activities to utilize it. His relegation to a dependent role encourages the "pseudojuvenilism" of the college. Second, education tends to take place in a *social vacuum,* since the student is abstracted from his home and the work community. Although Brownell's term is inexact in that life is a subsociety rather than a social vacuum, the crucial point is that the college social system does differ from the world experienced after graduation. Finally, tendencies to *divorce theory from practice* undermine the application and retention of learning. Focusing attention on the common patterns of events and thoughts is the unique contribution of higher learning. But the integration of theories within the circumstances of student life is an especially difficult task.

These principles are related to central curriculum issues: academic specialization versus liberal education, and vocational training versus general education. Specialization is most pronounced in graduate school but is also found in undergraduate concentrations. Advocates of liberal education see adverse consequences in narrowing perspective and raising barriers against common understanding among groups of specialists. Ideally, a liberal education emphasizes the common characteristics of all knowledge and art to develop a whole man through integration of learning. Similarly

[27] Burton R. Clark, "The 'Cooling-Out' Function in Higher Education," *American Journal of Sociology,* Vol. 65 (May 1960) pp. 569–76; Clark adapts the concept developed by Erving Goffman.
[28] Baker Brownell, *The College and the Community* (New York: Harper and Brothers, 1952), pp. 34–39.

vocational education emphasizes the relevance of learning to job performance. The college is seen as a source of the trained manpower required by the society at large. General education opposes this orientation. Instead of emphasizing the practical and concrete, general education would cultivate appreciation of the central values of the society and abstract principles.

Advocates of either side in these two sets of issues can marshal impressive arguments. Distinctions between the opposing views break down, however, as the college strives to cope with growing student bodies, multiple purposes assigned the university, and limitations of budgets. Concern for individuality and the human spirit conflicts with pressures to standardize the curriculum so as to simplify administration and to allocate personnel and other resources "efficiently." The human spirit is left to students and faculty, coping with a variety of knowledge too extensive for effective standardization. Thus the probability that a curriculum will be individualized and meaningful to the student depends largely on the quality of instruction in the classroom. Differences between academic specialization and liberal education as ideologies are blunted by the realities of classroom events and the vital contributions of competent and dedicated instructors.

Peer groups as influences

The extra-classroom environment is a vital influence on learning. The far-ranging and diverse objectives assigned to higher education call for acquisition of an impressive array of knowledge and for considerable revision of attitudes to produce graduates prepared to assume responsible positions in society. The relatively brief and largely formal interaction in the classroom is insufficient to fulfill these obligations. As suggested by Brownell's "corrupting principles," the qualities of the university's own social system raise obstacles against the aspirations of some universities and some of their instructors to take full advantage of the classroom experiences as means of viable learning and as a means of bringing extra-classroom experiences into support of classroom learning. Later, this chapter will describe experiments which reflect a formal recognition by the university of the importance of relationships among students in determining the outcome of campus experiences.

In their search for prestige and recognition among peers, members of the student body exert control over the behavior of one another. Similarities among students, which stimulate behavior outside the formal control of the university, reflect influences operating before students join the campus community, however. Various institutions of higher education differ in the kinds of occupations for which they prepare students, the prestige they enjoy in society as a whole, the characteristics of their academic programs, and the populations from which they draw students. The kind and intensity of selection of students among applicants for admission have an influence on the characteristics of a particular student body. Successful applicants, furthermore, bring to the campus expectations and attitudes which are bases for developing congeniality groups.

The similarities in norms found in congeniality groups leads some observers to speak of student subcultures.[29] However, the fluidity of student norms limits the usefulness of the concept to *description* of behavior and patterns of thought among categories of students. The concept has less merit in terms of the transmission through generations of students of uniform cultural patterns.[30] The wisdom of conceiving of student subcultures as a descriptive term is indicated by their failure to capture the meaning of student life in later years or on other campuses.

In describing student norms existing at the time of their analysis, Clark and Trow postulated four student "subcultures." [31] (They caution that the fluidity of student norms prevents the fitting of all behavior neatly into their categories.) The *collegiate subculture* is essentially anti-intellectual and resembles the stereotype of college life as a "playground" diverting the energies of promising adolescents temporarily from competition in the job market. In earlier decades films usually portrayed campus life as centered around the football "rah-rah" spirit, drinking, and "fun" dating within fraternities and sororities. In this subculture, study is tolerated for sake of staying in school, but lack of commitment to intellectual effort and future adult careers is suggested by preference for "snap" courses and "easy" curricula.

The *vocational subculture* emphasizes the instrumental value of training for an occupational career. Students tend to be ambitious and future-oriented. Many are married and must earn their livelihood while taking courses. The curricular requirements are obstacles to be cleared in a race for graduation. The intellectual demands of the courses and the fun culture of the campus are shrugged off as distractions which only slow progress toward qualification for a technical occupation providing security and prestige.

Identification with the intellectual concerns of serious faculty members is the central feature of the *academic subculture*. The pursuit of knowledge and ideas permeates activities outside the classroom. Typically, graduate or professional education is the objective. Scholarly and scientific habits of mind and work are internalized in an involvement with coursework beyond mere academic survival.

The *nonconformist subculture* places particular stress on off-campus

---

[29] For example, Burton R. Clark and Martin Trow, "The Organizational Context," in Theodore M. Newcomb and Everett K. Wilson (eds.), *College Peer Groups* (Chicago: Aldine Publishing Co., 1966), pp. 18–26.

[30] This distinction is made in regard to "subculture of poverty" in Chapter 7, pp. 174–76.

[31] Clark and Trow, "The Organizational Context," present the general dimensions of these typologies. However, they are not responsible for our interpretation.

affiliations and response to the currents of thought experienced in the classroom or from sources off campus. Students are variously labeled as "intellectual," "radical," "alienated," or "bohemian." A common bond is the image of the campus as a place of political freedom, comfortable living, and bohemian atmosphere. They share a common detachment from the college they attend and a generalized hostility to its administration. One of the categories within the more generalized nonconformist subculture is a drug subculture loosely linked to the campus. Later discussion of drug users among students will distinguish those oriented to the "straight" world from those alienated from it.[32]

Dissension and unrest on the campus

Campus unrest, sometimes expressed in aggressive protest, has many possible explanations. The participants themselves differ in motivation and characteristics. However, there is a common theme. Restlessness is associated with a belief, not always carefully thought out, that current educational practices and procedures are modeled after the needs of the 19th century and are irrelevant to the conditions that will be encountered after graduation.

Sometimes campus dissension is shrugged off as only an aggravated form of the hell-raising within the collegiate subculture. Immaturity and youthful exuberance used to be expressed in "panty raids" and rallies before the traditional football game. The tolerance by the outside community of such exuberance relegates students to the status of children who do not know what they are doing ("boys will be boys"). The *in loco parentis* policies of universities stem from the same assumption. Such tolerance becomes rather shaky when the student protesters raise fundamental issues, when the operations of the college are questioned, and when property destruction is widespread.

Another explanation for campus dissension centers around rebellion against constraints and authority. This rebellion is supposed to stem from the psychological characteristics of individuals and is felt to be related to intense hatred of male, parental, and societal authority. Radical students are seen as coming from families which epitomize the flatness and emptiness of middle-class life.[33] With their revolt against authority able to gain a means of expression in campus life, these students focus on ungearing the university as a device for shaping students to become personnel of "soulless and exploitative" organizations of the "establishment." This explanation exaggerates the importance of personal maladjustments in creating general student unrest, though the reference to middle-class families

---

[32] See Chapter 20, pp. 514–15.
[33] Kenneth Keniston, *Young Radical: Notes on Committed Youth* (New York: Harcourt, Brace & World, 1968), pp. 45–48.

appears to have more validity. Westby and Braungart find leftist students come predominantly from the upper-middle class. They explain that security permits these students the luxury of nonconformity—unlike social climbers, they do not suffer from status anxiety.[34]

Keniston sees two errors in most such explanations. First, dissent is equated with personality maladjustment. Second, two polar types of student dissent are regarded as identical. The *political activist* attempts to take a stand on some matter of general political, social, or ethical principle because he perceives injustice being done to *others* less fortunate than himself. His interest is in social action for the oppressed outside of traditional political institutions rather than in advancing any particular ideology. The *culturally alienated student* is too pessimistic and too firmly opposed to the establishment to engage in active protest. He "drops out" and limits his dissent to the private means of nonconformity in behavior and dress, of stress on subjective experience, and withdrawal from politics and conventional society. Because campus dissent draws on both types, Keniston raises the crucial question of whether or not eventual frustration of the aspirations of political activists will leave dissent to the culturally alienated and thereby deprive society as a whole of a reservoir of talented young Americans for constructive change.[35]

Because of backgrounds and motivations, only a small proportion of students, Keniston says, are inclined personally toward rebellion. When campus issues become of more widespread concern, other students are more likely to join the activists and abandon apathy and privatism. A campus cultural climate is an important element in this spread of support in that it must encourage faith that the protest will win support from graduate students and young faculty. Spread of activism, Keniston says, is more likely to occur in large universities with a reputation for superior academic quality than in technical and denominational colleges.[36]

Gusfield offers another interpretation which attributes student activism to discontent created by fundamental changes in the nature of the large university.[37] He contends that mass education has changed the qualities of the student population. Instead of drawing a privileged few, the universities have received a large number of students without exceptional talent or backgrounds congenial to becoming members of an aristocratic elite—students preparing for white-collar and technical jobs defy efforts to weed out the "unfit" according to "academic standards." Meanwhile, Gusfield says, growth has led to the complex bureaucracy of the "mass university,"

---

[34] David J. Westby and Richard G. Braungart, "Class and Politics in the Family Backgrounds of Student Political Activists," *American Sociological Review,* Vol. 31 (October 1966), pp. 690–92.

[35] Keniston, *Young Radical,* pp. 300–302, 324–25.

[36] Ibid., pp. 306–18.

[37] Joseph Gusfield, "Beyond Berkeley: High Noon on the Campus," *Trans-action,* Vol. 2 (March–April 1965), pp. 3–7.

to which students are unable to relate. Furthermore, career considerations have diverted faculty interests from teaching to research and to service to the off-campus community.

All of this, Gusfield declares, adds up to enormous pressure on students to win social and economic rewards through academic credentials as symbols of merit. Cut off from personal relations with the distant faculty and exposed to an impersonal academic organization, the student is clutched by fears that his grades will cost him the chance for rewards granted to persons found meritorious. Campus demonstrations by some previously politically apathetic students provide relief from these pressures and from the tedium of rote learning. For others, he says, campus dissatisfactions are excuses for their own personal failures.

What is being done about it

New organizational models have been suggested to solve the difficulties that come with increased size. New colleges have been developed within universities to encourage intimacy of student-teacher relationships while preserving the benefits of the greater resources of the large university. A key purpose is the creation of a vibrant intellectual climate. Examples are Monteith College of Wayne State University, New College of Hofstra College, and Oakland University of Michigan State University.[38]

Since 1930 Harvard has operated "enriched" dormitories with common rooms, libraries, dining rooms, and residential tutors. These houses are supposed to extend classroom experience into the routines of daily living, with shared meals and coffee breaks promoting spontaneous exchanges of ideas. As Jencks and Riesman point out, however, the size of the college's population is only one of the factors affecting degree of intimacy. Temperament affects the likelihood that an individual will respond to others, and temperaments are likely to be similar in the smaller colleges, each with its own admissions policy. They add that a residential house requires intimate contacts over a span of time before its own subculture emerges.[39]

Another strategy relies on independent study to individualize education. The student moves as rapidly as he chooses through a prescribed curriculum and takes examinations whenever he is prepared. Sometimes the student pursues his own course with the help of an instructor. In other versions of individualized instruction audio-visual materials are employed independently, some extramural project is pursued, or seminars are offered undergraduates. Preliminary and inconclusive evaluation suggests

[38] Lewis B. Mayhew, "The New Colleges," in Samuel Baskin (ed.), *Higher Education: Some Newer Developments* (New York: McGraw-Hill Book Co., 1965), pp. 1–25.
[39] Christopher S. Jencks and David Riesman, "Patterns of Residential Education: Reflections from a Case Study of Harvard," in Sanford, *College and Character*, pp. 195–201.

benefits in insight, problem-solving capacities, and attitudinal change.[40] (However, instructor-centered methods are superior in producing gains in information and mastery of a subject.)

New communication and information-processing technologies have also been introduced. Examples are television, films, language laboratories, audio and video tapes, and programmed learning systems. But for these, teachers and students must be taught to use the devices, formidable investments and problems are involved in preparing the materials, and the ultimate usefulness of the devices pivots on the skill of the teachers who employ them.[41]

JUNIOR COLLEGE: A RECENT DEVELOPMENT

A product of the 20th century, the junior college initially offered typical liberal arts college subjects to a few local students to provide the first two years of study for a bachelor's degree, before transfer to a senior college. Most junior colleges also provide vocational training and adult education, and sometimes they provide community services through technical consultation and cultural events.

The pressures of burgeoning enrollment and accelerating costs have caused senior colleges and universities to move toward raising of standards. The rapid development of higher education has brought adoption of various versions of statewide master plans in some states, including establishment of new community colleges. This development would orient the public junior college toward serving as the lower division of a bachelor's degree regime, with the student transferring to a senior college for the last two years of course work.

A central theme of the JC is the democratization of higher education. The financial barriers to securing at least two years of college education are lowered by permitting the student to live at home and by reducing or eliminating tuition. Through an open-door admission policy, the junior college provides the marginal student a chance to demonstrate that his questionable academic background is not a reliable index of his potential.

Marginal status and ferment of growth

The junior college is linked concurrently with local secondary education and the statewide system of higher education. Its terminal vocational curricula identify it with local concerns and the preparation of students

---

[40] Bruce Dearing, "The Student on His Own: Independent Study," in Baskin, pp. 50–56.
[41] C. R. Carpenter and L. P. Greenhill, "Providing the Conditions for Learning: The 'New' Media," Baskin, *Higher Education,* pp. 133–49.

for jobs in local industries. Because many junior colleges admit all applicants, their student bodies include a greater proportion of students without previous academic experience and motivational readiness to undertake the regimen most frequently associated with the standards of senior colleges. Its academic curricula involve it in the problems of transferability of credits to senior colleges. The junior college suffers an unfavorable reputation when its marginal graduates are found academically unprepared, but its attraction to student applicants is jeopardized if it openly acknowledges that it screens out those students unqualified for the usual senior college regimen.[42]

The junior college teacher is supposed to implement a policy of "education after high school for everybody who wants it." When there is no provision for screening applicants, the instructor confronts remarkable heterogeneity of backgrounds and aptitudes among students. He is usually challenged to prepare one student for college transfer while avoiding the loss of students with more limited aspirations. Because he and his students are commuters, campus life does not exist as a leavening process to supplement classroom experience. All the while, the campus may be still under construction. (Classes may even be held in temporary buildings as bulldozers clank outside.) Curricula and courses are in various stages of development. Class size and teaching loads are frequently excessive, and the forecast is for even a greater enrollment next year. Caught in the vortex of this growth, the instructor worries about his inability to keep current with developments in his field and to maintain affiliation with others of his discipline.

Some consequences of democratization

The junior college serves as a democratizing agent through providing inexpensive access to higher education. While senior college students represent a selection among applicants, public junior college students tend to represent a cross section of the community.[43]

A large-scale study of students transferred from junior colleges indicates that the junior colleges are performing rather well as a melting pot of higher education. Their graduates with an aptitude for college work and good high school records perform well in senior colleges—though the performance of students with serious high school deficiencies is less satisfactory. Because junior colleges are used to a great extent by students with financial difficulties, transfers tend to suffer especially from inadequate economic resources when they enter the senior college. The inadequacy of counseling in some junior colleges favors unrealistic vocational choices which

[42] Burton R. Clark, *The Open Door College: A Case Study* (New York: McGraw-Hill Book Co., 1960) pp. vii–ix.
[43] Roger H. Garrison, *Junior College Faculty: Issues and Problems* (Washington, D.C.: American Association of Junior Colleges, 1967).

bring disillusionment after transfer. Because they enter the senior college in midstream, transfer students are handicapped by lack of appropriate orientation to their new setting.[44]

Many junior colleges claim that one of their primary objectives is to prepare students for technical or semiprofessional pursuits. Critics have noted that their actual performance is not consistent with this claim. Two thirds of their enrolling students state they intend to prepare to enter a senior college, but two thirds of them actually become terminal students.[45] This reflects the function of the junior college as a screening device for senior colleges, but it tends to degrade the image of terminal programs designed for technical and semiprofessional occupations.

SUMMARY

Higher education is experiencing increased demands on its services to cope with various social problems. The greater scale of these demands has overwhelmed alma mater. Not all her professors are certain that she has the resources and capacities to meet the demands of the general community. Faith in education as a cure-all for the various ills of society clashes with the conception of higher education as *the* social elevator. The first objective emphasizes open admission on the basis of broadening the population receiving benefits. The latter objective tests applicants for capacity to perform in statuses providing rewards because of competent service. The problems of higher education also reflect a discrepancy between the ideals it professes and its practices in reality. By applying the intellectual capacities that are its chief stock in trade, the university *should* be able to work out its own problems while making its proper contribution to the urban society.

FOR ADDITIONAL READING

Joseph Axelrod, Mervin B. Freedman, Winslow R. Hatch, Joseph Katz, and Nevitt Sanford, *Search for Relevance: The Campus in Crisis* (San Francisco, Calif.: Jossey-Bass, Inc., 1969).

Joseph A. Califano, Jr., *The Student Revolution: A Global Confrontation* (New York: W. W. Norton & Co., 1970).

James Bryant Conant, *Shaping Educational Policy* (New York: McGraw-Hill Book Co., 1964), Chapters 3 and 4.

Charles Frankel, *Education and the Barricades* (New York: W. W. Norton & Co., 1968).

[44] Dorothy M. Knoell and Leland L. Medsker, *From Junior to Senior College* (Washington, D.C.: American Council on Education, 1965).

[45] Leland L. Medsker, *The Junior College: Progress and Prospect* (New York: McGraw-Hill Book Co., 1960), pp. 24–25.

Nathan Glazer, "Student Politics and the University," *Atlantic Monthly,* Vol. 224 (July 1969), pp. 43–53.

Ervin L. Harlacher, *The Community Dimension of the Community College* (Englewood Cliffs, N.J.: Prentice-Hall, 1969).

Lawton M. Hartman, *Graduate Education: Parameters for Public Policy* (Washington, D.C.: National Science Foundation, 1969).

Thomas Hayden, "Student Social Action: From Liberation to Community," in Mitchell Cohen and Dennis Hale (eds.), *The New Student Left: An Anthology* (Boston, Mass.: Beacon Press, 1966), pp. 270–88.

James D. Koerner, "The Life and Hard Times of Parsons College," *Saturday Review,* Vol. 52, (July 19, 1969), pp. 53–55, 64–65.

William H. Orrick, Jr., *Shut It Down! A College in Crisis* (Washington, D.C.: National Commission on the Causes and Prevention of Violence, June 1969).

Francis C. Rosecrane, *The American College and Its Teachers* (New York: Macmillan Co., 1962).

James W. Thornton, Jr., *The Community Junior College* (2d ed.; New York: John Wiley & Sons, 1966).

Ellen Kay Trimberger, "Why a Rebellion at Columbia Was Inevitable," *Transaction,* Vol. 5 (September 1968), pp. 28–38.

Laurence R. Veysey, *The Emergence of the American University* (Chicago: University of Chicago Press, 1965).

Nicholas Von Hoffman, *The Multiversity* (New York: Holt, Rinehart & Winston, 1966).

———— "The Class of 43 is Puzzled," *Atlantic Monthly,* Vol. 222, (October 1968), pp. 69–76.

George Williams, *Some of My Best Friends are Professors* (New York: Abelard-Schuman, 1958).

Parameters of race and ethnic relations 14

In recent decades, no social issue has raised more concern about the functioning of our society than race relations. At first glance, it would appear that 400 years of smoldering discontent among blacks has burst suddenly into flame. Actually, however, even though recent dramatic developments suggest a "black revolution," the surfacing of this discontent reflects a long-term development in our society as a whole.

The black American "revolution" is regarded by many observers as the most important series of domestic events of the postwar period in the United States. Well-disciplined organizations of blacks have established unprecedented alliances with religious groups and political parties, and the federal government has made commitments to the cause of black equality. A crisis is revealed by evidence that the black population is in serious trouble because of the effects of discrimination, injustice, and inadequacies of the social structure in giving Afro-Americans a place and function in the U.S. social order. Moynihan finds the family structure of the lower-class black approaching a breakdown in many urban centers.[1]

MINORITY RELATIONSHIPS AND SOCIAL PROBLEMS

The word "minority" means a smaller number of people than those constituting a "majority." The crux of problems associated with minority

[1] Daniel Patrick Moynihan, "The Case for National Action: The Negro Family," in Lee Rainwater and William L. Yancey, (eds.) *The Moynihan Report and Politics of Controversy* (Cambridge, Mass.: The M.I.T. Press, 1967), pp. 47–51.

groups, however, lies in an inferior power position, rather than simple numerical inferiority. The minority group has special physical or cultural characteristics which are supposed to distinguish it from others. These characteristics are evaluated negatively by the dominant group and all members of the minority group are arbitrarily lumped together as "inferior." Consequently, the life chances of the minority group member are affected profoundly simply because he is a member of the group.

Imposition of an extra handicap

Within any national society, there are various privileges and opportunities held out as rewards that may be attained through competition according to the norms of the society's culture. We have a social problem when the physical or cultural characteristics of a minority group are taken as a basis for arbitrarily denying these privileges and opportunities regardless of individual merit. Members of the minority group may resemble some members of the majority in some respects, including inferior education, low job opportunity, substandard housing, and inadequate medical care, but the central point is that the minority group's inferior power position gives it an additional handicap.

In sharing this extra handicap, the minority members are pressed toward identification with one another as a self-conscious social unit. Membership in the minority group is transmitted through birth on the basis of a socially invented rule of descent enforced by the majority. By choice or necessity, the minority tends to marry within its own group, to perpetuate its cultural and physical differences from the majority, and to *remain* in a inferior power position.[2]

Minority problems are actually majority problems. Myrdal points out that the white majority determines the black's "place" in the American society and that "the Negro problem" exists because of forces operating in the larger American society.[3] The black person's life style and his opinions on "his" problem are, in the main, secondary reactions to the pressures from the dominant white majority. The moral dilemma raised by discrimination, Myrdal says, goes on within people as well as between them. Minority relationships become recognized by the majority as a social problem when the members of the majority disagree as to whether the subjugation of the minority is socially desirable or in the ultimate interest of the majority.

In recent U.S. history, discrimination and segregation have received increasing attention from the majority population because of a rising level

[2] Charles Wagley and Marvin Harris, *Minorities in the New World: Six Case Studies* (New York: Columbia University Press, 1958), pp. 4–10.

[3] Gunnar Myrdal and assistance of Richard Sterner and Arnold Rose, *An American Dilemma* (New York: Harper & Brothers, 1944), pp. xlvii–lv.

of aspiration among the underprivileged. As members of the majority come to think in terms of the concept of relative deprivation, they become more concerned over the lot of the poor.[4] The blacks, Indians, and Spanish-speaking minorities are represented among the poor disproportionately to their share of the population.

Failure of the "melting pot"

A moral dilemma stems from the divergence of reality from American ideals. Peoples from many lands and diverse cultures have populated the United States, and on the pedestal of the Statue of Liberty, a poem proclaims: "Give me your tired, your poor, your huddled masses yearning to breathe free." An American "melting pot" was supposed to transform a heterogeneous mass of diverse peoples into a new American culture dedicated in principle to personal freedom together with an opportunity to demonstrate individual qualification for social and economic rewards. Presumably, the blending of cultures would justify the abandonment by newcomers of old ways in order to be assimilated into a national culture of high quality. A strong nation was to be produced through the full personal commitment of its citizens to the national culture, regardless of race, creed, or color. Actually, the "Americanization" process has tended to remodel newcomers into conformity with a white, Protestant, Anglo-Saxon culture.

Assimilation, as implied by the poem on the Statue of Liberty, is usually interpreted to mean that acceptance of the national culture brings benefits to the newcomer. Adoption of the host culture must be distinguished, however, from assimilation in terms of equality of status and opportunity, often denied to immigrants in the past as well as current native minorities. Both varieties of assimilation are retarded when minority groups are physically and socially separated from the majority.

Segregation is frequently interpreted as a social and physical isolation forced upon a minority by the dominant majority. It may also reflect the wishes of the minority in expressing their sense of peoplehood. The distinction between the sources of segregation is difficult to apply in daily social interaction, since discrimination by the majority influences the adjustments of the minority to their underprivileged status. In withdrawing from humiliating contacts with the majority, the minority develops habits, interests, and preferences for "our own people."

These points will serve as background for our study of the shifts in attitudes among blacks in regard to their assimilation within the American society. As Chapter 15 will indicate, high hopes, raised initially by the civil rights movement, have been dashed. Disillusionment and the development of a strong sense of peoplehood have moved Afro-Americans toward

[4] See Chapter 6, pp. 146–49.

separateness. The question arises: Can ethnic identity be balanced against the need for a viable national society involving all citizens?

BACKGROUND ON MINORITY GROUPS

In the United States minority groups have been distinguished largely on the basis of race, nationality, religion, and language. Minorities have tended to be composed of nonwhites, non-Protestants, and persons not speaking English as their primary language. Among the nonwhite races in the United States, the largest proportion are blacks. In order of size, the other large groups are American Indians, Japanese, Chinese, and Filipinos. In recent decades all of these groups have exceeded whites in their rate of population increase. In educational attainment, occupational status, and average income, the Japanese and Chinese compare favorably with whites. The Indians and blacks are clearly at a disadvantage.[5] Blacks will be the subject of the next chapter. Here we will briefly present the history and situation of other minorities.

Spanish-speaking groups

In the Southwest the Spanish-speaking people include Hispanos and Mexican-Americans. After the Mexican-American War in 1848, Mexico ceded a large territory to the United States, thus making a large number of Spanish-speaking people U.S. citizens. Their descendants call themselves "Hispano" to distinguish themselves from the Mexican-Americans who migrated later from Mexico and from the children of these later migrants. Predominately a rural people, the Hispanos have had limited contact with the outside world. Although their standards of living are low, they enjoy full political rights. Away from their home villages, they experience discrimination less intensively than the blacks.[6]

After the decline of immigration from Europe, the permanent immigrants from Mexico were supplemented by *braceros,* contract laborers performing temporary and seasonal work, largely on farms. There were also *wetbacks* who entered illegally. The importation of braceros was terminated in 1964. Mexican-Americans have become increasingly urbanized. Although found in all walks of life, they continue to be heavily overrepresented in the low-paid occupations. In rate of acculturation and

[5] Calvin F. Schmid and Charles E. Nobbe, "Socio-Economic Differentials among Nonwhite Races," *American Sociological Review,* Vol. 30 (December 1965), pp. 909–21.

[6] See Carey McWilliams, *North from Mexico* (Philadelphia Pa.: J. B. Lippincott Co., 1949), pp. 51–52; John H. Burma, *Spanish-Speaking Groups in the United States* (Durham, N.C.: Duke University Press, 1954), pp. 3–34; Clark S. Knowlton, "The Spanish Americans in New Mexico," *Sociology and Social Research,* Vol. 45 (July 1961), pp. 448–55.

assimilation, they are among the least "Americanized" of all ethnic groups.[7]

With relatively cheap air travel to New York, migration from Puerto Rico assumed mass proportions after World War II. Population pressure and insufficient job opportunity on the island have pushed migration. Although found through all the states, Puerto Ricans have settled chiefly in New York City, where they are employed in the garment industry and as service workers. Migrants have been drawn from the most productive age groups, the above-average in education, and urbanites of Puerto Rico. Although their earnings were above average in Puerto Rico, these migrants experience lower job status than other whites in New York and are subjected to slum conditions. The migrants are predominately white but include blacks who encounter racial prejudice in New York.[8] In Puerto Rico, class membership is more important than color in fixing status, and on the mainland, the migrants are puzzled by the higher priority given racial identity in determining acceptability in social gatherings, occupation, housing, and marriage. It is not clear what will be the outcome of this difference in conceptions. Some writers believe that the Puerto Ricans will split into those identified as whites and those identified as nonwhites. Fitzpatrick reports evidence that currently Puerto Ricans in New York are continuing to follow the deemphasis of racial distinctions prevalent on the island.[9]

Chinese in the United States

Earlier Chinese immigration was for labor in U.S. mines, for railroad construction, and for farm work. These immigrants soon encountered hostility, especially in western states, because of their willingness to work for low wages, and during periods of unemployment the racial and cultural distinctiveness of the Chinese made them targets for scapegoating. Mob violence was particularly characteristic of a number of Pacific coast towns in the 1880s. Later popular literature and movies in the "Limehouse" pattern presented stereotypes of the opium eater, treacherous "white slavers," and tong hatchetmen. The struggles of China against Japan before and during World War II brought about a more favorable image of a heroic people.[10]

[7] Celia S. Heller, *Mexican American Youth: Forgotten youth at the Crossroads* (New York: Harper & Row, 1950), pp. 22–87.

[8] C. Wright Mills, Clarence Senior, and Rose Kohn Goldsen, *The Puerto Rican Journey* (New York: Harper & Row, 1950), pp. 22–87.

[9] Joseph P. Fitzpatrick, "The Adjustment of Puerto Ricans to New York City," in Milton L. Barron (ed.), *Minorities in a Changing World* (New York: Alfred A. Knopf, 1967), pp. 285–87.

[10] These paragraphs are based on: S. W. Kung,. *Chinese in American Life* (Seattle, Wash.: University of Washington Press, 1962), pp. 31–45, 87, 171–78; Rose Hum Lee, *The Chinese in the United States of America* (Hong Kong: Hong Kong University Press, 1960), pp. 33–39, 273, 357–72.

In the early decades Chinese-Americans were concentrated largely on the West Coast; subsequently they have tended to disperse throughout the nation, though with a preference for larger cities. Immigration, made possible by amendment of immigration laws (as well as a natural increase from births), has increased their numbers since World War II. Changes in U.S. immigration laws permitted the arrival of more females to correct the sex-ratio imbalance which had favored growth of a "rooming-house" culture that hindered preservation of the family and other community institutions.

The Chinese have had fewer problems of racial discrimination in Hawaii than on the mainland, though even on the mainland they were not subject to the concentration camp ordeal imposed on Japanese-Americans during World War II. Chinese-Americans are, however, subjected to racial discrimination, as witnessed by the infrequency of intermarriage, relative superficiality of contacts with the dominant culture, and limitation of economic opportunities beyond technical and scientific fields. They continue to have a large lower class, but they have experienced recent social and economic progress. The intensity of prejudice in the 19th century slackened with the reduced flow of immigration because of the Exclusion Act of 1904, the retreat into Chinatowns in earlier decades, and the withdrawal of Chinese workers from competition for laboring jobs.

Japanese in the United States

Because of the unfriendly reception accorded to, and the legal restrictions imposed upon, Japanese migrants, Japanese migration to the United States was only a trickle until 1900. The unwillingness of Japanese-Americans to accept discrimination aroused the antagonism of native Americans, but the power of the Japanese government motivated the government of the United States to use diplomacy, rather than unilateral legislation, to restrict immigration. President Theodore Roosevelt negotiated the so-called Gentlemen's Agreement in 1907 whereby Japan would not issue passports except under certain circumstances.

Until the attack on Pearl Harbor in 1941, Japanese-Americans were heavily concentrated on the West Coast, with distinctive colonies outside of this region found only in Chicago and New York.[11] During World War II Japanese-Americans felt the impact of prejudice, war hysteria, and confusion among government officials. Free-floating fears of "fifth-column" activities extended beyond those Japanese in the United States who had strong loyalties and to their mother country to include *all* Japanese-Americans, and on March 2, 1942, the commander of the Western Theater of Operations established relocation centers to which West Coast persons

[11] Charles F. Marden and Gladys Meyer, *Minorities in American Society* (3rd ed.; New York: American Book Co., 1968), pp. 197–200; also see Bradford Smith, *Americans from Japan* (Philadelphia, Pa.: J. B. Lippincott Co., 1948).

of Japanese origin or descent were removed. Until liquidation of these centers in 1946, 110,000 Americans remained shut up in American concentration camps and suffered forced sale of their property and deterioration of their businesses and professional practices. The violation of their civil rights was paradoxical in that some 33,000 Japanese-Americans served in the armed forces of the United States, earning an impressive array of honors for bravery.[12]

Their return to California after the war met opposition, but a counter-reaction among West Coast whites made fair play the final, dominant response. The Japanese-Americans had to shift more to employment by non-Japanese, however, and they also dispersed to other parts of the country, although they continue to be concentrated in the western states.[13]

American Indians

In 1492 some million Indians of the United States and Alaska were fragmented into more than 600 distinct societies. Their persistent wars with one another were aggravated by their wish to deny to other tribes the highly valued utensils and weapons of the whites. Methods of extermination, appropriation of lands, and expulsion of tribes were employed by whites in order to take their land. Unable to mobilize in a common defense, the Indians were finally defeated in war by 1892. When the U.S. Supreme Court ruled that Congress could unilaterally revise treaties made by Indians, the way was opened for land-hungry whites, and by 1928 the 137 million acres of land held by the Indians in 1887 had melted to 50 million acres, and this was the least desirable land.[14]

The early policy of the government was to deal with the tribes as though they were independent sovereignties, although the Indians did not have a centralized authority and conception of property consistent with this policy. In contrast, the Spaniards regarded Indians as subjects of the crown and the church rather than as members of sovereign tribes. Both policies resulted in merciless exploitation, but only the Spanish policy fostered assimilation.[15]

[12] See Alan R. Bosworth, *America's Concentration Camps* (New York: W. W. Norton & Co., 1967); Alexander H. Leighton, *The Governing of Men* (Princeton, N.J.: Princeton University Press, 1945); Edward H. Spicer, Asael T. Hansen, Katherine Luomala, and Marvin K. Opler, *Impounded People* (Tucson, Ariz.: University of Arizona Press, 1969); Dorothy Swaine Thomas and Richard S. Nishimato, *The Spoilage* (Berkeley and Los Angeles, Calif.: University of California Press, 1946).

[13] James W. Vander Zanden, *American Minority Relations* (2d ed.; New York: Ronald Press, 1966), p. 262.

[14] See John Collier, *The Indians of the Americas* (New York: W. W. Norton & Co., 1947); Dale Van Every, *Disinherited: The Lost Birthright of the American Indian* (New York: William Morrow & Co., 1966); Paul A. F. Walter, Jr., *Race and Culture Relations* (New York: McGraw-Hill Book Co., 1952), pp. 279–80.

[15] Brewton Berry, *Race and Ethnic Relations* (3d ed.; Boston, Mass.: Houghton Mifflin Co., 1965), pp. 233–41.

The disillusionment of the Indians and their segregation on reservations brought destruction of tribal cultures. Hunting nomads could not take easily to the settled life of the farmer. To tide them over until they could adjust, government rations were distributed, thus serving to pauperize them. The destruction of tribal cultures was further advanced by a new "Americanization" policy in the 1880s whereby the communal ownership of reservation land was to be broken into individually owned parcels to assimilate Indians into American culture. Their religion was suppressed. English was to become their language. Through formal education, children were to be weaned from the ways of their forefathers, though never were adequate provisions made for enabling Indians to assume the role of citizen. In fact, only in 1924 were they granted American citizenship.[16]

RACE AND SOCIAL BEHAVIOR

Properly, *race* denotes one of the major divisions of mankind on the basis of hereditary physical characteristics such as shape of hair in cross section, stature, color of eyes and hair, blood group, and so on. This biological phenomenon is employed by racists to argue that their own race is "superior." As Dobzhansky puts it, race bigots contend that, the cultural achievements of different races being so obviously unlike, it follows that their genetic capacities for achievement must be just as different. Nobody can discover the cultural capacities of any population or race, he says, until there is equality of opportunity to demonstrate these capacities.[17]

Confusing biology and culture

Scientific classification of mankind into clear-cut races is a confusing task at best. The idea of a "pure" race is a fiction because of the impact of a variety of social factors on biological classification of peoples. Throughout history racial groups have sometimes been isolated from one another and sometimes have mixed their genes through great migrations. When isolated, they have preserved their biological types through endogamous mating. In addition to mergers through migration, biological differentiation of racial groups has been diluted through such sociocultural factors as changes in diet, preferences in selection of mates, and differential death rates as a consequence of war and disease.

Montague considers "race" to be one of the most dangerous and tragic myths of our time. By "myth," he refers to the belief that physical traits are linked with mental traits and cultural achievements. He reports that

---

[16] Ibid.
[17] Theodosius Dobzhansky, *Mankind Evolving* (New Haven, Conn.: Yale University Press, 1962), pp. 285–86.

available facts offer no scientific evidence of demonstrable difference in the structure of brains of members of different ethnic groups. The variability of brain size is such that it has no significance to cultural or intellectual development. Montague asserts that, given similar opportunities to realize their potentialities, the average achievement of members of each ethnic group is about the same.[18] Social-cultural differences cannot be attributed solely to bodily characteristics.

Nevertheless, the ideology of *racism* assumes that races can be ranked along a superiority-inferiority scale, one's own race placed at the top. "Inferior" races are supposed to be earlier, more primitive offshoots from the tree of biological evolution. Genetic mixing of the races is feared as destructive to the presumed high quality of the "superior" civilization.

Prejudice and discrimination

Prejudice is to pass a judgment in advance of due examination; to prejudge. The judgment *may* be unduly favorable, but in terms of our discussion a minority group suffers negative consequences. Allport defines *prejudice* as thinking ill of others without sufficient warrant. His definition has two elements: unfounded judgment and a feeling tone. The latter includes scorn or dislike, fear, and aversion.[19]

Ignoring both the differences among the members of the minority group and their similarities to himself, the prejudiced person applies *racial stereotypes* to assign identifies to *all* members of the group according to his perceived notions of what he believes them to be like and how he thinks they will behave. It is common practice in anonymous and mobile urban life to make quick judgments of strangers on the basis of their external qualities. In Goffman's terms, the stranger is given a "virtual social identity" regardless of his "actual social identity." [20] When the individual is assigned discreditable qualities in this virtual social identity, he suffers stigmatization as a consequence of the prejudgments applied to him.

There has been a tendency to reify prejudiced attitudes. As Raab and Lipset put it, these attitudes have been conceived as little mental packages tucked away in the corner of the brain, awaiting the proper stimulus to bring them to life. The prejudiced attitude is supposed to include both hostility and a stereotype. However, an individual can have a negative stereotype without hostility, hostility without a negative stereotype, or may have different feelings about two groups cloaked with the same negative stereotype. Furthermore, Raab and Lipset assert, an attitude is not a thing

---

[18] Ashley Montague, *Man's Most Dangerous Myth: The Fallacy of Race* (4th ed.; Cleveland, Ohio: World Publishing Co., 1964), pp. 23–24, 100, 363.
[19] Gordon W. Allport, *The Nature of Prejudice* (Reading, Mass.: Addison-Wesley, 1954), p. 7.
[20] Erving Goffman, *Stigma: Notes on the Management of Spoiled Identity* (Englewood Cliffs, N.J.: Prentice-Hall, 1963), pp. 1–5.

but a process involving all the factors in a social situation. Rather than prejudice operating as a state of mind to stimulate behavior automatically, evidence indicates that attitudes shape themselves to behavior. Changes in the environment within which interaction with minority groups occurs can modify specific attitudes. Conversely, the fountainhead of prejudiced attitudes and prejudiced behavior is the pattern of community practices within which the child's modes of behavior are learned and individual practices are shaped.[21]

In his report on data derived from the Cornell Studies in Intergroup Relations, Williams finds prejudices to be formulated obscurely and to be expressed most frequently within one's own group. Unless some concrete situation precipitates their expression, the prejudices remain disengaged.[22] Since a gap exists between prejudiced attitudes and the action of discrimination, there is the possibility of inhibiting the expression of prejudices. Private feelings may be inhibited from public action through development of new constraints derived from self-interest and changes in the circumstances under which discrimination had been facilitated. Later we shall consider the socioeconomic developments which have changed these circumstances.

In *discrimination,* categoric action is taken which denies to individuals or groups the equality of treatment they may wish. The word "discrimination" may refer positively to the ability to be discerning and perceptive in relationships with other people, but in minority-group relations, "discrimination" has a specialized and less attractive meaning. The prejudices held against minorities are converted into actions by individuals and groups to deny members of the minorities equal access to the opportunities and privileges which our system of beliefs asserts are available to all. Instead of judging the individual on his own merits, prejudice causes him to be placed arbitrarily in a social category ranked as inferior. Discrimination converts this categoric and negative judgement into social reality. The target of discrimination is excluded from certain types of employment, residential housing, educational and recreational opportunities, membership in religious and social organizations, political activities, and health services.

ASSIMILATION AND ETHNIC GROUPS

The ideals of the national society, it was noted earlier, call for the merger of peoples from diverse origins into a common culture. What is the proper basis for this merger—assimilation of all people into a single

[21] Earl Raab and Seymour Martin Lipset, "The Prejudiced Society," in Earl Raab (ed.), *American Race Relations Today* (Garden City, N.Y.: Doubleday-Anchor, 1959), pp. 29–48.
[22] Robin M. Williams, Jr., *Strangers Next Door* (Englewood Cliffs, N.J.: Prentice-Hall, 1964), p. 77.

culture or the development of a pluralistic culture? Would assimilation of all peoples under one cultural blanket bring social equality?

Cultural and structural assimilation

Gordon makes a useful distinction between cultural assimilation and structural assimilation. *Cultural assimilation* is the ultimate outcome of acculturation in that the newcomers adopt the patterned ways of thinking, feeling, and behaving toward one another which characterize the dominant culture of the host society. This does not necessarily involve *structural assimilation,* wherein the newcomers are absorbed into the intimate social life of the host society as implemented in its cliques and institutions. The concept implies that the newcomers seek, and are accepted by the members of the host society for, membership in the social groups of the host society. Cultural assimilation may result in the newcomers adopting the language and many of the cultural ways of the host society, but this cultural assimilation must be accompanied by structural assimilation to provide the newcomers full membership in the host society and their winning of the social and economic rewards of membership.[23]

When minority groups are separated from the majority group by differential participation within the social structure, the total society is compartmentalized regardless of the success of cultural assimilation in bringing similarities in general beliefs, values, and symbols of a common history. Integration within American society implies that every individual, regardless of ancestry, will be able to enter into relationships with other members of the society except for limitations based on ability, taste, and personal preference. Both cultural and structural assimilation would have to be advanced.

Peoplehood as a social bond

Many social groups may properly claim the right to decide who may become their members and enjoy the privileges provided by their group's activities. "Ethnicity," derived from the Greek word "ethnos," refers to identification of a person with his own people. Gordon employs *ethnic group* in that sense.[24] The growing dominance of urban life has weakened the bonds of kinship and has strengthened a reliance on more rational and explicit mechanisms of coordinating individual behaviors into large-scale organizations. Thereby, individuals have lost the full effectiveness of intimate groups in providing them a sense of belonging and clear guidelines as to expected behavior. Gordon argues that a sense of peoplehood per-

[23] Milton M. Gordon, *Assimilation in American Life* (New York: Oxford University Press, 1964), pp. 67–78.
[24] Ibid., pp. 23–28.

sists today, reflecting the urge to identify with some group smaller than a nation.[25] This sense of peoplehood may be based on race, religion, or national origin, but the ethnic groups, in Gordon's use of the term, reflect an urge for social affinity with a particular group.

Seeing the American social structure as a series of ethnic subsocieties enclosed within a national society, Gordon finds the ethnic subsociety serving several functions.[26] The sense of intimate peoplehood ties individuals together through group identification. A network of groups and institutions based on ethnic identity enables the individual to confine his primary relationships to his ethnic subsociety through the stages of the life cycle from birth through adolescence, marriage, and parenthood to retirement and death. It is comfortable to live among people like oneself. The ethnic heritage is a prism through which the national culture is refracted to provide a spectrum of subcultures based on a range of identifications with particular religions, nations of origin, and/or racial groups. The sharing of a national culture by otherwise diverse groups is pivotal to the "cultural pluralism" model of American society. In this view, through tolerance of differences found in subnational communal life, the stability of the national society is to be maintained in the face of a diversity of beliefs among its heterogeneous groups.

Earlier efforts to "Americanize" ethnic minorities following a *melting-pot conception* of cultural assimilation. The new American was supposed to emerge from the mingling of the best features of many ethnic heritages. In reality, schools and other agencies of cultural indoctrination pressed newcomers from southern and eastern Europe to continue the dominance of Anglo-Saxon culture. Thereby, "Americanization" became a process of remolding newcomers into conformity with a white, Protestant, Anglo-Saxon culture. Because of the positive contributions of the ethnic groups listed above, Gordon questions the melting pot's tendency to eliminate subcultural diversity in favor of standardization of culture according to the Anglo-Saxon model.[27] Furthermore, the ethnic subcultures exhibit strengths of potential advantage to the overall society. Speaking of the Mexican-Americans, Burma sees virtues in the Hispano culture within which people for three centuries have demonstrated a staying power against drought and flood, maintained community solidarity, and shown more family stability than "our own divorce-ridden one."[28]

To merge diverse ethnic groups into a harmonious society, loyalty to the ethnic group may not block identification of the individual with the all-encompassing society. Gordon proclaims the need for a society in which one may say with equal pride: "I am a Jew, or a Catholic, or a

[25] In Chapter 3, we discuss the urbanite's search for a social-psychological community and the persistance of primary groups.

[26] Gordon, *Assimilation in American Life,* pp. 37–38.

[27] Ibid., pp. 115–31.

[28] Burma, *Spanish-Speaking Groups in the U.S.,* p. 31.

Protestant, or a Negro, or an Indian, or an Oriental, or a Puerto Rican";
"I am an American"; and "I am a man."[29]

Factors retarding rate of assimilation

Merger of an ethnic group into the national society is impeded by
differences in language. However, language is most significant as evidence
of deep-seated differences in cultural orientations.

The assimilation of the Chinese-American has been hindered by certain
cultural themes. Indirect methods of social interaction, for example, conflict with the American preference for directness and frankness. Involvement of ethnic associations in personal problems conflicts with individualism. Covert measures of dealing with deviants obstruct police operations.
As culture bearers, the family can retard acceptance of American values.
Lee reports conflicts between parents and their American-born children
over such issues as grandparents' control over grandchildren, dating,
household chores, the speaking of Chinese, and marriage for love.[30]

Whether voluntary or imposed by the majority, segregation of the
minority retards acculturation. When the ethnic community resembles the
homeland, the migrant has little inducement to adopt new ways. A continual influx of new migrants revives old customs. When most of one's
activities occur within an ethnic island, there are few opportunities to
associate with persons outside one's own group. Spatial segregation may
reflect an occupational segregation in that the minority is assigned a kind
of work which isolates its members from usual community life.

Factors promoting rate of assimilation

Acculturation is promoted when the small size of the minority group
requires it to interact with members of the majority in employment and
gaining goods and services. The urban environment exerts pressures toward assimilation. The numbers and diversity of people encountered in
daily intercourse require new habits and behavior. (Usually, these challenges of familiar ways come with migration of the minority people, but
in the case of Mexican-Americans in the Southwest, Saunders says, it is
the westward expansion of the Anglo culture that has exposed the long-
term residents to cultural differences.[31])

Increased schooling of minority children inculcates urban values and
those of Anglo-Saxon culture. With proficiency in English and exposure
to the values of the dominant culture, the second generation is better
equipped to find a place in American society, barring discrimination, and
to move away from the ethnic culture.

[29] Gordon, *Assimilation in American Life,* p. 265.
[30] Lee, *The Chinese in the U.S.,* pp. 55–118, 126–34, 251.
[31] Lyle Saunders, *Cultural Differences and Medical Care* (New York: Russell Sage Foundation, 1954), p. 96.

Paradoxically, discrimination against an ethnic group results in pressing some of its members to accept the negative evaluations at least sufficiently to deny that they are part of the group. Within the Mexican minority the native-born of native-born parents distinguish themselves from the immigrants who are more likely to be darker in skin color and who place stress on their Mexican-Indian background. The native-born see themselves as Spanish-Americans and serve as a buffer between the immigrants and the Anglo-Americans into whose ranks they sometimes pass.[32] Similarly, New York-born-and-reared Puerto Ricans reject identification with recent migrants.[33]

Progress in cultural assimilation without concomittant structural assimilation contributes to personal disorganization among the second generation of migrants. Exposed to the influences of the dominant culture, Mexican-American youth in ethnic enclaves of metropolitan centers have become isolated from their parents. Without appropriate adult models in their marginal position, they form gangs. Furthermore, the ethnic community is left as largely lower class when those who do advance in economic and educational status divorce themselves from the community.[34]

DISCRIMINATION AND THE SOCIAL ORDER

In advancing theories such as scapegoating, psychologists emphasize the relationship of prejudice to the characteristics of individuals. Studies of prejudiced persons concentrate on how they acquire certain attitudes and beliefs, how certain cultural values are instilled in them, and how they express these attitudes and support these values in ways conducive to discrimination against minorities. Prejudice is alleged to satisfy some psychic need of the prejudiced person, or to compensate him for some personality defect. Reluctant to blame himself for his failures in the competition with his fellows, the prejudiced person vents his own frustrations, and projects his own fears and lusts on the "scapegoat" group. When he selects a target already disdained by his own group, he casts himself as a defender of his own group's values while expressing his own frustrations.[35] Although the sociologist shares a concern about these important matters, he gives greater emphasis to the forces external to the individual.

[32] McWilliams, *North from Mexico*, pp. 209–10.
[33] Elena Padilla, *Up from Puerto Rico* (New York: Columbia University Press, 1958), p. 59.
[34] Leonard Broom and Eshref Shevsky, "Mexicans in the United States—a Problem in Social Differentiation" *Sociology and Social Research*, Vol. 36 (January-February 1952), pp. 153–57; also see more recent discussions: Y. Arturo Cabrera, *Emerging Faces: The Mexican-Americans* (Dubuque, Iowa: William C. Brown Company, 1971; William Madsen, *The Mexican-Americans of South Texas* (New York: Holt, Rinehart & Winston, 1964).
[35] Allport, *Nature of Prejudice*, pp. 236–38, 335–68.

Norms, status, and power

Prejudice can be traced to the operation of the same processes which give order to society. Prejudice is translated into action largely because the norms of discrimination and segregation are built into the process of socialization and regularized social arrangements. Stereotyped descriptions of certain racial and ethnic groups are included in the cultural heritage which provides norms against which a child learns to judge persons, things, and ideas he encounters. Prejudice is thus developed through the same processes by which he learns to love his mother, to appreciate apple pie, and to be patriotic and religious. Individuals are prejudiced, Westie says, because they are raised in societies which have prejudice as a facet of the normative system of their culture. It is built into the notions of what "ought to be" and of ways members of the group "ought" to behave in relationships with members of certain outgroups.[36]

Race prejudice, Blumer says, is fundamentally a matter of defining oneself as belonging to one racial group and of assigning to another racial group those individuals against which one has prejudices.[37] The "racial" group does not necessarily exist except in the beliefs of the prejudiced group. Blumer sees prejudice as attributable to one of several feelings involving concern for the social position of one's own group in reference to the position of the other group. A feeling of superiority provides self-assurance. The feeling that the subordinate race is intrinsically different and alien is presented as justification for social exclusion.

However, it is a feeling of proprietary claim which is most active in arousing prejudice, Blumer argues. The dominant group believes that it has either exclusive or prior rights in many important areas of life ranging from land and jobs to positions of power and prestige. Another fourth feeling is that the subordinate race harbors designs on the prerogatives of the dominant race. Violent reactions of the dominant group are most likely when the minority's rejection of an inferior position is interpreted as an assault upon these prerogatives.[38]

The linking of racial conflict with social position focuses attention on caste. *Caste* is a rigid form of assigning individuals and groups to various levels of prestige and power according to their status at birth. A primary element is a categoric limitation on the upward mobility of the subordinate caste from the lowly position inherited at birth. Prohibitions against marriage outside the caste maintain this limitation. The community based on

[36] Frank R. Westie, "Race and Ethnic Relations," in Robert E. L. Faris (ed.), *Handbook of Modern Sociology* (Chicago: Rand McNally, 1964), p. 579.
[37] Herbert Blumer, "Race Prejudice as a Sense of Group Position," *Pacific Sociological Review,* Vol. 1 (Spring 1958), pp. 3–7.
[38] Allen D. Grimshaw, "Factors Contributing to Color Violence in the United States and Britain," in Allen D. Grimshaw (ed.), *Racial Violence in the United States* (Chicago: Aldine Publishing Co., 1969), pp. 254–55.

caste maintains a stable equilibrium when the etiquette of deference is observed by the subordinates. The equilibrium is in jeopardy when the subordinates, excluded from scarce awards they seek as much as do the members of the dominant caste, do not accept as proper the barriers raised against their participation in a competition based on individual merit. The ambitious subordinates arouse the resentments of the "superior" caste, whose members fear that its monopoly over rewards is threatened.

Permeation of institutional fabric

The lives of individuals are profoundly affected by social structures such as schools, hospitals, governmental agencies, factories, political parties, and so on. The term *institutional racism* refers to the embedment in these stable social arrangements of differential distribution of the benefits of a society according to racial status.[39] Career opportunities can be offered or withheld. Preparation for economic opportunities is not equally available to all. The protection of the law and provision of health service may be offered differentially to the various segments of the community.

The enforcement of a system of segregation, regardless of the interest and wishes of the subjugated minority, involves the question of political and economic *power*—the extent to which a party (person or group) can control the behavior of another. Segregation maintains the dominance of one group over another through traditions, socialization, and coercion.[40] The traditions support the alleged superiority of the dominant groups in terms of preferred cultural values, typical personality characteristics, and prestige. The "inferior" group is pictured as shiftless, deceitful, and ignorant. The beliefs of racism are indoctrinated into the young of both groups to prepare them for conduct appropriate to their place in the segregated society. The "inferiors" are expected to know their "place" and to act accordingly.

Segregation has been maintained by social control techniques ranging from naked coercion to more refined techniques. The Klan, the rural sheriff, the metropolitan police, the board of education, and the functionaries of similar organizations play roles in this control system. Another pattern has been the use of middle-class blacks as intermediaries between white leaders and the mass of blacks in enforcing the standards of segregation for the sake of personal advantages of the intermediaries.[41]

Discrimination is also maintained by "a series of uncoordinated though similar individual acts no one of which has more than short-run significance."[42] Individual whites refuse to associate with blacks and employers

[39] See Louis L. Knowles and Kenneth Prewitt (eds.) *Institutional Racism in America* (Englewood Cliffs, N.J.: Prentice-Hall, 1969.)
[40] R. A. Schermerhorn, "Power as a Primary Concept in the Study of Minorities," *Social Forces,* Vol. 35 (October 1956), pp. 53–56.
[41] Myrdal, *An American Dilemma,* pp. 768–80.
[42] H. M. Blalock, Jr., "A Power Analysis of Racial Discrimination," *Social Forces,* Vol. 39 (October 1960), pp. 57–58.

withhold desirable jobs to avoid inconvenient negative reactions of other whites. Instead of demonstrating some conscious "plot" to maintain segregation against blacks, the actions of most whites, Blalock says, maintain discrimination without conscious policies. Ending discrimination is difficult when formal policies and laws maintain it, but is even more difficult when "gentlemen's agreements" exist. For example, at the top echelons, craft unions have supported social legislation and the elimination of discriminative practices among unions, but at the local affiliate level exclusion of nonwhites from membership is characteristic of bricklayers, electricians, plumbers, and heavy equipment operators.[43]

The exclusion of blacks from apprenticeship opportunities in the skilled trades is a result of racial discrimination, but other factors are also involved. Black youth often lack adult models of their own race to interest them in such occupations, and they frequently do not have the educational prerequisites. Apprenticeship committees tend to favor friends and relatives even if racial discrimination could be ruled out, and even if he gains admittance, the black encounters discrimination among co-workers to complicate his learning.[44] In his careful study, however, Marshall finds union racial practices moving toward equalitarianism—but at a rate disappointing to most civil-rights advocates.[45]

The black's chief educational handicaps have been segregated schools and inferior instruction. In the *Brown* decision the Supreme Court outlawed segregated schools largely on the basis of the detrimental effect on black children. The separation of blacks from the social life of the white society has contributed to a distinctive subculture in ghettos derived largely from the patterns of lower-class Negro families. This family type is characterized by a high proportion of mother-headed households and ambivalence about the desirability of marriage. Black women can at least equal their men in obtaining marginal jobs and have greater access to welfare payments. The husbands and wives continue to operate rather autonomously in separate pursuit of their own interests.[46]

Costs and implications of discrimination

Because it is used as a biological concept, race has a profound impact on social relationships and, through prejudice and discrimination, imposes

---

[43] Whitney M. Young, *To Be Equal* (New York: McGraw-Hill Book Co., 1964), pp. 69–80.

[44] George Strauss and Sidney Ingerman, "Public Policy and Discrimination in Apprenticeship," Louis A. Ferman, Joyce L. Kornbluh, and J. A. Miller (eds.) *Negroes and Jobs: A Book of Readings* (Ann Arbor, Mich.: University of Michigan Press, 1968), pp. 305–15.

[45] Ray Marshall, *The Negro and Organized Labor* (New York: John Wiley & Sons, 1965), p. 311.

[46] Lee Rainwater, "Crucible of Identity: The Negro Lower-Class Family", *Daedalus,* Vol. 95 (Winter 1966), pp. 176–99.

heavy psychological costs on those persons assigned to inferior status. Bodily characteristics, especially skin color, become a central measure of moral and social worth. All of us have difficulties in determining who we are and how we fit into a complex, swiftly changing world. We search for answers by observing how other persons react to us. The minority-group member is judged arbitrarily and automatically on the basis of his skin color, regardless of his other social and personal characteristics. His difficulties in achieving a favorable conception of himself are aggravated by the messages of inferiority conveyed in his contacts with whites and dominant culture.

Recent socioeconomic progress among blacks may decrease special pressures on self-images, but a decade ago, a study found the Afro-American personality shaped in an atmosphere of a struggle for survival. Kardiner and Oversey reported a low capacity for relating with others because of an inner mistrust that anyone could love the black for his own sake. The black had an enormous problem of controlling aggressions, which were cloaked by laughter and ingratiation. As ineffective adaptations to bolster his self-esteem, the black disparaged status striving among his peers and employed magical aids such as gambling.[47]

In its 1954 decision against school segregation the Supreme Court found that blacks were deprived of equal protection under the Fourteenth Amendment, which provides that no state shall "deprive any person of life, liberty, or property without due process of law, nor deny to any persons within its jurisdiction the equal protection of the law." The principle of respecting the worth and dignity of every individual underlies the American way of life. The democratic process cannot operate in an atmosphere that is restrictive, coercive, or lacking in freedom. In keeping minorities in a subordinate status, the control mechanisms of segregation exact heavy psychological, emotional, and social costs on minority members through denial of major desires found in every normal human being.

Housing segregation has implications beyond undue restriction on choice of residence.[48] It creates and maintains segregation in schools, community services, employment, political participation, religious activities, and so on. At the same time, discrimination in housing is aggravated by other community problems: massive internal migration, expansion of suburbs, and the deterioration of central cities. Because the home expresses status and personal aspirations, the drive by blacks for equality in housing draws especially strong resistance and evasion.

[47] Abram Kardiner and Lionel Oversey, *The Mark of Oppression* (Cleveland, Ohio: World Publishing Co., 1962), p. 313–14; for a poignant description of the psychological costs to the Negro, see: Robert Coles, "It's the Same, but It's Different," in Talcott Parsons and Kenneth B. Clark (eds.), *The Negro American* (Boston, Mass.: Beacon Press, 1967), pp. 254–79.

[48] Adapted from Don J. Hager, "Housing Discrimination, Social Conflict, and the Law," *Social Problems,* Vol. 8 (Summer 1960), p. 80–81.

SUMMARY

assigned divviance statived

Minorities are involved in social problems because they are assigned arbitrarily an inferior position in society. Discrimination and forced segregation are the price they pay through an extra handicap assessed against their chances to benefit from promises held out by a society founded on the ideals of democracy. The ultimate consequences of the price they pay also have impact on the majority in undermining the moral and social cohesion of the national society. After summarizing the characteristics and place in American society of minorities other than blacks, we considered several concepts pertinent to the issue of whether or not discrimination would continue to divide the nation. These concepts were race, prejudice, discrimination, assimilation, and ethnic group. Because these concepts are associated with norms, the difficulties of minority relationships are social problems involving the workings of society itself. The next chapter builds on this foundation of concepts to take up the problems of Afro-Americans.

Can discriminate s being prejudiced

FOR ADDITIONAL READING

Aaron Antonovsky, "The Problem: The Social Meaning of Discrimination," in Bernard Rosenberg, Israel Gerver, and F. William Howton (eds.), *Mass Society in Crisis* (New York: Macmillan Co., 1964), pp. 408–24.

Gunther Barth, *Bitter Strength: A History of the Chinese in the United States, 1850–1870* (Cambridge, Mass.: Harvard University Press, 1964).

Gordon H. DeFriese and W. Scott Ford, "Verbal Attitudes, Overt Acts, and the Influence of Social Constraint in Interracial Behavior," *Social Problems,* Vol. 16 (Spring 1969), pp. 493–505.

Stanley Frost, *The Challenge of the Klan* (New York: AMS Press, 1969).

Ernest Galarza, Herman Gallegas, and Julian Samora, *Mexican-Americans in the Southwest* (Santa Barbara, Calif.: McNally & Loftin, 1969).

Nathan Glazer and Daniel Patrick Moynihan, *Beyond the Melting Pot* (Cambridge, Mass.: The M.I.T. Press and Harvard University Press, 1964).

Thomas F. Gossett, *Race: The History of an Idea in America* (Dallas, Texas: Southern Methodist University Press, 1963).

Harry H. L. Kitano, *The Japanese-Americans* (Englewood Cliffs, N.J.: Prentice-Hall, 1968).

Robert E. Lane, "Why Lower-Status People Participate Less than Upper Status People," in Lewis Lipsit (ed.), *American Government: Behavior and Controversy* (Boston, Mass.: Allyn and Bacon, 1967), pp. 87–97.

Raymond W. Mack, *Race, Class, and Power* (2d ed.; New York: American Book Co., 1968).

Joan W. Moore, "Colonialism: The Case of the Mexican Americans," *Social Problems,* Vol. 17 (Spring 1970), pp. 463–72.

Peter I. Rose, *They and We: Racial and Ethnic Relations in the United States* (New York: Random House, 1964).

James W. Silver, *Mississippi: The Closed Society* (New York: Harcourt, Brace & World, 1964).

Sidney M. Willheim and Edwin H. Powell, "Who Needs the Negro?" *Trans-action,* Vol. 1 (September-October 1964), pp. 3–6.

The American 15
black: Ferment
and change

Afro-Americans have played a central role in focusing national concern on the paradox of poverty and social injustice in the midst of unprecedented technological potential and rights and liberties rhetoric. Black marches, sit-ins, and other forms of black protest have been among the chief awakeners of the national conscience. Increasing black activism has signaled the abandonment by blacks of passive accommodation to racial discrimination and segregation, as well as attesting to their higher level of aspiration.

FORCES OF SOCIAL CHANGE

Why have minority relations attracted so much attention since World War II when the plight of the blacks has festered in this country for two centuries? Certainly the social injustice is not new—nor are expressions of concern over it. The unprecedented feature is the convergence of widespread concern with pressure by blacks for fundamental changes, and this is yet another facet of the changes wrought by the rise of contemporary urban society.

Today's patterns of minority relationships are being reshaped by urbanization, alterations in the economic system, greater population mobility, and a decline in regional isolation coupled with growing integration of the national economy, political response to discontent, improved communication—and changes in attitudes among blacks. Discrimination and segregation operate within a social system, and under the impact of changing conditions, the system has lost its effectiveness in keeping blacks "in their place."

Demographic factors

Behind the apparently sudden emergence of minority problems are a number of demographic conditions. For example, in 1910 about 90 percent of U.S. blacks lived in the South and 80 percent of these southern blacks lived in rural areas. But by 1970 the proportion of U.S. blacks in the South had dropped to 53 percent and by 1980 it will probably have dropped to 46 percent. In 1960, for the first time in history, the proportion of urbanities among blacks (73.2 percent) exceeded the equivalent share (69.5 percent) of whites. These data indicate a great shift out of the South and toward cities.[1]

The cities' demand for unskilled workers after World War I brought the first large-scale migration of blacks to the North. This migration was accelerated by agricultural trends in the South associated with boll weevil infestation, floods, and the mechanization of farming, together with the decline of the cotton economy, which undermined the previously dominant influence of plantation owners and contributed still further to the exodus from southern farms. World War II stimulated the migration even further, so that today black population bases in the North and West have reached such a size that black populations there will increase significantly in the future through births alone, regardless of easing of migration.

While city whites are moving to the suburbs, blacks are concentrating in metropolitan areas. In 1950 6.6 million blacks lived in central cities; a generation later, in 1970, this figure had risen to 13.1 million, a 98.5 percent increase—while in the same period the white population in the central cities increased only 5.8 percent. In 1950 10 percent of the population of New York City was black, but by 1970 21 percent was. Other major U.S. cities show similar increases over the same period; for example, Chicago's black population rose from 14 to 33 percent; Detroit's, from 16 to 44; Philadelphia's, from 18 to 34; Washington, D.C.'s from 35 to 71; and Los Angeles's, from 9 to 18.[2]

Urbanism and minority protest

Migration to the city provides minorities a broader—although usually still inadequate—range of economic and social opportunities than is found

[1] C. Horace Hamilton, "The Negro Leaves the South," in Russell Endo and William Strawbridge (eds.), *Perspectives on Black America* (Englewood Cliffs, N.J.: Prentice-Hall, 1970), pp. 206–11; and Bureau of Census Reports.

[2] United States Department of Commerce, Bureau of the Census, *The Social and Economic Status of Negroes in the United States, 1970,* Special Studies, Current Population Reports, Series P–23, No. 38, July 1971, Tables 6 and 11.

in rural areas. The city also has a more rapid rate of change than rural areas, and this undermines the stability essential to keeping blacks "in their place" so that they do not jeopardize the interests of the dominant majority. The city differs so greatly from the native environment of rural blacks who migrate to it that it releases them from the controls of the rural segregation system. (Discrimination and segregation of course exist in the city, but their operation is not readily apparent to the newcomer unacquainted only with local informal controls.)

Moreover, the maintenance of segregation does not necessarily correspond with the economic self-interests of a city's dominant whites. The cash registers of urban department stores are color-blind, and chain stores and nationwide industries usually find regional segregation policies contrary to their best interests in other sections of the nation.

Migration to the cities of the South as well as the North and other regions enables blacks to escape the white paternalism of farms and villages, since within an urban mass the individual concealed from the close observation of whites is able to gain a measure of freedom of action under the cloak of anonymity. As the size of the community grows, the white citizen knows less and less of life in the ghetto. Killian and Grigg recall, for example, the astonishment of some southern whites when they learned that Black Muslim temples existed in their own cities.[3]

The new social and economic aspirations which stimulated black migration, however, are frequently not gratified by an urban environment. There is a potential for alienation in the city, and though the black with high social position is more likely to identify with the values of the community in a large city than in a small town, Killian and Grigg found that individuals of low occupational status are as alienated in the big city as they are in the small town.[4]

When the city rewards only with despair after arousing hope, passivity may be abandoned when some previously ignored event is accompanied by violence. A familiar pattern in the city, for instance, has been ghetto aggression following a police arrest accompanied by brutality. It has been suggested that the comparative freedom of the city, coupled with the transfer of rural poverty to urban slums, favors the growth of protest groups and the involvement of previously noninvolved persons.[5]

Breakdown of regional isolation

Along with the rest of the nation, the South has felt the rising demand for governmental services which local and state governments cannot provide without assistance from Washington. Because it has, and because of

[3] Lewis M. Killian and Charles M. Grigg, "Race Relations in an Urbanized South," *Journal of Social Issues,* Vol. 221 (January 1966), p. 24.
[4] Lewis M. Killian and Charles M. Grigg, "Urbanization Race, and Anomia," *American Journal of Sociology,* Vol. 67 (May 1962), pp. 661–65.
[5] Killian and Grigg, "Race Relations in a Urbanized South," pp. 25–26.

its need to replace agriculture with industrial employment, white southern leaders have had to modify their regional society to make it more consistent with standards in the rest of the nation. The black sharecropper was dependent upon a single person, the plantation owner, in almost every aspect of his life, but the town worker's hourly pay, public welfare services, and increased shopping bring him into the impersonal market of the city.[6]

Compared with plantation owners, merchants and industrialists are under much sharper pressures against implementing racial discrimination. Their need for customers and their desire for as unrestricted a use of the labor force as possible operate against the expression of prejudicial beliefs. Moreover, with the development of the American economy on a national scale, the expression of regional racial mores becomes an obstacle to local industrial growth. Corporations find it inconsistent with their long-term interests to be identified with racial discrimination in hiring and other practices, and racial tension and discord are disruptive to economic tranquility and the network of cooperative arrangements essential to profitable business operations. Even southern businessmen, for example, were quick to recognize the implications for their expansion aspirations when Little Rock's rate of industrial growth dropped abruptly after the governor of Arkansas made a major effort in 1957 to forestall integration of Little Rock's Central High School.[7]

Political developments

The political power of minority groups, especially blacks, has been strengthened by several developments. For one, growth of a white, urban middle class in the South has weakened the landed gentry there. For another, in areas where they are numerically dominant, blacks have gained influence through heavier registration and voting, and the migration of Afro-Americans into northern industrial cities has given them a pivotal political power there.[8] Finally, with the rise of Third World nations in Africa, U.S. domestic practices of racial discrimination put a nation identifying itself with democratic principles in a very bad light.

Decisions of the Supreme Court declared the "white primary" illegal in 1944 and outlawed school desegration in 1954. Accelerating a movement initiated by the Roosevelt administration in the 1930s, the executive branch moved against job discrimination in government and among contractors with the federal government. Segregation in rail and bus terminals was abolished in 1961 and in 1964 the most comprehensive civil rights

[6] J. Milton Yinger and George E. Simpson, "Can Segregation Survive in an Industrial Society," *Antioch Review,* Vol. 18 (Spring 1958), pp. 16–17.

[7] J. Milton Yinger, *A Minority Group in American Society* (New York: McGraw-Hill Book Co., 1965), pp. 41–42.

[8] Ibid., pp. 50–51.

legislation since post-Civil War days was enacted with respect to voting registration, provision of facilities to serve interstate commerce, access to public facilities, programs of federal aid, and discrimination by employers and labor unions.[9]

Black middle class

Under urbanization, a black middle class has emerged that for the most part shares the dream of "the good life" of the white middle class—a home, a car, a regular vacation, and an education for the children.[10] With teachers its largest bloc, the black middle class is made up of doctors, lawyers, small businessmen, ministers, and postal workers. More recently, its ranks have been expanded to include technicians, politicians, labor leaders, minor government functionaries, and agency managers.

Although economic opportunities for blacks improved substantially after World War I, the most spectacular gains here were initiated with the manpower shortages of World War II; however, these relative gains do not cancel out the disproportionate representation of blacks in the less skilled blue-collar and service occupations which are particularly vulnerable to obsolence and unemployment.[11] The reduction of European immigration has benefited U.S. minorities, but, as Glenn says, future gains depend on a greater availability of high-status occupations through expansion of their share of all jobs.[12]

The relatively recent rise of protest movements in the United States is linked with the expansion of the black middle class in terms of the relative deprivation concept.[13] That is, in spite of their gains when compared with the lot of U.S. blacks of the past, members of the black middle class are frustrated by their failure to achieve even greater success in winning equality within the white social structure.[14] Instead of comparing their lot with the less fortunate members of their own race, black middle-class members compare their situation with that of whites who resemble them in education, occupational skills, and career aspirations. Their gains have whetted appetites for more progress, and their awareness of the less obvious barri-

[9] Arnold M. Rose, "The American Negro Problem in the Context of Social Change," *Annals of American Academy of Political and Social Science,* Vol. 357 (January 1965), pp. 5–9.

[10] C. Eric Lincoln, "The Negro's Middle-Class Dream," in Milton L. Barron (ed.), *Minorities in a Changing World,* (New York: Alfred A. Knopf, 1967), pp. 339–48.

[11] Joe L. Russell, "Changing Patterns in Employment of Nonwhite Workers," in Louis A. Ferman, Joyce C. Kornbluh, and J. A. Miller (eds.) *Negroes and Jobs: A Book of Readings* (Ann Arbor, Mich.: University of Michigan Press, 1968), pp. 92–107; M. Elaine Burgess, "Race Relations and Social Change," in John C. McKinney and Edgar T. Thompson (eds.), *The South in Continuity and Change* (Durham, N.C.: Duke University, 1965), pp. 345–46.

[12] Norval D. Glenn, "Changes in the American Occupational Structure and Occupational Gains of Negroes During the 1940's," *Social Forces,* Vol. 41 (December 1962), pp. 188–95.

[13] See Chapter 6 for the presentation of this concept.

[14] Wilbert E. Moore, *Social Change* (Englewood Cliffs, N.J.: Prentice Hall, 1963), pp. 83–84.

ers against their full equality is coupled with knowledge of the privileges accorded their white counterparts with whom they have communication. The social and economic progress of middle-class blacks frequently reflects an intellectual capacity to discern the hidden workings of institutional barriers to racial equality.

The general belief among many whites is that blacks typically set low life goals for themselves because their typical life situation discourages any belief that planning and hard work will improve their condition. However, there are signs that black youth are moving closer to white youth in their life plans and ambitions.[15] Social and economic progress has given the Afro-American middle class a capacity to implement protest that is unavailable to the most downtrodden elements of society, the helpless poor, whose passivity reflects their fatalism.

Changes in leadership patterns

If only by their presence in cities in greater numbers, blacks gained advantages in their struggle for opportunity and power. Large concentrations of minorities facilitate communication and organization to a degree not possible between scattered rural districts. Development of a new sense of group identification among members of minorities has impelled race relations in a more equalitarian direction, and even segregation has had an influence in turning them toward one another in relationships within the church, educational institutions, and political organizations. With the erosion of strict segregation, possibilities of shaping new kinds of leadership, have developed.

Under the social system of segregation, *Uncle Toms* serve as liaison between the white supremists and the blacks in a parasitic status in which the black begs for favors and the whites gain the labor of passive blacks.[16] Under such an arrangement, patience and accommodation in the face of economic and social adversity are emphasized. Today, however, more militant leaders have emerged to challenge this concept. In studying Tallahassee, Florida, Killian and Smith found the accommodative leadership style breaking down and "new" leaders refusing to compromise with segregation or to negotiate with whites in the traditional accommodating fashion. The new leadership type sought gains through formal demands, boycotts, lawsuits, and by voting. The black population rejected the "old"

---

[15] Burgess, "Race Relations and Social Change," p. 348; Bernard C. Rosen, "Race, Ethnicity, and the Achievement Syndrome," *American Sociological Review,* Vol. 24 (February 1959), pp. 47–60; Noel P. Gist and William S. Bennett, Jr., "Aspirations of Negro and White Students," *Social Forces,* Vol. 42 (October 1963) pp. 40–48; Robert G. Halloway and Joel V. Berreman, "The Educational and Occupational Aspirations and Plans of Negroes and White Male Elementary Students," *Pacific Sociological Review,* Vol. 2 (Fall 1959), pp. 56–60.

[16] Gunnar Myrdal with assistance of Richard Sterner and Arnold Rose, *An American Dilemma* (New York: Harper and Brothers, 1944), pp. 720–22, 768–70.

leaders as untrustworthy, and the city officials found these "old" leaders unable to gauge sentiment or to deliver results.[17] With the collapse of the strategy of accommodative relationships, segregationists found that they lacked means of dealing with blacks in the customary ways of control through evasion. With previous accommodative channels of communication between the races broken, a void appeared in interracial relations.[18]

Racial moderates among whites called for the reciprocal role among blacks of *racial diplomat*. Thompson describes this type of person as highly skilled in dealing with white leaders, rejective of segregation, knowledgeable in the customs affecting interracial relations, and dedicated to serving the community as a whole. Although the racial diplomat's accomplishments for his race may be significant and may win him respect as a "successful" member of the middle class, he is subject to the suspicion that he is "selling out to the whites."[19]

The militant is described as *race man* by Thompson. Vitally concerned with the welfare of blacks, the race man sees himself as a black symbol of mankind's struggle for dignity. Impatient with second-class citizenship, he refuses to work within the framework of a "separate but equal" doctrine as does the racial diplomat.[20] Congenial to cooperation with white liberals, however, Thompson's race man differs from those black militants who argue for separateness (see pp. 379–85).

STRATEGIES AGAINST DISCRIMINATION

How can the extra handicap of racial discrimination be erased to bring the scales of social justice closer to balance? Later we shall consider the strategies of protest and activism employed by blacks. Here we consider strategies frequently employed by a broader spectrum of reformers.

Appeals of mass media

Mass communication media have become formidable instruments for tying together the elements of this complex society, but their functions and limitations must be recognized in judging their pertinence to racial issues.[21] Appeals to the brotherhood of man are insufficient to eliminate deep-seated prejudices and discriminate practices in community institutions. At the same time that such appeals are least effective in reaching the preju-

[17] Lewis M. Killian and Charles V. Smith, "Negro Protest Leaders in a Southern Community," *Social Forces,* Vol. 38 (March 1960), pp. 253–57.

[18] Lerone Bennett, Jr., *Confrontation: Black and White,* (Chicago: Johnson Publishing Co., 1965), pp. 260–61.

[19] Daniel Thompson, "Patterns of Race Relations Leadership," in Endo and Strawbridge, *Perspectives on Black America,* pp. 336–43.

[20] Ibid., pp. 347–51.

[21] See Chapter 10, pp. 258–62.

diced persons, they encourage less prejudiced persons to believe that the mere expression of liberal views eliminates discrimination.

Mass media can reach large numbers of people simultaneously, but the communicator operates within the capacity of audience attitudes for change. In community disputes the media serve more as providers of information than as agents of direct and lasting persuasion. By expanding public awareness of the existence of discrimination and its consequences for other highly appreciated values, the media may strengthen control over racial extremists and over excesses of practices of segregation, but really effective influence comes through exploitation of preexisting behavior patterns or attitudes. Mass media messages must be supplemented by face-to-face communication.

Greater interaction among the races

Increased contact among the races is not in itself sufficient to alleviate racial dissension. In fact, increased contact may only increase awareness of the possible threats and alien qualities represented by the "majority" and the "minority." In summarizing common features of previous studies, Simpson and Yinger offer the following principles.[22] Prejudice is likely to be aggravated when the contacts are incidental to the rhythms of daily life, are involuntary, and are tension-laden. Better prospects for attitude change exist when individuals are placed in situations where they share some characteristics in such nonracial matters as social class, occupational interests, and educational attainment. Similarly, it is preferable that blacks are encountered in roles not usually associated with blacks, because then they are more likely to be judged as individuals who are, say, co-workers, fellow soldiers, alumni of the same school, or parents sharing one's own problems and perceptions. Along this line, there are special advantages in bringing the races together where they work in interdependent activities, with each group member relying on the efforts of the other members to get the job done.

Equal-status contacts have been advocated as those most congenial to the alleviation of racial differences. Allport, for example, believes that interaction of blacks and whites who hold the same level of job is more effective than relationships between whites and blacks of inferior-superior job statuses.[23] Persons of similar social position share similar perspectives derived from social class, work experiences, and common interests in task performance, of course, but like interests can also mean competition for job opportunities. Establishment of a firm policy prohibition of racial discrimination is more likely to change attitudes in work relationships, but

---

[22] George E. Simpson and J. Milton Yinger, *Racial and Cultural Minorities* (3d ed.; New York: Harper & Row, 1965), p. 510.
[23] Allport, *Nature of Prejudice,* pp. 261–65.

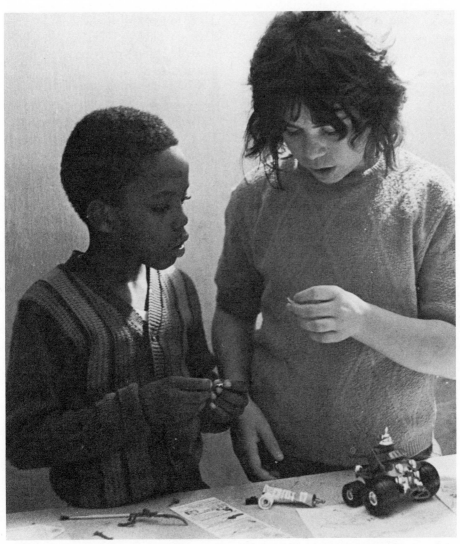

Bill Semich, Action for Boston Community Development, Inc.

Equal-status contacts as strategy. To alleviate the effects of racial differences, one strategy is to bring the races together in social relationships derived from common interests in task performance. At the Happy Hours Workshop in an East Boston apartment building, youngsters such as those above, build model airplanes, ships, and other vehicles.

equal-status contacts will still vary in effectiveness according to personality and social variables.[24] Secure persons respond more favorably than insecure persons, and whites are more likely to feel insecure when blacks are in numerical dominance, and blacks when whites are. Finally, compulsory contacts draw resentments not necessarily based strictly on racial prejudice.

Greater frequency of interaction reduces the possibility of prejudice, but Williams emphasizes the importance of distinguishing between the probability of frequent interaction among the races and the nature of interaction once contact has been established.[25] Personal choice has less influence on the frequency than on the nature of interaction, and opportunities for contacts are regulated by the rhythms of daily life according to the role and status of the individual in the community. The typical contacts of a person are regulated by activities characteristic of his work, recreational, and family routines. The anchoring of discrimination in the social fabric insulates individuals against contacts with minorities and thus the unprejudiced majority-group members must go outside of his familiar living patterns to establish interracial contacts. Thus, also, increased interracial contacts are least probable among the very persons whose racial attitudes the social reformer wants to change.

Increased contact is not necessarily constructive, however. A study of the 1965 Los Angeles riot in Watts reports that a high level of discontent prevaded the entire black enclave. Among those persons regarding the riot favorably, however, those in a more fortunate economic position exhibited antiwhite sentiment, while the less fortunate were motivated more by economic discontent. Since blacks in a more fortunate economic position tend to have more contracts with whites than those in a less fortunate economic position, Murphy and Watson hypothesize that discontent increases with an increase in contact between the races. In learning to compare themselves with whites, the more fortunate Afro-Americans raise their aspirations, and their gains fail to keep pace with these heightened aspirations.[26]

Can laws change behavior?

In the reconstruction era after the Civil War, laws that were passed to protect blacks proved to be without real force. Recent decades have brought new minority rights legislation, judicial decisions, and administra-

---

[24] George E. Simpson and J. Milton Yinger, "The Sociology of Race and Ethnic Relations," in Robert K. Merton, Leonard Broom, and Leonard S. Cottrell, Jr., *Sociology Today: Problems and Prospects* (New York: Basic Books, 1950), p. 398.

[25] Williams, *Strangers Next Door,* pp. 157–67.

[26] Raymond J. Murphy and James W. Watson, "The Structure of Discontent: Relationship between Social Structure, Grievance, and Riot Support," in Nathan Cohen (ed.), *The Los Angeles Riots* (New York: Praeger Publishers, 1970), p. 250.

tive action, and where existing laws have been a prop to inequality their influence has been removed. A central issue is raised: Can laws change the hearts and minds of men?

Proponents of civil rights legislation make certain assumptions. The first of these is that when behavior patterns are regulated by new norms, attitudinal patterns will also reshape themselves. Since prejudice is believed to be largely a matter of social habit and interests, rather than something firmly grounded in personalities, it is felt that by changing the normative climate, behavior can be changed without requiring immediate and direct action against the prejudiced attitudes of individuals. Through laws, then, norms can be inserted to block the expression of prejudice in discriminatory practices.

If the law is enforced and is directed specifically against the behavior to be changed, there will be uniform pressure on all persons to practice racial equality. If previously discrimination was the normative behavior, the law is employed to create a situation in which discrimination is defined as deviant behavior. An additional benefit of such law, Young says, is that it gives an opportunity for practice of racial equality to those already willing but previously fearful of the risk.[27]

A second assumption made by proponents of civil rights legislation is that counterpressures against discriminatory practices can be created if individuals (and organizations) are forced to choose between their own aspirations and their commitment to discrimination and segregation. People, Raab says, will tend to change their behavior toward blacks, without changing their attitudes, if highly cherished values are at stake.[28] The movement of blacks into the cities and changes in the economic structure have raised the price whites must pay for discrimination and segregation. For example, if a white parent must pay both taxes for public schools and tuition for his child in a private segregated school, laws have created a conflict between quality of education and the preservation of segregated education.

Proper legal controls, Berger says, fortify the unprejudicial and the believers in fair play and undermine the position of those who practice discrimination. In codifying high ideals, laws can withhold certain privileges from discriminators, can establish conditions discouraging expression of prejudices, and can make the state's influence and power available to the victims of discrimination.[29]

A third assumption is that the laws must be used. In broad areas such as voting, employment, and public facilities, a new law has an immediate favorable impace in eliminating the most overt symbols of discrimination

[27] Whitney M. Young, *To Be Equal* (New York: McGraw-Hill Book Co., 1964), p. 38.
[28] Earl Raab, (ed.), *American Race Relations Today* (Garden City, N.Y.: Doubleday-Anchor, 1962), pp. 23.
[29] Morroe Berger, *Equality by Statute: The Revolution in Civil Rights* (rev. ed.; Garden City, N.Y.: Doubleday & Co., 1967), pp. 225–26.

and segregation. Forces of resistance need time to cohere, and there have been instances of complete desegregation under the impact of civil rights legislation. Some local officials will find ways to evade the intent of the law, however, by limiting themselves to the elimination of only the most overt symbols, without substantially changing other practices. To achieve the potentiality of the law, the minority must employ it in a manner which will reshape community attitudes so that new relationships become a part of the mores of the community.

Fourth, limits of enforcement must be recognized. Civil and criminal litigation against large numbers of people is socially disagreeable and may even lead toward a police state. Effective enforcement in the face of determined and widespread opposition, Bickel notes, would require more or less continuous official scrutiny and more or less continuous coercion. An additional difficulty would be the refusal, or at least unwillingness, of some state and local officials to cooperate in the enforcement of federal laws unpopular in their constituencies. The realistic alternatives are reduction of opposition, inducement and persuasion, or abandonment of the law. Pronouncement of a new law, then, is only the first step in a persuasive and educational action to convince all of the morality and justice of the law.[30]

STRUGGLES FOR EQUALITY

Under slavery blacks had only a limited number of options to break their shackles: running away, sometimes a chance to purchase freedom, faithful service to the master in the hope of being freed, insurrection and revolt, or gaining freedom as a reward for service in war.[31] The Civil War ended slavery as a legitimate institution, but the struggle for true equality remained to be fought.

The options of protest and activism

Contemporary efforts of U.S. blacks to improve their situation have taken advantage of social changes, which have provided options between passive adaptation to discrimination and suicidal revolt. These intermediate options may be grouped roughly under the headings of protest and activism.

The *option of protest* involves attempts to change the structure of race relations through political and legal actions within the system. This option has been characterized as the "politics of order" because the courtroom,

[30] Alexander M. Bickel, *Politics and the Warren Court,* (New York: Harper & Row, 1965), pp. 112–15.
[31] Edward Peeks, *The Long Struggle for Black Power* (New York: Charles Scribner's Sons, 1971), p. 26.

legislative lobby, newspaper columns, and other means of reshaping public attitudes are employed in an effort to improve the situation of the minority group within the framework of a democratic society.[32]

The *option of activism* involves more direct confrontation of those practices and social arrangements which sustain discrimination and segregation. Three kinds of politics have characterized activism. First, what Waskow describes as the "politics of creative disorder," that is, those forms of activism which operate on the edge of the dominant social system while clearly aiming to change it. Such creative disorder includes sit-ins at segregated restaurants, wade-ins at beaches, kneel-ins at churches, public marches, school boycotts, rent strikes, and job blockades, in all of which the philosophy of nonviolent resistance is prominent. Second, the "politics of disorder," in which resort to mob uprising and other forms of violence reflects alienation from the dominant culture and disillusionment with the political system. Third, what Rustin calls the "politics of escape," in which radical energy and passionate rhetoric provide emotional release, but without advancing solutions for the problems of race relations.[33]

Nonviolent resistance

The boycott of segregated city busses in Montgomery, Alabama, in 1955 was the first large-scale use of nonviolent resistance. Because of it, the Reverend Martin Luther King, Jr., and the Southern Christian Leadership Conference were projected into the national scene. Another version of this same approach were the sit-ins which gained impetus in 1960 when four black college students staged the first by sitting down at a segregated lunch counter at a Greensboro, N.C., variety store. Refused service, they continued to sit. Joined by other students the next day, they eventually won their point. The strategy of a sit-in is to request service at a "white only" facility and to remain seated when refused. If manhandled, the sitter does not offer resistance. If ordered to move by police officers, he politely declines.[34]

Nonviolent resistance, Gregg says, is a sort of moral jujitsu in that the lack of physical opposition causes the attacker to lose his balance. The victim reacts to aggression with kindness, generosity, and voluntary suffering. The attacker is surprised that the other party does not exhibit the hostility which enables the "game" of violence to proceed. The attacker is further weakened by the diversion of his energy against himself through the arousal of his own sense of decency. Becoming convinced his oppo-

---

[32] Arthur I. Waskow, *From Race Riot to Sit-In, 1919 and the 1960's* (Garden City, N.Y.: Doubleday-Anchor, 1966), pp. 226–46.

[33] Bayard Rustin, "The Failure of Black Separatism," *Harper's Magazine,* Vol. 240 (January 1970), pp. 25–34.

[34] Bennett, *Confrontation,* pp. 251–54.

376 Social problems of urban man

nent is not a coward, the attacker fears his opponent will capitalize on mistakes, and thus the attacker becomes uncertain of his cause in spite of his superior power. Meanwhile, the nonviolent person gains moral initiative and the capacity to control the situation.[35]

Nonviolent resistance, Bennett says, solved the dilemma of the minority group caught between two alternatives, accommodation to segregation and suicidal revolt, by cloaking open revolt in the garb of love and forgiveness. Every individual, King argued, had the duty to break or ignore unjust laws in order to bring the confrontation necessary to effect change. By basing his rationale on religious traditions, King made nonviolent resistance attractive to his followers.[36] They were released from the inner conflicts between their own resentment toward whites and religious traditions requiring suppression of hostility. King told his followers that it was proper to engage in aggressive activities because they would be expressing "love" for their enemies.[37]

Riots and violence

In the 1960s the United States ranked first among 17 Western democracies in civil strife. Nevertheless, the relative stability of American society was reflected in the employment of violence to express protest rather than to engage in rebellion against the government. Graham sees this paradox explained by four factors. One, because governmental institutions historically have had less impact than private institutions on the lives of people, violence has not been directed against the state. Two, racial and cultural pluralism generate tensions between ethnic groups which can produce displaced aggression against scapegoated groups. Three, affluence is unequally distributed but apparently it usually reduces concern over public policy as suggested by relatively low voter participation. Four, U.S. material progress has reinforced faith in the legitimacy of the country's social institutions.[38]

In 1969 the National Commission on Causes and Prevention of Violence reported that 200 riots had occurred since the summer of 1964. These 200 incidents differed in style from race riots of earlier decades when white mobs had perpetrated most of the violence in direct clashes between blacks and whites. Now the pattern was black aggression against white-owned property—but not white people. White mobs were not pres-

[35] Richard B. Gregg, The Power of Nonviolence (New York: Schocken Books, 1966), pp. 44–47.
[36] Bennett, Confrontation, pp. 228–34.
[37] James W. Vander Zanden, "The Non-Violent Resistant Movement against Segregation," American Journal of Sociology, Vol. 68 (March 1963), pp. 546–47.
[38] Hugh Davis Graham, "The Paradox of American Violence: A Historical Appraisal," Annals of American Academy of Political and Social Science, Vol. 391 (September 1970), pp. 75–78.

ent. A possible explanation is that the whites had become more receptive to black demands and the blacks, with higher expectations, had become disillusioned at the snail's pace progress of improvement in their situation. Furthermore, the demographic and socioeconomic changes described earlier had isolated larger populations of blacks in urban ghettos.[39]

On occasion, public officials have declared riots to be "senseless" violence devoid of political and psychological meaning, but scientists deny that any social event can be without cause. Studies indicate that the more recent riots have been employed as a means of achieving desired goals when more legitimate means are either unavailable or have been unsuccessful. Evidence that patterns exist is offered by a survey of 24 racial disorders occurring in 23 American cities in the summer of 1967. About these the National Advisory Commission on Civil Disorders stated in part:

Violence usually occurred almost immediately following the occurrence of the final precipitating incidence, and then escalated rapidly. Disorder did not erupt as a result of a single "triggering" or "precipitating" incident. Instead it was generated out of an increasingly disturbed social atmosphere, in which typically a series of tension-heightening incidents over a period of weeks or months became linked in the minds of many in the Negro community with a reservoir of underlying grievances. At some point in the mounting tension, a further incident—in itself often routine or trivial—became the breaking point and the tension spilled over into violence. "Prior" incidents, which increased tensions and ultimately led to violence, were police actions in almost half the cases; police actions were "final" incidents before the outbreak of violence in 12 of the 24 surveyed disorders.

The proportion of Negroes in local government was substantially smaller than the Negro proportion of population. Only three of the 20 cities studies had more than one Negro legislator; none had ever had a Negro mayor or city manager. . . . Although almost all of the cities had some sort of formal grievance mechanism for handling citizen complaints, this typically was regarded by Negroes as ineffective and generally ignored.

Although specific grievances varied from city to city, at least 12 deeply held grievances can be identified and ranked into three levels of relative intensity: *First level of intensity:* police practices, unemployment and underemployment, inadequate housing: *second level of intensity:* inadequate education, poor recreational facilities and programs, ineffectiveness of political structure and grievance mechanisms; *third level of intensity:* disrespectful white attitudes, discriminatory administration of justice, inadequacy of federal programs, inadequacy of municipal services, discriminatory consumer and credit practices, inadequate welfare programs.[40]

[39] August Meier and Elliott Rudwick, "Black Violence in the 20th Century: A Study in Rhetoric and Retaliation," in Hugh Davis Graham and Ted Robert Gurr (eds.) *Violence in America: Historical and Comparative Perspectives,* (Washington, D.C.: U.S. Government Printing Office, 1969), Vol. 2, pp. 308, 311–12.

[40] *Report of the National Advisory Commission on Civil Disorders* (Washington, D.C.: U.S. Government Printing Office, March 1, 1968), pp. 344.

Why did violence occur?

Interracial friction occurs far more often than the small number of times when precipitating events result in riots, so why is it that violence occurs when it does? Studying 73 race riots in the United States, Lieberson and Silverman found riot cities differing from nonriot cities in work situations and patterns of local government but not in greater prevalence of ghetto dwellings. In riot cities whites were in more direct competition with blacks for laboring, domestic, and service occupations, and the percentage of blacks who were storeowners was slightly smaller than in nonriot cities. There was a smaller difference between the races in average income. Fewer blacks were on the police force, and representation of blacks on the city council was smaller.[41] In another analysis, Downes reports that larger and densely populated municipalities which had lost population (or gained very little) since 1950 were more likely to experience hostile outbursts than those which had not.[42]

A group of studies found that from a third to a half of ghetto residents express support for riots and civil rights militancy, but that only 10 to 15 percent reported they had participated in riots. The militant, particularly the rioter, was usually young and male. In spite of the commonly held view that the very poor are predominant among rioters, there was no significant difference in income between rioters and nonrioters. The average rioter tended to be a high school dropout and the average nonrioter an elementary school dropout. Rather than being from the hard-core unemployed, the rioters tended to be from the underemployed.[43]

Two theoretical approaches are prominent among the many efforts to explain the violent reactions of blacks. One approach emphasizes *alienation*.[44] This view holds that living in segregated ghettos, blacks feel isolated because of the lack of their structural assimilation within the institutions of the dominant white society. But in his investigation of the 1965 riot in Watts, Ransford found that alienation alone was insufficient to explain participation in violence. In addition to feeling a sense of powerlessness in controlling his own fate, the participant in violence was convinced that he was being mistreated on the basis of race. The violent individuals had lost faith in leaders and institutions and in the usefulness of organized protest. For them, violence was a means of communicating their anger to the whites.[45]

[41] Stanley Lieberson and Arnold W. Silverman, "The Precipitants and Underlying Conditions of Race Riots," *American Sociological Review,* Vol. 30 (December 1965), pp. 887–98.
[42] Bryan T. Downes, "Social and Political Characteristics of Riot Cities: A Comparative Study," *Social Science Quarterly,* Vol. 49 (December 1968), pp. 504–20.
[43] Nathan Caplan, "The New Ghetto Man: A Review of Recent Empirical Studies," *Journal of Social Issues,* Vol. 26, (Winter 1970), pp. 60–64.
[44] See Chapter 2, pp. 32–34.
[45] H. Edward Ransford, "Isolation, Powerlessness, and Violence: A Study of Attitudes and Participation in the Watts Riot," *American Journal of Sociology,* Vol. 73 (March 1968), p. 581–91.

The alienation or *anomie* approach points to the social structure as blocking the legitimate aspirations of blacks. Contradictions in the sociocultural organization are conducive to racial violence because materialistic success, presented as a proper cultural goal, is denied to blacks through the structure's failure to provide avenues for achieving these goals. In their review of evaluations of riots, Masotti and Bowen note recurrent reference to the notion of rioters that they are being deprived of status, power, learning, leisure, and other values being distributed to other groups. These feelings of deprivation were accentuated by disillusionment when the breaking of legal barriers to integration failed to end ghetto problems. There was just enough improvement to lift the blacks from the passivity of despair, but their expectations exceeded the capacities of the social system for rapid and fundamental change.[46]

ASSIMILATION VERSUS SEPARATENESS

Convinced that their blackness has shut them out of the rights and privileges of being an American, Afro-Americans exhibit a peculiar ambivalence. Their protest movements move simultaneously toward excluding themselves from the national society and toward finding a place in it.[47] But while black nationalism has in several efforts sought to go it alone, the civil rights movement has largely sought to obtain rights and equality through the integration of blacks within the goals and values of the majority society. This movement toward integration and assimilation has drawn the greatest support from the black middle and upper class, the least support from the lower class.[48] The relatively low social cohesion in the lower class, however, raises doubt as to what the outcome of the pressure for black autonomy will be. (We can recall here Rustin's expression of concern that the expenditure of radical energy on passionate rhetoric will provide emotional release without advancing solutions for the deep-seated problems underlying race relations.[49])

Split from liberal coalition

The achievements of the liberal coalition of whites and blacks which has pressed for civil rights statutes and abolition of racial distinctions, Danzig says, include reconstruction of the legal basis of civil rights, fixing of federal responsibility to intervene where possible to enforce civil rights,

[46] Louis H. Masotti and Don R. Bower (eds.), *Riots and Rebellion: Civil Violence in the Urban Community* (Beverly Hills, Calif., Sage Publications, 1968), pp. 21–25.
[47] Joanne Grant (ed.), *Black Protest: History, Documents, and Analyses* (Greenwich, Conn.: Fawcett Publications, 1968), pp. 9–14.
[48] John H. Bracy, Jr., August Meier, and Ellott Rudwick (eds.), *Black Nationalism in America* (Indianapolis, Ind.: Bobbs-Merrill Co., 1970), p. liv.
[49] Rustin, "Failure of Black Separatism," pp. 25–34.

and establishment of equality before the law as the public policy of the nation.[50] The cry of "black power," however, signaled a determination among blacks to run their own organizations.

Liberals had supported civil rights as a way of changing the overall moral order. They sought equal opportunity and equal treatment for all according to individual merits. They were repelled by the rise among blacks of a demand for a group solidarity based on color to force preferential treatment for blacks to compensate for past injustices. This shift in attitudes, Danzig says, represented a self-interest movement contrary to the liberal view that what is good for democracy is good for blacks. Disillusioned by the failure of the civil rights movement to justify their high hopes, however, many blacks responded to the appeal to build a minority solidarity.

Liberals were shocked by the advocacy of violence and revolutionary objectives by some black militants. Furthermore, the militants began to violate the rules of the game whereby the whites gain a sense of security through the predictable operations of administrative bureaucracies. From a white perspective the looting in ghetto riots threatened law and order, but it also provided evidence that blacks felt alienated from the sacred concept of private property as the bulwark of our social arrangements.[51]

The racial ghetto as a "colony"

The setting of race relations in the United States has been compared with that of a colony exploited by an alien power. Afro-Americans differ from other ethnic groups in that two centuries of slavery here introduced them into American life as a minority dominated by a racist social system. Their ghettos have been administered by representatives of a white society external to the ghetto. Ghetto businesses, law enforcement, and service agencies are manned largely by people who reside outside its boundaries. Discrimination based on institutional racism has a special impact on blacks which increases the possibility of ghetto residence extending through more generations than experienced by earlier ethnic residents of U.S. ghettos. Whereas the latter were able to choose ghetto life as a temporary way station on the route to a better life, blacks face a probability of experiencing the "slum of despair" as their permanent lot.

The American situation, Blauner points out, differs from world colonialism. The interracial relations are within a society, not between the colony and a mother country geographically separated from the colony. In colonialism a minority from the mother country exploits the majority in the colony, while in the United States blacks are a numerical minority treated

[50] David Danzig, "In Defense of 'Black Power,' " in Endo and Strawbridge, *Perspectives on Black America,* pp. 182–92.
[51] Robert Blauner, "Internal Colonialism and Ghetto Revolt," *Social Problems,* Vol. 16 (Spring 1969), pp. 399, 408.

as social outsiders because they entered the society originally as slaves. The status of Afro-Americans resembles that of residents of a colony exploited by a home country in that the people of a colony are usually of a different race and culture than those found in the mother country. The Afro-Americans, however, lack the group culture and social structure of a people subjugated by another nation. Furthermore, American blacks are more dispersed as a people and more universally relegated to a ghetto than in the conquered nation.[52]

The rhetoric of black nationalism and black power frequently cites the similarity between the racial ghetto and the colony exploited by a mother country. The linkage is especially significant in that the rhetoric represents attempts to build a social and cultural solidarity among Afro-Americans. The lack of such solidarity is an important distinction between Afro-Americans and the peoples colonized by an alien state. Both black and white colleges have felt the pressure from black students to provide black studies to advance awareness of their own race while preparing them through other courses for full participation in the national society.[53]

Black nationalism

Grouped under the rallying cry of "black nationalism" a variety of ideas obscures the precision of meaning of the various ideas to which the term refers.[54] *Racial solidarity* is one of these ideas, the organization of blacks for action on the basis of common color and oppressed condition. *Cultural nationalism* is another, connoting the sharing of a style of life and philosophy distinct from white Americans. *Religious nationalism* is another, expressing the contention that Afro-Americans are a chosen people. *Economic nationalism* is a fourth, alternatively in capitalist and socialist models and emphasizing improvement in economic opportunity through control of the black market, establishment of black businesses, or elimination of private property as the basis of the American economy. Finally, *political nationalism* is expressed in reform endeavors within the political and economic systems.

The concept of "nationalism" was introduced among blacks in the 19th century, when various movements argued that Afro-Americans should possess a country, that they share a common heritage from Africa, that an ethnic identity sets them off from other groups, that they should shape their own destinies, and that they should control their own social institutions.[55]

---

[52] Ibid., pp. 393–98.
[53] Henry A. Bullock, "The Black College and the New Black Awareness," *Daedalus,* Vol. 100 (Summer 1971), pp. 594.
[54] Bracy, Meier, and Rudwick, *Black Nationalism,* pp. xxvi–xxviii.
[55] E. V. Essien-Udom, *Black Nationalism: A Search for an Identity in America* (New York: Dell Publishing Co., 1964), p. 20.

Behind black nationalism lies a common experience of oppression that elicits an emotionally charged search for a heritage in which blacks can take pride and through which they can feel an affinity based on the very racial characteristics which were formerly targets of disparagement. Black nationalism gives special emphasis to the idea that blacks have a manifest destiny in political and/or religious terms to create a utopia outside of the "white world," with hostility toward existing social institutions explaining a self-imposed exile from American politics and, in some cases, the drive to establish a black nation. Black nationalism turns from Christianity to establish cults claiming roots in the Near East. As a psychological protection against negative self-images, history is revised to make today's blacks the descendents of glorious ancestors, all this despite the fact that—or perhaps because—American blacks long ago lost their cultural linkages to Africa and adopted the political and religious culture of the dominant American society.[56]

Black nationalism's rejection of "white culture" suggests a contraculture in which a deviant group reacts to rejection by the surrounding dominant culture by denying the values of the dominant culture. Yet while black nationalism carries within it the need for conflict with the values of the surrounding culture, the norms of its adherents can be interpreted as products of the relationships of blacks to that larger culture. Its group unity is, at least in part, a consequence of the sharing by members of frustrating experiences in reference to the surrounding culture.[57]

Elements of black power

As an ideology, black power contains several elements which place it between the goals of separateness, on the one hand, and integration, on the other.[58] It expresses disdain for all organizations which practice racial discrimination, but also for black-white liberal coalitions (which are regarded as a form of tokenism). The strategy of confronting segregation in terms of a specific issue (such as school segregation) is rejected, along with the goal of integration in general. Instead of issue-oriented leadership, black power concentrates on making Afro-Americans conscious of the explotation they are victims of and the injustice they endure. Blacks are exhorted to forge their own programs, create their own ideas, and form their own institutions. Because the black working class is conceived as an instrument for changing society, black power lends itself to tactics of

[56] Ibid., pp. 66–75; C. Eric Lincoln, *The Black Muslims in America* (Boston, Mass.: Beacon Press, 1961), pp. 43–46.
[57] See: Chapter 2, pp. 51–53, and Milton Yinger, "Contraculture and Subculture," *American Sociological Review,* Vol. 25 (October 1960), pp. 625–35.
[58] Raymond S. Franklin, "The Political Economy of Black Power," *Social Problems,* Vol. 16 (Winter 1969), pp. 286–92.

violence to force governmental action to correct ghetto conditions. Black power emphasizes the development of a positive self-image in black terms rather than in accordance with some model acceptable to whites. Black is beautiful and strong, not ugly and submissive. A black is supposed to become imbued with the ethos of self-discipline and commitment to a history-changing movement.

The fundamental premise, Carmichael and Hamilton assert, is that, "before a group can enter the open society, it must close ranks." [59] Other ethnic groups in U.S. society have raised themselves by first establishing a bargaining position of strength within a pluralistic society. Blacks (black nationalists argue) must do things for themselves, since even white allies unconsciously further white supremacy. Moreover, the goals of blacks are seen as not necessarily the same as those of the dominant, white society. Once black self-identity and self-determination is established, Afro-Americans will be able to participate fully in the decisions affecting their own lives.

Racial integration is rejected if it means simply the admitting of blacks into white middle-class society, since that would imply that blacks have nothing of their own worthwhile to contribute and that admission to a "white world" is their only route to improvement. Carmichael and Hamilton believe this kind of integration would simply siphon off those blacks acceptable to middle-class whites, thereby depriving the black community of much know-how and potential leadership. Since race is an overwhelming fact of life, they reject (as conducive to tokenism) the objective of being treated as individuals rather than as members of a race.

Black Muslims

With some 100,000 adherents, the Black Muslims are a tightly disciplined example of black nationalism which has drawn from the lower socioeconomic levels of Negro communities throughout the nation. The origin of the cult is traced to a mysterious person who appeared in Detroit in 1930 calling himself Wallace Fard Muhammad and proclaiming himself as Prophet from Arabia. He disappeared mysteriously to be replaced by his assistant minister, Elijah Muhammad.

Under the leadership of Elijah Muhammand, the Black Muslims withdrew from the dominant society to develop a black nation and wait for the "white devils" to destroy themselves, at which time the blacks will inherit the earth. Declaring themselves to be an integral part of Islam, the movement nevertheless departs from orthodox Moslem belief by its insistence that blacks must separate themselves from the abhorrent white race and by their belief in their manifest destiny to inherit the earth. The mem-

[59] Stokely Carmichael and Charles V. Hamilton, *Black Power: The Politics of Liberation in America* (New York: Random House, 1967), pp. 44–45.

bership is predominately young, male, lower class, and formerly Christian.[60]

For these population segments, the appeal of the Black Muslims lies in the exaggerated sense of consciousness of kind, the opportunity to identify with a power potentially capable of overcoming white domination, the tone of rebellion against the inaction of Christian churches in racial issues, the emphasis on youth and masculinity, and the black orientation of Muslim parochial schools. Perhaps the chief appeal, however, is the opportunity to cast off one's old self and assume a new identity, symoblized by the taking of a new name to signify rebirth from a "slave" status. As a Black Muslim, the recruit must demonstrate unrelenting self-mastery, unquestioned loyalty, and high standards of personal and group morality. He must also be steadily employed, and make financial contributions to the movement. In return, his dignity and self-reliance are strengthened, his energies are given a direction meaningful to him, and his resentments and aggressive feelings are given release. The movement has been particularly tolerant of criminals, drug addicts, and other social deviants, and it has been remarkably effective in the rehabilitation of such individuals.[61]

Black Panthers

The Black Panther Party was established by Huey P. Newton and Bobby Seale in 1966. Important converts later were Stokely Carmichael, for a time, and Eldridge Cleaver, who, as a prisoner, had written the sensitive book, *Soul on Ice.* The movement bases its philosophy on revolutionary black nationalism and what has been called "do-it-yourself Marxism-Leninism." A central theme has been that "the black colony" must be "liberated" from the "mother country" of white America, which is judged to be the equivalent of a colonial oppressor. Although recognition of origins in Africa is lauded, the idea of a return to Africa is ridiculed. Another Black Panther Party tenet is the destruction of capitalism and racism as interrelated phenomena.[62]

The Party presents this program: Blacks will not be free until they are able to determine their own destiny. Unless white businessmen give full employment, means of production must be taken from them and "placed in the community"; "robbery" by white men must be ended, and decent housing provided the black community; education must expose the "decadent American society" and teach "true" black history; all black men must be exempt from military service; "police brutality" and "murder" of black

[60] Lincoln, *Black Muslims in America,* pp. 22–27, 217–21.

[61] Ibid., pp. 27–32, 248–52.

[62] Theodore Draper, *The Rediscovery of Black Nationalism* (New York: Viking Press, 1970), pp. 97–102.

people must end and all black prisoners must be released from confinement; all black people brought to trial should be judged by their peer group or people from black communities; and, finally, a United Nations-supervised plebiscite should be held in "the black colony" to determine the will of black people as to their "national destiny."[63]

Advocating that "power grows out of the barrel of a gun," Black Panthers have been involved in a number of shoot-outs with the police, and have also been the victims of institutional violence. In Chicago in 1969, for example, Panther leaders Fred Hampton and Mark Clark were killed in an incident which outraged both white and black community leaders, who feared the incident marked the beginning of governmental suppression of dissenting voices in the United States. Trouble with the police reduced Panther ranks, and membership was estimated in 1970 at less than a thousand.[64]

RELATIVE CHANCES OF ESCAPING THE GHETTO

Immigrants from Europe to the United States were subjected to discrimination, poverty, and the hazards of the ghetto, but most eventually escaped the ghetto. The question is, will the U.S. blacks be able to duplicate such an escape?

Pertinent factors

Although European immigrants suffered discrimination, it can be argued that blacks face a much more stringent network of discriminatory practices and racist institutions. They are encountering an economy with declining demands for the unskilled labor which gave a foothold to European immigrants, and today's political machines are not as well equipped to dispense favors and a primitive form of social work assistance as those of the past.

European immigrants held visions of a better future which enabled them to accept less desirable work temporarily without feeling deprived. They brought a set of social institutions with them to give them a starting place for adjustment to an unfamiliar environment. Afro-Americans lack both of these advantages. Slavery and segregation denied them a functioning institutional life, including a strong family structure, and they also lack experience in managing money and in planning a long-term strategy for rising in status.

[63] "The Black Panther Party: A Ten-Point Program," in William M. Chace and Peter Collier (eds.), *Justice Denied: The Black Man in White America* (New York: Harcourt, Brace & World, 1970), pp. 534–37.
[64] Peeks, *Long Struggle for Black Power*, p. 401.

A less pessimistic view interprets the dilemma of the black as more a consequence of his lower-class position in society than of his racial identity. In this view, the disdain of the higher classes for the lower classes is given great weight in explaining social inequities. Although recognizing that slavery had great traumatic impact, Handlin, for instance, sees the black's recuperative potential as underestimated. He attributes the disadvantages of the contemporary urban black to the consequences of migration to the city, and argues that the situation of the blacks differs only in degree from that of earlier migrants, and is a consequence of the recency of their arrival, their greater numbers, and their greater concentration in a few cities. As for the problem of discrimination based on color, Japanese-Americans, to cite one example, have much less visibility today than in earlier decades, and, in fact, the emphasis on overcoming racial distinctions is misdirected, Handlin declares, because the fault lies rather in the inadequacies of our systems of political decision, employment, education, housing, and handling of deviants.[65]

Improvements in situation

On the average, blacks have made gains in educational attainment, occupational status, and income over the past two decades—on an absolute basis. For example, the percentage of blacks, 25 to 34 years old, with four or more years of college, increased from 4.3 percent in 1960 to 6.1 percent by 1970. The proportion of black college students attending other than predominately black colleges rose from 48.7 percent in 1964 to 72.4 percent by 1970. Gains in occupational status and income are shown by tables 15–1 and 15–2.[66]

Because of the great disadvantages the blacks inherited from the past, however, recent gains are insufficient to claim anything more than slight progress—for example, the proportion of black families with less than $3,000 family income has declined markedly in the last decade, and in the same period blacks have moved into the better-paying jobs at a rate exceeding that of whites. But these are statistical, not real gains. Blacks show gains when compared with their situation of the past, but they fail to show the rates of improvement reported for whites. In short, then, in spite of gains in socioeconomic status, the differences between the races is increasing, with the blacks' situation relatively worsening.[67]

---

[65] Oscar Handlin, "The Goals of Integration," *Daedalus*, Vol. 95 (Winter 1966), pp. 271–84; also see: James M. O'Kane, "Ethnic Mobility and the Lower-Income Negro: A Socio-Historical Perspective," *Social Problems*, Vol. 16 (Winter 1969), pp. 302–11.

[66] Data from the Bureau of the Census; see footnote to table 15–1 for source.

[67] For example, see Daniel P. Moynihan, "Employment, Income, and the Ordeal of the Negro Family," in Talcott Parsons and Kenneth B. Clark (eds.), *The Negro American,* pp. 147–52; and Thomas F. Pettigrew, *A Profile of the American Negro* (Princeton, N.J.: D. Van Nostrand Co., 1964), pp. 15–24.

TABLE 15–1
Distribution of families by income and race in 1947, 1960, and 1969
(adjusted for price changes, in 1969 dollars)

	Negro and other races			White		
	1947	1960	1969	1947	1960	1969
Number of Families (in thousands)	3,117	4,333	5,215	34,120	41,123	46,022
Percent	100	100	100	100	100	100
Under $3,000	57	38	20	21	14	8
$3,000 to $4,999	25	22	19	26	14	10
$5,000 to $6,999	9	16	17	24	19	12
$7,000 to $9,999	6	14	20	17	26	22
$10,000 and over	3	9	24	12	27	49
Median Income	$2,660	$4,001	$6,191	$5,194	$7,252	$9,794
Net change, 1947–1969:						
Amount			$3,531			$4,600
Percent			132.7			88.6

Source: United States Department of Commerce, Bureau of the Census, The Social and Economic Status of Negroes in the United States, 1970, Special Studies, Current Population Reports, Series P-23, No. 38, July 1971, Table 17.

TABLE 15–2
Employment by broad occupational groups and race: 1960 and 1966 to 1970
(numbers in millions — annual averages)

Year	Total		White-collar workers, craftsmen, and operatives		All other workers*	
	Negro and other races	White	Negro and other races	White	Negro and other races	White
1960	6.9	58.9	2.9	46.1	4.0	12.8
1966	7.9	65.0	4.0	52.5	3.9	12.6
1967	8.0	66.4	4.3	53.6	3.7	12.7
1968	8.2	67.8	4.6	54.9	3.6	12.8
1969	8.4	69.5	4.9	56.4	3.5	13.1
1970	8.4	70.2	5.1	57.0	3.4	13.2
Change, 1960 to 1970:						
Percent	+22	+19	+72	+24	−15	+3.2

*Includes private household and other service workers, laborers, and farm workers. Median usual weekly earnings were $50–$100 a week for these workers, compared with $100–$170 a week for white-collar workers, craftsmen, and operatives in March 1970.
Source: United States Department of Commerce, Bureau of the Census, The Social and Economic Status of Negroes in the United States, 1970, Special Studies, Current Population Reports, Series P-23, No. 38, July 1971, Table 46.

Major difficulties remain

The passage of civil rights legislation and the removal of the most obvious signs of segregation, Young warns, should not lull supporters of minority groups into thinking that the struggle is over.[68] Even if discrimination were eliminated overnight, the problems of the ghetto—poverty, underemployment, and family instability—would remain.

Another difficulty so far not mentioned may be described as the *pipeline factor.* Racial discrimination and segregation accumulate disabilities of inadequate education, insufficient job skills, and patterns of dependency and low self-esteem. Assuming elimination of the sources of these disabilities in future generations, it will still be necessary for the age cohort of better prepared blacks to move through the "pipeline" of population replacement. Because of these difficulties, Young calls for a domestic version of the postwar Marshal Plan, in which more than $17 billion were spent to rebuild war-ravaged Europe. He insists that an equivalent expenditure is necessary to close the economic, social, and educational deficiencies that separate blacks from other Americans.[69]

If the energies of activists are to have long-term consequences, they must be coordinated into effective political strategies. Civil rights groups emphasize social and economic self-help within a framework of equal opportunity. Since these goals require representation within political institutions, Laue predicts the movement will tend toward greater technical sophistication in the employment of legal and educational approaches to give long-term significance to the crises involving militants.[70]

The mercurial quality of black protest is indicated, however, by the rise of separateness since Laue made his interpretation. Calls for black power and black nationalism have replaced calls for integration and assimilation, with the goal of racial solidarity based on an awakening black consciousness. The central question is whether the search by blacks for autonomy as an ethnic group will destroy the possibility of fitting them into an amalgam of ethnic groups constituting a pluralist society. Peeks asks: "What do you do with minority or ethnic identity once it is recognized and established as a potential for group power in this pluralistic society?"[71]

Whites should recognize, Danzig cautions, that minority solidarity is more a defensive stance toward a hostile society than a plot to take over the country. Rather than *organized* blacks, the disorganized and the hopeless are the ultimate threat. Lacking a network of unifying social traditions and effective social institutions, the blacks, Danzig believes, must depend on political action through color consciousness to build group solidarity.

[68] Young, *To Be Equal,* pp. 15–16.
[69] Ibid, pp. 26–31.
[70] James H. Laue, "The Changing Character of Negro Protest," *Annals of American Academy of Political and Social Science,* Vol. 357 (January 1965), pp. 119–26.
[71] Peeks, *Long Struggle for Black Power,* p. 402.

In building a black community, separateness is not necessarily inconsistent with a pluralist society consisting of an amalgam of ethic groups. But, black power in and of itself, Danzig warns, risks the loss of essential allies if a black movement is based *exclusively* on self-interest.[72]

SUMMARY

A wide range of social, economic, and political changes have upset the system of segregation and discrimination whereby blacks were expected to undertake cultural assimilation without structural assimilation. Out of these changes has come a time of protest, activism, and incidents of violence in the blacks' struggle for civil rights and full participation in American society. Protest has depended on political and legal strategies. Activism has involved use of nonviolent resistance and various degrees of violence. Black nationalism and black power come in several varieties; some versions are intended to develop a power base to advance political and economic negotiations. These efforts toward racial solidarity have reversed the earlier search for assimilation within American society, a development that raises important questions about the future course of race relations.

FOR ADDITIONAL READING

Charles Abrams, *Forbidden Neighbors* (New York: Harper & Brothers, 1955).

Jacques Barzun, *Race: A Study in Modern Superstition* (rev. ed.; New York: Harper & Row, 1965).

Hubert M. Blalock, Jr., "Urbanization and Discrimination in the South," *Social Problems,* Vol. 7 (Fall 1959), pp. 146–52.

Leonard Broom and Norval D. Glenn, *Transformation of the American Negro* (New York: Harper & Row, 1965).

Eldridge Cleaver, *Soul on Ice* (New York: McGraw-Hill Book Co., 1968).

Robert Conot, *Rivers of Blood, Years of Darkness* (New York: Bantam Books, 1967).

Harold Cruse, *The Crisis of the Negro Intellectual* (New York: William Morrow, 1967).

Joseph S. Himes, "The Functions of Racial Conflict," *Social Forces,* Vol. 45 (September 1966), pp. 1–10.

Elliott Liebow, *Tally's Corner* (Boston: Little, Brown and Co., 1967).

Gary T. Marx, *Protest and Prejudice* (New York: Harper & Row, 1967).

Jisuichi Masuoka and Preston Valien (eds.), *Race Relations: Problems and Theory* (Chapel Hill, N.C.: University of North Carolina Press, 1965).

[72] Danzig, "In Defense of 'Black Power,' " pp. 191–92.

L. K. Northwood and Earnest A. T. Barth, *Urban Desegregation: Negro Pioneers and Their White Neighbors* (Seattle, Wash.: University of Washington Press, 1965).

James M. O'Kane, "Ethnic Mobility and the Lower-Income Negro: A Socio-Historical Perspective," *Social Problems,* Vol. 16 (Winter 1969), pp. 302–11.

Thomas F. Pettigrew, "Race Relations in the United States: A Sociological Perspective," in Talcott Parsons (ed.), *American Sociology: Perspectives, Problems, Methods* (New York: Basic Books, 1968), pp. 258–71.

Daniel C. Thompson, *The Negro Leadership Class* (Englewood Cliffs, N.J.: Prentice-Hall, 1963).

James W. Vander Zanden, *Race Relations in Transition* (New York: Random House, 1965).

Walter Williams, "Cleveland's Crisis Ghetto," *Trans-action,* Vol. 4 (September 1967), pp. 33–42.

Crime and criminals 16

A former prisoner, just out from behind bars, was asked to tell about himself in his own words.

"I am 49 years old with a long career in and out of penal institutions. I have spent 25 years in prisons, of which 18 months was in a juvenile reform school. Finally, I have developed enough maturity to realize how silly it is to be the professional convict I have been.

"At the age of nine I was placed in reform school in an eastern state. I was placed in a large dormitory with boys ranging from 9 to 14 in age. We worked on a farm in the morning, went to a sort of school for an hour, and then back to the farm for the rest of the day. Bedtime was eight o'clock. The so-called housemasters and housemothers thought nothing of knocking the boys down with their fists. I was placed in the training school because, since the age of five, I was constantly running away from home. The situation at home was not much to my liking. My stepfather and mother were constantly bickering. Of course, this is no excuse. I had a sense of adventure. I was declared a stubborn child and placed in the reform school until I was 12.

"My parents moved to New York City. There I ran away again and joined a circus. I was picked up by the police. They had no record of a lost boy under the name I was going under at the time. They sent me to an orphanage, and I ran away again. Again I was picked up by the police. Some smart social worker recognized my description and had the police notify my parents.

"Until 22 I led a fairly normal life in school, not getting into trouble, gaining a certain amount of education through the National Youth Administration and Civilian Conservation Corps. Then I went in the Army.

I rose to rank of sergeant. I got involved in a drinking party in a barracks one night. The place caught fire. I was court-martialed. I received 12 years for burning a building, to wit, an empty storehouse at a base hospital. This sentence was reduced by a military review board to five years. I was transferred to a federal prison as a military prisoner. There, I was constantly on the run, agitating, constantly on the move, always in some difficulties and scrapes. After two and a half years there, I was transferred to another federal institution where I finished out my five-year sentence, having served three years and nine months with loss of seventy days good time.

"Upon release I went home and immediately became involved in a series of fires. I was sent to a state mental hospital for 30 days observation which stretched into a year. Again I was sent to the court. For the crime of arson, I was sentenced to the state penitentiary for five to seven years. Within a year of release, I was back in prison again for another two and a half to three years for another fire. Released again, I was involved in another fire within 90 days in a midwestern state and got 7 to 15 years this time. Now I am out again.

"All my crimes were crimes of arson. Why did I set fire to buildings? It was a hatred of people. Why did I want to strike back at whole communities? That's a good question. Because I felt probably that the people didn't give me the break that I should have gotten. Today I realize that you make your own breaks in this world. You have to get somewhere by fighting for it. You just can't hate people because they're all like yourself in the long run. All fighting and scrambling for what they think is right and best. This hatred business started in my own home. My folks took me down and had me arrested as a stubborn child. When I came out I suppose it started then because I was the boy that had been in reform school.

"Often times you'll find society itself sort of drives you toward a crime. I went to work at a hospital as a surgical technician, perfectly willing to go straight and get this $360 a month they were paying me. When I walked into the personnel office, they handed me a questionnaire. I came to this question: 'Do you have a criminal record?' I put down 'no.' At the top of this questionnaire was a statement which said that, purely for civil defense reasons, would you please put your fingerprints at the bottom of the application. This was merely to identify you in case of an air raid. No use would be made of these fingerprints except for the fact you were caught in a disaster area you would be identified. I put my fingerprints at the bottom and went to work.

"Six weeks later, after going through the training where I'd reached the point where I was of real value to the hospital, I was called to the personnel office and told that through my fingerprints they had found out I was an ex-convict. Because they had court officials coming into the hospital, they would have to fire me for lying. These judges, lawyers, and so forth might resent an ex-convict working on them in the operating room. Now this was stupid and silly, but the fact was that they just didn't want any ex-cons working there. They 'graciously' allowed me to resign.

"I had been happy working there. It was the type of work I was interested in. I thought I was beginning to get my feet on the ground. It was a sort of shock to get my final check. I walked across the street to a bar and proceeded to get clobbered. The next morning I woke up and found there had been a fire across the street from my apartment. A week later I was arrested for this fire. Having a criminal record, I couldn't tell them whether I had or hadn't. I might have, but I had a complete blackout from drinking. It wasn't much of a fire; it was in a closet underneath the stairwell. It could've been a disastrous fire because it was an old apartment house."

IMPLICATIONS OF AUTOBIOGRAPHY

Some of the themes in this brief autobiography will be explored in this chapter and the next. The man's words remind us that convicted law violators are also human beings who have histories, are usually puzzled over their own behavior, and share the frailties and strengths found among members of any large-sized group. The visitor to a prison may want to see what "a murderer looks like." Murderers come in various sizes, shapes, colors, and personalities. The wifekiller, the barroom brawler who pulled a knife, and the robber-murderer represent distinct motives and social situations. Lumping all criminals into some vaguely conceived physical type encourages the false belief that they are all alike in ways which enable us to distinguish them sharply from noncriminals.

Riddle of criminal behavior

The former prisoner asked the question: "Why did I set fires to buildings?" He falls back on a vague sense of alienation engendered by what he implies was a disorganized home. He describes himself as a product of a cruel "reform school" but also as a footloose youngster with some sophistication in making his way in what he describes as a hostile world. He tells of a series of difficulties in the Army and in prisons where "I was constantly on the run, agitating . . ." It can be inferred that he encountered at least some authorities who were puzzled about what to do with the person who raised so many problems for himself and others. Some judge must have wondered whether psychiatry offered an answer, since the man was referred to a mental hospital for observation. Perhaps the course of his career would have been changed if the official response had been to treat an emotional difficulty rather than to define his behavior as simply criminal. Without reliable and essential information, the reasons for the man's committing arson cannot be investigated here, but with the advantages of hindsight, we can argue that his long period of imprisonment brought few desirable results.

The riddle of criminal behavior is a special version of the riddle of all human behavior. The problems of criminal behavior intersect the question of what to do about poverty, family disorganization, inadequate schooling, mental illness, alcohol and drug abuse, and the other social problems of our age. The explanation of criminal behavior involves us in a search among a wide range of social and psychological factors operating to produce the particular person standing before us. This is essentially the same search we must undertake when we have responsibilities in dealing with the other social problems.

System of criminal justice

The arsonist, murderer, and sex offender loom large in images of the criminal as an enemy of society conceived as requiring a "war" on crime. People who cry for "law and order" frequently justify extreme measures in terms of these "enemies" and descriptions of a "crime wave." As we shall see, the generalized fears of "the criminal" as a "dangerous enemy" are based on exaggerations. Violent criminals are only a small fraction of the total population of apprehended offenders, and even violent criminals are not universally dangerous enemies of the community. Furthermore, official statistics are unreliable evidence of a "crime wave"; they are more useful as measures of increased activities in the administration of criminal justice than of a greater proclivity for criminal behavior.

Instead of virtually exclusive attention to the offender as the crime problem, increasing recognition is being given the system of criminal justice itself as a factor in the persistence of criminal behavior. The involvement of the social structure in the generation and persistence of criminal behavior is one of the qualifications of crime as a *social* problem. Chapter 17 will be devoted to this subject.

In calling himself a "professional convict," the former prisoner implied that his experiences pressed him to adjust to the prison as a "human warehouse" in ways which emphasized his status as prisoner.[1] In being handled impersonally as a "thing," he was expected to adopt the ways of a "good prisoner" in marked isolation from the conditions of a normal community. Thereby, his adjustment to prison was channeled toward commitment to a prisoner role which, if the prison is intended to prepare for constructive behavior after release from confinement, would be temporary and transitional.

Heretofore, the hostility a former prisoner feels against the prison has been interpreted as evidence of his maladjustment. However, an encouraging development has been the increased recognition that the opera-

---

[1] The prison as "human warehouse" is discussed in Chapter 17, pp. 439–42.

A message from home for the exile. The prison is the instrument whereby the system of criminal justice applies its legal authority to punish the convicted offender. Will the exile return to the community with less probability of further criminal behavior? The answer depends partly on the quality of links he retains with that community.

tion of agencies of criminal justice are also at the heart of the problem of repeated crimes, and rising expectations for performance of correctional institutions are shared by many of the executives and personnel of the agencies. A pivotal question is whether these expectations are shared by a sufficient proportion of the public to lend vigor and persistence to the reform of the system of justice and the mobilization of the required resources.

LEGAL ORDER AND SOCIAL CONTROL

The criminal differs from other kinds of "problem people" in two important respects. First, he has been evaluated as a proper subject for the attention of the agencies which make up the system of criminal justice. Second, he has been thereby defined as a *criminal,* a status in which, as a subject of this system, he incurs the moral condemnation of the community and the added consequences of punishment. These consequences have impact on his self-image and his future relationships within the community.

Law as social engineering

As previously discussed, man is a social creature whose behavior is related with the behaviors of his fellows through a network of social norms.[2] His relationships with others are patterned into a meaningful whole because he conforms largely to the rules characteristic of his group. *Social order* connotes a state of peace and tranquility wherein the behaviors of individuals and groups are in keeping with some overall scheme which lends predictability to social transactions.

This order exists because the individual members of the groups share common meanings and values within a totality of social institutions such as the family, school, and church. Places of work and organizations for distribution of goods constitute social institutions in that they embody social rules to which the participants in their activities are supposed to conform to produce orderly and satisfactory transactions among persons. The social relationships are orderly and predictable because the participants are in common agreement on values and the social rules. In short, informal controls, derived from a sense of conscience and socialization to appropriate norms, are sufficient to produce expected behavior.

What if these informal controls are insufficient to produce social order or if individuals, such as our former prisoner, engage in behavior considered to be a threat to the community? The criminal law is a part of the structure of formal controls to which the community resorts to remedy

[2] See Chapter 1, pp. 13–17.

this breach in the social order. The resort to the criminal law suggests that the behavior it prohibits has been evaluated by lawmakers as a sufficient social problem to require drastic official action.

The legal order is placed by Roscoe Pound within the total order in terms of two general functions. First, it applies a system of rules and procedures to harmonize and reconcile controversies between individuals. Second, it restrains and deters antisocial acts threatening the general safety, health, peace, and economic order. Pound sees the criminal law as that part of the legal system which defines how duties are to be imposed upon all persons and which prescribes how these duties will be enforced through means of prosecutions and penal treatment. He emphasizes that the legal regime is only a portion of the regulative agencies which also include the family, church, and other social institutions. The law is a part of social engineering in that it has been contrived deliberately by human minds to serve a consciously implemented system of formal control.[3]

Uniqueness of criminal behavior

Criminal behavior differs from other forms of social deviance in that it is in violation of the legal rules promulgated by a political authority and is subject to punishments administered by the state. In this sense the police, courts and correctional agencies are instruments of the state in enforcing explicit rules of conduct formulated by lawmaking bodies and in administering the penalties provided in the criminal law. The legal rules are supposed to reflect the larger set of mores of the society in that the laws are intended to protect those values deemed highly important to its people.

An exact definition of criminal behavior is complicated by the relative inflexibility of written codes in the face of changing social conditions under which they are administered and the variations among the codes enacted among the jurisdictions. Usually, crime is defined as any behavior prohibited by a criminal law. Hart moves beyond this rather empty statement to note the implicit assumption that a conviction for a crime is a distinctive and serious matter. Then, a *crime* is conduct which, if duly shown to have taken place, will incur a formal and solemn pronouncement of the moral condemnation of the community and the added consequence of punishment.[4]

When the fate of a particular offender is examined, the image of criminals as unmitigated monsters usually dissolves. The story of our former prisoner is likely to evoke sympathy over his many years behind bars, the tribulations he encountered in childhood, and the stigmatization he experienced as a former prisoner seeking work. However, the serious threat

---

[3] Roscoe Pound, "Criminal Justice in the American City—A Summary," *Crime and Delinquency,* Vol. 10 (October 1964), pp. 419–21.

[4] Henry M. Hart, Jr., "The Aims of the Criminal Law," *Law and Contemporary Problems,* Vol. 23 (Summer 1958), pp. 404–5.

of the arsonist must also be considered. Some official action must be taken to end this threat.

The issue shifts from sympathy alone to other questions: Is resort to criminal law the most promising strategy for dealing with the particular kind of social deviation? For example, if arson expresses emotional difficulties, will the application of the coercive authority of the criminal law come to bear on these difficulties? Is the removal of the arsonist from the community sufficient to safeguard the community? Since removal of all convicted criminals from the community would require the construction of many more prisons, there must be some other justification for imprisonment beyond simple isolation of all convicted criminals from the free community. Then what are the objectives of criminal justice which are supposed to be accomplished by punishment?

GENERAL OBJECTIVES OF CRIMINAL JUSTICE

Ultimately, criminal justice is intended to create the general observance of the law regarded as tantamount to an orderly and satisfying society. There is less agreement on how this purpose is to be achieved. Traditionally, criminal justice has relied heavily on punishment of the law violator. Gaining greater public support is another set of strategies whereby the treatment is supposed to eliminate the criminality of the convicted offender. His attitudes are to be modified and his capacities strengthened to increase the probability that he will seek his personal goals within the boundaries of legitimate behavior. A third approach is crime prevention. Through correction of the adverse social circumstances and of the inadequacies of socialization processes, the development of delinquent and criminal careers is to be cut off at the source.

Reliance on punishment

The arguments supporting punishment stress retribution, deterrence, and incapacitation. The victim's desire to strike back at the offender has been taken over by the state under *retribution.* Oppenheimer suggests alternative explanations. Retaliation fulfills a religious mission to punish the criminal. It may resolve (through "paying the debt") the social disharmony created by the offense. Through his suffering the offender may "wash away" his guilt.[5]

Under *deterrence,* punishment is supposed to prevent future offenses. The offender will fear that penalties will be imposed again when he assesses the benefits of a new offense. Other persons are supposed to be deterred when the offender is punished for the crime *they* contemplate.

[5] Heinrich Oppenheimer, *The Rationale of Punishment* (London, Eng.: University of London Press, 1913), pp. 182–83.

When these arguments are not convincing, some penologists retreat to the concept of *incapacitation*. Granted that punishment is not efficient on either of the above scores, they argue, at least imprisonment temporarily prevents the criminal from preying on free society.

Impressive arguments are raised against punishment as a means of achieving long-term benefits for either the offender or the community. Indiscriminate and arbitrary penalization may produce hostility among offenders who believe they have been misused or who react with greater caution in future offenses. In either respect, punishment for its own sake contributes to the breeding of formidable foes for those agents of criminal justice who see themselves as conducting a "war" on criminal "enemies." Paradoxically, stubborn resistance to punitive policies may make the prisoner some kind of "hero." On the other hand, passive accommodation to confinement is the stuff from which dependency is made. The nerve of self-reliance is cut to make the prisoner a psychological vegetable needing someone to tell him what to do and to provide his means of physical survival.

Just as in the case of treatment, the fitting of punishment to the crime and to the offender requires careful study. This requirement is seldom met because sole reliance on punishment is likely to be associated with high volume of cases and the assumption that the expense of investigative and diagnostic services can be avoided. Probably the strongest counterargument is that application of punishment as an end in itself isolates the offender from the very social processes in which he is supposed to become more competent.

Sharp criticisms of punishment usually overlook two matters. First, elements of deprivation exist in most social transactions; even high-quality therapy includes experiences which the offender may regard as punishment. Second, punishment can influence behavior if used to a limited degree for a well-designed purpose.

Skeptics of the deterrent effect of punishment should take another look at the issue, Tittle suggests. He relates the prison admissions to number of crimes known to the police to measure the certainty of punishment for seven kinds of offenses. The severity of punishment was measured by the length of time served in prison. Among the states, he concludes that, with only slight exception, the rate of crime decreases as the level of certainty increases, regardless of the level of severity, for all offenses except homicide. Generally, the severity of punishment had little effect except as it was related to certainty. He sees the certainty of punishment also involving the informal penalties of conscience and censure of one's peers, whereas severity of punishment is less likely to enter the thinking of the offender before his crime.[6]

---

[6] Charles R. Tittle, "Crime Rates and Legal Sanctions," *Social Problems,* Vol. 16 (Spring 1969), pp. 407–23.

Treatment of convicted offenders

Treatment is a social process whereby the offender is supposed to be moved along a continuum of stages from his overt conflict with the law to his acceptance of the rules of legitimate society as his own. Treatment approaches vary, but all are intended to revise his attitudes about himself and his relationships with other persons or to improve his capacity to meet his personal goals without conflict with the interests of society. The focus of attention is upon his personal qualities and his social environment. His crime is significant for the cues it offers in explaining why he violates the law. Otherwise, chief attention is diverted from the crime per se and toward the deficiencies he has as a unique individual in coping with the problems of life without resort to crime.

In keeping with the treatment goal, courts distinguish between determination of guilt and the selection of the form of disposition most likely to halt further offenses. In lieu of imprisonment for sake of punishment, the judge would be provided alternatives to increase the probability that his decision would have constructive consequence. Probation involves the conditional release of the convicted offender in the community under supervision of an officer of the court in lieu of imprisonment. Some states provide the indeterminate sentence; the offender is sentenced to a range of years, such as 1 to 20 years, so that the correctional authorities may fit the length of confinement to the treatment requirements of the inmate.

Correctional institutions rely primarily on individualized treatment under the assumption that the sources of criminality lie within the bounds of the individual's personality, with environmental factors regarded as largely constant. The strategies include one-to-one psychological counseling, vocational training, academic education, religious counseling, and recreational activities.

Gaining increased attention are environmental approaches based on two assumptions. The first assumption is that the rise and persistence of criminality occurs within social groups. The second is that the correctional institution provides a setting which can have negative as well as positive influence on the inmate's subsequent behavior. One of the most frequent strategies is guided group interaction in which inmates and staff engage in free discussion of key issues in a supportive and permissive atmosphere to get at the roots of deviant behavior. Other strategies are discussed in the next chapter: therapeutic community, open institution, and community-based corrections. To speed the release of eligible prisoners, parole is employed to return prisoners to the community under guidance and supervision of representatives of paroling authorities.

Treatment programs operate under handicaps. The primary emphasis on punishment conflicts with the fundamental premise of therapeutic strategies that the client presents himself voluntarily for corrective services because he recognizes his need for those services. The convicted offender is an involuntary client and has been subjected to the degradation of formal conviction as a transgressor. He is likely to identify the therapist as a representative of the coercive system which has degraded him and is therefore reluctant to enter wholeheartedly into the rehabilitative process. Many offenders have a long history of failure and frustration that is difficult to overcome within available time and resources. All inmates have their unique characteristics. How can *the* fulcrum for behavior change be found for *this* man? The correctional agency usually lacks sufficient resources and personnel to mount a full-fledged treatment program. Its staff includes many employees who reject treatment objectives. Strong resistance is applied by an inmate culture centered around opposition to all officialdom. Finally, correctional agencies generally lack a consistent and fundamental philosophy to lend direction to their treatment activities.

Prevention of delinquency and crime

To forestall the disagreeable eventualities of delinquency and crime, a broad range of actions is taken to clear away the personal and social difficulties contributing to the occurrence of antisocial behavior. Acclaimed universally as more promising than subsequent efforts to halt a delinquent career, prevention attracts less unanimity concerning the approach and techniques to be applied. The field of crime prevention is characterized by a confusion of vague and naive ideas. There is a lack of precision in defining who is the target of the efforts and exactly what is supposed to be accomplished by a wide variety of techniques advanced as the solution.[7]

Sometimes the target population is seen as essentially "normal" youngsters who are kept on the "right track" by strengthening family life, providing "wholesome" recreation, or expanding a character-building program such as the Boy Scouts. At other times, the target population is described as socially maladjusted or emotionally disturbed youngsters whose proneness for antisocial behavior is to be overcome through school programs or mental health clinics. Other efforts center attention on the group already diagnosed as delinquent. Social group workers search out delinquent gangs to try to bring them into the regularized institutional life of the community. Finally, crime prevention tries to break the cycle of repeated offenses of individuals with a criminal record. Then the various strategies of law enforcement and corrections are employed to forestall future criminal behavior of persons already caught by criminal justice agencies.

In an attempt to give order to the many meanings of crime prevention, Lejins defines three concepts.[8] *Punitive prevention* uses the threat of

[7] For fuller discussion of crime prevention, see Elmer H. Johnson, *Crime, Correction, and Society* (rev. ed.; Homewood, Ill.; Dorsey Press, 1968), pp. 304–58.

[8] Peter P. Lejins, "The Fields of Prevention," in William E. Amos and Charles F. Welford (eds.) *Delinquency Prevention: Theory and Practice* (Englewood Cliffs, N.J.: Prentice-Hall, Inc., 1967), pp. 1–21.

punishment in an effort to deter transgressions. *Corrective prevention* assumes that antisocial behavior stems from environmental factors and psychological conditions which must be remedied if the tide of law violations is to wane. General societal policies may be manipulated to remedy the fundamental conditions contributing to delinquency and crime. Reform of education, unemployment compensation, social welfare programs, regulation of alcohol and drug traffic, and other similar measures are intended to reduce the probability of crime-producing circumstances. Based on behavioral science, diagnostic methods are employed in an effort to detect incipient delinquency. Sections with high rates of delinquency draw the special attention of preventive services and of programs intended to revitalize community life as insulations against antisocial behavior. *Mechanical prevention* attempts to make crime perpetration more difficult through burglar alarms, street lighting, police surveillance, and so on.

URBANISM AND POLICED SOCIETY

One irony of history, Morris declares, is that social "progress" carries with it the seeds of a greater volume of criminal behavior. Disturbed by the increasing tide of delinquency, representatives of the so-called underdeveloped nations asked him how they might curb this trend. He advised them to reject the techniques for building a modern nation. Their people should remain ignorant, bigoted, and ill-educated. Development of efficient communication and transportation systems should be avoided to insure that the villagers would remain isolated all their lives. Schools should not provide hope that children can rise above their father's level of achievement. As legitimate opportunities increase, so also do illegitimate opportunities.[9] In short, the fundamental characteristics and by-products of urbanization would have to be avoided, and the benefits of advanced technology would have to be given up.

Justice as a formal control system

The association between urbanization and the increased visibility of criminal behavior begets criminal justice as a formal control system. Urban society, consisting of tightly woven political, social, and economic systems, demands an unprecedented level of public order. Preindustrial communities relied on the informal controls of family, church, and neighborhood, supplemented by loosely organized policing by constables and sheriffs. With industrialization undermining this control system, the rising middle class felt threatened by the vicious, criminal, and violent elements of the population plus the rapidly multiplying poor of the cities.

[9] Norval Morris and Gordon Hawkins, *The Honest Politician's Guide to Crime Control* (Chicago: University of Chicago Press, 1970), p. 49.

In the middle of the 19th century there emerged the modern police as a bureaucratic and paramilitary organization interposed between the victim and the offender. The "policed society," as Silver calls it, arose when a public bureaucracy supplanted various kinds of self-policing by citizens and constituted a continual presence of centralized political authority in daily life.[10] A relatively small body of disciplined policemen was able to deal with a larger population of criminal or disorderly individuals. With increased reliance on formal actions by police, the disposition of cases established by arrest instigated greater activity by courts and correctional agencies as supporting elements of the "policed society."

Impact of urbanism on police work

The urban environment raises special needs for law enforcement and provides a setting appropriate for police strategies, but also creates difficulties for effective law enforcement. Stinchcombe's differentiation between public and private space is useful for explaining this statement.[11] Private space is controlled by families, schools, recreational organizations, and so on, which regulate the behavior of their members through their particular rules and goals. Outside of these private areas is public space, such as streets and marketplaces. The urban need for systematic policing stems from population concentrations in public space which insulate individuals from the personal controls of the more intimate groups once they enter the anonymity of public space. The police department becomes an essential control agency in contributing to the community's equilibrium.

This population concentration makes police patrol economically feasible on a basis of per capita costs. Similarly, standardized handling of clients and expensive equipment can be utilized. Conversely, the tasks of urban law enforcement are complicated by the concealment of transgressors by the greater size, heterogeneity, and mobility of population. The imposition of a broader spectrum of service tasks beyond crime suppression has added to the burden of police work. Too, police organizations are weakened by the defects of local government: duplication of duties among government units frequently lacking sufficient tax revenues to meet burgeoning demands for services, and vulnerability to control by municipal political machines. The rise of urban society has undermined the autonomy of the locality in providing goods and services. Similarly, crime frequently has regionwide and sometimes national ramifications, but law enforcement continues to be organized as though each unit of local government continues to be capable of policing its own jurisdiction.

---

[10] Allan Silver, "The Demand for Order in Civil Society: A Review of Some Themes in the History of Urban Crime, Police, and Riot," in David J. Bordua (ed.) *The Police: Six Sociological Essays* (New York: John Wiley & Sons, 1967), pp. 1–24.

[11] Arthur L. Stinchcombe, "Institutions of Privacy in the Determination of Police Administration Practice," *American Journal of Sociology,* Vol. 69 (September 1963), pp. 150–60.

The localization of law enforcement is a product of the special faith in and preference for local units of government traditional in the United States. However, this emphasis and the suspicion of strong police agencies have blocked systematic relationships among police bodies. Smith sees only a collection of police units which have some similarity in authority, organization, or jurisdiction, without any systematic relationship with each other.[12] Fears of centralization overlook the tendencies of local power structures to place their self-interest before democratic enforcement of the law. When covering a larger geographical area, the more elaborate police organization can withstand purely local pressures against equal enforcement. Even bureaucratic standardization of procedures is an insulation against differential enforcement. A larger organization can provide a better brand of police training and regularity of career opportunities to raise recruitment quality and chances of retaining officers capable of intelligent task performance.

Finally, the urban citizen is reluctant to take an active part in dealing with crime events suddenly involving him as a witness, but without background information on the meaning of the event. Under these circumstances, urban police must rely especially on their own presence and information to apprehend criminals, whereas rural police can depend more on the complaints of citizens.

Issues raised by urban disorder

The differentiation between private and public space is associated by Stinchcombe with a number of law enforcement issues.[13] The distinction is vital to maintenence of political rights, for example. Within his private space the individual is legally free of police supervision in that the processes of investigation and apprehension are restricted to assure the sanctity of the home and private property. The goal of police efficiency is balanced against the preservation of civil rights. Police work is less complicated in public places when the officer is more likely to be able to observe the transgression and is less restricted in the gathering of evidence and making arrests.

The effectiveness of enforcement is influenced by the place of crime occurrence. There are special difficulties in apprehending armed robbers in public places, but the rate of conviction after arrest is higher than that for rape and assault, which occur in private places. Burglary and larceny involve the criminal's invasion of the private space of others and result in higher conviction rates. Vagrancy, drunkenness, and disorderly conduct

---

[12] Bruce Smith, *Police Systems in the United States,* (2d ed.; New York: Harper & Row, 1960), pp. 20–21.

[13] Stinchcombe, "Institutions of Privacy in Determination of Police Administration," pp. 151–57.

are offenses especially associated with public space and have particularly high conviction rates. Illegitimate businesses in prostitution, gambling, and the like are able to cloak their operations in privacy and thus complicate law enforcement.

Finally, public disorder becomes a concern of special priority in urban law enforcement. Stinchcombe distinguishes between individual, collective, and structural disorder.[14] In *individual disorder* the "drunk and disorderly" person in public space draws police attention. He is less likely to do so if his offense occurs in private space. The police are thrust into the functions of "social sanitation" in dealing with beggars, common drunks, street prostitutes, and other offenders who violate moral sensibilities. This situation illustrates another major factor; those offenders without access to private places are especially vulnerable to arrest. Thus, social class prejudice is built into the system of criminal justice.

Riots and street demonstrations are examples of *collective disorder* which stems from the questioning by a segment of the population of the basis of the community's power structure. As the most visible representatives of that structure, the police become involved directly in the issues beyond law enforcement per se. Sometimes they are surprised to find some demonstrators describing them as a garrison force coercing a "conquered people."

Structural disorder refers to the unintended consequences of the assembling of population masses in relatively small space. That is, the metropolis is experiencing new regulatory needs in terms of smog, deterioration of the central city, public sanitation, and traffic congestion, which involve police as administrators of anonymous masses.

THE EXTENT OF CRIMINALITY

Annual reports of law enforcement agencies usually describe a mounting tide of crime as measured by number of arrests or some kind of crime rate. Increased concern is justified, of course, but the significance of the increase depends on what these data measure. Do they measure a greater proclivity for crime among persons in general, or do they simply reflect greater police efficiency in detecting that portion of the population most prone to break the law? A higher expectation of law observance among citizens presses the agents of criminal justice to be less tolerant in arrest decisions, sentencing by courts, and granting of parole by correctional authorities. Therefore, official statistics can indicate a higher incidence of crime when actually the amount or seriousness of noncomformity may be less today than in earlier days which are described by official rates as having less crime.

[14] Ibid., pp. 157–58.

Defects of official statistics

There is no reliable measurement of the total extent of crime. Information on arrests tells us about the offenses reported to the police and the successes of the police in identifying someone as a suspect. Some unknown proportion of offenses do not come to the attention of the police because the crime is unreported. If the public becomes more willing to report crimes, the number of arrests can increase without an actual change in extent of criminality. Time of special public concern can produce illusionary "crime waves" simply because of increased sensitivity to offenses and a decline in policemen's willingness to take actions short of formal arrest.

Official reports on the extent of crime are among the least satisfactory forms of social statistics. The *Uniform Crime Reports* of the Federal Bureau of Investigation comprise at this writing the most careful and systematic attempt to provide reliable and valid data on the number of arrests in the United States. Nevertheless, this commendable effort suffers from the inherent difficulties of arrest data obtained through voluntary reporting by local law enforcement agencies. Each local department gathers and submits its own set of figures, largely on its own. Their accuracy depends on how carefully the arrest events are counted and what is selected to include in the count. Changes in crime rates are affected by the differences in the identity of agencies reporting to the F.B.I. and the way the statistical gathering tasks are performed from year to year. Deliberately or inadvertent, a department can record a lower number of arrests because certain events are overlooked, or a department may neglect to submit its report, thereby changing the coverage of agencies from year to year. The individuals making the count may differ from year to year, altering the level of efficiency over time. Beyond differences in methods of tabulation, the comparability of arrest data among jurisdictions is undermined by the variation among the laws being enforced.

Higher crime rates may prove only that the police are more diligent, efficient, or less tolerant of the kinds of misconduct which had always come to their attention. In times of high public concern over crime, these agencies are more likely to be severe in their decisions on the people captured in their nets. The official crime rate can be increased simply by a greater tendency to make an arrest under circumstances in which previously the violater was released with a warning. Admissions to prisons can be doubled if judges make less use of suspended sentences or probation. Drug addiction, gambling, shoplifting, or homosexuality may arouse unusual public concern and increase police surveillance to bring greater arrest rates as new evidence to support the fears which initiated the process that provided the new evidence in the first place.

Specter of a crime wave

The fears aroused by the specter of unprecedented criminality overlook the extent of lawlessness in earlier eras. In early 18th century London, for example, disorder and crime ran rampant. In taverns, coffee houses, and shops, customers expressed fears, Tobias reports, that in the dark streets "their hats and wigs should be snitched from their heads" or "that they may be blinded, knocked down, cut or stabbed." The violent transitions wrought by urbanization in 19th-century England raised concerns also expressed today. Turnpikes and railways spawned bands of roving criminals. The adverse consequences of family disorganization, reflected in "latchkey children," were lamented. Display of goods in accessible places was supposed to encourage thefts akin to shoplifting today.[15] Elliott reports that laxities in business honesty and general disregard for the law characterized our frontier era.[16] General lawlessness is recorded in the histories of various American metropolises.[17] After examining early American history, Bell concludes that there probably is less crime today in the United States than there was 100 or even 25 years ago.[18]

Today's description of increased crime is counterbalanced by evidence of a reverse trend over the long term. Using arrest reports of Boston police from 1849 to 1951, Ferdinand finds a clear decline in rates for murder, assault, and larceny. The overall trend for burglary and robbery is downward, but these crimes have had periodic increases, and recent years have brought them to their highest level. Manslaughter increased at the turn of the century but has declined since. Only forcible rape has increased rather consistently because of the greater opportunity for such incidents with increased prevalence of automobiles and greater willingness of victims to report them. Ferdinand suggests that the increase in national crime rates is a symptom of the movement from low-crime rate, rural areas to high-crime rate, urban areas. Rural areas place less reliance on law enforcement in dealing with transgressors and have less portable property available for easy theft. With greater proportions of the American population in urban areas, the national crime rates would increase because of the lesser contribution of the low-crime rate, rural areas through their lower rates for most

---

[15] J. J. Tobias, *Crime and Industrial Society in the 19th Century* (New York: Shocken Books, 1967), pp. 22, 37, 46–48.

[16] Mabel A. Elliott, *Crime in Modern Society* (New York: Harper & Row, 1952), p. 272.

[17] Herbert Ashbury, *Gangs of New York* (New York: Alfred A. Knopf, 1928); Herbert Asbury, *Gem of the Prairie* (New York: Alfred A. Knopf, 1940); Carl Bridenbaugh, *Cities in Revolt: Urban Life in America, 1743–1771* (New York: Alfred A. Knopf, 1955); Robert Bruce, *1877: Year of Violence* (New York: Bobbs-Merrill Co., 1959); Philip Taft, "Violence in American Labor Disputes," *Annals of American Academy of Political and Social Science,* Vol. 364 (March 1966), pp. 127–40; and Irving Werstein, *July 1863* (New York: Julian Messner, 1957).

[18] Daniel Bell, *The End of Ideology* (Glencoe, Ill.: Free Press, 1960), p. 137.

crimes. Therefore, Ferdinand regards migration as the explanation for the apparent discrepancy between a long-term decline in urban rates and an increasing national rate.[19]

Official crime statistics overlook an unknown, but certainly large, quantity of law violations by the "respectable" middle and upper classes. The official data would have us believe that crime is almost exclusively lower-class behavior, and studies of convicted and imprisoned offenders reveal a skewing toward the lower socioeconomic classes. But there is reason to believe that this skewing is a product of the screening process of the system of justice, and that persons of higher status tend to evade the net of law enforcement and corrections. The offenses they perpetrate are less likely to be under the scrunity of police. Upper-status people have greater resources for evading punishment if apprehended. The greater impact of criminal justice on the lower levels of the social structure is indicated by a number of studies which demonstrate that the infractions of the middle and upper classes are grossly underestimated by arrest data. When selected samples of presumably law-abiding people are asked to recall their past law violations, the studies uniformly show delinquencies and crimes at all levels of society.[20]

VARIETY OF CRIMINAL BEHAVIORS

The crime problem is conceived largely in terms of the violent offenses of homicide, forcible rape, and various other sex trangressions. Special concern over violent crimes is justified by the high priority given to physical security and the protection of sex and family life among the fundamental values. Nevertheless, only about 8 percent of all arrests reported by police are for these crimes. Other kinds of crime constitute the primary work load of the system of criminal justice. Approximately 70 percent of reported arrests are for crimes suggesting personal disorganization; drunkenness, drunk driving, and disorderly conduct alone comprise about half the arrests made. Crimes against property draw about 22 percent of reported arrests; larceny-theft, burglary, breaking-entering, and automobile theft comprise 16 percent.

[19] Theodore N. Ferdinand, "The Criminal Patterns of Boston since 1849," *American Journal of Sociology,* Vol. 73 (July 1967), pp. 84–99.

[20] For example, see: John P. Clark and Eugene Wenninger, "Socio-Economic Class and Area as Correlates of Illegal Behavior among Juveniles," *American Sociological Review,* Vol. 27 (December 1962), pp. 826–34; Robert Dentler and Lawrence J. Monroe, "Early Adolescent Theft," *American Sociological Review,* Vol. 26 (October 1961), pp. 733–43; Martin Gold, "Undetected Delinquent Behavior," *Journal of Research in Crime and Delinquency,* Vol. 3 (January 1966), pp. 27–46; Fred J. Murphy, Mary M. Shirley, and Helen L. Witmer, "The Incidence of Hidden Delinquency," *American Journal of Orthopsychiatry,* Vol. 16 (October 1946), pp. 686–96; Albert J. Reiss, Jr., and Albert L. Rhodes, "The Distribution of Juvenile Delinquency in the Social Class Structure," *American Sociological Review,* Vol. 26 (October 1961), pp. 720–32; James S. Wallenstein and C. J. Wyle, "Our Law-Abiding Law Breakers," *Federal Probation,* Vol. 25 (March-April 1947), pp. 107–12.

Violent personal criminals

This class of offender perpetrates homicide, assault, forcible rape, and various other sex crimes in which physical injury is inflicted in a direct and personal confrontation. Long prison sentences and, more rarely, the death penalty are imposed usually for the violent crimes, especially for first degree murder and rape. Nevertheless, the violent offenders usually do not conceive of themselves as criminals and do not organize their lives around criminal values.

Rather than being highly individuated behavior, crimes of violence are shaped by general and cultural patterns. Crimes of violence are generally perpetrated against persons with whom the offender has had previous social relationships rather than against strangers. A very high proportion of these crimes involve other members of the family or at least casual acquaintances. The offender and the victim are highly likely to be of the same race and in places where both usually congregate.[21] Amir relates forcible rape to patterns of learning within a cultural context.[22] Contemporary culture is relatively more permissive toward sexual experimentation than in earlier decades, and the search for a "thrill" may be extended by some groups to tolerate sexual aggression. The themes of masculine dominance and the double standard grant special leeway to male sex transgressions.

Dealing chiefly with murders of passion, Wolfgang and Ferracuti develop a premise that psychological and social forces converge to produce a subculture of violence.[23] They see the probability of violence promoted when the individual operates in a cultural milieu supporting resort to physical combat as a measure of daring, courage, or defense of one's own sense of worth. When both parties share this tendency to employ violence in social relationships, there is a greater probability of physical assault and violent quarrels under provoking circumstances which other subcultures would regard as too trivial for such strong physical reactions.

Wolfgang and Ferracuti point to the expression of violence in various aspects of life: parent-child relationships, parental discipline, domestic quarrels, street fights, and so on. However, legitimatized violence is likely to be vicarious in the dominant culture and less prevalent than in particular subcultures. Even in the latter, the greater acceptance of violence as a response to aggravating situations does not imply that such drastic behavior always occurs. Individuals differ in their proclivity for violence even

[21] President's Commission on Law Enforcement and Administration of Justice, *The Challenge of Crime in a Free Society* (Washington, D.C.: U.S. Government Printing Office, February 1967), pp. 39–41.
[22] Menachem Amir, "Patterns of Forcible Rape," in Marshall B. Clinard and Richard Quinney (eds.), *Criminal Behavior Systems: A Topology* (Holt, Rinehart, & Winston, 1967), pp. 72–73.
[23] Marvin E. Wolfgang and Franco Ferracuti, *The Subculture of Violence* (London, Eng.: Tavistock Publications, 1967), pp. 153–61.

when their immediate groups are unlikely to disapprove of such responses. Nevertheless, the probability of violence is related to age, sex, ethnic or racial group membership, and socioeconomic status. Violent crimes are more characteristic of individuals in ages ranging from late adolescence to middle age and males are predominant. Residents of the ghetto have high rates of violence. Quinney reports higher murder and aggravated assault rates are associated with lower levels of schooling, family income, and proportion of males in occupations other than white collar.[24]

Occasional property criminals

The offenses of occasional property criminals include naive check forgery, "joyriding" automobile theft, amateur shoplifting, casual theft, and vandalism. These transgressors do not see themselves as criminals, lack sophistication in criminal techniques, and commit crimes irregularly and infrequently as acts incidental to their life organization.[25]

The "youthful prank" element in some occasional property crimes is illustrated by Wade's investigation of the destruction of property by young vandals. Usually vandalism is interpreted as a deliberate and wanton act. Wade sees it as spontaneous and unplanned behavior in conformity to pressures from peer groups. Preliminary to the act of vandalism, the juveniles are waiting for something to happen in an unstructured situation. Some spontaneous event occurs. One boy may throw a rock at a window. The group's attention is focused on the possibilities of play with destruction secondary to the purposes of excitement, demonstration of skill (accurate aim in rock throwing), and exhibition of courage to impress one's peers. In an atmosphere of mutual excitement, the initial testing of each other's eligibility for peer respect may grow into a veritable orgy of vandalism under the cloak of anonymity and the definition of the behavior as a prank or mere mischief. Subsequent guilt may be eased by rationalizations that the vandalism was a form of protest or an act of revenge against some villain.[26]

Crimes and personal disorganization

Criminal statutes are employed against conduct which outrages certain moral sentiments. The general morals are supposed to be safeguarded against excessive drinking, drug abuse, sexual misconduct, gambling, neg-

---

[24] Richard Quinney, "Structural Characteristics, Population Areas, and Crime Rates in the United States," *Journal of Criminal Law, Criminology and Police Science,* Vol. 57 (March 1966), p. 49.

[25] Marshall B. Clinard, *Sociology of Deviant Behavior* (3d ed.; New York: Holt, Rinehart & Winston, 1968), pp. 265–66.

[26] Andrew L. Wade, "Social Processes in the Act of Juvenile Vandalism," in Clinard and Quinney, *Criminal Behavior Systems,* pp. 94–109.

lect of children, and similar behavior. The punitive force of the criminal law is supposed to have remedial effect through pressing the deviant to abandon his misconduct and through using him as an example to deter others. These transgressors are regarded as victims of their own moral weakness and inability to organize their own lives constructively. Therefore, the use of the criminal law is defined as humanitarian in intent and ultimately beneficial to the offender from the perspective of moral stewardship. Under the Calvinistic stewardship tradition, the use of legal coercion is one of the acceptable means of overcoming the immorality of drinking, gambling, sexual irregularity, family nonsupport, and other behaviors censured as "sinful" by the keepers of the dominant morality.[27]

The remarkable but largely futile faith placed in moral coercion produces two thirds of reported U.S. arrests. The offenses include public drunkenness, drunken driving, drug use, homosexuality, liquor law violations, commercialized vice, gambling, vagrancy, disorderly conduct, and offenses against the family and children. A heavy volume of these cases is imposed on the system of criminal justice.

The resort to criminalization of behavior in an attempt to control these forms of deviance jeopardizes the widespread acceptance of the system of criminal justice as desirable and binding on the conduct of "good" citizens. In a multivalued and dynamic society, the diversity of moral sentiments undermines the community consensus essential to effective law enforcement. The police are in an advantageous position when the necessity to enforce the law is exceptional, because then law obedience is maintained by the force of the individual's own conscience. In the absence of such moral consensus, the police must rely largely on their own resources in eliminating what the framers of laws have defined as both immoral and illegal. In light of the great difficulties of law enforcement without strong and persistent support from the community, full enforcement would require a police force of a size beyond the available resources.

The bulk of the offenders arrested and jailed are drawn from the less privileged segments of the community because their behavior is less likely to coincide with the moral expectations of the dominant segment. In other words, laws expressing moral sentiments are potentially instruments for imposing the moral standards of one group on the behavior of other groups. In addition, to be thrust into the role of moral coercion, the police risk their own demoralization. A demand exists for illicit alcohol, drugs, sex, and gambling. When supplying this demand is prohibited by law, a market is created for criminal organizations which will endeavor to corrupt public officials to maintain the stability of their illicit operations. Furthermore, being propelled into the responsibility of dealing with persons suffer-

---

[27] Clifford S. Griffin, *Their Brother's Keepers* (New Brunswick, N.J.: Rutgers University Press, 1961), pp. 104–9.

ing from personal pathologies, the police, courts, and correctional institutions are pressed into service as processors of human "salvage," although the strategies of punishment are poor substitutes for the medical and psychological approaches required.

Consequently, a promising means of reducing the burden on the system of criminal justice would be the "decriminalization" of many forms of antisocial behavior now subject to criminal sanctions. For example, Morris and Hawkins make a strong case for elimination of drunkenness, narcotics and drug abuse, gambling, disorderly conduct and vagrancy, abortion, sexual activities between consenting adults in private, and those juvenile delinquencies which would not be criminal among adults. Believing that the prevention of harm to other persons is the only proper function of the criminal law, they see a highly moralistic system of criminal justice to be a particularly inept and costly instrument for coercing men toward virtue.[28]

Crimes related to occupations

The murderer, rapist, thief, and robber personify "the criminal" in the minds of many of us. The search for explanations of criminality often place great emphasis on poverty, ghetto neighborhoods, and psychological abnormalities, but these ideas are severely tested when we consider crimes associated with respectable occupations. Such offenses include embezzlement, fraudulent sales, false advertising, misgrading of goods, fee splitting, antitrust violations, tax cheating, medical prescription violations, and employee thefts.

In his characteristically colorful style, Ross years ago called attention to the moral insensibility and overwhelming threat of law violations of respectable, exemplary, trusted personages placed "at the focus of the spider web of fiduciary relations." Ross commented: "To strike harder at the petty pickpocket than at the prominent and unabashed person who in a large, impressive way sells out his constituents, his followers, his depositors, his stockholders, his policyholders, his subscribers, or his customers, is to 'strain at a gnat and swallow a camel.' " [29] Through his concept of white-collar crime, Sutherland has made the objective analysis essential to bringing these behaviors within the scope of criminology. He refers to crimes committed by a person of respectability and high status in the course of his occupation, the significant element being that the offenses are not associated with poverty or with the social and personal pathologies accompanying poverty.[30]

[28] Morris and Hawkins, *The Honest Politician's Guide to Crime Control,* pp. 2–28.
[29] Edward A. Ross, *Sin and Society* (Boston, Mass.: Houghton Mifflin Co., 1907), pp. 29–30.
[30] Edwin H. Sutherland, *White Collar Crime* (New York: Holt, Rinehart & Winston, 1961), pp. 9–10.

The expansion of study beyond white-collar occupations is advocated because offenses are perpetrated in other occupations holding less prestige and power in the social structure. Newman points out that farmers may water the milk, for example, or television repairmen may perform unnecessary work.[31] Violations of the criminal laws in the course of occupational activities are not conceived as criminal by the violators, however. Their membership in a legitimate occupation makes it likely that other persons will agree and abstain from strong disapproval. This withholding of public censure raises serious doubts about the moral health of the community because of the blurring of distinctions between "right" and "wrong" among persons and groups who identify themselves as pillars of the community.

The pertinence of the increasing size of organizations and impersonality of relationships in urban society is suggested by Smigel's study of public attitudes toward stealing from bureaucracies. He finds that most individuals, if obliged to choose, would prefer to steal from, and be more approving of others stealing from, large-scale, impersonal rather than small-scale, personal organizations. Two lines of reasoning are used. One is that stealing from large organizations is believed to be less evil because such organizations are supposed to be impersonal, powerful, and ruthless. The other is that theft from large organizations is considered less risky because the presumed inefficiency and anonymity of big business and big government provide greater opportunity to steal and to conceal the theft.[32] Where police surveillance methods are inefficient, embezzlement and tax fraud are concealed with the regular operations of the business. The victimized organization has the primary likelihood of detecting the offense and is usually more inclined to seek restitution of property rather than criminal prosecution. Businesses are frequently more willing to accept the risk of thefts from employees than to assume the costs of maintaining systems of prevention.

Professional criminals

The next two types of offenders differ from those already presented in that they follow criminal careers. The term *career* connotes a relatively orderly sequence in a person's life, with passage from one status to another. An occupational career is the succession of related jobs filled by an individual in an orderly series. The career provides a broad framework of incentives which motivate the aspirant to move through the sequence of statuses from novice learner to a full-fledged practitioner of techniques

[31] Donald J. Newman, "White Collar Crime," *Law and Contemporary Problems*, Vol. 23 (Autumn 1958), p. 737.
[32] Erwin O. Smigel, "Public Attitudes toward Stealing as Related to the Size of Victim Organization," in Erwin O. Smigel and H. Lawrence Ross (eds.) *Crimes Against Bureaucracy* (New York: Van Nostrand Reinhold Co., 1970), pp. 15–21.

of the specialized occupation and to gain acceptance of other specialists as a colleague.[33]

The criminal career is characterized by pursuit of crime for economic gain, as a primary or secondary means of acquiring income. Second, criminal activity is part of the individual's way of life in that he sees himself as a criminal and identifies himself with other criminals. Third, he follows a sequence of learning whereby knowledge and skill in criminal techniques is acquired progressively, much as any occupational specialist systematically improves his grasp of the techniques of his job. He tends to become especially proficient in a particular kind of offense, such as picking pockets, passing illegal checks, or burglary. Fourth, the perpetration of crimes reflects deliberate planning, assessment of odds of detection and punishment, and analysis of the crime situation. Thus, the career criminal differs markedly from the offender who breaks the law in the course of sharp departures from his usual course of behavior.[34]

The highest degree of commitment to a criminal way of life and the most sophisticated development of a criminal career are found among *professional criminals.* The term "professional" implies their progressive and extensive development of certain techniques and social skills, their recruitment through more or less conscious choice, their admission to a learning regimen by professional criminals who control learning opportunities, and their acceptance of a form of criminal activity as their primary occupational endeavor.

In analyzing the professional thief, Sutherland emphasized the essential characteristics of criminals who adapt crime as their primary occupation. They develop specialized abilities and skills in the planning and execution of particular kinds of crime to minimize the risks of apprehension, to ease the disposal of stolen goods, and to promote the fixing of cases to forestall the probability of severe punishment if apprehended. Through association with experienced professionals, they learn the skills and gain the acceptance of their peers as a colleague among professional criminals. Through this acceptance, they gain a sense of personal worth according to the standards of professional criminals rather than the standards of the legitimate society upon whose members they prey. This acceptance also provides protection against the agencies of criminal justice by schooling the recruit in techniques of evasion such as use of negotiated pleas, tactics of lawyers, bribery, and returning loot to persuade victims to drop charges.[35]

The professional represents only a small portion of the prison population because of his skills in evading detection and, when apprehended, in

---

[33] Everett C. Hughes, "Institutional Office and the Person," *American Journal of Sociology,* Vol. 43 (November 1937), pp. 409–10.

[34] See Clinard and Quinney, *Criminal Behavior Systems,* pp. 319–31.

[35] Edwin H. Sutherland, *The Professional Thief* (Chicago: University of Chicago Press, 1937).

avoiding imprisonment. He is an unlikely prospect for correctional strategies because he regards crime as natural a form of livelihood as legitimate business or craftsmanship and because he regards imprisonment as an occupational risk.

Some professional criminals carry out their activities as members of *crime syndicates* which resemble legitimate business combinations in the scale of their interstate operations, employment of skilled personnel engaged in a complicated series of interrelated transactions, and large amount of capital. Crime syndicates specialize in providing illicit goods and services which result in high profits. Naked force and threats of violence are employed to maintain stability of operation and to gain control of legitimate businesses and labor unions.[36]

There is strong disagreement concerning the origin and intensity of organization of crime syndicates. In one view a tightly knit, hierarchially organized society has roots in the Mafia of Sicily. In testimony before the Senate Permanent Subcommittee on Investigations in 1963, Joseph Valachi, a minor member of organized crime, brought forth a different term, *La Cosa Nostra* (Our Thing), in describing an organization of "families" controlled by a national body of governors.[37] A differing opinion is that a looser form of cooperation exists among criminal groups which have gained ascendary in various areas, cooperating in common defense and meeting from time to time to discuss problems of mutual interest. Cooperation avoids costly wars and provides security for operations.[38]

The financial tribute exacted by organized crime is diverted from legitimate commerce and the meeting of needs of high social priority such as medical care, support of dependents, and education. "Shylocking" (loan-sharking) and illegal gambling rackets are great drains on the poor. Narcotics traffic profits from degradation and encourages crimes by addicts to support their habit. Coercion, extortion, and fear have enabled racketeers to invade laundry services, distribution of alcohol beverages, food wholesaling, the garment industries, and other legitimate businesses for profit and for fencing of stolen property. Although the wish to avoid great visibility of their operations tends toward minimization of violence, mayhem by strong-arm specialists takes its toll of the public tranquility. Finally, the corruption of public officials is inconsistent with viable democratic institutions.[39]

[36] For further discussion of organized crime, see Don C. Gibbons, *Society, Crime, and Criminal Careers* (Englewood Cliffs, N.J.: Prentice-Hall, 1968), pp. 129–50; Elmer H. Johnson, *Crime, Correction, and Society,* pp. 248–58; and Herbert A. Bloch and Gilbert Geis, *Man, Crime, and Society* (2d ed.; New York: Random House, 1970), pp. 190–217.

[37] *Organized Crime and Illicit Traffic in Narcotics, Part I* (U.S. Senate Permanent Subcommittees on Investigations, 88th Cong., 1st sess., September-October 1963 (Washington, D.C.: U.S. Government Printing Office, 1963).

[38] Robert K. Woetzel, "An Overview of Organized Crime: Mores versus Morality," *Annals of American Academy of Political and Social Science,* Vol. 347 (May 1963), p. 2.

[39] Earl Johnson, Jr., "Organized Crime: Challenge to the American Legal System, Part I," *Journal of Criminal Law, Criminology, and Police Science,* Vol. 53 (December 1962), pp. 399–425.

Quasi-professional criminals

The quasi-professional criminal differs from the professional criminal by his lower order of skill and dexterity. He has knowledge of criminal activities, has criminal associates, and organizes his life around crime, but he is not accepted as a full colleague by the professional criminals because of his comparative clumsiness in technique, his lack of self-discipline, his proneness to arrest and incarceration, and his inability to settle down to one type of crime. Because he is denied full acceptance by the masters of crime, he lacks opportunity for systematic learning associations with more proficient criminals.[40] Therefore, the quasi-professional criminal tends to be at the bottom of the scale of the career criminal and to be a part-time offender.

He tends to have a history of truancy and delinquent gang membership from which he progressed into more frequent and substantial adult criminality. Most of his offenses are against property. The low degree of his skills raises the risk of apprehension, and incarceration, and he spends a considerable part of his early adult years in penal institutions.[41]

SUMMARY

Criminals are not as distinct from noncriminals as the image of "dangerous enemies" of society would suggest. As with all human behavior, criminal behavior emerges from many causes which are related to other social problems. The wide differences among the major kinds of crime demonstrate that there is no such thing as "the typical criminal." Rather than violent dedicated criminals, police stations and courts are in fact clogged largely by drunks, disorderly persons, and other "immoral" offenders.

Convicted offenders are unique in that they have been defined as proper subjects for imposition of the political authority of the state through punishment of behaviors prohibited by the criminal law. The accused offender, if convicted and sentenced, thus becomes involved with the police, courts, and correctional agencies. The development of urban society has brought a greater need for formal controls, including the system of criminal justice. In that sense, the expansion of this system has reflected increased recognition of the breaches in the social order brought about by the forces shaping urban society. The increased work load and the changing conditions under which urban society functions have complicated the responsibilities of the agencies of criminal justice. As we shall

---

[40] See Julian Roebuck and Ronald Johnson, "The Jack-of-All-Trades Offender," *Crime and Delinquency,* Vol. 8 (April 1962), pp. 178–79.

[41] Don C. Gibbons, *Changing the Lawbreaker* (Englewood Cliffs, N.J.: Prentice-Hall, 1965), p. 105.

see in the next chapter, the deficiencies of their administration are an example of the contribution of the social structure itself to the problems which weaken its efficiency in meeting human needs. The official crime rates attest to the greater administrative burden of these agencies, but the claims of increased general proclivity for criminal behavior are of questionable validity.

The system of criminal justice relies heavily on punishment in its efforts to remedy breaches in order. However, because of the shortcomings of sole reliance on punishment, there is growing support for therapeutic methods and the reshaping of this system in that direction. Crime prevention draws widespread acclaim, but the term is used in so many senses that a coordinated program is unlikely.

FOR ADDITIONAL READING

Donald J. Black, "Production of Crime Rates," *American Sociological Review,* Vol. 35 (August 1970), pp. 733–48.

Stuart Bowes, *The Police and Civil Liberties* (London, Eng.: Lawrence & Wishart, 1966).

Tom Buckley, "The Mafia Tries a New Tune," *Harper's Magazine,* Vol. 243 (August 1971), pp. 46–47, 50–56.

Ramsey Clark, *Crime in America* (New York: Simon and Schuster, 1970).

Marshall Clinard, "Cross-Cultural Replication of the Relation of Urbanism to Criminal Behavior," *American Sociological Review,* Vol. 25 (April 1960), pp. 253–57.

Robert L. Derbyshire, "The Social Control Role of the Police in Changing Urban Communities, *Excerpta Criminologica,* Vol. 6 (May-June 1966), pp. 315–21.

Werner J. Einstadter, "The Social Organization of Armed Robbery," *Social Problems,* Vol. 17 (Summer 1969), pp. 64–83.

William M. Evan, *Law and Sociology* (New York: Free Press of Glencoe, 1962).

Theodore N. Ferdinand and Elmer G. Luchterhand, "Inner-City Youth, the Police, the Juvenile Court, and Justice," *Social Problems,* Vol. 17 (Spring 1970), pp. 510–27.

Morris Ginsberg, *On Justice in Society* (Baltimore, Md.: Penguin Books, 1965)

Leroy G. Gould, "The Changing Structure of Property Crime in an Affluent Society," *Social Forces,* Vol. 48 (September 1969), pp. 50–59.

Fred P. Graham, "Black Crime: The Lawless Image," *Harper's Magazine,* Vol. 241 (September 1970), pp. 510–27.

F. H. McClintock, *Crimes of Violence* (New York: St. Martins Press, 1963).

Robert M. MacIver, *The Prevention and Control of Delinquency* (New York: Atherton Press, 1967).

John M. Martin, "Three Approaches to Delinquency Prevention: A Critique," *Crime and Delinquency,* Vol. 7 (January 1961), pp. 16–24.

David W. Maurer, *The Big Con* (New York: Signet Books, 1962).

Edwin I. Megargee, "Assault with Intent to Kill," *Trans-action,* Vol. 2 (September-October 1965), pp. 27–31.

Hank Messick, *The Silent Syndicate* (New York: Macmillan Co., 1967).

Raymond I. Parnas, "The Police Response to the Domestic Disturbance," *Wisconsin Law Review,* Vol. 1967, No. 4 (Fall 1967), pp. 914–60.

Arnold S. Trebach, *The Rationing of Justice: Constitutional Rights and the Criminal Process* (New Brunswick, N.J.: Rutgers University Press, 1964).

Gus Tyler, *Organized Crime in America* (Ann Arbor, Mich.: University of Michigan Press, 1967).

Gordon P. Waldo, "The 'Criminality Level' of Incarcerated Murderers and Non-Murderers," *Journal of Criminal Law, Criminology, and Police Science,* Vol. 61 (March 1971) pp. 60–70.

Marvin Wolfgang, *Patterns in Criminal Homicide* (Philadelphia, Pa.: University of Pennsylvania Press, 1958).

Administration of 17 criminal justice

In the introduction to the last chapter, a former prisoner told how half of his life had been spent behind the walls of penal establishments. Accused of arson, he became subject successively to the attention of police, courts, and correctional agencies. In other words, he was processed by the system of criminal justice.

"SYSTEM" OF CRIMINAL JUSTICE

From one point of view, the manifold activities of our system of criminal justice operated in conjunction to determine whether the former prisoner was guilty of the criminal charges filed against him, to determine the degree of threat he posed to the community, and to determine what official response to his behavior would be most likely to end the threat. From the perspective of the convicted offender, he had become caught up in a processing which operated largely regardless of his wishes. Impersonal forces were shaping the events he experienced: "They" had made decisions which "shipped" him out of freedom and demanded that he "shape up." It is understandable, to say the least, that he would find this processing as neither welcome nor constructive to his immediate interests.

Whatever the perspective, a central theme is a regular, orderly way of doing something. The word *system* implies this theme. In this sense the former prisoner was moved through a sequence of procedures handled by various agents who administer the work of criminal justice: arrest, police booking, detention, preliminary court hearings, arraignment, trial, sentencing, imprisonment, granting of parole, and so on. Each procedure is supposed to be a step toward accomplishing something. Each derives its justification by fitting into the overall set of processes.

Conflicts and strains

On a higher level of abstraction, the agencies and their components are supposed to constitute the system of criminal justice in that their activities are coordinated in orderly and efficient fashion to achieve clearly formulated goals that all hold in common. The last chapter demonstrated that the criminal law relies heavily on punishment of the law violator, the ultimate purpose being to create the general observance of the law, essential to an orderly and satisfying society. This use of the criminal law constitutes a resort to formal and official action when there is a breakdown of the controls that depend on a basic consensus of norms and values.

This chapter centers its attention on the workings of the "system" of criminal justice which has assumed increased responsibility for maintaining order in urban society. We will find illusionary any idea of one, single, highly coordinated and efficient system moving confidently and vigorously toward clearly delineated, common goals. There are conflicts and strains between the police, courts, and correctional agencies as each of these generalized administrative components of criminal justice pursue its specialized purposes. Each component processes the law violator without full awareness of what the personnel of other components actually are doing. For example, prison officials frequently comment on the small proportion of judges who have visited the correctional institutions to which they commit convicted offenders. Members of one component frequently hold reservations about the support they receive from personnel of another component. For example, policemen have complained about "lenient" judges and parole boards who "turn loose the criminals we catch after much hard work." Even within a component, there are major disagreements. Tensions exist between treatment and custody staffs of prisons, between prison and parole personnel, between "hard-line" and "community-oriented" police officers, and between "hanging" and "treatment-oriented" judges.

The agencies have inherited the difficulties of maintaining public peace and order through the complex techniques of formal control in an urban society. The increased heterogeneity and size of urban populations have complicated the tasks of these agencies at the same time that the complexity of relationships in large-scale organizations has raised the level of demand for order. Because of increased resort to formal control techniques, the system of criminal justice has a larger burden of cases. Concurrently, the system has been called on to expand its range of services without enjoying the benefit of universal agreement on its proper goals.

Functionaries untainted by incompetence and corruption find their efficiency sharply restricted by conditions beyond their control.

Sources and meaning of inefficiency

No matter how efficient an agency may be, its personnel will encounter dissatisfaction with their work. The law and its implementation will lag behind public expectations of how it should be employed. There will be disagreements among various interest groups about the objectives and functions of criminal law. Finally, people are particularly impatient when the force of the law is directed toward them.

Our own traditions place inconsistent expectations on our Anglo-American legal system.[1] The roots of our common law are derived from an individualism not consistent with conditions in an age of large-scale organizations. The irony of white-collar crime is that petty offenders are prosecuted while the social crimes of great organizations receive little attention. The traditional emphasis on crimes against persons continues to color the criminal law to lend persistence to this paradox. Individualism is also expressed in our reliance on the adversary system whereby trials become a kind of combat between the prosecution and defense. Nevertheless, we tend to see the passing of a law as the shortcut to social reform without assuming the soul-searching ordeals of changing our own behavior and the social structure itself.

The consequence is the placing of heavier work loads on the administrative apparatus of criminal justice agencies. Criminal law is pressed into the enforcement of morals to burden personnel of law enforcement, courts, and correctional agencies with handling persons accused of excessive drinking, drug abuse, sexual misconduct, and so on. The jails and prisons are clogged with persons there to be punished as "criminals" because they have exhibited forms of behavior which have been defined as personal disorganization of such magnitude as to constitute a social problem.[2]

Inefficiency of administration is also attributable to defects in the organization of the administrative apparatus. Law enforcement has been found to have serious management deficiencies: a lack of standards of education and achievement for administrators and middle managers, insufficient provision for training, diffusion of authority and responsibility, erratic leadership, improper grouping of functions, resistance to needed changes, and ineffective deployment and utilization of available personnel and material resources.[3] The organization of courts has been described as archaic and

---

[1] Roscoe Pound, "The Causes of Popular Dissatisfaction with the Administration of Criminal Justice," *Crime and Delinquency,* Vol. 10 (October 1964), pp. 355–71.

[2] See Chapter 9, pp. 245–48, and Chapter 16, pp. 410–12, for criticism of the resort to criminal law for this purpose.

[3] President's Commission on Law Enforcement, *Task Force Report: The Police* (Washington, D.C.: U.S. Government Printing Office, 1967), pp. 44–65.

wasteful. A multiplicity of courts preserves concurrent jurisdictions, clogging one court's calendar while another is largely free of cases, and there is excessive debate over technicalities.[4] Correctional agencies are burdened with too many obsolete facilities designed for punitive policies. Prisons isolate inmates from the outside world to which they are expected to adjust in keeping with the rehabilitative purposes. Staffing and organizational ideologies are heavily oriented to safekeeping as opposed to achieving programmatic conditions favorable to instilling new attitudes or new capacities for constructive integration of inmates into community life after release.

However, any demand for greater efficiency in the administration of criminal justice should be balanced against the prospect of cold, inhuman, and unlovable efficiency through universal application of abstract legal rules. Beyond the consequences of internal contradictions in the "system," Seagle points to the "painstaking deliberation" with which a democracy designs inefficiency into such administration to safeguard the rights of the individual.[5] In illustrating this designed inefficiency, Packer describes two competing models in the operation of criminal justice: crime control versus due process.[6]

Emphasizing repression of criminal behavior, the *crime-control model* is dedicated to efficiency of law enforcement as a safeguard for public order. Success requires a high rate of apprehension and conviction. Since the police and court establishments have resources insufficient for the volume of apprehended offenders, speedy processing is sought through reliance on informal and standardized procedures. A presumption of guilt enables the overall system to operate much like an assembly-line conveyer belt, with the cases processed at each of a series of stations. These stations represent prearrest investigation, arrest, postarrest investigation, preparation for trial, trial or entry of plea, conviction or acquittal, and disposition of the convicted offender. With the presumption of guilt stronger as the defendant moves farther along the sequence of stations, routine procedures are used for efficient handling.

The *due-process model* presumes innocence until proof of guilt. If the crime-control model resembles an assembly line, this model looks like a kind of obstacle course with impediments set up against the further progress of the defendant through criminal-justice processing. The reliability of fact finding is challenged recurrently against errors of witnesses, coerced confessions, and other possible distortions. Guilt is determined in procedurally regular fashion according to legal rules which must be satisfied

---

[4] Pound, "Causes of Dissatisfaction with Administration of Criminal Justice."

[5] William Seagle, *Law: The Science of Inefficiency* (New York: Macmillan Co., 1952), pp. 1–5.

[6] Herbert L. Packer, *The Limits of the Criminal Sanction* (Stanford, Calif.: Stanford University Press, 1968), pp. 154–73.

apart from the question of whether the defendant actually behaved as the charge alleges.

COURTS AND CRIMINAL JUSTICE

The outcome of criminal justice depends in large measure on the appropriateness of two interdependent processes of decision-making handled respectively by the police and the courts. The disposition of cases without trial represents a large share of these decisions, thereby meriting greater attention than it usually receives. Because the police are involved in this kind of disposition, the relationships between the police and the courts will receive attention here.

The policeman as gatekeeper

The policeman initiates the process of criminal justice through apprehension and arrest. The discretion in arrest decisions of this gatekeeper has a crucial effect on the efficiency of the overall system of criminal justice.

Because it is part of an overall system, the police agency operates in an environment of uncertainty about the outcome of its work. Although it is part of the executive branch, the agency is subject to a division of authority in which the eventual outcome of its arrest decisions is determined by the procedures of another branch of government, the judiciary. The work of the policeman would be simplified if he were free to collect evidence, apprehend suspects, and obtain confessions according to the necessities of efficient law enforcement *only*. However, this degree of control by the executive branch raises the specter of a police state and political corruption. Furthermore, the judiciary has a keen interest in the law enforcement procedures of acquisition of evidence, interrogation, arrest, and detention. These procedures must conform to the rules of legality if the court is to do its part as a bulwark for civil rights.

The courts breed their own discrepancies between the ideal and their practices. Population growth and increased reliance on legal controls have imposed greater work loads on the courts and aggravated perennial problems of delay, disparities in sentences, and differential justice according to the social class status of defendants.

Disposition without trial

Most criminal cases are disposed of without the trial our legal institutions assume will determine the outcome. Somewhere between a third and a half of cases initiated by arrest are dismissed by police, prosecutor, or judge. Of the cases prosecuted, as many as 90 percent of all convictions circumvent trial through a plea of guilty by the accused. Charge reduction to elicit pleas of guilty is a major device. This heavy reliance on nontrial dispositions raises doubts about the fairness of informal and subterranean procedures, fears that decisions are not preceded by collection of essential information, concerns over safeguards for the constitutional rights of defendants, and suspicions that the guilty are permitted to escape proper punishment.[7]

From prosecutors through courts to correctional agencies, the system of criminal justice depends on dispositions without trial to reduce the work load through more rapid processing of cases and diversion of convicted offenders from correctional facilities. Without this form of disposition, the agencies of criminal justice, already heavily burdened, would be overwhelmed. This rather expedient argument is given further support by evidence offered in Newman's report on the study of the American Bar Foundation that dispositions without trial enable judges to serve worthy purposes. When the original charge calls for an excessively stern sentence, reduction of charges on guilty pleas may individualize justice in light of the circumstances of the offense, special characteristics of the defendant, the normality of his conduct within the defendant's subculture, or the excessive impact of conviction on the defendant's future status. Furthermore, reduction of the charge enables the judge to control law enforcement abuses or counter adverse consequences of overly stern statutes.[8]

Through a guilty plea, the defendant may strike a bargain with the prosecution whereby he draws a lighter penalty through reduction of the original charge. By pleading guilty he avoids the publicity of a trial and the greater social visibility of his transgression as a blow to his reputation. When the victim of the crime is reluctant to testify, or the available evidence may not convince a jury, the prosecution may accept a guilty plea to gain assurance that some punishment will ensue. Finally, the bargain may induce the defendant to provide information essential to the solution of other crimes.

Effectiveness of juries

The selection of juries has been criticized on grounds that many qualified persons are exempt and that certain social, ethnic, and racial groups are overrepresented. Professional people, for example, are likely to be excused, even though the decision-making responsibility calls for competent jurors. Probably the chief doubt, however, is about the lack of qualification of the average juror.

Reporting on research on jury deliberations, James says there was little difference among jurors of varying educational attainment in terms of pertinence of opinion, accuracy in recall of testimony, ability to influence

[7] President's Commission on Law Enforcement and Administration of Justice, *Task Force Report: The Courts* (Washington, D.C.: U.S. Government Printing Office, 1967), p. 4.
[8] Donald J. Newman, *Conviction: The Determination of Guilt or Innocence without Trial* (Boston: Little, Brown and Company, 1966).

other jurors, or to be persuaded by them. However, the grade-school juror's interpretation of the judge's instructions were less accurate, and the college-educated group had more concern for facilitation discussion.[9] Although diverse strangers are thrust together to arrive at an important decision under unprecedented circumstances, the jurors develop a sense of collective responsibility to the public. One study found that in the jury room the evidence was fitted together, the disturbing details of an incest case examined without undue emotion, and the judge's instructions followed.[10]

Disparities among sentences

Sentencing policies have been shaped by two—frequently conflicting —objectives. The principle of equality before the law has been cited in defense of *identical disposition* of all persons convicted of the same offense. Under this principle, regardless of aggravating or mitigating factors, the convicted offender would draw the sentence predetermined as the proper measure of punishment for counterbalancing the effect of this kind of offense on the community's tranquility and for deterring repetition of the offense.

Because of the rigidity and possible harshness of completely uniform sentencing, the objectives of *individualized sentencing* are to base punishment on the personality of the convicted criminal and the specific circumstances of the offense. Ideally, the judge's decision takes into account the personal qualities, background, motivations, and rehabilitative potentiality of *this* offender as compared with other offenders. To achieve individualized sentencing, the judge is permitted a broad range of discretion. The potential weakness of this approach, of course, lies in the subjective basis of decisions and the differences in philosophies among judges.

Comparisons of median sentences for similar offenses show wide differences among federal district courts and time served by inmates released from various state prisons.[11] Furthermore, studies summarized by D'Esposito reveal extreme disparities from judge to judge in weighting common characteristics of crime or offender according to the judges' penal philosophies, judical personalities, social backgrounds, and temperaments. Sentence severity is affected by prior felony convictions and the offense charged, but there was little difference in terms of age, marital status, or

[9] Rita M. James, "Status and Competence of Jurors," *American Journal of Sociology,* Vol. 64 (May 1959), pp. 565–66.
[10] Rita James Simon, "Trial by Jury: A Critical Assessment," in Alvin W. Gouldner and S. M. Miller (eds.), *Applied Sociology: Opportunities and Problems* (New York: Free Press, 1965), pp. 294–307.
[11] *Federal Offenders in the United States District Courts, 1968* (Washington, D.C.: Administrative office of U.s. Courts, 1969); *National Prisoner Statistics—State Prisoners: Admissions and Releases, 1964* (Washington, D.C.: Federal Bureau of Prisons, undated).

educational level of offender. In addition to abuse of judicial discretion, the disparities can be attributed to failure of statutes to provide proper guidelines, the inadequate provision for appellate review of sentences, the inconsistent classification of crimes according to a logical evaluation of harm to society, and the differential impact of plea bargaining.[12]

Disparities among sentences obstruct the achievement of the ultimate objectives of criminal justice. Confidence in this system is shaken by violations of the idea of equal treatment under the law. Criminal corrections has an additional burden in its assigned goal of returning the released prisoner to the free world ready for good citizenship when excessively severe or grossly disparate sentences press parole boards to reduce sentences through commutation or to interpret parole policies according to reputation of judges for sentencing severity. Prison inmates tend to be embittered when they find others have received much milder sentences for offenses they regard as identical; already alienated by their compulsory isolation from the outside world, prisoners see additional justification for resistance against their keepers and opposition to the prison programs presumably designed to reorient their attitudes and behavior.

One major form of remedy would be to provide standards for exercise of judicial discretion. Various proposals for *model penal codes* would place primary focus on the offender rather than the nature of the crime. The wide range of crimes would be coped with by establishing three categories of felonies with penalties graduated to recognize severity of offense. Sentences for ordinary offenses would be reduced, and more careful statutory delineation of the qualities of dangerous offenses would restrict the possibility that judicial discretion would result in excessive sentences against the ordinary offenses. Another reform strategy is *appellate review* of sentences, in which a higher authority would require justification for each sentence according to an overall national scheme, would be able to bring the various sentencing decisions into a logical order, and would provide a forum for establishment of standards.

Since discretion in sentencing rests ultimately on the competence of the judge, a major dimension of reform is improvement of the training of judges through law schools and subsequent training sessions. The selection of judges also must be supportive of the raising of the standards of those men presently on the bench. In his nationwide survey of courts, James developed a typology of incompetent judges. Hacks are men without competence as judges who are appointed to the bench as a reward for faithful service to the political party. The retirees use the judgeship as semiretirement from practice of law; some of them keep unduly short working days for sake of their own leisure. Unable to earn a living in private practice, some failures as lawyers become judges. Inadequacies in per-

---

[12] Julian C. D'Esposito, Jr., "Sentencing Disparity: Cases and Cures," *Journal of Criminal Law, Criminology and Police Science,* Vol. 60 (June 1969), pp. 183–86.

formance included insufficient attention to the proceedings, lack of decorum, inadequate knowledge of law, failure to keep current with changes in laws, indecisiveness when making decisions likely to draw criticism, expression of various kinds of prejudice, and personality quirks inconsistent with the proper judicial temperament.[13]

COURTS AND INDIGENT DEFENDANT

The rules of due process are intended to give the defendant his day in court when he is supposed to have a full-fledged chance to refute the case of the prosecution. Under the adversary system the prosecution and defense confront each other to expend maximum energy in discovering and presenting the merits of its case and the weaknesses of the adversary's arguments. The sum consequence is supposed to be the uncovering of the truth. However, the defendant must have legal counsel if these rules of due process aere to be employed intelligently on his behalf.

Vulnerability is particularly great for the defendant without financial means of engaging legal counsel. Two courses of action are available to remedy this situation. Under the *assigned counsel* arrangement, if the accused offender appears in court without a lawyer or financial means to hire one, the judge appoints a lawyer for him, usually paid from county or state funds. In the *defender system,* salaried lawyers devote all or a substantial part of their time to representing indigent defendants.

Advocates of the assigned counsel arrangement believe it preserves the traditional role of the lawyer in close support of his client, whereas the defender as a public employee with many cases cannot provide individual attention. Assuming competent assigned counsel, the system is supposed to mobilize a wide participation among lawyers in the administration of criminal justice and to provide learning opportunities for young lawyers —although at the possible disadvantage to their clients. The costs to the taxpayer are greater for the defender system.

Advocates of the defender system claim assigned counsel are more likely to advise their clients to plead guilty, although—on the other hand —novice lawyers might very well place an undue pressure for nonguilty pleas so they could gain trial experience. The assigned counsel system has been criticized for not providing sufficient funds for proper investigation and preparation of a defense. The selection of assigned counsel has been evaluated as coming too late in the criminal proceedings and too prone to excusing experienced attorneys. The defender system is supposed to provide more competent counsel on a consistent basis and to sustain a more persistent relationship with the prosecution.[14]

[13] Howard James, *Crisis in the Courts* (New York: David McKay Co., 1968), pp. 6–10.
[14] Lee Silverstein, *Defense of the Poor in Criminal Cases in American State Courts* (Vol. 1; National Report) (New York: American Bar Foundation, 1965), pp. 18–33, 45–49.

Bail as a source of inequality

After arrest for a felony, the accused must be arraigned in trial court, where the charge is read to him and he is required to enter his plea. If he pleads not guilty, a trial date is set. Bail refers to the release of a person from custody under financial security to assure his appearance for trial. The fundamental assumption is that he is innocent of the charge until proven guilty. However, the court has discretionary power to decide the probability of the accused person's appearance for trial. The probability depends on the seriousness of the charge, the character of the accused, and the weight of the evidence against him. If not released pending trial, the defendant is detained in jail.

Although presumed innocent, the detained defendant is subjected to the conditions of the local jail and probably his dependents lose the support of a breadwinner. When the accused lacks financial resources for bail, he loses the freedom available to more fortunate defendants. This differential impact on the poor is aggravated by the greater probability of later conviction. Foote reports that for similar crimes, jailed offenders are more likely to be convicted and to receive longer sentences than those released on bail.[15] Beeley finds the amount of bail in a given case is determined arbitrarily, regardless of the personality, social history, and financial means of the accused. Often the bail is excessive. On the other hand, unreliable professional bailsmen are accepted and their bonds not forfeited when the defendant does not appear. Thus, the professional bondsman has undue influence in lower courts, exploiting unsophisticated clients and working in collusion with the police and court officials.[16]

For bail reform, the President's Crime Commission recommends more effective means be established for determining the defendant's reputation and ties within the community which would indicate low risk.[17] The Vera Foundation, a charitable institution, established the Manhattan Bail Project, an experiment in which New York University law students interviewed detained prisoners concerning their regularity of employment, family responsibility, residential stability, favorable references, and previous criminal record. Verifying the information through investigation, the project workers offered recommendations to the court. Of the first 2,300 defendants released without bail on such recommendation, 99 percent returned to the court as required.[18] The President's Crime Commission further recommends increased forfeiture of money bail, greater penalties

---

[15] Caleb Foote, "The Bail System and Equal Justice," *Federal Probation,* Vol. 23 (September 1959), pp. 45–47.

[16] Arthur L. Beeley, *The Bail System in Chicago* (Chicago: University of Chicago Press, 1927, second impression 1966), pp. 155–56.

[17] President's Commission on Law Enforcement, *Task Force Report: The Courts,* pp. 38–39.

[18] *Toward Justice for the Poor: The Manhattan Bail Project* (New York: Vera Foundation, 1964).

against absconders, and shortening of the average length of pretrial detention.

JUVENILE COURTS

The issues involving the juvenile court center around the conflict between what Dunham calls the social-agency and legal images.[19] In the *social-agency image* the juvenile court is supposed to understand the child, to diagnose his difficulty, to treat his condition, and to restore him to the community under circumstances likely to direct him toward responsible adult behavior. These objectives reflect an attempt to bring the behavioral sciences into play to fit justice to the overcoming of the emotional and social maladjustments behind the problems of the child in terms of his particular qualities and situation.

The courts also reflect the ideas of humanitarian reformers of the late 19th century that the corrosion of urban life must be countered through social work to strengthen the middle-class institutions of the family, school, and church, which were regarded as essentially sound.[20] Crimes of adolescents were regarded as temporary and reversible if they could be subjected to a rational social discipline at a tender age before the adverse affects of urban life become fixed. Under the concept of *parens patriae,* the court was given wide discretion to intervene in the lives of children in the spirit of benevolent parents dealing with dependent children. The juvenile delinquent was to avoid the stigma of a criminal record and, through informal and private hearings, be spared the travail of proceedings applied to adult defendants.

In the *legal image* the juvenile court is a part of the overall court system. The *social-agency image* places it in conflict with the other types of courts employing traditional legal procedures under the due-process model. The informality of juvenile court proceedings has drawn sharp attacks for violating the basic legal rights of the child and his parents. In 1967 the Supreme Court ruled in the *Gault* case to extend civil rights to youths before juvenile courts in terms of affording timely notice of charges, right to counsel, privilege against self-incrimination, and rights of confrontation and cross-examination of accusers.[21]

A perennial issue is the type of cases the juvenile court should handle. In most communities with social resources to care for the increasing num-

[19] H. Warren Dunham, "The Juvenile Court: Contradictory Orientations in Processing Offenders," *Law and Contemporary Problems,* Vol. 23 (Summer 1958), pp. 508–27.

[20] Anthony M. Platt, *The Child Savers: The Invention of Delinquency* (Chicago: University of Chicago Press, 1969).

[21] President's Commission on Law Enforcement and Administration of Justice, *Task Force Report: Juvenile Delinquency and Youth Crime* (Washington, D.C.: U.S. Government Printing Office, 1967), Appendix A.

ber of children requiring protection and care, the juvenile court has tended to assume responsibility for a growing volume of cases. This tendency was promoted by passage of laws requiring that certain types of children be cared for at public expense. The expansion of its activities has brought the juvenile court into matters also handled by educational and/or public welfare agencies: truancy, child neglect, acting-out behavior as evidence of psychological difficulties, and so on. Efforts by juvenile courts to apply therapeutic, rather than punitive, methods have brought demands that the older juveniles perpetrating the more serious crimes be tried in criminal courts.[22] Finally, the jurisdiction of the juvenile court has been criticized as encompassing too broad a spectrum of offenses and thus reflecting a moral imperialism. The President's Crime Commission recommends eliminating court action against smoking, swearing, disobedience, truancy, and so on.[23]

Although the social-agency objectives are worthy, the juvenile court lacks the range and quality of social service resources necessary to achieve them. Allen warns against raising unrealistic and unrealizable expectations in terms of public disillusionment, apathy, and even hostitity.[24] To fulfill its promise, the juvenile court must overcome the low quality of many of its judges and the inadequacy of many of its hearings.[25] Lurking in the background is the failure of most juvenile correctional institutions to erase the corrosive effects of imprisonment and to provide genuine therapeutic experience. Too often these institutions provide custodial keeping with little opportunity for properly designed educational and psychological intervention relevant to the needs and behavior of their young inmates.[26]

CONFLICTS IN POLICE WORK

Law enforcement carries stresses for the policeman because the assignment of social service tasks to urban police has aggravated the difficulties of accommodating the suppression of crime within a society based on democratic values. Although much of his training and his job expectations center around enforcement of criminal law, much of an officer's time is

[22] Robert G. Caldwell, "The Juvenile Court: Its Development and Some Major Problems," *Journal of Criminal Law, Criminology and Police Science,* Vol. 51 (January–February 1961), pp. 502–504.

[23] President's Commission on Law, Enforcement and Administration of Justice, *Task Force Report: The Courts,* p. 85.

[24] Francis A. Allen, *The Borderline of Criminal Justice* (Chicago: University of Chicago Press, 1964), p. 56.

[25] See: Shirley D. McCune and Daniel L. Skolar, "Juvenile Court Judges in the United States—Part II: A National Profile," *Crime and Delinquency,* Vol. II (April 1965), pp. 121–31.

[26] See: Edward Rolde, John Mack, Donald Scherl and Lee Macht, "The Maximum Security Institution as a Treatment Facility for Juveniles," in James E. Teele (ed.), *Juvenile Delinquency: A Reader* (Itasca, Ill.: F. E. Peacock, 1970) pp. 437–44.

consumed in peacekeeping where he lacks sufficient guidance beyond his own "common sense."

Service and control functions

The primary function of the policeman emphasizes the *guardian of society* role, wherein the state's authority is used legitimately to protect citizens against active criminals. This role assigns him control functions exemplified by the military officer or prison warden. Concurrently, the policeman is cast in the role of *social service humanitarian* when he performs duties such as finding lost children, recovering drowned bodies, referring individuals for emergency services, mediating family disputes, providing ambulance service, and so on.[27] The preponderance of such services is illustrated by a study showing only 16 percent of all telephone calls received by Detroit police in 1968 were related to predatory crime.[28]

The involvement of police in such services is attributable in large measure to the failure of other community agencies to provide around-the-clock service for an entire city.[29] The social service agencies tend to favor building-centered programs wherein clients are expected to present themselves voluntarily and ready to conform to agency-defined expectations. Since police are organized to work on the streets, they are more likely to contact the "hard-to-reach" potential client for social services. The flight of "respectable" people to the suburbs and the comparative failure of social agencies to serve the "hard-to-reach" cases has drawn the police into an institutional vacuum and they are the major representative of middle-class values among a population of underprivileged people.

The control orientation of police work and the lack of police resources for supportive social-welfare services undermine their effectiveness in dealing with problems of individuals in the ghetto. Patrolmen keep the ghetto peace through an aggressively personalized approach to residents in which coercion is employed to keep order within a world characterized by frustration, mistrust, and fortuitousness of daily events. The power of arrest is invoked to reduce the aggregate total of troubles rather than to decide individual cases strictly on legal merit. Guilt in a particular minor offense is less important than the risk of future disturbance of the peace.[30]

The effectiveness of the police agency is determined largely by the skill and discretion employed by personnel occupying the lowest level of positions in the organizational structure. In direct contact with clients, the man

---

[27] Elmer H. Johnson, "Police: An Analysis of Role Conflict," *Police,* Vol. 14 (January-February 1970), pp. 47–52.

[28] Thomas E. Bercal, "Calls for Police Assistance," *American Behavioral Scientist,* Vol. 13 (July-August 1970), p. 682.

[29] Elaine Cumming, Ian Cumming, and Laura Edell, "Policeman as Philosopher, Guide and Friend," *Social Problems,* Vol. 12 (Winter 1965), pp. 276–86.

[30] Egon Bittner, "The Police on Skid Row: A Study of Peace-Keeping," *American Sociological Review,* Vol. 32 (October 1967), pp. 699–715.

on the beat has major influence on whether the ultimate outcome of police activities will coincide with the avowed purposes of the agency. Under the crime prevention conception of police work, the initial contacts with delinquents and potential delinquents offer opportunities to divert them from serious future crimes. The handling of a moment of trauma for both officer and suspect calls for discretion, tact, and intelligent assessment of the situation.

Balancing efficiency and civil rights

The democratic emphasis on civil rights places the policeman in an awkward position when he is pressed strongly to suppress crime at all costs. The outcome of his work is monitored by the courts according to the due-process model. He is expected to maintain *order* in the dynamic environment of the streets and also to enforce the *law* as gatekeeper for the courts. Nevertheless, the identification of police with capacity to control disorder and unrest makes him a favorite target for criticism when he does not meet expectations for "law and order." Conversely, he draws hostility of the underprivileged who experience him more directly than the social forces creating unemployment and other frustrations. In summarizing the role of the patrolman, James Q. Wilson puts the idea thusly: "Sub-professionals, working alone, exercise wide discretion in matters of utmost importance in an environment that is apprehensive and perhaps hostile."[31]

Restrictions on arrest privileges, some police executives argue, hamper the police in preventing crime and in clearing cases through marshaling of evidence and apprehension of the perpetrator. Because most arrests are made at a critical moment not of police choosing, O. W. Wilson says police should be authorized to question persons whose actions arouse reasonable suspicion that the suspect may be seeking an opportunity to commit a crime. On reasonable grounds, the officer should be privileged to search a man he suspects possesses a dangerous weapon. O. W. Wilson believes that police should be authorized to hold an arrested person before bringing him before a magistrate for at least 24 hours, excluding days when courts are not in session. Arguing that freeing guilty defendants because of police overzealousness only punishes society and rewards the guilty, he prefers criminal prosecution and disciplinary actions as safeguards of police abuse of authority.[32] Presumably, their own discipline and the limits of public tolerance would reduce the social danger of police excesses, but Paulsen defends the exclusion of illegally acquired evidence as the most

[31] James Q. Wilson, *Varieties of Police Behavior: The Management of Law and Order in Eight Communities* (Cambridge, Mass.: Harvard University Press, 1968), pp. 30–31.

[32] O. W. Wilson, "Police Arrest Privileges in a Free Society: A Plea for Modernization," in Claude R. Sowle (ed.) *Police Power and Individual Freedom* (Chicago: Aldine Publishing Co., 1962), pp. 24–51.

practical way to maintain constitutional safeguards against police invasion of civil rights.[33]

Use of violence and coercion to extract a confession is known as the "third degree." Inbau agrees such tactics should be forbidden, but he objects to prohibition of psychological trickery and deceit in interrogation to obtain incriminating information from the guilty. He argues that in many cases even the most clever officers are unable to obtain physical clues. Inbau believes that provision of legal counsel immediately upon arrest would destroy the privacy the officers require if their psychological tactics are to be effective.[34] Weisberg retorts that the secrecy of interrogation creates the risk of abuses and undermines public confidence in law enforcement.[35]

Limited enforcement of the law

Full enforcement of the law is a practical impossibility and generally undesirable. Resources available to the agency are insufficient. Literal interpretation of the penal code would require the arrest of a broader spectrum of violators than the framers of the laws intended. As a safeguard against law enforcement beyond the level acceptable within community mores, the laws should not be applied mechanically to the wide variety of situations which they cover technically. The ambiguity in laws—put there by legislators to provide flexibility in enforcement—requires police discretion if the technical violator is not to receive the same punishment as the deliberate lawbreaker. Withholding of charges, furthermore, is useful to induce minor offenders to provide evidence against more serious criminals.[36]

Law enforcement is ideally intended to create a state of universal law observance, because full law enforcement and sole reliance on coercion are not feasible or desirable in a democracy. Law enforcement operates within a social sphere requiring coordination of police actions with the working of other social institutions in the community.[37] Therefore, attitudes of private citizens are a prime ingredient in law enforcement. An arrest ideally has an educational effect toward promoting future law observance. Full obedience to the law can be achieved only to the extent that community mores support the legal norms. The policeman faces

---

[33] Monrad G. Paulsen, "The Exclusionary Rule and Misconduct by the Police," in Sowle, *Police Power and Individual Freedom,* p. 97.

[34] Fred E. Inbau, "Police Interrogation: A Practical Necessity," in Sowle, *Police Power and Individual Freedom,* pp. 147–52.

[35] Bernard Weisberg, "Police Interrogation of Arrested Persons: A Skeptical View," in Sowle, *Police Power and Individual Freedom,* pp. 179–80.

[36] Herman Goldstein, "Police Discretion: The Ideal versus The Real," *Public Administration Review,* Vol. 23 (September 1963), pp. 140–48.

[37] Elmer H. Johnson, "Interrelatedness of Law Enforcement Programs: A Fundamental Dimension," *Journal of Criminal Law,* Criminology and Police Science. Vol. 60 (December 1969), pp. 509–16.

serious obstacles when called on to enforce a law which does not enjoy the benefits of moral and habitual compliance. As citizens themselves, policemen reflect attitudes prevalent in their community. When police brutality and corruption exist, they probably stem from the recurrent experiences of dealing with violent and corrupt persons, or from the patterns found in the police agency as a whole. Brutality and corruption cannot persist in volume, however, unless support is provided by major segments of the community.

Discretion versus bureaucratic discipline

Although effective law enforcement depends on the intelligent decision making of the officer on the spot, the bureaucratic and paramilitaristic organization of the urban department works against flexibility in his decision making. Skolnick sees the basic dilemma of law enforcement in a democracy in the conflict between the need for exercise of judgment by patrolmen and the pressure of bureaucracies on subordinates that they obey the rules to maintain organizational unity.[38]

The policeman is pressed by the public to produce tangible results in suppressing those criminals who pose either genuine or supposed danger to the community. However, this public pressure for tangible results is not matched by willingness of the public to participate in a "war on crime."[39] The officer is encouraged to believe he stands alone in this "war," a conception which heightens the image of danger in his work. The identification of police work with "war" provides support for a rationale pressing the officer to conform to the arbitrary rules of the police bureaucracy dedicated to the "efficiency" of the crime-control model. If he departs from rules imposed from authorities above him in this bureaucracy, the "foot soldier" jeopardizes the police organization's protection of him against danger. Furthermore, he risks administrative penalties if his departure is revealed by some incident in his daily work.

In either sense, the "foot soldier" is discouraged from employing his own discretion in keeping with the unique qualities of the specific incident. The due-process model is interpreted as inconsistent with the orderly functioning of the police organization as an end in itself, regardless of the consequences for the overall system of criminal justice.

Isolation from the public

Public ambivalence toward the police officer's work encourages him to see himself as a member of a vocational minority subjected to stereotyping.[40] Since police work is popularly supposed to be directed against

---

[38] Jerome H. Skolnick, *Justice Without Trial* (New York: John Wiley and Sons, 1966), p. 232.

[39] See introduction to Chapter 3 for examples of this issue.

[40] David H. Bayley and Harold Mendelsohn, *Minorities and the Police* (New York: Free Press, 1969), pp. 54–55.

criminals, the duties of traffic control and other noncriminal regulation are perceived as exposing the "good citizen" to stigmatization. Fear, mistrust, and disdain of dictatorships have influenced public suspicion of police in democracies. Carried to an extreme, police isolation can produce a mental set characterized by political conservatism, authoritarian attitudes, and suspicion of intellectuals.[41]

Tendencies toward isolation can be balanced in varying degrees by the general public acceptance of the need for law enforcement. Clark points out that outcries against the police demand reform not abolition. Fearing the negative consequences of total isolation of the police from the community's wishes, the public frequently makes overtures of support. Business and other groups especially dependent on police services are particularly likely to be accommodative. On the other hand, the police require a working relationship with the public, even criminals, to obtain information.[42] Law enforcement must operate in conjunction with the culture and living patterns of the community if it is to achieve law observance.

POLICE AND AGGRAVATION OF DEVIANCE

The labeling approach to deviant behavior emphasized societal reaction to the deviant. An implied issue is whether the reaction of police to juvenile misconduct can contribute to criminality through stigmatization of the technically guilty but noncriminalistic offender.

The labeling of youths as deviants, Black and Reiss find, operates in a more complex manner than suggested by the conception of the police as autonomous parties indiscriminately using their authority.[43] Their study of routine patrol work in three large cities determined that citizens directly initiate most police encounters with juveniles.

First, and overwhelmingly, the officers react to situations within which the moral standards of citizens dominate the definition of certain conduct as requiring police action. The probability that the juvenile will be taken to the police station is determined to a major extent by the complainant who provides information and whose willingness to sign a formal complaint is crucial to arrest. Black juveniles are more likely to be arrested than white juveniles when there is a complainant involved. This greater probability of a more severe decision for black juveniles existed in spite

---

[41] See: A. C. Germann, "Community Policing: An Assessment," *Journal of Criminal Law, Criminology and Police Science,* Vol. 60 (March 1969), pp. 92–93; also see Seymour M. Lipset, "Why Cops Hate Liberals and Vice Versa," *Atlantic,* Vol. 223 (March 1969), pp. 76–83.

[42] John P. Clark, "Isolation of the Police: A Comparison of the British and American Situations," *Journal of Criminal Law, Criminology and Police Science,* Vol. 56 (September 1965), pp. 309–10.

[43] Donald J. Black and Albert J. Reiss, Jr., "Police Control of Juveniles," *American Sociological Review,* Vol. 35 (February 1970), pp. 63–77.

of the fact that most complainants were black. The majority of the officers were white, but they were somewhat more lenient when they encountered the black juveniles alone, without involvement of a black complainant.

Second, the great bulk of police encounters pertain to matters of minor legal significance. Third, although probability of arrest increases with greater legal seriousness of the alleged offense, the probability of arrest is very low for juveniles.

In their study of police contacts with juvenile offenders, Piliavin and Briar find officers had limited information on the boys at the time they had to decide on initial disposition. For nearly all minor violators, and for some serious delinquents, the decision was based on the youths' personal characteristics and not on their offenses. The evaluation of their characteristics was related to cues which emerged from the interaction between the officer and the youth. The decision to take action was most likely for older juveniles, members of known delinquent gangs, blacks, youths with well-oiled hair and black jackets, and those who did not manifest appropriate signs of respect toward the officer.[44]

POLICE MANPOWER DEFICIENCIES

The high priority of intelligent discretion by the gatekeepers for the system of criminal justice demands qualified policemen. The diversity of social services beyond enforcement of the criminal law calls for a skilled management. Nevertheless, a Brookings Institution study finds a manpower shortage resulting from decades of political neglect, public apathy, and professional parochialism. Police agencies generally are understaffed and experience serious recruiting difficulties. A significant percentage of the men on any force are not suited to meet the responsibilities of modern law enforcement.[45]

Probably the quality of law enforcement has been improved compared with past decades, but the level of expectation and the necessities for more efficiency in social service tasks have been raised at an even faster pace. Niederhoffer, a knowledgeable and objective expert, believes the record of police on civil rights, except in the South, has improved substantially through better training in human relations, increased recruitment of minority group personnel, and continuation of psychiatric screening of police candidates.[46]

[44] Irving Piliavin and Scott Briar, "Police Encounters with Juveniles," *American Journal of Sociology,* Vol. 70 (September 1964), pp. 206–14.

[45] Charles B. Saunders, Jr., *Upgrading the American Police* (Washington, D.C.: The Brookings Institution, 1970, p. 35.

[46] Arthur Niederhoffer, *Behind the Shield: The Police in Urban Society* (Garden City, N.Y.: Doubleday Anchor, 1969), pp. 178–95.

Recruitment and retention

The President's Crime Commission reports that most departments fail to screen out the incompetent candidates for police jobs. However, almost all large departments in 1965 were below their authorized strength. Furthermore, there was a progressive decline in the proportion of candidates who were being accepted.[47] With an insufficiency of qualified candidates under the standards being used, there is little value in criticisms that standards are too low.

Retention of personnel is at least as important as recruitment. The fact that every year an average of 5 percent of a department's force leaves police service suggests the magnitude of the retention problem. Sole attention to recruitment as a solution also tempts one to draw the unwarranted conclusion that the incompetence of particular officers is the nub of the deficiencies of manpower quality. Actually, qualities of the police bureaucracy and the environment of police work should also be considered.

Departmental policies and practices, McNamara says, create uncertainties for police officers.[48] Police personnel are subjected to the discipline of a semimilitary organization; the violators of departmental rules are subjected to deprivation of pay, vacation time, and job. These penalties rest on the assumption that task failures stem from willful disobedience or negligence rather than errors of judgment. Police work calls for intelligent decision making at the time of the incident, but strict discipline imposed from above discourages the officer from using professional judgment on the spot. Career advancement also poses uncertainties. An adverse report in personnel files can block promotion. Finally, the written examinations do not necessarily test the officer on the basis of knowledge and skills which determine whether the successful applicant will demonstrate most competence in doing the job.

Although he usually starts without cynicism, the rookie soon confronts the divergence between the ideal standards voiced in training and the conditions of patrol out on the streets. Under the wing of veteran officers, the rookie is likely to be urged to be "tough." He is pressed, Niederhoffer says, to become cynical in two senses: a cynicism toward people in general encouraged by the corrupt and defeated people encountered in police work and a cynicism toward the police system itself raised by the divergence of its practices from the ideal. He reports the degree of cynicism is associated with length of service (leveling off after five or ten years); lower level of job position; greater expectation of promotion among col-

---

[47] President's Commission on Law Enforcement and Administration of Justice, *Task Force Report: The Police* (Washington, D.C.: U.S. Government Printing Office, 1967), pp. 9, 125–26.

[48] John H. McNamara, "Uncertainties in Police Work; Relevance of Police Recruits' Backgrounds and Training," in David J. Bordua (ed.); *The Police: Six Sociological Essays* (New York: John Wiley & Sons, 1967), pp. 177–90.

lege graduates; middle-class patrolmen as opposed to men from the working class; and members of the vice squad as compared with the youth
division.[49]

Education and training

Since the effectiveness of law enforcement depends ultimately on the
skills, ethics, and dedication of the men who meet the public and deal with
offenders, recommendations for reform usually emphasize education and
training. The President's Crime Commission has echoed the suggestion of
some police executives that all personnel with enforcement powers should
have baccalaureate degrees. Implementation of this recommendation requires a long-term program of raising the pay scales, regularizing the career
system to reward intellectual growth, and reducing the authoritarian and
bureaucratic barriers against discretion in arrest decisions.[50]

Advocates of a college education for police officers argue that the
college experience reduces conservative and authoritarian orientations
among policemen. Efforts to change police practices encounter serious
resistance from those patrolmen who see the community-relations brand
of law enforcement as "soft" and antithetical to the guardian-of-society
role.[51] Higher education is also supposed to produce a personal commitment to occupational ethics as a safeguard against abuse of power. The
increased sophistication of police management and technology calls for
grounding in scientific principles. Finally, law enforcement has an unprecedented opportunity to recruit from the ranks of college graduates. The
growing emphasis on "college for all" raises prospects that the present
labor market will be unable to absorb all the graduates without a new
spectrum of people-serving occupations.

Only in recent decades have colleges and universities shown serious
and widespread commitment to education for law enforcement. The rise
of two-year community-college programs has been especially noteworthy,
one of their attractive features being that their wide distribution enables
an officer to pursue an education while employed. The academic programs have not always been of proper quality, however, because of the
questionable competence of instructors and relevance of courses, and it
is doubtful that academic institutions can provide the necessary technical
instruction in forensic science, firearms, and so on. These subjects are best
left to agency in-service training or specialized facilities.[52]

---

[49] Niederhoffer, *Behind the Shield,* pp. 43–107.

[50] For a review of issues involved in education for policemen, see: Saunders, *Upgrading
the American Police,* pp. 79–116.

[51] See: Linda McVeigh Matthews, "Chief Reddin: New Style at the Top," *Atlantic,* Vol.
223 (March 1969), pp. 84–93.

[52] Elmer H. Johnson, "One Answer to Manpower Needs of Applied Criminology: Associate in Arts Degree," *Police,* Vol. 12 (May-June 1968), pp. 52–56.

THE PRISON AND PENAL TRADITIONS

In the last 200 years the prison emerged as an essentially American invention to cope with the crime problem. Although humanitarian abhorrence of capital punishment and other cruel punishments motivated many of its creators, the prison is grounded in the traditions of punishment and stigmatization of the convicted offender. In practice, these traditions have been associated with the isolation of the prisoners and the prison itself from the currents of life in the outside community.

The adverse effects of these traditions and this isolation stimulated the development of probation and parole to join the correctional institution as the major components of what we now know as the field of corrections. The increasing dominance of urban life has accelerated the growth of the numbers of convicted offenders and has promoted recognition that alternatives to punishment must be brought into play if the crime problem is to be managed.

Security prison: Order versus behavior change

Locking the convicted law violator behind prison bars for a protracted period has consequences highly likely to undermine the treatment purposes the contemporary prison is supposed to have. Few prison wardens today will speak openly of punishment per se as their central purpose. If they defend a punitive procedure, most wardens will explain it as a means to a rehabilitative end. Even in these instances, a reliance on punishment undermines the process of voluntary communication among staff and inmates essential to significant change in attitudes and future behavior of inmates.

When preservation of order in the prison is the primary purpose, the disciplinary policies suppress the emotional needs and individual qualities of the inmate for the sake of the general conformity of the "quiet" prison. When higher priority is given to resolving the inmate's inadequate capacity to deal with life's problems without law violation, he is expected to undergo the emotional travail of self-evaluation and personality change to produce greater self-discipline for new effectiveness in behavior when he returns to the community. Then his conformity to the letter of prison rules is secondary to the ultimate importance of his present experimentation with new ways of interpreting and responding to the problem events affecting him. A pertinent question is whether the supreme goal is immediate tranquility of the prison or maximization of the offender's willingness and capability to undertake the role of the law-abiding citizen.

Defects of the "human warehouse"

The maximum security prison is designed to maintain almost total control over inmates through concentration of power in the hands of ruling officialdom, a detailed set of regulations, routinization of behavior, and

The prison as a "fish bowl." The photographer uses his camera to compare the Honor Block, State Prison of Southern Michigan, with a fish bowl. In prison slang, the newly admitted prisoner is called a "fish."

constant surveillance.[53] The outside community operates on the principle that the followers are persuaded to accept the instructions of superiors through a sense of duty and self-identification with the family, work establishment, governmental unit, or other organization within which the individual's behavior is a part. The maximum security prison relies heavily on the coercion of the military conqueror over a defeated population.

In actual practice, Sykes points out, the total power in the hands of armed bureaucrats is eroded by the heavy financial costs of constant and detailed surveillance, the drain on effectiveness of coercion because of the guard's sympathy for the human beings subject to his authority, the skill of inmates in perverting situations to their own ends, and public ambivalence toward the authoritarian prison.[54]

For the sake of financial economy, custody prisons sometimes include such large numbers of prisoners that they qualify as *human warehouses* largely storing and processing human beings much as large-scale industries handle large quantities of material objects. The prison is an example of a *total institution* in which large numbers of people live together around the clock within a circumscribed space under a tightly scheduled sequence of activities imposed by a central authority.[55]

The "human-warehouse" prison stands in sharp contrast to normal life in the outside world. Most of us sleep, play, and work in different localities, each with its own kind of personalities and experiences. The prison does not differentiate these spheres of life. Its circumscribed physical space denies privacy and a range of choice in companions. The inmate is denied the monetary rewards emphasized in the outside world for motivating work and self-esteem. He is shut out from participation in the family life regarded as the core of adult responsibility.

Many prisoners feel deeply insulted by being lumped with the perverse personalities they find among inmates. The prisoner is part of blocks of people moved through various sequences of standardized procedures described as "classification," "education," "therapy," "inmate employment," or "disciplinary committee." The speed and ease of the work of officials is facilitated by handling inmates as though they were identical, but failure to recognize individual differences undermines treatment.

Finally, a basic split between the managers and the managed raises formidable barriers against the communication between staff and inmates essential to genuine therapy. Correctional officers are instructed to stand aloof from the people they guard in order to avoid corruption of their

---

[53] Gresham M. Sykes, *Society of Captives* (Princeton, N.J.: Princeton University Press, 1958), pp. 14–15.
[54] Sykes, ibid., pp. 48–58.
[55] Erving Goffman, "On the Characteristics of Total Institutions: The Inmate World" in Donald R. Cressey (ed.), *The Prison* (New York: Holt, Rinehart & Winston, Inc., 1960), pp. 16–22.

authority, yet correctional officers have more continual contact with inmates than any other class of employee. Their aloofness aborts the possible
usefulness of their opportunities for diagnosis and treatment of inmates.
Moreover, the overtures of inmates, even when motivated in response to
official invitations to accept prosocial values, are regarded with suspicion.
Officials are pressed toward pessimism about the moral worth and
rehabilitative potential of inmates. The social distance of inmates from the
staff encourages them to give support, although sometimes only tacitly,
to an inmate subculture centering around resistance to officials.

REVISING THE TRADITIONAL PRISON

The humanitarian impulse and the recognition of the weaknesses of
punishment have generally eased the severity of imprisonment. Many
correctional institutions have moved toward greater use of reeducation,
vocational training, and psychological intervention.

New organizational schemes

The President's Crime Commission refers to the recent appearance of
the *collaborative institution,* one structured around the active partnerships of all inmates and all staff members in the process of rehabilitation.[56]
In such an institution, the official rules are revised to ease the demands
for conformity for its own sake and to minimize regimentation. The traditional conflict between custodial and treatment staffs is reduced by placing
both groups on staff teams under a role system emphasizing their collaboration. Representing a large portion of the staff and a particularly persistent
contact with inmates, correctional officers are given a recognized place
in counseling activities and in serving as referral agents to bring their
experiences into the diagnostic and treatment resources. The direct involvement of inmates in the process of rehabilitation serves to strengthen
their own commitment to their own behavioral change, to enlist peer
groups in the process, and to mobilize the potential of some inmates to
be a constructive influence on others.

Specializing in those inmates psychologically ready and equipped to
participate actively in the rehabilitative process, the correctional institution
may be established as either the therapeutic community or open institution
models. In the *therapeutic community* the objective is to create an attitudinal climate whereby all social relationships between staff and inmates
contribute to the inmate's progress along the rehabilitation route.[57] Within

[56] President's Commission on Law Enforcement and Administration of Justice, *Task Force
Report: Corrections* (Washington, D.C.: U.S. Government Printing Office, 1967), p. 47–50.
[57] The introduction of this concept owes much to: Maxwell Jones, *The Therapeutic
Community* (New York: Basic Books, Inc., 1953).

such an institution, every form of activity is an opportunity for the inmate to evaluate his place and functioning within social groups of his past, present, and future. A supporting and nonrejecting environment provides opportunities for surfacing of inner feelings and for coping with them without retaliation from others. Although formal programs are offered, an effort is made to maintain spontaneity of relationships within the organizational shell. Without clear-cut rules, both the inmates and staff members must confront problems on the basis of their own evaluations and skills in social relationships. It is hoped that the experiences within the institution will be relevant to life after release.

The *open institution* is characterized by the absence of walls and the substitution of psychological controls for physical barriers against escape.[58] Similar to the therapeutic community, this institution is intended to resemble life in the free community as much as is feasible. Free movement within the grounds, family visits, and correspondence are encouraged. Work conditions and tasks are supposed to resemble employment outside. A small and carefully selected population is a key factor in the dependence on intimacy of inmate-staff relationships for control through self-discipline. Prospects for transfer to a custodial prison also serve as a deterrent to misconduct.

More akin to the traditional model are several kinds of facilities with small prisoner populations to overcome the "human warehouse" features of large prisons and to encourage greater intimacy between staff and inmates. Honor farms and forestry camps are assigned inmates considered unlikely to attempt escape. In some states, to bridge the gap between closed prison and the open community, inmates near the end of their sentence or scheduled parole are transferred to prerelease centers for reorientation and job preparation services. A promising development has been the establishment of work release for adult prisoners in 28 states in 1968 and 41 states and the District of Columbia in 1972.[59] The inmates are housed in a correctional facility and are subject to prison control but are employed for pay in jobs in the free community.

COMMUNITY-BASED CORRECTIONS

One promising recent development has been the growing popularity of *community-based corrections.* Ideally, the term refers to a fundamental reorientation of the several existing fields of corrections into a new structure. Now limited to probation, institutions, and parole, these fields would

[58] Charles Germain, "To What Extent Can Open Institutions Take the Place of the Traditional Prison?" *Proceedings of Twelfth International Penal and Penitentiary Congress, 1930,* Vol. 4, No. 2 (The Hague, 1951), pp. 11–12.

[59] Elmer H. Johnson, "Report on An Innovation—State Work-Release Programs," *Crime and Delinquency,* Vol. 16 (October 1970), pp. 417–26 (1972 data from subsequent survey).

lose their autonomy from each other and crime prevention activities would be added. The convicted offender now is handled successively by probation, institutions, and parole as though he essentially had no previous experiences within the system of corrections. Each of these agencies is excessively aloof from the other's activities. Community-based corrections would integrate their several activities to expose the convicted offender to *systematic* experiences. Instead of dealing with crime as a discrete problem, community-based corrections enters into an active alliance with other agencies responsible for overcoming the various social problems.

Local correctional centers

The central institution would be the *community-based institution,* the architectural and methodological antithesis of the traditional fortresslike prison which serves as a place of banishment. A small and informal structure, it would be located near the population center from which its inmates are drawn. Extensive screening and classification of inmates received from the courts would be the basis of alternative handling of sentenced offenders. Some would be placed immediately in community treatment programs: vocational education in local schools, mental health clinics, parole, work release. Another group would be provided short-term, intensive treatment before being assigned to a community program.

Diagnosis would result in a third category being referred to higher custody facilities required for long-term confinement of the more difficult and/or dangerous inmates. When completion of sentence provides no legal alternative to release, even these inmates would be returned to the local facility for reentry to the community. For all types of inmates, a properly staffed local facility would ease transition into the community as a means of reducing changes of further crimes.

This new kind of institution would reduce the unnecessary prolongation of confinement and avoid the adverse consequences of long-term imprisonment. The institution would provide diagnostic services to local courts to improve the effectiveness of sentencing and to maximize the intelligent use of probation as an alternative to incarceration.

Alternatives to imprisonment

Corrections is being pressed to try new ways of handling convicted offenders in lieu of imprisonment. Spiraling crime rates arouse public concern and involve the costs of adding to the bedspace of correctional facilities. Compared with other nations, the United States has a high proclivity for imprisoning convicted offenders. In 1960 for every 100,000 of population, Canada imprisoned 240 persons, the United States 200, Norway 44, and the United Kingdom 59.[60] Even if the crime rates and the imprisonment rates were to remain constant, growing total population adds to the burden of the system of criminal justice. The financial burden is especially great when expansion of custodial prisons is required.[61]

Delinquents may be placed with group-care foster parents, instead of sending them to institutions for juvenile delinquents. Under the supervision and care of substitute parents, the children are supposed to benefit from the security, guidance, and affection of a family setting.

Community-based corrections provides several means of diverting convicted offenders from correctional institutions through probation or speeding the release of inmates through parole. Beyond this, community-based centers offer other innovative ideas. Stark describes an experiment of the California Youth Authority in which intensive treatment in the community is substituted for traditional correctional institutions. Selected juveniles are released directly from the reception centers to an intensive parole program. Located in high-delinquency areas near the homes of the youngsters, the centers provide space for parole officers, school tutoring, group counseling, and recreation.[62]

Probation is conditional release of a convicted offender by the court under supervision by an agent of the court. Ideally, a judge's decision to withhold commitment to penal confinement is based on the officer's careful presentence investigation of the offender's background, social situation, and personal qualities. If the probationer's behavior is found to be unsatisfactory, he may be returned to the court for imposition of a sentence to penal confinement. Probation is advocated as a means of easing the stigmatization of being labeled as an "ex-convict," of avoiding the adverse consequences of imprisonment on the offender, and of utilizing the treatment and employment resources of the free community.

Parole involves early release from prison before completion of the full sentence but with the parolee subject to certain conditions and the supervision of a parole supervisor. Parole is under the authority of the executive arm of government, rather than the courts. Parole shortens exposure to penal confinement, and—theoretically—provides a means of returning the prisoner to the free community at the point in his prison career when his own attitudes and progress in institutional treatment are most favorable for successful adjustment to the community. Unfortunately, in practice, parole decisions emphasize matters other than the inmate's current attitudes. Inmates tend to be judged on the basis of public attitudes toward the crime for which they were convicted. Murder and rape, for example,

[60] John Hogarth, "Toward the Improvement of Sentencing in Canada," *Canadian Journal of Corrections,* Vol. 9 (April 1967), p. 124.
[61] An estimate for California is $22,000 a bed and an additional $400 per inmate for maintenance and treatment. See: Herman G. Stark, "Alternatives to Institutionalization," *Crime and Delinquency,* Vol. 13 (April 1967), pp. 328–29.
[62] Stark, "Alternatives to Institutionalization," pp. 325–27.

446   Social problems of urban man

draw particularly negative attitudes against parole early in a man's prison confinement. Absence of a favorable employment-residence plan for release also reduces parole prospects. Agencies usually avoid paroling a man with a short sentence because he is likely to resent parole supervision beyond the time he would otherwise have served in prison. Finally, failure to adjust to conditions of penal confinement does not necessarily indicate a prisoner is a poor prospect for parole, but a record of prison rule violations reduces chances for receiving parole.

SUMMARY

The police, courts, and correctional agencies compose what is known as the system of criminal justice. However, for a number of reasons, these components individually and collectively do not demonstrate the coordinated activities which justify a rigorous use of the term "system." In striving to cope with the crime problems of urban society, these components are sources of problems themselves.

Conflicts between the crime-control and due-process models are prevalent in each of the components of the system. The police experience disparate demands that they enforce the law and maintain the peace, that they suppress crime and perform social services, and that they be organizationally disciplined and show initiative in arrest decisions. The mounting case load of courts has aggravated problems such as delay in judicial procedure, dispositions without trial, disparities in sentencing, undermining of the civil rights of indigent defendants, and disputes over proper functioning of juvenile courts. Prisons are handicapped by the persistence of punitive traditions and isolation from the mainstream of community life.

This chapter has focused attention on the social structure of the criminal justice agencies as a source of discrepancies between expectation and practice. Emphasis is shifted away from the law violator, who usually is considered the primary source of "the" crime problem.

FOR ADDITIONAL READING

Carl Bakal, "The Traffic in Guns: A Forgotten Lesson of the Assassination," *Harper's Magazine,* Vol. 229 (December 1964), pp. 60–68.

Arthur J. Bilek, "State of the Art: The Administration of Criminal Justice," in Richard D. Knudten (ed.), *Crime, Criminology, and Contemporary Society* (Homewood, Ill.: Dorsey Press, 1970), pp. 242–57.

Howard G. Brown, "Juvenile Courts and the Gault Decision: I, Background and Promise," *Children,* Vol. 15 (May-June 1968), pp. 86–89.

George Edwards, *The Police on the Urban Frontier* (New York: Institute of Human Relations Press, 1968).

Daniel Glaser, *The Effectiveness of a Prison and Parole System* (Indianapolis, Ind.: Bobbs-Merrill Company, Inc., 1964).

Allen D. Grimshaw, "Police Agencies and the Prevention of Racial Violence," *Journal of Criminal Law, Criminology, and Police Science,* Vol. 54 (March 1963), pp. 110–13.

Lawrence E. Hazelrigg, *Prison within Society: A Reader in Penology* (Garden City, N.Y.: Doubleday Anchor, 1968).

Oliver J. Keller, Jr., and Benedict S. Alper, *Halfway Houses: Community-Centered Correction and Treatment* (Lexington, Mass.: D. C. Health and Company, 1970).

J. L. Lyman, "The Metropolitan Police Act of 1829," *Journal of Criminal Law, Criminology and Police Science,* Vol. 55 (March 1964), pp. 141–54.

Donal E. J. MacNamara and Edward A. Sagarin, *Perspectives on Corrections* (New York: Thomas Y. Crowell Company, 1971).

Jessica Mitford, "Kind and Usual Punishment in California," *Atlantic,* Vol. 227 (March 1971), pp. 45–52.

Richard A. Myren, "A Crisis in Police Management," *Journal of Criminal Law, Criminology, and Police Science,* Vol. 50 (March-April 1960), pp. 600–604.

Stuart S. Nagel, "Testing Relations between Judicial Characteristics and Judicial Decision-Making," *Western Political Quarterly,* Vol. 15 (September 1962), pp. 425–37.

Nial Osborough, "Police Discretion Not to Prosecute Students: A British Problem," *Journal of Criminal Law, Criminology and Police Science,* Vol. 56 (June 1965), pp. 241–45.

Robert S. Pickett, *House of Refuge: Origins of Juvenile Reform in New York State, 1815–1857* (Syracuse, N.Y.: Syracuse University Press, 1969).

Elliott M. Rudwick, *The Unequal Badge: Negro Policemen in the South* (Atlanta, Ga.: Southern Regional Council, 1962).

Mort Stern, "What Makes a Policeman Go Wrong?" *Journal of Criminal Law, Criminology and Police Science,* Vol. 53 (March 1962), pp. 97–101.

L. H. Whittemore, *Cop! A Closeup of Violence and Tragedy* (New York: Holt, Rinehart and Winston, 1969).

James Q. Wilson, "What Makes a Better Policeman," *Atlantic,* Vol. 223 (March 1969), pp. 129–35.

18 Trauma of medical care

The physician has been portrayed as one of our great cultural heroes: He is the "family doctor" who, as in the Fildes painting favored by the American Medical Association, sits by a sick child through an all-night vigil in a struggle to save life. In sharp contrast to this image, the nation's medical system has come under vigorous and widespread attack, and health care has been elevated to the stature of a full-blown national crisis.

The Ehrenreichs sketch the general dimensions of this health care crisis.[1] Some three million Americans seek medical care each day, but only some of them are helped. Health care is scarce, expensive, dangerously fragmented, and presented to the patient in an atmosphere of mystery. In both cities and rural areas, it is difficult to find the place for medical care and thereafter to receive prompt service. The patient must chop his way through a tangled jungle of medical specialization and organizational fragmentation. He has difficulty in learning the facts about his illness and what is being done about it. As a consumer, he lacks rights and protection when things go wrong. The burdens of poverty and racial discrimination follow him in his search for medical assistance.

QUALIFICATIONS AS SOCIAL PROBLEM

At first glance, illness would appear to be simply a physiological difficulty stemming from injury or change in the internal environment of the

[1] Barbara and John Ehrenreich, *The American Health Empire: Power, Profits, and Politics* (New York: Random House, 1970), pp. 3–15.

448

body. If this were so, social and cultural behavior would be absent and medical care would be disqualified as a *social* problem. However, as shown below, illness and medical care *do* involve social and cultural behavior.

Furthermore, the health care crisis is intimately related to developments within urban society which have strained the social structure supposed to serve individual and group needs. The inadequacies of medical care became increasingly apparent in the 1960s as another aspect of rapid urbanization—aspects which include decay of cities, struggles for human rights, and growing impatience with the burdens of poverty and discrimination. The medical establishment has felt the impact of a rising level of expectation for service that has exceeded the pace of any improvements it has been able to provide.

Paradoxes in the situation

Modern medical care holds several paradoxes which produce social problems. The accomplishments of public health and medical measures have brought spectacular declines in death rates, especially in the younger ages, but an increased proportion of the population is surviving to the senior years when chronic diseases are more prevalent and the individual's financial resources are less likely to be adequate in a crisis. The lives of some others are saved only to require expensive lifetime care. Medical advances have promoted recognition of diseases previously untreated and have expanded the number of symptoms contributing to disease rates.

Another irony is that medical progress adds to problems of disease control, although these problems are insufficient to cancel overall progress. For example, strains of microorganisms resistant to antibiotics pose special threats to hospitals formerly considered antiseptic and also populated by persons particularly unprepared to cope with infection. The X ray and the fluoroscope, great assets to medicine, raise concern over the consequences of radiation. Advanced medical care is characterized by an elaborate organization which depends on an intricate division of labor among specialists and on the hospital as the location of complex technology.[2] The doctor-patient relationship has lost the personal touch. The doctor's home visit has largely vanished, partly because the technology of medicine requires a central location.

Capturing the essence of a fundamental dilemma of contemporary medicine, Rosen suggests that the industrial revolution has finally caught up with the medical practitioner to create discrepancies between his traditions of individualistic practice and the demands that he discipline his behavior within medical care bureaucracies.[3] Once a highly respected

---

[2] Herman Miles Somers and Anne Ramsay Somers, *Doctors, Patients, and Health Insurance*, (Washington, D.C.: Brookings Institution, 1961), pp. 4–15.

[3] Quoted by Robert N. Wilson, "The Social Structure of a General Hospital," *Annals of American Academy of Political and Social Science*, Vol. 346 (March 1963), pp. 74–75.

healer working alone, the doctor is becoming a technical specialist working in coordination with other specialists in a medical team.

Along with the impressive advances in the efficiency of medical technology have come increased costs to the consumer. "Miracle" drugs and promises of further medical break-throughs lead patients to expect the latest version of treatment. Physicians, Ruthstein reports, now spend a great deal of time reassuring patients by attempting to undo false hopes engendered by careless public statements.[4] With higher expectations and, for some patients, the provision of medical insurance, even the higher costs of medical care do not eliminate the demand for services. One consequence is the continued provision of health care according to ability to pay.

In spite of great health progress, there are indications that the United States has not kept pace with certain other nations. Life expectancy has gradually increased in the last century, but in the last two decades this increase in the United States has tailed off. United Nations statistics show that between 1959 and 1966 the United States dropped in position among nations in average life expectancy rates from thirteenth place to twenty-second place for males and from seventh to tenth place for females. A similar situation exists for infant mortality.[5] Greenberg cites a slum neighborhood in Boston with a higher infant death rate (one out of nine) than reported in ancient, plague-infested Egypt (one out of ten).[6]

Two differing interpretations

The health care crisis has been assessed from several perspectives. From one point of view, the fundamental source of difficulty is the "American health industry" composed of hospitals, doctors, medical schools, drug companies, and health insurance companies. Health care is no more the top priority of this "industry," it is contended, than the production of safe, cheap, efficient, pollution-free transportation is a priority of the American automobile industry. The American medical establishment is described as both efficient and systematic in extracting profits in terms of differences between income and expenditures. Without fundamental change in the orientation of organizations involved in health services, even the diversion of all our military expenditures into such services would be insufficient to end the health care crisis.[7]

From another point of view, the shortcomings of private medicine are

[4] David D. Ruthstein, "At the Turn of the Next Century," in John H. Knowles (ed.) *Hospitals, Doctors, and the Public Interest* (Cambridge, Mass.: Harvard University Press, 1965), p. 302.

[5] David D. Ruthstein, *The Coming Revolution in Medicine* (Cambridge, Mass.: The MIT Press, 1967), pp. 11–46.

[6] Selig Greenberg, *The Quality of Mercy* (New York: Atheneum, 1971), p. 97.

[7] Ehrenreich and Ehrenreich, *The American Health Empire,* pp. vi, 21–22.

insufficient to explain the health care crisis. Schwartz argues that complex forces outside the control of any medical establishment are affecting differential infant mortality and life expectancy rates. Drug overdoses, heart disease, and lung cancer have their roots in the living patterns and habits of people beyond the control of medicine. The size of the United States and the heterogeneity of its population produce conditions which made invalid direct comparisons with health statistics of small and homogeneous nations. Agreeing that private medicine has flaws and is sometimes abused "as any human arrangement tends to be," Schwartz finds "astonishing" that, in an era of increasing disenchantment with big government, reformers "want to nationalize and bureaucratize American medicine." He argues that if the "revolutionary proposals for transforming American medicine are adopted and implemented, medical care in this country will cost more while providing less satisfaction and poorer treatment for millions." [8]

Illness as sociocultural behavior

The social factors in illness and medical care are indicated by the difference between the concepts of illness and disease. The concept of *disease,* as Coe indicates, refers to an objective phenomenon characterized by the altering functioning of the body as a biological organism.[9] Objective phenomena include those which can be placed under a microscope or otherwise tested to determine whether the patient's body is not functioning properly or to determine the organic basis for the body's departure from normal functioning.

By *illness,* Coe refers to a subjective phenomenon; that is, individuals perceive themselves as not feeling well, and therefore they may deviate from behavior which is normal for them. "Subjective phenomenon" concentrates attention on the importance of the individual's own perception of the state of his health. The individual may feel sick without a disease being present (or he may not experience illness even though a disease is present). Two persons with the same clinical symptoms may act altogether differently in degree and kind of concern expressed and whether and how they search for treatment.

Pain has physiological characteristics in terms of intensity, duration, and quality of sensation. However, pain is also included among the elements of illness as a subjective phenomenon. Individuals differ in their willingness to experience pain, but more crucial to our point, they tend to view disease, as defined above, from the perspective of their particular culture and to respond to disease in patterned ways. Group pressures may lead

[8] Harry Schwartz, "Health Care in America: A Heretical Analysis," *Saturday Review,* Vol. 54 (August 14, 1971), pp. 14–17, 55.
[9] Rodney M. Coe, *Sociology of Medicine* (New York: McGraw-Hill Book Co., 1970), pp. 91–100.

a person to deny feeling ill and to strive to meet work and other obligations in the usual fashion. The dependency of illness is repugnant in a group stressing rugged individualism. Conversely, when the individual experiences stress from competition with other persons, illness is often welcomed as freeing him from usual obligations and granting him sympathy and personal care.

The operation of cultural factors is suggested by a New York hospital study of three groups of Americans: Jews, Italians, and a native-born group. Jews were more skeptical of doctors and particularly anxious about the long-term implications of pain. Italians tended to have more confidence in doctors and to be more concerned about the immediate relief of pain. Both groups were less inhibited in exhibiting suffering than the native-born patients who viewed the body as a machine which should be fixed as promptly as possible. The last group derived a sense of security from the volume of activities initiated in its behalf—tests, examinations, injections and so on. The impersonal character of the hospital routine was less disturbing to it.[10]

Compared with persons of higher socioeconomic status, persons in lower-income groups have less information and knowledge about disease. They are less likely to recognize the signs of major illnesses, to understand body functions, or to practice prevention of ill health. They appear more likely than more privileged groups to respond to illness with fear, anxiety, and defensive refusal to acknowledge a medical problem. However, the relative importance of various causes of these differential responses is not clear: differential perception of symptoms, anxiety because of inadequate knowledge, simple fear, concern over medical costs in face of competing demands on slender economic resources, or inferior access to medical services. Lack of hospital insurance raises a special threat, as indicated by the narrowing differences among the social classes in utilization when medical services have been made available regardless of financial means.[11]

Routes to medical care

In considering illness as social behavior, Mechanic and Volkart distinguish between (1) stress factors which may produce physical symptoms and (2) the chances that an individual experiencing symptoms will seek treatment. In a population of university students, they found that those bothered by "loneliness" and "nervousness" made more frequent visits

---

[10] Mark Zborowski, "Cultural Components in Responses to Pain," in Herman D. Stein and Richard A. Cloward (eds.), Social Perspectives on Behavior (New York: Free Press, 1958), pp. 145–56.

[11] David Mechanic, "Illness and Cure," in John Kosa, Aaron Antonovsky, and Irving Kenneth Zola (eds.) Poverty and Health: A Sociological Analysis (Cambridge, Mass.: Harvard University Press, 1969), pp. 205–10.

to the medical clinic than those who were not.[12] Because individuals differ in the likelihood of their seeking medical care for physical symptoms, the people coming to the physician are different from the larger population of people who have the same physical symptoms.

Social, cultural, and psychological factors distinguish those who come from those who do not. Suchman describes five stages through which the sick person passes in deciding whether to seek medical help.[13] First, the individual perceives that something is wrong—a pain, rash, or blurred vision, for example. He evaluates the change in his functioning and responds in ways ranging from refusal to admit organic difficulties to acceptance that a problem exists. Probably he tries self-medication or folk remedies. Second, he assumes the sick role, turning to persons significant to him for confirmation that he should be excused from usual obligations. Third, he seeks professional advice to confirm his claim to the sick role and to obtain an explanation for his symptoms. Fourth, when he receives and accepts confirmation, he undergoes a treatment regimen within the professional care system. Fifth, varying with the nature and severity of his ailment, he undertakes recovery and rehabilitation to relinquish the dependent sick role and reassume normal role obligations.

These stages reflect the operations of two sometimes conflicting systems of decision making. The *professional referral system* comprises the treatment events implemented by the physician as gatekeeper to professional care. Friedson points to a *lay referral system* consisting of some kind of local folklore of medicine and a network of personal influence along which the patient travels on his way to the physician.[14] In his early reactions to some symptom, the patient is likely to exchange information with relatives, friends, neighbors, and fellow workers. These people offer advice drawn from their own medical experience and casual knowledge of folk remedies, patent medicines, significance of the symptom, and the relative merits of physicians in the area. If the symptom persists and the patient's worry increases, he is likely to seek assistance under terms shaped by his network of lay consultants. The lay referral systems differ among subcultures in the intensity of their influence in the time between the patient's first perception of the symptom and his decision to consult a physician.

The idea of lay referral system focuses attention on the way the client's entry into the channels of medical service is subject to sociocultural factors beyond the science of medicine and the professional authority of the physician. To some extent the lay referral system controls professional practice by determining whether the physician gets patients, whether he

[12] David Mechanic and Edmund H. Volkart, "Stress, Illness Behavior and the Sick Role," *American Sociological Review,* Vol. 26 (February 1961), pp. 51–58.

[13] Edward A. Suchman, "Stages of Illness and Medical Care," *Journal of Health and Human Behavior,* Vol. 6 (Fall 1965), pp. 114–28.

[14] Eliot Friedson, "Client Control and Medical Practice," *American Journal of Sociology,* Vol. 65 (January 1960), pp. 374–82.

holds them, and the accommodations to lay attitudes he must undertake to win patient cooperation with medical treatments.

Dissemination of public information on the prevalence of certain diseases, on their diagnostic clues, and on new medical discoveries enhances the probability that the individual will associate certain symptoms, sometimes erroneously, with particular ailments. The physician is pressed to accept or manipulate lay expectations through the administration of placebos and the substitution of "wonder" drugs for drugs unpopular among patients. However, with the failure of the lay consultants to remedy the patient's problem, Friedson says the patient becomes dependent on the expertise of the physician who is the gatekeeper for referrals to the specialized services of medical colleagues.

MEDICAL MANPOWER PROBLEMS

Major elements in the U.S. health care crisis are the insufficiency and maldistribution of medical manpower. Greenberg reports that 5,000 communities are without physicians and that by 1975 the nation will be short 80,000 of the number of doctors it will need. To provide an optimum level of hospital care, another 260,000 professional and technical workers would be needed. The ratio of dentists to population has been declining for some time.[15]

Maldistribution of services

The geographical distribution of physicians is out of keeping with the distribution of need as measured by disease and death statistics. The states with the lowest per-capita income and highest illness rates draw less than their share of physicians, pediatricians, and obstetricians. The Public Health Service presents data revealing the consequences: Infant mortality rates vary greatly among the states and the races. For whites the rate ranges from 14.9 (per 1,000 live births) in Hawaii to 24.9 in West Virginia in 1967. For nonwhites it ranges from 17.5 in Hawaii to 47.4 in Mississippi and 51.2 in Alaska. Regardless of level of family income, white mothers were more likely than nonwhite mothers to have health insurance coverage for hospital care. However, a 1964–66 study reports that only 28 percent of the white mothers had coverage when family annual income was less than $3,000 compared to 82.5 percent for the income level of $10,000 and over. For the period July 1966–June 1967 white children averaged 3.9 visits to doctors and nonwhite children only two visits. For families with income less than $3,000 there were 2.5 visits compared with 4.2 visits for children in families earning $7,000 and over. In 1968 the number of dental visits per child under age 15 ranged from .4 for families

[15] Greenberg, *The Quality of Mercy,* pp. 125–26.

with less than $3,000 income to 2.3 for families with income of $15,000 and over.[16]

Availability of medical services depends on the individual's residential location. Residents of rural areas, small towns, and low-income areas of cities are likely to find themselves in deserts as far as medical care is concerned. In addition to the failure of the supply of medical manpower to keep up with population growth, the increasing specialization of medicine has deprived neighborhoods of many of their general practitioners. Instead, doctors' offices usually cluster around hospitals and cater to certain kinds of medical problems to take advantage of the doctor's grasp of one segment of this century's increasingly complex medical knowledge. The physician also gains the benefits of more regular hours and superior income. Schwartz views as understandable the fact that many physicians would prefer to live and practice where it would be most advantageous and pleasant for them rather than in surroundings of poverty or of professional isolation.[17]

Insufficient supply of personnel

The demand for medical services has been inflated by their increased utilization, by population growth, and by the increasing share of the population represented by persons in senior ages when chronic diseases are most prevalent. In earlier eras the impotence of medicine evoked fatalism in the face of sickness even among those who could afford the luxury of the best medical care then available. With the development of effective public health and medical measures, this fatalism has been supplanted by a broadening expectation that adequate medical care is a universal right.[18] But the supply of medical personnel has not kept pace.

Paradoxically, the shortage of physicians is partly the indirect consequence of the upgrading of medical education in the decades immediately preceding the 1950s. Richmond explains that previously the education of physicians had been conducted by a loose collection of medical schools, many operated as private businesses, which were largely oriented toward nonscientific training. To incorporate the quality of training essential to utilization of improved medical knowledge and technology, medical schools were brought into the framework of universities early in this century. About a third of the schools were closed, and after 1907 the number of physicians per 100,000 population declined, not to begin a significant increase until after 1958.[19]

Another paradox is that the richest nation in the world is dependent

[16] *The Health of Children—1970,* (Washington, D.C.: Public Health Service, September 1970).
[17] Schwartz, "Health Care in America," p. 16.
[18] Somers and Somers, *Doctors, Patients, and Health Insurance,* pp. 133–45.
[19] Julius B. Richmond, *Currents in American Medicine* (Cambridge, Mass.: Harvard University Press, 1969), pp. 1–11.

for medical personnel on much poorer nations—nations where the personnel is much needed at home. About 14 percent of our medical manpower
is represented by foreign physicians trained abroad. In fact, more foreign
physicians have been entering the United States in recent years than are
being graduated from American medical schools. The greatest number of
medical graduates on hospital staffs in this country comes from five countries with much lower standards of medical education than the United
States—the Philippines, India, Korea, Iran, and Thailand.[20]

Two strategies, Mechanic says, are available to remedy deficiencies in
the supply of medical personnel.[21] First, the number of medical schools
and their number of graduates could be increased under the present educational organization. Disputing the more or less explicit charge that the
American Medical Association has been choking off the supply of doctors
for the sake of preserving its power, Schwartz contends that the medical
schools have produced a net increase of between 35,000 and 40,000
doctors just since 1965 through expanded enrollments, establishment of
new medical schools, and reduction of the length of training.[22]

Second, the available resources could be concentrated into programs
and forms of organization to increase the doctor's productivity, though
concentration on greater productivity runs counter to the personal relationships with clients so essential to the supportive functions of the physician. Already the contemporary physician renders more service than his
predecessor because of improved diagnostic equipment and chemotherapy and changes in the typical site of his work, and the telephone and
the patient's automobile enables him to concentrate his practice in his
office or hospital, with savings in the time he must devote to home visits.
Many physicians have adopted management and business practices to add
efficiency to their offices and free their time further. However, as Mechanic points out, the two strategies do not concentrate sufficiently on the
inadequacies of the current delivery system in distributing medical manpower according to the greatest need for services.

Differential utilization of services

The lack of preventive and outpatient services for the less privileged
segments of U.S. population is a fundamental deficiency of contemporary
medical care.

Surveys have shown that the greater burden of sickness and disability
falls upon lower-income groups, even though, the utilization of physician
services declines along with decreasing social class status. Ross suggests
explanations for this: Superior purchasing power among the more privi-

[20] Greenberg, *The Quality of Mercy,* p. 131.
[21] David Mechanic, "The Changing Structure of Medical Practice," *Law and Contemporary Problems,* Vol. 32 (Autumn 1967), pp. 709–11.
[22] Schwartz, "Health Care in America," pp. 15–16.

leged encourages utilization of medical insurance and services; low income curtails use of physicians for fear of high bills.[23]

Lower social classes have greater fear of illness and less desire to see a doctor than higher social classes. Koos' study demonstrates this difference among the social classes in typical interpretations of illness.[24] The upper and middle classes are more likely to understand and accept modern treatment methods, while the lower classes rely more on folk therapy. As an upper-class member, the physician has a vocabulary, demeanor, and insistence on formal procedures which are alien to the ways of lower-class persons.

Affluent citizens have been protected by voluntary insurance plans, usually tied to employment fringe benefits. Employers, government agencies, philanthropists, and voluntary insurance agencies have assumed a growing share of personal health care expenditures. Their orientation has been toward meeting catastrophic illness which requires hospitalization. The consequence has been the preservation of the fee-for-service method of physician compensation which is basic to the current system for delivery of medical services. When catastrophic illness and hospitalization are not involved, this system fails to induce improved otpatient service for diagnosis and disease prevention.

HIGHER COSTS OF MEDICAL CARE

Medical care costs have increased at a faster pace than the cost of living, and the price of hospital services has advanced at an even higher rate, partially because of increased use of expensive equipment and paramedical personnel. Fewer days of treatment are required usually; that is, hospital care has gained in effectiveness, and declines in average length of stay reduce the occupied bed time because of greater patient turnover. The net effect, however, is to increase per diem costs.

Factors in escalating costs

Drug prices and physician fees have increased less than the general medical index because of several factors. The drug price index has been held down by the increased purchases of hospitals to reduce the effect of more costly purchases by drugstore consumers. Prices of wonder drugs decline after they experience competition and more widespread use. Drugs have had some consequences which save money by shortening hospital stays, substituting home care for expensive hospitalization, and

[23] John A. Ross, "Social Class and Medical Care," *Journal of Health and Human Behavior,* Vol. 3 (Spring 1962), pp. 35–40.

[24] Earl Lomon Koos, *The Health of Regionville* (New York: Hafner Publishing Company, 1967), p. 32.

permitting a more speedy return to work. The relative stability of physicians' fees conceals developments which have increased the doctor's income through greater productivity; that is, the average time of contact with the patient is shorter and he makes fewer home visits.[25]

Paradoxically, increased costs reflect the unprecedented potential of medicine in saving lives and restoring health. Diagnosis and treatment have benefited from improved technology, but, at the same time, the heavy investment required for the various devices, their functional interrelationship, and the constellation of specialized technicians required for their operation mean that the patient must be brought to a central location. Hospitalization increasingly has replaced home care where the family could provide food, lodging, and household services. These are now provided by salaried personnel in special facilities. Increased specialization of medical occupations adds to the size of hospital staffs, their equipment, occupancy of space, costs of special training, and fees of consultation teams. The fixed costs of plant equipment and staff raise formidable budgetary problems for hospital administrators, especially when the improvements in rapidity and effectiveness of treatment shortens the average length of hospitalization. Increased patient turnover adds to the time when beds are not occupied, thus requiring a higher per diem charge to meet expenses. As a financial strategy, hospital authorities are tempted to prolong hospital stay and to provide nonessential treatment services. The insufficiency of overall hospital planning aggravates the situation by duplication of specialized services among hospitals in a given region.

Drug utilization and insurance

Major complaints of the Kefauver Committee against proprietary drug manufacturers were that their profits were excessive, that their production was heavily concentrated in a relatively few companies, that an undue emphasis was placed on sales and advertising, and that costs increased by differentiating products at a dizzy pace.[26] Because the "cream" of profits come before other companies can market a new drug, hard-sell promotion bombards the physician, and he has difficulty in keeping reliably informed on the relative merits of new discoveries. Rushing of new drugs to the market injects "planned obsolescence" into the situation and adds risks of unanticipated side effects. The manufacturer gains influence in decisions supposed to be limited to physicians. Emphasis on brand names adds to stocking costs, thus inflating prices, at the same time that increased drug utilization has made drugs a major portion of the family medical dollar (and contributed to the triviality and misuse of drugs).

[25] Seymour E. Harris, *The Economics of American Medicine* (New York: Macmillan Co., 1964), pp. 52–59, 75–77.
[26] Harris, ibid., p. 6.

Finally, the pharmacist's role has been converted from a compounder of prescriptions formulated by a local doctor to a person who transfers capsules from large to small containers.[27]

Increased medical costs are also associated with the growth of prepayment insurance which guarantees reimbursement to reduce the hospitals' concern over costs. Fire or life insurance is based on actuarial risk in that odds can be determined that the event insured against will occur. There is less predictability of when a patient will be sufficiently ill for hospitalization, how long his stay should be, or what services will be required. Because hospital expenses are covered and ambulatory services are not, the existence of insurance protection encourages the use of hospitalization even when the need does not justify it. This additional use and the expense of administering insurance inflates its cost beyond the services it is designed to cover because rates must cover the expenses. Another complaint is that the supplier of services increases charges beyond the amounts reimbursable by insurance. As a safeguard against overutilization, insuring agencies often impose part of the costs upon the insured through deductible features, waiting periods, and ceilings on benefits.[28]

Methods of remuneration

Critics of the higher costs of medical care usually begin by challenging the fee-for-service method of remuneration. Under the *fee-for-service* method, the practitioner sets fees for the specific services he delivers. Among alternatives is the *retainer method* whereby the physician receives the equivalent of a salary in advance of task performance to provide health services for a particular group of clients. The *capitation method,* similar to the salary method, stipulates that the physician will be paid a given amount to care for a person, sick or well, for a given period of time. Usually the agreement covers a large panel or a group of persons.[29]

Most favored by the medical profession, the fee-for-service method is defended on several scores.[30] It is supposed to relate the physician's reward to what work he does and to his degree of enthusiasm and competence. The physician with special skills or willingness to accept long hours can increase his income while providing service for more patients. Presumably, the inefficient or unpopular physician is penalized economically. Fee-for-service has been defended by its advocates as the most efficient method in meeting changes in kind of service. By altering the fee structure, changes in patterns of service would be encountered.

---

[27] Somers and Somers, *Doctors, Patients, and Health Insurance,* pp. 91–92, 208–12.
[28] Harris, *The Economics of American Medicine,* pp. 358–60, 377–78.
[29] Milton I. Roemer, "On Paying the Doctor and the Implications of Different Methods," *Journal of Health and Human Behavior,* Vol. 3 (Spring 1962), pp. 4–14.
[30] James Hogarth, *The Payment of the Physician* (New York: Macmillan Co., 1963), pp. 522–34.

Critics argue that the amount of the fee is determined by the provider of services who is not a disinterested judge of the value of his services, Hogarth says. By favoring quantity of tasks performed, fee-for-service tends to erode quality of service and to favor excessive services. Also, the interests of the physicians are not always consistent with the fee system. He is subjected to pricing his own services when his own self-image is that of an altruistic savior of troubled people. He may encounter the unpleasantness of controversies over bills, especially since the uncertainties of treatment undermine the forecasting of fee costs for a particular illness. The administration of his office is complicated by the necessity to handle each transaction.

Greenberg sees the fee-for-service method as a form of piecework renumeration rendered obsolete by fundamental changes in the character and cost of health services.[31] Because of the continued control of medical care by the suppliers of services, he cites the potentialities for abuse. Needless services and subversion of the coordination among specialists are promoted by excessive individualism. Voluntary insurance plans cover hospitalization rather than outpatient services; therefore, limitation of insurance protection to catastrophic illness provides greater assurance to the physician that his fee will be paid if his patient is hospitalized.

A key advantage of the retainer method is that the physician is given an economic inducement to keep his client well and to practice preventive medicine. Medical societies have opposed prepayment plans which put physicians on salary, contending that this arrangement degrades the physician and undermines the physician-patient relationship. They have denied society membership and hospital appointments to doctors participating in group plans.[32]

Critics charge that governmental medical service overworks the general practitioner, involves him in excessive paper work, encourages patients to demand care for trivial ailments, and generates a patient load beyond the possibility of proper care. In response, Gemmill reports that British physicians have found the greater paper work largely counterbalanced by the virtual disappearance of the billing of their private patients. Establishment of partnerships has reduced the work burden, provided regular time off, and permitted economical use of office staff. The issue of care for trivial complaints is complicated by the difficulty of determining—short of a medical examination—what is a trivial ailment. Gemmill concludes that if anyone is receiving inadequate care under the British National Health Service, it is not the seriously ill.[33]

[31] Selig Greenberg, *The Troubled Calling: Crisis in the Medical Establishment* (New York: Macmillan Co., 1965), pp. 18–19.

[32] Richmond, *Currents in American Medicine,* pp. 55–59.

[33] Paul F. Gemmill, *Britain's Search for Health* (Philadelphia: University of Pennsylvania Press, 1960), pp. 49–62.

CHANGES IN CONTEXT OF PRACTICE

Medicine is a profession chasing its own tail, says a medical school professor. Magraw finds medicine in a state of internal confusion and uncertainty in terms of patterns of medical care and in the roles of the professions involved in providing that care. Expanded knowledge and more complicated technology has given medicine unprecedented effectiveness, but it has also meant unprecedented specialization. In 1931 only 17 percent of U.S. physicians in private practice were full-time specialists, but by 1964 the figure had risen to 61 percent. The continuing expansion of knowledge requires doctors to avoid obsolescence through constant study. No longer is the typical physician engaged in solo practice predominately in his own office or in the patient's home. New "ancillary personnel" have appeared to make medicine a team effort. The hospital has become the dominant site for treatment, and between the patient and the physician new "third parties" have emerged in efforts to meet the financial burdens of major illness.[34]

Effects of specialization

Medical research has developed specialization in anatomy, physiology, cellular pathology, bacteriology, endocrinology, biochemistry, and brain surgery. Concurrently, medical practice has developed an increasing range of specialties among physicians, technicians, managers, and assorted paramedical occupations. The traditional medical team—physician, nurse, and laboratory technician—is frequently supplemented by the speech pathologist, engineer, psychologist, biostatistician, and so on. Medical school graduates are moving progressively toward specialization to gain the personal benefits of regular hours, greater income, prestige, and means of keeping current with a reasonable proportion of the avalanche of medical literature. With greater prevalence of specialization, affiliation with a hospital is essential if the physician is to have access to the more sophisticated medical technology and is to fit his specialized talents into a constellation of specialties.[35]

The structure of the delivery system has been profoundly affected by factors associated with specialization. The typical site of diagnosis and treatment has been shifted away from the patient's home to the physician's office and, increasingly, to the hospital, where a team of specialists is mobilized appropriately for the particular illness episode. The efficiency of medicine stems from the mobilization of an appropriate set of specialists to a succession of patients who share a need for particular services. The

---

[34] Richard M. Macgraw, *Ferment in Medicine* (Philadelphia: W. B. Saunders Company, 1966), pp. 1–6.
[35] Somers and Somers, *Doctors, Patients, and Health Insurance,* pp. 27–31.

patient is unlikely to have persistent association with his saviors in a serious crisis—he may not even know their names.

New relationships with patients

With his little black bag and kindly manner, the old family doctor was both healer and counselor. His bag was sufficient to contain the rather slender supply of instruments and drugs he had against illness and death. Although his resources were few, his close and persistent contact with many of his patients provided him with knowledge of them as total human beings and means of engendering their confidence and trust. As one of the consequences of many changes in the organization of medical practice, the central figures today have come to be highly trained medical specialists surrounded by the complex and expensive equipment of the hospital. The physician's relationships with his patients are undergoing significant changes.

Training for greater technical capacity tends to lead physicians to see medicine as exclusively a response to physical ailments. Heavy patient loads and pressures of time divert their attention from the supportive functions the mythical family doctor provided for his patients through a congenial "bedside manner." The fee-for-service method of remuneration, furthermore, makes it to the doctor's advantage to direct his attention to the ailment, with minimal recognition that a personality is linked with the body he is treating.

Extensive specialization has fragmented the patient in the sense that the response to his medical problem is diffused among specialists, with more attention devoted to the physical disorder than to the whole man. The emotional support and understanding provided by the family physician have been lost to an important degree. The patient may be left as his own diagnostician to decide what specialist to consult. He may seek out a pharmacist, or friend, or he may go to a hospital emergency room in lieu of consulting a family physician.

Persistence of an image

In spite of the growing formality and brevity of physician-patient relationships, the image of the physician continues to be charged with the ideas of solo practice and intimate relationships with his patients. The growing discontent of many physicians and patients can be attributed in part to the discrepancy between this image and the facts of the relationship. Why does this image persist?

In his busy practice, the physician confronts illness and disability in great specificity, as does the patient. The physician is likely to see the practice of medicine as a highly personal transaction in which his freedom to fit decisions to the patient's particular needs is paramount. In addition to the technical competence he brings to the disease crisis, the physician has a great treatment resource in the faith the patient places in him, a man personally and technically capable of safeguarding health and life in ways mysterious to the patient. The physician has a charismatic authority which stems from this faith.

Along with social workers, lawyers, and other supportive professionals, physicians have been pressed to meet the emotional needs of individuals who have lost much of the psychological support formerly provided by the family, church, and neighborhood. Today, with urban life mobile and anonymous, the physician is expected (beyond treatment of disease) to assist in dealing with psychosocial problems.[36] This demand is highly likely to be frustrated by the increased bureaucratization and fragmentation of medical care. The physician's specialization and the emphasis on his productivity shorten the duration of treatment and, thereby, his opportunity for contact with the patient.

From the perspective of the professional organizations of medicine, the image of the solo and friendly physician is an asset in power struggles over medical care. The image of selfless service to one's neighbors in solo practice stands in sharp contrast with the assumed cynicism of paid employees of a "soulless" organization. Presented as independent of any organization, the physician is supposed to be free of any obligations other than to the interests of his clients and the ethics of his profession.

Intervention by third parties

One of the fundamental changes in medical practice has been the increased involvement of "third parties." [37] Here, "third party" refers to the intervention into medical care issues of governmental agencies, labor unions, industrial enterprises, health cooperatives, and similar social institutions. The dominance of the medical profession over health care is challenged by these countervailing forces, and organized medicine resents the intervention as highly undesirable and dangerous to medical care. However, the increased involvement of third parties has come with the growing discontent with medical services, the scale of resources necessary to be mobilized for correcting deficiencies, and the overlapping of medical problems with other social problems. Too, labor unions and the federal government have become important third parties as purchasers of medical care.

Medicine is increasingly involved in third party relationships with other social institutions which are also concerned with a wide range of social problems associated with medical care.[38] Population problems, for in-

[36] Mechanic, "Changing Structure of Medical Practice," p. 712.
[37] Somers and Somers, *Doctors, Patients, and Health Insurance*, pp. 228–38.
[38] E. Blythe Stason, "The Role of Law in Medical Progress," *Law and Contemporary Problems*, Vol. 32 (Autumn 1967), pp. 565–67.

stance, involve physicians in the value-charged issues of family planning, birth control, artificial insemination, premarital genetic testing and counseling as a safeguard against birth defects, and abortion. Legal issues abound in homotransplantation (a part of one human body is removed and implanted in another). Medical research raises moral and legal issues concerning the use of human beings for experimentation. The complexity of modern medical techniques aggravates the problem of obtaining patient consent to therapy. In a highly mobile society the possibility of malpractice suits is a formidable deterrent to medical assistance for victims of automobile accidents or similar emergencies observed by a passing physician. (In 32 of our 50 states "good samaritan" laws provide legal protection to physicians in such situations.)

With the recent trend to define alcohol and drug addiction as diseases, physicians have been thrust into the difficulties of framing treatment programs in the face of persistent beliefs that addicts should be subject to the stigmatization and penalties of the criminal law. Here medicine becomes a participant in organizational responses to social deviance involving reshaping of public attitudes and modifying the structure of traditional societal responses to the deviant. This new necessity to participate with third parties in complex organizations is further illustrated by the development of Medicare and other large-scale programs intended to extend medical services to the underprivileged.

The medical organizations hold great power because of their effective discipline over members, unity of occupational sentiment, relative scarcity of medical personnel in face of greater utilization of medical services, and the high economic returns available to practitioners under fee-for-service and private entrepreneurial traditions. Changes in the structure of medical practice, Mechanic believes, have created special interest groups among medical specialities to reduce the solidarity of the medical professions, however. Interpreting the experiences of Great Britain, Mechanic argues that continued unconstructive opposition to government efforts to reform medical care will delay programs of change in the short run but will reduce the influence of organized medicine on the final solution.[39]

Medicare and Medicaid

The power of the medical community and the relative shortage of medical personnel explain the extreme caution that has been used in introducing new government programs. The struggle to enact Medicare legislation is an example of how this power has been used in opposition to legislation supposed to improve the quality of medical care.[40] *Medicare*

---

[39] Mechanic, "Changing Structure of Medical Practice," pp. 720, 723.
[40] For description of the legislative history of Medicare, including the opposition of the American Medical Association, see; Eugene Feingold, *Medicare: Policy and Politics* (San Francisco: Chandler Publishing Company, 1966), pp. 96–155; Max J. Skidmore, *Medicare*

legislation in 1965 provided protection for every person 65 and over without changing the traditional delivery system. *Medicaid* refers to provision of federal matching funds to states for medical care of the "medically indigent."

Although making possible care for more people, Medicare did not lift the financial burden from those persons unable to pay. The various services available under Medicare were only partially covered because of limitations set by deductible provisions and requirements that participants contribute to costs, and these deductible features work against prevention and early diagnosis. By accepting direct billing to the patient and permitting 80 percent of "reasonable" fees, the government has added to the average income of physicians while preserving the fee-for-service method.[41]

Medicare initially was bitterly opposed by the medical profession. Just before passage, there was talk of a "boycott" by physicians. Colombotos studied the changes in attitudes of physicians toward the provisions of Medicare for hospitalization of the elderly. By comparing attitudes at various points on a continuum of time from before to after the passage of the law, he found a progressively more favorable attitude toward these provisions with the passage of time.[42] In contrast, opposition to Medicaid persisted because physicians saw it as a "welfare" approach departing from the financing of medical care through insurance. Colombotos points out that Medicare is based on the insurance principle without controlling physicians' fees. In contrast, New York's version of Medicaid was particularly liberal among the state programs in attempting to control the quality of medical care through limiting free choice of physician and using fixed fees to hold down costs.

IMPACT ON THE HOSPITAL

The general hospital has become the focal point of medical care as it has changed from a custodial institution to a complex multipurpose institution. The transfer of the site of much medical care from the patient's home to the hospital is in response to the need for a physical setting where the miraculous devices of modern medicine can be mobilized. No longer do most people fear the hospital as a place where patients wait to die. Not only do the nuclear family and the smaller household have difficulty in caring for the bedridden patient, but the physician prefers the hospital in order to save his time and to promote his personal and professional con-

---

and the American Rhetoric of Reconciliation (University, Ala.: Univerity of Alabama Press, 1970); and Richard Harris, *A Sacred Trust* (Baltimore: Penguin Books, 1969).

[41] Theodore R. Marmor, "Why Medicare Helped Raise Doctors' Fees," *Trans-action,* Vol. 5 (September 1968), pp. 14–19.

[42] John Colombotos, "Physicians and Medicare: A Before-After Study of the Effects of Legislation on Attitudes," *American Sociological Review,* Vol. 34 (June 1969), pp. 318–34.

venience. In 1970 more than 28 million Americans (one out of seven) entered one of the country's 5,820 general hospitals. These hospitals' clinics and emergency wards handled 120 million outpatient visits. Overall, hospitals receive more than 40 cents out of every dollar spent on health care.[43]

Clinics and emergency wards

As evidence of the public's greater acceptance of the hospital as a place for treatment rather than death, there is growing use of hospital emergency rooms as a primary source of medical care. Macgraw reports on reasons found in studies.[44] Physicians there are on call at all times, whereas regular doctors require appointments during office hours. Mobile families are less dependent on house calls and may require medical assistance before they have established contact with a physician. Because their doctors may limit responsibility for their care, patients may take minor problems elsewhere. Hospital emergency fees may be lower than those of the physician. Diagnostic facilities and personnel are available in the hospital.

Between 1950 and 1965 inpatient admission rate rose 25 percent, but outpatient visits increased 40 percent in spite of lack of conscious planning by hospital authorities, great financial obstacles, and opposition by the medical profession. This remarkable increase in the use of clinics and emergency wards has been explained as a demand for instant care at the convenience of the patient rather than the physician. The emergency room enables the public to elude the professional "gatekeepers" against "improper" use of hospital services and to get around the private doctors who safeguard their own time through scheduled office hours.[45]

Traditionally, hospital ambulatory services have been identified with charity care of the urban poor and provision of cases for training medical personnel. In spite of the growing and new kind of demand for ambulatory services, dramatic differences persist in the quality of care offered by inpatient and outpatient facilities. General medical clinics have been described as a "grab bag of members of the private and house staffs, with assembly-line treatment and little personal relationship between doctors and patients." [46]

Lower-income groups depend largely on public clinics for more impersonal, episodic, and fragmented care in which treatment seldom goes beyond management of a specific symptom or complaint. The impersonal and bureaucratic structure of the clinic works against the psychological support the middle-class patient receives from the personal interven-

[43] Greenberg, *The Quality of Mercy,* p. xiii.
[44] Macgraw, *Ferment in Medicine,* p. 94.
[45] Herman M. Somers and Anne R. Somers, *Medicare and the Hospitals: Issues and Prospects* (Washington, D.C.: Brookings Institution, 1967), pp. 47, 72–73.
[46] Greenberg, *The Quality of Mercy,* p. 67.

tion of the family physician in the problem situation surrounding the illness.

Roth describes the negative attitudes of the staff of emergency clinics, where many of the poor receive unscheduled service. New clerks, aides, nurses, and doctors are indoctrinated to tolerate no "abuse" or "disobedience" from a clientele largely conceived of as "garbage." The patient waits until the staff gets around to him, is made to stand, even if ill or aged, while questioned, and is instructed peremptorily about rules and procedures: "Sit down over there!" "Put out that cigarette!" "You can't go back there!" He is questioned on matters regarded as private by middle-class standards: "Are you on welfare?" "Is there a father in the home?" "Are you able to pay for this visit?" [47]

Administrative issues

The dimensions of medical care problems are linked with the nature of the general hospital. The hospital has been intimately associated with developments in medical care which have received intense criticism: rising costs, increasing specialization of practice, and increasing bureaucratic impersonality in relationships of patients with physicians. The hospital is the refuge for the patient and the workshop of the physician—but it also is an educational center for medical personnel, a research facility, and a community health center.

To whom does the hospital belong? The trustees, who largely represent the philanthropists who supported hospitals in the past? The physicians, who employ it as their workshop? The community served by the hospital as a health center? The funding agencies external to the local community which are becoming increasingly important to the financial support and regional coordination of services? Or the hospital administrators charged with keeping this complicated operation in some kind of order?

The difficulties of administrating these diverse and sometimes conflicting activities are further complicated by the "guest" status of two vital groups. The patients provide the major share of a hospital's income, but they have little influence over its operations. As the other "guest" category, physicians use this expensive workshop—which is supported financially by others. As fiercely independent professionals controlling expert knowledge, a constantly changing group of physicians are the mavericks who complicate the work of the constantly present but less prestigious administrators.

Without a competent medical staff, the hospital is a hotel for sick people, but even the best hospital must furnish the services offered routinely by a large hotel populated by successive waves of transients.[48]

[47] Julius A. Roth, "The Treatment of the Sick," in Kosa, Antonovsky, and Zola, *Poverty and Health,* pp. 216–33.
[48] Wilson, "Social Structure of a General Hospital," p. 71.

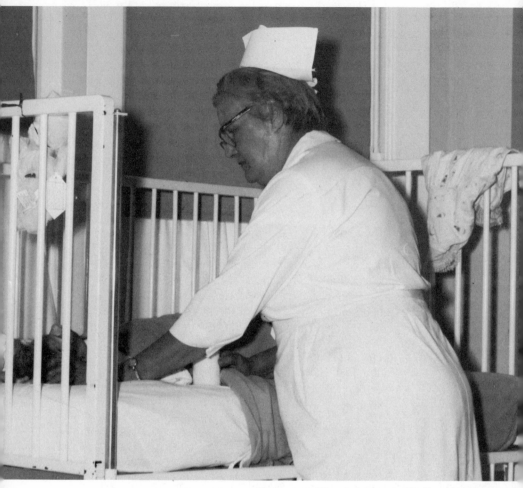

Wisconsin Department of Health and Social Services

Can a bureaucracy sustain tender, loving care? The increased capacity of medicine to forestall death has brought greater demand for its services and changed the context of its practice, with the general hospital now the focal point of medical care. An important issue is whether administrative efficiency can be achieved without losing sight of the anxieties of the patient.

Dependent on the hospital for the facilities he must have, the physician encounters here pressures to reshape his professional role from that of the independent entrepreneur in solo practice to the role of participant in a highly organized team effort coordinated through disciplining of individual specialists within a bureaucratic framework.

Problem of depersonalization

The relative concentration of treatment in the hospital has made it the focus of the problem of depersonalization of medical care, because it is in the hospital that the patient's need for supportive responses during the illness crisis collides most obviously with the impersonality of the medical bureaucracy. Here we see in accentuated form the conflict between the subjective illness perspective of the patient and the objective disease perspective of the medical practitioner. When the efficiency of the hospital staff and its technology are given virtually exclusive priority, the patient is subjected to the environment of a "human warehouse." [49]

The patient confronts an alien environment while subject to pain, apprehension, anxiety, and fear as shaped by the definitions of his particular subgroup. The behavior of the inhabitants of this strange environment differs markedly from those of his family. His new status as patient raises problems of adjustment. Admission to the hospital strips him of his identity. He is no longer an individual with accomplishments in the world outside, but only the occupant of Room 34. He becomes a body between sheets to be moved, inspected, and injected. The familiar environment of his home and family is replaced by a strange world inhabited by unfamiliar people engaged in unfamiliar activities. His care involves the appearance of different staff persons who perform sharply circumscribed tasks and then withdraw. Inadvertently he may not be told of their experiences during and after treatment because the staff assumes he already knows what they know. His complaints about a cold meal or noise in the corridor may be dismissed by personnel with many tasks to perform. [50]

Prolonged hospitalization exposes the chronically sick and aged poor to what Henry calls *depersonalization,* the process of depriving an individual of the factors that attach him to his social system. [51] Unable to care for themselves, they are sent to an institution with low budgetary allocations per patient in which respect for the individual as a unique

---

[49] The concept of "human warehouse" is applied to the custodial prison in Chapter 17, pp. 439–42.

[50] Esther Lucille Brown, "Meeting Patient's Psychosocial Needs in the General Hospital," *Annals of American Academy of Political and Social Science,* Vol. 346 (March 1963), pp. 117–25.

[51] Jules Henry, "Personality and Aged with Special Reference to Hospitals for the Aged Poor," in John C. McKinney and Frank T. de Vyver (eds.), *Aging and Social Policy* (New York: Appleton-Century-Crofts, 1966), pp. 281–97; also see: Julius A. Roth, "The Public Hospital: Refuge for Damaged Humans," *Trans-action,* Vol. 3 (July–August 1966), pp. 25–29.

personality is undermined by a number of mechanisms. Symbolic means involve handling of his body as though it were an inanimate object and talking about him in his presence as though he were not there. Personal shame is attacked through exposure of private areas of the body and exposure to experiences usually associated with disgust, such as lying in excreta. Routinization of daily life deprives him of individuality of habit in eating, dress, making beds, and even taking medication. Protection is lost against pilfering, changes in temperature, and even unsanitary conditions. Prevention of disturbances among patients suppresses their inclination to assert their personal wishes. Finally, the comfort and convenience of the staff is likely to overshadow the interests of patients.

NEED FOR COORDINATION

The complexity of health and medical care services has raised formidable problems in organizing and coordinating a wide variety of specialists and social institutions. Earlier in the century, the physician in solo practice could handle the medical care available to his community. Now even the physician is more likely to work with others in some form of association, partnership, or group practice. A network of public health agencies at all levels of government has developed to provide preventive services, training, public education, and research. Voluntary health agencies range from groups concentrating on specific diseases or health problems to fund raising. Major systems of health insurance, medical equipment production, and pharmaceutical industries have emerged.

Why the need for coordination?

Increased specialization of services presents difficulties in treating the patient as a total personality rather than simply as the carrier of a disease or disability. The high costs of medical care are attributable in part to duplicated equipment and services. Effectiveness of medical care is weakened by controversies between the free enterprise and public utility models for delivery of services. Our present shortage of medical personnel could be alleviated through coordination of new kinds of subprofessionals to free physicians from more routine tasks.

In the face of these needs for coordination, Ruthstein finds the medical care system is comprised of conflicting and duplicated activities with gaps in service.[52] The location of doctors is only incidentally related to the geographical distribution of medical needs. Community requirements are subordinated in hospital growth to financial resources, interests of medical staff, and pride of the board of trustees. The catch-as-catch-can structure

[52] Ruthstein, *The Coming Revolution in Medicine*, pp. 49–50, 74–76.

of the system reflects the inadequacy of research into its proper dimensions. The vast expansion in hospital facilities, especially under the Hill-Burton program, has kept pace with population growth, improved the quality of their services, and provided better geographical distribution, but Ruthstein cites the waste inherent in the concept that every general hospital should provide every service to every patient. The haphazard distribution and relatively small size of most hospitals results in the wasteful duplication of highly specialized services for relatively few patients.

Coordination of medical services, Ruthstein suggests, calls for the weaving of medical facilities into regions centered around large teaching hospitals affiliated with medical schools.[53] Such a development would be initiated by precise definition of medical needs and an inventory of medical care resources. The central hospital would include facilities for the care of a spectrum of chronic diseases. A mental disease unit would be accessible to patients, their families, and their physicians. All of the physicians on the central staff would comprise a group practice unit providing ambulatory care in offices on the hospital grounds, impatient treatment in hospital wards, and quick access to specialists. The gap in preventive services would be filled by units located at the hospital and in community centers at appropriate places in the region. A voluntary health organization would be located at the hospital to lend direction to the present proliferation of individual health agencies.

Efforts to personalize practice

To counter the depersonalizing effects of increasing bureaucratization and specialization of medical practice, various remedial actions have been proposed.

A citizen's commission, sponsored by the American Medical Association, suggests a new role of *primary physician,* serving as first contact for intelligent entry into the medical service system, because the term *family physician* does not properly emphasize training to deal continually with the total personality of the patient within a comprehensive medical care system. The patient brings to the physician problems which have physiological, anatomical, psychological, social, economic, genetic, and other aspects. As gatekeeper to the medical care system, the primary physician would provide a breadth of view to individualize the total response and integrate the set of specialized tasks.[54]

Through specialized graduate training and provision of better connections with hospitals, the general practitioner would be made more qualified and his inferior opportunities for income corrected to entice more physi-

[53] Ruthstein, ibid., pp. 117–32.
[54] "Defining the New Physician," *Saturday Review,* Vol. 50 (January 7, 1967), pp. 122–25.

cians into this area.[55] The curriculums of some medical schools have been "humanized" to advance a conception of comprehensive care as encompassing the patient's emotional and family problems within the totality of his socioeconomic environment.

More promising than either of these strategies is the revision of the institutional setting of medical care to facilitate a coordinated approach to the patient. A broad range of formally organized group practices have emerged whereby the skills of physicians are combined to react to the patient as an entity. Solo practice is being given up by groups of three to several hundred physicians to share physical facilities, income, and responsibility for the same patients. Group practice varies in purpose from one extreme of specialized diagnosis and treatment of a particular disease after referral to the other extreme of comprehensive care of a continuing clientele. Staffs may be full-time or part-time. Some of these new groups are propriety on a fee-for-service basis; others are sponsored by a labor union or health cooperative.

SUMMARY

Medical care is a social enterprise extending beyond the application of techniques by the physician in solo practice. Its social aspects are indicated by the distinction between *disease* and *illness*. As primary human values, preservation of health and overcoming of illness are embedded in the rising concern over social deprivation and inequities in life opportunities. The organization, distribution, and economics of medical care loom large among the social problems of an urban age. The dimensions of the medical care problem involve maldistribution of services, inadequate supply of personnel, and rising costs. These dimensions are related to paradoxes in an age of unprecedented medical care efficiency and rising dissatisfactions with the characteristics of its delivery system. These paradoxes are products of fundamental changes in the context of medical practice because of expanded specialization of techniques, greater complexity of medical care institutions, and their exposure to the dehumanizing influences of bureaucratization. The study of medical care again provides evidence of the profound effects of urbanization and technological change on the strategies employed to meet human needs.

FOR ADDITIONAL READING

Robert J. Bazell, "Health Radicals: Crusade to Shift Medical Power to the People," *Science,* Vol. 173 (August 6, 1971), pp. 506–9.

[55] Somers and Somers, *Doctors, Patients, and Health Insurance,* pp. 37–41.

Ann Cartwright, *Patients and Their Doctors* (New York: Atherton Press, 1967).

Matt Clark, "Miracles and Mishaps: Closing the Quality Gap," *Atlantic,* Vol. 218 (July 1966), pp. 88–94.

Stephen M. Creel, "Our Backward Medical Schools," *Atlantic,* Volume 217 (May 1966), pp. 46–50.

Raymond S. Duff and August B. Hollingshead, *Sickness and Society* (New York: Harper & Row, 1968).

Eliot Friedson, *Profession of Medicine: A Study of the Sociology of Applied Knowledge* (New York: Dodd, Mead and Co., 1970).

John Fry, *Medicine in Three Societies: A Comparison of Medical Care in the U.S.S.R., U.S.A. and U.K.* (New York: American Elsevier Publishing Company, 1970).

E. Gartley Jaco (ed.), *Patients, Physicians and Illness* (Glencoe, Ill.: Free Press, 1958).

David Mechanic, *Medical Sociology* (New York: Free Press of Glencoe, 1968).

Emily Mumford· and J. K. Skipper, Jr., *Sociology in Hospital Care* (New York: Harper & Row, 1967).

Talcott Parsons, "Social Change and Medical Organization in the United States: A Sociological Perspective," *Annals of American Academy of Political and Social Science,* Volume 346 (March 1963), pp. 21–33.

Marion K. Sanders (ed.), *The Crisis in American Medicine* (New York: Harper & Brothers, 1961).

W. Richard Scott and Edmund H. Volkart (eds.), *Medical Care: Readings in the Sociology of Medical Institutions* (New York: John Wiley and Sons, 1966).

Anselm L. Strauss, "Medical Ghettos," *Trans-action,* Vol. 4 (May 1967), pp. 7–15, 62.

Roul Tunley, "America's Unhealthy Children—An Emerging Scandal," *Harper's,* Vol. 232 (May 1966), pp. 41–46.

Glenn M. Vernon, *Sociology of Death* (New York: Ronald Press, 1970).

Irving Kenneth Zola, "Culture and Symptoms—An Analysis of Patients' Presenting Complaints," *American Sociological Review,* Vol. 31 (October 1966), pp. 615–30.

19 Mental illness as a social problem

In his 1963 message to Congress, President John F. Kennedy outlined the dimensions of the country's "most critical health problems," mental illness and mental retardation. He described the peculiar public toleration of the heavy anguish imposed on mentally ill persons and their families, and referred to the inadequacies of social arrangements for care of the mentally ill. In both respects his message is an appropriate introduction to our examination of the "insanities" of society's typical responses to mental disorder. In part, President Kennedy said:

> Mental illness and mental retardation . . . occur more frequently, affect more people, require more prolonged treatment, cause more suffering by the families of the afflicted, waste more of our human resources, and constitute more financial drain upon both the Public Treasury and the personal finances of the individual families than any other single condition.
>
> There are now about 800,000 such patients in this Nation's institutions—600,000 for mental illness and over 200,000 for mental retardation. Every year nearly 1,500,000 people receive treatment in institutions for the mentally ill and mentally retarded. Most of them are confined and compressed within an antiquated, vastly overcrowded, chain of custodial State institutions. The average amount expended on their care is only $4 a day—too little to do much good for the individual, but too much is measured in terms of efficient use of our mental health dollars. In some States the average is less than $2 a day.
>
> The total cost to the taxpayers is over $2.4 billion a year in direct public outlays for services—about $1.8 billion for mental illness and $600 million for mental retardation. Indirect public outlays, in welfare costs and in the waste of human resources, are even higher. But the anguish suffered both by those afflicted and

by their families transcends financial statistics—particularly in view of the fact that both mental illness and mental retardation strike so often in childhood, leading in most cases to a lifetime of disablement for the patient and a lifetime of hardship for his family.

This situation has been tolerated far too long. It has troubled our national conscience—but only as a problem unpleasant to mention, easy to postpone, and despairing of solution. The Federal Government, despite the nationwide impact of the problem, has largely left the solutions up to the States. The States have depended on custodial hospitals and homes. Many such hospitals and homes have been shamefully understaffed, overcrowded, unpleasant institutions from which death too often provided the only firm hope of release.[1]

IMPLICATIONS FOR URBAN SOCIETY

As one of the major examples of personal disorganization, mental illness has a particular potential for disrupting social relationships within the delicately balanced and complex urban society. Mental illness is especially difficult for any group to handle because such behavior defies usual logic or conventional modes of understanding. Its social impact is aggravated when the individual is more visible and his role performance more essential in a densely populated and socially complex urban social system compared with a rural setting. The impact varies, of course, according to the degree of threat to tranquility and social order his unusual behavior and his departure from expectations constitute. Violent behavior stirs greater concern than passive withdrawal from social intercourse. Mental illness of the breadwinner has special impact on his dependents, and incapacitation of the business executive or political leader exacts heavy costs on the organizations they are expected to direct. The departures from social expectations of mentally ill persons jar the predictability of behavior essential to the blending of individual behaviors into a social concert.

Psychological and economic costs

As President Kennedy noted, mental illness exacts a heavy toll of suffering on patients and their families. In addition, the burden for both individuals and society is made even heavier through its involvement in the fabric of society. Research of recent decades has revealed, Clausen says, that "the relationship between social factors and mental illness is vastly more complex than most of us had assumed."[2] Mental illness differs from physical illness, Carstairs declares, in its intimate dependence on social

[1] Message to the 88th Congress, 1st. Sess., House of Representatives, Document No. 58, February 5, 1963.
[2] John A. Clausen, "The Sociology of Mental Illness," in Robert K. Merton, Leonard Broom, and Leonard S. Cottrell, Jr., (eds.), *Sociology Today: Problems and Prospects* (New York: Basic Books, 1959), p. 487.

factors and because the sane also share many of the symptoms of insanity. The very definition of a person as a psychiatric case involves the attitude of other persons in his environment that his behavior is intolerable.[3]

Mental illness has great impact on the economy because it removes workers from the production of goods and services and because their care imposes financial costs. One valiant attempt to estimate these costs estimated the expenditures by government, philanthropic organizations, and individuals on the care, cure, and prevention of mental illness in 1956 at $1.7 billion. Even this high figure fails to include such elusive costs as capital construction and depreciation of hospital buildings, specialized medical care of patients with psychological complaints, and private psychiatric care. Another $700 million at the very minimum was added to the estimate for loss in production by reason of the denial to the economy of the labor of the mentally ill.[4]

Society and management of tensions

Psychological discomfort is inevitable to some degree in every society because the stress placed on individuals reflects the demands that they perform their roles for the sake of the effective functioning of society. Soldiers are expected to place duty before their personal interests. Competition for academic excellence and production of competent graduates expose university students to the frustration of failure. By keeping achieved rewards below the level of aspiration, workers are supposed to be motivated to effective labor.

Usually societies provide for management of tensions to minimize conflict between the interests of individuals and the interests of the group. Frustration may be forestalled by socializing the young to identify their own interests with the adult roles they will enter. The social institutions may provide roles to ease the tensions created by other roles. For example, the patriarchal father maintains his authority by remaining aloof from his children, but the tensions inherent in this situation are given relief through the love functions of the mother.[5]

Rituals also may ease tensions attending characteristic crises. Funeral customs cushion the shock of loss of a loved one, distract the bereaved person by requiring observance of the passage of the loved one into the heavenly community, permit the expression of sorrow, and provide the embalmer's "memory-image" to offset the reality of death.[6] For relief of tensions in general, religious practices may reassure the frustrated person

[3] G. M. Carstairs, "The Social Limits of Eccentricity: An English Study," in Marvin K. Opler (ed.), *Culture and Mental Health* (New York: Macmillan Co., 1959), p. 377.

[4] Rashi Fein, *Economics of Mental Illness* (New York: Basic Books, 1958).

[5] Charles P. Loomis, *Social Systems* (New York: D. Van Nostrand, 1960), pp. 70–71.

[6] Thomas D. Eliot, "Bereavement: Inevitable But Not Insurmountable," in Howard Becker and Reuben Hill (eds.), *Family, Marriage and Parenthood* (Boston: D. C. Heath, 1948), pp. 657–58.

that a better life lies in the hereafter. Another means is provision of special holidays when individuals are permitted to "break loose" from their usual role demands.

The social structure of a particular society may provide shelter for its eccentric, vulnerable, and disturbed members. In the Middle Ages, religious communities served this purpose. The "tramp" and "hobo" have represented more or less organized vagrancy which is tolerated when laws are not openly flaunted. Village life provides shelter and even employment within their limitations for some individuals not regarded as fully responsible. In cities a few eccentrics are able to contribute their special talents within the shelter of universities and the other social institutions of the arts and sciences.[7]

Consciously designed institutions for the mentally ill include day hospitals, halfway houses, sheltered workshops, and ex-patient organizations to provide easier transition into community life.

Urban life and tensions

Frequently, urban life is seen as particularly conducive to mental disorder because of social complexity, impersonality, anonymity, and a high rate of social change. As discussed earlier, the size and density of urban populations color the way people behave toward one another.[8] The sense of personal identity can be weakened in the urban environment, inhabited as it is largely by persons with whom one does not have lasting or intimate associations. The individual may experience a sense of powerlessness in affecting the events impinging upon him from within large-scale organizations, and in a social order characterized by a heterogeneous population and diversity in behavioral codes, his capacity to make moral judgments may be overstrained when the cultural norms contradict one another.

Earlier we noted that the advanced technology of our society has raised problems of effective use of leisure time and substitution of some new form of motivation for the work ethic. Other sources of tension have been created as by-products of technological triumphs: the monotony of repetitive work, restriction of tasks to the narrow confines of one's work function within an intricate division of labor, rapid obsolescence of job skills, vulnerability to unemployment because of events outside the sphere of the individual's direct observation, and difficulty in relating one's own narrow activities to the achievement of some ultimate purpose.[9]

The relationship between social change and mental disorder has been explained through the concept of *anomie*, the central thesis of which is that rapid social change undermines the cohesiveness of society by bring-

[7] Kenneth Soddy (ed.), *Cross-Cultural Studies in Mental Health: Identity-Mental Health and Value Systems* (Chicago: Quadrangle Books, 1962), pp. 97–99.

[8] See Chapter 3, pp. 68–74.

[9] See Chapter 4; pp. 101–4, and Chapter 11, pp. 276–79.

ing traditional norms into question.[10] The individual is caught by the contradictions between what the norms tell him is the proper way to behave and the realities he encounters in social situations. From a general impression that his world is without any meaningful rules, the individual is more likely to become confused and engage in bizarre behavior. Such contradictions may have differing impacts on persons in various social positions (sex, age, occupation, etc.). Accordingly, the strains resulting from anomie will vary in different types of social structures.

Modern society produces alienated individuals who become candidates for deviancy including mental illness. However, Rose says, there is no reason to believe that our society produces more stresses than other societies, and there is no evidence that our society produces more mental illness.[11] The earlier "simpler" societies are commonly regarded as carefree, but Eaton and Weil found otherwise when they examined the prevalence of mental disorder among the Hutterites, an isolated religious sect in Canada. Psychoses and other forms of mental disorder occur with regularity among them in spite of their relatively uncomplicated way of life. The Hutterite was pressed to live up to rather austere standards.[12] Similarly, caught in the stresses of the industrial revolution a century ago, Massachussets in 1885 had about the same rate of first admissions to mental hospitals for patients less than 50 years of age as in 1940. Furthermore, the earlier period had a greater proportion of patients with severe derangement.[13]

The relationship between mental illness and urban conditions is complicated by the great variability among individuals in what they experience as stress. What constitutes a stressful situation for one person, may be taken in stride by another.[14] A host of factors are involved as sources of stress and frustration as interpreted by the individual. In relationships with other persons, every event of the day has a possibility of frustration. The significance of a given event is likely to be affected by the age, sex, race, occupation, prestige level, and other statuses occupied by the individual. Shaped by his previous experiences, the personal needs of the individual are brought to the event to affect its meaning to him.

After reviewing a number of studies on the relationship between social change and mental health, Fried concludes that mental health inheres in the relationship between the individual and his immediate environment— not solely in the individual. Individual needs and goals are fulfilled or

[10] See Chapter 2, pp. 48–51.

[11] Arnold M. Rose, "Sociological Studies on Mental Health and Mental Disorder," *International Social Science Journal,* Vol. 20, No. 2 (1968), p. 278.

[12] Joseph W. Eaton and Robert J. Weil, *Culture and Personality Disorders* (Glencoe, Ill.: Free Press, 1955), pp. 209–10.

[13] Herbert Goldhamer and Andrew Marshall, *Psychoses and Civilization* (Glencoe,, Ill.: Free Press, 1953), pp. 91–97.

[14] Louis P. Thorpe, Barney Katz, and Robert T. Lewis, *The Psychology of Abnormal Behavior: A Dynamic Approach* (New York: Ronald Press Company, 1961), p. 61.

frustrated by the reciprocal patterns of interpersonal relations within roles. Emotional disturbance and major mental disorders are associated with failure to handle conflicts acceptably, withdrawal from social relations, marital difficulties, and so on. Collectively, these signs of mental illness can represent the impact of social change in creating social disorganization.[15]

Fried sees this social disorganization as the consequence of the simultaneous failure of individuals to adapt psychologically to the new circumstances wrought by social change and the failure of the individual's environment to provide him resources for adaptation. The individual may lack sufficient internal resources to cope with crises raised by migration, technological unemployment, disruption of family life, and so on. External resources may make up for overstrained internal resources through guidance, education, formal controls, and provision of alternatives to familiar but now outmoded ways of meeting personal needs. External resources will be insufficient for some individuals who, lacking capacity for readjustment to new conditions, experience intolerable frustration. However, despite the disturbing effects of change in urban life, there is a wide range of alternative methods for coping with these effects, especially when the external environment provides means for effective adaptation.

FUNCTIONAL DISORDERS

Psychiatrists employ a classification of diagnostic groups to categorize patients. Some psychiatrists see these labels as denoting different disease conditions, while others see the labels as describing patterns found among patients in reacting to stress, rather than denoting disease. This difference in perspective raises issues over whether the "disease model" or the "psychosocial model" is most valid in defining mental illness and in mobilizing treatment.

Broad categorization of disorders

The diversity and range of psychiatric classifications are beyond the scope of our discussion here. Because our interest is in mental illness as a social problem, delineation of the general nature of three classifications should provide a basis for consideration of the social implications of the alternative models of mental illness. At the highest level of abstraction, the American Psychiatric Association[16] distinguishes between:

1. Those conditions associated with impairment of brain tissue. In these

[15] Marc Fried, "Effects of Social Change on Mental Health," *American Journal of Orthopsychiatry*, Vol. 34 (January 1964), pp. 3–28.

[16] Committee on Nomenclature and Statistics, *Diagnostic and Statistical Manual: Mental Disorders* (Washington, D.C.: American Psychiatric Association, 1952).

organic disorders mental disturbances are attributed to injury to the central nervous system because of high fevers, nutritional deficiencies, drug intoxication, brain tumors, or accidents. Infectious diseases include paresis (from syphilis), epidemic encephalitis, epidemic cerebrospinal meningitis, and senile brain disease.

2. Mental deficiency.

3. Disorders without clearly defined clinical cause. In the absence of known organic sources, these conditions are called *functional disorders* in that they appear to express psychogenic causes related to social experiences in the early life of the individual. This chapter centers attention on the functional disorders, where the influence of social factors is most apparent.

In functional disorders psychological and sociological factors converge and become interdependent. The individual aspires and behaves, but he also has a particular place in a social structure and has been conditioned to a particular set of cultural beliefs.[17] The social environment shapes the needs, aspirations, and typical responses of the individual as he strives to gain satisfactions through cooperative relationships with other persons. In the course of his personality development, he learns to seek the rewards and possessions to which his culture gives high priority. His self-image is shaped by attitudes others take toward him. Gratification of his wishes to belong and to be accepted as a worthy person is related to his ability to discipline his behavior within a set of social expectations. Social rebuff may aggravate his sense of inadequacy or hostility. His relationships with others may provide him with feelings of security and personal accomplishment. His biological needs, including sex, are transformed into social needs to be appeased through conformity with acceptable ways of gratifying them.

Functional psychoses and psychoneuroses

The American Psychiatric Association further subdivides the functional disorders into: (1) psychotic disorders; (2) psychophysiologic, autonomic, and visceral disorders; (3) psychoneurotic disorders; (4) personality disorders; and (5) transient situational personality disorders. Among these ambiguous subcategories, psychoses and psychoneurotic disorders are most germane to this chapter. The functional psychoses include schizophrenia, manic-depressive disorders, and paranoia. In psychoses the patient manifests severe decompensation (exaggerated and deviant defensive patterns), marked distortion of reality, and loss of contact with reality. The schizophrenic has a strong tendency to retreat from reality. Through delusions and hallucinations, he is likely to exhibit marked disturbances in thought processes. The manic-depressive shows extreme fluctuations in mood with

[17] Marvin K. Opler, *Culture, Psychiatry, and Human Values* (Springfield, Ill.: Charles C Thomas, 1956), pp. 16–17.

related disturbances in thought and behavior. Paranoid disorders involve delusions of persecution and/or grandeur, but the patient otherwise maintains a relative intact personality structure—a fact that may complicate recognition of his mental illness.

Psychoneurotics (also called neurotics) are unhappy and anxious individuals who do not exhibit the gross falsification of external reality and loss of contact with reality found among psychotics. Not requiring hospitalization, psychoneurotics feel basically inadequate, exhibit anxiety, are painfully aware of themselves, but lack insights into the causes of their difficulties in forming satisfying relationships with other persons. Examples of psychoneurotic behavior are diffuse anxieties without a particular threat, lack of enthusiasm, complaints of aches and pains, paralysis, or loss of hearing without organic cause, amnesia or somnambulism, persistent and irrational thoughts and impulses, and prolonged dejection.

DISEASE MODEL OF MENTAL ILLNESS

Described as the "disease model" is a set of beliefs, imported from medicine, that usually is applied to mental illness.[18] Each condition of mental disorder is supposed to be marked by a unique set of observable symptoms. A malign process within the organism is supposed to persist over time to deprive the sick person of control of his behavior. Some pernicious agent—physical, chemical, intrapsychic, genetic, interpersonal, or social—is seen as the source of mental illness. Some kind of therapy is deemed to be essential to alleviation of the "disease."

Mental health as absence of symptoms

From practical considerations the physician treating the physically ill would conceive health as the absence of physical symptoms and pains which would bring patients to him. As a branch of medicine, psychiatry would be prone to extend this idea of absence of symptoms to define "mental health" as a residual category of persons left over after the mentally ill persons are removed.

The conventional view of mental illness emphasizes symptomatology. Mental illness may be defined reliably when grossly observable symptoms are present. In applying symptomatology to identify mentally healthy persons, the clinical professional speaks of the harmonious blending of diverse elements of the mental apparatus. Ideally, the mentally healthy person is supposed to exhibit self-esteem, to be successful in synthesizing what he has done with what he wants to do, to progress in achieving his higher

[18] Merlin Taber, Herbert C. Quay, Harold Mark, and Vicki Nealey, "Disease Ideology and Mental Health Research," *Social Problems,* Vol. 16 (Winter 1969), pp. 349–57.

goals in life, to be independent of the social forces impinging upon him, and to master the problems experienced in the major spheres of love, work, and play.[19]

Difficulties of the disease model

Under the disease model, premises of medical practice have been extended to include mental illness. Application of the disease model to mental illness raises objections. First, mental illness does not produce the clear-cut symptoms whereby organic disease can be diagnosed and treated. Second, mental illness does not produce the identifiable and progressive course of disease.[20] The presence and course of physical disease can be traced frequently through laboratory analysis of body fluids or the functioning of organs. Organic disorders lend themselves to such analysis, but functional disorders involve social relationships of the patient which elude precise laboratory analysis. Increasing doubt has been expressed that some identifiable malign process within the individual produces a distinct set of observable symptoms. The search for a single cause of mental disorder has been a frustrating experience because of the multitude of possible physical, chemical, genetic, intrapsychic, and social sources of a wide variety of mental illnesses.

The crucial test of the disease model, Mechanic believes, is whether a disease theory for a mental condition provides a correct diagnostic decision which leads to correct action. In medicine a diagnosis of pernicious anemic for a patient suffering from tuberculosis does not produce correct action. Similarly, psychiatric diagnosis under the disease model must be reliable and produce a specific treatment for the given disorder. Electroshock therapy appears to be more useful for depressive psychoses than for schizophrenia; furthermore, different psychiatric drugs are appropriate for each of the two forms of psychoses. However, when the disease model yields little useful information, Mechanic says, serious disadvantages ensue. The disease perspective adds a burden of shame to the patient with a relatively mild mental condition. The disease orientation implies a release of the patient from personal responsibility for undertaking corrective effort. Search for a more promising treatment strategy is impeded by an overgeneralized faith in the disease model.[21]

Subject to many vicissitudes, symptoms may remain latent or become obvious under varying circumstances. Coleman distinguishes between the psychiatric symptom and the patient's feeling of distress. He suggests persons seek help because they experience feelings of distress, not be-

[19] The meanings of such criteria of positive mental health are elaborated in Marie Jahoda, *Current Concepts of Positive Mental Health* (New York: Basic Books, 1958), pp. 22–64.
[20] Taber et al, "Disease Ideology," pp. 350–52.
[21] David Mechanic, *Mental Health and Social Policy* (Englewood Cliffs, N.J.: Prentice-Hall, 1969), pp. 18–20.

cause they are disturbed by the symptoms. It is likely that what undergoes spontaneous remission is the state of distress. When the patient feels better, the symptoms tend to recede from his awareness.[22] The person may have feelings of persecution which do not interfere with his functioning until some crisis episode imposes unusual stress, or he may have gross psychiatric symptoms interfering with his interpersonal relations without experiencing distress, or stress in a particular situation may evoke behavior unusual for him without entailing protracted psychiatric disability. A psychiatric examination at that time could exaggerate the significance of temporary symptoms and thereby raise doubts in the individual and his close associates which would make the diagnosis itself a factor in subsequent mental difficulties.

These several possibilities are evidence of the complexity of psychiatric evaluation when there is an absence of gross symptoms. Redlich suggests caution against arbitrarily labeling an individual as psychiatrically abnormal on the basis of symptoms.[23] The motivation for a given act may make it normal; thus one may need to distinguish between a wish for cleanliness and a compulsive washing as an expression of a latent conflict. The context in which the act occurs may render it socially relevant. Wearing swimming trunks on a summer beach is not the equivalent of parading down a New England street similarly clad in a snowstorm.

SOCIAL NORMS AND MENTAL ILLNESS

In the "disease model" a common assumption is that some neurological defect is the basis of all disorders of thinking and behavior. Just as diseases affect other parts of the body, physiochemical maladjustments are supposed to affect the brain to create symptoms of mental disease.

Psychosocial model of mental illness

In advancing several arguments, Szasz objects to this arbitrary equating of mental illness with organic disease.[24] Problems of living associated with deviant beliefs are not attributable solely to defects of the nervous system. Instead of anatomical and genetic factors, mental illness involves the patient's conceptions of himself and his communications with other persons.

---

[22] Jules V. Coleman, "Social Factors Influencing the Development and Containment of Psychiatric Symptoms," in Thomas J. Scheff (ed.), *Mental Illness and Social Processes* (New York: Harper & Row, 1967), pp. 158–67.

[23] Frederick C. Redlich, "The Concept of Health in Psychiatry," in Alexander H. Leighton, John A. Clausen, and Robert W. Wilson (eds.), *Explorations in Social Psychiatry* (New York: Basic Books, 1957), pp. 145–46.

[24] Thomas S. Szasz, "The Myth of Mental Illness," in Stephan P. Spitzer and Norman K. Denzin (eds.) *The Mental Patient: Studies in the Sociology of Deviance* (New York: McGraw-Hill Book Co., 1968), pp. 22–26.

Physical illness is a deviation from normal functioning of the body; mental illness connotes a deviation from social expectations. In this regard, the response to the mentally ill person constitutes an effort to safeguard the rules which lend order and predictability to behavior of individuals and groups.

The "labeling" theorists argue that "deviance is not a property *inherent* in certain forms of behavior; it is a property *conferred* upon these forms by audiences which directly or indirectly witness them."[25] In the study of mental illness, attention is diverted from the behavior of the person evaluated as being mentally ill and toward the processes whereby he comes to be so evaluated.

The candidate for the status of the mentally ill person moves through a series of stages in social interaction with other persons whereby his departure from expectations becomes recognized as qualifying him for that status. His deviant behavior alone does not qualify him; mental illness is a *social* phenomenon in that defining him as a mentally ill person involves evaluation in comparison with the norms of his audience. The chances that a given kind of deviant behavior will be considered mental illness are affected by the degree that his daily activities in the family, work place, or other sites depart from expectations. The chances are increased when his behavior constitutes a visible threat to the interests of others. However, the norms of his particular group also affect the probability that his behavior will be explained as mental illness or be tolerated as merely unusual or "queer."

An important characteristic of the mentally disordered person is his inability to communicate effectively with others. His behavior does not make sense to others. This breakdown in communication can be interpreted from two polar perspectives. Usually, mental illness is attributed to faulty adjustment of the individual with little, if any, recognition given to the possibility of error in the standards whereby his behavior is assessed as "maladjusted." He is among the social deviants who fail to measure up to the mark presumably set by society. From another point of view, attention is diverted from the faults of the individual to the confusion among, or conflict between, the norms against which his behavior is judged.

Residual deviance

The evaluation of a deviant act varies according to the priority given a particular norm and the judgment applied to the deviant himself. The deviant may be seen as merely uncouth or ignorant, as criminal or sexually

---

[25] Kai T. Erickson, "Notes on the Sociology of Deviance," in Howard S. Becker (ed.), *The Other Side: Perspectives on Deviance* (New York: Free Press, 1964), p. 11; also see our Chapter 2, pp. 55–57.

perverted, or as a personally disorganized drunk or drug addict. When he cannot be categorized under one of these familiar lablels, there is what Scheff calls *residual deviance*. When earlier societies could not account otherwise for strange, bizarre, and frightening behavior, they were likely to attribute it to witchcraft or possession by demons. Scheff sees the labeling of such deviants as "mentally ill" to be a contemporary example of residual deviance.[26]

The prevalance of residual deviance is much greater than the number of persons who receive treatment for mental illness. Apparently, Scheff says, many persons are not defined as insane, nor do they conceive of themselves as insane, even though they may hear voices or exhibit other grossly deviant behavior. Their bizarre conduct may be recognized, may be ignored, or may be explained as eccentricity.

The contribution of the reactions of others is suggested by the fact that much residual deviance is only transitory and is terminated when the stresses of a particular situation are removed. Scheff cites evidence that combat neurosis of soldiers and strange behavior of children is frequently ended when the deviants are kept within their familiar groups and only superficial medical attention is afforded.

Role of the mentally ill person

Why do some individuals exhibit their strange behavior over a protracted period? The usual explanation is to attribute this persistence to factors characteristic of the individual. Scheff cites a second possibility: The reaction of the other persons (the "audience") is to regard the individual as mentally ill and to place him in the role of the mentally ill person.

The folklore about mental disorder emphasizes the possibility that symptoms of mental illness can be pretended for the sake of hidden purposes, such as avoidance of criminal prosecution. In addition to the possibility of calculated shamming, Scheff notes the pressure of groups that the patient behave according to special expectations applied to the mentally ill. Even when he considers this role obnoxious, the patient finds conformity can simplify his relationships with others. Furthermore, his behavior is a mixture of genuine symptoms and a cynical use of them. The consequence is that the stereotyped meaning of being "crazy" is learned. In constantly encountering evaluations of other persons in terms of these stereotypes, the patient is exposed to continual reaffirmation of his eligibility for the role of the mentally ill.

Even in treatment, he is rewarded for playing this role by being commended for "insight" gained by accepting professional diagnosis of what

[26] Thomas J. Scheff, "The Role of the Mentally Ill and the Dynamics of Mental Disorder: A Research Framework," *Sociometry,* Vol. 26 (December 1963), pp. 436-53.

his symptoms mean. The crisis he experiences tends to make the patient even more susceptible to suggestion under pressures of shame, confusion, and anxiety. Thereby, Scheff says, the residual deviance, interpreted by the audience as mental illness, becomes confirmed in the role of the mentally ill person. What could be only a transitory episode is transformed in effect into the individual assuming the role of the mentally ill.

Criticisms of labeling approach

Contending that the labeling theorist have overstated their case, Gove argues that the vast majority of persons who have become patients have a serious disturbance involving an untenable situation requiring commitment to a mental hospital. Drawing on data of several studies, he points out that public officials rejected hospitalization for a portion of those persons who came before them. Furthermore, he argues, the debilitating processes associated with hospitalization have been exaggerated; introduction of tranquilizers, the open door policy of hospitals, and reduction in the average length of hospitalization have changed the mental hospital so as to erase much of the debilitating effects of the traditional insane asylum. In short, he believes the labeling theorists exaggerate the probability that commitment itself promotes the severity of the mental disturbance.[27]

Also finding "little evidence that such labeling processes are sufficiently powerful to be major influences in producing chronic mental illness," Mechanic considers the approach useful, nevertheless, for underscoring the importance of the impressions conveyed to the patient in determining whether he adopts a sick role. It is absurd, Mechanic says, to believe that certain patterns of behavior will disappear simply because they are ignored (that is, the "labeling process" is withheld). However, prevention of mental illness does entail communication of the expectation that the patient will continue to perform conventional roles satisfactorily and that his difficulty is a problem in living rather than a demonstration that he is a pathological being.[28]

PATHWAYS TO TREATMENT

The behavior of the mentally ill person becomes an element in the social problem of mental disorder when it becomes visible to others who decide something must be done to correct his deviation from their expectations. The symptoms he exhibits become grounds for moving him along path-

[27] Walter R. Gove, "Societal Reaction as an Explanation of Mental Illness," *American Sociological Review,* Vol. 35 (October 1970), pp. 873–84.
[28] Mechanic, *Mental Health and Social Policy,* pp. 47–48.

ways which lead toward hospitalization or other forms of treatment. These pathways are social in the sense that they involve contingencies shaped by attitudes and institutionalized procedures which are stimulated by the definition of him as mentally ill.

Stages in becoming a patient

The patient moves through the stage of first recognition that he is out of step with expectations when he is included among the clientele for professional treatment. Spitzer and Denzin distinguish four major events in the prepatient stage.[29] The *behavioral event* consists of the individual engaging in some public action or set of actions. In the *definitional event* an evaluative process results in the behavior being defined as deviant, unacceptable, and qualifying as mental illness. The disturbed individual constitutes a social problem when his behavior disturbs the social system for other persons. However, patients seeking treatment also speak of interpersonal problems such as employment difficulties and inability to "get along with people."

When the individual continues to fail to meet the expectations of evaluators in his intimate groups and community agencies, the *treatment decision* is expressed in persuasive pressures that he seek psychiatric help. (Sometimes the individual seeks help without such external pressure.) The *legalistic definition* is provided by the official processing whereby he becomes a patient through legal or voluntary commitment to a hospital.

Variation in tolerance

In the definitional event and the treatment decision, the individual is subjected to a folklore regarding mental illness. This folklore affects the probability that the behavioral event will initiate the valuation culminating in classification of him as mentally ill. The probability is shaped by the norms characteristic of his family, work, friendship, and neighborhood groups. In various social situations, there is variation in toleration of deviant behavior. Physical aggression or exotic language is more characteristic of certain groups. Dress or demeanor considered pathological in an isolated and conservative community is more likely to be accepted in a culturally heterogeneous urban area. Failure to maintain regular employment is more subject to negative evaluation as willful malingering in a subculture emphasizing the work ethic, but may possibly be seen as a search for "higher" values than materialism in a subculture emphasizing individuality.

Unusual behavior is more likely to be overlooked when it is related to

---

[29] Norman T. Denzin and Stephan P. Spitzer, "Paths to the Mental Hospital and Staff Predictions of Patient Role Behavior," in Spitzer and Denzin, *The Mental Patient,* p. 335.

some crisis, such as death of a loved one, which is defined as a proper time for exemption from usual role demands. Definition of deviance as only eccentricity is less likely as the behavioral event acquires greater visibility, intensity, and frequency of aberration. Tolerance is eroded with greater perception of the behavior as damaging to the tranquility of social relationships and threatening to the welfare of the groups and of the deviant himself.

Sensitivity and rejection

Research indicates that only a minority of the families of mental patients are so sensitive about illness of a family member as to withdraw from relationships with other persons in the community or to strive to conceal the illness. The degree of sensitivity increases with the continued bizarre behavior of the released patient and with higher class status of the family. Members of the upper and middle class are influenced toward tolerance of mental illness by their higher formal education, but concern about maintaining their class position arouses fear of a derogatory evaluation by the rest of the community.[30]

The choice of the source of help affects the degree of public rejection experienced by a mentally ill person. In a study of attitudes in a New England town, Phillips finds that the quest for assistance drew negative evaluation of the person. The degree of rejection was least when assistance was not sought. Furthermore, the degree of rejection increased according to type of assistance sought in this order: clergyman, physician, psychiatrist, and mental hospital. When the behavior was not described as markedly abnormal, the individual was expected to accept responsibility for his recovery. Resort to a psychiatrist or to a mental hospital was associated with identification of the person as a genuine mental case.[31] The degree of rejection also varies, however, with the visibility of the behavioral deviation from what the respondents expected, regardless of the extent of pathology from a psychiatric perspective.[32]

ATTITUDES TOWARD MENTAL ILLNESS

Tuberculosis and cancer used to be regarded as somehow shameful, but the trend has been away from such stigmatization and toward a more matter-of-fact classification of the ill person as simply a victim of disease.

[30] Howard E. Freeman and Ozzie G. Simmons, "Feelings of Stigma among Relatives of Former Mental Patients," *Social Problems,* Vol. 8 (Spring 1961), pp. 312–21.
[31] Derek L. Phillips, "Rejection as a Consequence of Seeking Help for Mental Disorders," *American Sociological Review,* Vol. 28 (December 1963), pp. 963–72.
[32] Derek L. Phillips, "Rejection of the Mentally Ill: The Influence of Behavior and Sex," *American Sociological Review,* Vol. 29 (October 1964), pp. 679–87.

However, mental illness continues to carry implications of moral fault and social transgression. There is a vague suspicion that the mentally ill person is a willful rebel against the social order because he does not fit neatly into the role of the physically sick. Psychotics do not behave as ordinary sick people who want help, nor do they participate in the processes intended to alleviate their condition.

The social reactions to mental illness intermingle fears of the insane and humanitarian concern for their welfare. Madness, inexplicable to ordinary people, arouses generalized fears calling for detention of the insane for the sake of the security and tranquility of the community. The early history of public attitudes toward mental illness emphasizes neglect, persecution, and the isolation of mentally disturbed persons. They were thrust into jails and poorhouses and subjected to chains, straitjackets, and padded cells. In the early 19th century, physical restraint was the normal method of dealing with disturbed patients.

The "normalizing theme"

The ambivalence in public attitudes toward mental illness is significant in several ways. These attitudes differ from those of public health professionals and present possibilities of either aggravating or reducing the burden of mental illness on individuals and the community. Differences of public beliefs about mental illness from the concepts of professionals lend a degree of uncertainty to hopes that public education will provide a community climate congenial to effective use of diagnostic and treatment programs. The fears aroused by the "insane" increase the stigmatization of the mentally ill person and his continued isolation from the community. Willingness of his family to accept his need for treatment is impeded and thus complicates the discovery of patients early in the development of his emotional difficulties. When fear generates the conviction that mental illness is incurable, "treatment" is more likely to be purely custodial hospitalization which isolates the patient from the community under the equivalent of a life sentence. Involuntary commitment to a mental hospital raises the possibility that the protection of the community from strange and "dangerous" individuals becomes the paramount consideration. Then the diagnostic functions of mental health professionals can be converted into what may be called "psychiatric injustice."

However, the public attitudes toward mental illness are not fully described when elements of fear are emphasized. In evaluating the deviant behavior of the persons they know, lay people demonstrate a reluctance to define them as mentally ill. In an experiment intended to change attitudes toward mental illness in a Canadian community through a public education campaign, Cumming and Cumming encountered unexpected hostility, apathy, and withdrawal of cooperation. To explain these reactions, they cite a *normalizing* theme whereby lay people tend to dismiss psychological symptoms as a "quirk." This theme is related to a striving by the sane to interpret the unusual behavior of their associates as "normal" in the sense of being essentially consistent with the social expectations of the community.[33]

The Cummings found that lay and professional people use different criteria in judging whether behavior is "abnormal." Lay groups *do* have methods of defining mental illness without assistance of psychiatrists, the two researchers say. While professionals use specific psychological symptoms for such definition, lay people see mental abnormality in terms of highly visible deviations from behavioral standards they consider essential to the effective working of the family, neighborhood, or other important social group. Professionals see a range of psychological states between excellent mental health and psychoses. The man on the street identifies mental illness as psychoses requiring hospitalization; otherwise, behavior short of this is seen as fairly normal.

In initial confrontation of mental illness, the lay person denies that deviation actually exists. Usually he makes every effort to explain the deviation as being consistent with expectations and to define the individual as continuing to function as a group member. When denial is no longer feasible, however, this tolerance usually disappears and the mentally ill person is subjected to social and physical isolation. Hospitalization is the physical isolation which expresses the social isolation of the mentally ill, an isolation through which the sane reaffirm the solidarity of the social system that has been undermined by the unpredictable behavior of the mentally ill person.

Cumming and Cumming identify resistance to the rule breaker as both a hope for and an obstacle to the reintegration of the mentally ill person into the fellowship of the community. The initial reluctance of society to see the mentally ill person as such offers the possibility that his movement toward greater abnormality will be forestalled by his continued acceptance as a fully functioning member. Moreover, within the range of behavior tolerated in his particular social environment, his unusual behavior may raise no serious personal and social difficulties. Individuals under situational stress may also escape the stigma of being labeled as mentally ill, but, this tolerance can impede early treatment and preventive measures which the subsequent course of the mental illness may reveal to have been desirable.

Reshaping of public opinion

Gradually over the last 200 years public opinion concerning mental disorder seems to have been reshaped. A 1950 poll of Louisville, Ky.,

[33] Elaine Cumming and John Cumming, *Closed Ranks* (Cambridge, Mass.: Harvard University Press, 1957), pp. 103–9, 121–34.

residents suggests that folk attitudes toward victims of mental disorder are giving way to concepts based on modern science.[34] A later study in Baltimore found only 15 percent of the respondents expressing a desire to isolate or reject the mentally ill.[35] Convergence of lay attitudes with a psychiatric point of view, however, appears to be greater with increased level of education and when the mental illness is exhibited grossly. Otherwise, tolerance of mental illness is associated with lay perception of the overt threat the behavior presents.[36]

The years after World War II particularly brought attitude changes. Attention to mental illness had been aroused by the rejection for military service of huge numbers of men classified as psychiatrically unfit. Mental hospitals had deteriorated during the Great Depression, and then WW II bled them of their professional personnel and prolonged their budgetary undernourishment. Albert Deutsch and others in the 1940s described mental hospitals as chambers of horror to arouse public concern over these centers of neglect.

The introduction of electroconvulsive and other forms of physical treatment in the 1930s and after paved the way for public recognition that mental disorder is amenable to treatment. The introduction of tranquilizing drugs in the 1950s was an important factor in reducing hospital case loads and reducing the need for physical restraints. Increased coverage by mass communication media of the mental health problem, and more public contacts with hospitals, removed some of its mystery. Physical facilities and standards of hospital staffing could be upgraded. With speedier discharge of patients, the identification of hospitalization with a "life sentence" lost its validity.[37]

Changes in institutional treatment

Four phases in the history of responses to the mentally ill are delineated by Bockoven.[38] The *moral treatment phase* made the patient comfortable, aroused his interest in purposeful activity, invited his friendship, and

[34] Julian L. Woodward, "Changing Ideas on Mental Illness and its Treatment," *American Sociological Review,* Vol. 16 (August 1951), pp. 443–54.

[35] Paul V. Lemkau and G. M. Crocetti, "An Urban Population's Opinion and Knowledge about Mental Illness," *American Journal of Psychiatry,* Vol. 118 (January 1962), pp. 692–99.

[36] Bruce P. Dohrenwend and Edwin Chin-Shong, "Social Status and Attitudes Toward Psychological Disorder: The Problem of Tolerance of Deviance," *American Sociological Review,* Vol. 32 (June 1967), pp. 417–32.

[37] Kenneth Robinson, "The Public and Mental Health," in Hugh Freeman and James Farndale (eds.), *Trends in the Mental Health Service* (New York: Macmillan Co., 1963), pp. 13–16; George Rosen, *Madness in Society: Chapters in the Historical Sociology of Mental Illness* (Chicago: University of Chicago Press, 1968), pp. 274–88; Leonard J. Duhl, "The Changing Face of Mental Health," in Leonard J. Kuhl (ed.), *The Urban Condition* (New York: Basic Books, 1963), pp. 66–67.

[38] J. Sanbourne Bockoven, *Moral Treatment in American Psychiatry* (New York: Springer Publishing Company, 1963), pp. 103–13.

encouraged discussion of his troubles. Today the word "moral" suggests some kind of religious approach. Moral treatment, however, was intended to apply the psychological ideas then current that the physical environment could be used "scientifically" to influence the patient's mental state.[39] Bockoven explains "moral" was used in the sense of "morale" (zeal, hope, spirit, and confidence), or in the sense that the insane are not morally responsible for their acts. In sum, "moral treatment" indicated compassionate and understanding treatment of innocent sufferers.

The moral therapist acted toward his patients as though they were mentally well. He believed that kindness and forbearance were essential. By the Civil War, this phase ended under the pressure of an insufficiency of therapists, a sharp growth in patient populations, and the appearance of patients with foreign backgrounds with whom psychiatrists lacked cultural affinity.

The *custodial nontreatment phase* was characterized by impersonal and routine administration for the sake of "efficiency" and "economy" of operations, with minimum allowance for personal peculiarities of staff or patients. Bockoven sees this "human warehouse" perspective as an outgrowth of the medical view of the times that mental disease is incurable, and also as an outgrowth of the managerial emphasis on efficiency in industry. Mental hospitals had become receptacles for the poor, old, mentally deficient, and other problem people for whom the community did not otherwise provide. The location of the hospitals in remote areas, and their rigid administrative structure, blocked communication of patients with the outside world.

The *custodial reeducation phase* brought some modification in the medical attitude that mental disorder is incurable. Patients came to be regarded as teachable in that they could learn to behave *like* rational human beings. Instead of representing a genuine commitment to treatment of mental disorders, however, teaching involved occupational and industrial skills useful to the operation of the mental hospital. The regime continued to be authoritarian and stratified. The patients were the "lower class" and were subjected to the austerity and deprivation considered proper for the less "worthy" class. As the "upper class," hospital personnel imposed principles of punishment to control and train patients to achieve "efficiency" in peformance of work necessary for daily operations and to minimize disruption of the routines of hospital life.

The custodial hospital has been criticized for promoting chronicity among patients by failing to orient its efforts toward treatment. A survey of patients of one state distinguished between "legitimate involuntary patients" (properly confined for treatment of protection of the community), "illegitimate involuntary patients" (patients rated as slightly or moderately

[39] Gerald N. Grob, *The State and the Mentally Ill* (Chapel Hill, N.C.: University of North Carolina Press, 1966), p. 10.

impaired and not likely to endanger themselves or others), and "transitional patients" (voluntary admissions and/or patients for whom there were release plans). First admissions usually went to receiving hospitals. The transfer hospital was custodial in nature, with most of the patients hospitalized more than 10 years. The survey found 29 percent of receiving hospital patients were illegitimate involuntary patients without plans for release or prospects for helpful treatment.[40]

The *therapeutic research phase* emerges, Bockoven believes, when the findings of the behavioral sciences are beginning to be applied. Already there appears to be erosion of support for the belief that the mentally ill should be banished from society into large custodial institutions. A mental hygiene movement has crusaded for prevention and early treatment of disorders and for greater emphasis on short-term psychiatric care.

Recently, remarkable developments have occurred among hospitalized mental patients, Zusman declares. For example, schizophrenia (once a label for an inevitable deterioration into complete social disability) has come to represent a serious but treatable condition. Although schizophrenics compose the majority of hospitalized mental patients, similar change has occurred for all types of patients. As described earlier in this chapter, mental hospitals have unlocked doors, have introduced tranquilizing drugs, and have provided a more homelike atmosphere. Zusman explains the change among patients as a consequence of the changes in the hospitals. Humane treatment and social pressure on patients to act in a socially acceptable way have countered the previous influences of institutions in strengthening the further social breakdown of patients. The central idea is that many symptoms of mental illness are the results of conditions under which the mentally ill are treated, and not a part of primary illness.[41]

RESPONSES AND SOCIAL PROBLEMS

President Kennedy's message to Congress quoted at the beginning of this chapter reflects increasing recognition that mental illness constitutes a serious *social* problem and that custodial institutions have become a scandal. The growth of community psychiatry is encouraging in that the segregation of the mentally ill is being broken and the exclusive attention to the patient as an individual is being supplemented by recognition of the importance of the social environment within which he endeavors to cope with the problems of living. However, there are formidable difficulties in determining the proper role for the mental health professional in dealing

[40] Thomas J. Scheff, "Legitimate, Transitional, and Illegitimate Mental Patients in a Midwestern State," *American Journal of Psychiatry,* Vol. 120 (September 1963), pp. 267–69.
[41] Jack Zusman, "Some Explanations of the Changing Appearance of Psychotic Patients," *Milbank Memorial Fund Quarterly,* Vol. 44, Part 2 (January 1966), pp. 363–65.

with problems of living which have ramifications beyond mental illness in and of itself.

Rise of community psychiatry

Through a marriage of social and behavioral science, community psychiatry constitutes a movement beyond the individual's psychiatric problems to include his family and work setting and the larger community environment. The concern for the family and work settings brought an interest in extending the area of treatment from the isolated mental hospital to scattered mental health units more accessible to these settings. A central argument is that the mentally ill person should be treated within his total personal and social environment, not cloistered in a specialized and isolated institution.

In the last decade mental health professionals have moved toward greater recognition that mental illness is a socially defined condition constituting a social problem. Psychiatry is demonstrating stronger concern for preventive and therapeutic services requiring changes in the community as a social system, rather than concentrating on the individual patient. Under community-oriented programs, psychiatrists express needs to extend services to populations previously without accessibility to treatment and to mentally ill persons before a crisis occurs; to change the community's mental health climate through cooperation with schools, courts, and other service agencies; and to add the community itself as a unit of treatment beyond the individual patient or family.[42]

Passage of the 1963 Community Health Centers Act represented a national commitment to a mental health facility close to its clientele and involved in community life for referral of patients and financial support. Involvement of the local community is preferred to make the facility a factor in shaping the response to mental disorder. This objective exposes community psychiatry to the difficulties of overcoming the fragmentation of local government, inadequate tax bases, the fitting of a new service into the established governmental structure, and the barriers to efficient service raised by outmoded jurisdictions of governmental units. The movement also faces problems of an insufficiency of professional personnel and their unequal distribution across the nation.[43]

Obscurities in role of psychiatrist

When mental health becomes an important public policy issue, the psychiatrist is moved out of his clinic and into the arena of competing claims for national resources. In diagnosing and treating the patient, he

[42] Leonard J. Duhl and Robert L. Leopold (eds.), *Mental Health and Urban Social Policy* (San Francisco: Jossey-Bass, 1968), pp. xii–xii, 3–4.

[43] Robert H. Connery et al., *The Politics of Mental Health* (New York: Columbia University Press, 1968), pp. 502–9, 529–36.

is relatively free to concentrate on the individual with incidental attention to the environment within which the patient endeavors to solve the problems of living. As we have seen, the psychiatrist has difficulties in applying conventional methods of assessing symptomatology and in finding the best means of relieving the psychological distress of his patient. However, he has more opportunity in the clinic to express humanitarian concern for the patient's need than when he calls for heavy public investment in services for large groups of people whom he defines as mentally ill. His clinical skills are less germane in debates over the merits of heavy investment in unproven strategies in mental health programs at the cost of education, highways, urban renewal, public housing, and so on.

With his grounding in the highly prestigious status of physician, the psychiatrist has impressive stature when he presents himself as an expert in dealing with social problems such as crime, family disorganization, and drug abuse. Perhaps his credentials are accepted more readily because his clinical background is more likely to orient him toward changing the personalities and inclinations of individuals rather than changing the structure of society. Then the psychological difficulties of blacks, the poor, and law violators may be interpreted as more a matter of their maladjustment and less a matter of the conditions determined by the social structure.

Are the professionals trained in treating typical psychiatric conditions such as schizophrenia, Mechanic asks, also the appropriate experts for dealing with the problems resulting from environmental impoverishment, cultural deprivation, social change, social discrimination, and other conditions stemming from the social structure? Furthermore, he wonders, in the light of limits on available psychiatric manpower to handle hard-core mental illness, whether it is fruitful to extend the boundaries of the problem of mental illness to include other major problems requiring development of social, economic, and educational services.[44]

Another area of role conflict centers around the use of psychiatric diagnosis to determine mental competence in situations involving issues beyond mental illness in and of itself. The situations are determination of competency to stand trial and involuntary commitment to a mental hospital. If the defendant is unable to understand proceedings because of a mental disorder, the courts regard trial on criminal charges to deprive him of the rights accorded all defendants. Determination of incompetency is complicated by absence of clear-cut criteria and differences between psychiatric and legal interpretations. Persons suffering from mental illness frequently deny they are mentally ill and require treatment. Assuming that these persons require treatment for their own sake and constitute a threat to the community, legal procedures are provided for commitment to a mental hospital regardless of their wishes.

Szasz distinguishes between the psychiatrist's service as an agent for

[44] Mechanic, *Mental Health and Social Policy,* pp. 31–33.

the patient and as an agent for the patient's relatives, a school, military services, court of law, or some other organization. In the latter role, the psychiatrist performs social and legal services which, Szasz fears, can be instances of depotism in the humanitarian concern for the patient. By relieving the law violator of criminal responsibility because of mental disorder, the psychiatrist is supposed to be excusing the defendant from inappropriate punishment. However, Szasz says, the ultimate consequence is that hospitalization loses a therapeutic meaning and becomes another version of punitive custody. Similarly, involuntary commitment skirts the issue of civil rights guaranteed all citizens to become a form of social control of deviants "under a facade of medical and psychiatric jargon." [45]

Concept of "surplus" population

Once the person has been identified as mentally ill, hospitalization serves constructive purposes by possibly promoting remission of his disorder, protecting him against the possibility of behavior injurious to the interests of himself and others, and removing him from sources of stress in the community. On the other hand, hospitalization also removes the patient from his social circle and relegates him to a place traditionally remote from the community. The unintended consequences of this isolation can be to strengthen beliefs that his disorder is incurable and, by withdrawing the patient from public attention, to permit or encourage neglect rather than therapy.

Through these unintended consequences, the mental hospitals may be collection centers for the rejected people of society who constitute a *surplus population* defined as "useless" and a burden on the "useful" people. The possibility is germane to urban society wherein surplus populations are created by such developments as automation, efforts of labor unions to control job opportunities, cultural disadvantages, poverty, racial prejudice, vocational incompetence, and so on. The complex organizations of urban society require personnel with competencies and personalities congenial to the tasks necessary to maintain their operations. However, as Goode shows, in facing the problem of how to utilize the services of the less able, every society is subject to opposing factors toward protection *of* the inept and protection of the community *from* the inept. In fact, he argues, our social system is more productive because bureaucracy and the intricate system of specialized tasks permit more efficient utilization of the inept. [46] The mental hospitals operate as collection centers through a screening process whereby only some of the inept are hospitalized.

[45] Thomas S. Szasz, *Law, Liberty, and Psychiatry* (New York: Macmillan Co., 1963).
[46] William J. Goode, "The Protection of the Inept," *American Sociological Review,* Vol. 32 (February 1967), pp. 5–19.

In applying the concept of surplus population to mental retardation, Farber refers to two themes in the screening process through which marginal persons may become vulnerable to commitment to institutions. The *theme of incompetence* refers to the inability of the persons found inadequate to attain the level of conduct the organizations of the community require for their own continued existence. Going beyond inadequacy in and of itself, the *theme of deviance* adds the implication that the surplus population constitutes some kind of threat to the community. Whereas incompetence implies inability to conform to accepted standards, deviance suggests some motivation to act contrary to the norms of the organization.[47]

Social factors in commitment

In moving along the pathway to the stages of treatment decision and the legalistic definition, the individual reaches the point where he is evaluated as qualifying for the status of mentally ill person. Considerable study has been devoted to the processes through which the officials of courts and mental hospitals decide whether a person should be committed to a mental hospital. Are their screenings of candidates based solely on the mental disorder or do other factors also influence the decision?

The psychiatric diagnosis of the individual as mentally ill does not, in and of itself, result in his commitment to a mental hospital. Rather, as Lemert points out, the legal proceedings are initiated because the individual's behavior has deviated from expectations to such an extent that attention has been drawn to him as a major disturber of relationships within the family and his other social groups. The commitment action is less a response to his behavior in itself and more to his status within his group. Commitment is more likely when his deviant behavior is particularly destructive to the functioning of the group and places special strain on the tolerance of other members.[48]

Studies of commitments to mental hospitals indicate the importance of relatively unrecognized decisions before the involuntary patient is admitted to the mental hospital. Mechanic suggests this importance by noting that the arrival of the involuntary patient in the hospital is usually regarded as sufficient evidence of psychiatric impairment because the professionals lack the time and resources in the crowded hospital to make a rigorous psychiatric diagnosis. Unless there is insufficient bed space to absorb new admissions, the patient seldom is told that he does not require treatment.[49]

[47] Bernard Farber, *Mental Retardation: Its Social Context and Social Consequences* (Boston: Houghton Mifflin Company, 1968), pp. 9–13, 23–24.

[48] Edwin M. Lemert, *Human Deviance, Social Problems, and Social Control* (Englewood Cliffs, N.J.: Prentice-Hall, 1967), pp. 67–68.

Nature of decision-making process

The formal legal procedure is supposed to be a means of arriving at a rational decision on appropriateness of hospitalization. Through application of due process and scientific principles, the court is supposed to weigh complex and uncertain factors in reaching a decision derived from intelligent insight. If the decision is to be objective and rational, five conditions must be present, Scheff asserts.[50] First, there must be sufficient time for deliberate consideration of the facts. The enormous case load of urban courts and the brevity of many prehearing psychiatric examinations counterindicate the provision of sufficient time. Second, the notoriety of a given case must not be a factor in the decision. Public sentiment is less likely to be aroused by erroneous commitment than by the release of a patient who subsequently endangers the tranquility of the community. Third, the judge should not be personally acquainted with the patient; he should follow impersonally the psychiatric facts. Fourth, because the judge lacks technical knowledge of mental disease, he must guard against manipulating the situation to shift the blame for a wrong decision to the psychiatrist. Fifth, the decision should not pivot on whether the patient has financial means for legal counsel or a capacity for demanding his legal rights.

In their study of hearings of one county lunacy commission, Miller and Schwartz found the proceedings to be rather perfunctory, as though an earlier decison was being rubber-stamped.[51] The proceedings did not measure up to Scheff's conditions for objective and rational decision making. Although the judge did reverse a medical recommendation for commitment to a mental hospital in nearly one fourth of the cases, the demeanor of the defendants at the hearing had great bearing on the outcome. Miller and Schwartz describe four typical situations:

In *defiance assignments* the defendant resisted commitment to a mental hospital in intensities ranging from silent disdain and verbal protest to assaultive violence. Appearing to be especially aware of their circumstances, these defendants were likely to protest their loss of liberty and rights. Half of them were either released or held for further study. Their success was more likely when they questioned the validity of the complainants' case, because challenge of the professionals' judgment was universally futile.

Bewilderment assignments involved aged, physically incapacitated, or

[49] David Mechanic, "Some Factors in Identifying and Defining Mental Illness," *Mental Hygiene,* Vol. 46 (January 1962), pp. 66–74.

[50] Thomas J. Scheff, "Social Conditions for Rationality: How Urban and Rural Courts Deal with the Mentally Ill," *American Behavioral Scientist,* Vol. 8 (March 1964), pp. 21–24.

[51] Dorothy Miller and Michael Schwartz, "County Lunacy Commission Hearings: Some Observations of Commitments to a State Mental Hospital," *Social Problems,* Vol. 14 (Summer 1966), pp. 26–35.

socially retarded patients who did not appear to understand the events they were undergoing. The complainants were family members who often exhibited distress as they recited reasons for inability to care for the patients. The tone of the proceedings was vague reassurance and a blunting of the reality that confinement in a mental hospital was the issue. With exception of two releases to a nursing home, all these patients ended up in a mental hospital.

In *nonparticipation assignments,* the patients remained mute and paid little attention to the proceedings. They tended to be treated as a nonperson and to receive no defense. The complainant and examining doctors cooperated ritualistically in brief hearings which usually resulted in commitment.

In *volunteer assignments* the patients, complainants, and examining doctors cooperated in an atmosphere of mutual admiration and good fellowship. The patients accepted the role of psychiatric patient which they were accorded if there was evidence that they had held jobs, been socially adjusted, and otherwise avoided social deviation. Because of previous failure to abandon alcoholism, two patients were not committed on grounds they, as malingerers, would not benefit from treatment.

PARADOX OF SOCIAL CLASS

A noteworthy paradox is that, although they appear to be particularly vulnerable to mental illness, the lower social classes have inferior access to effective treatment. In a survey of pertinent studies, Fried finds powerful evidence that the lowest social classes have the highest rates of severe psychiatric disorder. Furthermore, blacks suffer greater prevalence of severe psychiatric disorders than whites even when intervening factors such as migration, education, and occupation are controlled.[52]

Stress and access to care

The Midtown Manhattan Study found that the lower classes differed from the higher classes in matters related to stress: deficient interpersonal affiliation, increasingly greater proportion of psychotics with increasing stress, greater impairment per unit of stress, inability to postpone gratification, and more explosiveness in face of frustration. Lower-class persons were found to be more likely to act on impulse, to be submissive toward strong personalities, and to be more sadistic toward the weak. A greater proportion of lower-class persons revealed feelings of futility, alienation,

[52] Marc Fried, "Social Differences in Mental Health," in John Kosa, Aaron Antonovsky, and Irving Kenneth Zola (eds.), *Poverty and Health: A Sociological Analysis* (Cambridge, Mass.: Harvard University Press, 1969), pp. 113, 136–37, 141–44.

depression, resignation, social isolation, and concomitant distrust of others.[53]

The lower the social class status of the mentally ill person the less available to him is effective psychiatric care.[54] In their important research, Hollingshead and Redlich find the appraisal of abnormal behavior as psychiatrically disordered is highly influenced by the individual's class position. The first decision that a person requires psychiatric care, whether a neurotic or a psychotic, comes increasingly from police and courts as the social class status declines. In the higher classes the referral is more likely to come from the patient, his family, or his friends. Furthermore, the researchers report, the patients from the higher classes are induced to see a psychiatrist through gentle and "insightful" prodding, whereas those of the lower class are subjected to direct and authoritarian coercion.[55]

One analysis of the themes in mental health pamphlets reveals a dominance of middle-class orientations. The mentally healthy person is identified as skillful in getting along with others within organizations, competent in overcoming problems, motivated for satisfaction in his work, able to control his emotions, future-oriented in striving for preestablished goals, and a participant in community organizations and activities. Since lower-class orientations are diametrically opposed to each of these qualities, the researchers conclude that the mental health movement unconsciously supports the maintenance of middle-class social structure. To the extent that the middle-class way of life is unavailable to lower-class people, the themes of the "mentally healthy" model block adjustment to the realities of lower-class life.[56]

Orientation of clinical staff

The differences in class orientations influence the probability that a patient will be admitted for treatment and that he will receive intensive treatment. An investigation of all referrals to a psychiatric clinic for a year reveals that the higher a patient's social class status the more likely he was to be accepted for treatment, to be treated by highly trained personnel, and to be treated intensively over a long period. The researchers suggest that the patterns reflect staff assessments of the patient's motivation for psychotherapy. Since lower-class patients do not share the psychiatrist's conception of the therapeutic process, the psychiatrist's values would

[53] Thomas S. Langer and Stanley T. Michael, *Life Stress and Mental Health* (New York: Free Press of Glencoe, 1963), pp. 467–72.

[54] James T. McMahon, "The Working Class Psychiatric Patient: A Clinical View," in Frank Riessman, Jerome Cohen, and Arthur Pearl (eds.), *Mental Health of the Poor* (New York: Free Press of Glencoe, 1964), p. 284.

[55] August B. Hollingshead and Fredrick C. Redlich, *Social Class and Mental Illness: A Community Study* (New York: John Wiley & Sons, 1958), pp. 185-92.

[56] Orville R. Gursslin, Raymond G. Hunt, and Jack L. Roach, "Social Class and the Mental Health Movement," in Frank Riessman, et al., *Mental Health of the Poor,* pp. 57–67.

affect the likelihood of acceptance of the patient. Furthermore, the differences in values and patterns of communication may hamper the establishment of the therapeutic relationship.[57]

Many lower-class individuals equate mental disease with severe psychoses and are particularly likely to avoid voluntary hospitalization to supplement the mental health professional's reluctance to undertake their treatment on a long-term basis. However, along with the greater possibility that the lower-class disturbed person will be committed to a state mental hospital, he is more likely to be relegated to custodial care unless he responds quickly to treatment. Accordingly, one study of the long-term population of a hospital found 93 per cent of the low-income patients still in the hospital after ten years although almost all patients in the middle- and upper-income groups had been released.[58]

The relationship between social class status and mode of treatment appears to be more than simple inability to pay. A study of a clinic specializing in patients unable to pay finds a significant relationship between social class and whether or not a patient was accepted for treatment.[59] Brill and Storrow report that the lower class patients had lower estimated intelligence, less education, a tendency to see their problem as physical rather than emotional, a desire for symptomatic relief rather than overall help, and a lack of understanding and desire for psychotherapy. They conclude that the social class differential in acceptance for treatment is a product of the therapists' emphasis on psychotherapy as the preferred mode of intervention since lower class patients are less favorable candidates.

The social problem of mental illness also entails the adequacy of the system for delivering services necessary to its alleviation. One discrepancy is the concentration of psychiatrists in private practice serving persons who are the less severely handicapped but who have generally greater ability to pay fees. Another discrepancy is the location of psychiatrists versus the location of the bulk of the most seriously ill mental patients. A large proportion of psychiatrists are in private practice whereas psychotics under treatment are concentrated in understaffed mental hospitals.

SUMMARY

Mental illness constitutes a social problem in that deviation from social expectations obstructs the blending of individual behaviors into a social

[57] Jerome K. Myers and Leslie Schafer, "Social Stratification and Psychiatric Practice: A Study of an Out-Patient Clinic," *American Sociological Review,* Vol. 19 (June 1954); pp. 307–10.

[58] Frank Riessman and Sylvia Scribner, "The Under-Utilization of Mental Health Services by Workers and Low Income Groups," *American Journal of Psychiatry,* Vol. 121 (February 1965), pp. 798–801.

[59] Norman Q. Brill and Hugh A. Storrow, "Social Class and Psychiatric Treatment," in Riessman, *Mental Health of the Poor,* pp. 68–75.

502 Social problems of urban man

order. In an urban society the management of tensions is particularly complex, but there is no evidence that severe mental disorder is especially prevalent. Of two alternative conceptions of mental illness, the disease model and the psychosocial model, the latter is more useful to analysis of mental illness as a social problem. Social norms operate in the definition of some deviant behavior as mental disorder and in the movement of persons through the several stages whereby they become defined as a patient. The complexities of lay attitudes toward mental illness become apparent in an analysis of the concepts of residual deviance and the normalizing theme. The hospitalization of mental patients raises the issues of adverse consequences of custodial institutions, involuntary commitment, and the paradox of the lower social classes with their limited access to treatment and their vulnerability to mental illness. Recent decades have brought increased recognition of social factors in the appearance and treatment of mental illness. Changes in public attitudes, treatment strategies, and new emphasis on prevention offer prospects for more effective responses to the problem.

FOR ADDITIONAL READING

Marshall B. Clinard, *Sociology of Deviant Behavior* (3d ed.; New York: Holt, Rinehart & Winston, 1968), Chapter 12.

Albert Deutsch, *The Shame of the States* (New York: Harcourt, Brace, 1948).

Leonard J. Duhl and Robert L. Leopold (eds.), *Mental Health and Urban Social Policy: A Casebook of Community Actions* (San Franciso: Jossey-Bass, 1968).

H. Warren Dunham and S. Kirson Weinberg, *The Culture of the State Mental Hospital* (Detroit: Wayne State University Press, 1960).

Michael Foucault, *Madness and Civilization* (London: Tavistock Publications, 1965).

Howard E. Freeman and Ozzie G. Simmons, *The Mental Patient Comes Home* (New York: John Wiley & Sons, 1963).

Richard E. Gordon, Katherine K. Gordon, and Max Gunther, *The Split-Level Trap* (New York: Bernard Geis Associates, 1961).

J. Hoenig and Marion W. Hamilton, *The Desegregation of the Mentally Ill* (New York: Humanities Press, 1969).

Daniel Offer and Melvin Sabshin, *Normality: Theoretical and Clinical Concepts of Mental Health* (New York: Basic Books, 1966).

Marvin K. Opler, *Culture and Social Psychiatry* (New York: Atherton Press, 1967).

James W. Rinehart, "Mobility Aspiration—Achievement Discrepancies and Mental Illness," *Social Problems,* Vol. 15 (Spring 1968), pp. 478–88.

Edwin M. Schur, "Psychiatrists Under Attack: The Rebellious Dr. Szasz," *Atlantic,* Vol. 217 (June 1966), pp. 72–76.

Ailon Shiloh, "Sanctuary or Prison—Responses to Life in a Mental Hospital," *Trans-action,* Vol. 6 (December 1968), pp. 28–35.

Harry Silverstein (ed.), *The Social Control of Mental Illness* (New York: Thomas Y. Crowell Company, 1968).

Alcoholism and 20
drug abuse

Some people regard the drinking of beverage alcohol as a sign of moral disintegration and social irresponsibility. Similarly, many persons associate "drug abuse" with crime and unconscionable revolt against sacred principles. At the other extreme of opinion, drinking is associated with good fellowship and relief from tensions, and with social practices maintaining a healthy society, and drug use is defended as an expression of personal freedom and the individual's right to search for alternative styles of life in an age of impersonal bureaucracy.

QUALIFICATION AS A SOCIAL PROBLEM

These differences of opinion reflect a recognition that actual behavior departs significantly from legal or traditional social expectations. For some people, the use of drugs may be the discrepancy; for others, the discrepancy may be in the efforts to undermine the freedom of the users. The debate flourishes because all parties believe something can be done to remedy the discrepancy each sees, but there is little agreement on *what* to do or *how* to do it.

These value conflicts and general concern over the effects of alcoholism and drug abuse qualify these related topics as social problems. This chapter will first treat drug abuse and alcoholism separately and then consider them together in regard to three major strategies in societal reaction— prohibition and suppression, treatment, and education and prevention.

The use of drugs raises fundamental disagreements. Some groups interpret it as simple but extreme antisocial behavior calling for prohibition and suppressive measures against "criminal" users and traffickers. Other groups see the issue as one of personal maladjustment by troubled individuals requiring medical or psychological intervention. Still others focus attention on the flaws in social and cultural arrangements that produce frustrations and resort to intoxicants. Even if agreement can be reached on the proper measures to undertake, however, fundamental disputes emerge over which agency or profession should assume primary responsibility. For example, should the courts or medical establishment be the coordinators of an organized community response?

Drugs considered dangerous have been, or are, prohibited by law, thus qualifying this social problem as one of the *crimes without victims.* Features of this concept are willing exchange among adults of strongly demanded but legally prohibited goods or services.[1] (One major exception would be those persons who are tricked into drug use.) The addict himself appears to be the victim, but he is a "willing" partner in the transaction. It may be argued that he must be rescued from the harm he inflicts on himself, but is the self-harm sufficient to justify imposition of the force of the criminal law to save him from himself?

Addiction shares some of the features of the social problems already considered in this book. The strongly negative evaluation of the drug addict suggests the patterns of segregation and prejudice imposed on racial minorities. Most pertinent are the issues of overcriminalization of deviance, the weaknesses of the crime control model in serving treatment purposes, and conflicting purposes imposed on the system of criminal justice. The problem of drug abuse raises issues also involved in the delivery of medical care services, the obscurity of diagnosis in mental illness, the impact of urban life on psychiatric disorders, and the typical societal reactions to mental illness.

DEFINITION OF ADDICTION

Addiction is thrust into the area of public controversy by the subjective ways in which it is defined. When high emotionalism is engendered, drug use is indicted indiscriminately and all users are lumped together. But should the former or occasional user be differentiated from the habitual user? Is one shot of heroin sufficient to qualify a former user as a relapsed addict? Does addiction include the taking of drugs which have been "cut" sufficiently to forestall physical dependence? Is the status of the addict to be defined as that of a criminal or that of a medical patient? Is the use of

[1] Edwin M. Schur, *Crimes without Victims* (Englewood Cliffs, N.J.: Prentice-Hall, 1965), p. 169.

alcohol at a New Year's Eve party to be approved but smoking of mild marijuana to be considered moral degradation? The answers to these questions depend largely on the personal values of the individual, and indicate the difficulty of defining addiction objectively.

Physical and psychological dependence

Popularly the term "addiction" is identified with a compelling appetite which increases with each momentary satisfaction. Casual initial indulgence is supposed to be replaced with habituation which drives the user of drugs into increasingly antisocial behavior as a victim of his own cravings. Some theories assume an underlying predisposition of particular individuals toward addiction because of basic psychic disturbances.

The recent tendency is to substitute the term "physical dependence" for "addiction" and the term "psychological dependence" for "habituation," the aim being to lend greater precision to analysis.

Physical dependence involves tolerance and withdrawal illness. Tolerance refers to the condition in which the body adapts itself to the drug so that larger doses are progressively required to produce the effects obtained originally. When the body becomes accustomed to the drug, the absence of the drug produces pains, known as withdrawal illness; when the user is unconstrained, these distressing symptoms tend to lead to a search for drugs to alleviate the discomfort.

Psychological dependence refers to the impact of the drug experience as distinct from physical dependence per se. Lindesmith asks: What is the experience in which the craving for drugs is produced? As an answer, he suggests the characteristic craving is generated in the repetition of the experience of using drugs to relieve withdrawal distress provided the user learns to identify the absence of drugs with his discomfort.[2] The initial administration of drugs may have been part of medical treatment and the patient may not have been aware of that part of the treatment; or the naïve user may be unprepared for the experiences such use is expected to produce. In either case, he is unprepared for the withdrawal symptoms. The novice requires instruction from a physician or an experienced drug or the withdrawal symptoms. The novice requires instruction from a physician or an experienced drug user to identify drug abstinence as the source of his difficulty, and, therefore, learning within a social setting is injected into the dependency situation.

Marijuana and learning

Because marijuana does not produce the ineradicable craving characteristic of opiates, Becker reports that marijuana is used occasionally for

[2] Alfred R. Lindesmith, "Problems in the Social Psychology of Addiction," in Daniel M. Wilner and Gene O. Kassebaum (eds.), *Narcotics* (New York: McGraw-Hill Book Co., 1965), pp. 133–34.

the pleasure the user finds in it.[3] Becker distinguishes this "recreational" user from those few who smoke "pot" for its alleged prestige value. The "recreational" novice ordinarily does not smoke in a fashion that insures a dosage sufficient to produce the real symptoms of intoxication which provide pleasure. Additionally, he must learn to associate the symptoms of being high with the drug. Thirdly, he must learn to enjoy the effects he has learned to experience because at first these effects may be perceived as physically unpleasant or at least ambiguous. By completing this learning process, he finds marijuana consumption a pleasure. In undergoing the process he acquires a new orientation to the world. In this fashion, Becker makes a case against the argument that the marijuana user had some predisposing psychological trait accounting for his resort to the drug.

In an experiment where users were compared with subjects previously unexposed to marijuana, the naïve users did not get high after smoking in a setting devoid of peer group instruction on what to expect from the drug. In the same setting regular users did get high. Depending on the strength of the dose, the naïve users did show impaired performance on simple intellectual and psychometer tests, whereas some regular users even improved their performance slightly after smoking marijuana.[4]

Commonly drug addiction is explained by the occurrence of drug-induced euphoria, a feeling of well-being, relaxation, and happiness. However, this romanticized conception of habitual drug use should be distinguished from the hopeless dependence on the drug implied by the term "being hooked." Wikler doubts that euphoria explains continued use. Tolerance to the euphoric effect of morphine develops quickly, and the addict is beset by remorse and anxiety. He would have to balance any benefits of euphoria against the misery of physical dependence. Wikler prefers to explain persistent drug use in terms of unconscious motivations related to environmental circumstances. "Being hooked" involves the addict in sustained "hustling" for drugs to prevent boredom and to hold the approval of other addicts. Recurrently he experiences discomfort as· the dose wears down, and this drives him to repeat the dose to abolish the discomfort.[5] (It seems reasonable to assume, however, that the opiate addict in the agony of aggravated withdrawal illness is more concerned with gaining access to drugs than winning the approval of other addicts.)

DRUGS: THEIR NATURE AND IMPACT

American attitudes toward use of drugs are ambivalent. The remarkable contemporary developments in pharmacology are part of the technologi-

---

[3] Howard S. Becker, "Becoming A Marihuana User," in John O. O'Donnell and John C. Ball (eds.), Narcotic Addiction (New York: Harper and Row, 1966), pp. 109–22.

[4] Andrew T. Weil, Norman E. Zinberg, and Judith M. Nelson, "Clinical and Psychological Effects of Marijuana in Man," Science, Vol. 162 (December 13, 1968), pp. 1235–38.

[5] Abraham Wikler, "Conditioning Factors in Opiate Addiction and Relapse," in Wilner and Kasselbaun, Narcotics, pp. 86–88.

cal revolution promising to bring relief to sick bodies and troubled minds. Previous chapters have summarized the possibilities of opening new frontiers of knowledge in medical care and in framing more promising approaches to mental illness than custodial hospitalization.[6] However, pharmacology also raises difficult issues in the potential use of personality control drugs as weapons for despotism, excessive costs and dangerous administration of drugs, and framing of policies for distribution of drugs in ways assuring their beneficial use and avoiding adverse consequences for the individual and his community.

Problems for the United States

One of the remarkable features of drug abuse in the United States has been its relatively recent recognition as a major problem. Part of the answer lies in the spread of marijuana use into segments of the community outside the ghetto. However, even more basic, is what we shall call "hyperemotional evaluation."

Into the beginning of the 20th century, Lindesmith and Gagnon point out, addiction was rarely mentioned in connection with juvenile delinquency, had little relationship to the criminal underworld, and was largely identified with opium smoking by some Chinese immigrants and a few underworld persons. Around the turn of the century, a change in the situation emerged with the beginning of legal measures against drug use.[7] Furthermore, the patterns of drug use changed, particularly in the United States. During the 19th century, addiction appeared to be less concentrated among males, blacks, lower social classes, and younger age groups than it is today.

Why, Lindesmith and Gagnon ask, the changes in the population of drug users between the 19th century and today? Earlier, middle-aged urban and rural women of the middle classes were heavily represented, and blacks were relatively immune to this influence. Accordingly, these authors find unsatisfactory the current explanation of drug use as reflecting simply a loss of a sense of meaning in life for individuals caught in the frustrations of urban disorganization.

The missing ingredient in this explanation, they argue, is that in this century our nation has developed policies for the control of drug abuse through reliance on the suppressive tactics of criminal law enforcement. In nations where addicts have access to legal drugs and illicit traffic is minimal, the characteristics of addicts resemble those in America in the 19th century. With the shutting off of access to legal drugs, however, a lucrative market for criminal organizations emerged in areas of the large

[6] See Chapter 4, p. 101; Chapter 18, pp. 449–50; and Chapter 19, pp. 493–94.
[7] The Alfred R. Lindesmith and John H. Gagnon, "Anomie and Drug Addiction," in Marshall B. Clinard (ed.), *Anomie and Deviant Behavior* (New York: Free Press, 1964), pp. 163–65, 171–74.

cities, usually port cities, where law enforcement is particularly inefficient. The conditions for profitable illicit transactions shaped the patterns whereby illicit drugs were available. In short, the policies taken toward drug use affected the current dimensions of drug abuse as an urban problem largely concentrated, until relatively recently, in the ghetto.

An important virtue of this analysis is that it focuses attention on the *social* dimensions of drug abuse, which frequently are interpreted as only the sum of a large number of disorganized *individuals*. However, regardless of the interpretation, the problem merits great concern. Richards and Carroll summarize several studies to show the dimensions of the problem.[8]

The number of narcotic addicts in 1969 has been estimated at about 109,000, but this figure is believed to be short of the actual number. Derived from the number of deaths attributed to heroin, another calculation estimates 90,000 to 104,000 heroin addicts in New York City alone in 1969 and approximately 200,000 in the nation. It is believed that marijuana use has increased rapidly since 1965. Some 8 to 12 million Americans have had some experience with marijuana; about 10 percent are chronic users, 25 percent occasional users, and the remainder one-time "tasters." There is evidence, however, that the number of marijuana users declined in 1970, and fragmentary information suggests less use of LSD since 1968 among college and high school students.

The uncertainty of estimates, Richards and Carroll explain, stems from a number of difficulties in obtaining reliable data. Information is derived largely from one-time studies in scattered locations with various sampling techniques. The only source of national statistics is the reporting system of the Bureau of Narcotics and Dangerous Drugs, which utilizes voluntary reports, largely from law-enforcement agencies. Health and social agencies appear to be reluctant to provide names of drug users because of the confidentiality of the doctor-patient relationship and the possibility that the names will be used for law-enforcement purposes. Therefore the accuracy of BNDD information is questionable.

The psychological and physiological impact of drug use on the individual varies according to a number of factors. Blum summarizes some of the evidence.[9] In some instances even chronic users of mind-altering drugs do not appear to suffer damage to health or personal adjustment, but there are notable exceptions. One-time users have suffered psychosis; one-time overdoses of morphine, barbiturates, and other psychoactive substances have caused death. The possibility of damage increases with greater size of dose and length of time of use. The degree of effect varies with the social and medical history of the individual. Poverty-stricken males are among the groups most vulnerable to ill-effects of heroin, in-

[8] Louise G. Richards and Eleanor E. Carroll, "Illicit Drug Use and Addiction in the United States," *Public Health Reports,* Vol. 85 (December 1970), pp. 1035–41.
[9] Richard H. Blum, "Drugs, Behavior, and Crime," *Annals of American Academy of Political and Social Science,* Vol. 374 (November 1967), pp. 141–42.

dicating that the social setting affects the physiological and psychological consequences. Similarly, the degree of damage appears to be related to whether the person has learned to use drugs safely. Teaching includes information on safe dosage, the benefits such use is supposed to obtain, and the kinds of relationships with other persons associated with use. Self-medication for "escape" from problems is more dangerous than use of drugs for social facilitation or specific medical problems under competent supervision.

Opiates and cocaine

Statutes refer to opiates and cocaine as narcotic drugs, although a dictionary definition of "narcotic" would include the wider range of drugs which induce sleep, dull the senses, or relieve pain. (Some states also include marijuana as a narcotic.) The opiates include opium, morphine, their derivatives and compounds, and their synthetic equivalents. The social problem of drugs in the United States largely involves heroin, a morphine derivative. Cocaine is not the problem it once was.[10]

A white powdered substance, heroin is derived from opium. Usually it is injected. The person becomes flushed and experiences a tingling sensation. Gradually, he lapses into a state of reverie known as euphoria. With regularity of administration, he becomes dependent on the drug and gains tolerance so that a heavier dose is required to create the same level of effect he experienced originally. If the addict does not receive his daily supply, he develops withdrawal symptoms of stomach cramps, diarrhea, and muscular pains. As a stimulant produced from coca leaves, cocaine is a white, odorless, bitter-tasting powder which is either sniffed or injected. It produces fleeting pleasurable sensations, but cumulative dosages bring hallucinations and disagreeable symptoms such as heavy perspiration and tremors. Its unpleasant symptoms and anxiety reactions have reduced its use.[11]

When supplied with drugs, the opiate addict appears and feels relatively "normal" in the sense of his own satisfactions in the short run. There is considerable doubt that his life is "normal" in the sense of responsible participation in the organized life which makes human beings distinctive among animals, however. He suffers more than his share of physical disease, but major tissue pathology does not seem to occur, and some addicts live to advanced age.[12] As a depressant, the opiate in the short

---

[10] President's Commission on Law Enforcement and Administration of Justice, *Task Force Report: Narcotics and Drug Abuse* (Washington, D.C.: U.S. Government Printing Office, 1967), p. 2.

[11] David W. Maurer and Victor H. Vogel, *Narcotics and Narcotic Addiction* (2d ed.; Springfield, Ill.: Charles C Thomas, 1962), pp. 62–63, 115–16.

[12] Alfred R. Lindesmith, *The Addict and the Law* (Bloomington, Ind.: Indiana University Press, 1965), p. X.

term relieves anxiety and tensions and reduces the sex and hunger drives. In the long run, the opiate interferes with a self-sustaining life by producing apathy, inability to concentrate, and reduced physical activity.

Marijuana

Coming from the female cannabis plant, whose stem produces the fiber for hemp rope, marijuana consists of the dried tops of the uncultivated plant. A resin is secreted around the flowers of the female plant, and the drug's potency depends on how much of the resin is included and on the conditions under which the plant is grown. In eastern countries cultivated cannabis produces more potent drugs, with hashish consisting of pure resin with some five or eight times the strength of marijuana.[13]

The effects of marijuana range from mild to dramatic alteration of consciousness, depending on the potency of the preparation and the amount consumed. The immediate physiological effects are somewhat minimal. Pulse rate and blood pressure increase, the pupils of the eyes become larger, blood sugar level rises, the ability to coordinate muscles decreases. Perception of time and distance and thought processes are distorted. The user generally describes feelings of euphoria and enhanced senses of taste and touch. Some users experience feelings of being separate from their bodies or other fantasies which can stimulate panic. Very occasionally, temporary psychotic reactions are experienced.

Grinspoon concludes there is abundant evidence that marijuana is not addictive. Cessation of its use does not bring withdrawal symptoms, and the user feels no need to increase dosage. Tobacco and alcohol have greater habituation potential than marijuana.[14] Nevertheless, habitual use of marijuana for "escape" is associated with loss of motivation for achievement; this consequence for youth is devastating in the long run if opportunity for career preparation is lost because advancing age places him beyond the "point of return." Inexperienced users have had panic reactions which clear up in a few hours or days, but the weaker doses of marijuana scarcely ever produce such an effect.[15]

Hallucinogenic drugs

LSD (lysergic acid diethylamide) is derived from a fungus attacking rye and wheat. As all hallucinogenic drugs do, LSD causes some individuals to see colors, shapes, and objects that are really not there. In this respect

[13] William H. McGlothlin, "Marijuana," in Margaret O. Hyde (ed.), *Mind Drugs* (New York: McGraw-Hill Book Co., 1968), pp. 26–30; and Weil, et al., "Clinical and Psychological Effects of Marijuana," pp. 1235–38.

[14] Lester Grinspoon, "Marihuana," *Scientific American,* Vol. 221 (December, 1969), p. 21.

[15] McGlothlin, "Marijuana," pp. 32–33, 39–40; for answers to frequent questions about effects of marijuana, see: E. R. Bloomquist, *Marijuana* (Beverly Hills, Calif.: Glencoe Press, 1968), pp. 167–212.

it is more powerful than other hallucinogens such as psilocybin and mescaline. Psilocybin is derived from certain mushrooms; mescaline, from peyote cactus. The objects seen by users of "hallucinogens" should not be confused with "hallucinations," which refer to the conviction of the perceiver that he sees an object or event for which other observers can find no objective basis. Usually the user of hallucinogens can distinguish between the action of the drug and reality.[16]

The subjective effects of hallucinogens depend on the properties and potency of the drug itself, the personality traits and current mood of the user, and the social and psychological context. The experiences are never the result of the drug alone. In fact, sometimes a nonuser, observing someone else taking the drug, will behave as though under its influence. However, in experimental situations, the subjects taking an inactive substance can be distinguished by their answers to questions and physiological responses. Excitement of the sympathetic nervous system is indicated in dilation of the pupils, higher blood pressure, spinal reflexes such as knee jerks, and a general arousal of alertness. Because the drugs are not physiologically addicting, there are no withdrawal symptoms.

An apparent recent increase in the use of hallucinogens out of curiosity has caused a number of experts to call for firmer controls. The taking of the drugs without knowledgeable persons present appears to have increased the incidence of "bad trips." The hazards of the drugs are related to one of their possible benefits to mankind; medical researchers suspect that these drugs stimulate the early stages of schizophrenia and may shed light on some chemical cause.

DRUGS AND SOCIETY

The conception of a drug addict as a fiend, a pervert, and a threat to civilization emerged in the United States soon after the Civil War. The myth of the "dope fiend" as a sexual menace has been kept alive by suggestive references to "dope parties" and "vicious crimes," although opiates actually depress the sexual appetite. Because of the force of the propaganda, however, it is extremely difficult to gain a hearing for the presentation of objective facts on the nature of drug addiction.[17]

Hyperemotional evaluations

Heroin, cannabis, and hallucinogens are popularly described as treacherous and demoniacal in power to tempt and destroy beyond alcohol. The

[16] Duke D. Fisher, "LSD for Science and Kicks," in Hyde, *Mind Drugs,* pp. 67, 73; Frank Barron, Murray E. Jarvik, and Sterling Burnell, Jr., "The Hallucinogenic Drugs," *Scientific American,* Vol. 210 (April 1964), pp. 29–37.

[17] Lawrence Kolb, *Drug Addiction* (Springfield, Ill.: Charles C Thomas, 1962), pp. 152–66.

Drug Abuse: A Personal Problem and a Public Issue. Beyond the implications of physical and psychological dependence for the individual user, drug abuse involves normative conflicts and a major public issue—whether this individual should be treated as a criminal or a patient.

treachery is seen in their false allure of pleasure. Blum wonders whether the notion of private pleasure stirs particular rejection in a society oriented to work and self-discipline according to norms of the dominant culture.[18] Similarly, noting that Britain demonstrates less punitive attitudes toward drug users, Schur asks whether Americans see the addict as "un-American" because of his characteristic passivity and nonproductivity in violation of the preferred activism and work ethic dominant in American culture.[19] Since they are more likely to abide by these norms, alcoholics in general would draw less general censure than drug addicts.

In western culture the religious mystic is suspected of heresy or madness; the chemical mystic draws similar suspicion. A society geared to moderation, Blum suggests, rejects the ecstasy and orgiastic frenzies attributed to the drug experience.[20] The recent broadening concern over marijuana is also explained in part by its spread into the community beyond the black, Puerto Rican, and Mexican-American ghettos.[21]

Drugs are employed because the user believes he gains benefits from them. They dull unpleasant or intolerable inner feelings and provide temporary escape from the pressures of competition in a complex world. They alleviate boredom or indecision and they delay fatigue. When taken in the company of peers, they may provide a sense of belonging. They have been employed to induce religious experience. Claims have also been made that drugs stimulate creativity and intellectual innovation, but these claims have been tested with marijuana, especially in the area of musical performance, with uniformly negative results (although the use of drugs may make for more spontaneity).[22]

Conversely, narcotic addicts appear to have a mortality rate considerably higher than their ages in the twenties and thirties would indicate.[23] Overdoses are fatal, reliance on illegal suppliers risks the absence of quality control as a safeguard against adulterants and unreliable dosage, concentration of effort on obtaining drugs favors neglect of one's health in other regards, and there is the danger of contaminated needles causing hepatitis, tetanus, tissue infections, and skin abscesses.

Lasagra protests the emotionality, hysteria, and exaggeration which have blocked a reasonable approach to addiction. He calls for recognition that some drugs in proper dosage provide relief for medical patients, may normalize behavior, and prevent conflict. Some undetected addicts have functioned well in spite of daily drug use. Furthermore, the legitimate use

[18] Richard H. Blum, "On the Presence of Demons," in Richard H. Blum and Associates, *Society and Drugs* (San Francisco: Jossey-Bass, 1969), pp. 332–34.
[19] Edwin Schur, "Attitudes Toward Addicts: Some General Observations and Comparative Findings," *American Journal of Orthopsychiatry,* Vol. 34 (January 1964), pp. 80–90.
[20] Blum, "On the Presence of Demons."
[21] Grinspoon, "Marihuana," p. 21.
[22] McGlothlin, "Marijuana," p. 41.
[23] Charles E. Cherubin, "The Medical Sequelae of Narcotic Addiction," *Annals of Internal Medicine,* Vol. 67 (July 1967), pp. 23–33.

of drugs in medicine raises little prospect of addiction of patients given morphine for short-lived painful states.[24]

Goode is impressed with the function of marijuana as an ideological symbol for moral values held before the debate over legalization of marijuana. Those who approve legalization, Goode argues, identify with a glorification of the irrational over logic, bursts of insight over chains of thought, and disruption of traditional forms of behavior in a search for creative experience. Conversely, the opponent tends to see the drug as evil before he resorts to arguments that it stimulates crime, immorality, and mental breakdown.[25]

Drugs and subculture

The most prevalent explanation for the spread of drug use is the personality weaknesses of the drug user. Eldridge considers this explanation to be misleading in two respects.[26] It suggests that there is something unique about the weaknesses of the addict which leads to addiction. Further, it implies that drug use leads to these infirmities, whereas in actuality the prior existence of personal problems more likely stimulated the drug use as a mode of adjustment. Eldridge prefers to see the explanation in terms of the individual personality structure or the social structure of the users' communities which tended them toward this mode of adjustment.

In slums, Feldman believes, the movement of a large minority of youth into drug use grows from an ideological seed bed which confers high status and prestige upon the *stand-up cat*.[27] In the folklore of the street, he is characterized by daring, strength, predilection for excitement, and toughness. The first drug users in the slums seem to be the older adolescents who have earned stand-up cat reputations. They serve as distributors for underworld suppliers and as models for younger aspirants to the stand-up cat status. Feldman sees the aspiration for this status to be at the core of the spread of drug use among slum youth.

The spread of drug use outside of the ghetto appears to be related to the social functions it serves for satisfying curiosity and gaining new experience, and as an aspect of intergenerational conflict and a means for displaying apparent sophistication. Why do otherwise conforming middle-class youths use marijuana in spite of the penalties they risk? Examining attitudes of high school students, Mauss finds evidence that such youths

---

[24] Louis Lasagra, "Addicting Drugs and Medical Practice: Toward the Elaboration of Realistic Goals and the Eradication of Myths, Mirages, and Half-Truths," in Wilner and Kassebaum, *Narcotics,* pp. 5, 62–63.

[25] Erich Goode, "Marijuana and the Politics of Reality," *Journal of Health and Social Behavior,* Vol. 10 (June 1969), pp. 83–94.

[26] William Butler Eldridge, *Narcotics and the Law* (New York: New York University Press, 1962), pp. 23–24.

[27] Harvey W. Feldman, "Ideological Supports to Becoming and Remaining a Heroin Addict," *Journal of Health and Social Behavior,* Vol. 9 (June 1968), pp. 131–39.

identify marijuana use as part of a collegiate way of life. Conversely, students not planning to go to college and those of lower social class status had lower rates of marijuana use.[28] Among college students, Suchman reports marijuana use is more prevalent among those who adhere to a "hang-loose" ethic which repudiates the values of conventional society.[29]

In one study of a drug subculture attached to a university campus, Carey describes the users as regular students, part-time students, dropouts, and a few who never attended college.[30] The campus environment attracted them as a place of political freedom, comfortable living, and bohemian atmosphere. *Experimental users* try marijuana chiefly because of some form of disillusionment with society and because the student is placed in a setting where drugs are available. Fear of being found out by authorities or his family is a paramount concern. *Recreational users* move on to regular use as a pleasant adjunct to many social situations without becoming dependent on drugs. Continuing to prepare for a career, they see themselves as especially intellectually oriented, sensitive, and open-minded. The *heads* take drugs frequently and in variety. They are the most open in centering their lives around drugs separate from the "straight" world.

In light of the subcultural basis for the spread of drug use, it has been argued that current strategies for control of addiction are based on a faulty premise.[31] While these strategies emphasize getting the user off drugs through treatment and law enforcement, the proper emphasis would be on the emergence of a self-image and way of life built on narcotics. Recognizing that he is dependent on drugs and assimilated into a culture of drug-users, the individual identifies himself as an addict.

Characteristics of drug users

Large cities with minority-group populations concentrated in ghettos are the prime environment within which drug use has flourished in the last several decades. More recent years have shown a decline in average age of users and in strength of the opiate dose. The users tend to be more sociable in congregating with other users.[32] In California, arrests remained at about the same number between 1962 and 1966 for drugs other than marijuana. For marijuana, arrests increased greatly, with the gains concentrated among whites and the young. This trend also held for other states.[33]

[28] Armand L. Mauss, "Anticipatory Socialization toward College as a Factor in Adolescent Marijuana Use," *Social Problems,* Vol. 16 (Winter 1969), pp. 357–64.
[29] Edward A. Suchman, "The 'Hang-Loose' Ethic and the Spirit of Drug Use," *Journal of Health and Social Behavior,* Vol. 9 (June 1968), pp. 146–55.
[30] James T. Carey, *The College Drug Scene* (Englewood Cliffs, N.J.: Prentice-Hall, 1968).
[31] Isadore Chein, Donald L. Gerard, Robert S. Lee, and Eva Rosenfeld, *The Road to H: Narcotics, Delinquency, and Social Policy* (New York: Basic Books, 1964), pp. 14, 26–27.
[32] Charles Winick, "Epidemiology of Narcotics Use," in Wilner and Kassebaum, *Narcotics,* pp. 9–10, 16.
[33] Carey, *The College Drug Scene,* pp. 44–46.

Information was gathered on drug users, ages 16 to 20 years, from case files of courts and municipal hospitals in three boroughs of New York City. Of the 1,558 census tracts covered by the study, 15 tracts contributed 83 percent of the cases although they had only 29 percent of the total population aged 16 to 20 years. The researchers report that the drug-epidemic areas were characterized by high concentrations of blacks and Puerto Ricans, high percentages of wives separated from husbands, particularly low incomes and average education, a disproportionate number of men in unskilled jobs or unemployed, and similar factors associated with slums.[34]

Opiate users are primarily young adults. Winick explains the relatively few older users in several ways. Unsterilized hypodermics cause infections fatal to some already weakened by malnutrition, for example, and overdoses, inadvertent taking of wrong drugs, and accidents related to drug use add to death rates. Winick also advances a *maturing out hypothesis* which suggests that the need for drugs declines in the ages in the thirties. The frustrations of school, sexual adjustment, vocational choice, and establishment of a family press some adolescents and young adults to use drugs, but with the reduction of these urgencies, the older individual is more likely to accept some place in the established order and contacts with drugs become briefer.[35]

SHOULD MARIJUANA BE LEGALIZED?

Through the Marijuana Tax Act of 1937, Congress outlawed the sale, possession, or use of marijuana largely because of arguments that it leads to aggression, insanity, sex crimes, and idleness. Now this decision is being questioned. The debate preceding enactment of the 1937 law and the current dispute over removal of legal prohibition are significant because the use of marijuana has become a symbol of a host of conflicts in our society.

Assessment of frequent arguments

The debates over legalization, Kaplan says, involve users as well as nonusers because the issues extend beyond marijuana to obscure objective evaluation of any effect of the drug itself. In the minds of many people marijuana is identified with a life-style of immediate gratification, blunted competition for material values, and the pursuit of pleasure. Proponents of legalization are likely to argue that marijuana use expresses personal

[34] Chein, et al., *The Road to H.,* p. 39, 55.
[35] Winick, "Epidemiology of Narcotics Use," pp. 7–9.

freedom and enhances artistic creativity. Opponents are likely to identify the drug with political radicalism, erosion of respect for authority, and social permissiveness. There are obscure fears that the drug has something to do with violent crime, unrest among racial minorities, undermining of the moral values of the dominant culture, loss of "law and order," and behavior of some youths which arouses outrage of the "silent majority." [36]

Legal prohibition of marijuana is defended on grounds that cannabis releases suppressed wishes and counters inhibitions, thus making criminal behavior more likely. Conversely, prohibition is opposed on grounds that its use produces a "cool," passive feeling. Kaplan states that neither explanation is proven because the expectation of the user influences the effect of the drug. Nevertheless, most users expect a passive feeling, and this is what they get. Furthermore, controlled laboratory experiments, although not conclusive, do support the view that the effect is antiaggressive.[37] Police files frequently are cited to indicate that marijuana users represent an undue share of violent criminals. However, there is insufficient evidence that the offender actually is a user, that he was under the influence of marijuana at the time of the crime, or that marijuana use was the cause of the crime.[38]

One assumption is that marijuana use is a step toward later use of heroin. While it is true that the majority of heroin users coming to the attention of authorities have had prior experience with marijuana, this fact does not demonstrate that marijuana leads to heroin use. Beckett argues that the legal prohibition unjustly lumps marijuana users who smoke "pot" for pleasure only and without danger with the minority who move on to heroin.[39] The majority of youthful drug users, Blumer says, have no association with heroin users and have no access to heroin. Those youthful users who do have access primarily come into contact through "hustling," that is, the gaining of income without working. Some of these "entrepreneurs" try heroin, including a portion who get "hooked." [40]

In a sample weighted heavily with frequent users and middle-class subjects, Goode finds two thirds of the marijuana users had taken at least one other drug at least once. However, only 13 percent had used heroin and only 5 percent more than three times.[41] Rather than indicating that marijuana causes heroin use, multiple-drug use suggests that those persons

[36] John Kaplan, *Marijuana—The New Prohibition* (New York: World Publishing Company, 1970), pp. 3–18.

[37] Kaplan, ibid., p. 136.

[38] President's Commission on Law Enforcement and Administration of Justice, *Task Force Report*, p. 13.

[39] Dale Beckett, "Should We Legalize Pot?" in Erich Goode (ed.), *Marijuana* (New York: Atherton Press, 1969), pp. 148–49.

[40] Herbert Blumer, "Attitude Toward Addiction," in Goode, ibid., pp. 85–88.

[41] Erich Goode, "Multiple Drug Use among Marijuana Smokers," *Social Problems,* Vol. 17 (Summer 1969), pp. 48–64.

predisposed to use drugs will experiment with various drugs until they find the one most satisfactory to them. Since marijuana is more accessible than other drugs, they are likely to start with it.

Kaplan contrasts the relative absence of heroin use among those student groups using marijuana with the concurrence of both drugs among poor urban blacks and Spanish-speaking Americans, where heroin use is concentrated. This pattern runs counter to any causal connection. He argues that prohibition of marijuana makes its use as criminal as heroin use and thereby drives the users of a relatively mild drug underground to increase the number of law violators with which police must deal. Thus, the suppression of heroin is made even more difficult. Furthermore, the identification of marijuana with heroin undermines the credibility of public-education efforts to forestall movement from marijuana to heroin.[42]

Another concern is that legalization of marijuana would undermine the cultural attitudes against drug use in general. Rather than providing a neutral attitude toward marijuana use, legalization could stimulate a cultural legitimation which might favor such use, and with the elimination of the function of marijuana use as a gesture of rebellion against the "establishment," this function may be transferred to genuinely dangerous drugs.

The protagonists of marijuana argue that such use is a choice consistent with personal freedom. Since alcohol drinkers and tobacco smokers have such freedom of choice, why not "pot" smokers? In refutation, Beckett points out the minority bear a responsibility for considering the consequences on other persons, including loved ones. The comparison with alcohol and tobacco smoking is weakened by the latent assumption that one form of potential health danger justifies another. Furthermore, arbitrary identification of marijuana use with individual freedoms overlooks the possibility of license among the wide variety of motives for its use and of the situations within which it may be used.

Regulation as a solution

As opposed to prohibition, regulation of marijuana holds superior promise for orderly control of its quality and conditions of its sale. Violation of constitutional guarantees and the criminalization of users would be avoided. Furthermore, McGlothlin and West say, the legalization of marijuana is in keeping with the increasing acceptance of pleasure for its own sake in an age of abundance.[43] Because marijuana does not involve physical dependence and long-term physical effects, a system of regulatory control is consistent with a trend toward greater personal freedom when the social interests are not endangered.

---

[42] Kaplan, *Marijuana,* pp. 259–60.
[43] William H. McGlothlin and Louis J. West, "The Marijuana Problem: An Overview," *American Journal of Psychiatry,* Vol. 125 (September 1968), pp. 376–78.

Under a "licensing model" of marijuana control recommended by Kaplan, marijuana would be sold by licensed dealers without impediment as long as certain conditions were met. This model is essentially the way the liquor trade is regulated under the open license system. Unlicensed sale would be criminal. Quality of purity and potency would be controlled. The price would be controlled through taxation to provide revenue to pay for drug control and education. Sales to children would be prohibited; prices would place it largely out of their reach. Kaplan admits licensing probably would increase use of the drug, but present trends indicate that such an increase is inevitable. The disadvantages he believes, would be outweighed by the social costs of making marijuana use a crime.[44]

ALCOHOLISM: NATURE AND IMPACT

Usually alcoholism is defined as a condition in which the individual has lost control over his alcohol intake in that he is consistently unable to refrain from drinking once he begins. Elements in problem drinking would be excessive intake of alcoholic beverages, the individual's increasing worry over his own drinking, the disturbance of his functioning in his social world as indicated by troubles with the police, his wife, his boss, and so on; and his loss of control over his own drinking.

Qualification as social problem

Abuse of alcohol is related to social problems both directly and indirectly. Similar to drug abuse, alcoholism is a major health problem which interferes with the efficiency of the drinker as a family member and employee. Depending on the degree of drinking and the moral stance of his groups toward drinking, he can receive negative evaluation by family and other individuals or groups, often producing penalties such as job loss or general ostracism. His family and associates may suffer from his ostracism and his inefficiency in meeting his role obligations. Drinking scandals can discredit the organizations with which he is identified—employing organizations, colleges, fraternal groups, and so on. The criminalization of drinking also places him in the status of a law breaker, thus complicating the tasks of the system of criminal justice and raising the difficulties suggested by the concept of crimes without victims.

Problem drinking is a drain on the economic system through on-the-job accidents and worker absenteeism. The impact is particularly great in the productive ages 35 to 50 years when an employee is likely to develop specialized skills or supervisor status in which his efficiency is crucial to

[44] Kaplan, *Marijuana,* pp. 349–50.

the employer. However, some alcoholics claim they are especially cautious in avoiding accidents, that they are absent from jobs when they would be most accident-prone, and that their habitual work routines enable them to manage the effects of alcohol in repetitive jobs.[45]

Background on alcohol and drinking

A great variety of foods can be converted into alcohol easily and at low cost. Alcohol can be stored for long periods and transported with facility to simplify bootlegging and smuggling when it is prohibited by law. Through a metabolic process, alcohol provides energy and calories. High-strength alcohol can injure the mucous membranes, but a mild irritant action stimulates the flow of gastric juice to induce appetite for a good meal. Alcohol acts primarily on the nervous system but probably affects all cells. The effect on the body depends on the level of alcohol concentration in the body; alcohol can result in death when its concentration in the bloodstream reaches 0.7 percent.[46]

Drinking reduces discrimination, affecting judgment and control of the user's faculties. Although it is a depressant, alcohol has been described as a stimulant because it tingles the tongue, causes a slight burning sensation, and releases inhibitions. Long-term drinking has its most noticeable effect on the digestive system in terms of gastritis and cirrhosis of the liver and on the nervous system as manifested in memory lapses, hallucinations, and extreme tremor.

The aggregate per capita consumption of alcohol in the United States has increased, but the gain reflects a wider prevalence of drinking in the population rather than greater consumption per drinker.[47] Consumption of alcohol is a typical behavior among Americans. A sample survey of continental United States indicates only 22 percent have never used such beverages.[48] Of the consumers, only 32 percent drink no more than once a year. Another 15 percent are infrequent users, averaging less than once a month. Drinking at least once a month, low-quantity light drinkers represent 28 percent of the consumers; medium-quantity moderate drinkers, 13 percent. The remainder, 12 percent, are heavy drinkers, defined by this survey as taking at least five drinks a month. The highest proportions of heavy drinkers were found among men aged 30 to 34 and 45 to 59 and among women 21 to 24 and 45 to 49. Among the drinkers, 26 percent of the men and 5 percent of the women were heavy drinkers.

[45] Harrison M. Trice, "The Job Behavior of Problem Drinkers," in David J. Pittman and Charles R. Snyder (eds.), *Society, Culture, and Drinking Patterns* (New York: John Wiley & Sons, 1962), pp. 493–510.

[46] Chauncy D. Leake, "Good-Willed Judgment on Alcohol," in Salvatore P. Lucia (ed.), *Alcohol and Civilization* (New York: McGraw-Hill Book Co., 1963), pp. 16–19.

[47] Leake, ibid., p. 3.

[48] Don Cahalan, Ira H. Cisin and Helen M. Crossley, *American Drinking Practices* (New Haven, Conn.: College and University Press, 1969), pp. 184–85.

ALCOHOL AND SOCIETY

The proper place of beverage alcohol in society draws diverse and conflicting evaluations. It may be associated with the dregs of society and seen as a moral failing. Another response is to accept drinking but to censure the man who cannot "hold his liquor," including the alcoholic.

Norms and alcohol consumption

A particular group may forbid drinking of alcoholic beverages (*proscriptive norms*), and another group may spell out the ways in which consumption may occur (*prescriptive norms*) without violating expected standards. Research indicates that heavy drinking is more characteristic of persons introduced to drinking while members of groups with proscriptive norms than among persons drawn from groups with prescriptive norms. For example, Snyder finds that the intoxication rate is higher among drinking students drawn from ascetic Protestant and Mormon groups than among Jewish students who are not subject to religious prohibitions. In traditional Judaism, drinking is integrated into the rituals of holy days, festivals, and the recognition of changes of status. Drinking is learned in a ritualized manner under family control.[49] Mizruchi and Perrucci point out that the prescriptive norms are more flexible in that a degree of conformity is expected rather than total abstinence and that explicit guidance is provided for behavior.[50]

The distinction between the heavy drinker and the alcoholic varies with the level of tolerance found in the particular subculture. When the group accepts heavy drinking, recognition of true alcoholism in early stages is delayed because the group is less likely than an abstinent group to see the heavy drinker as a deviant.[51] The norms of the particular group affect the distinction made between the heavy drinker and the alcoholic. The unwritten rules involve level of consumption permitted, emphasis placed on fulfillment of roles such as breadwinner or parent, and what is considered to be proper in drinking behavior.[52]

Social ambivalence toward drinking

In our culture the conflict between asceticism and the search for pleasure creates what Myerson calls *social ambivalence.* Controversies ranging around alcohol, he says, reflect conflict between the values of hedonism

[49] Charles R. Snyder, *Alcohol and the Jews* (Glencoe, Ill.: The Free Press, 1958), p. 189.

[50] Ephraim H. Mizruchi and Robert Perrucci, "Norm Qualities and Differential Effects of Deviant Behavior: An Exploratory Analysis," *American Sociological Review,* Vol. 27 (June 1962), pp. 391–399.

[51] The labeling process is considered in Chapter 2, pp. 55–62.

[52] Margaret J. Sargent, "The Concept of Alcoholism as a Mental Illness," *Quarterly Journal of Studies on Alcohol,* Vol. 29 (December 1968), pp. 974–78.

and values demanding an austere and self-denying life. Extolled in song, drinking in fellowship is identified with maintenance of social ties. Raising the glass symbolizes sharing of experiences with one's fellows at a wedding celebration, sealing a business contract, or serving as good host. Opposing this interpretation, ascetism urges us to regard beverage alcohol as subverting duty, religion, work efficiency, and psychological equilibrium.

Myerson sees effective control of alcoholism endangered by the excesses of either set of values. Excessive ascetism denies the reality of the pleasure principle in human life and the usefulness of temperate drinking in relaxing tension and releasing good fellowship. Conversely, extravagant hedonism would legitimatize antisocial consequences, personal disorganization, and unrestricted quest for profits in the liquor trade.[53]

From the perspective of persons morally certain that alcohol consumption is an unmitigated evil, the persistence of drinking among Americans must be a frustrating puzzle. Probably the simplest popular explanation is that drinkers are perverse and somewhat antisocial people who place their personal and immediate satisfactions before the social and long-term interests seen by the opponents of drinking. This explanation overlooks the grounding of alcohol consumption within social institutions and within the web of social life. In equating moderate drinking with alcoholism, temperance groups have placed themselves in opposition to other subcultures and economic interests.

Sociocultural environment and alcohol

The relationship between drinking and sociocultural environment is suggested by the distribution of alcoholism. For example, a sample survey of residents of the Borough of Manhattan indicates that the groups most vulnerable to alcoholism are widowers, divorced or separated persons of both sexes, blacks of both sexes, the least educated, and persons with the lowest incomes. Jews show a remarkably low incidence. On the basis of various psychological measures, alcoholics show marked psychological stress.[54]

Some segments of the public are especially concerned about drinking among college students because they believe that alcohol plays a dominant part in an unconventional life style which "perverts" decent young people. The arbitrary identification of campus life with heavy drinking illustrates the conflict between images of hedonism and ascetic values

---

[53] Abraham Myerson, "Alcoholism: The Role of Social Ambivalence," in Raymond G. McCarthy (ed.), *Drinking and Intoxication* (New Haven, Conn.: College & University Press, 1959), pp. 306–12.

[54] Margaret B. Bailey, Paul W. Haberman, and Harold Alksne, "The Epidemiology of Alcoholism in a Urban Residential Area," *Quarterly Journal of Studies on Alcohol,* Vol. 26 (March 1965), pp. 19–40; also see Genevieve Knupfer and Robin Room, "Age, Sex, and Social Class as Factors in Amount of Drinking in a Metropolitan Community," *Social Problems,* Vol. 12 (Fall 1964), pp. 224–40.

which characterize value conflicts over drinking. Perhaps college students are held particularly suspect because, as potential leaders of the future, they are supposed to be ascetic. However, the image of them as heavy drinkers is overdrawn. Only a small proportion of students drink frequently and heavily. Although a survey of 27 American colleges found 74 percent of the students drink, only 21 percent of the men and 10 percent of the women drink more than once a week. The example of their parents was highly related to whether the students drank. The majority who drink had started their drinking before entering college.[55]

As another example of the integration of drinking behavior within the social structure, the production and distribution of alcoholic beverages constitutes a significant business enterprise and source of tax revenues. These economic interests raise a value dilemma because the socially desirable quest for profits becomes entangled in a trade which can promote excessive drinking, alcoholism, and corruption. Attempts to control these pathological consequences are complicated by the wish to preserve economic advantages.

Public drinking houses

Commercial establishments comprise still another example of the development of a social structure based on drinking behavior. The public drinking house is a social institution in western society which comes in several types.[56] Skid-row taverns largely serve homeless men with cheap liquor. (Chapter 7 noted the recent decline of skid row.) Patronized by white-collar and business groups, downtown cocktail lounges are sites for business transactions and occupational sociability. In the business districts or near the city limits, drink-and-dine taverns cater to small groups seeking food and music. In similar sites nightclubs and roadhouses add a floor show. Neighborhood taverns cater to local clientele, largely "regulars," by providing a meeting place for congenial relationships, recreation, and talking over personal problems.

When patronized by "regulars" who have been long-term residents of the neighborhood, each tavern sets its own norms as to the degree of inebriation or boisterousness tolerated.[57] By providing a comfortable place for drinking, the tavern has been called a cause of alcoholism, but serving primarily as a meeting place, the tavern in its several versions actually reflects the moral standards of a segment of the community. In the minds of some persons the skid-row tavern and operations of criminal rings link some drinking houses with the sordid aspects of community life, but even

[55] Robert Straus and Selden D. Bacon, *Drinking in College* (New Haven, Conn.: Yale University Press, 1953), pp. 57, 85, 101, 116.

[56] Marshall B. Clinard, "The Public Drinking House and Society," in Pittman and Snyder, *Society, Culture, and Drinking Patterns*, pp. 270–92.

[57] David Gottlieb, "The Neighborhood Tavern and the Cocktail Lounge: A Study of Class Differences," *American Journal of Sociology*, Vol. 62 (May 1957), pp. 559–62.

in the slum the neighborhood tavern serves as a center for social life unrelated to criminal behavior.

CRIME AND ALCOHOL OR DRUG USE

Several purposes may involve the criminal law in the control of alcohol and drug use. To raise revenue through taxes on alcohol, the state prosecutes bootleggers and others who deal in nontax-paid liquor. Under the assumption that use should be limited to adults, sale of liquor to minors is prohibited. When the protection of health is considered to be a paramount factor, the distribution or misuse of medical prescriptions becomes a law violation. The criminal law is also employed to deal with the behavioral consequences of intoxication. Drunken driving involves a threat to the life and property of others, and disorderly conduct offends public taste and disturbs the peace. Finally, the criminal law may be invoked with special force against users under the assumption that addiction is essentially a criminological issue.

Association with offenses

Beyond the definition of possession of intoxicants or addiction as crimes, the addict is supposed to engage for several reasons in behavior considered to be criminal. To appease an appetite denied a legal supply of drugs, the addict is said to engage in money-making crimes to pay for the illegal and expensive drugs supplied by criminal traffickers. Furthermore, drugs are supposed to produce feelings of courage and to counter inhibitions, thus increasing the possibility of crime.

Studying addicts in a United States Public Health Service Hospital, O'Donnell finds a recent increase in proportion of addicts with a criminal record prior to addiction.[58] The offenses committed after addiction were more numerous than before addiction, with most later crimes perpetrated for money, especially those by addicts using illicit drugs. O'Donnell reports that the subjects with the greatest number of post-addiction crimes depended mostly on illegal sources of drugs. He believes that the increase in crime after addiction is a product of the way of life forced on the addict and should not be attributed directly to drug use.

Urban delinquency and drugs

In urban areas where drug use is most prevalent, property crime also is likely to be high. This relationship is one aspect of the spatial distribution

[58] John A. O'Donnell, "Narcotics and Crime," *Social Problems,* Vol. 13 (Spring 1966), pp. 374–85.

of addicts within the urban community. Although drug use has tended to diffuse, it is concentrated heavily in disadvantaged areas also characterized by low income, delinquency, high infant mortality, and other social problems. As a novel practice, drug use would be diffused more rapidly within the "street-corner society" with its restless search for excitement and new experiences to counter a pessimism engendered by the conditions of the urban ghetto.[59]

Delinquency and narcotics are independent symptoms in that they are alternative forms of adjustment. Original drug use may lead to delinquency to raise money to support the habit. Delinquent gangs seem to resist immoderate drug use, however, since it undermines reliability and attracts police scrutiny, and regular users tend to form cliques that sap the cohesiveness of the gang. Furthermore, gang norms inhibit exploitation of fellow members through tempting them into narcotic addiction.[60]

Among the forms of traditional crime, addicts tend toward arrests for nonviolent property offenses to a greater extent than other offenders. Among military offenders, Bromberg and Rodgers found marijuana users to engage in the nonaggressive crimes.[61] Chein and his associates also argue that increased drug use does not result in an overall gain in juvenile crimes if violation of narcotics laws are ignored. The larger number of property crimes is counterbalanced by fewer rapes, assaults, automobile thefts, and instances of disorderly conduct.[62]

PROHIBITION AND SUPPRESSION

As social problems, the use of alcohol and drugs stimulate societal reactions which, in themselves, may aggravate the conditions the reactions are supposed to alleviate. Already we have considered this possibility in studying such problems as crime, mental illness, race relations, and sexual deviation. Because alcohol and drug use are of high visibility among American moral concerns, we would expect that the societal reaction would include resort to law enforcement as the means of problem solution.

Suppression as narcotics policy

With increased concern over narcotics use after World War II, legislation to suppress it was passed by almost all states. The legislation, Allen

[59] Harold Finestone, "Narcotics and Criminality," *Law and Contemporary Problems,* Vol. 22 (Winter 1957), pp. 71–72.
[60] Chein, et. al., *The Road to H,* pp. 11–12.
[61] Walter Bromberg and Terry C. Rodgers, "Marijuana and Aggressive Crime," *American Journal of Psychiatry,* Vol. 102 (May 1946), pp. 825–27.
[62] Chein, et. al., *The Road to H,* p. 11.

points out, has a number of common features.[63] The strongly prohibitive regulations rely heavily on the system of criminal justice, with penalties becoming increasingly severe. Because drug use involves both a willing buyer and a willing seller, the victim of addiction is thrust into a criminal status and the possibility of police abuses increased. The definition of possession of drugs as a criminal offense erodes the distinction between the user and the trafficker. As a consequence, drug control becomes involved in the conflicts between the crime-control and due-process models we discussed earlier.[64]

Prohibition of all narcotics for addicts and the use of criminal statutes are the central features of the *suppressive reaction* which employs vigorous police activity and stern judicial measures for the sake of community protection. Any evidence of criminal tendencies draws predominant attention when the addict is conceived of as an antisocial personality. Thereby, he is judged to be unqualified as a medical patient undergoing the travail of addiction, and if a physician attempts medical measures, he risks being judged as a collaborator in criminal behavior. Moreover, addiction loses its significance as an extenuating factor for criminal acts such as would be provided by the medical definition of the addict as a victim of a disease.[65]

Prohibition and regulation of alcohol use

The prohibition of liquor under the 18th Amendment is a classic case of the inadequacy of the criminal law as an instrument for imposing one brand of morality on a population composed of diverse cultural groups. The strategy sacrificed the constructive aspects of moderate drinking, and the heterogeneity of interests blanketed within the temperance movement undermined the certainty of purpose in enforcing prohibition. The absence of universal moral support for prohibition undermined the effectiveness and invited the corruption of law enforcement.

Even after repeal, the "moral crusade" of prohibition had its adverse consequences by fostering social ambivalence toward drinking. Trice cites the maze of half-truths and invectives which cripple the objective study of the causes of alcoholism and the organization of effective community response.[66] Examples are the identification of alcoholism with the skid-row bum, the overlooking of the constructive aspects of drinking groups

---

[63] Francis A. Allen, "Current Tendencies in American Narcotics Legislation," in Wilner and Kassebaum, *Narcotics,* pp. 21–29.

[64] See Chapter 17. For a review of the difficulties of narcotic law enforcement, see Rufus King, "Narcotic Drug Laws and Enforcement Policies," *Law and Contemporary Problems,* Vol. 22 (Winter 1957), pp. 113–31.

[65] Finestone, "Narcotics and Criminality," pp. 79–81.

[66] Harrison M. Trice, *Alcoholism in America* (New York: McGraw-Hill Book Co., 1966), pp. 13–27.

in bars and in the home, and a failure to recognize the fundamental differences among cultural groups in the significance of drinking. The persistence of social ambivalence fosters the isolation of the drinker from the social situations essential to his rehabilitation.When it regards excessive drinking as a moral fault, the criminal justice system reacts particularly punitively against those convicted offenders who were intoxicated. If intoxication is the result of addiction as a disease, Moore argues that the courts should consider the medical condition as a possible mitigating factor.[67]

With the collapse of the prohibition model, governmental control has withdrawn to the regulation of the "liquor trade" as primarily a state and federal responsibility. A few states provide "local option" laws whereby local citizens vote their community "wet" or "dry." Under the open license system the states leave the alcoholic beverage trade to private enterprise under licensing and regulation, the nominal public objectives being to limit the number of competitors, eliminate people with criminal or questionable financial histories, and control the physical location of public drinking houses. Regulations attempt to control advertising, sales to minors or "habitual drunkards," hours for sales, and activities such as prostitution and gambling. In monopoly states the trade is conducted by the government to varying degrees, usually including the retail sales.

TREATMENT REACTIONS

Because of its complex physiological, psychological, and social bases, addiction is a difficult problem for medical treatment or other forms of therapy. The dependency and benefits sought in the use of alcohol or drugs make the addict an unlikely prospect for easy and voluntary acceptance of the role of patient, and the strong punitive reactions of agents of criminal justice aggravate the difficulties of winning his genuine participation. The alcoholic occupies an uncertain role because staffs of hospitals and community agencies have negative and pessimistic attitudes toward accepting him as their client. The services available in the community have a merry-go-round quality, especially for alcoholics caught in a cycle of arrest, incarceration, release, then arrest again. Casework agencies regard psychiatric treatment as essential, but psychiatric clinics handle few alcoholics. Psychiatric programs see intensive casework required, but casework agencies are reluctant to work with alcoholics. The net effect is the breakdown of referral systems.[68]

[67] Robert A. Moore, "Legal Responsibility and Chronic Alcoholism," *American Journal of Psychiatry,* Vol. 122 (January 1966), pp. 748–56.
[68] David J. Pittman and Muriel W. Sterne, "Analysis of Various Community Approaches to the Problem of Alcoholism in the United States," in David J. Pittman (ed.), *Alcoholism* (New York: Harper and Row, 1967), pp. 206–8.

Addiction as a disease

When considered as a disease, alcoholism becomes a medical problem rather than a result of moral degradation or a sole subject for legal suppression as a crime. Since disease implies a condition outside the control of the victim, this definition implies the inappropriateness of indicting him as a moral transgressor. Therapeutic advantage may be gained by releasing the individual and/or his wife of self-guilt by shifting blame to impersonal forces out of personal control.

The definition has the fundamental error, however, of assuming that addiction is a homogeneous entity caused by specific biochemical or physiological disturbances. Furthermore, the emphasis on medicine invites exclusive attention to biological factors and the secondary physiological effects in terms of malnutrition, liver damage, and endocrine disturbances. Such exclusive attention risks overlooking the psychological, cultural, and sociological factors. The "sick person"—particularly the mentally sick person—is particularly unattractive in a culture placing heavy emphasis on individual responsibility and self-reliance. Mental illness in itself draws an adverse evaluation. McNamara suggests that a superior approach would be to interpret addiction as a problem of social adjustment or learning of alternative ways of living.[69]

Medicine applies the disease model to alcoholism in differing ways. Siegler and her associates distinguish two versions.[70] In the *"old" medical model,* alcoholism is considered a serious, progressive, and eventually fatal disease incurred through immoral behavior. The patient is seen as perverse in his persistent destruction of his body and failure to observe the physician's instructions. This model moves outside the proper sphere of medical competence to add moral imperialism. The *"new" medical model* sees alcoholism as a progressive disease stemming from physiological, psychological, and sociocultural factors. Probably physiological factors, such as defects in metabolism, are given priority because medicine emphasizes the physical organism. The emphasis is placed on the necessity for improving the effectiveness of therapeutic strategies, rather than demanding that the alcoholic patient conform to moral standards. In fact, past failures are considered no justification for abandonment of therapeutic effort or retreat into moral indictment of the alcoholic for his deviance.

Treatment of alcoholism

Physiological treatment includes conditioned reflex therapy, administration of certain drugs, and use of adrenocorticotrophic hormone (ACTH)

[69] John H. McNamara, "The Disease Conception of Alcoholism: Its Therapeutic Value for the Alcoholic and His Wife," *Social Casework,* Vol. 41 (November 1960), pp. 460–65.
[70] Miriam Siegler, Humphry Osmond, and Stephen Newell, "Models of Alcoholism," *Journal of Studies on Alcohol,* Vol. 29 (September 1968), pp. 571–91.

and adrenocortical extract (ACE).[71] In conditioned reflex therapy, an aversion for alcoholic beverages is developed by inducing vomiting through a noxious stimulus in a fashion which causes the patient to associate the beverage with unpleasant reactions. Similarly, disulfiram (Antabuse) induces sensations of being on fire and suffocating when alcohol is ingested. Benzedrine, amphetamine, and tranquilizers have been administered to establish rapport for psychological intervention through relief of pessimism and hostility. Under the theory (now seriously questioned) that alcoholics suffer from adrenal cortical insufficiency, ACTH and ACE are supposed to remove addictive urges and alleviate withdrawal symptoms of alcoholics.

Psychological and environmental methods cover a wide and heterogeneous range from punitive confinement in jails to psychotherapy. Somewhere within this range are prolonged hospitalization, religious conversion, pastoral counseling, and social casework. The jail has been described in terms of "revolving doors" because short-term and repetitive confinement, without effort other than coercive response to the persistence of drinking, deals with symptoms rather than the sources of behavior. Pastoral counseling and social work hold more promise when they focus on the difficulties within the total family situation. Similarly, psychotherapy has the merit of concentrating on the sources of pathological drinking behavior, but the high cost of prolonged one-to-one treatment and the avoidance of lower-class clients are disadvantages.[72]

A fellowship group of compulsive drinkers, *Alcoholics Anonymous,* was established in 1936 by a stockbroker and a physician in an effort to end their own alcoholism. As a primary group based on the status of the sober former drinker, AA affords intimacy, mutual acceptance, and identification with a common struggle for sobriety. Expressed in "the twelve steps," the subculture emphasizes admission that the individual is powerless over alcohol, recognition of need for help of a power greater than himself, confession of past wrongs, effort to amend the injuries to others, and devotion to helping other alcoholics.

One of AA's strengths, Maxwell says, is the hope given the disillusioned alcoholic by the example of its members.[73] Furthermore, a prerequisite to membership is a readiness to seek and accept help. The alcoholic joins a primary group with a subculture providing a new orientation toward alcohol and its relationship to his problems of living. His work with other alcoholics provides persistent follow-up lacking in most other treatment strategies. In this special fellowship, his alcoholic rationalizations are dis-

[71] Morris E. Chafetz and Harold W. Demone, Jr., *Alcoholism and Society* (New York: Oxford University Press, 1962), pp. 205–11.

[72] Factors in the underutilization of clinical psychiatric services by lower-class alcoholics are suggested in the discussion of "The Paradox of Social Class," in our Chapter 19.

[73] Milton A. Maxwell, "Alcoholics Anonymous: An Interpretation," in Pittman and Snyder, *Society, Culture, and Drinking Patterns,* pp. 577–85.

sected and exposed. He is given social rewards previously sought through the bottle, but these rewards are predicated on persistent sobriety. The status of *former* alcoholic becomes a symbol of triumph over degradation. Trice and Roman see as the central contribution of AA the cancellation of the stigmatizing label of drunkard and its replacement with the label of former and repentant deviant.[74]

The compulsion to drink, it has been suggested, is converted into a compulsion to follow the AA way in the fervor of proselytizing new members and in cultlike participation in group activities. Furthermore, AA principles draw on the values of emotional control, strength, and godliness to point the way back to the American middle-class way of life.[75] Its middle-class orientation, however, obstructs participation by lower-class alcoholics. Seeing the group as a religious cult, Cain questions the dogmatism of the movement as a source of dependency to AA retarding full participation in community life as a recovered alcoholic.[76] Furthermore, Ellison says that the national headquarters has been captured by an ultraconservative clique and that a reverence for past accomplishments has deprived AA of its once acknowledged leadership in knowledge of alcoholism.[77]

Treatment of drug abuse

Drug treatment strategies have been listed as medical-psychiatric in a hospital setting, the religious approach, rational authority, chemotherapy, the community approach, and the communal approach.[78] In hospitals devoted to addicts, *medical-psychiatric* treatment includes detoxification, some rebuilding of bodily health, and involvement of some patients in therapeutic relationships with various treatment professionals. These therapies usually rest on the assumption that addiction should be treated as a physical disease.

Regarding addiction as essentially sinful, the *fundamental religious perspective* would provide an intense religious experience to convert addicts into missionaries to save others and to bring a profound involvement in a more socially acceptable way of life. Convinced that most addicts will not voluntarily sustain a prolonged treatment regimen, *rational authority* is employed to keep them in a treatment setting long enough for effective

---

[74] Harrison M. Trice and Paul M. Roman, "Delabeling, Relabeling, and Alcoholics Anonymous," *Social Problems,* Vol. 17 (Spring 1970), pp. 538–46.

[75] Chafetz and Demone, *Alcoholism and Society,* pp. 161–63.

[76] Arthur H. Cain, "Alcoholics Anonymous: Cult or Cure?" in Judson R. Landis (ed.) *Current Perspectives on Social Problems* (2d ed.; Belmont, Calif.: Wadsworth Publishing Co., 1969), pp. 80–89.

[77] Jerome Ellison, "Alcoholics Anonymous: Dangers of Success, *Nation,* Vol. 198 (March 2, 1964), p. 214.

[78] Louis Lieberman, "Current Trends in the Rehabilitation of Narcotics Addicts," *Social Work,* Vol. 12 (April 1967), pp. 53–59.

outcome. Probation and parole may involve social casework techniques or involvement of the addict's family under firm presentation of the legal powers held over him as a convicted offender.

The *community approach* places the addict within the community setting in terms of the development of his addiction and its treatment. Both the addict and the community are subject to a wide variety of efforts. Services range through social welfare, religion, employment assistance, psychological intervention, and development of community resources. The organization of services and the revision of institutional arrangements is as much subject to attention as the treatment of the addict as an individual. The attitudinal climate and socioeconomic opportunity structure of the community are deemed crucial factors in both the rise and resolution of addiction.[79]

Chemotherapy employs methadone and cyclazocine and naloxone to counter the effects of heroin. Methadone, an addictive drug, has milder abstinence symptoms and permits the addict to become stabilized and amenable to other therapies. Cyclazocine and naloxene, neither of which are addictive, appear to have similar benefits but do not satisfy the addict's craving for drugs. Most treatment programs using these narcotic antagonists are restricted to patients who appear to be highly motivated to stop using drugs. Even with these patients, however, problems include a high dropout rate in early phases of treatment, use of other drugs, and the necessity that the addicts face the realities of their situations. Chemotherapy has been criticized for providing only a crutch to a patient without dealing with his basic problems. Proponents argue that the urgency of the drug problem requires giving immediate assistance to the addict "down in the gutter" rather than awaiting the ideal solution.[80]

Narcotics clinics, dispensing drugs free or at a nominal cost, have been advocated to eliminate criminal traffic and to remove the criminal sanctions obstructing treatment efforts. The hope would be that elimination of peddler proselyting would reduce recruitment of new addicts. The low costs of legal drugs would reduce the crime of addicts for the sake of income.

Such clinics are the basic element of the drug program in England where no direct link between crime and addiction is reported. The monthly amounts of prescribed heroin have continued to drop. In the mid 1960s heroin use reached epidemic proportions when some American experts declared the clinics had failed. However, May reports, in 1969 the number of new addicts began to decline after the government limited prescribing to special treatment centers. He explains the narcotics crisis as the careless

---

[79] See Richard Brotman and Alfred Freedman, *A Community Mental Health Approach to Drug Addiction* (Washington, D.C.: Office of Juvenile Delinquency and Youth Development, U.S. Department of Health, Education, and Welfare, 1968).

[80] Allen L. Hammond, "Narcotic Antagonists: New Methods to Treat Heroin Addiction," *Science,* Vol. 173 (August 6, 1971), pp. 503–6.

overprescription of a few "junkie doctors" who operated like drug pushers.[81]

Critics of narcotics clinics contend that insufficient drugs would be provided to sate the addicts' desire for euphoria. Since the recruitment of new addicts is not largely a result of peddler proselyting, it is doubtful that clinics will be sufficient to stem the growth of addiction. Furthermore, the clinics do not alter the social and psychological causes of addiction; hence, their low-cost drugs may only perpetuate the problem.[82]

Under the *communal approach,* the addict places himself in a special subcommunity structured socially and culturally to expose him to new way of life. Day-by-day contact with other residents becomes a socialization process by means of group therapy sessions and imposition of informal controls by other persons fighting addiction. By maintaining drug-free days he gains status within the group as he is exposed to a new orientation toward what he previously regarded as a "square world." [83] The most prominent example of this approach is Synanon, established in 1958 by Charles E. Dedrich.

EDUCATION AND PREVENTION

If the recruitment of new alcoholics or drug addicts can be forestalled to a significant extent, the problems of addiction can be reduced to reasonable magnitude. This worthy objective requires a revision of basic attitudes and practices for a larger population than the minority of current users.

Restructuring context of drinking

Addiction is an indicator of tensions, anxieties, and unfulfilled needs which the individuals are not able to alleviate through socially approved mechanisms. The dimensions of the addiction problem suggest a discrepancy between the addicts' needs and the means of gratification provided by socially approved arrangements. This interpretation suggests the possibility that the needs satisfied by drinking or drunkenness could be fulfilled through other activities. At a superficial level this possibility might be sought through luring the drinkers into other entertainment and hobby activities. At a more profound and difficult level, the structure of community life would be reshaped to reduce drinking problems.

---

[81] Edgar May, "Drugs Without Crime," *Harper's Magazine,* Vol. 243 (July 1971), pp. 60, 61–65.

[82] Eldridge, *Narcotics and the Law,* pp. 108–110; and David P. Ausubel, "Controversial Issues in the Management of Drug Addiction: Legalization, Ambulatory Treatment, and the British System," in O'Donnell and Ball, *Narcotic Addiction,* pp. 195–209.

[83] Joseph A. Shelly and Alexander Bassin, "Daytop Lodge: Halfway House for Drug Addicts," *Federal Probation,* Vol. 28 (December 1964), pp. 46–54.

Wilkinson would combine control of the alcohol trade and public education.[84] He assumes, first, that deep-seated attitudes toward alcohol consumption affect probability of drinking and open the door to revision of an individual's reliance on alcohol to cope with stress. His second premise is that deliberate policy measures can reshape drinking behavior when they are consistent with drinking patterns which are associated with low rates of alcohol consumption. He would use the law and public administration within these existing constructive patterns rather than try to impose one drinking pattern, such as abstinence, on American society. Wilkinson would distinguish sharply between drinking per se and drunkenness, in order to emphasize clear guidelines for moderate use. Tax differentials would favor light over strong drinks. He endorses the idea of drinking with food to link drinking with other constructive living patterns and to forestall drunkenness caused by drinking on an empty stomach.

Most people who are going to drink, Wilkinson contends, should learn to manage alcohol at an early age and with their families. He would drop the legal age for purchase of alcoholic drinks to 18 years and would eliminate age limitations when accompanied by parents or guardians at establishments serving meals. Reduction of the legal age is supposed to eliminate the "forbidden fruit" appeal of public drinking and to encourage public drinking within a family context favorable to learning how to control drinking. Public education, ranging from television documentaries to less formal efforts, would emphasize the enjoyment of moderate use, the immaturity demonstrated by drunkenness, and the worthiness of abstinence.[85]

Forestalling drug addiction

The New York Academy of Medicine offered in 1955 a useful program for dealing with the problem of narcotics abuse. The program emphasized that public attitudes should be reshaped to regard the addict as a patient rather than as a criminal, and that the full weight of law enforcement should be applied to traffickers. An educational program should be undertaken to make potential addicts aware of the danger of narcotic drugs, and reliable research should be begun to determine the facts on the number of addicts and the nature of addiction, in order to eliminate the confusion and distortion arising from arbitrary definition of addiction as simply a criminological problem.[86]

The advocates of a vigorous law enforcement approach also urge education and prevention, but place a greater emphasis on limiting the supply of drugs through control of manufacture and distribution from abroad

[84] Rupert Wilkinson, *The Prevention of Drinking Problems* (New York: Oxford University Press, 1970), pp. 5–8.
[85] Wilkinson, ibid., pp. 105–21.
[86] "The Academy's Proposals," in O'Donnell and Ball, *Narcotic Addiction*, pp. 188–95.

through international agreements. The reduction of the availability of drugs is deemed a key answer to prevention. Another answer is to provide information on drugs to youngsters to forestall curiosity and to warn of the ultimate consequences of drug use. Parents, teachers, and leaders of youth groups would employ brochures giving information to reduce vulnerability.[87] However, the effectiveness of such education is doubtful because it lacks impact on the social conditions and the peer-group attitudes resistant to the conventional values expressed by adults.

SUMMARY

Because of the social ambivalence with which consumption of alcohol is regarded in American society, the control of the adverse consequences of its use is particularly difficult. Identification of the precise nature of drug addiction is also severely handicapped by heated debates. These normative conflicts qualify the use of alcohol and many drugs as one of the major social problems, but they have blurred the objective facts on the physiological and psychological costs to the user and obstructed treatment efforts by stigmatizing the user. Why is the user so stigmatized and why does social ambivalence exist as a barrier to concerted and effective action to remedy the problems? In attempting to find answers, we have traced the roots of the problem through the fabric of society itself. In reviewing various suppressive and therapeutic strategies, we suggested that the answers lie in revision of the organized responses to the addict and in the handling of addiction as only one aspect of the several social problems considered in earlier chapters.

FOR ADDITIONAL READING

Howard M. Bahr and Stephen J. Langhur, "Social Attachment and Drinking in Skid-Row Life Histories," *Social Problems,* Vol. 14 (Spring 1967), pp. 464–72.

Howard S. Becker, "History, Culture and Subjective Experience: An Exploration of the Social Bases of Drug-Induced Experience," *Journal of Health and Social Behavior,* Vol. 8 (September 1967), pp. 163–76.

Richard Blum and Associates, *Utopiates* (New York: Atherton Press, 1968).

Daniel Casriel, *So Fair A House: The Story of Synanon* (Englewood Cliffs, N.J.: Prentice-Hall, 1963).

Sherri Cavan, *Liquor License: An Ethnology of Bar Behavior* (Chicago: Aldine Publishing Company, 1966).

Morris E. Chafetz, *Liquor: The Servant of Man* (Boston: Little, Brown and Company, 1965).

---

[87] Maurer and Vogel, *Narcotics and Narcotic Addiction,* pp. 164–65.

Edgar Z. Friedenberg, "The Synanon Solution," *Nation,* Vol. 200 (March 8, 1965), pp. 256–61.

Allen Ginsberg, "The Great Marijuana Hoax," *Atlantic Monthly,* Vol. 218 (November 1966), pp. 104–12.

Joan K. Jackson, "Alcoholism and the Family," in Jeffrey K. Hadden and Marie L. Borgatta (eds.), *Marriage and the Family* (Itasca, Ill.: F. E. Peacock, 1969), pp. 575–88.

Julius Klein and Derek L. Phillips, "From Hard to Soft Drugs: Temporal and Substantive Changes in Drug Usage among Gangs in a Working-Class Community," *Journal of Health and Social Behavior,* Vol. 9 (June 1968), pp. 139–45.

Donald E. Larsen and Baha Abu-Laban, "Norm Qualities and Deviant Drinking Behavior," *Social Problems,* Vol. 15 (Spring 1968), pp. 441–50.

Julian Roebuck and S. Lee Spray, "The Cocktail Lounge: A Study of Heterosexual Relations in a Public Organization," *American Journal of Sociology,* Vol. 72 (January 1967), pp. 388–95.

Earl Rubington, "The Bottle Gang," *Quarterly Journal of Studies on Alcohol,* Vol. 29 (December 1968), pp. 943–55.

William Simon and John H. Gagnon, "Children of the Drug Age," *Saturday Review,* Vol. 51 (September 21, 1968), pp. 60–63, 75–78.

Charles R. Snyder, "Inebriety, Alcoholism, and Anomie," in Marshall B. Clinard (ed.), *Anomie and Deviant Behavior* (New York: Free Press, 1964), pp. 189–212.

Lewis Yablonsky, *Synanon: The Tunnel Back* (Baltimore: Penguin Books, 1965).

21 Coping with social problems

Is urban man capable of managing the social problems of his day? The pessimist replies no—too much is out of gear in the urban social machinery. The optimist replies yes—everything is possible to the resolute human spirit and to technology.

In bringing this book to a close, I hope to show that means *are* available to cope with our difficulties. A book of this sort has first a responsibility to analyze the nature of social problems, and I have endeavored to apply the research and interpretations of a wide range of social scientists in capturing the essence of the problems. But in focusing attention on the failures of the social machinery, this endeavor has perhaps encouraged the impression that contemporary urban society is out of joint to the exclusion of a second responsibility of this kind of book—to suggest means of dealing with the problems. In responding now to this second responsibility, I hope to correct any impression that urban society today is in such general chaos that it is beyond human control.

GROUNDS FOR A MEASURE OF OPTIMISM

A social problem becomes the subject of collective and organized remedial effort after a reasonable degree of agreement has been reached that something is wrong and that something can be done. A condition is defined as constituting a discrepancy between what *is* and what is *expected* to be. When economic want, inequality among the races, inadequate medical care, and other such problem conditions arouse widespread concern, demands are made that something be done to correct their conflict with American ideals—but there are disagreements over what should be done. (Some few Americans would even deny that the conditions actually are undesirable.) Nevertheless, the definition of certain kinds of private "troubles" as public issues indicates that there is a general agreement that collective and organized efforts should be undertaken for reform.

Evidence of faith that reform is possible

The appearance of public issues implies a measure of optimism among Americans that means can be found to overcome the difficulties. Otherwise, the previous passivity in the face of undesirable but "inevitable" conditions would have remained. The very emergence of disagreement and dissension signals a continued, or perhaps reawakened, conviction that a better life is attainable within the general framework of contemporary society. Conflicts within the community are evidence of the vitality of its life, as Coleman says, because controversy goes hand in hand with membership participation.[1] Controversies suggest that there *is* something about which to disagree. That is, when previously passive groups become active over once dormant issues, this is evidence that the dissemination of increased amounts of knowledge has broadened the recognition of certain conditions as undesirable and the awareness that something can be done to correct them.

Expectations that something should be done appear today to be increasing. Because of their visibility and immediate threat, some problems attract greater concern than other issues which are also vital to the community. Opinion surveys, for example, report widespread public concern over domestic problems of race relations, crime, and education. That is, Americans express many fears about personal safety in walking alone at night in their urban neighborhoods.[2] But this "urban unease," as Wilson calls it, is aroused more by those problems which are visible in public places and which are directly disturbing to persons in their immediate environment.[3] In his poll of Boston homeowners, Wilson found the greatest degree of unease to be aroused by such diverse behaviors as trampling on precious rosebushes, public drunkenness, reckless driving, political demonstrations, and street crimes. His respondents placed lesser emphasis on problems of housing, transportation, pollution, and urban

[1] James S. Coleman, *Community Conflict* (New York: Free Press, 1957), pp. 3–4.
[2] See: President's Commission on Law Enforcement and Administration of Justice, *The Challenge of Crime in a Free Society* (Washington, D.C.: U.S. Government Printing Office, 1967), pp. 49–51.
[3] James Q. Wilson, "The Urban Unease," *Public Interest,* No. 12 (Summer 1968), pp. 25–28.

renewal—which are anchored in the institutional framework of society.

A basis for cautious optimism today is the growing consciousness among human beings that they are subject to the influences of *man-made* social systems. There appears to be a dawning recognition that, since these systems are man-made, they are also vulnerable to changes by man. The greater visibility of urban problems, then, is partially a product of more widespread knowledge that alternatives to the status quo are possible. Today's wider distribution of knowledge reflects the development of mass communications, the upsetting of traditional ways of life through population mobility, and other kinds of social change, and also of increases in levels of formal education. Boulding sees this growing consciousness as a development of the last two hundred years, which has been accelerated in the present generation.[4]

A further justification for a measure of optimism rests on the idea that, rather than undergoing collapse as a human community, urban society is developing a new basis of harmony among its component groups. This development is necessitated by the reduced importance of territorial anchorage in the urban community. Stein speaks of the "eclipse of community" through the weakening of the social psychological bonds among residents of a given physical locale. The processes of urbanization, industrialization, and bureaucratization have made individuals dependent on large-scale business enterprises and governmental bureaucracies which extend beyond the confines of local communities. Community ties, Stein says, have become "increasingly dispensable, finally extending even into the nuclear family."[5]

This evaluation, however, may be mistaking the processes of social change for a process of general social deterioration. Opposing this evaluation, there is evidence that primary groups persist in urban society.[6] Furthermore, as Martindale notes, the community may properly be defined as a set of groups sufficient to solve all of the basic problems encountered in ordinary life—that is, the community does not necessarily have some fixed point on the earth's surface.[7] Considered in this light, changes in the nature of the community as a social system (less anchored to a fixed point in space) may be interpreted as evidence of the need for a new basis of harmonizing groups in a way relevant to contemporary human requirements. Strategies outlined later in this chapter may preserve the social psychological community through facilitation of participation in its affairs

[4] Kenneth E. Boulding, *The Impact of the Social Sciences* (New Brunswick, N.J.: Rutgers University Press, 1966), pp. 4–7.

[5] Maurice R. Stein, *The Eclipse of Community* (Princeton, N.J.: Princeton University Press, 1960), pp. 107, 329.

[6] See Chapter 3, pp. 74–76.

[7] Don Martindale, "The Formation and Destruction of Communities, in George K. Zollschan and Walter Hirsch (eds.) *Explorations in Social Change* (Boston: Houghton-Mifflin Company, 1964), pp. 61–87.

and improved delivery of the services a community should provide its members.

Reform of the social order

As opposed to revolution, *reform* regards the foundations of the existing social order as essentially healthy. Reform's objective is to correct the flaws described as social problems, rather than to strike at the roots of the existing social order. Revolution offers the illusion of an easy "solution" through abolishment of the existing social system, but it usually conceals the difficulties of building a new social order under some new rules. Reform raises the complications of "social surgery" in removing the unsound elements of social institutions without undermining the social order generally accepted by the members of the society.

Within a democratic and highly complex society such as ours, the tasks of reform are particularly difficult.[8] Because democratic traditions demand respect for the right of every citizen to participate in the determination of his own affairs, controversies are more likely to arise among interest groups over whether or not a given condition *is* a problem meriting reform, whether or not its correction should receive *high* priority, and whether or not a particular reform strategy *should* be implemented. In the face of the complexity of our present-day problems and their involvement with many aspects of urban life, special expertise is frequently required in community problem solving, but controversies among special-interest groups may block the maximum utilization of this expertise. Finally, the distribution of power among groups in the community has great influence on whether or not a given reform will be undertaken and, if it is, the nature of the outcome.

Often reform is seen as a moral and humanitarian endeavor undertaken by the altruistic members of the groups holding power in the community or society. Recognition should be given to humanitarian considerations, of course, but the basic force behind reform is more likely to come from some degree of self-interest. The limited and hesitant emergence of the "welfare state" in the United States, for example, may be attributed to recognition that the loyalty of neglected citizens must be retained and that their underprivileged status is a drain on the vitality of the society.[9] Agents of change are likely to find that moral apathy and political cynicism weigh against successful use of conscience alone in persuading people in power to give up immediate advantages voluntarily for the sake of underprivileged groups. Clark believes moral force has greatest effect when

---

[8] See Peter Marris and Martin Rein, *Dilemmas of Social Reform* (New York: Atherton Press, 1967), pp. 7–10.
[9] See Chapter 6, pp. 145–46.

combined with practical advantage; for example, a need among employers for trained manpower can be used by blacks to get vocational training.[10]

Effecting change through accommodations

From the perspective of the leadership in a society, reform is a process of mobilizing power and resources to attain the goals of the society. Because underprivileged groups lack power and resources to overcome the problems embedded in the social structure, the reform startegy would be to convince the powerful groups that their own interests are also involved in the achievement of the proposed changes. Social reform has been described as a *sounding-out process*.[11] The participation of other parties is required if the reform proposed is to become reality, but initially the reformer states his proposal rather vaguely because he does not know how the other parties will react. If his proposal is rebuffed, its initial vagueness permits the reformer to reformulate it in terms more likely to win acceptance. Through a series of such actions and reactions, the proposal can be reshaped to attract broad-based support.

Elsewhere we use work-release as an example of this strategy.[12] To obtain statutory authority to place selected inmates on paid jobs in the free community, the North Carolina Department of Correction initially accepted inadequate legislation to gain the support of sentencing judges, potential employers, and the state legislature. The pilot phase provided experience and reassurances which permitted amendment of the statutes. Through a series of accommodations within the social system of state government and the social system of the prison department alone, an effective program was developed over the long term.

This accommodative version of the reform process means that the reform movement must include experts in the assessment of the sociocultural environment within which the desired changes are to be implemented, as well as experts in the technical knowledge pertinent to the given public issue. For this reason, we will consider the nature and functions of social planning, community organization, and social action. Along this line, an additional justification for measured optimism that social problems can be overcome is what Moynihan calls the *professionalization of reform*. He argues that a large body of professional persons and professional organizations has recently given impetus to reforms initated from within government. This development has been spurred by availability of resources for social purposes because of greater capacity to manage

[10] Kenneth B. Clark, *Dark Ghetto* (New York: Harper & Row, 1965), pp. 202–3.
[11] James D. Thompson and William J. McEwen, "Organizational Goals and Environment: Goal-Setting as an Interactive Process," *American Sociological Review,* Vol. 23 (February 1958), pp. 23–31.
[12] Elmer H. Johnson, "Work Release—A Study of Correctional Reform," *Crime and Delinquency,* Vol. 13 (October 1967), pp. 521–30.

economies, the assessment of public policies by professionals who emphasize independent judgement, and the growth of knowledge germane to
governmental response to the changing needs and desires of the electorate.[13]

DEMOCRACY AND PLURALISM

As a form of government, democracy is organized according to principles which suggest that, under circumstances of contemporary urban society in the United States, widespread participation in political processes
is desirable and essential to successful management of social problems.
The principle of *popular sovereignty* would distribute governmental decision-making power among all members of the community, rather than
reserving it for particular persons or groups. *Political equality* implies that
all members of the community have the same opportunity to participate
in selecting among genuine alternative solutions to public issues. ("Opportunity," however, does not guarantee that all members actually will participate.) *Popular consultation* refers to institutional machinery whereby officials learn public preferences and act accordingly rather than in keeping
with the officials' personal preferences. In controversial issues within a
democracy, however, popular consultation does not necessarily set out
clear guidelines.[14]

Participation: Crucial to democracy

Participatory democracy involves the processes by which citizens influence or control those persons who make major decisions affecting them.
This participation implies the will among citizens to exert influence beyond
mere ceremonial support or voting. Citizens acquire knowledge on public
issues, attend public meetings, and engage in other attempts to influence
decisions among alternative measures through active interaction with decision makers. The emphasis is on *attempts* to influence, because participation does not guarantee that one's views become the basis for decision.[15]
In a time of a high rate of change, the stability of a democracy rests on
a continued faith that existing political institutions are the appropriate ones.
This faith is more likely to be sustained when groups rising in power have
access to places in those institutions. With governmental activities having
great importance to the delivery of an unprecedented variety of vital

[13] David Patrick Moynihan, "The Professionalization of Reform," in Joseph R. Gusfield
(ed.), *Protest, Reform, and Revolt* (New York: John Wiley & Sons, 1970), pp. 245–58.
[14] Austin Ranney, *The Governing of Men* (rev. ed.; New York: Holt, Rinehart & Winston,
1966), pp. 88–95.
[15] Sidney Verba, "Democratic Participation," in Bertram M. Cross (ed.), *Social Intelligence for America's Problem* (Boston: Allyn and Bacon, 1969), pp. 126–43.

services, participatory democracy is a valuable means of establishing social goals and determining in a legitimate fashion the priorities for utilizing resources insufficient to meet all competing claims.

Furthermore, as Lipset explains, political stability depends on "give-and-take" politics in which all parties accept the "rules of the game" intended to preserve a basic consensus through limiting the intensity of conflict which otherwise would forestall solution to critical issues. The rules call for peaceful "play" of power, adherence of the "outs" to the decisions made by the "ins," and the recognition of the "ins" of the rights of the "outs." All parties are supposed to recognize competing ideas and prevent the excessive accumulation of unresolved issues.[16]

Participatory democracy has been described as a valuable means of dealing with the disadvantages experienced by the poor and other underprivileged groups.[17] The Economic Opportunity Act of 1964, for example, called for "maximum feasible participation of the residents of the area and the members of the groups served." Inclusion of the poor in decision-making processes has been advocated as a means of assimilating them into the mainstream of American society and of countering the "colonialism" of social service programs imposed on the slum by agencies controlled from outside the slum. The poor are supposed to gain sufficient political power for effective negotiation of their grievances against landlords, exploitive merchants, and unresponsive welfare agencies. Through participation in programs intended to serve their needs, underprivileged people are meant to gain a sense of community, thus countering alienation and apathy.

Differences in degree of participation

Characteristics of individuals and groups affect their degree of participation, of course. A high rate of participation requires access to information, skill in using that information, control over the material resources which provide power, and membership in influential organizations. Even when the individual has these assets, however, he still must want to participate because he believes such activities are worthwhile and germane to his own interests.[18] Many Americans belong to no associations, and of those who do belong, only a minority participates.

Social class status is an important predictor of participation because position in the social structure is related to access to information, verbal facility, experience in organizational activities, and perception of benefits to be gained through participation. Present-day leadership of established

[16] Seymour Martin Lipset, "Some Social Requisites of Democracy: Economic and Political Legitimacy," in Nelson W. Polsby, Robert A. Dentler, and Paul A. Smith (eds.), *Politics and Social Life* (Boston: Houghton-Mifflin Company, 1963), pp. 541–68.

[17] Sumati N. Dubey, "Community Action Programs and Citizen Participation: Issues and Confusions," *Social Work,* Vol. 15 (January 1970), pp. 76–84; also see our Chapter 7.

[18] Verba, "Democratic Participation."

organizations and of the political system is heavily concentrated among people of the higher social classes. Participation of lower-income people is inhibited by high rates of residential mobility, the shattering of neighborhood institutions by urban renewal projects, intergroup tensions—and resistance to their participation by entrenched organizations. Their experiences with community organizations lead them to believe that they are more likely to be targets for the actions of others than the initiators of actions themselves. Persons in lower socioeconomic positions are apt to see civic and political organizations as forces external to themselves which shape and control them. They are apt to be paralyzed by an inherent pessimism—a conviction that their conditions cannot, or will not, be improved.[19]

Moreover, high rates of political participation by members of each of several contending groups encourage dissension and complicate decision making. Thus, advocacy of widespread participation in the name of democracy actually runs counter to rapid and orderly decision making when compared to the relative efficiency, in this regard, of elite society. *Elitism* is a pattern of decision making characterized by limited mass participation in community issues and by domination by small groups of leaders.[20]

Great differences among groups in participation invite elitism to a degree, thus often straining the legitimacy of claims that a community is democratic. Public issues frequently call for specialized knowledge, sustained attention, and careful study—characteristics which are uncommon among average citizens. The issue is rather one of the proper place and function of elites in a democracy, not of insistence upon their absence. With a broader participation in decision making, the functions of elites would be determined by their competence. Within the range of the functions of elites as specialized experts, Key believes, the health of the democratic order hinges on their beliefs, standards, and competence in lending direction to collective efforts to deal with social problems.[21]

Pluralism and voluntary associations

Political pluralism traditionally has been presented as the answer to undemocratic elitism. It has been defined as a sociocultural system in which the power of the state is divided among the branches of government and shared between the state and a multitude of private groups and in-

[19] George Brager, "Organizing the Unaffiliated in a Low-Income Area," *Social Work,* Vol. 8 (April 1963), pp. 35–37; Edgar S. and Jean Camper Cahn, "Citizen Participation," in Hans B. C. Spiegel (ed.), *Citizen Participation in Urban Development* (Washington, D.C.: NTL Institute for Applied Behavioral Science, 1968), pp. 215–18; George Crowell, *Society against Itself* (Philadelphia: Westminister Press, 1968), pp. 68–100; John M. Foskett, "The Influence of Social Participation on Community Programs and Activities," in Marvin B. Sussman (ed.), *Community Structure and Analysis* (New York: Thomas Y. Crowell Company, 1959), pp. 314–27.
[20] Robert Presthus, *Men at the Top* (New York: Oxford University Press, 1964), p. 24.
[21] V. O. Key, Jr., *Public Opinion and American Democracy* (New York: Alfred A. Knopf, 1967), p. 558.

dividuals.[22] Political pluralism was conceived as a means of curbing the power of a centralized government and promoting the freedom of individuals to participate in community decision making. Voluntary groups are supposed to be the means whereby the freedom of individuals will be converted into effective participation. Providing a more formal structure and a more permanent system of relationships than a spontaneous collection of individuals, each voluntary association is composed of the proponents of a given view on a public issue. Examples are trade associations (such as the National Steel Institute and the Automobile Manufacturers Association), labor unions, religious organizations, medical and other professional societies, and recreational organizations. Voluntary associations operate outside the sphere of government but, in addition to their other functions, they strive to influence public policy through providing information, lobbying, and mobilizing their memberships as pressure groups. Through a multitude of voluntary associations, diversity of participation in public affairs is supposed to be promoted.

Questions have arisen recently, however, that cast doubt on the wide acclaim for voluntary associations as instruments of democracy. Powerful voluntary associations administered by their own elites without accountability to the citizenry as a whole have raised serious challenges to the kinds of political decision making appropriate to a genuine democracy. In government itself, for example, the size of bureaucracies and the span of their activities have expanded tremendously. Even so, government has not grown as fast as some other nongovernmental institutions. Drucker, for example, compares the power landscape of 1900 to the Kansas prairie—it was completely flat, except for the hillock of government.[23] Now political government has become a Mount Everest, but there also are towering mountains of giant corporations, labor unions, farm blocs, large universities, professional and trade groups, and even the more organized churches. In the face of this plurality of great power centers, Drucker lists three interrelated challenges. Government must be made capable of governing—of having policies and pursuing them; the new partial power centers within society must be prevented from usurping the functions of government and encroaching upon individual freedom and citizenship; and the freedom of the individual must be safeguarded and strengthened.

SOCIAL PLANNING

The search for means of attaining such objectives must operate within the context of a contemporary urban life which has strengthened the need

---

[22] Presthus, *Men at the Top*, pp. 10, 17–18.
[23] Peter F. Drucker, "Individual Freedom and Effective Government in a Society of Super-Powers," in William V. D'Antonio and Howard J. Ehrlich (eds.), *Power and Democracy in America* (Notre Dame, Ind.: University of Notre Dame Press, 1961), pp. 3–23.

for social planning. As a general term, *social planning* constitutes a rational and orderly application of the methods of science to the study of social problems and, secondly, the framing of an appropriate strategy to effect changes indicated by the study.

Members of large organizations and political entities collectively seek enduring solutions to the problems that affect them. Earlier we described social problems as developing over time through the several stages of awareness, policy determination, and reform. That is, instead of arising full-blown, social problems emerge in controversy over whether or not a given social condition qualifies as a public issue and, if it is a public issue, the kind of remedies to be undertaken.[24] Planning implies the philosophical principle that concerted action by society is essential to the solution of problems that defy unguided social processes of individuals and personal groups. Reform requires collective and systematic effort organized around identification of common goals through careful and objective analysis. The emotionalism of controversy obstructs this effort; planning is supposed to substitute careful thought for emotionalism. Ideally, planners use the methods and objectivity of science to produce a well-delineated policy as a framework for establishing goals and choosing the means to stimulate actions necessary for their orderly achievement.[25]

Probably the adjustment of social institutions to new conditions can be left to the natural interplay between the social units when such units are small and self-contained, but, Mannheim argues, contemporary industrial technology and the sociological characteristics of urban society require democratic planning in place of laissez-faire or totalitarian regimentation. He calls for planning for freedom and social justice, subjected to democratic control to forestall regimentation and prevent restrictions that will favor the narrow self-interests of a particular group.[26]

The laissez-faire philosophy assumed that the social order of a large-scale and heterogeneous society could be maintained by a variety of voluntary associations whose interaction was supposed somehow to have "natural" consequences congenial to the general good. Dispersal of public authority was supposed to restrict the exercise of government to those spheres of action enjoying agreement among at least most groups. The clash of self-interest groups was supposed to produce just policies automatically.[27]

In the United States, laissez-faire doubts about government have been

[24] See Chapter 1, pp. 5–8.
[25] For discussion of relationship between planning and policy, see Howard E. Freeman and Clarence C. Sherwood, *Social Research and Social Policy* (Englewood Cliffs, N.J.: Prentice-Hall, 1970), pp. 2–6.
[26] Karl Mannheim, *Freedom, Power, and Democratic Planning* (New York: Oxford University Press, 1950), p. 29.
[27] Henry S. Kariel, *The Decline of American Pluralism* (Stanford, Calif.: Stanford University Press, 1961), pp. 2, 181; also see Michael D. Reagan, *The Managed Economy* (New York: Oxford University Press, 1963).

modified toward a more recent conception of the state as the only viable means of ensuring economic and civil liberty.[28] Earlier chapters in this book described the rise of the welfare state, the intervention of government in race relations and medical care, the "war on poverty," and similar illustrations of the more recent conception of the state as a balance wheel for integrating a diffuse socioeconomic system and as an agent for encouraging innovative responses to social problems.

This greater reliance on social planning reflects the scale and complexity of today's urban society. Anchored in habits of daily life and the network of social institutions, social problems defy simple, direct, and short-time "solutions." More long-term and deliberate mechanisms for coordinating resources and influencing human behavior are required than in earlier societies in which relationships were more personalized, the population more homogeneous, and the techniques for converting natural resources to serve human needs less complex.

In confronting the difficulties of managing urban society, the planner expresses the view, sometimes overstated, that man's ingenuity should enable him to cope with social problems if he has the will to do so, but this ingenuity is exposed to a special challenge by democratic planning. The conception of government as the balance wheel of a diffuse socioeconomic system lends new emphasis to the importance of widespread political participation among the groups making up a pluralistic society. Democratic principles encourage people to expect the workings of American society to be in keeping with the "self-evident truths" enunciated in the Declaration of Independence "that all men are created equal, that they are endowed by their Creator with certain unalienable Rights, that among these are Life, Liberty and the pursuit of Happiness." These expectations lend special relevance to such social issues as those of civil rights, equal opportunity to qualify oneself for social and economic rewards regardless of race, access to medical care, and so on. These expectations imply that participation in the processes of decision making is crucial to the workings of our society and the well-being of its citizens.

In public issues involving complicated technology, the planners are usually expected to have technical expertise. For example, competing solutions for environmental pollution must be tested against the capacities and side effects of their technological support systems. The democratic model further requires sociological expertise to frame goals consistent with the values of the people presumably to be benefited by the reform, to win the consent of the varied groups involved in the proposed change, and to accommodate unpredicted developments when plans are applied to heterogeneous groups. Under the conception of reform as an accommodative process, planners must discover leverage points for the desired

[28] Presthus, *Men at the Top,* pp. 17–18.

change within a complex system for most efficient outcomes at least social cost.

Without losing sight of the ultimate general objectives, planners must respect the fundamental values of a democracy. Instead of striving to complete a preconceived scheme, democratic planning is seen as an on-going process in which adjustments are made in response to the reactions of the people for whom the plan has been designed. This conception reflects increasing recognition that the outcomes of plans are fundamentally affected by the responses of the target population and the agencies serving these people.[29] The encouragement of broad participation to obtain such feedback, Duhl says, is the difference between "a society that plans" and a "planned society." [30] It is the difference between democratic planning and totalitarianism.

In a pluralistic society with a diversity of cultures among social classes and ethnic groups, Berger argues, planning should be done for specific types of people with distinctive cultural styles—not for "faceless densities" with a given amount of disposable income.[31] He objects to emphasis on elements of the physical environment as the leverage point for changing living styles. Attempts to wipe out social class and ethnic differences in favor of a homogeneous "American" culture are resisted by the attachment of underprivileged people to their own subculture. This attachment lends a stability to their lives offering a means for promoting orderliness in urban society, although it can also be a barrier to their adjustment to changing conditions. Displaced by urban renewal or similar urban planning, most people will take their culture with them, thus frustrating planners who seek to promote a homogeneous, embracing urban culture. Because underprivileged people are also concerned about the quality of urban life, Berger prefers planning emphasis on preservation of cultural differences to build a loose and heterogeneous urban community composed of more or less autonomous groups and neighborhoods.

Arguments for incrementalism

In a society characterized by technological complexity and cultural diversity, the framing of plans for broad sectors of public affairs is especially difficult. Fully rational and comprehensive planning is beyond full realization and, in most circumstances, futile, Dahl and Lindblom argue.

[29] John C. Bollens and Henry J. Schmandt, *The Metropolis: Its People, Politics, and Economic Life* (2d ed.; New York: Harper & Row, 1970), pp. 228, 234–36.

[30] Leonard J. Duhl, "The Parameters of Urban Planning," in Stanford Anderson (ed.), *Planning for Diversity and Choice* (Cambridge, Mass.: M.I.T. Press, 1968), pp. 71–73.

[31] Bennett M. Berger, "Suburbs, Subcultures, and the Urban Future," in Sam Bass Warner, Jr. (ed.), *Planning for a Nation of Cities* (Cambridge, Mass.: M.I.T. Press, 1966), pp. 151–54, 157–62.

Under their conception of incrementalism, reform would be accomplished through a series of increments of change, each within the limitations of reliable estimates of what the consequences will be. The scope of each increment would be determined by the feasibility of reasonably accurate prediction for the given problem area. When incremental planning is not adequate to the situation, calculated risks would have to be taken through abandonment of scientific analysis.[32]

Dahl and Lindblom see incrementalism as an effective strategy for rational calculation when the consequences of alternative solutions are difficult to predict. Because man has many goals, rational action for the attainment of one goal risks conflict with other equally vital goals. A narrower and less drastic change enables the reformer to issue more detailed instructions and hold more effective control over subordinates who implement the change in detail. Errors in planning are less costly because decisions can be modified, and other existing organizations are less subject to fundamental revision.

COMMUNITY ORGANIZATION AND ACTION

The implementation of a plan involves *community organization,* a process through which a community identifies a social problem, ranks the needs or objectives involved, develops the will to cope with these needs or objectives, and takes action to deal with them.[33] This definition resembles the stages of awareness, policy determination, and reform through which problems become targets for collective action.[34]

Two approaches to community organization

The process occurs in two general sets of circumstances, Ross and Lappin explain. First, it may involve a *geographical community* embracing the residents of an area such as a village, neighborhood, or a section of a city. The effort is directed toward the residents themselves, toward strengthening their sense of social solidarity and degree of participation in community affairs, or toward improvement in the delivery of services to them. Focusing his attention on action as one of the aspects of community organization, Moynihan applies the term *experimental action* to efforts to include the poor among the community decision makers through expansion of their power or by confronting the established power structure. The ideological commitment is to social change rather than stability,

---

[32] Robert A. Dahl and Charles E. Lindblom, *Politics, Economics and Welfare* (New York: Harper & Row, 1953), pp. 82–85.

[33] Murray G. Ross and B. W. Lappin, *Community Organization: Theory, Principles, and Practice* (2d ed.; New York: Harper & Row, 1967), pp. 40–43, 51–52.

[34] See Chapter 1, pp. 5–8.

to recognition of cultural diversity rather than to perservation of current community consensus, and to meeting social problems rather than maintaining order in governmental affairs.[35]

Second, the process may involve a *functional community* composed of professionals and agencies specializing in the handling of a particular social problem. Here the focus is more on the coordination, or development, of programs drawing the specialized interest of professionals and agencies. Again referring to the action component of community organization, Moynihan calls *action for efficiency* the approach which emphasizes the coordination of diverse but related efforts to maximize their impact. The poor are expected to carry out the program designed by the professionals and agency executives. Under the assumption that a satisfactory community consensus exists, the objective is to strengthen the stability and efficiency of programs developed largely by government and operated within the existing power structure.

Community action and participation

The encouragement of citizen participation is frequently advocated as a means of overcoming alienation of the underprivileged from schools, criminal justice, welfare agencies, and similar institutions. "Citizen participation," however, has differing meanings. It may be only ritualistic, without the surrender of decision-making power by the agency bureaucracy or the existing community elite. It may mean the inclusion of some new group in the decision making (such as the middle-class–oriented residents of a slum) but the continued exclusion of other groups (such as the lowest strata of the poor suffering most from the demolition of slum housing). Finally, it may mean the inclusion of the clients of welfare, criminal justice and other services among those who have a real voice.[36] The resistance of the community elite and bureaucratic inertia make the first two versions more common, the third version particularly difficult to implement.

In terms of increasing parent participation in improving ghetto schools, for example, Bloomberg and Kincaid list some of the difficulties. Organized residents must acquire understanding and skills in dealing with underlying problems not susceptible to mere rhetoric and protest. Their efforts must be persistent. Teachers and administrators must be receptive to such participation. The new participatory decision-making process must be relevant to school issues.[37]

[35] Daniel Patrick Moynihan, *Maximum Feasible Misunderstanding* (New York: Free Press, 1969), pp. 77, 147,168–69; also see his "What Is 'Community Action'?" *Public Interest,* No. 5 (Fall 1965), pp. 5–7.

[36] Elliott A. Krause, "Functions of a Bureaucratic Ideology: 'Citizen Participation', " *Social Problems,* Vol. 16 (Fall 1968) pp. 129–43.

[37] Warnen Bloomberg, Jr., and John Kincaid, "Parent Participation: Practical Policy or Another Panacea?" *Urban Review,* Vol. 2 (July 1968), pp. 5–11.

The *self-determination action approach* espoused by the late Saul D. Alinsky would organize slum neighborhoods by capitalizing on the resentments of the residents against the outside world they distrust. Community conflict is used deliberately and raw issues are exacerbated to arouse and rally previously passive residents. Through concerted action, the poor are supposed to gain power for hard-nosed bargaining with an "establishment" not otherwise amenable to making the changes sought. To involve all elements of the neighborhood, militancy is emphasized in demonstrations, picketing, boycotts, rent strikes, and publicity.

Assessment of conflict as a strategy

In the face of apathy in the slum as a response to a hostile environment, Silberman emphasized the significance of the agitation in making residents see themselves as persons of worth and substance. In witnessing the impact their agitation has on "city hall," they become willing to accept the assistance they need because it is a product of their own power, not charity.[38] The deliberate use of conflict has been defended as more likely than a cooperative policy to effect desired changes, more likely to gain influence for the otherwise powerless groups, more likely to shake up ossified bureaucracy, and more likely to rejuvenate organizations by redistributing power.[39]

Violence in the community, Coser argues, may serve three social functions.[40] The expression of frustrations may serve as a danger signal of serious social maladjustments and thereby provide a means whereby frustrated people can make a claim on authorities that reform measures be undertaken.

Second, shut out from legitimate means of achievement, lower-status individuals may turn to violence as an alternative means to compensate for inferior social position, absence of legitimate means of gaining social satisfactions, and inadequate access to occupational rewards. In this function, Coser distinguishes between realistic and nonrealistic conflict. *Realistic conflict* arises from frustration of specific demands within a given relationship and from estimates of gains the participants hope to win from the groups toward which aggression is directed. Although directed against some target group, *nonrealistic conflict* is more a matter of tension release than pursuit of some specific purpose.

Finally, violence may serve as a catalyst to arouse revulsion against

[38] Charles Silberman, *Crisis in Black and White* (New York: Random House, 1964), pp. 346–48.
[39] Lyle S. Schaller, *Community Organization: Conflict and Reconciliation* (Nashville, Tenn.: Abington Press, 1966), pp. 76–86.
[40] Lewis A. Coser, "Some Social Functions of Violence," *Annals of American Academy of Political and Social Science,* Vol. 364 (March 1966), pp. 8–18; and Lewis A. Coser, *The Functions of Social Conflict* (New York: Free Press, 1956), p. 49.

societal arrangements previously regarded as sacred. Police reactions to civil rights demonstrators or suppression of a prison disturbance, for example, may exceed public tolerance and make the system of criminal justice subject to doubts among an unprecedented proportion of the population.

A central difficulty with conflict is its short life as a basis for new persisting relationships. The rancor stimulated by conflict and the temporary emotionalism of participants are inferior foundations for the cooperation essential to orderly implementation of new arrangements. New institutional patterns after the conflict ends require attention to detail in policy-making and administrative practices which lend themselves to the sabotage of persistent change once the heat is off. Hunter suggests that, in addition to militancy, the self-determination approach must include persuading the bureaucracy to identify itself with the changes.[41] Wilson sees the approach as effective in winning concession on specific issues but risking the destruction of broad plans calling for fundamental changes. In exacerbated conflict, the approach may alienate the neighborhood from the city as a whole.[42] To effect lasting change and to gain public funds in the long term, the program of community action for reform depends on the support of the established leadership, and Marris and Rein see the championing of "radical democracy" as opposed to winning this support.[43] Finally, the conflict may be directed against the wrong "enemy," one who lacks the power to remedy the situation being protested.

FACILITATING COMMUNITY PARTICIPATION

Without popular participation in democratic decision making, Mydral warns, the increasing reliance on government to deal with social problems will result in a widespread complex of officials uncontrolled by their memberships. He believes that a greater degree of participation is probable with the advances toward national integration in the United States as a consequence of high population mobility and the decline of the cultural heterogeneity existing when immigration was at high tide.[44] Chapter 2 cited the vital importance of two-way communication between the leaders and the membership of giant political and economic structures if democracy is to be a reality. The following pages present and assess some of the strategies for encouraging greater participation.

[41] David R. Hunter, *The Slums: Challenge and Response* (New York: Free Press, 1964), pp. 179–81.

[42] James O. Wilson, "Planning and Politics: Citizen Participation in Urban Renewal," in Roland L. Warren (ed.), *Perspectives on the American Community: A Book of Readings* (Chicago: Rand McNally & Company, 1966), pp. 482–83; for further criticisms, see Frank Riessman, *Strategies against Poverty* (New York: Random House, 1969), pp. 3–15.

[43] Marris and Rein, *Dilemmas of Social Reform,* p. 183.

[44] Gunnar Myrdal, *Beyond the Welfare State* (New Haven, Conn.: Yale University Press, 1960), pp. 49–55.

Volunteer action against problems

Recent decades have brought increased voluntary participation in efforts to meet social problems. Youth and young adults have been recruited into the Peace Corps, VISTA, and direct-action programs such as voter registration, civil rights, and other mobilization of slum dwellers. Retired professionals have enlisted in mental health, welfare, recreation, probation work, and educational projects. Senior citizens have remained active through similar contributions of their time and effort. The lower levels of the social class structure produce fewer recruits, but the trend is toward reducing the differences among the classes and age groups.[45] Volunteer work, Cohen contends, promises to be a building block for urban democracy through its provision of meaningful participation and its intensification of social responsibility.[46]

Naylor distinguishes between the *administrative volunteer,* who serves on a committee or board in a policy-making capacity, and the *operational volunteer,* who performs tasks such as putting out the agency newsletter, stuffing envelopes, acting as a receptionist, preparing school lunches, and so on.[47] Here we are primarily interested in the operational volunteer who increases his participation in the direct interactions of community life. Sometimes the volunteer assumes the interviewing, counseling, and other tasks usually performed by full-time staff. The tasks of the operational volunteer may approach those of the professional, depending on the functions of the program and the agency's conception of the volunteer as a personal resource. Volunteers have been used in such diverse programs as probation of offenders, hospital care, and service to persons released from mental institutions.[48] The volunteer serves as a link to the outside community for clients. In supplementing the professional staff, he contributes time and enthusiasm to improve the impact of programs in tasks for which he can be trained rather quickly or which utilize his special talents.

Professionals, however, are apt to regard volunteers as a mixed blessing.[49] The agency requires each of its salaried specialists to perform his tasks on schedule if the overall organization is to carry out its work. The employee is expected to give highest priority to his job during working

[45] Harriet H. Naylor, *Volunteers Today—Finding, Training and Working with Them* (New York: Association Press, 1967), pp. 12–13.

[46] Nathan E. Cohen, "Citizen Participation the Backbone of Democracy," in Nathan E. Cohen (ed.), *The Citizen Volunteer* (New York: Harper & Brothers, 1960), pp. 28–33.

[47] Naylor, *Volunteers Today,* pp. 24–28.

[48] Ivan H. Scheier, *Using Volunteers in Court Settings* (Washington, D.C.: Office of Juvenile Delinquency and Youth Development, 1969); Keith J. Leenhouts, "The Volunteer's Role in Municipal Court Probation," *Crime and Delinquency,* Vol. 10 (January 1964), pp. 29–37; Winifred Overholser, "The Volunteer in Psychiatric Rehabilitation," *Mental Hygiene,* Vol. 45 (April 1961), pp. 163–66.

[49] Bernard Barber, "Bureaucratic Organization and the Volunteer," in Herman D. Stein and Richard A. Cloward (eds.) *Social Perspectives on Behavior* (New York: Free Press, 1958), pp. 606–9.

hours. Salary is a major inducement for demonstrating the self-discipline with agency expectation, but because the volunteer is motivated by enthusiasm for social service and is nonsalaried, his personal preference plays a large part in determining his work performance. When obligations to his family and his own job conflict with his volunteer work, there is less certainty that he will be present to carry out his assigned function. The volunteer has to be continuously "sold" on the job since he always is free to leave. Finally, since jobs often call for special skills, the selection of volunteers among applicants and the provision of special training are crucial.

New careers and indigenous workers

Since many social problems are associated with income deficiency, the *new career* approach would provide economic opportunity to the poor by restructuring professional jobs and by providing educational upgrading for the poor to qualify them. It is argued that new kinds of aide jobs can be created, requiring minimum training for entry. Aides would be involved in teaching, family planning, health services, probation work, research, recreation, child care, and so on. Performing relatively simpler tasks, the aide frees the professional to concentrate on more demanding functions and thus eases the qualitative and quantitative shortage of manpower in human-service fields. The aide's on-the-job training would be supplemented by formal education to enable him to qualify for movement up a career ladder designed to bridge the currently formidable gap between the untrained person and the full professional. In short, jobs are provided first, diplomas later.[50]

The professional functions could be broken down into a team of specialists. Gordon says the professional in a community agency could have the support of a team composed of specialists in contacting potential clients, dealing with other community agencies, providing sympathetic assistance of applicant-clients at case intake, administering psychometric tests, or home visiting.[51] Such a breakdown of tasks would simplify short-term training and would lend significance to the slum dweller's familiarity with his neighborhood and its people.

Although he is an essential element in new careers, the indigenous worker may be employed as a separate concept. The *indigenous worker,* a staff member drawn from the ranks of the area's residents, would involve the poor directly in the given program. His employment adds to the economic opportunites of slum dwellers, and his participation in the agency's affairs enhances his self-image. It is assumed that, because he works

[50] Riessman, *Strategies against Poverty,* pp. 21–25.
[51] Jesse E. Gordon, "Project Cause, The Federal Anti-Poverty Program, and Some Implications of Subprofessional Training," *American Psychologist,* Vol. 20 (May 1965), pp. 334–43.

on his native turf, the indigenous worker can contact and communicate with slum dwellers more ably than middle-class professionals. His acceptance by his neighbors draws formerly unreached clients into the agency and qualifies him as a role-model for other residents. However, only residents with certain characteristics hold promise as indigenous workers. Expertise in the program's area is required (examples of needed skills are homemaking, experience as parents, or sustaining of constructive interpersonal relationships), and preference is given individuals who identify with other working-class members without rejecting the nonstriving residents. A personal conviction that action will solve problems is necessary.[52]

Both the new careers and the indigenous worker concepts involve the slum dweller in role conflicts. As a nonprofessional working with professionals, he observes the greater economic and psychic rewards granted the professional, and his personal ambition may then lead him to identify with professionalism and to reduce his emotional affiliation with clients; if this happens, the advantages of using the indigenous worker are lost.[53] These concepts also impose strains on the agencies and their professionals by challenging the professional's self-image as being competent through hard-won skills.

Self-help organizations

In the health and welfare fields, self-help organizations originate through the activities of parents and relatives of ill or handicapped children. The core ideas are *self-organized* and *mutual aid* as these people strive to learn more about the nature of the child's difficulties and to improve the treatment received. The sharing of a common problem motivates the establishment of the group and nonmembers. Typically, this sharing places the group members in peer relationships with one another which lends a spontaneity that minimizes the development of formal authority and prestige rankings. However, self-help groups have developed extensive national organizations; for example, the National Association for Retarded Children, the United Cerebral Palsy Association, the Muscular Dystrophy Association of America, the National Cystic Fibrosis Foundation, the National Multiple Sclerosis Society, and the National Hemophilia Association. The complexity of these organizations creates a need for professionals in administrative and expert tasks to lend greater formality to the organization at those levels.[54]

---

[52] George A. Brager, "The Low-Income Professional," in George A. Brager and Francis P. Purcell (eds.), *Community Action against Poverty* (New Haven, Conn.: College and University Press, 1967), pp. 163–67.

[53] Perry Levinson and Jeffery Schiller, "Role Analysis of the Indigenous Nonprofessionals," *Social Work,* Vol. 11 (July 1966), pp. 98–99.

[54] Alfred H. Katz, "Self-Help Organizations and Volunteer Participation in Social Welfare," *Social Work,* Vol. 15 (January 1970), pp. 51–60.

Beyond fund-raising, self-help groups provide a wide variety of volunteer activities in maintaining centers for the handicapped, providing transportation, supporting research, and increasing public knowledge of the particular problem. Self-help, Katz suggests, can be interpreted in two ways. Individuals not included among the target problem population are motivated by public service, probably also by concern for a friend or relative in the target population. The concern for the particular problem condition tends to draw participants across social class lines and to circumvent motives to promote one's personal career. Participants afflicted with the problem condition receive advantages of "self-help" in face-to-face interaction with their peers which promotes a sense of social identification with others in a sphere of common interest. Helping oneself becomes a means of countering alienation and the depersonalizing influences of urban structure in a relationship resembling the extended family.

DELIVERY OF SERVICES

In the years after World War II, the United States became the world's first "service economy." In other words, it became the first nation with more than half of the employed population engaged in work other than the production of food, clothing, housing, automobiles, or other tangible goods. The service economy includes wholesale and retail trade, finance, insurance, real estate, general government, and services of a professional, personal, business, and repair nature. Between 1947 and 1967 total U.S. employment rose from 57 to 74 millions, and virtually all of the net increase occurred in the service economy. For instance, the *increase* in employment in health services between 1950 and 1960 exceeded the total employees in automobile manufacturing in either year.[55]

Patterns in delivery of services

Democratic ideals suggest that such an expansion would herald a broadening of the consumption of services *throughout* the population, but previous chapters of this book have documented the differential distribution of the benefits of health care, mental health services, education, leisure-time activities, and social services. The greater expectations of the underprivileged and the concept of relative deprivation have underscored this discrepancy. Not only is the delivery of services distributed differentially among the social classes, but the place of delivery is usually located where the underprivileged find access difficult. Public assistance, employment, and medical care offices are likely to be remote from lower-class

[55] Victor R. Fuchs, *The Service Economy* (New York: Columbia University Press, 1968), p. 1.

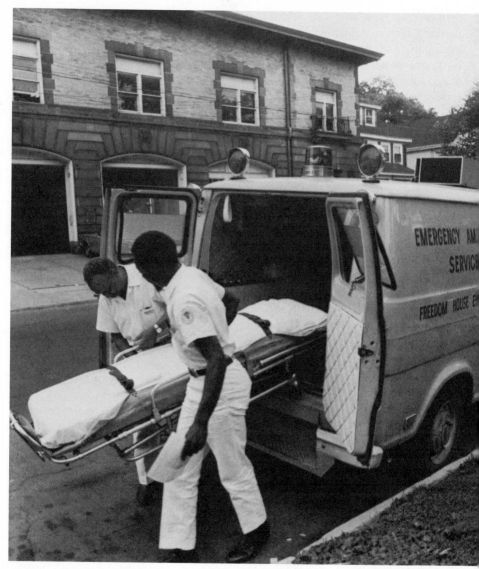

Improving the delivery of services. Ambulances represent jobs as well as delivery of services to the sick. Among slum residents both are in short supply. As a pilot project in the "Hill" area of Pittsburgh, a black-owned ambulance service was funded by government and private foundations and blacks have been trained to administer emergency medical care.

residential areas. The well-to-do have private rooms in hospitals, travel first class, employ expert legal counsel, and have cultural and educational choices. The poor occupy charity wards, receive no or inadequate legal assistance, and are restricted in economic, cultural, and educational opportunities.[56]

How do the social service agencies deliver services to the persons who become their clients? Addressing herself to care for the mentally ill, Cumming describes two models.[57] In the *pinball machine model,* a group of agencies is coordinated through their generalized agreement rather than through a central plan or organizational structure. The applicant for services approaches or is taken to one of the agencies. Depending on how functions are distributed among the agencies, he is sent to what is regarded as the appropriate agency for his problem. Not subject to a centralized authority, the agencies are free to accept or reject the referred applicant. The agencies may overlap each other in services provided, but each has its own policies and standards. Therefore, the rejected applicant must find another agency in a random fashion similar to a ricocheting pinball. This model can conceivably favor greater attention to the individual client in the absence of an umbrella of coordinating procedures among agencies, but its reliance on informal consensus promotes the opposition of vested interests to introduction of new service activities which cut across the domains of other agencies.

The *dispatcher model* postulates an overall plan and policy which governs who shall be treated and where a given kind of service will be delivered. Through a centralized authority, "traffic officers" find and coordinate the treatment resources required for the particular client among the interdependent agencies, each of which has its functions within the overall division of labor. Ideally, the model is oriented to the patient's treatment and only secondarily to his income and reputation or which agency gains a favorable image in a competition for prestige. This model's advantages of overall planning and coordination of services reduce duplication of activities and gaps in services delivered to clients. Such centralization, however, conflicts with American values of individualism by its restrictions on the autonomy of agencies and the influence which theoretically the client has on his treatment experience.

Some innovative approaches

Outside of the more usual modes of delivering social services, a number of approaches have been introduced to broaden the distribution of health care, mental health assistance, and other services. These approaches in-

---

[56] Adam Yarmolinsky, "The Service Society," *Daedalus,* Vol. 97 (Fall 1968), pp. 1264–68.

[57] Elaine Cumming, "Care for the Mentally Ill, American Style," Mayer N. Zald (ed.), *Organizing for Community Welfare* (Chicago: Quadrangle Books, 1967), pp. 125–33.

volve improvement of the coordination among agencies, introduction of new worker roles, third party intervention, rise of advocacy roles, extension of legal services, and the ombudsman.

Coordination among agencies may be improved through such schemes as the case conference or coordinating councils. In the *case conference,* representatives of agencies meet regularly to consider cases which concern several agencies so that action can be coordinated and responsibility fixed. The sessions are useful for determining gaps in services and establishing procedures for handling similar cases.[58] *Coordinating councils* also include representatives of existing community agencies, but they operate at the executive level.

The polyvalent worker and the detached worker are less orthodox strategies which move the services out of the confines of a building-centered program. The *polyvalent worker* is an all-purpose social worker who provides information and referral services for people with special problems or who are unable to find the usual administrative channels for services among a range of agencies. This worker may be located in neighborhood information centers or may regularly come to certain places in the neighborhood.[59]

Similarly, the *detached worker* searches out clients not likely to be drawn into building-centered programs. This category specializes in delinquency prevention. The social group worker or recreation worker goes out in the streets to present himself as a friendly adult to predelinquents. The subcultures of the gangs and of slum life in general are recognized as realities influencing the attitudes and behaviors of their members, and the worker strives for acceptance within the values of those subcultures as a neutral person unidentified with the welfare agencies, police, and other organizations seen by slum people as symbols of alien authority. By gaining the acceptance of street-gang members, he attempts to build bridges between the isolated and alienated members and the community's institutions, such as the schools, employers, police, and courts.[60]

Third party intervention

Third party intervention refers to individuals or organizations which attempt to improve the conjunction of systems of service delivery and the individuals in need of those services. The objective is to reduce the fragmentation of the components of the delivery system and of the amorphous mass of present and potential clients. To organize and increase the demand

---

[58] Alfred J. Kahn, *Theory and Practice of Social Planning* (New York: Russell Sage Foundation, 1969), pp. 287–88.

[59] Kahn, ibid., pp. 279–80.

[60] Saul Bernstein, *Youth on the Streets* (New York: Association Press, 1964; and John M. Gandy, "Preventive Work with Street-Corner Groups," *Annals of American Academy of Political and Social Science,* Vol. 322 (March 1959), pp. 114–16.

for services, efforts are made by the third-party groups to reach out into the community to connect the client with the service agencies through provision of information on the availability of services appropriate to his problem and by referring him to the proper agency. Neighborhood centers increase accessibility and counter the impersonality of bureaucracy. Improved coordination is designed to reduce discrepancy between needs and the actual delivery of services.[61]

The *neighborhood information center* provides the local residents with information on where a service can be obtained, initial explanation of the meaning of pertinent laws or regulation, and referral to an appropriate agency through helpful contact. It also offers suggestions to agencies for improving their policies and procedures, and educates the public on the availability of services in the community. To serve as an effective intermediary between potential clients and the people-serving system, the center ideally conveys a friendly open-door atmosphere while offering a wide range of services confidentially, flexibly, and expertly.[62]

As another means of decentralizing services, *multiservice centers* bring to the neighborhood the representatives of housing, employment, visiting nurses, and other offices. As an outpost, the center integrates the services of the various agencies which would otherwise be involved segmentally in the several problems of some families. They provide for consolidating the several cases of these agencies and for fixing responsibility among agencies. The functions of the neighborhood information center and advocate may be added.[63]

Advocate of the underprivileged

Agencies may employ a *coordinator* who is a predominately neutral middleman between the agency and its clients to expedite the delivery of services. His intermediary role tests his neutrality in that his loyalty to the agency and his associations with fellow employees tend to operate against persistent identification with clients. The *advocate* negotiates with agencies for the client to secure an entitlement or right which has been obscured or denied. Unlike his client, the advocate knows the laws, regulations, and administrative procedures relevant to the issue. He uses his knowledge to compel attention and action by subordinates in the target agency because he is prepared to go above them to their superiors.[64]

[61] Martin Rein and Frank Riessman, "A Strategy for Antipovery Community Action Programs," *Social Work,* Vol. 71 (April 1966), pp. 3–10.

[62] Alfred J. Kahn, Lawrence Grossman, Jean Bandler, Felicia Clark, Florence Galkin, and Kent Greenwalt, *Neighborhood Information Centers* (New York: Columbia University School of Social Work, 1960), pp. 112–19.

[63] Alfred J. Kahn, *Studies in Social Policy and Planning* (New York: Russell Sage Foundation, 1969), pp. 284–87.

[64] Richard A. Cloward and Richard M. Elman, "Advocacy in the Ghetto," *Trans-action,* Vol. 4 (December 1966), pp. 27–35.

Rather than helping a man to help himself, the advocate fills in a power deficit on the man's side by providing him with a knowledgeable and dedicated defender in negotiations with an organization.[65]

The social worker may take three professional approaches. In the *process orientation* approach, the professional does not have preconceived goals in guiding interactions of his client with agencies and other persons. Ideally he is neutral, without a personal stake in the outcome; the goals are supposed to emerge in the course of the interaction. The *clinical orientation* approach involves the professional in the responsibility of diagnosing the client's problem and determining the appropriate course of treatment. The *social reform orientation* approach seeks to make an impact on social problems by influencing change in organizations and institutions. Although some degree of advocacy may be found in any professional interaction in which a client's interest is opposed by some person or institution, Brager declares, advocacy must be a part of the social reform orientation.[66]

Advocacy planning takes the view that planning is pluralistic and partisan, requiring representation of any group whose interests are at stake. In this view, the planner would represent private citizens or organizations outside of private or public bureaucracies by preparing plans for his clients and arguing for their adoption much as a lawyer pleads for his client. By being able to draw upon the planner's technical competence, the clients would be able to participate in planning more effectively, rather than being forced into the limited and defensive stance of protest against the proposals of bureaucracies. Critics of the advocacy role claim it paralyzes action by politicizing planning and encouraging conflicts between special-interest groups. Although proponents of advocacy planning are likely to recognize inefficiencies in short-term decision making, they argue that these inefficiencies are justified by the opportunities given to articulate the interests of all people and to counter any tendencies toward despotism.[67]

Lawyers of the poor

The legal problems of the underprivileged are most visible in reference to the criminal law. Low-income groups are more subject to police surveillance and the inequities of law enforcement—especially the differential enforcement of laws that define "public order" and "moral conformity"—

[65] Hettie Jones, "Neighborhood Service Centers," in Harold H. Weissman (ed.), *Individual and Group Services in the Mobilization for Youth Experience* (New York: Association Press, 1969), pp. 44–45.

[66] George A. Brager, "Advocacy and Political Behavior," in John S. Morgan et al., *Changing Services for Changing Clients* (New York: Columbia University Press, 1969), pp. 109–13.

[67] Lisa R. Peattie, "Reflections on Advocacy Planning," in Hans B. C. Spiegel (ed.), *Citizen Participation in Urban Development* (Washington, D.C.: NTL Institute for Applied Behavior Science, 1969), Vol. 2, pp. 237–50; Bollens and Schmandt, *The Metropolis,* pp. 240–41.

than high-income groups. Inferior access to legal counsel, bail, and proba-tion exact undue penalities from the poor—and the criminal justice system represents only a *portion* of the legal problems of the poor. For example, insufficient access to legal counsel makes the poor man vulnerable to the unfair credit practices of unscrupulous merchants, and Appleby cites the obscurity of public assistance procedures, invasion of individual privacy, and the practice of administrative discretion which make welfare law a proper subject for the services of lawyers. Tenant-landlord relationships, evictions, and allocation of public housing space also involve legal mat-ters.[68] In family law, the well-to-do are able to shield their delinquent children from the juvenile court through restitution to the victim or private therapy. They can obtain divorces in Reno or fight legal battles for custody of their children, while lack of money bars access to such means for the poor, whose family problems are aggravated by their very poverty.[69]

To estimate the nature and extent of the legal needs of lower-income people, a sample of 402 Denver households was studied. Although 232 respondents believed they had no legal problems, about half of them were evaluated by a panel of lawyers as being in need of legal help. While, legal problems tended to become more numerous as increased income gener-ated more difficulties about buying and using possessions, nevertheless, 62 percent of the Denver households studied which were below the poverty line had legal problems.[70]

Sykes offers three arguments for legal assistance to the poor through a neighborhood law office. The location in the neighborhood is a possible remedy for the reluctance of the poor to seek services from an agency in a downtown location far from their environment; the case overload of the usual legal aid societies forces them to limit their services in quantity and time (the neighborhood law office constitutes an additional resource); and, finally, the neighborhood law office implements the notion that the poor have legal *rights,* thus countering any tendency of the legal establish-ment to regard the legal rights of the poor as a privilege.

Ombudsman: Official tribune

Introduced in the 1809 Constitution of Sweden, the *ombudsman* typi-cally is appointed by the Swedish legislature to receive citizens' com-plaints, to be an impartial and independent investigator, and to make suggestions for redress and reform of administrative actions. Direct, infor-mal, speedy, and cheap handling of grievances is emphasized. The om-

[68] Michael Appleby, "Overview of Legal Services," in Harold H. Weissman (ed.), *Justice and the Law in the Mobilization for Youth Experience* (New York: Association Press, 1969), pp. 26–30.

[69] Monrad G. Paulsen, "The Legal Needs of the Poor and the Family Law," in Jeanette Stats (ed.), *The Extension of Legal Services to the Poor* (Washington, D.C.: U.S. Government Printing Office, 1964), pp. 19–21.

[70] Gresham M. Sykes, "Legal Needs of the Poor in the City of Denver," *Law and Society,* Vol. 4 (November 1969), pp. 255–77.

budsman has the power to criticize and publicize, but he cannot reverse the actions of any agency he investigates beyond the force of public censure. In the face of the slowness and impersonality of bureaucracy, he provides rapid and personal responses to the individual caught in a tangle of red tape.[71]

Recently, the idea has drawn interest in the United States as a means of enhancing the responsiveness of local, state, and national governments.[72] (Sometimes, however, the applications depart from the concept to confuse it with advocacy or other grievance procedure.) Some metropolitan newspapers, for instance, have special columns which respond to the complaints of readers through providing information and intervention with the businesses or agencies involved in the grievances. In other applications, the "ombudsman" is made an arm of the executive of a private or public organization, but his subjection to the authority of the executive deprives him of the full independence basic to the ombudsman role.

The ombudsman approach is useful in the American situation as one means of reducing the inequities of administrative justice without the expensive and time-consuming resort to court procedures. Instead of simply eliminating administrative agencies, recourse could be made to a personalized and nonlegalistic review of their decisions by an independent ombudsman who relies on the voluntaristic support of the agency as pressed by the force of generalized public opinion. Critics see the approach as more appropriate for small units of government or delimited spheres of administration than the great geographical span and complex business of a large and heterogeneous nation. In the latter instance, the volume and diversity of cases operates against personalized and rapid handling, and thus state and local government would be a more appropriate setting. Furthermore, it is feared that our political and administrative culture lacks the traditions of neutrality among civil servants that is present in the Scandinavian countries. Finally, the ombudsman is seen as a threat to the separation of legislative and executive powers which is already a special problem in achieving orderly and consistent government.[73]

SUMMARY

The foregoing survey of methods useful in coping with social problems was intended to provide evidence that a measure of optimism is justified

[71] Donald C. Rowat, "The Spread of the Ombudsman Idea," in Stanley V. Anderson (ed.), *Ombudsman for American Government* (Englewood Cliffs, N.J.: Prentice-Hall, 1968), pp. 9–10, 36; and Henry S. Reuss and Stanley V. Anderson, "The Ombudsman: Tribune of the People," *Annals of American Academy of Political and Social Science,* Vol. 363 (January 1966), pp. 45–48.

[72] Donald C. Rowat, *The Ombudsman: Citizen's Defender* (2d ed.; Toronto: University of Toronto Press, 1968), pp. xii–xvi.

[73] Samuel Krislov, "A Restrained View," in Rowat, ibid., pp. 246–55.

in assessing prospects of reducing the impact of our present problems. These methods must operate under the ideological imperatives of democracy as it functions within a large-scale and pluralistic society. In keeping with the principles of democracy, the methods presented and analyzed were grouped under two categories—facilitating participation and improving the delivery of social services. The principles of democracy also influence the application to social problems of the techniques of planning, community organization, and community action. All methods of reform pose difficulties in application to a complex urban society, of course, but the very definition of certain conditions as proper targets for societal action and the existence of controversies over what to do about them attest to the vitality of American society.

FOR ADDITIONAL READING

George A. Brager, "Institutional Change: Perimeters of the Possible," *Social Work,* Vol. 12 (January 1967), pp. 59–69.

Lee J. Cary (ed.), *Community Development as a Process* (Columbia, Mo.: University of Missouri Press, 1970).

Kenneth B. Clark and Jeanette Hopkins, *A Relevant War Against Poverty: A Study of Community Action Programs and Observable Social Change* (New York: Harper & Row, 1969).

Terry N. Clark (ed.), *Community Structure and Decision-Making: Comparative Analyses* (San Francisco: Chandler Publishing Co., 1968).

Marshall B. Clinard, *Slums and Community Development* (New York: Free Press, 1966).

Richard A. Cloward and Frances Fox Piven, "We've Got Rights! The No-Longer Silent Poor," *New Republic* Vol. 157 (August 5, 1967), pp. 23–28.

Irwin Epstein, "Professional Role Orientations and Conflict Strategies," *Social Work,* Vol. 15 (October 1970), pp. 87–92.

Amitai Etzioni, " 'Shortcuts' to Social Change," *Public Interest,* No. 12 (Summer 1968), pp. 40–51.

David W. Ewing, *The Human Side of Planning* (New York: Macmillan Company, 1969).

William A. Gamson, "Rancorous Conflict in Community Politics," *American Sociological Review,* Vol. 31 (February 1966), pp. 71–81.

Alfred J. Kahn, *Theory and Practice of Social Planning* (New York: Russell Sage Foundation, 1969).

Clarence King, *Working With People in Community Action* (New York: Association Press, 1965).

Rensis Likert, *Human Organization: Its Management and Value* (New York: McGraw-Hill, 1967).

Carol H. Meyer, *Social Work Practice: A Response to the Urban Crisis* (New York: Free Press, 1970).

Robert Morris and Robert H. Binstock, *Feasible Planning for Social Change* (New York: Columbia University Press, 1966).

Cynthia R. Nathan, "Why Public Welfare Needs Volunteers," in Malvin Morton (ed.), *Can Public Welfare Keep Pace?* (New York: Columbia University Press, 1969), pp. 151–62.

Marvin E. Olsen, "Social and Political Participation of Blacks," *American Sociological Review,* Vol. 35 (August 1970), pp. 682–97.

Arnold M. Rose, *The Power Structure* (New York: Oxford University Press, 1967).

Alan Shank, *Political Power and the Urban Crisis* (Boston: Holbrook Press, 1969).

George B. Thomas, "Tension: A Tool for Reform," *Saturday Review,* Vol. 52 (July 19, 1969), pp. 50–52 ff.

Henry Wechsler, "Patterns of Membership in a Self-Help Organization in Mental Health," *Mental Hygiene,* Vol. 45 (October 1961), pp. 613–22.

Author index

Subject index